WORLD WAR II

For my mother, Lillian Matanle, who was so excited by the prospect of this book, but died before it could be completed.

Author
Ivor Matanle

Photographs © 1989 **The Keystone Collection**, London (from the libraries of Keystone Press, Central Press and Fox Photos)

Picture research by
Anne Matanle

Designed by
Philip Clucas MSIAD

Maps drawn by
Sally Strugnell

Publishing Director
David J. Gibbon

Commissioning Editor
Trevor Hall

Production Director
Gerald Hughes

3570
This edition published in 1997 by Colour Library Direct
© 1989 CLB International, Godalming, Surrey
Printed and bound in China
ISBN 1-85833-333-4

ACKNOWLEDGEMENTS

The Publishers acknowledge with grateful thanks the contribution made in verifying the textual and pictorial content of this book by **Terry Charman** of the Imperial War Museum, London, and **Andrew Preston**, who also researched the map showing the concentration camp system.

The map showing airfields at the time of the Battle of Britain is based on material supplied by the Royal Air Force.

All remaining maps are based on material supplied by the Daily Telegraph plc.

Opposite: the huge losses of men and women, both military and civilian, created enormous numbers of orphan children throughout the world. This little girl, like countless others, was fed and cared for temporarily by the Red Army after the Germans had been driven back from the village where she lived.

WORLD WAR II

IVOR MATANLE

FOREWORD BY
Viscount Montgomery of Alamein CBE
Oberbürgermeister Manfred Rommel
John S. D. Eisenhower

CONTENTS

Dwight D. Eisenhower

World War II, the greatest paroxysm that has ever seized the human race, was an event so enormous and so tragic as to defy the imagination. Millions died in Britain, France, Germany and Japan — and tens of millions in the Soviet Union. The United States, though spared the worst of the horrors, also made her sacrifices. Indeed, since it encompassed the entire globe, one feels humble in attempting to address World War II in its larger scope, and senses the understatement of hoping that it was the last civil war of Western Civilization.

Unlike many other major conflicts, World War II began with no illusions. In World War I, for example, both sides expected a short war and an easy victory. In contrast, the generation that came of age in 1939 was well aware of the trials and costs ahead. My own vivid memory of my youth, I believe even more vivid than the experience of Pearl Harbor Day, dates back to September 3, 1939, when I sat with my parents in the Manila Hotel, as we all strained our ears to hear Prime Minister Neville Chamberlain's simple, grim words: "Now Great Britain is at war with Germany. You can imagine what a bitter blow this is to me." The phrase "war with Germany" was fateful indeed.

At that time, we in the Philippines, along with peoples all over the world, hoped that the period of inactivity following the declaration of hostilities — what some called the "Phoney War" — would continue indefinitely. But it was not to be. In early May, 1940, Western Europe — then, later, Eastern Europe and the Far East — were caught up in a series of events the like of which had never been seen before.

But in the tragedy that befell millions certain developments gave hope for the future. Britain and the United States were successful, to an unprecedented degree, in forging what Prime Minister Winston Churchill early visualized: "two nations, marching shoulder to shoulder, in a noble brotherhood of arms." Those two nations were joined later by France and others, and in conjunction with the Soviet Union, they liberated Europe, including the people of Germany, from the yoke of Nazism. Naturally, I am proud of the role my father played in this effort, while one of my own compensations for advancing years is the feeling that I, among millions of others played a miniscule part.

World War II has been documented and was photographed extensively, but the hunger for more information on the subject remains. It is my hope that this book, portraying sacrifice and nobility on both sides of a European War that developed into global strife, will contribute to the mutual understanding between former allies and antagonists that is so necessary to the future of the civilized world.

John S.D. Eisenhower

Bernard Law Montgomery

It is a popular fallacy that generals, who achieve fame and significant recognition only through war, are themselves warlike. In the 1914-18 War, a cataclysm which very nearly destroyed the flower of British manhood, my father was a young officer in the trenches in France until he was very badly wounded. After recovering, he returned to the front and served on the staff. These early experiences taught him that it was essential to conduct military operations so that the loss of life was kept to a minimum.

In the Second World War, when my father first commanded the Eighth Army in North Africa, Sicily and Italy, and then the 21st Army Group in North-West Europe, he was able to put into practice what he had both learned in the first conflict, and studied in great detail between the wars. The largest military operation ever undertaken in the history of warfare was the invasion of Normandy in June 1944, when my father commanded all the ground forces of the Allied Armies. Then, as always, the morale of his troops was one of his foremost preoccupations, and he would comment that "there are no bad soldiers, only bad generals". Perhaps it was this characteristic, together with a clear recognition of the efficiency and professional skills of his opponents, that made him one of the last great captains.

In his final message to the troops from Luneburg Heath in May 1945 my father concluded with the words: "We have won the German war. Let us now win the peace". This is the constant lesson of history, and worthy of study by both young and old. To maintain peace in the aftermath of the Second World War, it was essential for the free democratic nations of the Western economic systems to form a strong alliance, and to sustain it against all opposition.

It was this consideration which led to the formation of NATO, which ensured the continuing presence in Europe of the United States of America. The Federal Republic of Germany, once our opponent, has for many years been an important ally, and the alliance has grown with the gradual inclusion of most countries in Western Europe. NATO has given strength through unity, created dialogue between diverse nations, and is our main hope that peace will prevail.

Viscount Montgomery of Alamein CBE

Erwin Rommel

The Second World War, in which Hitler's power reached its zenith as well as its end, was a world drama in which millions of people lost their happiness, their health and their lives. We can only hope that it will prove the last major war, for another conflict of comparable dimensions would probably, in the light of advanced arms technology, endanger the survival of the whole of humanity.

Despite initial military successes, Germany lost the Second World War. In the Soviet Union, her armed forces were pushed further and further back following the Battle of Stalingrad of 1942-3. Her position in North Africa was surrendered after Field Marshal Montgomery's victory at El Alamein. The successful landing of the American and British troops in Italy opened up a further front on European soil. And finally, the invasion of Normandy under General Eisenhower and Field Marshal Montgomery developed into one of the greatest military victories in history. It was after this that the strength of the German armed forces flagged, owing ultimately to the successive blows dealt by the American and British air forces to the supply of raw materials, to the armaments industry, and to the transport system of the Third Reich.

After the war ended, the German people had to come to terms with the fact that it was Adolf Hitler who was responsible for its inception. Once the full extent of the Nazi atrocities had become evident, they even accustomed themselves to the conviction that it was better to have lost the war under Hitler than to have won it with Hitler. It was not a realisation that came easily to anyone in the face of four million dead soldiers, but it was imperative to embrace it in order to regain self respect.

Americans, Britons and Frenchmen showed themselves to be magnanimous victors. Within their respective occupation zones, they helped the Germans restore the democracy which Hitler's dictatorship had supplanted in 1933. The Federal Republic of Germany was founded and accepted into the family of free peoples as an equal member, and as an ally within the framework of NATO. May these associations fulfil their objectives to secure our future freedom and peace.

And may the remembrance of the Second World War stay alive in the hearts of the defeated as a warning against ideologies hostile to liberty, while at the same time encouraging all democratic nations to continue their progress along the path they have since trod in the interests of human dignity and peace in our world.

Oberbürgermeister Manfred Rommel

A striking and memorable study of a German soldier dismally
surveying the desolation that his army is leaving behind.

INTRODUCTION

Hardly anyone on Earth can have an entirely unbiased view of the causes, course and aftermath of the Second World War, nor of the manner in which they should be presented in a single-volume history. No book could possibly please everybody, nor escape criticism from many.
This will be no exception.

Nonetheless, I have set out during the seven years that this book has been in preparation to write a concise military history of the conflict from as balanced a viewpoint as I can achieve. I have tried to judge military actions and generalship, and the character of the principal leaders and combatants, from the position of a neutral observer aided by hindsight. The fact that the distinguished sons of outstanding opposing commanders of the war have been prepared to write forewords and put their names to this concept suggests that I have, in part at least, been successful. However, neutral observation does not preclude conclusions that might be deemed controversial. Those who disagree with my conclusions will doubtless accuse me of bias. But that is life.

It is important to recognise that this is a military history, with only such political historical content as I have felt to be necessary if the military course of the war is to be understood. This book does not — indeed could not in one volume — pretend to be a complete history of the period, and consequently deals very little with the non-military barbarities of the Nazi period in Europe, with the plight of prisoners of war in Europe and Asia, or with the status and activities of apparently neutral countries. I should perhaps also add that, in many ways, this is not an academic book, and that I have not been ashamed to allow a little humour and occasional personal reminiscence to creep into the text and the captions to the photographs.

To me, the glory of the book is the wealth of pictures, many of them unseen since their first airing in wartime newspapers, which have been unearthed by the unfailing efforts of the picture researcher for this project, my wife, Anne Matanle. Although there are many great photographs which connoisseurs of the genre will have seen a number of times before, there are more which have been little published, if at all, and which reveal new aspects of life amidst the chaos of war. Our thanks are due to the staff of The Keystone Collection in London's dockland, now one of the world's most exciting collections of news pictures, for their help during the years of preparation.

I should also like to thank Mr Terry Charman of the Imperial War Museum in London for his considerable efforts in checking the text and captions for accuracy, and for his extremely helpful suggestions which have improved this work considerably. Thanks are also due to a great many friends, acquaintances and people who don't know me from Adam who have wittingly or unwittingly helped me with information and suggestions for sources for this book.

Finally, I should like to thank you, in advance, for reading it,
and to express my hope that you find it enjoyable.

Ivor Matanle

Ivor Matanle

CHAPTER 1

CAUSE AND EFFECT
VERSAILLES TO POLAND AND THE PACT OF STEEL

Events cease to be of our own time, and acquire the perspective of history, suddenly yet unobtrusively. To those who fought against, or suffered under the tyrannies of the Second World War, or who were brought up during those turbulent years, the transition happened quite recently — perhaps during the late Sixties or early Seventies. For those born since the greatest war man has yet known, images and recollections of the Second World War seem quaintly old-fashioned; as much a thread of the tapestry of time as the Black Death or the Spanish Armada. In either case, the sense of detachment that historical perspective provides makes it possible to view both the war itself, and the events that led to its outbreak, with a degree of balanced judgement and impartiality that would have been impossible when the War was still part of the world's immediate experience.

Yet, although the Second World War has undeniably become part of the fabric of history, its effects and consequences shape the very structure of our lives and the politics of the governments under which we live. No previous conflict has had as great an influence upon subsequent events and thought. Most of the wars of history have resolved a dispute, asserted sovereignty, or suppressed rebellion without causing major long-term changes to the course of world history,

public opinion in Britain and France to the justness of Versailles was, in turn, a powerful argument for inaction by those countries when Hitler's still embryonic army invaded the demilitarised Rhineland in 1936 — and the essentially flabby and indecisive nature of the League of Nations both stifled the individualism and decisiveness of its members, and strengthened the resolve of the Fascist powers to take what they coveted by force. The political structure created after the Great War in a spirit of peace by President Wilson, Clemenceau, Lloyd George and their successors was in fact a blueprint for conflict and disaster.

Even worse, from a political standpoint, were the efforts of the British and French politicians of the mid-Thirties to uphold that structure and maintain the peace at all costs. Paradoxically, by 1938, the only cost at which peace could be maintained was the certainty of subsequent war, and it is clear, with hindsight, that the very weakness displayed by Britain's Neville Chamberlain and Lord Halifax at the time of the Munich Agreement in September 1938 was Hitler's most powerful incentive to march on Czechoslovakia in the Spring of 1939, and to plan the attack on Poland, first for August, then for September. Hitler believed that Britain and France would not go

1 It is not easy to decide just how much of the unanimity of rejoicing that shines out of this and other pictures of Hitler's tour of the Sudetenland after occupation was carefully orchestrated propaganda, and how much was genuine. Events of the time showed that there was real enthusiasm among many of the Sudeten Germans, but it surely cannot have been as totally uniform as this picture suggests.

culture or political thinking. The Second World War was the War that nobody wanted, that everybody expected, and from which only the USSR gained territorial advantage, albeit at huge cost. So how did it happen?

There was no one cause, no one train of events, no single course of political thought that alone brought about the greatest single human tragedy the world has known. The causes of the Second World War are to be found in the combined and coincidental influences of three principal trains of events. The first of these is the political; the consequence of the Great Powers' failure after the First World War to take advantage of the opportunities offered for the creation of a new, stable order. By imposing upon the German people, who never considered that they had lost the war, unrealistic terms under the Treaty of Versailles, they ensured the political and military humiliation of Germany, which with the Weimar Republic's leaders responsibility for its acceptance, was the greatest single plank upon which Hitler built his popular support. The ambivalent attitude of

2 Hermann Goering, later to be one of the architects of Nazi Germany and *Reichsmarschall* commanding the *Luftwaffe*, flew fighters for the German Army Air Service from 1915 to 1918, and was awarded the coveted 'Ordre pour le Merite', known as the Blue Max, in May 1918. He became the last commander of von Richthofen's JG1 'Flying Circus'.

3 Lenin, whose real name was Vladimir Ilyich Ulyanov, speaking in Petrograd, formerly St Petersburg, against the revolutionary government in March 1917. Lenin's Bolsheviks (the word means 'great', and was used to mean 'majority') swept to power on November 7th 1917 in the October revolution, the Russian calendar of the time being out of step with that of other countries.

4 On November 11th 1918, the Armistice that effectively ended the Great War was signed in a railway coach in a wood at Compiegne. In 1940, Hitler was to have the identical railway coach taken from a museum back to the same wood for the signing of the surrender of France. Here, Marshal Foch, Allied Commander in Chief, stands to receive the German plenipotentiaries in 1918.

5 Like Adolf Hitler, Mussolini loved to pose and posture, although unlike Hitler, in his early years of power, he projected an image of a cultured performer and family man. Here, in an undated picture from the twenties, Mussolini is revealed as the musician.

Cause and Effect

to war in defence of Poland, and that Poland could be defeated in isolation as Czechoslovakia and Austria had been before.

The second stream of events to make a major contribution to the coming of the Second World War was the succession of economic crises of the Twenties and Thirties, and their aftermaths. The willingness of the Weimar government to print money to meet ever-growing demands on its resources caused devastating inflation that ravaged Germany throughout 1922 and 1923 and reduced the value of the mark catastrophically. In 1921, a reasonably stable currency had stood at 75 marks to the dollar. By January 1923, the mark was 18,000 to the dollar; by November one dollar was worth 4 billion marks. The savings and investments of a traditionally thrifty and comparatively wealthy German middle class became worthless. Not surprisingly, they blamed the Weimar government — and their dis-affection provided a fertile seedbed for Hitler's later promises of a new German prosperity and industrial might.

Perhaps an even greater economic contribution to the coming of war was made by the financial crisis and subsequent Great Depression of 1929 to 1933. Not only did the spectacle of the great powers writhing in economic disarray provide a credible background to Hitler's assertions of a viable National Socialist alternative in Germany, but the coming of Roosevelt and the New Deal, by galvanising a new self-assertiveness and confidence into American life, greatly increased the power of the American isolationist lobby.

1 The economic upheaval in Germany following the end of the war, the humiliation of Versailles and the disastrous economic policies of the Weimar Republic brought about monstrous inflation. A rash of news pictures portraying the worthlessness of the currency appeared – this one shows boys with their kite made of banknotes.

2 Benito Mussolini, the son of a blacksmith from the Romagna, was born in 1883, and founded Europe's first fascist regime in October 1922 after the 'March on Rome' in the previous March. This picture dates from March 1928, and shows him addressing a rally to celebrate the ninth anniversary of the founding of his Fascist Party in 1919.

3 The Wall Street Crash of October 1929, itself a symptom of widespread international financial instability, caused reverberations through the economic structure of Europe. Alongside the other economic crises that bedevilled the industrialised world at the turn of the decade, the Wall Street Crash played a part in creating the attitudes among German industrialists that enabled Hitler to gain their support.

16

To Hitler, watching from afar a succession of Neutrality Acts pass through Congress, it seemed certain that America would never go to war in Europe, and he miscalculated accordingly. Those who campaign in Europe for unilateral nuclear disarmament in the Eighties might pause to consider the lessons in the workings of human nature offered by the Thirties.

The third great course of events that drove the world inexorably to war was the growth of militant totalitarian nationalism. In Russia in 1917, first the February Revolution, which led to the government of Alexander Kerensky, then the Bolshevik October Revolution led by Vladimir Ulyanov, known as Lenin, swept the autocratic Tsarist monarchy from power and established the first of many oligarchic and undemocratic 'democracies' in Europe. Under the Bolsheviks, Russia proselytised the principles of the International. Yet, under Lenin's successor, Josef Stalin, who became General Secretary of the Communist Party in 1922, and achieved supreme power after ousting Trotsky in 1927, Mother Russia became inward-looking, reeling under a scale of tyranny unknown since Torquemada as the Communist government consolidated its hold on the vast confederation of states now known as the USSR, before seeking to extend its horizons.

The success of the Russian revolution in dispensing with the old order inspired Communist revolutionary movements in most of the countries of Western Europe, particularly Germany, Italy, France, Austria and Hungary. Indeed, Communist governments held power briefly in both Budapest and Bavaria after the First World War. It was in the backlash response to these revolutionary pressures that the extreme right-wing Fascist and Nationalist movements were born.

The first was in Italy under Gabriele D'Annunzio, who, in 1919, marched on and took Fiume on the Adriatic, then claimed by Yugoslavia, to the universal approval of the Italian press and the qualified disapproval of the Italian Government. Public adoration of

6

7

4 Japan's invasion of Manchuria following the so-called Mukden incident of September 18th 1931, and the creation of Japan's puppet 'Empire of Manchukuo' began the protracted struggle between China and Japan that lasted throughout the thirties and formed a background both to the rise of the military government in Japan and to the polarisation of US attitudes to Japanese aggression. Japan left the League of Nations on March 27th 1933.

5 At the end of January 1933, years of political manoeuvre and intimidation by Adolf Hitler brought to reality his cherished dream of the Chancellorship of Germany. Here the aged President Hindenburg, the hero of the First World War, shakes hands with the man whom he never trusted, and whose aspirations to chancellorship he had opposed.

6 The fire that destroyed the German Reichstag on February 27th 1933 was in fact started by Goering's agents, but was blamed on Communists to provide an excuse for the suspension of civil liberties and the taking of the first steps towards the creation of the one-party police state. A half-witted Dutchman named Marinus van der Lubbe was tried and convicted for starting the fire.

7 On March 16th 1935, Hitler introduced conscription for young men of military age in Germany, thereby contravening totally the Treaty of Versailles. In September, a new flag incorporating the Swastika was awarded to the armed forces. Here, on 8th November 1935, the sea of steel helmets belongs to new recruits swearing their oath of fealty to Hitler and to the flag outside the Feldherrnhalle in Munich.

the 'new Garibaldi' was such that another ex-servicemen's leader, Benito Mussolini, ever one to emulate the success of others, though not always with equal achievement, sought to give Italy the Nationalist government it seemed to want. In 1922, Mussolini 'marched' on Rome at the head of his Fascist Party (in fact he travelled by train), and gained enough support from those in power to be appointed Prime Minister by King Victor Emmanuel.

His success inspired the already active National Socialists in Bavaria, led by Adolf Hitler, to dream of a March on Berlin, an ideal that seemed possible in October 1923. The state government of Bavaria, led by Gustav von Kahr, had declared a State of Emergency in defiance of the Berlin government led by President Ebert and Chancellor Stresemann and seemed ready either to proclaim its

independence of Germany, or to support a National Socialist coup in Berlin. Hitler, who in September 1923 had scored a major political triumph by being seen beside General Ludendorff, a disgruntled hero of the Great War, on the platform at a Bavarian rally of the *Deutscher Kampfbund* — the German Fighting Union — had led his followers to believe that the moment of power was at hand. When the situation between von Kahr and the Berlin government became less bellicose at the beginning of November, Hitler feared that von Kahr would opt for Bavarian independence rather than revolution against the central government. He believed that this would deprive the National Socialists of their chance of power, and him of his credibility with his party. The result was the ill-advised and poorly planned Munich beerhall putsch, which earned Hitler nine months of peace in

Cause and Effect

Landsberg Prison to write *Mein Kampf*, gained him national fame for his sensationally effective oratory at his trial in April 1924, and conferred upon the National Socialist party five years of obscurity.

By the end of 1933, the political scene was set for the rise to war and the devastation of Europe. Josef Stalin was subjugating the USSR and speculating on the possibility of expansion westward. Adolf Hitler had finally achieved the Chancellorship of Germany, would in the following year gain absolute power, and was dreaming of his advance eastward. Mussolini was the dictator of Italy nurturing territorial ambitions in Africa and the Balkans. Roosevelt had embarked upon his spectacular first Hundred Days, and had begun the process by which the USA would grow in economic strength and ability to arm, yet would seem to onlookers implacably neutral. In

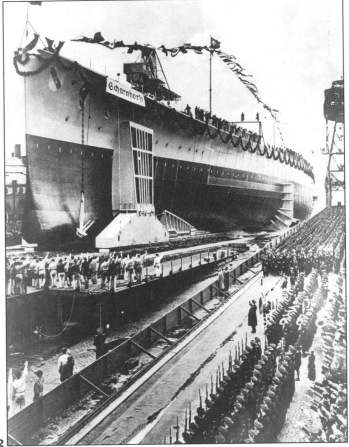

the Far East, Japan had invaded Manchuria, and was turning a baleful eye on China and South-East Asia. Sadly, Britain and France, who should have provided the balancing mechanism and the strength that alone could have averted eventual war, lacked the political direction and will necessary to bring lesser nations to their call and keep the dictators at bay.

Thus began the succession of ever more daring adventures by the Nationalist leaders and by Japan, each countered by little more than admonition and a wish to compromise. In July 1934, Chancellor Dollfuss of Austria was brutally and callously murdered by Austrian Nazis. Mussolini, to his credit, or perhaps because it suited his political needs not to have Hitler baying at his borders, threatened

military intervention, and the threat of Nazi takeover was temporarily averted. In March 1935, the German *Luftwaffe* was officially established in flagrant contravention of the Treaty of Versailles and Britain and France did nothing. On October 3rd 1935, Italy invaded Ethiopia. The League of Nations attempted to impose economic sanctions, which were hopelessly ineffective, and in December the Hoare-Laval plan for exchanges of territory between Italy and Ethiopia without reference to the League was leaked, thus weakening forever such influence as the League had ever had, and causing Parliamentary and public outrage in Britain.

In March 1936, Hitler took a massive gamble, and backed his hunch that the signatories to the Treaty of Versailles would do nothing

1 When Germany's rearmanent became open, the training of pilots became intensive. This is in fact a 1939 picture, and shows pilots at a Luftwaffe training school at which, according to the original news agency caption, cameras were used on the aircraft to record the success or otherwise of attacks carried out during training in aerial combat.

2 Hitler was conscious of the importance of sea power to his intended conquest of Europe, and began the building of a new Kriegsmarine in the mid-thirties. The *Scharnhorst*, a battle-cruiser of almost 35,000 tons, was launched at Wilhelmshaven on October 3rd 1936, and her sister ship *Gneisenau* was launched two months later.

3 The Nuremberg Party Congresses or rallies that took place each September were a major feature of the thirties in Nazi Germany, used as a focus for the German love of pageantry and as a means of expressing through spectacle and mass acclaim the power of the new Germany. Hitler never missed the opportunity of making a major policy speech at Nuremberg, and here is addressing units of the German Army, watched by thousands of the faithful.

4 Hitler's entry into the Rhineland in March 1936 was a bold step taken in the belief, proved correct by events, that the governments of Britain and France would do nothing that endangered peace, and would therefore not take military action despite the contravention of the Treaty of Versailles. In fact, the German troops were ill-trained and prepared, and would not have withstood a determined attempt to repulse them. This picture shows German mobile forces crossing the Hohenzollern Bridge in Cologne.

5 An interesting comparison with the previous picture, this photograph, also taken in Cologne, is a pointer to the very great dependence of the German army (and indeed most other armies) on the horse.

that in any way endangered peace. With hopelessly ill-supported and poorly trained troops, he occupied the Rhineland, specifically declared a demilitarised zone by the Treaty, and awaited developments. None came. Hitler had gained as never before the measure of his opponents.

Other nationalist movements had sprung up around Europe in response to the activities of militant Communist parties. Some, like Sir Oswald Mosley's blackshirts in Britain, were noisy yet ineffective, but, as the political stage was set in the Thirties for the rise to war, a third major Nationalist force arose in Spain under General Franco. In July 1936, Franco led an uprising to unseat the Republican government. Hearing after a performance of one of Wagner's operas at Bayreuth of the outbreak of the Spanish Civil War, Hitler conferred

hastily with Goering and von Blomberg, his War Minister, and decided almost on the spur of the moment to support Franco. Germany supplied aircraft, tanks, technicians and money valued at half a billion marks, and detached a large part of the emergent *Luftwaffe* for what amounted to training in active service. Known as the Condor Legion, this German air force killed hundreds of Spaniards when it bombed Guernica, and perfected in Spain the dive bombing and heavy bombing of civilian areas that were to be so significant a feature of later *Blitzkrieg* advances across Europe. After the Civil War, Germany had a corps of battle-trained airmen that no other Western nation possessed, a resource that was to prove of immense value in the training of the world's most powerful air force.

Mussolini was committed to the Spanish Civil War to an even

6 The strength of Russia under Josef Stalin in the East became a major concern for Adolf Hitler in the late thirties. Unless he could be sure that Russia would not retaliate, he could not risk advances eastwards. Here, Stalin in 1935 receives a deputation of workers.

7 Although Germany and Japan had signed an Anti-Comintern Pact in November 1936, Japan rescinded her membership of the Pact after the cynically motivated Non-Aggression Pact between Germany and Russia had been signed in August 1939. But, following the signing of a new ten-year alliance between Germany, Italy and Japan in September 1940, at talks with Japanese Foreign Minister Yosuke Matsuoka in the Spring of 1941, Hitler drastically miscalculated American armed strength and made a secret promise to declare war on the USA if hostilities occurred between the USA and Japan. In December, that promise was honoured after Pearl Harbour.

greater degree than Hitler, and, recognising this, one of Hitler's primary objectives in his support of Franco was to keep the war going, hoping thereby to maintain a state of emnity between Mussolini and the politicians of Britain and France. For Hitler knew that, whether or not there was to be war, he needed Mussolini on his side. In October, after a successful visit to Hitler in Berchtesgaden, Count Ciano, Mussolini's son-in-law and Foreign Minister, signed a protocol that set out a common policy for Germany and Italy in the field of foreign affairs. This was the Berlin-Rome Axis, the beginning of the alliance that was to secure Mussolini's downfall.

In the following month, Germany and Japan signed the Anti-Comintern Pact against the Communist International, and, in July 1937, as the Spanish Civil War raged on, the Japanese used the Marco Polo Bridge incident, a skirmish near Peking, as a pretext to invade China. Sensing the way things seemed to be going, Italy joined the Anti-Comintern Pact in November 1937, and the following month the Japanese killed some 150,000 people, mostly civilians, around Nanking.

The following year was a fateful landmark in the progress towards war. On November 5th 1937, Goering and the service chiefs had been

8 Franklin Roosevelt became the thirty-second President of the United States on March 4th 1933 at the age of fifty one years and thirty-three days. He took power at a time of economic crisis – seventeen million unemployed, and the nation's banking in a state of near-collapse – and restored comparative confidence and direction with remarkable speed. This picture was taken in 1938, as he began to steer American thinking away from its traditional isolationism.

1 On March 13th 1938, German troops entered Austria and annexed Germany's neighbour, and Hitler's native land, into the Reich. This picture shows troops of the 61st Infantry Regiment passing beneath a raised customs barrier at Kufstein.

2 Hitler entered Austria on March 13th, visited Linz, where he had lived during his schooldays, and laid a wreath on the grave of his parents in the churchyard at Leonding. He received a rapturous reception wherever he went and on March 16th entered Vienna to scenes of wild enthusiasm on all sides.

3 The enthusiasm of vast crowds that welcomed Hitler to Vienna – this scene was photographed in the Heldenplatz on 16th March 1938 – was fuelled by the announcement that, on April 10th there would be a national plebiscite to establish the Austrian people's view of union between Austria and the Reich. The plebiscite produced a ninety-nine per cent vote in favour of Anschluss.

told by Hitler in committee that war was inevitable, but that it would come at a time of their choosing. As 1938 began, Hitler took steps to annex Austria, believing, correctly, that once again Britain and France would do nothing. The annexation –*Anschluss* – was completed in a matter of hours on March 13th. Threats against Czechoslovakia arising from Hitler's claim to the Sudetenland, an area of Czechoslovakia inhabited mainly by German-speaking Czechs, led Europe to believe during April and May that it was on the brink of war. After further threats, Hitler secured from Britain's Prime Minister Neville Chamberlain and the French Premier Edouard Daladier at the Munich Conference in September complicity in forcing Czechoslovakia to cede the Sudetenland and some of her most valuable mineral resources to Germany. The willingness of Chamberlain to co-operate in Hitler's territorial ambitions when peace was threatened confirmed Hitler's belief that his military adventures would continue to go unchallenged.

Only six months after guaranteeing in return for the Sudetenland that Czechoslovakia would not be attacked, Hitler's armies occupied Bohemia and Moravia on March 15th 1939 and annexed Memel, a city of Lithuania inhabited by ethnic Germans, on March 23rd. Once again, Britain and France did nothing, but, at last, Chamberlain spelt out clearly in Parliament British condemnation of Hitler's latest aggression and made it clear that an attack on Poland would not be

5

6

7

4 Hitler's political gambit that had impressed Mussolini most was the way in which he had ridden roughshod over Prime Minister Neville Chamberlain of Great Britian and Premier Daladier of France at the Munich Conference to determine the future of the Sudetenland in September 1938. Here, Chamberlain and Mussolini are in earnest conversation at that conference, on 30th September.

5 All smiles at the Munich conference, Chamberlain was quite taken in by the apparent willingness of Adolf Hitler to sign a scrap of paper guaranteeing peace in return for Britain and France not opposing Germany's occupation of the Sudetenland area of Czechoslovakia. Six months later, German troops occupied the remainder of Czechoslovakia in defiance of the Munich Agreement.

6 On his arrival back in England, Neville Chamberlain made an oft-quoted speech promising 'Peace in our time'. As he spoke, he waved the piece of paper that Hitler had that morning absent-mindedly signed. On the same morning, Hitler and Mussolini had agreed informally that the time would come when they would fight side by side against Britain and France.

7 The ceding of the Sudetenland to Germany (without consultation with the Czechs, who were not even invited to the Munich Conference) had cost Czechoslovakia 11,000 square miles of her country, two thirds of her coal and eighty-six per cent of her chemical resources. Hitler was greeted with great enthusiasm when he visited the newly-occupied Sudetenland in the autumn of 1938.

tolerated. On 30th March, Chamberlain drafted the British guarantee of Poland's independence which was to become the pivot of war. This was accepted by Joseph Beck, Polish Foreign Minister, and consented to, after the event, by France. On April 26th, after Italy seized Albania, Britain reintroduced conscription, a clear indication that, at long last, the British policy of appeasement was being abandoned. Despite this, Hitler was firm in his belief that there would be no retaliation from Britain and France if he attacked Poland.

On May 22nd, Mussolini finally decided to throw in Italy's lot militarily with Germany, and the Pact of Steel was signed, committing each nation to join the other at war. Hitler felt that he had tied up one more loose end, but he was anxious to be sure that Russia would not intervene if Germany attacked Poland. In 1938, the Soviet Union had

stopped its aid to the Republicans in Spain, and had thereby secured Franco's victory. Hitler therefore had cause to believe that Stalin wanted no quarrel with Germany, but was concerned at the clear fact that Russia was engaged in protracted negotiations for a treaty with Britain and France. Something had to be done.

In May, after a major speech from Hitler which lacked his usual attacks on 'Bolshevik Jews', Stalin suddenly replaced Litvinov, the Western-orientated Russian Foreign Minister with the tough, uncompromising and seemingly indestructible Molotov. A few days later, a new Russian ambassador arrived in Berlin. Stalin, playing both sides against each other, gave Hitler hope of a treaty without breaking off negotiations with Britain and France, thereby hoping to obtain from Hitler concessions which would enable Russia to occupy the

Baltic states of Latvia, Estonia and Lithuania without intervention from Germany. Early in August, the British and French military missions found themselves being delayed in their attempts to conduct talks with Marshal Voroshilov in Moscow, and on August 21st 1939, Stalin announced his intention of signing a Non-Aggression Pact with Germany.

With the signing of this Pact on August 23rd, Hitler's way to Poland seemed open. But, on August 25th, the signing of the Anglo-Polish alliance was announced in London, and Hitler realised that his attempt to isolate Poland had failed. Less than twelve hours before the deadline, the planned German invasion of Poland on the 26th August was halted. On the 27th, Hitler, now less confident about the future of his enterprise, but committed to it, set a new date for the invasion of September 1st. On the 28th, Britain formally rejected Hitler's arrogant and bombastic offer of 'protection' for the British Empire in return for non-intervention by Britain if Poland were attacked, thereby declining to take part in a re-enactment of the fiasco

1 This shot of the two motorcycle troops being greeted by the crowd has the characteristics of an arranged picture. Although the people in the immediate foreground are obviously delighted with their German conquerors, those in the background are less certain.

2 Hitler put many more troops into the Sudetenland than would have seemed appropriate for a peaceable occupation with which the population was in full accord. This column marched into Rumberg, to the usual accompaniment of cheers and raised arms – but note the proliferation of official-looking photographers.

3 In April 1939, German aircraft production was at full stretch, and pictures showing the extent of German achievement and technology were issued almost daily as part of the Reich Propaganda Ministry's drive to influence world opinion.

4 As war approached, meetings between the dictators and their advisers took place frequently, although rarely as publicly as this picture suggests. In the front row are (left to right:) Goering, Mussolini, Hitler and Count Ciano, Mussolini's son-in-law and Foreign Minister. Rudolf Hess is between and behind Mussolini and Hitler; Heinrich Himmler is between and behind Hitler and Ciano.

5

6

5 Until Germany had succeeded in gaining the Soviet Union's signature to a non-aggression pact, Hitler dared not move against Poland. This picture shows Joachim von Ribbentrop, German Foreign Minister, meeting Josef Stalin for a discussion before the signing of the pact.

6 Albert Forster, *Gauleiter* (District Leader of the Nazi Party) in Danzig, who orchestrated much of the dissension in the Free Port of Danzig between the Poles and the Germans who sought to intimidate them. Forster was summoned to Berlin on August 7th 1939 to experience the wrath of Hitler at the failure of the Nazi threats to intimidate Polish officials in the city.

7

8

7 On September 1st 1939, the German armoured columns and infantry, preceded by dive bombers, advanced into Poland. They began their attack in the small hours of the morning – a little later, grinning soldiers tore down the Polish frontier barriers for the camera.

8 The final act in the pre-war saga of alliance between the axis powers in fact came a year after hostilities in Europe had commenced, when, on September 27th 1940 Germany Japan and Italy signed in Berlin a ten-year military, political and economic alliance. Seated (left to right) are Count Ciano, Italian Foreign Minister, Joachim von Ribbentrop, German Foreign Minister, and Saburo Kurusu, Japanese envoy in Berlin.

of Munich. But, because Britain also advised Germany that both Britain and Poland were prepared to meet to negotiate, Hitler believed he detected signs of weakness. He thought he saw evidence that Britain would not, after all, act if Poland were attacked. He therefore demanded that a Polish emissary be sent to Berlin with full powers to negotiate and settle. Knowing that this implied a Polish surrender, the Poles refused.

Thus, on September 1st, the German tanks rolled, the guns roared, and the *Wehrmacht* moved forward into Poland. The Second World War was now virtually inevitable. Germany greeted the news with silent resignation; there was no rejoicing as there had been in 1914.

At 9am on September 3rd, Britain's ambassador Sir Neville Henderson in Berlin delivered an ultimatum. Hitler's worst fears were confirmed; this time Chamberlain was not prepared to compromise. The ultimatum said that, unless satisfactory assurances of German action to call off the attack on Poland were received by 11am, a state of war would exist between Britain and Germany. Hitler had gone too far, was too arrogant, too aware of his own political vulnerability to retreat. He did not reply to the ultimatum.

At 11.15am on September 3rd 1939, Neville Chamberlain announced to a hushed nation and an appalled world that Britain was at war with Germany. It was the beginning of the greatest conflict the world has yet seen.

CHAPTER 2

THE WORLD WATCHES AND WAITS
POLAND, FINLAND AND THE PHONEY WAR

By evening on September 3rd 1939, both Britain and France had declared war on Germany. Both countries — indeed most of the world — expected events to gather speed; for a state of war such as had been known a generation earlier in France rapidly to be re-established. Hitler had snatched and held the political initiative for so long that he was expected by almost everybody to seek to retain it in the West, even as his armies subjugated Poland in the East. For, phoney as the war might have seemed in Birmingham or Rouen, in Detroit or Toronto, to the hard-pressed Poles the war was terrifyingly real. By the time France declared war on the evening of 3rd September, the Poles had been in battle for almost three days.

The German technique of *blitzkrieg* — lightning war — was used for the first time in Poland, and proved to be devastatingly effective. At 0430 hrs on 1st September, 48 divisions, six of them armoured, with 1,400 aircraft, invaded on three fronts, from East Germany, East Prussia and Slovakia. The master plan for the invasion, Case White, called for rapid neutralisation of Polish communications, airfields and troop concentrations, and the Junkers 87 'Stuka' dive bomber was used with deadly effect as a form of airborne artillery, taking over the role of harassing enemy positions that had previously been carried out by more vulnerable land based guns. Nonetheless, an early attempt on September 1st to dispose of the Polish Air Force, which had a total of 842 largely obsolete aircraft, only 400 of which were

battle-worthy, succeeded only in part, and the Polish airmen fought on heroically and with surprising effectiveness throughout the campaign.

On Sunday September 3rd, after days of bombing of Warsaw by German He 111 twin-engined bombers, and successful bombing raids by the Poles on German armour in the Radom-Piotrkow area, to the South West of Warsaw, the 1st and 4th *Panzer* divisions crossed the River Warta, and German forces captured Czestochowa. In the North West, the Polish Corridor, which had been a major cause of the dispute between Germany and Poland, was severed. By September 5th, the Germans had broken through to the Vistula and had taken Bydgoszcz in the North West, had destroyed the town of Sulejow by

1 Within minutes of Prime Minister Neville Chamberlain's radio announcement to a hushed Britain of the state of war with Germany, the silence was broken by the howl of London's air raid sirens. Civilians rushed for cover, inadvertently rehearsing what would later become depressingly normal – but it was all a false alarm.

2 On September 3rd 1939, this London newspaper seller passed into popular history by becoming the subject of one of the most used pictures of the Second World War. His placard says it all.

3 In London, the expectation of war had been high for many months since the Munich agreement of 1938 had delayed hostilities. This picture of Piccadilly Circus was taken in April 1939 – note the exhortation to enrol for National Service on the protective boarding erected around the famous statue of Eros.

4 As the probability of war increased, Britain's long standing plans for the evacuation of children from London to country areas away from the danger of bombing and expected gas attacks were put into action. Here, on 1st September 1939, police and railwaymen help some of the 800 children who went, without their parents, to undisclosed destinations.

5 The characteristic wing profile and fixed undercarriage of the Junkers 87 Stuka dive bomber became feared throughout Europe, particularly in Poland, where the population was the first to experience the horrors of dive-bombing before an armoured advance that was characteristic of Blitzkrieg.

6 Heroism was almost universal among Polish defenders of their homeland against the Nazi onslaught, and many Polish soldiers and airmen escaped to fight on with the Allies. These soldiers were not so lucky – they were captured on 7th September 1939 after heroic defence of the Westerplatte.

7 Possibly the first picture of Hitler as warlord, an increasingly common representation as the war developed. In this shot, taken on 18th September 1939, are (left to right) Goering, Bodenschatz, Keitel, Hitler and Foreign Minister Ribbentrop.

8 At six a.m. on 17th September 1939, Russia took advantage of the concentration of Polish effort against the German invader in the West to invade, with German connivance, from the East. These troops entering Poland were the first of many who were to make use of Hitler's war to achieve the subjugation of Eastern Europe. On October 4th, Nikita Kruschev, Secretary of the Ukrainian Communist Party and later to aspire to greater fame, announced the Communisation of East Poland.

concentrated bombing, and had forced the Polish High Command under Marshal Edward Smigly-Rydz to order a retreat. The advance on Warsaw seemed unstoppable, and on September 5th the Polish Government left Warsaw for Lublin.

By September 8th, the Battle of the Bzura, West of Warsaw, had begun in earnest. The 4th *Panzer* Division, which had advanced 225km in 7 days, lost 60 tanks in an attempt to storm the outer defences of the capital. Recognising that they had a tougher fight on their hands than had been anticipated, the *Wehrmacht* moved substantial reinforcements to Poland for the final assault on Warsaw, and by the 15th, the capital was surrounded. Despite ultimatums on the 16th and the 25th, mass air attacks on the city and huge fires, the

Poles fought on until the 27th, when after a massive indiscriminate artillery bombardment of Warsaw the Polish garrison commander was forced to offer to surrender.

Meanwhile, Russia had invaded Poland from the East on 17th September, advancing 100km with virtually no resistance, and the Polish Government and all surviving Polish aircrews had decamped to Rumania.

So, in Poland, the war was anything but phoney. By the time Hitler arrived for his victory parade in Warsaw on October 5th, 10,572 Germans had died in the fighting and 30,322 had been wounded. Some 217 German tanks and 285 planes had also been destroyed. The Poles had lost about 50,000 dead, some 750,000 prisoners of war to

The World Watches and Waits

Germany plus about 217,000 to the USSR, and 333 aircraft. 105,000 Poles escaped abroad to fight again. Although fast, the German victory was not easy.

Away from the agony of Poland, to those on land there seemed to prevail an uneasy peace. Britain and France had mobilised from September 1st, and the British Expeditionary Force was landed in France during September and October. On September 9th, Marshal Smigly-Rydz had appealed to General Gamelin of France for decisive action in the West to divert some of the force of the German assault away from Poland, but to no avail. The French Army demolished three bridges over the Rhine during minor skirmishes east of the Moselle, but elsewhere the armies waited. Hitler, in his mountain retreat at Berchtesgaden, had at first intended that his attack in the West, on Holland, Belgium and Luxemburg, should be mounted in October 1939, but drew back and deferred the assault until 1940.

The lack of action was not for want of decision on the part of the great powers. The United States, saddled with the Neutrality Acts of the Thirties, had officially announced her neutrality on September 5th, and had established with the Latin American states a Pan American Security Zone by which military operations were forbidden within 1,000km of American shores. But Australia, New Zealand and British India had declared war on the same day as Britain and France. South Africa had declared war on Germany on September 6th; Canada had followed suit on September 10th. But all remained quiet — except at sea.

The seaborne war had begun almost as soon as Chamberlain had risen from his microphone in Downing Street. A single RAF Blenheim aircraft had photographed the German Fleet at Wilhelmshaven on September 3rd, and 29 RAF Blenheims and

1 On September 17th, HMS *Courageous*, an ageing aircraft carrier of the Royal Navy, was torpedoed and sunk by the German submarine U-29. This picture had been taken in peacetime, in the mid-thirties.

Above Poland invaded and partitioned.

German Attacks 1-18 Sept.
Russian Attacks 17-18 Sept.
To Germany
To Russia
Pripet Marshes
Agreed Boundary of the German-Soviet Partition 29 Sept. 1939

2 Unlike the Germans, whose arms were virtually all new and manufactured since Hitler's repudiation of the Treaty of Versailles, the French had many large guns that dated from the Great War. This heavy gun, in position awaiting the expected German advance across the Rhine, is an example.

3 Along the Rhine, the fortifications of the Westwall, or Siegfried Line, were large enough to make possible artillery operations from within the concrete emplacements. This picture is dated 27th September 1939.

Wellingtons had attacked the fleet both at Wilhelmshaven and on the Kiel Canal on September 4th, with a loss of 7 aircraft. On September 14th, a German submarine, the U-39, attacked Britain's HMS *Ark Royal*, and was depth charged by accompanying destroyers. Three days later U-29 sank another British aircraft carrier, HMS *Courageous*, and on October 14th the *Kriegsmarine* scored a spectacular success when U-47 penetrated the Royal Navy's 'impregnable' anchorage at Scapa Flow and sank the battleship HMS *Royal Oak*. Two days later, 9 of the new Junkers 88 twin-engined fighter bombers, pride of the *Luftwaffe*, dive-bombed Royal Navy warships at Rosyth in the Firth of Forth, and HMS *Southampton* survived only because a bomb that penetrated her decks failed to

explode. Next day, a similar raid on Rosyth crippled HMS *Iron Duke*.

In December, the German pocket battleship *Admiral Graf Spee*, which had been tracked by British and French ships all autumn, was brought to battle off the River Plate Estuary by the British cruisers *Exeter*, *Ajax* and *Achilles*. The badly damaged HMS *Exeter* was obliged to retire to the Falkland Islands, and was replaced by HMS *Cumberland*, and the three ships lay off the Plate and waited for the *Graf Spee* to emerge. She never came. On Sunday December 17th, her Captain scuttled his ship in the Plate Estuary, where the wreck, later bought by the British for a sight of her radar, burned for a week.

Alarming as these events were, they could not be claimed to be the all-out war that had been expected, not least by Hitler's Generals.

4 By October, Poland was crushed and the Germans organised a major victory parade in Warsaw before turning their attention to the Western Front. Hitler was present in person to take the salute as his conquering divisions marched past.

5 As the continued inactivity on the Western front began to play on the morale of the British public, great efforts were devoted to producing pictures that emphasised Allied friendship and readiness to defeat the foe. This obviously posed picture shows a French officer shaking hands with a British corporal.

6 British troops were on their way to France, expecting quickly to be in action, by the third week of September 1939.

The World Watches and Waits

For, when the 1939 balance of power is studied, Hitler did not have things all his own way.

The Allies had, for a start, considerable naval superiority over Germany. Britain and France between them had 676 ships built or launched; Germany had 130, including 57 U-boats under the command of Commodore, later Admiral, Karl Doenitz, eventually to be Hitler's successor as Fuehrer. Most of the U-boats were short-range Class 1 and 2 boats, intended for coastal operations, and unsuitable as Atlantic raiders.

In the air, the *Luftwaffe* had considerable superiority. At the beginning of September 1939, Goering could claim, and put in the air, no less than 4,700 aircraft, including a formidable fleet of 552 of the sturdy and reliable Junkers 52 three engined transports, and nine squadrons of the Ju 87 Stukas. Against this, the Royal Air Force could muster only 3,600 aircraft, of which a great number were obsolescent, or even downright obsolete, a sad situation that resulted from a lack of defence spending by the government of appeasement in the late Thirties. The French had virtually no modern bombers or fighters, and the Poles, although beginning the war with over 800 largely obsolete aircraft, lost most of them in the terrible fighting in their own country.

Comparison of land forces is not so easy. The Germans had 53 divisions in the field at the outbreak of war, every one of them

1 By December 1939 there had been some degree of integration of the British Expeditionary Force and the French troops, and this picture was issued at the end of the year as 'the first photograph of British and French troops together in the Maginot Line', preparing to drink a toast to the New Year.

2 His Majesty King George VI visited the Maginot Line in France during the phoney war period. This picture shows him, in December 1939, being shown the facilities and equipment of the Maginot Line by General Gamelin.

3 Some British soldiers were given the task of helping French farmers, both to keep them busy and provide a useful propaganda picture! This one is dated 22nd November 1939.

4 Considerable damage was inflicted on Helsinki by Russian air raids. This picture shows a block of flats severely damaged by Russian air attack.

5 The Russians attempted to subdue the Finns in the early winter of 1939/40 by employing the techniques recently demonstrated by the Germans in Poland – heavy bombing, followed by armoured advance. The civilian population of Helsinki were warned to evacuate their homes and this policeman with a megaphone is directing evacuees outside Helsinki's main railway station.

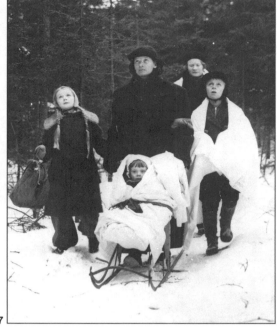

6 The remarkable Field-Marshal Mannerheim, Commander-in-Chief of the Finnish Army, leaving an army HQ with members of his staff on 20th October 1939. Mannerheim was already seventy-two at this time, yet successfully led the defence against vastly superior Russian invaders by employing local knowledge.

7 This poignant picture illustrates the fear held by families in Finland of the Soviet air attacks.

superbly equipped with up-to-date weapons, as one would expect of an army created virtually from nothing in five years. Although the French had 28 divisions, they were, by comparison, poorly equipped with weapons dating mainly from the First World War. The Poles were similarly equipped with rifles and automatic weapons from the Twenties and earlier. The British Army, although professional in outlook, was also sadly ill-equipped, and suffered from too great a belief in the trench warfare tactics which, while they had not won the Great War, could at least be argued not to have lost it.

Why the Allies did not attack Germany in the West when the *Wehrmacht* was preoccupied in Poland has been the subject of much debate, but the answer almost certainly rests in the slowness of French mobilisation, in a mistrust by both French and British of the principles of the mobile war (later espoused earnestly) and in a correct assessment of the strength of German air power. At the Nuremberg War Trials after the War, General Jodl and Field Marshal Keitel asserted that an attack in the West would have 'encountered only feeble resistance', but this has been questioned by many historians and will doubtless be debated many times yet.

The world's attention was diverted from Hitler's war, or the lack of it, when, at the end of November 1939 the USSR renounced its 1932 Soviet-Finnish Non-Aggression Pact and invaded Finland, with the intention of adding the land of the Finns to its expanding empire. Thus began the Winter War, one of the world's great examples of the triumph of local knowledge and sheer tenacity over brute force.

A redoubtable veteran of 72 years, Field-Marshal Mannerheim, was appointed Defender of Finland and Commander in Chief. He set about defending his country with 400,000 men (9 divisions), 145 aircraft, 2 coastal defence vessels and 5 submarines against Soviet forces amounting to 30 divisions, 1,200 tanks, 696 aircraft, 28 surface warships and 11 submarines. The Russians sought to emulate the Germans' tactics of *Blitzkrieg*, bombing Helsinki repeatedly, believing that, once the Finnish government had been subdued, it

8 The gallant Finns, although greatly in the minority, held the Russians at bay throughout a severe winter and inflicted several major defeats. These Finnish soldiers, well camouflaged and properly equipped for the conditions, are awaiting a Russian column.

9 The Finns were not without assistance from soldiers of other countries, although they came in quite small numbers. These men are foreign volunteers, taking a warm drink in the snow. Each man was equipped with a thermos flask as standard issue.

would be straightforward to march across Finland to the Gulf of Bothnia. Field-Marshal Mannerheim knew otherwise. Realising that the Finnish winter would inhibit drastically any army's attempt to cross the country North and East of Lake Ladoga, he withdrew the majority of his forces to defend a line drawn across the narrow Karelian Isthmus and across the area to the North of Lake Ladoga. All told, there were five divisions in the Isthmus, two divisions on the other side of the lake, a mere nine battalions covering the considerable area of Central Finland, and four battalions in independent Lappland.

1 Britain's war cabinet during the phoney war period was unsettled and ridden with disagreement originating in the policy of appeasement which had so recently been proved disastrous. Back row, left to right: Sir John Anderson (Home Secretary), Lord Hankey (Minister without Portfolio), Hoare Belisha (Secretary for War), Winston Churchill (First Lord of the Admiralty), Sir Kingsley Wood (Air Minister), Anthony Eden (Secretary for Dominions), Sir Edward Bridges (Cabinet Secretary). Front Row: Lord Halifax (Foreign Secretary), Sir John Simon (Chancellor of the Exchequer), Neville Chamberlain (Prime Minister), Sir Samuel Hoare (Lord Privy Seal), Admiral Chatfield (Minister of Defence).

2 There was outrage in Finland when the Russians bombed hospitals. This picture was taken shortly after just such a raid, which took place while peace talks between the reluctant Finns and the Russians were being held, in March 1940.

3 Finnish troops pose beside a captured Russian tank in January 1940.

During December, the Soviet Army began to learn the folly of taking on the Finns in an abnormally cold winter. The Soviet 7th Army was stopped dead in the Isthmus; the 8th Army fared no better on the other side of the Lake. Two divisions were utterly destroyed by the Finns at Tolvajarvi on December 12th. The day before, the 163rd Russian division was cut off near Oulu; on the 28th, the 44th Division was ambushed and destroyed. It is estimated that in the first phase of the Winter War, the Russians lost some 27,500 men against Finnish losses of 2,700.

Now the Russians began to recognise their inability to beat the Finns at their own game and changed their tactics. According to Mannerheim, no less than 45 Soviet divisions were deployed on the Finnish front for the second phase of the war at the beginning of 1940, and the tough Marshal Timoshenko was put in command. By mid-February, the Mannerheim Line had been breached, and by early March, as the weather improved and the Finns' natural advantage diminished, Mannerheim had to advise his government to sue for peace. On March 12th, the Russo-Finnish Treaty was signed in Moscow. Finland ceded the Viipuri and Salla districts and a part of Lappland, and was obliged to meet other conditions, but her moral triumph was undiminished. The Soviet position was condemned by the United States, France, Great Britain, Denmark, Norway, Sweden, Belgium, Hungary and Italy. Only Hitler's Germany failed to condemn the attack and remained non-partisan, and, to the fury of Count Ciano, forbade the transport across Germany of arms to be supplied by Italy to the Finns.

On the Western front, however, the winter had passed with only occasional skirmishes and air attacks. Six months after the outbreak of Hitler's war, there remained little war to see. On March 20th, the French Prime Minister Daladier resigned, and was succeeded by Paul Reynaud. On April 3rd, Winston Churchill, who had been appointed First Lord of the Admiralty on September 3rd 1939, became Chairman of the British Government's Military Commitee, another step towards the destiny that was to have a profound effect upon the conduct of the war. On April 4th, Neville Chamberlain told a Conservative Party meeting in London that Hitler, by failing to take advantage of his military superiority in September 1939, had 'missed the bus'.

Just five days later, Hitler invaded Norway. The real war had begun.

CHAPTER 3

THE BATTLE FOR NORWAY
AND THE FALL OF DENMARK

Control of Norway was crucially important to Germany's ability to use its sea power effectively against the Allies, particularly Britain. While Norway was at peace, and unoccupied by either of the fighting powers, there was no threat. But the weakness of Norwegian coastal defences, and the inability of her field army to resist effectively a determined invasion by a stronger power were clear. Admiral Raeder had pointed out several times in 1939 the potential danger to Germany of Britain seizing the initiative and launching its own invasion in Scandinavia — if the powerful Royal Navy had bases at Bergen, Narvik and Trondheim, the North Sea would be virtually closed to Germany, and the *Kriegsmarine* would be at risk even in the Baltic.

At the end of 1939, there had been negotiations between Raeder and Vidkun Quisling, the head of the Norwegian Najonal Samling (National Unity) Party, and a plan had been hatched for a takeover of Norway by political bloodless revolution, following which Quisling would have asked Germany for 'protection'. But, because Quisling, whose name has become synonymous with 'traitor', had only around

4 This picture of Vidkun Quisling, traitor of Norway, in conversation with Adolf Hitler in fact dates from April 1943, but the expression on Quisling's face says much about his total acceptance of the Nazi creed.

5 On April 8th 1940, the day after the Royal Navy force sailed from Scapa Flow, the destroyer HMS *Glowworm* met the 16,000 ton German heavy cruiser Admiral Hipper at sea and was attacked. This picture taken from the Hipper shows the *Glowworm* making smoke.

6 The *Glowworm* was no match for the mighty *Hipper*. As his ship began to sink, the captain of the *Glowworm* radioed that the German fleet was at sea, then used his ship to ram his German attacker, which survived to be scuttled at the end of the war. The radio message diverted the British fleet away from the German landings in Norway to a fruitless chase after German ships, and ensured the success of the German operation.

7&8 As intelligence had led the British government to suspect, the Royal Navy boarding party found a large number of British Merchant Navy prisoners aboard the *Altmark*. Some of the 299 rescued men, with two naval ratings, one with a captured *Kriegsmarine* cap, are shown on their return to safety.

10,000 Norwegians behind him, that idea was abandoned and, on January 27th, Hitler ordered detailed contingency planning of 'Operation Weser', the taking of Norway. At that stage, there was no commitment to the attack on Norway that was to follow in the spring, but two events moved Hitler to the point of action in April.

The first was the USSR's second, and successful assault on Finland, which threatened to put Russia within striking distance both of Swedish mineral resources and of the Norwegian ports. The second, which finally committed Hitler to action, was the interception by HMS *Cossack*, a British destroyer commanded by Captain Philip Vian, of the German ship *Altmark*, officially the supply ship to the *Graff Spee*, which was carrying 299 British Merchant Navy prisoners back to Germany. When the Norwegians had searched the vessel at Bergen, they had not found the prisoners,

who were battened down below decks. But, on the direct orders of Winston Churchill, Captain Vian informed the Norwegians that he was stopping the *Altmark*, boarded the prison ship in Jossing Fjord on February 16th, and released the prisoners, bringing them back to Britain. This made it clear to all concerned that the Norwegians were powerless to act when either power breached international law in Norwegian waters, and emphasised to Hitler the validity of Raeder's fears about a British occupation of Norway. The result was the issuing of two Fuehrer Directives, on February 26th and March 1st, which both appointed a commander for the Norwegian operation, General Nikolaus von Falkenhorst, and made clear that Denmark was to be occupied as part of the same operation.

The invasion of Norway, originally set for March 20th, but postponed to April 9th, was the first major test for the *Kriegsmarine*.

The Battle for Norway

The plan required five major naval groups to take part, respectively taking Narvik, Trondheim, Bergen, Kristiansand/Arendal, and Oslo. Most of the *Kriegsmarine's* available warships were actively involved, and the five groups sailed at various times between the 6th and the 8th of April so as to arrive off their targets simultaneously. Two army corps went with them, the 21st for Norway and the 31st for Denmark. Over a thousand German aircraft were committed to the assault. Amazingly, the Norwegian Government had been provided via a friendly Dutch military attache on April 4th with advance warning of the attack, but had not acted upon the information — if they had mobilised in time, history might have been somewhat different.

The assaults on Trondheim and Bergen went well for the Germans, aside from the damaging by shellfire (and subsequent sinking by the British Fleet Air Arm) of the light cruiser *Konigsberg* at Bergen. The *Karlsruhe* was torpedoed and sunk at Kristiansand by a British submarine (the *Truant*). At Stavanger, the paratroops took Sola airfield and the town without difficulty.

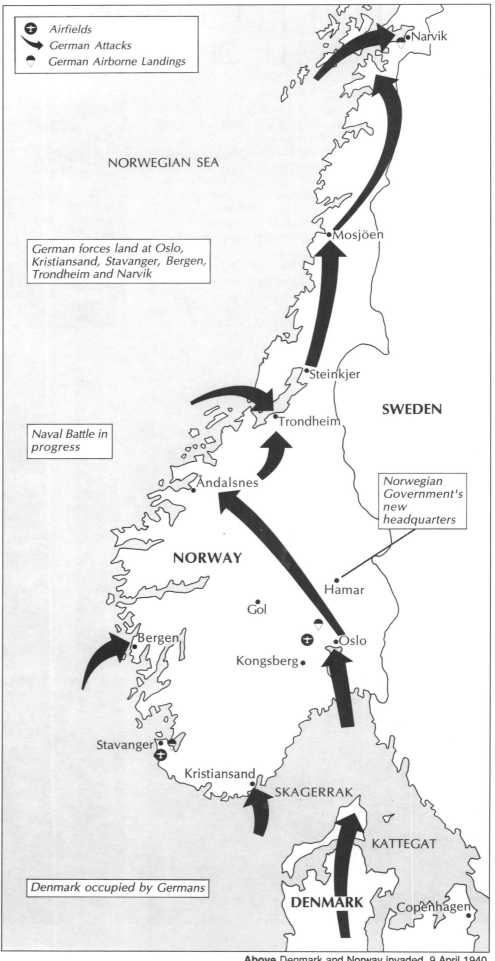

Key:
- ⊕ Airfields
- ⟶ German Attacks
- ▽ German Airborne Landings

NORWEGIAN SEA

German forces land at Oslo, Kristiansand, Stavanger, Bergen, Trondheim and Narvik

Naval Battle in progress

Norwegian Government's new headquarters

Denmark occupied by Germans

Narvik · Mosjöen · Steinkjer · Trondheim · SWEDEN · Åndalsnes · NORWAY · Hamar · Gol · Oslo · Kongsberg · Bergen · Stavanger · Kristiansand · SKAGERRAK · KATTEGAT · DENMARK · Copenhagen

Above Denmark and Norway invaded, 9 April 1940.

Narvik was taken quickly, but not without incident, and largely by treachery. Commodore Paul Bonte's German destroyers demanded the surrender of two Norwegian coastal defence vessels, the *Eidsvold* and the *Norge*. When their commander refused to surrender, his ships were blown out of the water. Almost immediately, Lieutenant-General Dietl led his 3rd *Gebirgsjager* Division into the town, and received its surrender from a Quisling, Colonel Konrad Sundlo.

The assault on Oslo was not so easy. The pocket battleship *Lutzow* was badly damaged by the Norwegian shore batteries in the fjord, and the *Blucher* was sunk by shore-launched torpedoes with the loss of 1,600 lives before the 163rd division managed to capture a large part

of Oslo, the arsenal at Horten and the airfield. But for this daring enterprise by Major General Engelbrecht, the battle would have lasted much longer, for it was the ability to land paratroops in Ju52 aircraft on that airfield, late on April 9th, that determined the course of events in favour of Germany.

Although Norwegian intentions were good, and the willingness of King Haakon, his government and country to fight was evident, Norway's organisation was less than effective and rendered the effort expended on defence largely valueless. General mobilisation was announced only after the invasion had begun. The Commander in Chief was unfit for service, and had to be replaced after the invasion on April 11th by Colonel Otto Ruge, who was hastily promoted to

1 King Haakon of Norway, much respected throughout the world, remained in Norway until the very last moment, and escaped to London on June 8th, 1940 as German armies invaded.

3

4

2 During March 1940, the month after the *Altmark* incident, Mr Sumner Welles, US special envoy, toured the capitals of Europe on a fact-finding mission, meeting the Fascist leaders as well as the governments of Britain and France. In London he is pictured with Joseph Kennedy, US Ambassador to Britain (and father of the late President Kennedy), and Winston Churchill, then still First Lord of the Admiralty.

5

3 The Norwegian coastline seen from the right hand seat of one of the invaders' Junkers Ju52 three engined transport aircraft as Germany's might swept across Norway in April 1940. The *Luftwaffe* had 552 of these reliable transport aircraft at the beginning of the war.

4 Vidkun Quisling proclaimed himself head of the Norwegian government but was replaced after five days by an Administrative Council. Quisling was nonetheless appointed puppet Premier of Norway by Hitler in 1942.

5 German infantry had a difficult time during the battle for Norway, and were often subject to attack by Norwegians employing local knowledge of the mountains. These troops are keeping their heads down under fire on a mountain road.

6 Operation Weser Crossing North, the German invasion of Norway, was carried out with six regiments, one parachute battalion, 1,000 aircraft, twenty-four surface ships and thirty *U-Boats*. Initial German land losses were light, although naval losses were considerable. These German troops are aboard an unidentified warship off the Norwegian coast.

6

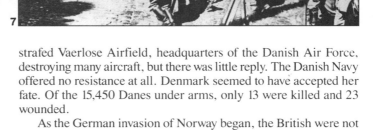

7

7 On April 9th, the same day as the invasion of Norway, a comparatively small force of German troops – two divisions, a brigade group and a battalion of airborne troops with sixty aircraft – swept into Denmark, meeting minimal resistance. These soldiers were disembarking in Copenhagen.

General. The command structure was hopelessly inadequate to deal with a situation as desperately demanding of strong military action. As the evacuation of 24,000 allied troops from Narvik and Harstad was completed two months later, King Haakon and the Norwegian Government were to escape narrowly from Tromso to England aboard HMS *Devonshire* on June 8th and Vidkun Quisling was to proclaim himself the head of the Norwegian Government, saying 'I shall be called the big traitor'. In that at least he was right.

Denmark caused the Germans less difficulty than Norway. King Christian X and his government yielded to the German ultimatum, although there was Danish military resistance at Jutland, and the Royal Guard made a stand at the Amalienborg Palace. The *Luftwaffe* strafed Vaerlose Airfield, headquarters of the Danish Air Force, destroying many aircraft, but there was little reply. The Danish Navy offered no resistance at all. Denmark seemed to have accepted her fate. Of the 15,450 Danes under arms, only 13 were killed and 23 wounded.

As the German invasion of Norway began, the British were not standing idly by, but the Allies' reaction was appallingly late, disastrously ineffective and disorganised. Admiral Sir Charles Forbes had sailed from Scapa Flow on the evening of the 7th, three days after news of the invasion had been leaked to the Allies. His force of two battleships, one battle-cruiser, four cruisers and 21 destroyers headed for Norway to provide cover for minelaying operations, but with orders that suggested the threatened invasion might be a blind for a break-out of the blockaded German fleet to the Atlantic. On April 8th, one of the destroyers, HMS *Glowworm*, met the *Hipper* and was severely damaged. With tremendous courage, her captain used his doomed ship to ram the *Hipper*, radioing as he did so that the German Fleet was at sea.

As a result, the British Admiralty did exactly what the Germans hoped it would do by instructing Admiral Forbes not to follow the German fleet into Trondheim, which would have been tactically sound, but to intercept the *Scharnhorst* and *Gneisenau*, which were operating as an independent battle squadron, and were in fact functioning as bait to keep the Royal Navy away from the landings in Norway. By the evening of April 9th, Germany was in control of the most important strategic positions in Norway and Denmark, and Hitler had achieved his easiest bridgehead yet. In Britain, Prime

1 The First Battle of Narvik on April 10th claimed two British and two German destroyers. On April 19th, the survivors of one of the British ships, HMS *Hardy*, met Winston Churchill at the Admiralty. Here Churchill makes a speech heard throughout Britain emphasising the resolution of Britain in combatting the forces of *Blitzkrieg*.

Minister Neville Chamberlain, who only days earlier had announced that Hitler had missed the bus, was in deep trouble.

2 The day after the invasion of Denmark, the Icelandic Parliament (the Althing) severed its constitutional links with Denmark. On April 13th, the Danish government of the Faeroe Islands agreed to accept British protection, and on May 10th, as Germany invaded the Low Countries, British troops occupied Iceland.

Britain now joined battle in earnest. On April 10th, the First Battle of Narvik brought 5 British destroyers into conflict with 10 German destroyers, and cost each side two destroyers and one senior commander. The Royal Navy also sank 8 German merchant ships and the ammunition carrier *Rauenfels*. On the 11th, the RAF attacked Sola airfield, Stavanger, and lost 1 Wellington out of 6. On the 13th came the Second Battle of Narvik, and a significant victory for the Royal Navy. HMS *Warspite* and 9 destroyers attacked 8 German destroyers and sank or disabled all of them. By the 14th, the British North Western Expeditionary Force had begun to land at Harstad, the 24th Guards Brigade arriving on the island of Hinnoy, near Harstad, some 96km from Narvik, and separated from the port by a sea channel and snow-covered mountains, on the 15th. On the 16th, the 146th Infantry Brigade landed at Namsos, and on the 17th the 148th landed at Andalsnes. The Germans were now isolated in Narvik, although with plenty of captured Norwegian weapons in addition to their own, and with a 'Mountain Marine' unit of 2,600 men, survivors of the

annihilated destroyer fleet, to use the Norwegian rifles and machine guns. This force was ordered to 'hold out for as long as possible'. Each day, the RAF attacked German military installations, and the sea war continued with losses on both sides.

The traitor Quisling, meanwhile, had been ousted on April 15th, and replaced by an 'Administrative Council' of Norwegian bureaucrats and lawyers. Suddenly and belatedly, this government, on April 18th, declared war on Germany. On the 19th, the British 146th Infantry Brigade, advancing South from Namsos, reached Verdal, 80km from Trondheim, and the French *Chasseurs Alpins* — fully trained mountain troops — landed at Namsos. The plan was that these forces would advance on Trondheim and link up with the Norwegian forces retreating northwards, but the arrival of substantial reinforcements for General von Falkenhorst's army, despite the attempt at a blockade of German shipping by Allied submarines in the Skaggerak, made the Allies look again at the weaknesses of their position.

3 Air raids and fighting on the ground caused extensive damage to civilian property in Trondheim, Bergen and Narvik.

4&6 These pictures date from 1939, but show something of the techniques used by German troops on mountain roads to booby-trap passing vehicles. The hinged board was hidden just beneath the surface of the road and was connected to a detonator which blew a mine when the vehicle passed over it. Picture **4** shows smaller charges, also blown by the same passing vehicle, which brought down trees to block the road.

5 Air operations were never easy for either side during the Norwegian campaign, as the snow and ice of an exceptionally severe winter had lingered unusually late. These men of the *Luftwaffe* are 'bombing up' an aircraft on a frozen lake.

7 Germany found the Norwegian campaign more difficult to win conclusively and quickly than had been expected, and continued to pour in men and equipment to reinforce those who had formed the initial invasion. These troops were landed at Oslo on April 27th.

7

1 Anti-aircraft and machine gun emplacements around harbour installations and airfields began to assume a look of permanence as the German Occupation became established.

2 This RAF crew is loading a bomber with leaflets for a flight over Germany, in the hope of influencing the population against the Nazi government.

3 Between May 7th and 10th, Britain's House of Commons debated the debacle of Norway, and Prime Minister Neville Chamberlain came under devastating criticism – 'In the name of God, go!' cried Leo Amery. Three days later, on the day that Germany invaded Holland, Neville Chamberlain resigned, and Winston Churchill became Britain's Prime Minister for her darkest hour.

The British troops in Norway were not properly equipped or trained for the position in which they found themselves. Because of the poor organisation of their embarkation, they had not even their full complement of stores and equipment. The German army was well-organised, well-trained and recently reinforced. It quickly became clear that the British plan to retake the centre of Norway could not work and, as if to emphasise the point, on April 26th the German 196th Division, on the right of the 21st Corps, succeeded in joining up with the 181st Division on the left, south of Trondheim.

All Allied efforts were now concentrated on Narvik, and the blocking of the vital route for iron resources through the port. British and French troops withdrew from Andalsnes and Namsos, King Haakon and General Ruge (and the Norwegian gold reserves) headed for Tromso, and the final phase of the Norwegian battle began on April 26th. It lasted effectively until May 28th, when the French 13th Foreign Legion Demi-Brigade finally recaptured Narvik, although by then other events in the Low Countries and France had captured the news. The Germans expected the Allies to try to make their stay in Narvik permanent – but on June 7th the French and British departed, having covered the evacuation of the Allied armies from Norway. Norway and Denmark were totally in German hands.

The pull back to Narvik on April 26th had also marked the beginning of the final phase of Neville Chamberlain's career as British Prime Minister. A motion of censure in the House of Commons debated on May 7th and 8th brought about his resignation, and on May 10th 1940, Winston Churchill, one of the greatest of Englishmen, became Prime Minister. On that same fateful day, Hitler unleashed his long-awaited *Blitzkrieg* in the West, and the attention of the world shifted from Scandinavia to Holland, Belgium and France.

CHAPTER 4

INVASION OF THE LOW COUNTRIES, AND THE LITTLE SHIPS OF DUNKIRK

On May 10th 1940, when the much-postponed and frequently amended *Fall Gelb* (Case Yellow) plan for the invasion of Holland, Belgium and France was put into effect, the land forces of Germany totalled 157 divisions, 49 more than there had been when Poland had been attacked at the beginning of September 1939. Seven were fighting in Norway, one was occupying Denmark, ten were keeping watch between the Carpathians and the Baltic. Three more were still training in Germany. The remaining 136 were committed to the great offensive in the West that was to prove to be France's greatest humiliation.

The *Luftwaffe* remained dominant in the air, being able to put into action 3,634 front line aircraft, of which 1,016 were fighters and the rest, 1,562, bombers. The latest French fighter aircraft − the sleek, fast Dewoitine 520 and the Bloch 151 − were both too few and too late to be effective in the battle, and most of the fighters of RAF Fighter Command were at home awaiting the inevitable attack on Britain − there were in fact 130 RAF fighters and 160 British

bombers in Europe, many of them hopelessly out of date and outclassed by the modern aircraft of the *Luftwaffe*.

Allied land forces totalled 135 divisions against the 136 fielded by the Germans − 94 French, 10 British, 22 Belgian and 9 Dutch − but, according to military observers of the time, many of the French divisions were made up of poorly trained, ill-disciplined and unwilling conscripts. Thus the balance of power was not as the figures suggest. France had, at that time, mobilised one man in eight. Britain, by contrast, had mobilised one in forty-eight "but her army was more effective, professional in outlook and prepared to fight."

At dawn on May 10th, General Kurt Student's 7th Airborne Division, General Albert Kesselring's *Luftflotte II*, and General Graf von Sponeck's 22nd Infantry Division began the mighty attack that was to complete the subjugation of continental Europe and humiliate France. The *Luftwaffe* raided airfields and towns in Holland, Belgium and Northern France, and Student's airborne troops took the important Moerdijk bridges across the Maas estuary to prevent their

4 Even during the phoney war period, the German army had been practising for the crossing of rivers and canals by every conceivable means. Here, a unit of German troops used inflatable rubber boats for an exercise in the snow.

4

5

6

5 One of the most daring and original military escapades of the Second World War was the capture at the outset of the campaign against the Low Countries of Fort Eben-Emael, at the junction of the Albert Canal and the River Meuse. While paratroops landed on the roof, German commando troops stole up silently in rubber boats to attack from the Canal.

6 The German paratroops who captured Fort Eben-Emael on the Meuse by landing gliders on the roof were feted as heroes by Hitler, who awarded Iron Crosses to the men who had led the raid. Goebbels' propaganda ministry made much of the event and of this photograph taken after the investiture.

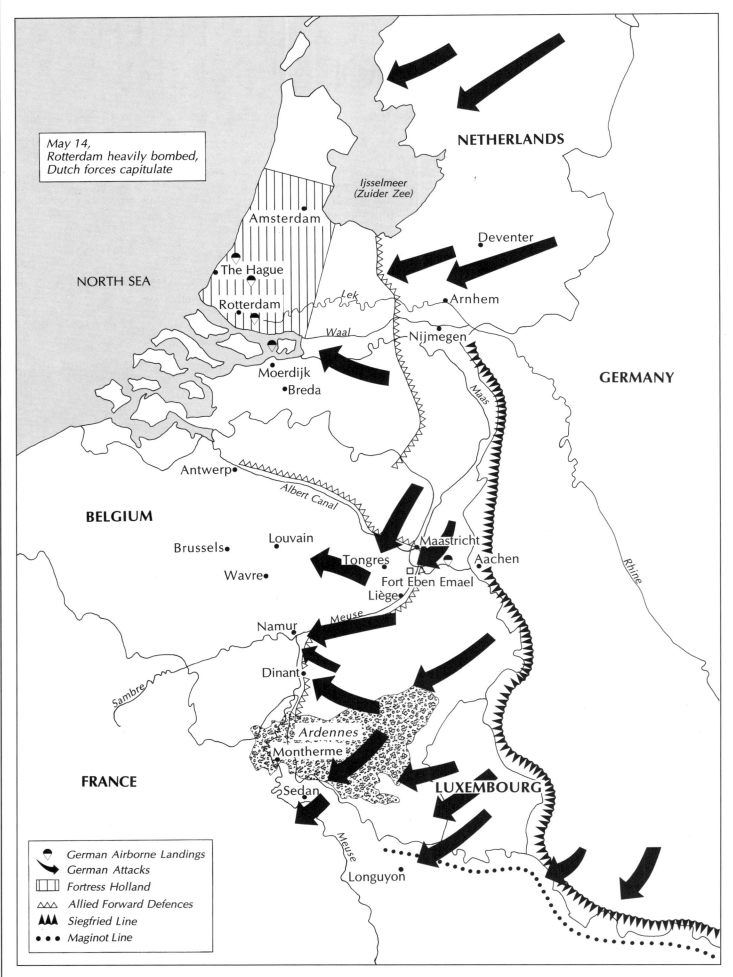

May 14,
Rotterdam heavily bombed,
Dutch forces capitulate

NETHERLANDS

Ijsselmeer
(Zuider Zee)

Deventer

Amsterdam

The Hague

NORTH SEA

Rotterdam

Lek

Arnhem

Waal

Nijmegen

GERMANY

Moerdijk

Breda

Maas

Antwerp

Albert Canal

BELGIUM

Louvain

Maastricht

Brussels

Tongres

Aachen

Wavre

Fort Eben Emael

Liège

Rhine

Namur

Meuse

Dinant

Sambre

Ardennes

Montherme

FRANCE

Sedan

LUXEMBOURG

Meuse

Longuyon

German Airborne Landings
German Attacks
Fortress Holland
Allied Forward Defences
Siegfried Line
Maginot Line

Left Belgium and Holland invaded.

1 Queen Wilhelmina of the Netherlands left Holland for London when the Dutch were forced to capitulate to the advancing Germans. From Britain, the Queen provided constant support for the underground movement in Holland – this picture was taken in London, and shows Queen Wilhelmina reading underground papers.

2 General Heinz Wilhelm Guderian (wearing headphones), the creator of the Panzer divisions, commanded 19th Panzer Corps during the advance through the Low Countries, and achieved the decisive breakthrough at Sedan on the Meuse against the French 2nd Army. In July 1940, after the fall of France, he was promoted Colonel-General.

3 The German onslaught on Brussels was a tragedy for such a fine and ancient city. Vast quantities of incendiary bombs were dropped, and many gems of European architecture were destroyed.

destruction, the banks of the Maas at Dordrecht and parts of Rotterdam. The airborne troops also succeeded in capturing Waalhaven airport.

General Von Sponeck's 22nd Infantry Division was given the task of taking The Hague and securing the co-operation, or the person, of Queen Wilhelmina or both. It is said that the General was so confident that he set out in full dress uniform, so that he would be properly dressed for his audience with the Queen. In the event, things did not go too well for him. His troops encountered the Dutch I Corps, who put up a fierce fight, recapturing the airfields earlier taken by the paratroops of the 22nd Infantry Division as part of the plan to encircle the capital. Von Sponeck was wounded, 1,000 of his men

were shipped off to England as prisoners that evening, and he never did get to meet the Queen.

The most sensational event of May 10th and May 11th was the capture by glider-borne paratroops of the fort at Eben-Emael on the junction of the Albert Canal and the Meuse. Regarded as impregnable, Fort Eben-Emael was defended by 1,200 well trained men who had been taught to expect a traditional attack at ground level. The paratroops instead landed on the roof in gliders, and systematically fought their way down through the building, which was not designed to enable its defenders to cope with such an assault. The outcome was that eighty men under the command of a sergeant silenced the mightiest guns on the Meuse, and made possible the capture of the 1,200-strong garrison, all within thirty hours.

Three *Panzer* Corps, Heinz Guderian's 19th, Reinhardt's 41st and Hoth's 20th, attacked at lightning speed through the Ardennes forest in South Belgium and Luxembourg, heading for the Meuse and the battle with France. The Belgian forces withdrew from the Ardennes in the face of this assault to a position behind the Meuse, leaving 2 infantry companies with the thankless task of holding up Guderian's 1st *Panzer* Division with road blocks.

The Anglo-French Army Group 1, of which the British Expeditionary Force formed part, crossed with a strength of 32 divisions into Belgium, thus putting into action the French C-in-C

1

4 A German 150mm howitzer in action on a Belgian road. The original caption reveals the popular viewpoint of the time towards King Leopold's sudden surrender by stating 'this advance would have been stopped but for the treacherous action of King Leopold'.

5 Large numbers of horses were used by the Germans during the invasion of the Low Countries. This pontoon bridge was built over one of Belgium's rivers, and clearly carried a great deal of traffic, since the build-up of mud is considerable.

3

4

6

6 The German armies did not have things entirely their own way during their advance towards the French coast. This German transport column had been attacked by the RAF on a Belgian road, and was severely damaged.

5

General Gamelin's brainchild, the Dyle Plan. From his HQ at Vincennes — which, incredibly, had no radio transmitter — Gamelin sought to launch an Allied counter offensive between the Ardennes and the Moselle. Sadly, not all his subordinates had sufficient confidence in the plan to do as they were bidden, and, in any event, Gamelin had neither the quality nor the quantity among his French troops for the plan to work. The German success at Eban-Emael had already taken the Albert Canal and key points on the Meuse. It would take more than the Allied Army Group 1 to do any more than defend. Even that proved difficult.

Although the French 7th Army had reached Breda on May 11th, by the 12th it was in retreat under pressure from Guderian's *Panzers*.

The Invasion of the Low Countries

Later that day the *Panzer* units reached the Meuse along a 130km front, from Dinant to Sedan. They had advanced 120km in three days. The French 7th Army fell back to Antwerp.

Next day, the Battle of the Meuse began. The three *Panzer* Corps established bridgeheads over the Meuse at Sedan, Montherme and Dinant, destroying the French 9th Army and opening an 80km gap in the Allied line. At Tirlemont, the French 2nd and 3rd Light Mechanised Divisions fought fiercely all day against 16th *Panzer* Corps, but were forced to fall back. On the 14th, Guderian's 1st *Panzer* Division crossed the Meuse at Sedan in force, and by nightfall the next day the French Army was in full retreat.

In Holland, fierce resistance around and in Rotterdam angered the Germans sufficiently for Hitler to order on May 14th the reprisal bombing of the city. Despite the fact that the garrison had already agreed to surrender, 100 Heinkel 111 bombers were not turned back, and the bombing went ahead. Tremendous fires in the fats and margarine stores of the port caused enormous destruction, nearly 1,000 people were killed and 78,000 were made homeless. The next day the Dutch Army formally surrendered, although isolated units held out until the 17th. The Dutch Army had lost 2,890 dead, 6,889 wounded. Some 2,500 Dutch civilians had lost their lives. Many more would follow during the grim days of occupation.

Friday May 17th saw the entry of the Germans into Brussels. At Montcornet, Colonel, later General, de Gaulle's 4th Armoured Division attacked Guderian's 19th *Panzer* Corps fiercely but was driven back, and later that day the 16th and 33rd *Panzer* Corps were

1 On May 17th 1940, following a withdrawal by the Anglo-French-Belgian armies from the Dyle Line to the Scheldt Line, west of Brussels, and the Belgian government's move to Ostend on the 16th, the German Army entered Brussels. The Mayor of Brussels had no alternative but to surrender to a delegation of German officers.

2 Two German soldiers stand at the foot of the flagstaff on the roof of the City Hall in Brussels as the swastika is hoisted.

3 On May 24th, Hitler and von Rundstedt ordered Guderian's lightning Panzer advance towards Calais and Dunkirk to stop at Gravelines, and on the 26th, the evacuation of Dunkirk began. By the time the Panzer advance recommenced on May 26th, the Allied forces had regrouped. The Wehrmacht resorted to air attacks in an attempt to halt the evacuation – this oil refinery at Dunkirk was hit by Stuka dive-bombers.

4 With a burning refinery in the background, a Lockheed Hudson of RAF Coastal Command patrols along the shallow beach from which the remains of the British Expeditionary Force had to be embarked.

detached from the German 6th Army in Belgium and sent to join the forces on the Meuse. Next day, Guderian's *Panzers* reached Peronne on the Somme. Disaster was clearly in the air for the Allies and, on Sunday May 20th, General Gamelin was dismissed and replaced by General Weygand. Colonel de Gaulle seemed almost to celebrate by having another go at Guderian, this time almost taking the General's Headquarters before being driven back by Stuka attacks from the air.

Next day, Guderian raced for the Channel coast along the Somme, and despite fierce resistance from the British 12th and 23rd (Territorial) Divisions, the 1st *Panzer* Division captured Amiens at midday, and the 2nd Division reached Abbeville and Noyelles at the mouth of the river by evening. They had advanced 386km in only eleven days.

By Wednesday May 22nd, Guderian was striking north to attack the encircled British troops at Boulogne, Calais and Dunkirk, and by the next day, as the Germans crossed the River Scheldt at Oudenarde and the British Expeditionary Force in Belgium was put on half rations, the forces on the Channel beaches were hemmed in.

At Boulogne, 6 British destroyers evacuated 4,400 troops under heavy fire, and the French destroyers *Jaguar* and *Orage* were sunk. The situation was desperate.

Then, on Friday May 24th, there occurred one of the strangest events of the war. Hitler and Field-Marshal Gerd von Rundstedt, to the intense frustration of the *Panzer* generals, ordered the *Panzer* Divisions to halt at Gravelines, South West of Dunkirk. Why this order was given remains the subject of intense speculation, but, whatever the reason, it resulted in what has become known as 'The Miracle of Dunkirk'. At Boulogne, the British were less fortunate – 5,000 British and French troops were captured on Sunday 25th May. At Calais the British garrison rejected a call to surrender and repulsed attack after attack.

All through Sunday 25th, massive preparations had been under way along the British coast to mount one of the strangest and greatest seaborne rescues of all time. On Monday 26th, and for the next week, every vessel that could cross the English Channel to collect men did so—fishing boats, pleasure boats, small sailing boats, even the Thames paddle steamer

5 Some of the total of 338,226 men who were evacuated from Dunkirk (120,000 were French or Belgian) wait in ranks stretched across the vast beaches for the extraordinary variety of ships that were to take them to England.

6 As they waited for rescue or capture, the men of the British Expeditionary Force showed great courage, firing at aircraft of the *Luftwaffe* as they passed overhead. Fortunately, the RAF had retained some of the initiative in the air over Dunkirk, and the troops on the beaches were spared the worst of air attack.

7 Many troops were out of their depth and swam desperately in full kit for the ships that would take them home. Helpers lined the sides of rescue vessels to pull them aboard.

1 Although historical
hindsight tells us that the
Dunkirk evacuation was
relatively little hindered by
air attack, there was no
rest at the time for the
anti-aircraft gun crews,
who expected attacks
constantly. This gun is
ready as more soldiers
wade out to the waiting
ships.

2 Home at last! British
soldiers evacuated from
Dunkirk arrive at a
London railway station
looking decidedly pleased
to be back.

3 After the adventures of
the Dunkirk evacuation,
many of the surviving
small pleasure craft
needed repair, and
dozens of them were
towed up the Thames for
the work to be done.
Surviving 'little ships' that
took part still fly the
pennant of the Dunkirk
Little Ships Association,
and are saluted by ships
of the Royal Navy as a
mark of respect.

Gracie Fields. Many small vessels, and all the naval ships that survived
the fierce bombardment to which the flotilla was subjected returned
several times, braving the most appalling conditions to rescue the British
and French soldiers marooned on the beaches.

When Hitler and von Rundstedt realised what was afoot, on the
26th, the *Panzer* Divisions were given the order to attack, but the
respite had provided the stricken Allies with the opportunity to mount
a ring of artillery around the besieged army, and the *Panzers* were
unable to penetrate to the beaches and prevent the evacuation.
Between the 26th and June 4th, 338,226 men, including some 120,000
French and Belgians, were evacuated from Dunkirk by a total of 861
ships and private craft. Sadly 243 vessels were sunk. The *Luftwaffe*
lost more than 130 aircraft, the RAF 106, with 87 pilots either dead
or captured. When the Germans took Dunkirk on June 4th, they
captured large quantities of abandoned British and French equipment
and vehicles – 2,472 guns, 84,427 vehicles and 657,000 tons of
ammunition and stores.

Meanwhile, on May 28th, King Leopold of the Belgians had
announced the surrender of the Belgian Army against the wishes of
his cabinet and many of his people. On Friday May 31st, the French
1st Army surrendered near Lille after a 4-day siege.

Dunkirk marked for the people of Britain an end and, in a
different way, a beginning. But for France the agony continued. The
Battle of France was about to begin.

CHAPTER 5

THE HUMILIATION OF FRANCE
THE AVENGING OF VERSAILLES

The army that had been at the end of the First World War indisputably the greatest in the world, and which had started the Second World War as Germany's most feared opponent, had come to a sorry pass. Badly led, ill-trained, the victim of endless political crises which had stifled military planning throughout the Thirties, the French Army had been inflated to unmanageable ill-disciplined proportions by over-hasty mobilisation. The largely amateur colossus that sought to bestride the most professional mechanised army the world had seen seemed to know its deficiencies; to know it could not win; it seemed almost to be committed to losing even before its leaders urged it to successes it could not achieve. Low morale is the most pernicious of diseases in an army open to infection.

4

In fact, the French Government was on the way to overcoming many of the underlying problems of supply from which the French armed forces — notably the *Armee de l'Air* — suffered. Nationalised in 1936/37, the French aircraft industry had designed new aircraft but had produced few of them before 1940. Nonetheless, between January and June 1940, production increased to an extraordinary extent. By June 1940, the Dewoitine D.520, the French competitor to the Spitfire and a worthy opponent for the Messerschmitt 109, was being produced at the remarkable rate of one per hour, but there were too few pilots to fly them. The situation was too far gone. France must still be the only power in history to have emerged from losing a campaign with more aircraft than she had had when she started it.

With Dunkirk taken, the German Army turned its attention to the capture of the remainder of France — Operation Red. General Weygand, Allied C-in-C, had 66 divisions available to him — 65 French and 1 British — and found them facing a reinforced German army of 120 divisions in the line with a further 23 in reserve. Hitler and the OKW staff moved to a temporary headquarters in the Belgian village of Bruly-de-Pesche, and a new plan was devised to enable the predominantly armoured Army Group to make the best use of the terrain. The mass *Panzer* assault was to be made across the plains of Picardy, XV *Panzer* Corps from Longpre, and Kleist's *Panzergruppe* from Amiens and Peronne.

On June 5th, the Battle for France began, and the Germans found

that, despite their numerical superiority, they made little progress and suffered considerable losses. By nightfall on the first day, General Erwin Rommel, later to be known as the charismatic 'Desert Fox', and at this time in command of the 7th *Panzer* Division, was only 13km South of the Somme. For days, although some progress was made, the French managed to contain the German forces and inflict great damage upon them. Weygand's army was well dug-in, defending every street corner and hedgerow, and fighting with great tenacity and spirit. Somehow the spirit of Verdun had returned.

On June 6th, Rommel broke through West of Amiens, despite the fierce resistance, and advanced 32km. On June 7th he reached Forges-les-Eaux, near Rouen; on the 8th he advanced 72km and

5

6

7

4 General Gamelin, Allied Commander in Chief at the time of the German invasion of the Low Countries and France in 1940, with Marshal Badoglio of Italy in 1935. The events of 1939 and 1940 made them enemies.

5 The scale of devastation seemed to become greater as the German advance continued. French towns and cities suffered dreadfully during May and June 1940 as the Germans sought vengeance for what they saw as the humiliation of Versailles.

6 British officers inspect one of the picturesquely-camouflaged bunkers of the Maginot Line, which was to have been France's defence against invasion from Germany, but which just did not go far enough towards the northern coast of France to be effective.

7 On Sunday, May 19th, General Gamelin, Allied C-in-C, (third from right) was dismissed and replaced by General Weygand. Gamelin, it was felt, had been fighting the wrong war.

The Humiliation of France

arrived at the Seine. Meanwhile, on the left of the German front, the German 9th Army had made progress across the wooded country of the Chemin des Dames, and on the right the 15th *Panzer* Corps had broken through the French 10th Army. Numerical strength was beginning to show dividends. The progress of the Germans forced General Besson to order General Frere to pull back the 7th Army to create a cohesive line with the 6th and the 10th, thus yielding a great deal of territory and sacrificing both men and weapons. Meanwhile, Rommel had swung back to the Channel at Fecamp, trapping General Ihler's IX Corps. On 12th June, Ihler was forced to surrender, and 46,000 French and British troops became prisoners.

On June 9th, Field-Marshal von Rundstedt's Army Group A had entered the campaign, against the French 4th Army and units of the French VII Corps. Seven French divisions fought gallantly against twice their numbers of fresh troops, inflicting heavy losses, and maintained high morale despite mounting odds. Their demeanour, skill and appetite for the fight could not have been more different from that of the earlier battles on the Somme. Throughout June 9th and 10th, the Germans made little progress, and were admiring of the quality of the French soldiers in their diaries and despatches. Then, inevitably, VII Corps' stand collapsed, and Guderian's *Panzers* crossed the Aisne and made South. On the evening of June 12th, he reached Chalons-sur-Marne.

By this time Weygand had only 27 divisions left in the field, Kleist's *Panzergruppe* had broken through from Peronne and Amiens, and the position was becoming irrecoverable without strategic withdrawal. On June 12th Weygand ordered a retreat to a line from Geneva to Caen; a far longer line to defend with 27 divisions than he had been defending only a week before with 66. On the 14th, the Germans entered Paris and found it almost empty. Only 700,000 people remained of a population of 5 million. The remainder had taken to the roads. Recognising the seriousness of the situation, and anxious to retain every soldier possible for the next crucial battle, Churchill ordered the immediate evacuation of all remaining British troops in France.

The French Government, which had earlier moved to Tours, now moved again for Bordeaux. Premier Paul Reynaud made a desperate appeal to President Roosevelt to declare war on Germany and come to the rescue of France, but his plea fell on ears that, one suspects, would have liked to have heard but could not. In his reply on June 15th, President Roosevelt promised every aid short of military intervention. On June 15th, as 30,600 British troops were evacuated from Cherbourg, and the Germans captured Verdun, the French Army GHQ moved to Vichy. The next day, Guderian captured Besancon, and it became clear that events were moving swiftly towards an inevitable conclusion. Premier Paul Reynaud resigned, and the veteran Marshal Petain, the hero of Verdun in the Great War,

1 The French Prime Minister, Edouard Daladier, had resigned on 20th March 1940, reputedly at the insistence not only of Marshal Petain, but also of Daladier's successor Reynaud's domineering mistress Countess Portes. Daladier remained in the cabinet as Minister for War; de Gaulle became Under-Secretary for Defence.

2 Despite the heroic efforts of some parts of the French armaments industry, notably the aircraft manufacturers, much of the defence of France was entrusted to obsolete weapons like this First World War gun, in action in June 1940.

3 Even the small villages of France were not immune to the damage that everywhere marked the path of the German advance. These German infantrymen are sprinting for cover under fire.

44

formed a new government. The next day, June 17th, Petain asked the Germans and Italians (Mussolini having declared war on Britain and France on June 10th) for terms for an armistice. On the 18th, Rommel captured Cherbourg, and the 5th *Panzer* Division took Brest. The last RAF squadrons left France. All towns of more than 20,000 inhabitants were declared 'open' and were ordered to surrender without resistance. Most, but not all, did just that. At Saumur, 2,300 cadets of the Cavalry School put up an epic fight under the command of Colonel Michon, and prevented the German 1st Cavalry Division from crossing the Loire for 48 hours. 200 cadets died. The 220,000 French troops holding the Maginot Line, the great fortification stretching from the Swiss border at Basle to Luxembourg, and which had been built to protect France from Germany, held out until June 25th. Sadly, the French governments of the Thirties had never found the budget or the political will in respect of Belgian and Dutch political sensibilities to extend the Maginot Line to the Channel, and the German armies, by taking Holland and Belgium before France, simply went round it.

4 Destruction and fire were everywhere across northern France as the beleaguered French army struggled to defend its homeland. A German self-propelled gun crew in action on a devastated railway crossing, firing blind into billowing smoke.

5 General Guderian, commander of '*Panzer* Group Guderian' during the Battle of France, created both the concept of *Panzer* warfare and the methods of training that proved so successful in Poland and France. Here he visits a training centre before the conflict began.

6 On Friday, June 14th, the German army entered Paris, and General von Bock, Commander of German Army Group B, reviewed great victory parades in the Place de la Concorde and at the Arc de Triomphe. Incredibly, the Germans succeeded in capturing intact the Renault tank factory at Billancourt.

7 On Monday, June 17th, a day after the resignation of Reynaud as premier, Marshal Petain, the new head of government, requested armistice terms from Germany. Hitler was determined that France should be as thoroughly humiliated by the signing of the Armistice as Germany had been in November 1918, so had the railway coach in which the 1918 document had been signed brought from a Paris museum to Compiegne. Afterwards, the carriage was exhibited in the Lustgarten, Berlin, where this picture was taken.

During the period when British and French troops that could escape to Britain were being evacuated from the Atlantic and Channel ports, every worthwhile warship or supply vessel that was unable to put to sea was scuttled and put beyond service for the German invader. Five submarines, the destroyer *Cyclone*, tankers and fleet auxiliaries, and many smaller vessels that might have helped the enemy were ruthlessly put out of commission by the French. The battleships *Paris* and the *Courbet*, seven submarines, four destroyers, six torpedo boats and thirteen gunboats managed to reach Britain. The newly completed battleship *Richelieu* escaped from Brest and sailed to Dakar; the incomplete *Jean Bart*, after a breathtaking escape from St Nazaire under heavy Stuka attack, and fuelling at sea under fire, ran the gauntlet of the U-boats in the Bay of Biscay and reached

The Humiliation of France

Casablanca. They were not all so lucky. The French troopship *Champlain* was seriously damaged by a mine in the Bay of Biscay, and was subsequently finished off by U-65 on June 21st.

While tragedy without equal in the long and glorious history of France was unfolding in the North, one French General was succeeding in his objective far to the South. General Olry, commanding the French 14th and 15th Corps, was facing invasion by the Italians. Mussolini, who customarily waited until the horses were in the home straight before placing his bets, ordered the Prince of Piedmont, who had until that moment been under orders to conduct a defensive strategy, to attack in the Alpine region between Mont Blanc and the Mediterranean. Despite protests from Marshal Badoglio, Mussolini insisted, and the Italian 1st and 4th Armies, some 450,000 men, attacked the 185,000-strong Army commanded by General Olry on 20th June. During the next five days before the Government of Marshal Petain concluded an armistice with the Italians at Villa Inchesa, near Rome, on the 25th, the Italians made little progress against the magnificently trained and disciplined

French Army of the Alps. The Italian 1st Army reached Menton, some two miles beyond the French initial line, but only by vast superiority of numbers. Once in Menton, the Italians became bogged down. At the Little St Bernard, the *Alpini* Corps failed even to take the French advanced positions. In the Maurienne Valley, after taking two villages, the Italian 1st Corps ground to a halt before French 75mm guns. On the Col de Mont Genevre, the 4th Corps made minimal progress, but took the Chenaillet redoubt, described by Mussolini with soaring hyperbole as one of the key positions in 'the Maginot system of the Alps'. He omitted to mention that the French artillery had inflicted appalling damage on the Italian fort at Chaberton. The Italian armour never managed to get into action. It was General Olry's victory. Despite the Armistice and Petain's capitulation, Olry's stand saved South-East France from Axis occupation. Remarkably, despite being outnumbered two to one, his forces had lost only 37 killed, 42 wounded and 150 missing. The Italians lost 631 killed, 2,631 wounded and 616 missing. Their performance did not please Adolf Hitler.

Nonetheless, France had fallen. The impossible had happened. As German formations completed the task of subjugating the French nation, de Gaulle broadcast to his country from London, where he was establishing the Free French forces to fight on. Churchill broadcast to Britain a message of indomitable courage and touching simplicity:

'Let us so bear ourselves that, if the British Commonwealth and Empire last for a thousand years, men will say, "This was their finest hour!"'

1 On June 22nd, the 'armistice' – effectively the surrender of France – was signed in the presence of Hitler at Compiegne. Marshal Petain and his Vichy government held power only as the puppets of Hitler, and their remaining armed forces thereby became a threat to Britain. Here, Hitler and Petain shake hands after the armistice, watched by the scheming Ribbentrop, Germany's Foreign Minister.

2 While in Paris for the signing of the French Armistice, Hitler, who had seldom been outside Germany and Austria before, toured the sights of the city in his new-found role of conqueror of France. With the Eiffel Tower and a considerable proportion of the officer corps of Germany behind him, he is seen here with Albert Speer, his friend and architect, and later head of Organisation Todt and the Armaments Ministry.

3 Hitler meets his mentor. Standing above the tomb of Napoleon Bonaparte in the Hotel des Invalides, the *Fuehrer*, who saw himself as Napoleon's successor in the conquest of Europe and Russia, reflects on the certainty of success.

4 The Vichy leaders established ever-closer ties with the German leaders during the first two years after the fall of France. This picture dates from the Autumn of 1941 and shows Marshal Petain (centre front) with *Reichsmarschall* Goering on his left and Admiral Darlan on his right.

5 This picture is a still from a cinema newsreel. The film from which it was taken, covering the signing of the Armistice at Compiegne, shows in its original form Hitler stamping his foot in delight. In the interests of Allied propaganda, an American film editor craftily cut several copies of the sequence of frames together, so that Hitler appeared to be performing a ridiculous dance, and the still picture was consequently issued to the press with a caption referring to 'Hitler's little dance'.

6 During 1941, posters such as these in German and French made their appearance in France. These examples conveyed the chilling news to citizens of occupied France that Yves Coantin of Saint-Adrien had been condemned to death for 'acts of violence against the German Army' by a German military court. Such posters were used as propaganda in an attempt to subdue resistance.

BEKANNTMACHUNG

Der Schlächter

Yves COANTIN

aus Saint-Adrien (C.-du-N.)

ist wegen Gewalttaten gegen die deutsche Wehrmacht am 22. März 1941 durch das Feldkriegsgericht

zum Tode verurteilt

und am Morgen des 9. April 1941

ERSCHOSSEN

worden

Der Feldkommandant des Departements Côtes-du-Nord.

ARRÊT de la Cour Martiale

LE BOUCHER

Yves COANTIN

de Saint-Adrien (C.-du-N.)

CONDAMNÉ A MORT

par le Feldkriegsgericht, le 22 Mars 1941, pour ACTES DE VIOLENCE contre l'armée allemande.

Il a été passé par les armes le 9 Avril 1941 au matin.

Der Feldkommandant des Departements Côtes-du-Nord.

BEKANNTMACHUNG

AVIS

7 By mid-1942, German reprisals and threats against French citizens had become savage in the extreme. Saboteurs and 'trouble-makers' were promised by this poster that, when they were caught, all their close adult male relatives would be shot, their womenfolk would be condemned to forced labour and their children sent to a German-organised institution.

8 At the border between the German-occupied area of France to the north, and Vichy France to the south, German border guards scrutinised papers carefully before civilians were allowed through.

As Britain braced itself for the ordeal that was to come, Hitler planned the final humiliation for France, and his vengeance for the terms and manner of the Treaty of Versailles. For the signing of the Armistice on June 22nd, he had the original railway carriage in which the 1918 Armistice had been signed brought from the museum in Paris to the Forest of Compiegne, and set up exactly as it had been in 1918. And there he made General Huntziger sign with General Keitel the armistice that gave two thirds of France over to German occupation and disarmed and demobilised the proud French army. The final stroke was the requirement that France pay the costs of the German army of occupation.

The real cost to France was incalculable. The Battle of France had cost between 82,000 and 94,000 French lives and about a quarter of a million wounded. Almost 2 million French soldiers were prisoners of war. The British had lost 3,475 dead and 15,850 wounded since the invasion on May 10th, plus many thousands more to German prisoner of war camps. Germany had suffered the loss of 27,074 dead and 111,034 wounded.

Now Britain waited for invasion. On a clear day, the Germans could see Dover from Calais across the 22-mile-wide straits. How long would it be before they crossed?

CHAPTER 6
THE SUMMER OF 1940, AND THE BATTLE OF BRITAIN

Europe basked in almost continuously magnificent summer weather as the temporary lull in large-scale hostilities caused all the combatant nations to take stock, regroup, redefine their priorities and discuss what the other side would do next. In France on July 1st, the French Government moved once again, this time to the town that was to become synonymous with French collaboration with Hitler – Vichy. Nine days later, on the 10th, the French National Assembly at Vichy gave Petain full powers to govern by a massive majority of 569 votes to 80 with only 17 abstentions. The next day, President Lebrun resigned, and Petain proclaimed himself 'Head of the French State', abolished the 1875 constitution and dismissed the Senate and the Chamber of Deputies.

On July 3rd came the 'Mers-el-Kebir affair'. Believing with some justification that Hitler's and Mussolini's guarantees of the neutrality of the French fleet, given as part of the Armistice agreements, were not to be relied upon, Churchill ordered Royal Navy 'Force H' under Vice-Admiral Sir James Somerville to secure for the Allies the naval squadron of Admiral Gensoul, currently at Mers-el-Kebir in Algeria, or sink them. After protracted negotiations, the French Admiral

refused to join the British fleet, and, at 1656 hrs, the British ships opened fire. The French battleship *Bretagne* was sunk, with the loss of 977 lives, and the *Dunkerque* was badly damaged with 210 lives lost. *Provence* ran aground; *Mogador* was badly damaged. Only the battleship *Strasbourg* escaped to Toulon.

A similar tragedy could have happened at Alexandria, but for the good sense and co-operation of the two admirals concerned, Cunningham of the British Royal Navy, and Godfroy of the French. Despite his orders from Churchill to achieve results by nightfall on July 3rd, Cunningham held his fire and continued to negotiate. Godfroy, despite the appalling news from Mers-el-Kebir, did the same. On July 4th, agreement was reached. Godfroy's eleven ships were to be immobilised in Alexandria Harbour and land their fuel

1 Goering (left) inspects an anti-aircraft unit 'somewhere in Germany'. Very much the professional airman despite his extravagances and excesses, Goering liked to demonstrate his ability to mix successfully with his officers.

2 This striking portrait of Hermann Goering shows him in his uniform as *Reichsmarschall* of Germany, and yet seems to portray a much younger Goering than the fatter and flabbier commander of the time of the Battle of Britain. Perhaps it is a triumph of the retoucher's art, but, in any event, the picture shows something of the spirit that had earned Goering the leadership of the Richthofen squadron of the *Luftwaffe* at the end of the First World War.

stocks, and the breech blocks of their guns and the detonators of their torpedoes were to be handed over to the French Consulate in Alexandria.

Nearer home for Churchill and England, French ships in British ports were seized on July 3rd, with some fighting on board the giant submarine *Surcouf* and the destroyer *Mistral*. Not surprisingly, the Vichy government in France was not happy, and on July 5th Petain broke off diplomatic relations with Britain. On the same day, as a reprisal for the Mers-el-Kebir incident, Vichy French warships captured three British merchant ships.

The U-boat offensive was beginning to bite. On June 30th, the British cargo liner *Avelona Star* was sunk by U-43. On July 2nd, another British liner, the *Arandora Star*, carrying 1,500 Italian and German internees and POWs to Canada, was sunk by the U-47 off Ireland with the loss of 670 lives. Three days later, HMS *Whirlwind*, a destroyer, was sunk by U-34 south west of Ireland, and the soon-to-be famous U Boat base at Lorient received its first boat, the U-30. Then, between July 6th and August 2nd came a series of devastating blows to the Royal Navy. No less than five British submarines were sunk off Norway – the *Shark*, *Salmon*, *Thames*, *Narwhal*, and *Spearfish*. In August, British submarine operations in the area were temporarily suspended.

Germany moved to occupy its first and, it proved, only British territory of the war. On Sunday June 30th, German troops landed on Guernsey in the Channel Islands, and, on the following day, occupied Jersey and the remaining principal inhabited islands. To assert

5

6

7

8

3 Filed in February 1941 at a British news agency, this picture shows Goering (centre) visiting Channel coast installations in France. Note his commemorative cuffband (right arm) which indicates his membership of the Richthofen squadron 1917-18. To Goering's left (right of picture) is General Hugo Sperrle of the *Luftwaffe*, commander of *Luftflotte III*, and in the background at the extreme left of the picture is General Lörzer.

4 This picture was issued by Allied news agencies in August 1940. *Reichsmarschall* Goering and the newly-promoted (19th July) Field-Marshal Albert Kesselring (nearest camera), commander of *Luftflotte II*, are said to be surveying the English Channel, across which they anticipated shortly to invade England. There was, in fact, considerable disagreement between *Luftwaffe* commanders at this time as to the best approach for the assault on England.

5 The Junkers 88 twin-engined light bomber was one of the most adaptable and successful German aircraft of the Second World War. Although prototypes flew in 1936, first deliveries to the *Luftwaffe* were made in September 1939, and 10,774 were built before the end of the war. The Ju88 played a significant role in the Battle of Britain, and Goering pinned great hopes on its performance.

6 At the Algerian port of Mers-el-Kebir on July 3rd 1940, British ships of Force 'H' under Vice-Admiral Sir James Somerville, acting on Winston Churchill's orders, fired on a French naval squadron. In this picture, the *Provence* (left) and the 30,000 ton battleship *Strasbourg* prepare to return fire. The *Strasbourg* was the only ship of the French squadron to escape the encounter.

7 The saga of British attacks on French warships did not end with the incidents in July 1940. The French passenger liner *Tacona*, used, as most passenger liners were, as a troopship, was set ablaze in Dakar harbour in September 1940 when the Royal Navy again attacked a French squadron.

8 French warships lying in British ports were seized on July 3rd 1940, as part of Churchill's policy of denying the Vichy French arms which might be used by Germany. Fifty-nine major warships were captured, plus a variety of smaller naval craft.

The Summer of 1940

German power and establish a suitable fear of the Fatherland, the Germans had bombed and strafed both Jersey and Guernsey on June 28th, killing 33 people and injuring 40.

Meanwhile, on June 27th 1940, Britain had announced a general blockade of the European coastline from the Bay of Biscay to the North Cape of Norway. In the air, the Allies had scored some successes, balanced by some devastating failures. Sunderland flying boats of the RAF, between 27th and 29th June, worked with destroyers of the Royal Navy to sink 4 Italian submarines and damage three more in the Eastern Mediterranean. On July 1st, Guy Gibson, later to become famous as the leader of the attack by 617 Squadron RAF on the Ruhr dams, dropped a 2,000lb bomb near the *Scharnhorst*, and his companions hit *Prinz Eugen* with two small bombs. The next week, on the 9th, a small force of 12 RAF Blenheims made a heroic attack on Stavanger airfield in Norway, from which not one returned unscathed. Seven aircraft were lost, five were damaged.

The Battle of Britain Begins

The comparative hush that had descended upon Europe with the Fall of France was not to last long. Hitler was already planning Operation Sealion, the invasion of Britain, and was studying closely the entirely

1 On 10th June 1940, having watched from the wings as Hitler conquered most of Western Europe, Benito Mussolini finally decided to enter the war, and added the considerable strength of the Italian armed forces to Hitler's already mighty war machine. This picture dates from the latter part of 1939, and shows part of the Italian Fleet during a review at Naples.

2 A German crew check through last-minute details of their briefing before take-off during the summer of 1940.

3 The Dornier 17 twin-engined bomber, originally developed in the mid-thirties as a six-passenger mail-plane for *Lufthansa*, was operated by the German 'Condor Legion' during the Spanish Civil War, at which time its speed outclassed all opposition. By the time of the Battle of Britain, the Dornier 17 could be caught and outfought by the Spitfire and the Hurricane, and sustained considerable losses.

4 The Junkers 87 *Stuka* dive-bomber, although by 1940 vulnerable to air attack, was nonetheless one of the principal weapons of German *Blitzkrieg* tactics. A skyful of *Stukas*, as shown in this picture, was a sight to be feared by those unlucky enough to be on the ground as they attacked.

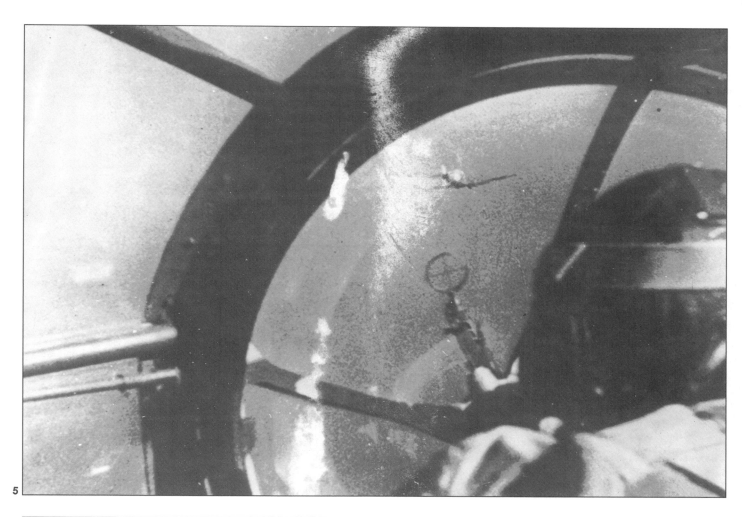

5 An interesting shot of a *Luftwaffe* gunner's-eye-view of a Royal Air Force Spitfire, as seen from the nose of a Heinkel 111 bomber. The Heinkel was equipped with one twenty mm cannon in a ventral gondola below the fuselage, and a total of five 7·9mm MG 15 machine guns in the nose, ventral, dorsal and beam positions.

6 Perhaps the most famous of *Luftwaffe* commanders, Adolf Galland (left) led III *Gruppe* of *Jagdgeschwader* 26 during the Battle of Britain, and became in November 1941 *General der Jagdflieger*, or General of Fighters, in succession to Werner Molders, after the latter's death in action. Credited with 104 Allied aircraft destroyed, he was at thirty the youngest General of the German armed forces. On the right is Field-Marshal Erhard Milch.

6

7

had been able to claim in 1805. The crippling naval losses of the operations in Norway had brought the German Navy to a low ebb, with only one pocket battleship, four cruisers and a dozen destroyers. The Home Fleet, based at Scapa Flow, was enormously superior, but had already bitter experience of the strength of the German U-Boat fleet as an adversary, and of the devastating effectiveness of *Luftwaffe* dive bombing against slow-moving ships. Hitler knew that it was very unlikely that the Admiralty would risk its big ships in the Channel, where manoeuvrability would be limited and vulnerability high.

Hence, he reasoned, the matter would be decided by air power. The *Luftwaffe* remained the finest air force in the world. Goering, always a powerful influence upon Hitler in matters concerning air power, believed it to be invincible, and promised Hitler that the *Luftwaffe* would not be beaten. On paper, it seemed likely that that prediction would be fulfilled. Hitler therefore resolved to pit the *Luftwaffe* against the Royal Air Force to secure mastery of the Channel for the invasion of England, set at this stage for shortly after August 25th.

The date of the beginning of the Battle of Britain is a matter of some debate. To the Germans, August 13th was designated *Adlertag* — the Day of the Eagle. Historically, that date marked the beginning

7 The Polish fighter pilots operating with the RAF gained a well-deserved reputation for daredevil heroism and, in many cases, great flying skill. These Polish pilots were photographed during the Battle of Britain beside one of their Hurricane fighters.

new set of strategic considerations that such an assault made necessary. Comparisons between Hitler's career and that of Napoleon Bonaparte are both inevitable and, perhaps, hackneyed, but there can be little doubt that, when approaching the problem of invading England, both recognised the same difficulties, each attempted to solve them, and both failed.

For both, a successful invasion of Britain could be achieved only if mastery of both the English Channel and the North Sea could be attained. In 1940, that implied mastery of the skies, as well as of the seas, and Hitler had to weigh the comparative strengths and strategic ability to fight of both his own *Kriegsmarine* and the Royal Navy on the one hand, and of the *Luftwaffe* and the Royal Air Force on the other. At sea, Hitler lacked the comparative strength that Napoleon

of the Battle. And yet the availability of aircraft, the morale and tenor of the crews, was determined on both sides by air operations against England that began on July 10th. On that Wednesday, *Luftwaffe* raids on the British mainland began in earnest, with 60 Junkers 88 twin-engined fighter bombers attacking the ports of Falmouth and Swansea, the Pembrey Royal Ordnance factory in South Wales, where 30 people were killed, and Martlesham airfield near Ipswich. On the same day, 25 Dornier 17 twin-engined bombers attacked a convoy near Dover, which produced the loss of one ship. Two days later, on Friday July 12th, night raids on Aberdeen caused 60 casualties, and Cardiff was bombed.

Amidst the growing threat, the recently arrived Poles and French pilots who had escaped from the German invasions of their countries began to form the Free Polish and Free French squadrons of the Royal Air Force. The first Free Polish Squadron, No. 302, was formed on July 13th, equipped with Hurricanes, and was rapidly to be drawn into the battle. Having experienced the terrors of Nazi invasion at first hand, the Poles particularly were fearless, dedicated, almost fanatical in their opposition to the *Luftwaffe*. Many had lost their families, their homes, everything to the German invasion, and had but one wish — to kill Germans. This made the Polish squadrons magnificently brave to the point of recklessness, but almost uncontrollable in battle, drowning conventional RT procedure with Polish language broadcasts on what they regarded as the dubious parentage of their opponents.

On July 18th, RAF Bomber Command struck back for the bombing raids on United Kingdom targets with night raids on the Krupp armament works at Essen, on targets at Bremen and on the

1 As Britain alone faced the onslaught of the intended German invasion, civilians all over the country collected scrap metal for the armaments factories. These boys of Liverpool Farm School, Newton-le-Willows, in the northwest of England, helped the local council pull down railings, and even donated the old aircraft fuselage in which they had been given elementary flying training.

2 Over 500 of these Messerchmitt Bf 110 twin-engined fighters were in service with the *Luftwaffe* at the end of 1939. As a fighter-bomber it was fast and effective; as a fighter it was not a success, mainly because of its lack of manoeuvrability and 'heavy' control characteristics. So many were lost flying bomber escort duty during the Battle of Britain that the *Luftwaffe* sent the faster and more manoeuvrable single-engined Messerchmitt 109 fighters to escort the escorts. Despite these shortcomings, over 6,000 Me Bf 110 aircraft (in all versions) were built by the end of the war.

Map

Legend:
- ◉ R.A.F Bases
- •••• Group Boundaries
- ---- Sector Boundaries
- △ Group Headquarters
- ▲ Command Headquarters
- ᛋ Luftwaffe Bases
- ◢ Kesselring's Advance H.Q.

NORTH SEA

TWELVE GROUP

Fowlmere
Duxford
Martlesham
Debden
North Weald
Stapleford
Rochford
Bibury
Uxbridge
Northolt
Hendon
LONDON
Hornchurch
Heathrow
Eastchurch
Croydon
Gravesend
Manston
Biggin Hill
Middle Wallop
Kenley
West Malling
Hawkinge
Worthy Down
Redhill
Lympne
Dover
ELEVEN GROUP
Dungeness
Dunkirk
Calais
Wissant
Oye Plage
Westhampnett
Tangmere
Marquise
Ford
Wilmington
Boulogne
St Omer
Samer
Tramecourt
Étaples
Le Touquet
Montreuil
St Pol
ENGLISH CHANNEL
Crécy
Abbeville
Dieppe
Aubin
Amiens
Arques
Barley
Montdidier

Left the Battle of Britain.

3 Although originally captioned simply 'Battle of Britain pilots at Biggin Hill' (one of the most important RAF fighter stations in the defence of London), this picture in fact shows legless air ace Wing-Commander (later Group Captain) Douglas Bader (top right, standing), and another famous top-scoring pilot who lived to tell the tale in some excellent postwar books, Wing-Commander Stanford Tuck (seated right).

4 The Polish fighter squadron of the RAF was credited with no fewer than 126 German aircraft definitely destroyed in six weeks of fighting during 1940. The squadron was commanded by a British officer, Wing Commander R.G. Kellett, DSO, DFC.

5 Pilots of the RAF were on constant readiness for long hours every day in July, August and September 1940. They were often 'scrambled' by their Group Operations Room several times a day, racing to their aircraft to do battle, then landing only for long enough to refuel and rearm before taking off again to fight the next wave of German aircraft.

Hamm marshalling yards. The next night, Dornier 17 bombers hit the Rolls Royce aero engine factory at Glasgow. Each day, air raids by each side on shipping and land targets continued, and the pressure on the aircrews mounted. In late July, Goering formed the *Luftwaffe's* first night fighter squadron with Messerschmitt 110 twin-engined fighters, and claimed the first night fighter 'kill' of the war — an RAF Whitley bomber over North West Germany. On July 22nd, only two days later, the RAF night fighters claimed their first night 'kill', a Dornier 17 near Brighton, shot down by a Blenheim using the new AI radar.

By July 28th, the battle was warming up. The South African fighter ace 'Sailor' Malan, based at Biggin Hill, shot and wounded Germany's top fighter pilot Molders, who crash-landed (and survived) in France. At the end of July 1940, Germany had lost 139 aircraft during the month; the RAF had lost only 52.

By August 1st, Hitler's provisional date for the invasion of Britain had been put back one month to September 15th. During the first two weeks of August, the pattern of air attacks on convoys at sea, attacks by night on primarily military targets, and occasional skirmishes between rival fighter formations continued. Then, on August 13th came the beginning of Goering's mighty thrust to destroy RAF Fighter Command, and clear the skies over the Channel for the invasion of Britain. The Battle of Britain had begun in deadly earnest.

In fact, Goering's much-vaunted assault that was to destroy the

The Summer of 1940

Royal Air Force in four days began more with a whimper than a roar. The early morning raids on Britain that were to launch the attack were cancelled, and the only enemy action to disturb the English forenoon that Tuesday was the arrival of 70 unescorted Dornier bombers that dropped their load on Eastchurch airfield near the Thames. A squadron of Junkers 88 fighter bombers that were scheduled to dispense high explosive medicine to Farnborough failed to find their target.

By afternoon, the *Luftwaffe* was beginning to get its act together, and another raid made up of Junkers 88 aircraft started a number of fires in Southampton Docks, but a Spitfire squadron claimed 9 Stukas over Hampshire, thereby leaving the RAF with the day's honours. In fact, on the first day, the German air force lost 42 aircraft, the Royal Air Force 13 fighters. The ratio of losses was even more in the RAF's favour on the following day 19 German to 4 British aircraft destroyed.

On August 15th came the first major show of strength by the *Luftwaffe* over Britain. *Luftflotten* 2, 3 and 5 arrived in force to attack airfields from the South Coast to the Tyne, in North-East England. *Luftflotte* 5, coming from Scandinavia to the Northern parts of the country, was soundly defeated by the RAF, but in the South of England much damage was done. One of Goering's elite units, *Erpr. Gr. 210*, bombed Croydon Airport with considerable effect, killing 62 people. My mother, who lived nearby at the time, recalled watching from her bedroom window as the German aircraft approached, and realising with stark amazement that the objects falling from them were bombs. Despite the damage done, even this first-class Group lost 6 Messerschmitt 110 aircraft and its commanding officer during

1 Although much-maligned, the anti-aircraft gunners deployed in the defence of London did score a number of successes, and damaged many more aircraft than were actually shot down. This Heinkel 111 bomber ended its career on common land in Surrey, south of London, on the night of 23rd September 1940, a victim of 'ack-ack'.

2 A fine German *Propaganda-Kompanie* picture of a Ju87 *Stuka* being bombed-up in France for a raid over Britain.

3 A remarkable picture taken from behind the gunner in the nose of a Heinkel 111 as he lined up his 7·9mm machine gun on an RAF Spitfire.

4 Some wartime captions to military pictures were triumphs of misinformation. The caption to this shot claims that it shows 'Nazi airmen in the control cabin of their bomber machine, showing one about to release the plane's load of bombs'. In fact, the aircraft is clearly on the ground, and the *Luftwaffe* NCOs are either checking instruments or just idly examining the cockpit.

5 A remarkable shot of the bomb falling away from a Junkers Ju87 *Stuka* as it banks and climbs after releasing its payload of death and destruction. One wonders whether this was a specially-arranged picture, or whether another pilot was a keen and effective amateur cameraman with his Leica.

the raid. Total *Luftwaffe* losses on August 15th were not the 144 aircraft gleefully claimed by Britain's most vocal newspaper, the *Daily Mirror*, but 76. The Royal Air Force had had a bad day, with 50 aircraft destroyed.

Next day, RAF Tangmere in West Sussex, in the extreme South of England, and 7 other RAF stations were bombed. Captured records show that the *Luftwaffe* Command Staff estimated the RAF to be down to 300 aircraft by this stage, probably because each destroyed RAF aircraft was being claimed by the gunners of several different German aircraft. In fact, the RAF had some 700 fighters still in active service, and most of them were in the air again on Sunday August 18th when the *Luftwaffe* once more launched fierce raids on Air Force bases and various other targets in South East England. Again the *Luftwaffe* came a poor second when the cost was counted, for they lost 19 Stukas, 8 out of an escort of 50 Messerschmitt 109 aircraft, and many others. By evening, 62 German aircraft had failed to return to their bases, and 34 British planes had been lost.

After a summer that had so far been almost unremittingly dry, sunny and clear for the deadly business of war, the few days from August 19th to 23rd were wet and dismal, with plentiful low cloud. Although there were intermittent raids, the pilots of the RAF were able to take some desperately needed rest. Ground crews worked feverishly to repair damaged aircraft and equipment, runways were patched, grass airfields were levelled and the craters filled. In Germany, Goering fumed at the wasted time.

By Saturday August 24th, the respite was over, the sun shone, and the *Luftwaffe* resumed its assault with massive raids on airfields across the South East of England, the area designated for Field-Marshal von Rundstedt's forces to land when the invasion began. RAF Manston in Kent had to be evacuated. Hornchurch, across the Thames in Essex, was badly damaged. Residential areas in coastal towns Portsmouth and Ramsgate were bombed. Most significantly, London was hit by incendiary attacks from a group of aircraft who were targetted to attack the Short flying boat factory at Rochester, but

6 Aged twenty-one, yet with the eyes of a veteran, this RAF officer, Pilot Officer Eric Lock, had fought through the Battle of Britain and the winter of the London Blitz when this picture was taken in 1941. He had just been taken from hospital to Buckingham Palace to receive the Distinguished Service Order, and the Distinguished Flying Cross and Bar from King George VI. He had destroyed twenty-two German aircraft, and had nine 'probables' to his credit.

7 The Focke-Wulf 190 was delivered too late for the Battle of Britain, but was used extensively for low-level hit and run raids over Britain in 1941 and 1942. It was one of the most successful fighters built for the *Luftwaffe*, and was used with considerable effect in North Africa and on the Russian Front.

8 During the night of August 1st/2nd 1940, Germany carried out its first leaflet raid on Britain, dropping these broadsheets headed 'A Last Appeal To Reason by Adolf Hitler', and containing the text of Hitler's speech on the futility of British resistance, which he had made in the *Reichstag* on 19th July. The civilian in the steel helmet is a member of ARP (Air Raid Precautions), the organisation that bore the brunt of organising civilian defence and rescue during the London Blitz and German bombing raids on other British cities.

9 The timeless lines of R. J. Mitchell's Supermarine Spitfire silhouetted against an evening sky – a squadron flies in close formation.

became lost because of British radio countermeasures. The consequences of this single mistake can be argued to have lost Germany the Battle of Britain, and ultimately the war. For the implications of the swell of public and government anger that followed the accidental bombing of London, and of all the events that followed, were immense.

Winston Churchill, incensed at the attack on non-military targets in London ordered the RAF to bomb Berlin, a hazardous long-range task for the aircraft then available. Of the 81 twin-engined bombers that took off for the raid on the night of August 25th, only 29 reached the German capital, (the remainder got lost on the way) and the actual damage done was comparatively slight when compared with the loss of the 8 RAF men who were killed and the 29 that were wounded. But Hitler, who had been specifically promised by Goering that no enemy would bomb Berlin, was put into a towering rage, and made the first of many emotional and ill-conceived strategic decisions that were against Germany's military interests. Forgetting the strategy of concentrating all *Luftwaffe* effort on the annihilation of RAF Fighter Command, he ordered that London be subjected to airborne *blitzkrieg*, as Warsaw and Rotterdam had been before. The preparation for this campaign of terror bombing, and the raids themselves, which began on September 7th and continued for 57 appalling days and nights, dispersed *Luftwaffe* effort, and took the pressure off RAF Fighter Command.

relieved of his command shortly after his pilots had won their heroic battle.

Hypothesise as one will as to what might have happened had Hitler maintained his original strategy, the facts are that he did not, and that the diverting of resources to the London Blitz enabled Fighter Command to gain the upper hand in the battle for mastery of the Channel airspace. In the last days of August there were daylight raids by the *Luftwaffe* on airfields across the South, around London and in Essex, air battles overhead to entertain the population every day, and a gradual increase in German night raids on civilian targets. Birmingham, Coventry and Plymouth were bombed on August 26th/27th, Liverpool on August 28th, Liverpool and Merseyside again on August 31st/September 1st. The crews and aircraft of RAF Bomber Command were not idle, and bombed Berlin again on the 28th, the 30th and the 31st.

September opened with another major assault on Fighter Command bases, with Biggin Hill in Kent badly damaged on September 1st, and Detling, Eastchurch, and Biggin Hill again hit on September 2nd. The RAF celebrated the first anniversary of the start of the war on September 3rd with the first of nine raids during the month on Berlin. On the same day, Hitler postponed the invasion of Britain from September 15th to September 21st. The 4th and 5th saw heavy and successful German attacks on the Vickers aircraft factory at Brooklands in Surrey, stopping production of Wellington bombers

In fact, after a bad start during the August 13th-17th period, when Germany lost 255 aircraft, the *Luftwaffe* had been set to win the Battle from the 24th onwards. Although more German aircraft than British were being lost daily, the *Luftwaffe* had started from a better base (1,137 fighters against 620 Hurricanes and Spitfires), and many of the planes that were being lost were bombers. Hence, the fighter strength of the *Luftwaffe* by comparison with the RAF was becoming greater as the 1,000 pilots with which the RAF was left by the end of the third week of August became progressively more tired. For as long as Goering could keep up the pressure on the airfields of the South East corner of England, there was little doubt that the RAF would go under eventually. Air Chief Marshal Sir Hugh Dowding, head of Fighter Command, accepted that this was the case, and was on record as informing Churchill of the fact. Perhaps this contributed to his being

1 On May 14th 1940, Anthony Eden, Secretary of State for War, broadcast an appeal for 'Local Defence Volunteers' to defend Britain against possible parachute invasion. By July 23rd, 1,300,000 men had volunteered, and the force was renamed 'Home Guard'. Although the subject of affectionate derision, the Home Guard was an effective supplementary force which became better armed and trained as the war progressed. This picture of 'Dad's Army' was taken in 1942.

2 Because Britain is a relatively small island, with its capital on a broad river and estuary quite close to the sea, land-based anti-aircraft defences left a major gap in fire-power through which German air formations could attack by flying up the River Thames. To combat this problem, forts were built in the estuary, and guns were mounted on them.

3 German bomber losses during the Battle of Britain were too great to be sustained. This Dornier 17 was shot down on August 18th; three days earlier, on August 15th, the *Luftwaffe* had lost seventy-six aircraft, which compares with RAF losses of fifty. London's *Daily Mirror* newspaper claimed that 144 German aircraft had been shot down on that day.

4 The Royal Observer Corps played a crucial role in Britain's defence, both in spotting approaching German aircraft formations as they crossed the coast, and in plotting the overall position and concentrations of the attacking *Luftwaffe*. Much of the plotting was carried out by women, who were in touch by field telephones with the observation posts.

5 On the night before this picture was taken, on the morning of 10th September 1940, 370 people were killed and 1,400 injured in London. The street sign at top right identifies the scene as Watling Street in London EC4, close to St Paul's Cathedral, but the censor has put his red pen through the street name so that enemy agents could not gain information on damage from newspaper pictures.

5

6

13 pilots. Bombs fell all over London; even Buckingham Palace was hit on September 13th.

The next day was strangely quiet in the RAF control rooms. Little happened. On the 17th, it seemed that the pressure might be on again, as large formations of Messerschmitt 109 aircraft carried out sweeps over Kent. But as the day turned to evening, and the 18th came and went without the massive attacks that RAF personnel had come to regard as normal, everybody realised that the men of Fighter Command whom Winston Churchill had called 'The Few' had indeed won a great victory and vanquished a mighty enemy.

On that same day, Hitler put off Operation Sealion indefinitely. The postponement was a historic decision of considerable magnitude and far-reaching consequences. The invasion of England was the only amphibious invasion that Hitler planned, and the only invasion that he planned and did not execute. By failing to take England, and therefore failing to complete his domination of Western Europe before turning East, he committed Germany to war on several fronts. By failing to quash the spirit of defiance that had sustained England through its ordeal, he unwittingly inspired the world particularly the USA to recognise that he could, and would, be defeated.

The Battle of Britain was the first setback for Hitler as assuredly as the Battle of Midway was later to prove the first setback for the Japanese in the Pacific. As the summer of 1940 became autumn, the world waited anxiously to see what would happen next.

6 Hundreds of homes in London, particularly in the east and southeast inner residential areas, were destroyed by German bombs before the Battle of Britain was over. As more and more families were, in the jargon of the time, 'bombed out', their children were moved into the schools, where they lived and slept until found temporary homes.

7 All through the battle of Britain, as aircraft fought overhead and bombs fell, the children of Britain, particularly in the heavily-bombarded southeast, learned a new hobby – collecting shrapnel. These boys in the southeast are hunting through a small bomb crater.

7

8 The Battle of Britain was over on September 15th 1940, but the ordeal of London was only just beginning. The presence of King George VI and Queen Elizabeth, who remained in London despite the considerable danger, was a great boost to Londoners' morale. The King frequently inspected the damage for himself – in this picture he and the Queen walk past a bombed cinema.

for four days, and again on Biggin Hill and Detling. The 6th brought the bombers to the Hawker aircraft factory at Weybridge in Surrey.

Then on the 7th September, the London Blitz began, and the daylight raids on the airfields and military installations slowed markedly. But there was to be one last major assault before the *Luftwaffe* acknowledged that the Battle of Britain was lost. On 14th September, the *Luftwaffe* had considerable success with daylight raids on Southern England, and met with comparatively weak resistance. Encouraged, Goering decided to launch an all-out offensive on Sunday, September 15th, the nearest Sunday to which is now commemorated each year in Britain as 'Battle of Britain Day'. Two major raids in daylight on London were massacred by the RAF fighters, which claimed in its enthusiasm 185 aircraft shot down the actual number was 53, with 16 damaged. The RAF lost 26 planes and

8

CHAPTER 7

THE BLITZ
THE BOMBS RAIN DOWN

On 30th August 1940, the German News Bureau announced to London 'The attacks of our *Luftwaffe* are only a prelude. The decisive blow is about to fall.'

For once, the German propaganda machine spoke the truth. At 4.56pm on the fine, late summer afternoon of Saturday September 7th, London's air-raid sirens later to be known less than affectionately as 'Moaning Minnies', announced the arrival of 375 German bombers and supporting fighters. They came up the Thames to London from the sea and set the London docks ablaze. As darkness fell, the fires burnt fiercely all over East London, and illuminated the efforts of a London Fire Brigade that was to have no rest for almost two months. This was the beginning of the London Blitz, and the only mass daylight raid of a campaign of terror that was characterised by the undaunted spirit of the civilian population. Although the daylight bombers were gone by 6pm that evening, the fires were still burning fiercely when the night raiders arrived to inflict more damage at 8.10pm.

1 Tower Bridge is outlined against the smoke as London's dockland blazes after the first great raid of the London Blitz, on September 7th 1940.

2 The area around St Paul's Cathedral seemed to act like a magnet for German bombs and British press photographers alike. The fires that burned nightly wreathed the famous dome in smoke – on the left is the tower of St Brides, another of London's many famous churches.

3 In the early stages of the London Blitz, people living in the worst-hit areas of east London travelled nightly to the fashionable West End, where the underground railway stations were open all night, to find shelter from the bombs far below street level. In the autumn of 1940, the government ordered that other inner London underground stations should remain open to provide protection for anyone who cared to use them. Here Herbert Morrison, Home Secretary and Minister of Home Security, visits Bethnal Green underground station.

4 Stories of lucky escapes from the effects of the bombs were legion. This house in a southeast coastal town received a direct hit while a ten year old girl and her mother slept in bed upstairs. When the house collapsed, the bed and its occupants were deposited neatly in the rubble. The little girl was totally unhurt, and her mother was merely scratched.

The raid lasted until 4.30am. Seemingly endless sticks of incendiary bombs and high explosive rained down. By dawn London had nine major conflagrations huge spreading areas of flame nineteen fires that would normally have called for thirty pumps or more, forty ten-pump fires, and nearly a thousand lesser fires, any one of which would have made the front pages in peace time. Thousands of houses in the inner suburbs along the Thames were destroyed or damaged in one night. 430 men, women and children were killed. 1,600 were seriously injured.

The next night, the German bombers came again, this time attacking the ancient square mile of the City of London, financial capital of the world, as well as the London docks. For nine and a half

5 A *Luftwaffe* pilot's eye view of the Silvertown area of London's dockland, just north of the Thames and east of Tower Bridge. West Ham greyhound stadium can be seen near the centre of the picture between the aircraft, which are Dornier 17 twin-engined bombers.

6 Children set about rebuilding their homes, destroyed by a German bombing raid on a coastal town in the northeast of England in 1941.

7 On 19th November 1940, 350 German aircraft attacked Birmingham, leaving many major fires to be fought. The bravery of the fire and ambulance services during the Blitz attacks all over Britain cannot be over-emphasised.

8 Hospitals, always at the centres of populations in great cities, continued to be hit, and many patients and nurses were killed and injured. Two London hospitals were bombed on the night of 14th November 1940, the night of the devastating raid on Coventry. These nurses were photographed retrieving valuable equipment and supplies from the wreckage of one of the hospitals.

9 The sadness of the suddenly-homeless was everywhere, and seemed especially poignant when it affected those of advancing years. This lady and her grandson were collecting together such belongings as they had been able to rescue from the wrecked family home.

hours, 200 bombers droned overhead, causing no less than twelve conflagrations, putting the railway network to the South of London out of action and destroying hundreds of houses. A further 412 civilians were killed, and 747 were seriously injured.

On Monday night, 370 were killed and 1,400 injured. On Tuesday a similarly frightening trail of destruction was left by another mighty raid. But on Wednesday London began to fight back, as the anti-aircraft batteries in the middle of the great sprawling city opened up with their reassuring racket. No aircraft were destroyed, but casualties were fewer and damage reduced.

Every single night for the rest of September the bombers came, the fires burned, and the death toll mounted. By the end of the month, 5,730 people had been killed and nearly 10,000 badly injured. Roads were cratered, telephone systems crippled, gas mains fractured, electricity supplies destroyed. Hospitals all over Greater London were damaged, some severely.

October seemed to produce a lessening of the scale of the attack. On the 6th, only one bomb fell. But still the bombers came every night, people died, and homes burned. The 15th full moon was to

1 In December 1940, the Palace of Westminster, which includes both Houses of Parliament, was bombed. The House of Commons was destroyed on the night of 10/11th May 1941, and for the remainder of the war the Commons met in the chamber of the House of Lords.

2 All who knew London during the war years remember the searchlights fingering the sky in their search for raiding aircraft, and the harsh staccato rapping of the ack-ack guns as they fired on the German bombers overhead. Through it all St Paul's stood almost unmolested, a symbol of hope.

5

prove hard on Londoners who had already endured almost six weeks of continuous bombing. Over 400 bombers arrived and dropped more than a thousand bombs. 430 were killed, 900 badly hurt. The pattern, the grisly monotony, continued until the nightly raiders left after their attack on the night of November 2nd, the 57th consecutive night of the Blitz. Wearily, London fought its fires, sought its dead, picked through the rubble and waited for nightfall to bring the next lot. But miraculously the raiders did not come. The spell was broken.

There were, in fact, only three nights in November when London was not bombed. Once again, the German crews celebrated the time around full moon with the biggest raid of the month, on the 15th, but, on the previous night, another terrifying raid had been directed, not against the capital but against Coventry, an attractive Midlands city in the industrial heartland of England. We now know that Churchill had been told in advance of this raid, because the secret intelligence centre at Bletchley Park had been able to decode monitored *Luftwaffe* orders with its captured German 'Enigma' coding machine. Despite this terrible knowledge, Churchill had been unable to increase Coventry's defences or give warning, lest the Germans discovered

3 The London docks area was characterised by its tall buildings clustered tightly together with narrow roadways, often made of wood blocks, between them. The tarred wood blocks themselves frequently burned fiercely, so that even the road was alight and impassable for fire appliances.

4 As the London holocaust continued, civilian organisation became ever more efficient, and street fire parties were formed to work with the Fire Service. Here, civilians and firemen are silhouetted against the flames as they tackle massive fires in February 1941.

5 This picture is undated, but the original caption tells how the boy, Donald Prout, aged ten, was at home with his parents in a town in the southwest of England when the bungalow received a direct hit. Donald worked with his father to rescue his mother, who was trapped.

6 One of the best of many pictures taken by London's pressmen during the London Blitz, this shot somehow exemplifies the weariness and bravery of the Fire Service. It has many of the qualities of a fine statue.

6

7 In May 1941, Westminster Abbey, in which William the Conqueror was crowned on Christmas Day 1066, almost fell victim to the madness of war. Despite damage to the roof, and the loss of the magnificent canopy here being examined by the verger, the Abbey survived almost unscathed.

8 The work of the Civil Defence and ARP volunteers was extremely dangerous, and many were killed and injured. These men had been working all night to rescue the injured during a raid in February 1941, only to have their own ARP post bombed when they returned to it.

7

8

that the Allies were able to decode their signals. The priceless secret of 'Ultra', as the decoding operation was known, was somehow preserved, not only until the end of the war, but for decades after it. Few intelligence operations in history have been so successful, or have yielded so much strategically valuable information. But that was no comfort to the people of devastated Coventry, who, on 14th/15th November 1940, lost their cathedral, their homes, and, in many cases, members of their families.

By the end of November 1940, 12,696 civilians in the London area had died, about 20,000 had been seriously injured, and approximately 36,000 bombs had fallen on England's capital. After November, the German Command realised that the strategy of total destruction and the crushing of Britain's will simply could not work, and the pattern of bombing became more widespread, though no less destructive. There were great fire raids on the City of London in December, and more raids in January 1941, but the force of the London Blitz was for the time being spent. Across Britain, the raids continued until May 1941, by which time 40,000 British civilians had been killed, 46,000 had been seriously injured, and over 1 million homes had been destroyed or damaged. In the Battle of Britain and the Blitz combined, the *Luftwaffe* had lost 2,400 aircraft, without achieving any of its objectives.

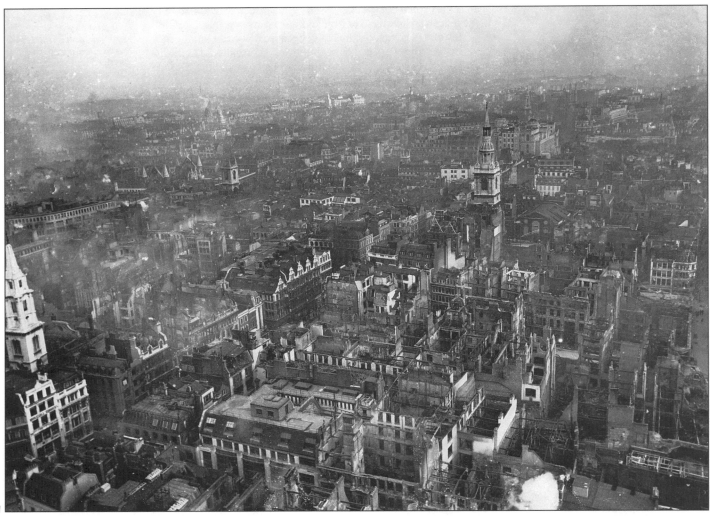

1 By New Year's Day 1941, this was the scene that met the eye looking east from the undamaged dome of St Paul's Cathedral. The destruction that surrounded Sir Christopher Wren's masterpiece was awe-inspiring. Bow Church is at right centre; all around it are dozens of gutted buildings.

2 The invention of the first airborne radar gave British night-fighters an ability to find German bombers at night that the Germans could not at first understand. To mislead the gullible, a rumour was started that John Cunningham, the Royal Air Force's most successful night fighter pilot, had developed phenomenal night sight by eating large quantities of carrots.

3 Attacks on towns and cities continued intermittently even during the periods of the war usually thought of as lulls in the bombing. This picture of bombing in the shadow of Canterbury Cathedral was released in June 1942.

CHAPTER 8

NEUTRALITY AS A WEAPON
THE U.S.A. TAKES A HAND

Although by spring 1941, as the Blitz in London passed its peak, the USA was still neutral, President Roosevelt's administration, usually but not always with the consent of Congress, was taking an increasingly active role in Britain's lone struggle to resist the onslaught of Nazism in Europe. His doing so was, in traditionally neutral America, something of a political hot potato. To understand the events of the time, it is necessary to look back a little at the nature of America's view of European conflict.

The involvement of the United States in the First World War had been a major psychological trauma for a nation reared and developed on the concept of isolationism. Then, far more than now, the United States was a nation of immigrants, still retaining close nationalistic

ties with their homelands. When the Great War began in 1914, and throughout 1915, thousands of Americans left their now-native shores to return to Europe and fight for the Kaiser. Nonetheless, the nation as a whole wished wholeheartedly to remain neutral; to keep clear of a conflict that could benefit them nothing, but damage them greatly. Despite this wish, Americans could not restrain their anger at the reports of German brutality in Belgium and France which repeatedly reached the press in the USA, probably with assistance from (and exaggeration by) the Allied propaganda machine.

Despite clear preference for the British and French cause expressed almost daily by some, though not all, members of the US administration, and in American newspapers, the US government,

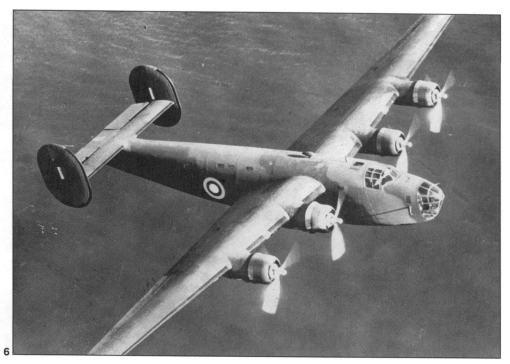

for reasons that are now not easy to understand, expected Germany to honour American unilaterally declared neutrality. The Wilson administration was incensed when Germany announced unrestricted submarine warfare, and its anger made it inevitable that the USA would enter the war, despite Woodrow Wilson's avowed intention to keep his country out of it.

After the Great War, public opinion in the USA could not forget that the US involvement in the conflict had been the result of political mismanagement (from the isolationist standpoint). There was great pressure on Congress progressively to define in far greater detail than hitherto the nature of US neutrality. In 1935, Congress enacted a law which authorised the President to prevent the shipment of arms and prohibit US citizens from travelling on foreign ships, except at their own risk. As the European political situation drifted towards war, and the US became nervous of the alliance between Japan and Germany, a Neutrality Act of November 1939 repealed the arms embargo element of the earlier legislation and instituted what became known as the 'cash and carry' arms system, designed to help friendly nations who were attacked by the tyrannies of Europe while keeping America out of the battle.

4 The great Mayor Fiorello la Guardia of New York, on his return as a Major after the US participation in the 1914-18 war. Public opinion had by 1917 demanded American participation in the Great War, despite Woodrow Wilson's intention of remaining neutral. When the USA entered the Second World War, la Guardia became a Brigadier General.

5 As German pressure on Britain increased in 1940, the USA began to rearm, and in September 1940 a State of Emergency was declared and the draft was instituted. The aid that was sent to Britain was not only in the form of arms: this picture, taken in Coventry in April 1941, shows a 'Queen's Food Convoy' vehicle, provided in this case by American organisations.

6 The 'Arsenal of Democracy' was supplying aircraft to Britain even before the Lend Lease Act became law in March 1941. This picture of a Consolidated B24 Liberator was issued for publication in January 1941 to announce the release by the USA of both B24 Liberator and B17 Flying Fortress bombers.

7 In London, at the height of the Blitz in 1940, fifty mobile canteens for air raid relief were supplied by American organisations through the Allied Relief Fund in response to an appeal from Lord Woolton, Minister of Food.

Neutrality as a Weapon

The USA was now beginning to show signs of the same philosophy that had caused the problems in 1916 the wish to help one side in a war while remaining neutral. Despite protests from midwestern isolationists and right wing senators, America began to sell arms to Britain and France. By so doing, Roosevelt made American neutrality wholly dependent upon the Axis powers' acceptance of the principle that a neutral power had the right to sell arms to Axis enemies. Clearly, it was a position that was tenable only for as long as Hitler and his Axis allies wished it to be.

By the time Nazi Germany had taken Norway, Denmark, the Low Countries and France, Roosevelt was advising the American nation to "have done with fears and illusion". In the year following the May 1940 German invasion of North West Europe, Congress appropriated $37,000,000,000, more than the total US expenditure on the Great War, for rearmament and aid to the Allies.

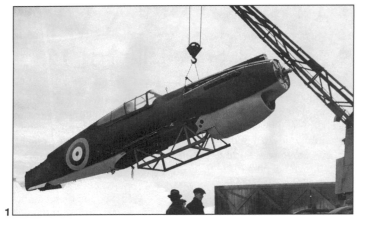

1 After the losses of the Battle of Britain, and the subsequent period of the Blitz, fighter aircraft were desperately needed for the defence of the British Isles. The USA supplied 340 of the Curtiss P-40 Warhawk fighter, renamed by the RAF as the 'Tomahawk I'. Some were shipped in, as in this picture, others were flown across the Atlantic.

2 As the aircraft began to be available from the USA, there was a shortage of pilots to deliver them, and the planes emerging from factories in Britain, to their units. Women pilots had been recruited into the Air Transport Auxiliary to ease the position, and quickly proved themselves as daring and capable as the men they released for service. Pauline Gower, the commander of the women's section of the ATA, is shown here arriving for the service in memory of the pre-war record-breaker Amy Johnson, who vanished while delivering a warplane as an Air Transport Auxiliary pilot.

3 Lend Lease remained the basis of arms supply between the USA and her Allies throughout the war. This British cruiser, its bow almost hidden by the spray, is pictured in 1943, ploughing through heavy seas to return to service after being repaired in a US port under the Lend Lease arrangement.

Public opinion in the USA was sharply divided. On the one hand William Allen White's Committee to Defend America by Aiding the Allies urged that the USA should become Britain's non-belligerent ally. On the other, the America First Committee, whose policy was one of pacifism, isolationism, anti-Semitism and dislike of almost anything British gained the strong support of many public figures, including Charles A. Lindbergh. Because Germany and Russia were signatories to a Non-aggression Pact, following the August 1939 agreement, pro-Nazis and pro-Communists joined in an unlikely alliance to keep the USA out of the war.

On June 10th 1940, Roosevelt, in a famous speech at Charlottesville, Virginia, warned the US people that they could not risk becoming 'a lone island in a world dominated by the philosophy of force', and promised to 'extend to the opponents of force the material resources of this nation'. At the end of July, by the Act of

4 At the end of March and beginning of April 1941, sixty-five German and Italian ships that were in American ports were seized by the US authorities. Four of them were at Gloucester, New Jersey, and the Italian seamen cheered and waved happily to the camera as their flag was pulled down, while armed US soldiers stood by.

5 Another famous woman aviator with distinguished wartime service was Jacqueline Cochran (right), the first woman to pilot an American bomber across the Atlantic. Here she was visiting an RAF fighter station as a guest of the Women's Auxiliary Air Force, now the WRAF.

6 This view of part of the final assembly department of the Curtiss-Wright Corporation aircraft production plant at Buffalo, N.Y., shows the number of P-40 Warhawk and Tomahawk aircraft that were being built at one time in the spring of 1941. Three more such factories were built by Curtiss-Wright alone by the end of 1941 as part of the massive US rearmament.

7 As the Battle of the Atlantic increased in ferocity during 1941, ex-American destroyers manned by the Royal Navy and, later, US ships with US crews, played a vital part in getting the food, fuel and arms through to besieged Britain. This picture was taken from the bridge of one of two ex-American destroyers that formed part of the escort to a convoy in May 1941.

8 An unusual picture in that the Stars and Stripes flies behind a group made up entirely of RAF officers – but it is the Second Eagle Squadron, and every man in the picture except Squadron Leader Powell (centre, with the small dog) is an American.

Havana, the USA announced its protection of Latin America, and thereby prevented Germany from taking control of French and Dutch colonies. Then in September, as America reeled with shock at Britain's struggle in the Battle of Britain, Roosevelt declared a State of Emergency on September 8th, instituted the draft and called up 800,000 men.

In August, after some delay and somewhat contentious negotiation (see next chapter), the USA had provided Britain with 50 desperately needed destroyers, all but three of which were of First World War vintage. Roosevelt had called this "an epochal and far-reaching" act of preparation for continental defense in the face of danger, because he had been able to justify the action politically by securing in exchange 99-year leases on seven British bases from Guiana to Newfoundland.

Now the country prepared openly for war, retooling the factories and retraining the workers for the production of munitions. An Office of Production was established to co-ordinate defence output and do everything possible to expedite aid to Britain ('short of war'). The USA had now become what Roosevelt was to call at the end of the year 'The Arsenal of Democracy', and the Presidential election of

Neutrality as a Weapon

November 1940 was fought against the background of the world crisis, with Roosevelt running for a third term on the grounds that the crisis demanded it. His campaign platform remained one of support for Britain but non-participation in foreign conflicts. Elected once more to the Presidency, Roosevelt found himself leading a country whose mood was changing fast. Americans had grown to admire Britain's desperate stand; to detest the tyranny of the jackboot. Sensing that the time was right to extend more help to Britain, Roosevelt proposed in January 1941 the Lend-Lease programme.

Lend-Lease came as a replacement for the "cash-and-carry" arms policy just in time for Britain, whose reserves of gold, dollars and US investment were almost exhausted by the cost of the war. When the bill, with the curiously patriotic designation HR-1776, became law in March, Roosevelt had been given the greatest discretionary authority ever given to an American President. An initial appropriation of $7,000,000,000 was authorised by Congress, and arms, ships, and aircraft began to cross the Atlantic with the least possible red tape and official hold-up. RAF pilots were sent to the

1 According to the original news agency caption, this picture shows 'some of the US destroyers for Britain', referring to the deal struck by Churchill for fifty aged US destroyers. This is patently not the case, as the vessels shown are battleships. This is possibly an example of the freehand use of available pictures to make a propaganda point.

USA to train. American warships began convoy escort duties, and inevitably became involved in actions against U-Boats. As a neutral nation, America now lacked a certain credibility. As an ally in the battle against Nazism, she was a prize without price.

Meanwhile, the USA had become increasingly the principal obstacle to Japan's expansionist aims. All through the Thirties, as Japan first invaded Manchuria, then attacked China, then became Hitler's ally, the relationship between the USA and Japan had become progressively more strained. In the summer of 1940, as support for Britain's war effort was stepped up, sales of strategic materials to Japan were banned. On September 27th 1940, Japan joined Italy and Germany in a tripartite pact that required each to come to the others' aid should the USA enter the war, and, the following April, Japan signed a Neutrality Pact with Russia, who was, it should be remembered, still a party to a non-aggression pact with Germany.

The tightening stranglehold on trade with Japan, and the increasingly evident readiness to fight displayed by the USA put pressure on Japan to expand and find new resources by colonial acquisition. On July 2nd 1941, 50,000 Japanese troops occupied Indo-China, until then administered by the Vichy French government. Britain and the USA froze all Japanese investment assets, and the slide towards war in the Asian theatre had begun. In July of 1941, as German armies fought their way across Russia, President Roosevelt's envoy Harry Hopkins flew to Britain to see Churchill, and flew in a PBY Catalina to Moscow. He took to Stalin a letter from Roosevelt offering assistance to Russia 'in its magnificent resistance to the treacherous aggression by Hitlerite Germany'. This resulted in a protocol signed on October 1st by Averill Harriman, US lease-lend

4

2 As America's entry into the war drew near, there was constant emphasis, in pictures and captions issuing from the US Navy, on the strength and readiness of the American fleet. This picture was supplied to the press after President Roosevelt's speech on Navy Day 1941, in which he made clear the willingness of the US Navy to fight if necessary.

3 The Eagle Squadrons, volunteer units of American airmen flying as part of the Royal Air Force, were an extremely practical demonstration of American support at a time when Britain needed it most. This picture shows some of the pilots of the second of three Eagle Squadrons, formed in August 1941, which was commanded by Squadron Leader Powell DFC, RAF, (second from left), and flew Spitfires. The Intelligence officer on the left is Sir David Assheton-Smith, whose great grandfather was War Minister during the Crimean War. Pilot Officer Bill Fiske of the Eagle Squadron was the first American to die in the Second World War.

4 The meetings between Winston Churchill and President Roosevelt on board the USS *Augusta* and HMS *Prince of Wales* between 9th and 12th August 1941 resulted in the signing of one of the most historic documents of the twentieth century – the Atlantic Charter. In this shot, Churchill seems to be enquiring 'Is that one of ours?'.

representative, Britain's Lord Beaverbrook and the Russian Foreign Minister Molotov, by which it was agreed that a huge volume of supplies would be sent to Russia.

Meanwhile, on August 9th–12th, Roosevelt had conferred with Churchill at Argentia Bay Newfoundland, exchanging visits aboard their warships *Prince of Wales* and *Augusta*. This conference produced a remarkable document that will be a part of history for centuries to come – the Atlantic Charter. Essentially a statement of the principles for which the war was being fought, and of the shape of the world that they hoped would emerge from the war, the Charter was drafted by Churchill, and amended and developed by the two statesmen together. Subsequently incorporated into a Declaration of the United Nations, the Atlantic Charter is, in its way, as historic as Magna Carta, or the American Declaration of Independence. It was also an act of true friendship between men and between nations.

Thus the USA, without declaring war, without going to war, became deeply implicated in the greatest war man had yet known. The stage was set.

5

5 President Franklin D. Roosevelt and Winston Churchill enjoyed an excellent working relationship, and Roosevelt frequently found Churchill's use of the English language irresistible. One wonders just what Churchill was stating so adamantly that could have amused Roosevelt so well. Behind the two leaders are General George C. Marshall, US Army, and General Sir John Dill, Chief of the Imperial General Staff.

CHAPTER 9

THE BEGINNINGS OF THE SEA WAR,
AND THE STALKING OF THE GRAF SPEE

We have already, in this book, noted some of the events of the war at sea in the context of other episodes and battles that took place before the end of 1940. It now seems right to take a brief yet detailed look at the course of the sea war from September 1939.

For the first three weeks of hostilities, the German Navy was kept tightly in check. Commanders were ordered to follow the rules of the London Convention of 1936 to the letter — and that meant that attacking passenger ships or French vessels was outlawed. Hitler was anxious not to repeat the mistakes of the First World War, when the sinking of the *Lusitania* in 1915 had become a significant factor in the entry of the United States into the conflict, although the British liner SS *Athenia* was torpedoed and sunk by U-30 on 3rd September 1939 with the loss of 112 lives. On September 24th, Nazi Germany's unaccustomed pretence of adhering to the rules was abandoned, and the ban on attacks on French ships was lifted. By the end of the month, the pocket battleships *Graf Spee* and *Deutschland* had sailed to their holding positions in the Atlantic, and the Allies awaited developments.

Most of the significant naval attacks of the period September — December 1939 have been mentioned earlier; suffice it to say that, despite the considerable naval inferiority in terms of both ships and training of the German Navy, they finished 1939 only marginally the loser. German U-Boats had sunk 114 Allied and neutral merchant ships, and would have sunk many more but for the reintroduction of the convoy system, which had saved many ships and lives in the First World War, and for the extraordinarily inefficient magnetic trigger mechanisms of the German torpedoes. But for these defective triggers, the aircraft carrier *Ark Royal*, later to be 'sunk' so many times by Goebbels' propaganda, would actually have gone to the bottom on September 17th. Similarly, on October 30th, the battleship *Nelson* was hit three times by torpedoes, none of which exploded.

The British (and later the Americans) started with the clear advantage of having Asdic, the submarine detection equipment that the US Navy called Sonar. The Germans had no equipment like it, and U-boats were frequently located, although in the early stages rarely destroyed, by British ships uttering the pinging signal of the Asdic transmitter. Nonetheless, nine U-boats were sunk during 1939, six of them ocean-going vessels.

Hitler had placed great reliance upon the big guns, vast fuel capacity and enormous range of his pocket battleships, and had

1 The 11,700 ton armoured cruiser *Deutschland*, launched in 1931 and renamed *Lutzow* in 1939, was sister ship to the *Admiral Graf Spee*. The Versailles Treaty had limited the size of German armoured ships to 10,000 tons; *Deutschland* and *Graf Spee* had been designed around powerful diesel engines to achieve the greatest possible power and range without breaking the Versailles limit too obviously.

2 The *Admiral Graf Spee*, here seen dramatically afire in the River Plate estuary, was launched in 1934, and was slightly larger than her sister ship *Deutschland* or *Lutzow* at 12,100 tons. She was also better armoured, had more fire power with a total of 38 guns (*Deutschland* had 26) and was equipped with eight 21" torpedo tubes instead of the six 19·7" tubes of the *Deutschland*.

3 In October 1939, there was a series of attacks on British warships at anchor in Scapa Flow, Orkney Isles, and at Rosyth in the Firth of Forth. Most were carried out by Junkers 88 twin-engined bombers. This picture of a German Blohm und Voss Bv138 flying boat was captioned at the time as showing 'one of the aircraft which was brought down in the sea after taking part in the recent air attack on the British Fleet'. The British destroyer from which the picture was taken rescued the crew.

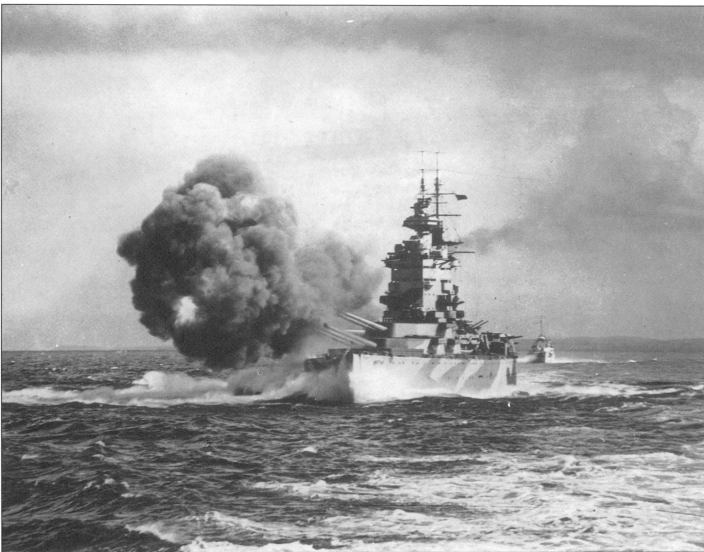

4 On December 13th 1939, *Admiral Graf Spee* was attacked by the cruisers *Exeter*, *Ajax* and *Achilles* under Commodore Harwood near the River Plate estuary. This picture by a sergeant in the Royal Marines, in his words, shows '*Ajax* firing her foremost turrets at 0740 as *Graf Spee* was on a bearing of approx Green 35 degrees. *Ajax* is making high speed, and is approximately 600 yards away'.

5 The 8,400 ton cruiser HMS *Exeter* was completed in 1931, and carried a crew of 630 men. Her six 8" and four 4" guns were no match in either range or fire-power for the six 11" guns (thirty-eight guns in all) of *Admiral Graf Spee*, and *Exeter* was quickly disabled, although her captain fired torpedoes until the last moment, severely damaging the German pocket battleship. *Exeter* survived this encounter, but was sunk during the aftermath of the Battle of the Java Sea in February/March 1942.

6 The 34,000 ton British battleship *Nelson*, here photographed in August 1942 during service in the Mediterranean, survived being hit by three defective torpedoes in October 1939, and went on to play an important role in the hunt for the *Bismarck*. The *Nelson* had three triple 16" gun turrets and six twin 6" turrets.

frequently expressed the belief that their value as ocean raiders would give Germany command of the seas and the ability to enforce a blockade. In practice, the pocket battleships were a disappointment. The *Deutschland*, renamed *Lutzow* after her first cruise of the war because of Hitler's deep-seated fear of a ship named 'Germany' being sunk, disposed of only 7,000 tons of small-scale shipping in her two months at sea from August 24th to November 1st.

On November 23rd, the *Scharnhorst* and the *Gneisenau*, ordered to lay on a show of force in the North Atlantic to draw some of the attention of the Allied Navy from the *Graf Spee* in the South, had surprised and overwhelmed the armed merchantman *Rawalpindi*, which sank with considerable loss of life. Among the dead was her commander Captain Kennedy, the father of Britain's well-known author and TV personality Ludovic Kennedy. But even this was a lone incident in an otherwise inglorious career for the pocket battleships.

The *Graf Spee* had more success in her first couple of months. Ordered to commence hostilities against Allied shipping while off Brazil on September 27th, she sank over 50,000 tons of shipping

before meeting her Waterloo in the form of Commodore Harwood's Royal Navy South Atlantic cruiser squadron, near the estuary of the River Plate, at dawn on December 13th, an action mentioned in an earlier chapter of this book.

Commodore Harwood's force consisted of the cruisers *Exeter*, *Ajax* and *Achilles*, whose 8" and 6" guns were hopelessly outclassed by the six 11" guns of *Graf Spee*. The German ship was also better armoured, and was equipped with radar, which Commodore Harwood did not have on any of his ships. Despite these disadvantages, Harwood went straight into action, sending the *Exeter* in for a head-on confrontation, while *Ajax* and *Achilles* skirted the battle to attack on the flank. Before *Ajax* and *Achilles* could bring their guns to bear, Captain Hans Langsdorff of the *Graf Spee* had brought the full force of the 11" guns down on the *Exeter*, knocking out all her guns, holing the hull and making the ship largely unmanoeuvrable. Even with this terrible damage, the captain and crew of the *Exeter* maintained the attack by firing torpedoes right to the last moment, but had to break away and limp smoking out of range at 7.15am.

The Beginnings of the Sea War

Ajax and *Achilles* kept fighting as best they could with their light guns, but in the effort to get close enough to do some damage, *Ajax* had most of her guns knocked out, so Commodore Harwood decided that discretion was the better part of valour, and retired to an honourable distance. On board the *Graf Spee*, 36 men had died, and 59 were wounded. The ship was not at risk, but was quite seriously damaged superficially, and Langsdorff decided, perhaps over-cautiously, not to attempt the home run through the northern seas in winter, but to put in to Montevideo, in neutral Uruguay, for repairs.

The Uruguayan Government was less than enthusiastic about the appearance of a German armed raider in the River Plate, and allowed Langsdorff only the 72 hours' grace that the strict letter of international law permitted. This was not long enough for the repair work to be carried out, and on December 17th, Langsdorff sailed from Montevideo. Believing entirely unfounded rumours that Britain's battle cruiser *Renown* and the aircraft carrier *Ark Royal* were waiting for *Graf Spee* out in the Atlantic, Langsdorff scuttled his ship in the Plate estuary. Perhaps because he felt unable to face the fury of Hitler, or possibly as a result of the humiliation he had suffered, he shot himself on December 20th.

A more serious hazard to Allied and neutral shipping in the early stages of the war was the magnetic mine, a massive semi-submerged or submerged bomb detonated by the magnetic field of a ship passing over it. Germany laid thousands of these mines from aircraft and U-boats, and sank 59 Allied and neutral ships with them before the end of 1939.

The salvation of the Allies' shipping came in the form of a magnetic mine washed up at Shoeburyness, on England's Thames estuary, on the night of November 22nd/23rd. Defusing this unexploded monster was a daunting and extremely dangerous task, for the techniques of coping with unexploded bombs were still in their infancy by comparison with the level of expertise a year or two later. Nonetheless, Commander J.G.D. Ouvry, Royal Navy, tackled the job and succeeded. As a result, scientists were able to understand how the mines operated, and devised a countermeasure known as degaussing. An electric cable carrying a current was passed around the ship, effectively neutralising the vessel's magnetic field. By March 1940, most Allied ships had been degaussed, and the peril of the magnetic mine was largely past.

In the first quarter of 1940, the Allies were more or less in control

1,2&3 Captain Hans Langsdorff took the battered *Admiral Graf Spee* into the neutral harbour of Montevideo, Uruguay. He was allowed only seventy-two hours before being required to leave, far too short a time for repairs to be effected. On December 17th 1939, believing that a substantial Royal Navy force was awaiting his appearance in the Atlantic, Langsdorff took the disabled *Admiral Graf Spee* out into the River Plate estuary and scuttled her. These pictures show clearly the sad state of a once-proud ship as she sank ingloriously into South American mud.

4 The captain of the *Graf Spee*, Captain Hans Langsdorff, showed qualities of honour and bearing that belonged to an earlier and perhaps more noble war. In none of the nine merchant ships his raider had sunk during its cruise had a single British life been lost, and, having chosen to scuttle his ship rather than surrender it, Langsdorff chose also an honourable death by his own hand rather than the court-martial and dishonour that he knew must follow in Hitler's Germany.

5 In February 1940, the *Exeter* returned to Plymouth for repairs and was welcomed by Winston Churchill and Sir John Simon. Churchill is seen here congratulating the ship's company on their achievements. It is interesting that the censor noticed the presence, in the background of this picture, of the battle-cruiser HMS *Repulse*, and wrote in red ink the instruction 'block out'.

6 The 22,000 ton HMS *Ark Royal*, which entered service in January 1939, just before the war began, carried a crew of 1,636, including the aircrew for her sixty Fairey Swordfish biplanes. This view from an escorting destroyer shows a Swordfish just after take-off. The *Ark Royal* sank after being torpedoed in November 1941 off Gibraltar.

of the situation at sea. There were as yet relatively few ocean-going U-boats, the terror of the magnetic mine had been overcome, and the convoy system was proving reasonably effective in protecting merchant ships from those submarines that were at sea. Nonetheless, 108 merchantmen were sunk between January 1st and March 31st 1940, almost 350,000 tons in the three months, at a time when British shipbuilders were constructing new ships at the rate of 200,000 tons every month. Naval convoy escorts sank eight U-boats during the same period, and the British and French navies felt they had matters well in hand.

The German invasion of Norway in April 1940 took most of Admiral Doenitz's U-boats out of the Atlantic raiding business for two months, and the merchant convoys had eight weeks of comparative respite. During that time only 20 Allied merchant ships totalling about 88,000 tons were sunk. Defective torpedo detonators continued to dog the efforts of the German submarine commanders, and Doenitz is on record as having said that the magnetic trigger problem

7 Briefing aboard a Royal Navy carrier, probably the *Ark Royal*, although the print is not captioned or dated. The Fusiliers officer is giving part of the briefing; the Lieutenant-Commander standing on the right is probably the squadron commander. The readiness board on the right reports the condition of each of three flights of the squadron.

spared an entire Royal Navy battle squadron — the battleship *Warspite*, seven cruisers, seven destroyers and five transports. Meanwhile six U-boats were sunk in the North Sea between April 10th and May 31st.

June brought a wave of appalling destruction to the merchant fleets, as the U-boats were released after Germany's victory in Norway, and returned to the task of sinking merchant ships. Fifty-eight vessels were sunk by U-boats in one month, and the *Luftwaffe*, from their newly-acquired bases in Holland, Belgium and Northern France, claimed forty-four more. More than half a million tons of Allied shipping — 144 separate ships — were sunk by the end of the month.

Now the balance of naval power shifted sharply in Germany's favour as the Italian Navy entered the war on Germany's side, and the

1 The *Ark Royal* turning to confuse the aim of German aircraft bombing the ship during the Norwegian campaign – a still from British Movietone News footage shot in May 1940. *Ark Royal* took part in the Norwegian campaign from April 23rd through to mid-June, and was then transferred to Force H in the Mediterranean.

2 Claimed at the time to be the first Second World War picture of a convoy under attack from German shellfire, this photograph was filed on 23rd August 1940. Taken from a ship in the convoy as it passed through the Straits of Dover, it shows a salvo from a German battery on the French coast just failing to achieve a hit.

3 On November 11th 1940, 21 Fairey Swordfish biplanes from the carrier HMS *Illustrious* carried out a surprise torpedo/bomb attack on the Italian Fleet at Taranto. The *Conte di Cavour*, pictured here, was one of two Italian battleships sunk; another was severely damaged.

4 Much of the Royal Navy's communications in port was still achieved by traditional signalling methods at the start of the Second World War. This picture was taken at the Central Signal Station, Portsmouth, in 1940.

5 Admiral Doenitz visiting a warship of the German fleet in the latter part of the war, after he had succeeded Raeder as Grand Admiral in January 1943. Doenitz was a popular leader, autocratic but usually fair to his men, who somehow retained the loyalty and trust of Hitler to the end. He was the last *Fuehrer* of the Third Reich, named as successor in Hitler's will, and negotiated the surrender of the German forces in the West.

6 Much of the escort duty to the convoys was carried out by the specially designed escort destroyers, which had reduced speed, torpedo and surface armament by comparison with conventional destroyers, but which were fitted with increased anti-submarine and anti-aircraft weaponry. This is the Royal Navy's HMS *Intrepid*, in 1940.

French Navy was effectively put out of the fight by the Fall of France. Maintaining the pressure on the Italian fleet in the Mediterranean, formerly a problem left to the French, was now entirely in the hands of Admiral Somerville's Force 'H', based at Gibraltar. The Royal Navy had only a limited choice of bases in Britain and elsewhere, whereas the Germans had the facilities of every Atlantic port between Tromso and St Jean-de-Luz. Britain had a naval base outside the British Isles only because, on May 10th 1940, following the German occupation of Denmark, Britain had occupied Iceland and the Faeroe Islands, until then Danish territory. Thus, although the Royal Navy could no longer blockade the North Sea between Scapa Flow and Norway, it was able still to maintain coverage of a line from the Orkneys and Shetlands, through the Faeroes to Greenland.

The reinforcement of naval strength as a result of German

7 Life in the convoys of small ships in the North Sea was hard, unglamorous and, unlike that in the more dramatic Atlantic and Russian convoys, little publicised. The North Sea weather is notorious among seamen, and the added hazard of enemy attack made service aboard the ships of a vital coastal convoy of colliers such as this suitable only to the brave and hardy.

conquest did not all flow Germany's way. A thousand ships of the Norwegian merchant fleet, totalling four million tons, and much of the Dutch and Belgian merchant marine had escaped the clutches of the Germans, and had been put at the disposal of Britain after May 1940. This additonal tonnage was considerable — equivalent to some 34% of the total British merchant marine in September 1939. As a result, Britain was able to face the Battle of the Atlantic with almost 30 million tons of shipping.

Admiral Karl Doenitz was not slow to seize for his U-boat fleet the benefits of the new bases that were available to the German Navy. As early as July 7th, the port of Lorient received its first U-boat for refuelling and rearming, and by August, when Doenitz established the headquarters of the U-boat fleet at Kernevel, just outside Lorient, work on refitting the port with the most up-to-date equipment in the world was well under way.

The subsequent successes of the German submarine fleet owed much to the dedication with which German scientists had pursued advanced radio technology, and to the readiness of the German Navy to accept what were then new scientific ideas. German radio direction finding had become very sophisticated by mid-1940, and the new installation at Lorient was capable of establishing a position from the briefest of transmissions by a convoy at considerable range. German codebreaking was also very effective, and the records suggest that Doenitz's team were usually able to decipher signals to convoys from British Western Approaches Command. Most important of all, the development for the *Wehrmacht* of what was for the period an immensely powerful radio that enabled whole tank formations to be

controlled in a cohesive manner — something that the Allies could not yet do — made it possible for the Lorient U-boat headquarters to be provided with radio transmitters able to communicate directly with U-boat commanders at great range, and direct several submarines on to the same target. This was the origin of the infamous 'Wolf Pack', that was to wreak such terrible havoc on Allied convoys.

As the new Lorient HQ was brought into commission, the U-boat fleet was still not large — 57 boats in September 1940. In the first year of war, the Germans had lost 28 submarines, and had commissioned

8 The German submarine building programme was put under heavy pressure by significant losses during the spring of 1940, and the German yards were pushed to ever-greater efforts. *U-Boats* came closer to winning the war for Germany than any other weapon, and in June 1940 sank fifty-eight British merchant ships.

9 Second World War submarines, unlike modern, nuclear powered vessels, were obliged to spend significant periods of time on the surface in order to recharge their batteries. At these times, *U-Boats* were at their most vulnerable, and often took the opportunity of escort if a surface vessel was nearby. This *U-Boat* is keeping company with a German minesweeper.

The Beginnings of the Sea War

1 Many of the *U-Boat* commanders and their officers were particularly committed Nazis, a fact partly due to the success of the Marine Hitler Youth in training young men in the Thirties. These Hitler Youth, aboard the German submarine supply ship *Saar* for an exercise shortly before the war, were inspected by Admiral Raeder, and would have been ready volunteers for the dangerous yet glamorised submarine service.

2 As Germany occupied the coast of Northwestern Europe from the Arctic Circle to the Bay of Biscay, no time was lost in building huge submarine pens at Lorient, Brest and several other locations. These formed the bases for the attacks on shipping in the Western Atlantic and the Channel approaches.

exactly the same number. Because the training of a submarine crew took (and still takes) a long time, Doenitz was rarely able at this time to put more than nine U-boats into the Atlantic West of Ireland. That his hand-picked and dedicated commanders managed to maintain an average of 920 tons of shipping sunk per U-boat, per day during October 1940 is an indication of just how effective his crews and his organisation were.

In the face of this efficient offensive force, Britain was desperately short of convoy protection and anti-submarine vessels. Until the destroyers and corvettes ordered during 1939 and 1940 were available, Britain needed more ships, and fast. In May 1940, Churchill had asked President Roosevelt for help in the form of some 50 American destroyers built at the end of the First World War. By July, having heard nothing and with an ever-more pressing need, Churchill tried again, with a further request on July 11th. Although a majority of American public opinion was in favour of helping Britain, and was sympathetic towards both the magnitude of her problems, and the fortitude with which she withstood them, there was great concern about the possible reprisals that such help might exact from Germany and Italy. Fears were expressed that the USA would be dragged into a war for which its industrial production facilities were as yet ill-prepared.

Roosevelt sought a compromise by offering Churchill an alternative deal that would have a direct benefit to US security. In return for the 50 destroyers, proposed Roosevelt, the USA would be allowed to establish bases in Guiana, the Antilles, Bermuda, the Bahamas and, given the agreement of Canada, in Newfoundland for 99 years. London accepted these terms, but objected sharply when Roosevelt attempted to make a further condition that the British Government declare that Britain's fleet would be sailed to America

if it could not be maintained in Home waters. Churchill curtly pointed out that the risk of having to scuttle or surrender the Fleet was one to which the German navy, or what was left of it, was more subject than the British.

Thus Britain approached the sea war of 1941 and 1942 with growing strength, but little effective means to fight the menace to merchant convoys posed by the U-boat. The terror of the wolf-pack was to prove one of the most fearsome chapters of the war. But, for the moment, let us return to the land-based war, and the warmer waters of the Mediterranean.

3 A stern view of one of Germany's Type VII *U-Boats*, of which 705 were built, 437 were sunk, 165 were scuttled and 103 surrendered at the end of the war. This boat, according to the original caption, was renamed by its commander 'Westward Ho!' after victories against British shipping.

CHAPTER 10

GAMBLE IN NORTH AFRICA
MUSSOLINI'S VENTURE ~ HITLER'S INTERVENTION

In June 1940, when Mussolini at last cast his hand for war, Italy had already in North Africa some 236,000 troops, over 1,800 guns, 150 aircraft and some 340 light tanks. These were divided as the Italian 5th Army to the West of Libya, and the 10th Army to the East, the two together amounting to a total of 14 Italian divisions. Ranged against them, but not yet in action, were eight French and five British divisions, the British under the command of General Sir Archibald Wavell. Of the 100,000 British troops, only 36,000 were in Egypt and ready to fight if their positions were attacked. The remainder were to the rear.

The armistice with the French at the end of June altered the balance significantly, taking the French army out of the calculation, and, on the other side of the coin, destroying the Italian commander

4 The British Commander-in-Chief in North Africa when Mussolini's adventure began was General Sir Archibald Wavell (centre). In November 1941, Wavell was replaced in North Africa by a Churchill impatient at the lack of effective offensive, and Wavell became British C-in-C India.

5 Marshal Rodolfo Graziani (right), here seen with Crown Prince Umberto of Italy, assumed command of the Italian forces in North Africa after Marshal Balbo's untimely and entirely avoidable death on June 28th 1940. He was a sound and practical, though less than brilliant, commander, and was immediately in conflict with Mussolini's often irrational and usually impractical orders.

Marshal Balbo's hopes of taking the Tunisian port of Bizerta to simplify his line of supply. To keep the Italians at a disadvantage, the British 7th Armoured Division began to make daily armoured raids across the Libyan frontier, the success of which, although in fact due to superior British training and discipline, was interpreted by the Italian Army as being the result of the inferiority of Italian weapons.

On June 28th, when it became clear that French North Africa would remain loyal to the Vichy government of Marshal Petain, the Italian Supreme Command ordered Balbo to invade Egypt. On the same day, having not received the order, Balbo suffered a fate that justified the Germans' worst fears about their tempestuous allies — he was shot out of the air over Tobruk by his own anti-aircraft gunners and killed. This was neither the first time nor the last that the Italian forces employed the 'own goal' as a technique in warfare, but it was the only occasion when they used it to dispose of their own Commander in Chief.

Balbo's command was assumed by Marshal Rodolfo Graziani, and the date for the invasion was set for July 15th 1940. The difficulties presented by the enterprise were formidable. There was but one supply route available across the desert from the Libyan frontier to Alexandria, and that route included two British bases, Sidi Barrani and Mersa Matruh. Graziani, sensibly, decided he was not prepared to begin the advance until he had sufficient trucks and water transport to keep his forces supplied. He asked approval to defer the assault until October 1940. Mussolini, predictably, refused to countenance such a practical suggestion. Knowing that Hitler intended to invade Britain on the 15th September, he was determined that Italy should take Egypt from Britain on the same day. Throughout July and August there were fierce disputes, inflammatory telegrams and endless problems between Mussolini and the Supreme Command, and between Mussolini and Graziani.

Eventually, still ill-prepared, Graziani was obliged to launch the might of Fascist Italy's 10th Army on the pitifully small British defending force on September 13th. Four divisions and an armoured group under General Bergonzoli advanced slowly across a hostile landscape in temperatures of up to 122 degrees Fahrenheit (50 degrees Celsius), succeeding in covering only some 12 miles a day. On September 16th, the crack '23rd of March' Blackshirt Division occupied Sidi Barrani, the 7th Armoured Division having been ordered to fall back before the advance. The Italians were now 60 miles into their 315-mile journey to their objective, Alexandria. Mersa Matruh lay 75 miles ahead.

To Mussolini's intense chagrin, Graziani, who was a veteran of desert operations, decided to pause, repair the damage done by the retreating British Army, set up a fresh water pipeline and stock Sidi Barrani so that it could be effective as a forward supply base. Wavell, like Mussolini, was disappointed, although for different reasons. He had hoped to see the Italians overextend their line of supply. Graziani knew that his equipment was inadequate, that he had too few men for the assault with which he had been entrusted, and that unless he

6 The 36,000 British troops (of a total of 100,000) that were in position to resist an Italian advance on Mersa Matruh were having to live and wait in extremely hot and unpleasant conditions, with temperatures reaching 50° C. These British soldiers are keeping their heads down during an air raid.

ensured adequate support, his army would stand no chance at all in the latter stages of the advance. Had Mussolini not retained in Italy for his forthcoming assault on Greece most of the troops that had recently been in action in the Alps, things might have been very different.

Graziani's pause lasted into October. At the Brenner Pass Conference on October 4th, at which Hitler, Mussolini, Ribbentrop and Count Ciano met to discuss strategy, the possibility of eventually sending a German armed detachment to North Africa was discussed, but Mussolini made it quite clear that Italy could handle North Africa alone for the time being without German assistance. In Mussolini's opinion, German *Panzer* support would be required only when the third stage of his conquest of Egypt was reached, the advance from Mersa Matruh to Alexandria. By October 21st, Mussolini was warning Graziani in some exasperation that, if the march on Mersa Matruh did not commence shortly, Graziani's resignation from his command would not come amiss. Graziani, who had been waiting

for the arrival of three motorised battalions, armoured cars and additional water trucks, was not disposed to put his troops at risk. Because of the imminent Italian campaign in the Balkans, there was little prospect either of those reinforcements arriving, or of the request for Graziani's resignation being enforced. Mussolini had other things on his mind.

In fact, the blame for the defeat at Sidi Barrani that was inflicted by Wavell on December 9th should not be laid entirely at Mussolini's door. The Italian 10th Army was deployed, in a manner that had obvious and exploitable weaknesses, in two separate groups fifteen miles apart with an undefended gap between. Two Libyan native divisions under Graziani's command were holding positions along the coast, and the 4th Blackshirt Division was to the rear of Sidi Barrani.

The British plan for the attack was daring. Lieutenant-General Sir Richard O'Connor's Western Desert Force was to penetrate the gap between the two halves of the 10th Army, and attack the coastal units from the rear, while the British 7th Armoured Division would advance towards Buqbuq to cut Italian communications and prevent reinforcements reaching the army under attack. An additional secondary brigade-strength attack under Brigadier Selby was to keep the coastal camp at Maktila busy. All told, only 36,000 British troops were taking on a force of almost five times as many men.

The attack on December 9th came as a surprise to the Italians, who had wrongly interpreted aerial reconnaissance information that British troops were on the move as evidence of a weary army being relieved. The 4th Indian Division, and the Matilda tank battalion,

1 The Italian Air Force was relatively well-equipped in the early stages of the war, and flew many raids against the British and French soldiers in Libya. This unclassified wreckage seems to be the tailplane of a Macchi C202 fighter, which entered service with the *Regia Aeronautica* in the summer of 1941.

2 The Bofors anti-aircraft gun was to be found in every theatre of the Second World War, on land and at sea. The Western Desert was no exception – this British Bofors crew is spotting aircraft through binoculars in the midst of a sea of sand.

3 Italian artillery was, by comparison with the larger and better equipped guns of the British and German armies, more than a little antiquated at the beginning of the North African campaign. Nonetheless, the guns that the Italians did have available were used effectively.

4 Although Italian soldiers of the Second World War did not always enjoy the best reputation as fighting men, this was undoubtedly due in part to severe doubts held by many of them about the cause for which they were fighting. These troops, however, seem to be taking the job seriously, in action in Libya.

together part of O'Connor's force, attacked Nibeiwa, and took 2,000 prisoners for the loss of 56 men. The 7th Armoured division reached the sea by evening, and cut off the retreat of the 2nd Libyan Division. Graziani ordered XXI Corps to withdraw to the frontier, and one division made it without difficulty. The other, the 'Catanzaro' Division, was less fortunate, and was almost annihilated. In a few short hours the Italian army had lost 38,000 prisoners, 237 guns and 73 tanks, against British losses of 624 dead.

At this crucial stage, General O'Connor had the victorious 4th Indian Division taken from his command for action against the Italians in Eritrea, and was awarded the 6th Australian Division as a replacement. He decided not to wait, and instead gave chase to the disorganised and humiliated Italians. On December 14th, O'Connor crossed the Libyan frontier at Capuzzo, swung north and attacked Bardia, defended by 45,000 Italian troops and 430 guns. On the 18th December, General Mackay and the Australian 6th Division arrived, ready for a fight. They celebrated the New Year with another victory. Bardia was captured on January 5th. The Italians lost a further 45,000 men as prisoners, and saw another 130 of their tanks captured.

By now Hitler was becoming increasingly worried at the antics of Mussolini, who had during the autumn launched his ill-prepared armies upon Greece without first advising Germany of his intentions (see below), and was now about to improve British morale and ruin the image of the all-victorious Axis with a devastating defeat in North Africa. In preparation for German intervention, *Luftwaffe X Fliegerkorps* was sent to Sicily at the end of December 1940, and by

5 The strength of the Royal Air Force in Libya was built up steadily during the first year of fighting, and the Italian troops were frequently subjected to raids by RAF bombers. These aircraft were bombing Italian artillery positions that threatened the line of the British advance.

6 A picture that somehow speaks volumes about the dust and discomfort of the desert war – Italian infantry taking up positions for the first battle of Tobruk in January 1941. General O'Connor took 25,000 Italians prisoner after this battle, and used captured Italian tanks to augment his own meagre armour in order to win it.

7 The Second World War will probably prove to have been the last great war fought mainly by men on foot. Some stages of the North African campaign, particularly in the early stages, were in many ways like trench warfare, characterised by the seizing and holding at considerable cost of insignificant positions after a brief advance. These Italian troops are lying flat along a ridge, under fire from British troops beyond.

Gamble in North Africa

February 6th, after the fall of Tobruk to O'Connor's all-conquering 7th Armoured Division, General Erwin Rommel was being briefed by Field Marshal von Brauchitsch to command the *Afrika Korps*, scheduled to land in North Africa by mid-February.

In Libya, O'Connor had, even before the fall of Bardia at the beginning of the month, detached the 7th Armoured Division to cut the communications of Tobruk, a vital deep-water port capable of providing a far more efficient means of landing supplies for the Allied force than the long overland route from Alexandria. At dawn on the 21st of January, a full scale-attack on Tobruk was mounted by the 6th Australian Division, who, because they were down to only 12 Matilda tanks, put captured Italian M-13/40 light tanks into action against their former owners. By the following afternoon, 22nd January, O'Connor was embarrassed with a further 25,000 Italian prisoners and had added 208 guns, 23 medium tanks and 200 trucks to his growing arsenal of alien equipment. Because of the speed of the advance, the Allies captured the vital sea-water distillation plant intact, and the port installation was sufficiently little damaged to be operating again within four days. In addition to the port of Tobruk, the victory brought

1 Italian armour on the move – the sheer size and emptiness of the desert is brought home by the column of vehicles snaking into the distance.

2 Marshal Pietro Badoglio, Chief of Staff at *Comando Supremo*, (left), seen here in conversation with Crown Prince Umberto of Italy, suffered an uneasy relationship with Mussolini, and in December 1940 was relieved of his post 'at his own request' after disagreement with Mussolini about *Il Duce's* ill-judged campaign in the Balkans. Badoglio was later appointed Prime Minister after Mussolini was deposed by King Victor Emmanuel III following the adverse vote of the Fascist Grand Council which unseated Mussolini in July 1943. Badoglio subsequently sought peace with the Allies.

3 Tobruk was captured by the Allies on January 21st 1941. The 9,200 ton cruiser *San Georgio*, armed with four 10" guns, had been badly damaged by the RAF a year earlier in January 1940, and had been used subsequently as an anti-aircraft gun platform. Shortly before the end of the Battle of Tobruk, the cruiser was again badly hit and sank. The hulk is here just showing above the water as fires on the shore continue to burn.

the bonus of the airfield at El Adem, another vital link in the supply chain which, like Tobruk, was to be in the news more than once in the months to come.

Graziani now set about a half-hearted defence of, and retreat from, Cyrenaica, the desert area that lay between O'Connor's forces and Benghazi, the next target that would be on the Allies' shopping list. Despite Mussolini's instruction to defend it, Graziani was more concerned to fall back to what he considered to be a defensible position. By January 27th, the 7th Armoured Division was at Mechili, some 140 miles from Beda Fomm, near the Gulf of Sirte, South of Benghazi. In appalling conditions, as the Italians retreated along the

much lengthier but better coast road, the *Via Balbia*, the 7th Armoured cut straight across the desert towards the coast. By 3pm on February 4th, the 11th Hussars were at Msus, some 60 miles from the *Via Balbia*, and at noon on the 5th they reached Beda Fomm, half an hour before the Italians retreating from Benghazi down the *Via Balbia*. By February 7th, Generals Cona and Babini had been captured, General Tellera was dead, and O'Connor had another 20,000 Italians to look after. The British had also reached El Agheila at the foot of the Gulf of Sirte, a position commanding the 15-mile-wide access to the sea from the desert. The British were poised to invade Tripolitania. And Rommel was about to arrive in North Africa.

CHAPTER 11

THE BALKANS
RUMANIA, GREECE, YUGOSLAVIA AND CRETE

The fall of France in June 1940 had brought to the surface a dispute which had smouldered for years and which, although not in itself directly connected with the war between the great powers, was about to exert a major influence upon it. This was the territorial disagreement between Hungary and Rumania, which arose from the Treaty of Trianon in 1920. This Treaty had, following the defeat of Austria-Hungary in the Great War, caused Hungary to cede Transylvania, beloved of all followers of Dracula, to Rumania – a not unreasonable boundary change in most respects, since the majority of the inhabitants of Transylvania were, in any case, of Rumanian origin.

There were however, within Transylvania, some 2 million people of the Magyar race, known as the Sicules, who had no wish to be Rumanian, and who persistently refused to accept their change of nationality. When France fell, the Hungarian Government made approaches to King Carol II of Rumania, but it soon became apparent that Rumania was immoveable on the issue. War seemed inevitable, but Hitler, whose reliance upon the oil wells at Ploesti caused him to put a high priority upon the maintenance of access to Rumania, intervened. Hungary, whose government had a sympathetic ear in Italy, agreed, if Rumania was also agreeable, to submit to Axis arbitration on the dispute. As a result, Ciano and Ribbentrop presided over arbitration proceedings in Vienna in August 1940. Their verdict was that Transylvania should be partitioned, the west going to Rumania. Hungary was to gain the area occupied by the Sicules, plus the extension of her 1920 frontier to the Moldavian Carpathians. This had the effect of putting three million Rumanians into Hungary, a neat reversal of the previous position.

The Rumanians resented their government's acceptance of this proposal deeply, and General Antonescu, appointed Premier by King Carol II on September 4th, rapidly forced King Carol to abdicate and established Carol's son Prince Michael on the throne. Antonescu

4 King Carol II of Rumania and his son, Crown Prince Michael, arriving to entertain King George VI and Queen Elizabeth to dinner at the Rumanian Legation in London in November 1938. King Carol's resigned acceptance in 1940 of the partition of Transylvania, decided upon by Ciano and Ribbentrop, the Axis Foreign Ministers, brought about revolution and his abdication.

5 Prince Michael was keenly interested in matters military, and, during the visit in autumn 1938 with his father, took the opportunity to visit RAF Odiham in Hampshire, where he inspected one of the latest fighters.

6 German troops parade in Bucharest in the manner that had been seen several times in other capitals and was shortly to become sadly familiar in the cities of Northwestern Europe. Unlike the scenes in Vienna two years earlier, there are no hands raised in the Nazi salute to be seen in the Bucharest crowd.

1 Mussolini, creature of impulse that he was, invaded Greece on 28th October 1940 in a fit of pique at the success of the German coup in Rumania. His love of publicity and wish to be seen as the military and political equal of Hitler were not matched by his ability to accept his generals' advice or to recognise an impending military disaster when it faced him.

2 The Greeks surprised the Italians as much by their military skill, bravery and determination as by the extent of the resistance from the civilian population, who regarded the invading Italians with derision. These Greek soldiers are artillery spotting – local knowledge of the hills and mountains was a crucial factor in the Greeks' success against the Italians, and subsequent guerilla operations against the German invaders.

3 When, in December 1940, the Italian campaign in Greece had become a near-rout, Mussolini arrived to survey the progress of the battle with apparently uncomprehending bravura.

asked Hitler to provide military assistance to Rumania, and on October 7th the 13th German Motorised Division began to arrive in Bucharest.

Mussolini was indignant at the occupation, particularly since his allies had not told him of it before it took place. He resolved to reward Germany in kind, and to the horror of his Generals, who had, only three weeks before, demobilised 600,000 men on the Duce's orders, instructed them to prepare to invade Greece on October 26th. Count Ciano, Mussolini's son-in-law and Foreign Minister, believed that neither Yugoslavia nor Turkey would come to the aid of Greece, to whom they were allied by the Balkan Pact, and that Bulgaria would approve of Italy's actions. Lieutenant-General Jacomoni, in command in Albania, told the planning conference on 14th October 1940 that everyone in Albania was anxious to settle the account with Greece. Faced with universal approval of Mussolini's scheme, Marshal Badoglio, who had severe doubts as to its military practicality, gave way and agreed, subject to an extension of the deadline for the attack for two days to October 28th.

On the morning of that day, having been warned by the German Ambassador that Italy was about to invade Greece, Hitler travelled to Florence to try and prevent the rash act that was to extend the Axis front and create new potential for defeat. He was greeted by a Mussolini wreathed in smiles, who obviously expected Hitler to be equally happy at his master stroke. 'Fuehrer' he is reported to have said, 'we are on the march! At dawn this morning our Italian troops victoriously crossed the Albanian-Greek frontier.'

4 Pulling their capes over their British-style steel helmets in an attempt to keep warm in the appallingly cold conditions of the Albanian mountains, these Greek soldiers were advancing on foot in pursuit of the Italian armies in Albania.

Early in the Italian campaign, it became clear that many of Ciano's political bases for the strategy were hopelessly wrong. Above all, the Italians had misjudged totally both their own standing with the Greek people, and the Greeks' patriotism and preparedness to fight. The plain fact was that the Greeks loathed Mussolini, his regime, his army and his ideas. They had seen the cruelty of Fascism, and they wanted none of it.

As soon as the invasion took place, the Greek Prime Minister, General Metaxas, ordered general mobilisation, which provided the commander of the Greek forces, General Alexandros Papagos, with 15 infantry divisions, 4 infantry brigades and a cavalry division, which together were assembled as five Army Corps. Although a head count gave the Italians the advantage, the mountainous terrain, the

determination of the Greeks, the essentially flabby nature of the Italian troops and the communications advantage enjoyed by the Greek army fighting on its own ground gave the defenders the edge. The Greeks also benefited from the extremely wet weather, which slowed down the invasion from the start, and made it virtually impossible for the Italian Air Force to give effective cover.

On the left of General Visconti-Prasca's invading army, the Alpine Division managed by November 2nd to break through the advanced Greek positions and take the village of Vovoussa some 25 miles from the border, but a Greek counterattack on the following day drove them back whence they came in considerable disarray. In the centre, the armour and infantry that were headed for Yanina were held up totally. On the right, the Siena Division took Filiates and Paramithia, and

5 In an effort to counteract the advantages enjoyed by the Greeks, the Italian army enlisted the aid of large numbers of pack mules to transport their supplies and equipment on the narrow mountain paths and roads. Although it is almost certainly an illusion, the impression given by this picture is entertaining, for it would seem if one studies it closely that the troops are going round in circles!

6 Mussolini's army was never good at standing its ground when the going got rough, and during the ferocious attacks launched by the Greeks many Italian units abandoned their equipment in their haste to retreat. The Greeks, being without armour of their own, were quick to turn this to their advantage – these Greek soldiers are driving recently-captured Italian light tanks into battle against the vehicles' former owners.

7&9 Some idea of the difficulty of even the foothill Albanian terrain for troops not accustomed to mountain warfare can be gained from these two pictures. 7 Italian troops are having to advance uphill across scrubland offering virtually no cover against small arms fire. 9 The Italian artillery piece is on a ridge with, again, no cover and no camouflage, and the crew must simply keep their heads down and hope that the enemy artillery observation posts do not get their range.

8 The Italian Alpine Division, which had seen some action in the Alpes Maritimes during the period of the fall of France, was sent to Albania to introduce some mountain battle experience into the misguided Italian attempt at conquest. These men of the Alpine Division had been flown in by trimotor transport aircraft.

The Balkans

looked able to take Yanina. But the weather raged on, the Italian Air Force was unable to prevent the Greeks from completing their mobilisation and concentration, and General Papagos made the most of the situation. By November 12th, Papagos could claim 100 battalions ranged in mountainous country they knew well, against 50 Italian battalions who wished they were elsewhere. He decided that the time had come to counterattack.

On November 14th, five days after the Italian command passed from General Visconti-Prasca to General Ubaldo Soddu, the Greeks attacked along the entire front, from the Ionian Sea to Lake Prespa.

Almost immediately, the Greek 5th Corps under General Tzolakoglou broke the Italian line at Mount Morova. Eight days after commencing the attack, Tzolakoglou crushed the Italian 9th Army at Koritsa, taking 2,000 prisoners, 80 field guns, 55 anti-tank guns, and 300 machine guns from the 'Tridentina' Mountain Division and two infantry divisions.

November 21st saw the Greek 2nd Corps under General Papadopoulos cross the Albanian frontier to take Ersëke and Leskovik. On December 4th, the 3rd Corps occupied Pogradec, and the following day the 2nd took Permet, 23 miles inside Albania. The 1st Corps under General Kosmas meanwhile chased the Italian 11th Army down the Dhrin valley, and were greeted delightedly by the very Albanian people upon whose loyalty the Italians believed they could count totally. The 1st had also taken Sarande.

Now the weather, and the almost total lack of Greek armour, began to take a hand in the campaign. While the Greeks were able to fight in the hills they could win. Once on the plains they were no match for Italian tanks. Eight new Italian divisions had been sent to Albania between the end of October and December 31st, but the Greeks had no reinforcements, either from their own or British sources. The weather was bitterly cold, and the troops of both sides were suffering from a shortage of adequate winter equipment and of food. For a time there was virtual stalemate.

1 Italian prisoners taken by the Greeks were, on the whole, treated well. These Italian soldiers look as tired and dispirited as most prisoners do, but were well fed and had their wounds tended.

2 The Athens Conference on February 22nd 1941 had decided that British arms should be re-established in Europe by the despatch of a British Expeditionary Force to Greece if Germany entered the war in the Balkans. After Bulgaria joined the Tripartite Pact on March 1st, Germany crossed the Danube, and the decision taken at Athens was put into action. In this picture, some of the Bren carriers and light tanks that had been landed at Piraeus and Volos from March 7th onwards are blessed by the Bishop of Canea.

3 The winter of 1940/1941 was harsh in Europe, and even in the Balkans the mountain snows persisted longer and with greater depth than is usual, thereby helping the Greeks significantly. These Greek soldiers are in fact outside their tents, but the snow has effectively camouflaged both soldiers and tents to such an extent that the Italians would be unlikely to spot them.

4 On April 6th 1941, the *Blitzkrieg* that was to overwhelm Yugoslavia began. Fifteen divisions, including five *Panzer* Divisions and 800 aircraft, began a campaign of terror and destruction. Some 17,000 people were killed in Belgrade between April 6th and April 8th. This artillery crew is firing on the vastly outnumbered and outgunned Yugoslav defenders.

5 The Yugoslav Army, here seen on manoeuvres in March 1941, just before the German onslaught, was well equipped with heavy artillery, and substantial Allied hopes were pinned on the ability of the big guns to save the day when the invasion came. In the event, the sheer scale of the German firepower unleashed upon Yugoslavia was so great that the hapless Yugoslavs had little chance of success.

The Implications of Taranto

It is necessary at this stage to take a look at the Mediterranean sea war, for the highly successful torpedo bomber attack on the Italian fleet in its base at Taranto by Admiral Cunningham's Mediterranean Fleet had a profound influence upon the Italian campaign in the Balkans. In the latter part of October, Cunningham and Rear-Admiral Lyster, commander of the Royal Navy's aircraft carrier force in the Mediterranean, had planned an attack on the Italian fleet, which was showing a marked disinclination to come out and fight. On November 11th, air reconnaissance established that all six Italian battleships were in port at Taranto, and 21 obsolete Swordfish biplanes armed with torpedoes (eleven aircraft) and bombs (the other 10) took off from the *Illustrious* to attack in two waves. Fortune was to some extent fav-

In his place, General Cavallero became Chief of Staff of *Comando Supremo*.

Meanwhile Hitler, who had been preoccupied with plans for 'Operation Felix' to take Gibraltar, destined to come to nothing because Spain's General Franco refused to throw in his lot with the Axis, had decided that Germany could not stand by and watch Mussolini and his compatriots annihilated. If he allowed the Balkan campaign to go to the Allies, the Rumanian oil fields would be threatened. Something had to be done. A date of March 15th was therefore set for a German invasion of Greece.

On December 29th, Cavallero arrived in Albania to take over personal command of operations from General Soddu. He had orders to go on to the offensive, and to prove that German intervention in

5

6

7

ouring the attack — the protective balloon barrage around the anchorage had been damaged by storms, and the Italian torpedo nets extended only 26 feet down into the water, whereas British torpedoes ran at 30 feet depth. Nonetheless it was a daring attack, carried out in slow-moving aircraft in the face of 21 batteries of 100mm guns and 200 light anti-aircraft guns, plus the guns of the ships they were attacking. Six torpedoes scored hits, putting *Littorio* and *Duilio* out of action for six months and sinking the *Cavour*. The Royal Navy lost only two aircraft, with one crewman dead and three prisoners, despite the Italians having fired no less than 8,500 shells.

The Italians responded to the Greeks' successes in the Balkans, and to the loss of half their capital ships at Taranto, with an orgy of blame and recrimination, refusing as always to accept that the true cause of the disaster was the incompetence, mismanagement and sheer vanity of Mussolini. Badoglio, who had warned against the militarily unsound Balkans attack in the first place, was pilloried in the press and on the radio, and resigned in disgust on November 26th.

8

6 A German SdKfz 222 armoured car provides cover for advancing infantry during the conquest of Yugoslavia, its 20mm cannon pointing menacingly at Yugoslav defenders. The SdKfz 222 was the standard German four-wheel armoured car, and was used extensively by the *Wehrmacht* in Europe and North Africa throughout the war.

7 As in Greece, the Yugoslav civilian population played an active role in the battle against the invaders, and after the surrender and German occupation the Yugoslav partisans became the most successful of the armed resistance organisations. This picture is undated, but shows women and children being rounded up, presumably for assisting the partisans. German propaganda presented the same picture under the heading 'Come back! Your village is now free from the Bolsheviks'.

8 Under the watchful eye of a guard of the *Waffen-SS*, two Yugoslav prisoners are taken to a German prison camp in April 1941. A total of 343,712 Yugoslav soldiers became prisoners of war during the German conquest of their country, which ended on April 17th with the capitulation of the Yugoslav Army.

The Balkans

Albania would be unnecessary. To achieve this he had 16 divisions spread across a largely mountainous front of 156 miles, made up of troops in poor health, with inadequate equipment and an over-extended supply line. The Greeks had roughly 13 divisions, and were on the offensive, although on a strictly limited-objective basis, taking a position here and a position there, with occasional dramatic success. An example was their defeat of the 'Wolves of Tuscany' division at Klisura. Nonetheless, Cavallero meant business, and between December 29th and March 26th, brought in reinforcements of 10 divisions and 4 machine gun battalions, plus 3 legions and 17 battalions of Blackshirts from Italy. The Greeks' inability to fight offensively became more and more apparent as the weather improved, as the Italian Air Force was increasingly brought into action, and as the lack of Greek armour made any form of modern attack impossible.

1 The weather conditions in Yugoslavia in the spring of 1941 were appallingly wet – as so often happens, the heavy snow of winter was followed by flooding, landslips and rain. Mud was everywhere, and both sides had constant difficulties with vehicles on the poor roads.

2 The enormous number of Yugoslav prisoners taken by the Germans – these are a few in just one transit camp among many – posed considerable food and supply problems for the invaders. King Peter of Yugoslavia just managed to escape being captured, and was flown out of Kotor in an RAF Sunderland flying boat on April 17th.

3 German artillery on the move in Skopje, Yugoslavia. The half-track personnel carrier acts both as a gun-tractor and as a tender for ammunition and supplies. The corporal on foot, who appears to be going the other way, bears a remarkable resemblance to Heinrich Himmler.

With his reinforcements in place, and much of his supply problem rectified, Cavallero went on to the offensive on March 9th with an attack on three divisions of General Papadopoulos' 2nd Corps between the rivers Apsos in the North East, and the Aoos in the South West. Against them beneath the Trebesina mountains were ranged no less than eleven divisions of Italian infantry and the 'Centauro' armoured division. After two days of fighting, with well dug in Greek artillery using their ammunition sparingly yet tellingly, the Italians had failed to break through, despite their great superiority of numbers, and were losing a great many men. General Papagos managed to reach Papadopoulos' Corps and reinforce his force with a further two divisions, and by the 15th March the Italians were no further towards their objective than they had been on the 9th.

Finally, on the 15th, Mussolini, who had watched the sorry affair of the Trebesina offensive in person with Cavallero, called off the attack and returned to Rome. The Italian Army had lost 12,000 dead and wounded for no very obvious gain. Meanwhile the tough and uncompromising General Metaxas had died in January, and had been replaced as Greek Prime Minister by Petros Koryzis. The British, approached by him to aid the Greeks in their fight against the Axis, consulted General Wavell, Air Chief Marshal Longmore and Admiral Cunningham, who all expressed doubts as to the capability of the RAF to hold Salonikan airspace against the *Luftwaffe*, if, as expected, Germany entered the Balkan struggle. At a conference in Athens on February 22nd 1941, attended by King George of Greece, British

Foreign Secretary Anthony Eden, Prime Minister Koryzis and Generals Dill and Wavell, there was extensive discussion as to the expected attitude of still neutral Yugoslavia to the anticipated German offensive, and of the reaction of Yugoslavia if the Greeks were obliged to withdraw from Salonika. Eventually the conference made the dangerous decision to attempt to re-establish a British presence in Europe by sending an expeditionary force to Athens should the Germans take action in the Balkans.

On March 1st 1941, Bulgaria belatedly allied herself with Germany, whereupon the German 12th Army crossed the Danube and triggered the plan for the British landings in Greece. From March 7th onwards the force, commanded by General Sir Henry Maitland Wilson, landed at Piraeus and Volos. Some 57,000 men and 100 tanks were put ashore, a force made up of the 6th Australian Division, the 2nd New Zealand Division and the 1st Armoured Brigade. By the end of March, Maitland Wilson's formations were established and had acquired, after protracted negotiations, three Greek divisions. But his forces were seriously under strength, mainly because he had been allotted the 7th Australian Division and the 1st Polish Brigade, neither of which was actually sent to Greece.

Germany attacks Yugoslavia

The establishment of German garrisons in Bulgaria gave Yugoslavia problems. No less than three countries were making claims upon Yugoslav territory: Italy, Hungary and Bulgaria. If Yugoslavia did not

4 After the surrender of the Yugoslav Army on 17th April, it took two weeks or more for the Germans to round up and disarm the majority of the remaining soldiers. Some simply escaped to the mountains and became the basis of the partisan groups who remained a severe problem to Germany for the rest of the war. These Yugoslav soldiers were less lucky, and were forced to surrender their rifles to the Germans.

5

now agree to join the Tripartite Pact, and ally herself with Germany, the probability was that Germany and Italy would see to it that the country was divided among their allies. Since Hitler had given assurances that German armies would not pass through Yugoslavia to invade Greece, it seemed inescapably opportune that she should now give in and join. On March 25th, the Regent, Prince Paul, and his Prime Minister did just that. This capitulation set in motion a military plot which, on March 27th, overthrew Paul and his government, proclaimed the young King Peter's majority and put General Simovic in power. Yet, despite this sudden action, the new government did nothing to anger the Third Reich, nothing to change policy in any significant way. This provided Germany with the opportunity to do what Germany was best at — seizing the initiative by force of arms.

A massive force of two Armies plus General Kleist's *Panzer*

6

7

8

9

Group was detailed for the assault, which took just twelve days to defeat Yugoslavia. On April 6th 1941, the *Luftwaffe* hit Belgrade with massive bombing raids, while Kleist's *Panzers* began the attack on the ground. By April 13th, Kleist and General von Wietresheim's 14th Motorised Corps, which had advanced 312 miles in seven days, met General Reinhardt's 41st *Panzer* Corps in Belgrade. Now the 46th *Panzer* Corps under General von Vietinghof captured by surprise a vital bridge over the River Drava at Bares, and opened the way to the rendezvous with the Italians at Karlovac. Sarajevo was occupied on the 15th April, and on the 17th the Yugoslav army surrendered. 6,028 officers and 337,684 NCOs and men became prisoners of war. But some 300,000 men escaped and took to the mountains, where they continued to fight and harry the Germans throughout their uncomfortable stay in Yugoslavia.

5 A major contribution to the speed of the German victory in Yugoslavia was made by the far greater mobility of the German Army by comparison with most others. This is part of a German motorised division, which used motor-cycles, cars, trucks, specialised radio vehicles (note the aerial arrays on the roofs) and armoured personnel carriers to get troops to their target.

6 The invasion of Greece by five German divisions under Field-Marshal List, which began on April 6th, encountered the same appalling weather conditions that bedevilled the Yugoslav operation. Extensive use was made of pack mules, both to carry supplies when conditions were too bad for motor vehicles, and also to drag military vehicles out of the mire.

7 In an attempt to restrict the movement of German troops and supplies, the Greeks blocked and blew up railway installations and roads at key places, sometimes, as in this case, by using explosives to create rock-falls to block the railway line. The Germans, never lacking in engineering expertise, rapidly cleared the worst of the rubble, and then used the railway tracks as a reliable route for their motor vehicles.

8 The Germans were not always able to overcome the problems put in their way by determined Greeks in possession of explosives. This *Panzer* officer has encountered a massive crater blown in a mountain road by Greek patriots, and can take his tank no further. If a column of vehicles was thus hindered on a narrow mountain road, getting the column back to a point where it could turn round could take hours or days, and this was a major delay to the German advance.

9 When Germany invaded Greece, Field-Marshal Sigmund Wilhelm List crossed from Bulgaria with five divisions from Germany's XXX Corps. Here, Field-Marshal List is in conference with a Bulgarian staff officer.

Tito's Partisans

The principal architect of the *Wehrmacht's* considerable discomfort in Yugoslavia was Josip Broz, known as Tito, a Croatian communist who narrowly escaped German arrest when he left Zagreb, his accustomed political base, in May 1941. Tito was a revolutionary leader of long standing who believed passionately in the Comintern and already led a substantial body of communist sympathisers before the German invasion of Yugoslavia.

By the end of May, Tito, by this time in Belgrade, believed that the Germans were about to invade the Soviet Union, and saw in this and the already complete German occupation of his country a potential opportunity for power. The three German divisions plus one regiment, commanded by Field Marshal von Weichs, which had remained in Yugoslavia after the capitulation, were removed late in April and early in May and were replaced by three divisions of older men more suited to occupation than to battle. Tito's belief that trouble for Stalin was afoot was turned into certainty by intelligence, gained by a White Russian from a German officer, that Russia was 'about to be liberated'.

The announcement of the German invasion of the Soviet Union on 22nd June 1941 brought celebration among Yugoslav communists, for it released them from the Comintern ban on military action imposed as a result of the Soviet/German non-aggression pact of August 1939. On 3rd July, Stalin issued an appeal for guerilla activities by all those behind the German lines, and Tito's Comintern controller Dimitrov issued more specific orders.

1 As the Germans took Albania and Greece, they were able to release many of the Italian prisoners who had earlier been captured, and took full propaganda advantage of the fact.

2 This picture, taken by a photographer of the *SS Propagandakompanie* named Peterseim, is captioned 'Freedom over Greece!'. The caption goes on to explain that the victory of the German armed forces has ousted the English warmongers from the European mainland. The caption fails to explain how the Greek vehicles came to be in the ditch, possibly because that was the result of German warmongering.

3 In just one day, Lieutenant-General Vieil and his 2nd *Panzer* Division dashed fifty-six miles from the Yugoslav/Greek border to Salonika, entering the port on April 8th. The Mercedes in the foreground looks decidedly second-hand after the Yugoslav campaign and this advance, evidence of the arduous road conditions and flood conditions that the German army had encountered.

"The peoples of Yugoslavia now have the opportunity to create a general liberation struggle against the German invader. It is a vital necessity to undertake all actions to assist and facilitate the just war of the Soviet people.... Remember that at present it is a question of liberation from Fascist domination, and not a question of Socialist revolution".

Tito issued a proclamation, printed on the Yugoslav party's already established secret press, and on 27th June 1941 set up a General Headquarters of National Liberation Partisans' Detachments. Individual acts of sabotage began to take place throughout the country, as yet largely uncoordinated and boosted by another major proclamation from Tito on 12th July. On 7th July, a Yugoslav veteran of the Spanish Civil War, Zikica Jovanovic, urged a crowd in the village of Bela Crkva, in Serbia, to resistance, shot two policemen and escaped. This incident marked the beginning of the great uprising.

Tito's most able and trusted lieutenants were sent to each of the regions to organise revolt under Tito's control. Some party groups, notably in Montenegro, did not accept that their role was solely to fight Germans rather than create a Socialist revolution, and, for some weeks, Tito had problems in establishing control. From his Belgrade headquarters, nonetheless, Tito controlled a rapidly expanding field army of small Partisan detachments, mostly living in the hills and keeping Tito's Intelligence Chief, Alexander Ranković, supplied with detailed information on Axis troop movements and concentrations. In return, Tito organised the capture and distribution of arms and ammunition and provided a headquarters training operation. Ranković's career was, in fact, almost brought to an early end in July, when he was arrested by the Gestapo as he planned to blow up Radio Belgrade. However, on 29th July, forty Partisans armed with revolvers and grenades freed him from a hospital where he was being held, without any of his rescuers being killed. Ranković went to the party headquarters in Western Serbia, and Tito himself had to leave Belgrade on 16th September. He was not to return until October 1944.

4 A Greek army captain urging his gun crew on as they move their artillery piece to bring it to bear on German formations near Epirus, hours before they were pressed back to surrender. The original caption to this picture is a masterpiece of propaganda, beginning 'Valiant Greeks, facing death with a smile ...'

5 A PzKpfw III Battle Tank leads an armoured column into Salonika in April 1941. In the foreground left are two hands raised in Nazi salute, which was interpreted by the Allied news media of the time as evidence of 'Fifth Column' treachery in Greece making the German invasion easier than it might otherwise have been. In fact, the salutes are far more likely to have been evidence of the philosophy 'If you can't beat 'em, join 'em'.

6 Captioned at the time simply with the words 'Nazis killed his father', this picture of a miserable little boy and his tearful mother in Athens summed up much of the sadness of the time for the Greeks.

7 On Tuesday April 22nd 1941, General Tzolakoglou (right), against his orders from Athens and without the approval of his immediate superior General Drakos, entered into negotiations for surrender. Here he is seen on his way to the negotiations with a German staff officer.

The Balkans

Within the six months between July and the end of 1941, Tito created an army of 80,000 men under arms, the nucleus of a force that was later to be estimated by the Germans, in late 1943, to total 111,000 men. His policy was to set out to clear the Axis troops from specific areas of the country, to call those areas 'liberated territories' and to use them both as operational bases and as footholds for eventual Communist power. By the end of August 1941, the Serbian insurrection, organised by Tito, had cleared the German army from almost two thirds of the Serbian countryside and the Germans had begun to re-think their attitude to the Partisans. Although the Partisans subsequently lost much of that initial territorial gain as the three long years of guerilla warfare got under way, the Germans were never again to believe that holding Yugoslavia would be easy. At its peak, the Partisan Army was to tie down more than twenty Axis divisions in the retention of a country which Germany had expected to occupy comparatively peacefully.

The Četniks

In organising resistance against the Axis invaders, Tito did not initially appear to have things all his own way. As early as April 1941, officers and men of the defeated Royalist army had begun to live and fight in the woods of Serbia under various leaders. But from them emerged Colonel Dragoljub Mihailović, who went to Western Bosnia when Yugoslavia capitulated and was in mid-Serbia by the middle of May 1941.

Intensely pro-Serb and anti-Croat, like many army officers, Mihailović was not a communist and had a low opinion of Tito, regarding him as (perhaps justifiably at the time) no more than an

upstart Croat revolutionary. Mihailović resisted German domination purely for reasons of pride and Serbian nationalism. By the end of September 1941, there were 5,000 Četniks. As Tito sought aid, arms and ammunition from the Soviet Union, so Mihailović looked for help from Britain. Initially, little came from either source to either leader and, at talks between Mihailović and Tito in October 1941, it became apparent that the Četniks were more opposed to communist domination under a Croatian leader than they were to the German occupation.

By the beginning of November, the Četniks were attacking Tito's Partisan positions, although without conspicuous success, for Mihailović had significantly underestimated the military capability of Tito's forces. Nonetheless, at this stage in events, the British, influenced by their commitment to the Yugoslav Royalist government in exile, seemed genuinely to believe Mihailović's assertions that Tito

1 This heavily (and badly) retouched picture of the moment of Greek surrender on April 22nd by General Tzolakoglou at Larisa includes the Mayor of Athens (left). Sixteen Greek divisions were surrendered, a total of 140,000 men. The Greeks had lost 15,700 soldiers dead and missing, and 218,000 as prisoners of war during the course of the campaign.

2 On April 19th, a conference between the Allies was held in Athens, when King George II and Generals Papagos, Wavell and Maitland Wilson were unanimous in deciding upon the evacuation of mainland Greece by the British Expeditionary Force. The King made a last appearance on a balcony at army headquarters and spoke to the people of Athens before leaving the country.

3 Within sight of the Acropolis, these German anti-aircraft gunners have quickly made themselves at home as the privations of the winter and spring amid the Balkan campaign gave way to summer sunshine in Greece.

6

7

8

was a fraud who did not represent the Yugoslav people, and on 15th November had the BBC announce that Mihailović had been made 'Commander-in-Chief of Yugoslav forces in the Fatherland'. Less than a week earlier, Mihailović had received his first parachuted supplies from the British, and on 12th November had been on the verge of losing his headquarters to the Partisans, who came within one mile of Ravna Gora, where the Četniks prepared for hasty evacuation.

At the height of this drama, Mihailović was at a meeting with German officers proposing joint operations against the Partisans, in return for which Serbia would be returned to the control of the Četniks. He assured the Germans that his main aim was to save the majority of his people from annihilation. The Germans did not fully trust him, and did not at this stage enter into an agreement, recognising that he was not the power he claimed to be and that Tito and his Partisans were far more dangerous.

While Mihailović was discussing terms with the Germans, two of his officers were holding talks with the Partisans, and reached a nine-point agreement to end hostilities. At the end of November, when major German response to earlier Partisan successes in Serbia had pushed the Partisans into retreat, Mihailović refused an offer from Tito of joint leadership and operations, stating that he was the only recognised leader of Yugoslav resistance. By the end of 1941, Mihailović had decided to make agreements with the occupiers and fight only against the communists. Only then did the British government realise something of the true situation and begin to think of Mihailović as being more of a master of compromise and prevarication than a Resistance leader.

Nonetheless, it was not until early 1944 that the British government, committed by its agreement with the Yugoslav Royalist government in exile to support of the Četniks, finally lost patience with Mihailović and withdrew the British liaison officers who had been seconded to the Četniks throughout the period when Tito's

9

Partisan Army had been doing battle with the Axis. Not until mid-1943 was significant, though qualified, Allied support given to Tito, and not until the summer of 1944, only months before his victory in Yugoslavia, was the Partisan Army fully recognised by the Allies. Tito's cool, resourceful leadership and considerable grasp of military strategy and tactics enabled him to keep an Axis force more then three times the size of his Partisan Army busy for more than three years.

Greece Invaded by Germany

When the Greeks heard of the Yugoslav signing of the Tripartite Pact on March 25th, General Papagos had ordered withdrawal from Salonika, but he changed his mind and issued orders to stand firm when news of the overthrow of Regent Paul on the 27th reached him. On the night of April 4th/5th, he conferred with Britain's Anthony Eden, General Dill and the Yugoslav General Jankovic on the border

4 This German *Propagandakompanie* picture by a photographer named Krempel, filed in June 1941 with the Weltbild agency in Berlin, shows ships sunk by air attack in Piraeus harbour. Considerable damage to harbour installations can be seen in the original picture.

5 Anthony Eden, later Lord Avon, British Foreign Secretary during the Second World War, took a major part in the negotiations with Greece which led to the landing, and subsequent evacuation, of the British Expeditionary Force. Here he is seen leaving No.10 Downing Street on 11th April 1941 with Mr A.V. Alexander, First Lord of the Admiralty.

6 Mugs of tea for some of the 50,732 British, Australian and New Zealand troops that were successfully evacuated from mainland Greece by the naval force under Rear-Admiral H.T. Baillie-Grohman. The evacuation was carried out under the nose of the *Leibstandarte Adolf Hitler SS Panzer* Division, which had reached Naupaktos and was crossing the Gulf of Patras.

7 These Australian nurses narrowly escaped capture by the advancing German armies during the evacuation of the British Expeditionary Force from Greece. During their retreat to the coast, they travelled by night along roads that were heavily machine-gunned and bombed during the day.

8 New Zealand soldiers, about to be embarked and obviously relieved to be getting away from Greece just in time. In fact, they were far from out of the wood, although they did eventually escape, for the Germans were trying to cut off their route to the open sea.

9 A corner of the ship upon which the last British subjects to leave Greece had been embarked. Women and children lived on deck for three days and nights without adequate food or shelter, and with very little water. The ship also evacuated 150 German prisoners taken by the Expeditionary Force.

1 As Greece fell, and German plans to take Crete were finalised, Hitler addressed the *Reichstag* in the Kroll Opera House, Berlin, stating that Germany had no further territorial aims. At the right of the front row of seated members, turning to look at Hitler, is Rudolf Hess, friend, secretary and confidante of the *Fuehrer* for almost twenty years. Just one week later, on May 10th 1941, Hess flew himself to Scotland in a Messerchmitt Me110 and crash-landed on the estate of the Duke of Hamilton, thereby entering upon the life of imprisonment in Britain and Germany which lasted until his death in 1987.

2 The beautiful, mountainous and militarily-forbidding island of Crete in 1941, as it would have been seen by the men of General Kurt Student's 7th Paratroop Division as they approached their drop zone. A total of 493 transport aircraft and seventy two gliders were used to deliver the parachute troops to their target. Almost 700 other aircraft were used in the invasion.

Legend:
- ▲▲▲ *Extended Limit of the German Advance Dec. 1941*
- •••• *Furthest Limit of the German Advance Oct. 1942*
- *Non Axis Occupied Territories*
- *Neutral Nations*

FRANCE *Unoccupied until Nov. 1942*

3 A dramatic picture of the German paratroops descending on Crete from their Junkers 52 transport aircraft, one of which has been hit by anti-aircraft fire and is spiralling to the ground in flames. Note the bomb burst to the left of the picture. The triple parachutes among the singles are supporting vehicles and guns being dropped for the assault on Heraklion.

4 The hundreds of parachutes dropping on Crete made an impressive sight in the area around Maleme on May 20th 1941. The RAF had only four Hurricane and three Gladiator biplanes available on the island to combat the German armada, as *Luftwaffe* bombardment before the invasion had destroyed twenty-eight of the thirty-five aircraft that had been serviceable on the island as recently as May 1st.

Left Axis power in Europe, October 1942.

between Greece and Yugoslavia. Papagos tried to persuade Jankovic to defend with the Greeks the short front necessary to prevent the Germans advancing to Greece if they entered Yugoslavia. Jankovic would have none of it. On April 6th, Papagos, knowing that the German invasion was imminent and that the defence of the full frontier was impossible, ordered the demolition of installations between the Bulgarian border and the forward Greek positions.

At 5.15am on the 6th, as *Panzer* Group Kleist entered Yugoslavia, Field-Marshal List crossed the border between Bulgaria and Greece with five divisions from the German XXX Corps in the East and the XVIII Mountain Corps in the West. Overhead, Stukas of the *Luftwaffe* attacked the fortified Metaxas Line, receiving as they did so a nasty surprise, for alone among such fortifications in Europe, the Metaxas Line had 37mm guns, which did a great deal of harm to the Ju87 aircraft. The Greeks held out with enormous courage and no little success. The Germans suffered substantial losses at the Nevrokop Basin, and in the Rupel Pass, and at no point found their advance easy. The Greeks were a tougher opponent than most that Germany had encountered. Nonetheless, sheer force of numbers and armaments ensured that the Germans advanced towards their objective, and gradually the Greek units began to surrender when they could do nothing more.

On April 8th, Lieutenant-General Vieil and his 2nd *Panzer* Division, after a lightning advance through Yugoslavia, crossed the border into Greece and dashed 56 miles in the day to occupy Salonika. General Bakopoulos was surrounded and, without communications, was forced to surrender. His 70,000 men were taken prisoner. By April 11th, the Yugoslav army having collapsed, the German 12th Army found itself in contact with General Sir Henry Maitland Wilson's Anglo-Greek formation. The British 1st Armoured Brigade had only 100 largely obsolete tanks to field against Field-Marshal List's 500-plus, and was unable to hold its position. The 2nd New Zealand Division, fighting every inch of the way, had to withdraw, thereby enabling German units to get between the British Expeditionary Force and the Greeks retreating from Albania.

On April 21st, the crack SS Division *Leibstandarte Adolf Hitler* captured Yanina to the rear of the Greeks. Going against orders from his government in Athens, the Greek commander General Tzolakoglou negotiated with the Germans, and surrendered sixteen Greek Divisions, the instrument of surrender being signed at Larisa by a representative of the Greek Parliament and Field-Marshall List.

Mussolini was not pleased, and felt that he should have been present to gloat over the surrender, despite his army's almost total failure to contribute to the victory that made it possible. To gratify his ally's ludicrous vanity, Hitler therefore ordered a further signing ceremony to be set up for April 24th, and at that entirely bogus

The Balkans

ceremony Mussolini attended the demise of the independent Greek state. On April 19th it was decided that the British Expeditionary Force must be evacuated from mainland Greece. Rear-Admiral Baillie-Grohman, entrusted with this hazardous task, managed on April 25th to get almost 51,000 British, Australian and New Zealand troops out despite the efforts of German paratroops landing along the Corinth canal and the arrival of the *Leibstandarte Adolf Hitler* on all sides. This near-miraculous escape, more daring than Dunkirk, and at the time almost as valuable in terms of resources saved, was pulled off with the loss of only four transport vessels and two destroyers. It stands as one of the major achievements of the Second World War.

The Expeditionary Force had lost 12,712 men either killed, wounded or taken prisoner, and had no military advantage, although the political benefits of their brave attempt to save Greece from occupation were to be felt. when Britain's involvement in the resolution of the Greek Civil War (1944-45) and the return of the

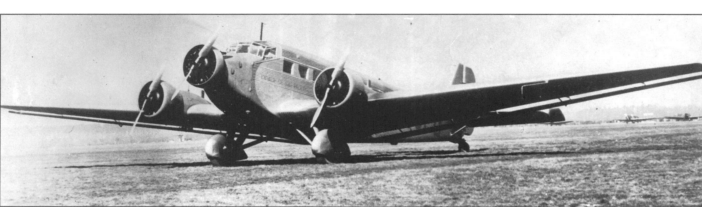

1 Much of the written propaganda perpetrated by both sides seems absurdly childish four or five decades on. This picture of a German officer questioning an admittedly scared Cretan civilian, said to be the burgomaster of a small village captured by the Germans in the early stage of the battle, was captioned by the British '...the brutal faces press round him as they demand information. This can happen here, but the moral is "Be like Dad; keep Mum"'.

2 Large quantities of weapons, supplies and ammunition were dropped with the German 7th Airborne Division in these cylindrical metal canisters. Once down, every weapon had to be checked and serviced at the first lull in the fighting. These German paratroops are resting in a dried-up river bed and checking their weapons.

3 The Junkers Ju52 three-engined transport was the universal maid of all work for the German armed forces, and formed the bulk of the fleet of aircraft from which the German paratroops descended upon Crete. Ugly and rudimentary it may have been, but the Ju52 was an extremely successful and reliable aircraft. The capture of Maleme airfield was achieved by courageous pilots crash-landing eighty Ju52 aircraft on to the heavily shelled airfield itself, bringing a regiment of mountain troops to seize the perimeter, under shellfire from British ships at sea.

4 The fighting for Crete was hard and bitter and was characterised by the use of a number of new weapons, notably small, portable flame throwers of a new type. The soldier in the foreground on the right has one of these weapons – note the tank on his back.

Government was accepted by the Greek people. Militarily, Greek adventure was a disaster for Britain when it could not afford setbacks of any kind.

The Invasion of Crete

Now, to prevent the RAF from having an easy base to attack his oil resources in Rumania during the invasion of Russia that was about to commence, Hitler turned his attention to Crete. On April 25th 1941, General Kurt Student, mastermind of the German paratroop forces, was given the task of planning the invasion of the little island in the Mediterranean that was so strategically placed.

Student planned a predominantly airborne invasion by the 7th Paratroop Division, reinforced by three infantry regiments, and backed by the air support of 228 bombers, 205 dive bombers, 233 fighters and 50 reconnaissance aircraft. The airborne units were to be dropped from 493 three-engined Ju52 transports, although some were to make a glider borne landing in a force of 72 gliders. A force of 63 small ships was hastily requisitioned to ferry the infantry units, and the Italian Navy provided a destroyer and 12 torpedo boats to escort them.

The Allies, because of their secret ability to decode Enigma signals, were well aware of the plan to attack Crete, and resolved to hold the island if at all possible. There were 42,500 men already in position, of whom 10,300 were Greeks. There were 6,540 Australian and 7,700 New Zealand troops who had been evacuated from Greece, but these units were very short of vehicles, arms and supplies because of the haste of their departure. Thus the force was far less formidable than it seemed on paper.

The RAF had 35 operational aircraft on the island on May 1st, but the heavy bombardment by the *Luftwaffe* during the run up to the attack left only four Hurricanes and three Gladiators in a fit condition to take off and fly to Egypt on the 19th May.

5 The sinking of the British 1,760 ton K-Class destroyer HMS *Kelly* along with HMS *Kashmir* by Ju87 Stuka dive-bombers off Crete touched a chord in the heart of the British nation, because the *Kelly* was commanded by Lord Louis Mountbatten, a cousin of the Royal Family and son of Prince Louis of Battenberg, who had been First Sea Lord prior to the First World War. Here, survivors of the *Kelly* row for safety.

5

6

7

6 After the evacuation of the British Expeditionary force from Greece, the Germans had lost no time in completing their conquest – this picture shows British soldiers captured by Germans as they took Corinth.

7 Even the sunny island of Corfu was subjected to the terrors of *Blitzkrieg*. These peasant victims of German air attack were in the care of the sisters of the hospital on the island.

The British forces were commanded by General Freyberg, an able and brave commander, but one who had arrived on the island only on April 30th, three weeks before the German attack came on May 20th. Throughout that day, the German 7th Airborne were dropped at Maleme, west of Canea, and around Heraklion and Rethimnon. There was bitter fighting, and the Germans had an unlucky day for losses of commanders — at Maleme, General Meindl was seriously wounded and had to hand over his command to Colonel Ramcke; at Rethimnon the Germans arrived without a commander at all, for General Sussman had been in a glider that had crashed en route.

The key to the battle lay with the Navy's effort to destroy the flotilla of small ships that was bringing the infantry reinforcements to the island. In this Cunningham's fleet was less than successful, losing in quick succession two cruisers and four destroyers, among them HMS *Kelly*, commanded by Lord Louis Mountbatten, and seeing *Warspite* and *Formidable* so seriously damaged that they had to be taken out the action. Although much pressure was applied from

London, Cunningham knew when he was beaten, and pulled back. On the 25th, the German infantry under Lieutenant-General Ringel succeeded in breaking out from the Maleme perimeter, and General Freyberg decided on the 27th that the time had come to evacuate the Allied troops from the island and asked the Mediterranean Fleet to take them off. The evacuation through the little port of Sphakia took every minute of the time from the night of May 28/29th to dawn on June 2nd. The anti aircraft cruiser *Calcutta* and two destroyers, *Hereward* and *Imperial* were lost, and 260 men were killed and 280 wounded on board *Orion* by a German bomb.

When the losses of the Crete operation were added up, the Commonwealth forces had lost 1,800 dead, and about 12,000 captured out of 32,000. The Royal Navy lost 1,828 killed and 183 wounded. 18,000 troops were successfully evacuated. The Germans lost almost 4,000 killed and roughly 2,500 wounded, all of them fully trained top-quality combat troops, and most of them hard-to-replace paratroops. Neither side had found Crete easy.

1 Hitler's Germany undertook very few seaborne invasions. As a result, good pictures of German landing craft in action are rare. This one shows the German army invading the island of Cos in the Aegean.

2 Although the Germans had effectively conquered Greece and Yugoslavia, they frequently wished they had not, so effective were the partisans and saboteurs in both countries. These white-cowled troops in snow camouflage are German alpine troops, in operation against partisans high in the mountains.

3 The Yugoslav partisans in particular kept substantial German forces tied down to anti-guerilla activity, and thereby reduced the strength of German forces in other theatres of war. These German Grenadiers are using the cover of a tank during winter operations against partisans in the mountains of Bosnia.

4 The constant battle between the German occupying power and the partisans inevitably caused the Germans, as in other occupied territories, to take harsh measures. These Yugoslav patriots were shot beside a common grave and, whether dead or not, allowed simply to tumble into the pit.

5 Substantial German armour was used in the battle against the partisans. This light tank is high in the forests of Yugoslavia seeking out the saboteurs who did so much damage to German communications from their mountain hideouts.

CHAPTER 12

BARBAROSSA~HITLER'S INVASION OF RUSSIA AND ADVANCE ON MOSCOW

From September 1939 until June 1941, the Second World War was, like the First, essentially a European war. Unlike the Great War of 1914-18, it was also a war founded on opposing concepts of politics, moral values and even religious outlook. The armies of both sides were not just patriotic and willing — they fought with a strong moral conviction.

Since 1924, when he dictated *Mein Kampf* to Rudolf Hess while imprisoned at Landsberg Prison, Hitler had made no secret of his loathing of Communism, and of his wish to annihilate the 'Bolshevik Jews'. By 1937, the principle of *Lebensraum*, of finding new 'living space' to the East, was well established in Nazi philosophy, and it was generally assumed that this implied a threat to Soviet Russia — hence Churchill's reference to the signing of the Non-aggression Pact between Russia and Germany on August 23th 1939 as 'this unnatural act'. The Pact seemed to indicate an uncharacteristic change of heart by Hitler — and yet it is clear that, when Britain was on the verge of defeat in 1940, Hitler hoped for an alliance with Britain against the

6

7

9

Bolsheviks. As early as July 29th 1940, Colonel-General Alfred Jodl, chief of Operations, had announced to an assembly of staff officers that Hitler had decided — to attack the USSR in the Spring of 1941. — On July 31st, Hitler himself said at a briefing "Wiping out the very power to exist of Russia! That is the goal!"

The simple truth was that the Non-Aggression Pact was no more than a device to buy time to defeat the Western democracies before turning East. It had always been Hitler's intention to attack Russia once all in the West had gone to plan. Now, in the summer of 1941, the whole of continental Europe with the exception of the neutrals (Sweden, Switzerland, Spain, Portugal) was either occupied or ceded to a puppet government — as was the case with Vichy France. Only Britain remained undefeated.

It seems likely that Hitler greatly underestimated both Britain's ability to recover from the military defeats she had suffered, and the extent to which the USA, even as a neutral, was prepared to supply arms and munitions. He also miscalculated totally the likelihood of

8

6 Josef Stalin was a uniquely successful tyrant, a Georgian from Tiflis who ruled the USSR with calculated ferocity, consummate skill and considerable political acumen. His judgment of the value of Hitler's signature and assurances was, however, sadly lacking, and most of the Soviet Air Force fell victim to Stalin's unwillingness to listen to warnings of German aggression and the total lack of preparedness of the Russian armed forces. William Shirer quotes an exchange of radio messages between a Russian frontier artillery unit and military headquarters on the night the invasion began. 'We are being fired on. What shall we do?' asked the artillerymen. 'You must be insane. Why is your signal not in code?' replied headquarters.

7 A German soldier and a Rumanian sailor, photographed doing guard duty together on the Black Sea border just a few days after Germany and Rumania together betrayed the Russo-German non-aggression pact by invading the Soviet Union.

8 Field Marshal Walther von Brauchitsch, Commander in Chief of the German Army, had been briefed by Hitler as early as July 21st 1940 to prepare for an assault on Russia. At that time, he told Hitler that the campaign would take 'from four to six weeks', a view he was to amend substantially before the attack began eleven months later on June 22nd, although not to the point of equipping his army for the awful cold it was to endure.

9 At 4 a.m. on June 22nd 1941, the day of Germany's surprise assault on the USSR, the Soviet Ambassador to Germany, Vladimir Dekanozov, had been summoned to the German Foreign Office in the *Wilhelmstrasse* to be told that, under false pretexts of retaliation against supposed border violations, German troops were at that moment invading the Soviet Union. This picture shows the scene in the Foreign Office as Ribbentrop formally read out Germany's Declaration of War on Russia.

the USA entering the war as a combatant, largely because his Japanese allies were not prepared to brief him in advance on their intentions.

Certainly, Hitler thought, at the end of 1940, when his Directive No.21 — Barbarossa — was issued to the High Command, that he could expect to remain in control of the war despite opening a new front, that the British were now largely a spent force, and that there was no reason to expect an expansion of the geographical compass of the war beyond his own attack on his allies in Russia.

In fact, as we now know, 1941 was the year when the essentially European nature of the Second World War evaporated, and it became a genuinely worldwide conflict. The year was to see Asia, America and Africa plunged into war, and the first signs of the Axis being pointed inexorably towards defeat. It was also the year when much wider polarisation of beliefs and cultures entered into the conflict; the Communist versus the Fascist; the Oriental opposing the Occidental.

1 The German Army advanced into Russia with only summer kit, believing that the campaign could not possibly last into the Russian winter. Initially the pace was typical of Nazi *Blitzkrieg*, and allowed the bemused Soviet forces and civilians little opportunity to regroup. But Russian resistance was nonetheless effective, and these German soldiers had to fight every metre of the way.

2 The Soviet T-34 medium tank, first used against the advancing German Army at Smolensk, was faster and more manoeuvrable than existing German tanks, and was effectively resistant to German anti-tank weapons of the time. Because it was diesel, rather than petrol, powered, it rarely caught fire when hit, and crews frequently escaped to fight another day. This particular vehicle belongs to a platoon leader. The slogan on the turret reads 'For the Motherland', a commonly-seen marking during the war.

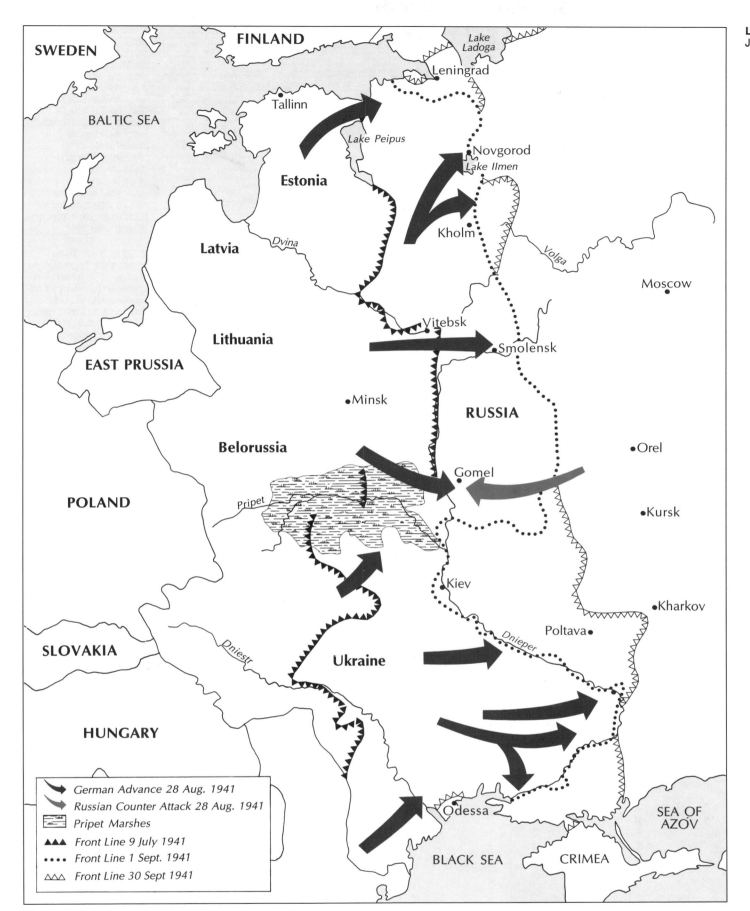

SWEDEN

FINLAND

Lake Ladoga

Leningrad

BALTIC SEA

Tallinn

Lake Peipus

Estonia

Novgorod

Lake Ilmen

Kholm

Latvia

Dvina

Volga

Moscow

Lithuania

Vitebsk

Smolensk

EAST PRUSSIA

•Minsk

RUSSIA

Belorussia

•Orel

Gomel

POLAND

Pripet

•Kursk

•Kharkov

SLOVAKIA

Dniestr

Ukraine

Kiev

Dnieper

Poltava•

HUNGARY

Odessa

SEA OF AZOV

BLACK SEA

CRIMEA

German Advance 28 Aug. 1941
Russian Counter Attack 28 Aug. 1941
Pripet Marshes
▲▲▲ Front Line 9 July 1941
•••• Front Line 1 Sept. 1941
△△△ Front Line 30 Sept 1941

At the beginning of the year, Hitler was at the pinnacle of his power; the architect of the greatest conquest the world had ever known; personally responsible for strategic decisions that his generals had said would be disastrous, and which had instead been outstandingly successful. When he said that Russia would be taken by Autumn 1941, there was, although logic was not on the side of his assertion, little reason for disbelieving him.

Yet, despite Hitler's long stated hatred of Bolshevism, Josef Stalin showed no sign of apprehension. Stalin had on May 7th 1941 added to his Secretaryship of the Communist Party of the USSR the Chairmanship of the Council of People's Commissars, a job he took over from Molotov, and evidently had no inkling of the likelihood of attack by Germany, then only six weeks ahead. Winston Churchill recalled in his 'The Second World War' that intelligence reports from the Balkans and Germany had convinced him by March 1941 that Hitler intended to attack Russia, and that by May he was certain of it. Churchill tried, with a short sharp telegram, to warn Stalin, but

3 Hitler's instruction to his armies to regard the Soviet population as sub-human and unfit to live was taken literally by many of the more convinced Nazis among the German soldiers. This picture, one of a series found in the pocket of a dead German soldier in the Ukraine, shows two Russian civilians who were about to be hanged. Note that the soldiers are not *SS*.

3

Barbarossa

the Kremlin responded with a communique dictated to *Tass*, the Russian News Agency, accusing Britain of spreading ugly rumours about Germany, and doing everything possible to appease Hitler. Stalin did not wish to be confused with facts, an act of stubborness that was to cost the USSR a large part of the Soviet Air Force, destroyed on the ground in the first wave of the attack.

June 22nd 1941

Thus when the fateful day of Barbarossa dawned, the Soviet armed forces were prepared neither for the fury of the treacherous attack launched upon them, nor for the barbarity of the treatment meted out by the German forces to Russian civilians and prisoners of war on the direct orders of Hitler, who instructed his armies to regard their Russian enemy as less than human. The assault brought into conflict

3,400,000 Germans and 4,700,000 Russian troops. The sheer scale both of the armies involved, and of their appalling losses, has no equal in any war in history.

Barbarossa began at 3.15am on that June morning along a front of no less than 2,900 kilometres, from the Baltic to the Black Sea. Into the attack went 153 divisions of the 208 that Germany had available, 120 of the 153 being thrown into the actual assault, the remainder being held in reserve. There were 29 *Panzer* and motorised divisions, with a total of 3,090 tanks. Four air fleets of the *Luftwaffe* were deployed on the new Eastern Front, bringing with them 1,945 aircraft.

By comparison, the Red Army, still unconcernedly engaged upon its summer manoeuvres when the blow fell, was sadly inadequate. Stalin had, since 1937, remorselessly 'eliminated' any major military

1 The first great pitched battle of the Russian campaign took place at Smolensk over a period of almost a month between July 11th and August 8th 1941. When Colonel-General Guderian's *Panzer* Groups eventually defeated Marshal Timoshenko's and Lieutenant-General Eremenko's armies, much of Smolensk was destroyed or on fire. This picture was received in London via New York on August 12th 1941.

2 German armour crossed the River Dnieper on July 11th. It had been preceded by infantry and engineers, who had crossed the river in rubber dinghies and rigged temporary bridges for the tanks and supply vehicles to cross.

3 Some 2,500 of the Soviet Union's 3,000 aircraft were destroyed on the ground by bombing on the first day of Barbarossa, and the fighters that remained were no match for the Messerchmitt 109 and Focke-Wulf 190. But many of the Russians' twin-engined bombers survived to fight on – this picture of a Soviet aircraft being bombed-up for a raid was taken some three weeks after the German invasion.

4 The great distances that the Germans advanced in Russia, often over extremely flat territory, made supply convoys vulnerable to Russian dive-bomb attack. The Germans developed a technique of harnessing barrage balloons on cables to vehicles in the convoy, which helped to prevent aircraft swooping low enough for effective dive bombing.

5 The retreating Russians emulated those that had fallen back before Hitler's predecessor Napoleon by destroying as much as they could – installations, crops, buildings – so that the invaders should take as little as possible. This dam on the Dnieper was blown as the Germans arrived; here a German officer is observing the damage through his binoculars.

figure who showed initiative, disagreed with his policies or attempted to wield influence. He had thus encouraged mediocrity, and brought to high command mainly incompetent sycophants who knew little other than when to keep their mouths shut. There were exceptions, whose names ring forth from the history of the Russian War — notably Malinovsky, Konev and Zhukov. But, in the opening weeks of the campaign, the military ineptitude of the majority of the Russian High Command killed almost as many Russian soldiers as did the fighting proficiency of the *Wehrmacht*.

Numerically, the Russian forces were not at any severe disadvantage. In terms of training, equipment, and, above all, quality of military leadership, they were no match for the might of the world's most experienced and efficient fighting machine. Only in July 1940 had previous resistance to the use of large scale tank formations been

6 Kiev, principle city of the Ukraine, was a major propaganda prize for the Germans on their way to capture Moscow and (Hitler had decided) Leningrad. This picture was radioed from Berlin to New York to show that German soldiers were actually before the Citadel in Kiev.

7 As Soviet resistance hardened, German troops had to clear every building in their path — every building that the Russians had not destroyed before them.

8 Marshal Budenny (left) knew that his army's position at Kiev could not be held, but was not allowed to withdraw until it was too late. Kiev fell to the Germans on September 18th and some 600,000 men were captured.

Barbarossa

1 Field-Marshal Fedor von Bock, who commanded Army Group Centre in the push for Moscow during the Autumn of 1941, was increasingly ill with stomach pain as the problems multiplied, and had to be replaced on December 18th by Field-Marshal von Kluge. A week later, on Christmas Day, Colonel-General Guderian, who had originated the *Panzer* warfare that had brought Germany so far, was relieved of his command for ordering a retreat without permission, and General Erich Hoeppner, also a brilliant tank commander, was stripped of his rank and forbidden to wear uniform on similar grounds.

reversed, and mechanised and armoured divisions been formed. Many of the inexperienced tank units were annihilated during the first few weeks of the campaign, and only those equipped with the new T-34 medium tank, and the KV-2 and T-35 heavy tanks were able to give the Germans any show of real resistance. These tanks were, in fact, the strongest features of the Soviet military profile – they were actually better than anything the Germans could put in the field. The T-34 in particular has been likened to Britain's Spitfire fighter in its importance to Allied success against Germany. With its 33 mph speed, 7.62 cm gun, low fire risk from its 500 hp diesel engine and cleverly shaped armour that was impenetrable to current German anti-tank weapons, the T-34 tank was to remain a major problem to the German army throughout the campaign and the war – but,

although 1,225 had been produced by the time Barbarossa began, the T-34 was not actually fielded against the German armies until they reached Smolensk. On the debit side of the account was the fact that, in June 1941, only 29% of Russia's tanks were in a fit condition to fight. Incompetent organisation had ensured that spares for the older tanks were in short supply and that maintenance had been inadequate.

The tremendous speed with which the German armour advanced into Russia is not therefore as remarkable as it first seems. By the evening of the first day, Colonel-General Guderian's *Panzer* divisions in the 'Army Group Centre' area had reached Kobrin and Pruzhany, almost 50 miles into Russia. Colonel-General Hoth's *Panzer* divisions were 59 miles from their starting point, and had taken the bridges over the important River Niemen intact. In the North, Field-Marshal von

2 General Georgi Zhukov, who galvanised the morale and resistance of the Leningrad defenders and population to withstand the most terrible siege in military history, and subsequently turned the battle of Moscow and the Russian War against Germany. Zhukov was a master tactician and leader of men; like Rommel, a soldier much respected by both sides.

Leeb's *Panzergruppe IV* under Colonel-General Hoeppner had also progressed 50 miles and had successfully taken the viaduct across the Doubissa gorges at Airogala.

Successful German bombing raids had destroyed a large proportion of the Soviet Air Force on the ground during the first hour of Barbarossa, and those that were left gave the *Luftwaffe* little trouble. Field-Marshal Albert Kesselring, commanding the *Luftwaffe* on the Eastern Front, reported that the Russian pilots were 'innocents to the slaughter', and his pilots had an easy campaign in the early stages, despite the Russians having 3,000 aircraft in the frontier regions on the day before Barbarossa began. The success of the initial bombing raids destroyed some 2,500 aircraft, and many more were shot down in combat on the first day. By June 23rd, resistance in the air was minimal.

Because Russian communications were almost non-existent, the High Command had no means of appreciating what was happening in such a modern high speed war. Their already inadequate grasp of tactics was rendered utterly useless by this lack of effective radio. Thus each Russian commander was taking separate, independent and often conflicting decisions against an enemy that was under the total and effective control of its High Command. Inevitably, gaps in the defensive line opened of their own accord for the Germans to sweep through; vital positions, bridges, installations were not destroyed before the Russians were forced to retreat.

The lightning advance continued. By June 25th, Guderian had reached Baranovichi, and Hoth was in Molodechno. The next day,

the two *Panzergruppen* made contact and pushed on to Minsk, where, on the 29th they closed with a pincer movement behind the unfortunate defenders. By July 8th, General Halder was noting in his diary that 32 of the 43 divisions of the Soviet 3rd, 4th and 10th armies had been virtually annihilated. The Germans had taken nearly 290,000 prisoners; captured 2,585 tanks, 1,449 guns, 246 aircraft.

July 11th saw the German armour cross the Dnieper, and Army Group South approaching Kiev. Not until mid-July, when a second pincer movement by *Panzergruppen* 2 and 3 brought massive forces to bear at Smolensk, did the Germans encounter any really successful resistance. The Russians trapped by the pincer fought furiously and well to break out, while, from the outside, Marshal Timoshenko and Lieutenant-General Eremenko fought hard to break in and relieve the besieged army. The battle went on until August 8th, when Marshal Timoshenko was defeated at Roslavl. Guderian took 38,000 prisoners, 300 tanks and 300 guns. Almost immediately, Smolensk fell, and German Army High Command (OKH) announced the taking of 310,000 prisoners, the capture or destruction of over 3,000 armoured vehicles, and 3,000 artillery pieces.

German armour at Elnia was now only 200 miles from Moscow. German casualties at August 13th had reached, since the beginning of the campaign, 389,924 officers and men, of whom 98,600 were killed or missing. Compare that with comparable German figures for the whole war to May 31st 1941 — 218,109 casualties, of whom 97,000 were killed. It had been a devastating seven weeks for the cream of German manhood, as well as for Russia. The pace of the advance,

3 At the end of August 1941, Mussolini visited Hitler at Rastenburg in East Prussia, and was then taken on a tour of the recently-conquered Ukraine by the *Fuehrer*. Close to Hitler in the picture is Field-Marshal Keitel, who seems appreciably more interested in the knocked-out tank than Mussolini, who is striding on ahead.

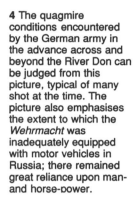

4 The quagmire conditions encountered by the German army in the advance across and beyond the River Don can be judged from this picture, typical of many shot at the time. The picture also emphasises the extent to which the *Wehrmacht* was inadequately equipped with motor vehicles in Russia; there remained great reliance upon man- and horse-power.

5 A German artillery unit fires on already burning Russian positions in the town of Kaluga, southeast of Moscow. Winter was already overtaking the German soldiers, who were becoming desperate to conclude the first phase of the campaign, and take Moscow, before they risked being frozen to death.

6 Two *Waffen SS* infantrymen cautiously approach an apparently disabled Russian BA-10 six-wheeled armoured car, ready to drop stick grenades through the ports and finish off the occupants. The BA-10 carried a crew of four, had a fifty hp petrol engine providing a road speed of thirty-four mph and a range of 188 miles, and was armed with a 45mm main gun plus two 7·62mm machine guns.

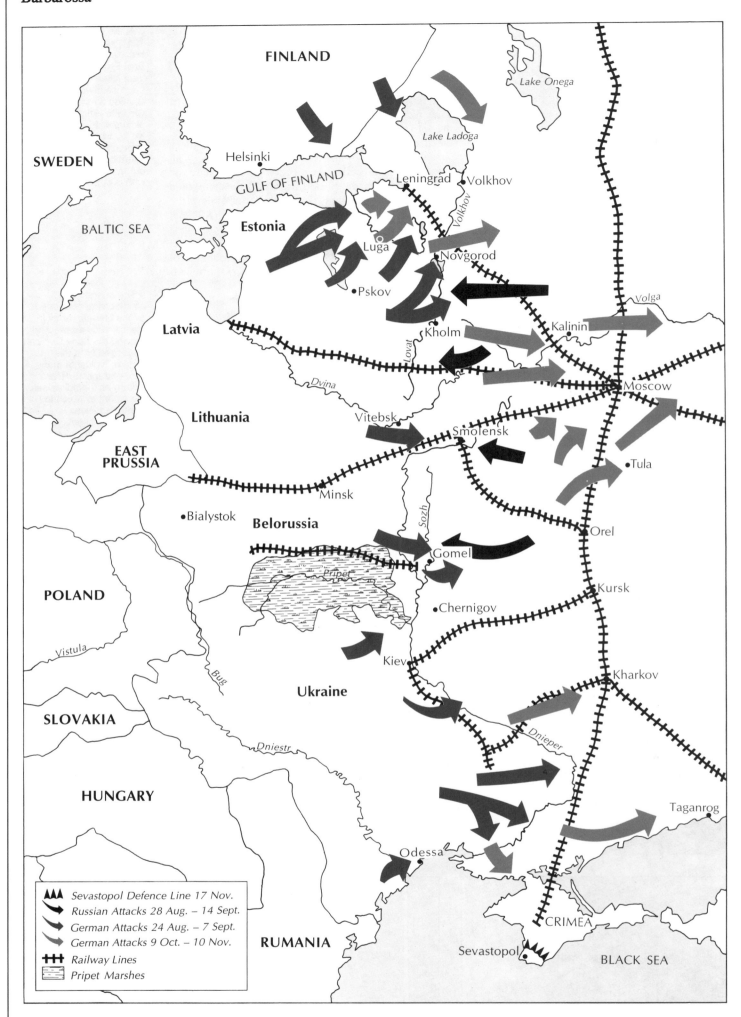

Left the siege of
Leningrad and
Sevastopol, 1941.

FINLAND

Lake Onega

SWEDEN

Helsinki

Lake Ladoga

GULF OF FINLAND

Leningrad • Volkhov

BALTIC SEA

Estonia

Volkhov

Luga

Novgorod

• Pskov

LATVIA

Volga

Kholm

Kalinin

Lovat

Dvina

Moscow

Lithuania

Vitebsk

Smolensk

EAST
PRUSSIA

Tula

Minsk

• Bialystok

Belorussia

Sozh

Orel

POLAND

Pripet

Gomel

• Chernigov

Kursk

Vistula

Bug

Kiev

Ukraine

Kharkov

SLOVAKIA

Dniestr

Dnieper

HUNGARY

Taganrog

Odessa

Legend:
- ▲▲▲ *Sevastopol Defence Line 17 Nov.*
- *Russian Attacks 28 Aug. – 14 Sept.*
- *German Attacks 24 Aug. – 7 Sept.*
- *German Attacks 9 Oct. – 10 Nov.*
- ✝✝✝ *Railway Lines*
- *Pripet Marshes*

CRIMEA

RUMANIA

Sevastopol

BLACK SEA

1 Back in the summer of 1941, when trainloads of Russian soldiers had been railroaded to the front, the Germans believed that there were few reinforcements to follow them. When Zhukov's great December offensive began, the Germans were amazed to find that the Russians were able to conjure up divisions of men and armour that the German High Command had believed could not exist.

2 The Russian plain offered very little cover for an infantry attack, and the Red Army trained its soldiers extensively in the subtle arts of minimal camouflage. These men are training on an exercise, and are approaching a target for grenade attack. The picture is interesting in that it provides some idea of the equipment issued to the Russian soldiers of the time.

the appalling road and rough country conditions, and the abrasive dust were having a serious effect on the mechanical condition of the German armour. Try as they might, the Germans were slowing down.

Now Hitler took a personal hand in the campaign in his role as military tactician, a pursuit for which he was fast proving himself manifestly unsuited. His Directive No.34 of August 12th 1941 changed the whole strategic plan of Barbarossa by insisting on what he saw as a tactical move to take Leningrad and the North, plus the Crimea and the Donets coal and industrial basin before winter. In vain did Field Marshal Brauchitsch, and Generals Halder and Guderian

express their belief that the army should continue its advance and take Moscow. Hitler was adamant. As usual, the Generals bowed to his will. From that time on, the campaign in Russia was doomed. Not one but two factors brought about the change of fortune. Barbarossa had been scheduled originally for May 1941, but Hitler had postponed it for more than a month because of the Balkan campaign. Even then Brauchitsch had predicted disaster in Russia when winter came. Now, Hitler's diversion of the attack wasted more of the vital summer weather.

But the effect was not immediate. In late August, Field-Marshal von Rundstedt's 11th, 17th and 6th Armies established four bridgeheads on the left bank of the Dnieper and on September 11th, Kleist linked up with Guderian at Kremenchug. In the South, Marshal Budenny requested permission to evacuate the Kiev pocket. Stalin rejected his request. By the 17th, when the armies were at last given permission to withdraw, they were encircled and could go nowhere. On the 18th, Kiev fell, and the commander, General Kirponos was killed. Vast numbers of men and machines were captured. The numbers are still the subject of dispute, but it is reasonably certain that over half a million men, more than 750 tanks and some 3,500 guns were captured. By the end of September, Russian losses since June amounted to 2,500,000 men, 22,000 guns, 18,000 tanks and 14,000 aircraft.

In the north, Leeb's Army Group North had reached the shores of Lake Ladoga, east of Leningrad, on September 8th, and had begun the siege that was intended to realise Hitler's intention of taking Leningrad for the winter. To the West of their positions, Marshal Mannerheim's Finns were recapturing the positions they had lost in the Winter War of 1940, and were in control of the Karelian Isthmus,

1

2

3

4

3 Soviet infantry attacking the advancing German invaders while under heavy shellfire. Although Soviet casualties were great at this early stage of the Eastern campaign, the Germans had lost more men in the first seven weeks of their Russian invasion than they had previously lost in almost two years of war.

4 An interesting picture of the German crossing of the River Beresina which shows how their vehicles were rafted across the broad waters of the river. Note the troops in the rubber assault craft right of centre.

but refused to assist Germany in the expected final assault on Leningrad. On September 11th, Stalin moved General Zhukov to take over the defence of Leningrad from the inscrutably mediocre Marshal Voroshilov, and, not for the last time, Zhukov pulled a garrison together, regenerated the Russians' morale and self discipline, and began the erection of stronger defences. By the 16th September, Hitler had ordered a major artillery and *Luftwaffe* bombing offensive against Leningrad and the nearby naval base in Kronstadt Harbour, and over the next few days one Russian battleship was sunk, and 2 battleships and 2 cruisers were seriously damaged at Kronstadt.

By the 30th September, the siege of Leningrad had claimed 4,409 civilian lives, an appalling death toll resulting from 200 artillery bombardments and 23 air raids in one month. Still the city did not surrender. As winter closed in famine gripped the city, and the citizens of Leningrad ate their pets, their wallpaper, their hair oil — anything that promised to sustain life. Not until January 1943 were the Russians able to open a rail link to the city, and not until January 1944 did the German bombing and shelling of the city finally stop. More than a million civilians died in what must surely be the most vicious siege in history. But they never surrendered.

Barbarossa

As the German advance in the other sectors slowed, the Red Army began, despite its losses, to regroup, and to assemble artillery, rockets and new infantry weapons. Belated reorganisation of the command structure began, and some semblance of morale and resurgent military discipline gave the Russian troops new heart. During the first two weeks of October, a massive offensive was launched by the Germans to take Moscow, and by October 20th, Bock was within forty miles of the capital. A massive evacuation of the government, foreign diplomats and much of the civilian population was under way; only Stalin and his military command remained in the Kremlin. On the night of October 14th-15th, it seemed to the Russian defenders that the crunch had come, as German armour attacked with great force, breaking through the perimeter of Moscow at one point, and coming within sight of Moscow's famous Khimke water tower.

At this crucial moment, Stalin replaced Timoshenko, with Zhukov, who had revitalised the defence of Leningrad. An able tactician, Zhukov recognised the German army's vulnerability to the cruel Russian winter, and contented himself with holding the line until the snow, which was already falling, took hold and bogged down the *Wehrmacht* in a misery of perpetual wet boots and temperatures far below zero. As the snow alternated with torrential rain, the German army became virtually immoveable. Judging his moment to a nicety, Zhukov chose December 6th to go on to the offensive. From now on, the Germans would never again be truly in the ascendant on the Eastern Front.

1 Rather than allow vehicles and equipment that had to be abandoned to fall into German hands in good condition, possibly to be used against them, the Soviet Army disabled or destroyed everything it could. These German troops (note the bicycle with the briefcase on the crossbar, and the steel helmet on the carrier) were going forward on foot, and could doubtless have made good use of the mangled vehicles they are passing.

2 Although the Red Army was lacking in defences against air attack at the time of the German invasion, production was increased dramatically during the first year of the Russian war. This is a Soviet anti-aircraft battery, probably during 1942, although the picture itself is undated.

3 An SdKfz 10/5 flak wagon pulls off the road into the cover of the trees. Armed with a 20mm cannon, this was just one of the many specialised vehicles that the German army developed as part of their *Blitzkrieg* tactics.

4 German infantry stop for a breather and a bite to eat after the capture of Vitebsk. The retreating Russians had ensured once again that the invaders gained little from the capture of the town, and the Germans were greeted by burning buildings all around them.

The Russians Fight Back

Throughout the great German offensive into Russia, the *Wehrmacht* had seemed invincible; better equipped, infinitely better led, better trained, more experienced in every field of conflict. But that was in summer and autumn. So confident had Hitler been that his mighty army would subdue Russia by October, that millions of German soldiers and airmen had gone to the Eastern Front with only summer kit. Now, in December, the temperature fell to twenty, sometimes more than thirty, degrees below zero. With little shelter, inadequate food and nil achievement since winter came, the morale of the *Wehrmacht* sank lower than ever before.

By contrast, the Red Army had regrouped, using the comparative lull in the campaign to bring up artillery, armour and reserve manpower. The coming of Zhukov had an effect on the defenders of beleaguered Moscow not unlike that later to be seen when General Montgomery took command of the British Eighth Army — morale was boosted for no very logical or explicable reason other than the sheer magnetism of the commander and the respect his troops held

for him. Above all, the Russian soldiers were properly equipped with warm quilted winter coats, waterproof boots and clothing designed to minimise wind chill.

German morale was not helped by Hitler's adamant refusal to permit tactical withdrawal. Hitler ordered that not an inch of ground be given. His commanders were bitter about this decision, believing that tens of thousands of German lives might have been saved if a limited withdrawal to positions affording some shelter had been permitted. Ultimately, this decision was to prove one of the principal reasons for the failure of Hitler's Russian campaign. Frozen almost, and in some cases actually, to death, his troops were no match physically or mentally for the counter offensive when it came. And come it did, on December 6th.

Initially, the ferocious onslaught of Zhukov's offensive set the German army reeling, although it fought bravely, as always, and just managed to hold its line. The Russians were now, entirely unexpectedly to the Germans, able to field 160 Divisions against Bock's 68, and were to go on to reinforce their strength with a further 60 divisions in the first six months of 1942. Production of the new

5 The German Engineer units became increasingly effective at repairing and replacing bridges blown by their retreating enemy as the war developed. In Russia they had plenty of practice – these engineers are studying the problems set them by a bridge over the River Narwa. The date is November 1941.

6 The enormous area of Soviet territory that the German army was required by its own objectives to capture, and the width of the rivers they encountered, frequently made it impossible for river crossings to be made via bridges, whether existing or specially built. Whole divisions crossed major rivers by simple rafting and inflatable boat techniques, a procedure which imposed considerable delays on the progress of the invasion.

7 As the time for the Russian counter-offensive before Moscow drew near, Stalin was obliged to replace Marshal Voroshilov, from whose incompetence Zhukov had rescued Leningrad, by sending Marshal of the Soviet Union Timoshenko (right) to the Caucasus. Zhukov was brought from Leningrad to Moscow, and revitalised the spirit of the Russian Army just at the moment when German morale was at its lowest.

8 As the Russian winter took hold, German soldiers, most of whom still had only their summer kit, froze, often to death. Men were unable even to relieve themselves without fear of injury due to freezing, and a large proportion of the German army suffered frostbite. Small wonder, therefore, that when the Soviet counter-offensive came, on December 6th 1941, the German Army was hard-pressed to hold its line.

tanks was now outstripping the rate at which the Germans were able to destroy them, and by the time the Battle of Moscow began, 1,853 T-34 tanks had been delivered to the Red Army. On December 20th, aware that without the opportunity to make a tactical withdrawal, eventual defeat was certain, Colonel-General Guderian left for Hiler's Eastern headquarters at Rastenburg, in East Prussia, to try and obtain the Fuehrer's agreement to a retreat. No permission was forthcoming. Hitler insisted on an attack that was manifestly beyond the army's capability.

Now, at what was already their worst hour, the Germans began to suffer an appalling loss of experienced commanders. On the 16th December, Field-Marshal von Bock asked to resign – a decision made necessary by a combination of ill-health and inability to agree with Hitler – and was succeeded by Kluge. On December 19th, Field-Marshal von Brauchitsch, who had had a heart attack in November, left the Army High Command (OKH), and Hitler took the opportunity of assuming his role as Commander in Chief of the Army. Then, on December 26th, Guderian was relieved of his command, being replaced by General Schmidt, and, at the beginning

of January, Colonel-General Hoeppner was disgraced for ordering the *4th Panzerarmee* to disengage, and was replaced by Colonel-General Hoth. On January 18th, Field-Marshal von Reichenau suddenly died – and Bock was brought back to active service against his wishes, with the luckless General Paulus being ordered to take over the Sixth Army. In the North, Field-Marshal von Leeb requested permission to retire, and was replaced as commander of Army Group North by Colonel-General von Kuchler.

To stiffen the German line, which at the beginning of 1942 showed every sign of breaking, Hitler began to bring in 22 infantry divisions from France and Germany in the first three months of 1942, but the Russians forestalled their arrival with further orders to Generals Konev and Zhukov, commanding the Kalinin and West Fronts, to attach and annihilate German Army Group Centre, which had so recently expected to celebrate Christmas in Red Square.

Thus began, on January 9th and 10th 1942, the offensive that was to lead to the appalling defeat of Stalingrad, and ultimately to the subjugation of Eastern Europe. The Bear had awakened.

CHAPTER 13

PEARL HARBOUR
THE UNITED STATES GOES TO WAR

If Hitler's assault on Russia had, in mid 1941, taken the Second World War beyond its European boundaries, then it was the infamous attack by Japan upon the US naval base at Pearl Harbour, on Oahu in the Hawaiian Islands, that finally made the war global in scale. For the devastating Japanese raid was the first roll of the dice in a mighty strategy which encompassed the whole of South-East Asia, and which almost succeeded.

The background to Japan's assault upon Pearl Harbour and the Pacific stretched back into the Thirties to the beginning of her protracted war with China. In that conflict, her troops had gained experience, her pilots had seen active service, her aircraft had gained in reliability. As Germany launched the Second World War in Europe, with a not dissimilar background of experience in the Spanish Civil War behind her, Japan saw clearly the triumphs that could be won by sheer brute force and military skill allied with audacity, surprise and speed. The lesson of *Blitzkrieg* was not lost on the subjects of Hirohito. Suddenly the world of the East seemed open to Japan, and she resolved to take her opportunity, and the wealth it could bring. Only the United States of America stood in the way, for America was neutral, and, unlike Britain, was not already irrevocably locked in European combat. Even Russia did not count as a threat for, although Russia had the manpower to fight on several fronts, Japan and Russia had signed a mutual non-aggression pact which, uncharacteristically, both Japan and Russia honoured until the very last days of the war.

The plan was first to destroy the American Fleet, then, while the USA was unable to put to sea with its armies, to overrun the whole of South-East Asia at a pace reminiscent of German *Blitzkrieg,* seizing in concurrent assaults Thailand, Burma, Malaya and Singapore, plus the Philippines and Dutch East Indies archipelagoes. Once the Pacific and Indian Ocean nations between Burma in the West, New Guinea in the South, and the Aleutians and the Gilbert Islands in the North and East were under the Rising Sun, Japan

1 On Tuesday May 27th 1941, in the East Room at the White House on a sweltering hot Washington night, President Roosevelt had proclaimed a national emergency, and had placed the USA on a war footing.

2 This 1937 aerial picture of part of the United States Pacific Fleet at anchor in Lahaina Roads, Hawaii, after manoeuvres at sea, gives an impression of the kind of target that the Japanese pilots were sent to attack at Pearl Harbour – ships in close proximity, with no camouflage or attempt at concealment.

3 A young Isoroku Yamamoto when he was a fast-rising officer in the Imperial Japanese Navy in the twenties. Japan's most brilliant naval planner and strategist, Admiral Yamamoto was Minister of the Navy from May 1938, and Commander of the First Fleet in 1939. He both planned and executed the attack on Pearl Harbour.

4 Links between Japan and Germany, while never close or trusting, had been forged to a greater degree than ever before during 1941. In March, a Japanese military mission visited Berlin to learn something of the German techniques of *Blitzkrieg* that had conquered most of Europe. On March 10th, General Yamashita (on Hitler's left) introduced the *Fuehrer* to the officers of his mission.

planned to throw a defensive perimeter around the newly-won territories, and exploit the mineral, natural and human resources of a vast area of the earth upon which the rest of the world had until then relied heavily. This ambitious programme was ratified by the Japanese government at a Supreme War Council held on September 6th 1941, not eleven months after the near-murder of Prime Minister Prince Funimaro Konoye, who had urged restraint and compromise with the USA. Konoye resigned on 16th October 1941, and was replaced by the warlike General Hideki Tojo, who was bent on war as a means for Japanese expansion.

In April 1941, five months before the Japanese made their irrevocable decision to wage war, an allied plan known as ABC-1 for the defence of South-East Asia had been agreed between the British and the Americans in Washington. Believing that the recently appointed Far East Commander, General Douglas MacArthur, would be able to retain control of the Philippines in the event of an attack by the Japanese, the planners agreed on a concentration of force against Germany, and a relatively low-key holding operation against Japan. Despite the fact that, as early as January 1941, US Ambassador Joseph Grew had reported from Tokyo the belief that the Japanese might attempt a surprise attack on Pearl Harbour, no allowance was made in the plan for an attack on the US Navy in the Hawaiian Islands. As late as November 1941, American aircraft were still parked undispersed and wing to wing on Hawaiian airfields, a perfect target for bombers.

The detailed plan for the attack from the air that was to give the world its first truly global war was worked out by a naval staff under

5

7

6

8

5 Burning oil streaming from a bomb-blasted oil storage tank almost obscures the capsized *Oklahoma*, in which were entombed 415 crew, and another of the American battleships. This picture was taken from the naval air station flying boat landing point.

6 Not until a full year after the Japanese wrought such fearful damage at Pearl Harbour was this picture of the fury of the attack allowed to be released. In the centre of the picture, with a huge plume of smoke rising from it, is USS *Arizona*, just hit by a 1,760 pound bomb. The black puffs are American anti-aircraft shells bursting.

7 The sad sight of the USS *California*, standing out clearly against the pall of smoke, listing to starboard after being hit by bombs.

8 Hundreds of US sailors pour over the side to safety as their ship lists and burns. They were among the lucky ones – 2,403 Americans were killed during the Pearl Harbour attack.

Pearl Harbour

the gifted Admiral Isoroku Yamamoto, Commander in Chief of the Japanese Navy. He had six aircraft carriers, with a strong force of 14 protective surface ships and 3 submarines, plus a total of 432 bombers, torpedo bombers and fighter aircraft with which to carry out the surprise assault. In November, Yamamoto announced the plan to his assembled officers on board the old 30,000 ton battleship *Nagato*. He told them not to underestimate the American armed services, and assured them that Japan needed a great victory if she was to be seen as a great power. Soon after, on November 25th, the task force under Vice-Admiral Nagumo left the Kurile Islands, and on December 2nd the signal "Climb Mount Niitaka" gave the fleet the irreversible order to proceed with the attack; Operational Order No.1 was to be put into effect.

Incredible as it seems to us now with the benefit of hindsight, Admiral Kimmel and General Short, the US commanders at Hawaii, were warned of the likelihood of imminent war on November 27th, but did virtually nothing to improve the security of the fleet, most of which was at anchor in Pearl Harbour, nor to protect the aircraft

1 Smoke and debris are everywhere as US sailors look helplessly at one of the capsized ships after the attack. Observers said that the sky was almost as black as night, so dense was the smoke from the major explosions on all sides.

2 During the attack on the air base at Hickam Field, one of the airfields hit by the Japanese as part of the Pearl Harbour raid, a US pilot was able to get these pictures of two of the Japanese fighter bombers carrying out the attack.

parked undispersed on the ground. There was a total failure to accept or recognise the possibility that an attack might be directed against Hawaii. Maybe it just seemed too nice a place.

When, at just before eight o'clock in the morning on December 7th, the 214 aircraft of the first of two waves came speeding in from the Pacific to the attack, the entire establishment was enjoying a typical peacetime Sunday. The formation of aircraft had been spotted at 7.15 am on radar, but the young Air Force officer to whom it was reported did nothing with the report because he was expecting a formation of B17 Flying Fortresses at the same time and place. If he had raised the alarm, the eight battleships and the other 86 vessels around them in Pearl Harbour would have had half an hour to recover their crews from their weekend ashore. As it was, they had only their watches on board. The aircraft were not armed. Even the anti-aircraft guns were not fully manned; their ammunition boxes were locked; the crews did not have the keys.

The next two hours were mayhem. Although the defenders reached their posts as quickly as they could in the circumstances, and put up a good fight, the damage was already done. A 1,760 pound bomb blew up the forward magazine of the USS *Arizona*, which quickly sank with 1,106 of her crew plus Rear-Admiral Isaac C. Kidd, and is still on the bottom of Pearl Harbour today. The *Nevada* was hit by two bombs and a torpedo, but maintained a magnificent fight

3 Although not identified by the original news caption (as was usually the case in news pictures of the period), this battleship appears to be the USS *Nevada*, which was comparatively lightly damaged during the Pearl Harbour attack. Here, her crew are fighting the fires after the Japanese aircraft had left.

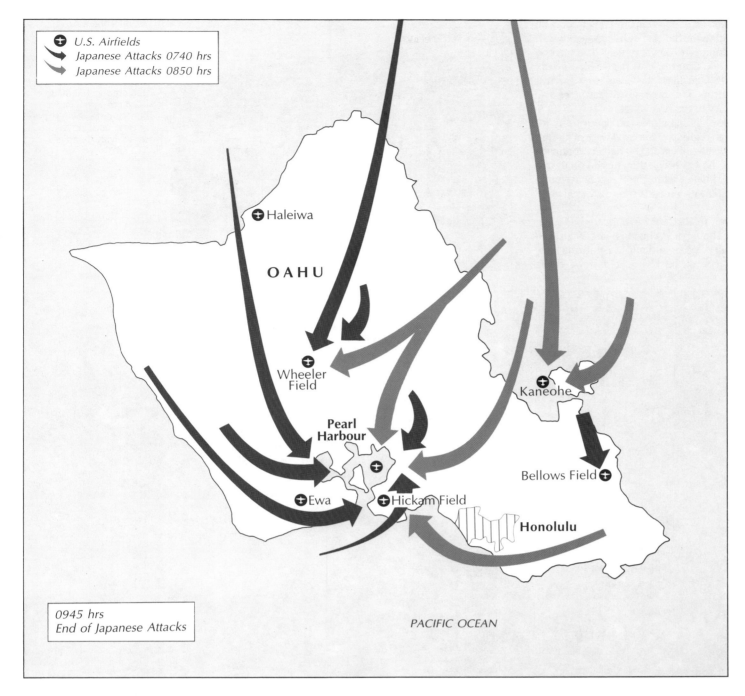

U.S. Airfields
Japanese Attacks 0740 hrs
Japanese Attacks 0850 hrs

Haleiwa

O A H U

Wheeler Field

Kaneohe

Pearl Harbour

Bellows Field

Ewa

Hickam Field

Honolulu

0945 hrs
End of Japanese Attacks

PACIFIC OCEAN

4 The battleship USS *Pennsylvania*, in the background, was in dry dock with the destroyers USS *Cassin* and USS *Downes*, shown in the foreground, badly damaged, when the attack took place.

5 That the Japanese comprehension of the psychology of the US serviceman was somewhat lacking early in the war is clear from this Japanese drawing, found in a crashed Japanese aircraft, shot down during the Pearl Harbour attack. The English statement 'You damned! Go to the devil', supported by crude drawings of damaged ships, is backed up by the inscription in Japanese, which adds 'Listen to the voice of doom. Open your eyes, blind fools'.

6 Another dramatic shot, as the men of the USS *Maryland* in the foreground crowd to the rails and watch helplessly the efforts to reach the few survivors of the USS *Oklahoma*, which had capsized, leaving only a part of her hull above water. Beyond is the dense black smoke pouring from the stricken *Arizona*.

6

Pearl Harbour

despite being in desperate straits. *Oklahoma* capsized after being hit by five torpedoes, trapping within the hull 415 of her crew. Some of them were still alive, though doomed to die, seventeen days later on Christmas Eve. *West Virginia* and *California* were also hit, as were *Tennessee* and *Maryland*, although these last two were far less severely damaged. Three cruisers and three destroyers were also partially disabled by the ferocity of the first attack.

One hour after the first wave, giving almost no opportunity for the defenders of Pearl Harbour to regroup, the second wave of aircraft attacked. The 54 bombers, 80 divebombers and 36 fighters continued the destruction of the pride of the US Navy, then turned on the air force bases at Wheeler and Hickham Fields, the flying boat station at Kaneohe and the naval installations on Ford Island. A total of 65 aircraft were destroyed.

By 10am the attack was over. In all, 2,403 Americans had died, and 1,178 had been wounded. The Japanese had lost just 29 aircraft and 55 airmen, a relatively small price for inflicting a significant blow on the ability of the US Navy to strike back. It would, however, be

1 Under the wing of a US naval aircraft caught on the ground by the Japanese attack, this gun crew mounted an improvised defence with a gun on a mount made of a length of pipe. Note the burned-out aircraft in the background and the extensively damaged hangar.

unwise to adopt the view, often set out in books discussing the attack on Pearl Harbour, that the damage to the US fleet and its strategic capability was as significant as Yamamoto had hoped. The plain fact is that the loss of two battleships, and the disabling of six others, did not leave the US Navy without teeth. The fleet's three aircraft carriers had not been in port and were intact. Experience was to show that their destruction would have been infinitely beneficial to the Japanese strategy. No less than 20 cruisers and 65 destroyers were undamaged and ready to fight. Almost as, or perhaps even more, important was the failure of the Japanese to attack the oil storage depots on the Hawaiian Islands, without which the US Navy would have been immobilised for months.

Interestingly, Admiral Chester Nimitz offered in his postwar memoirs an analysis of the losses of Pearl Harbour which actually argued that the element of surprise had worked to the advantage of the USA. He wrote:

'No one regrets more than I our 3,000 dead. . . . But if Admiral Husband Kimmel . . . had had information of the attack 24 hours in

2 One of the fuel storage tanks at Ford Island Naval Air Station receives a direct hit during the bombing of Pearl Harbour and other nearby installations, and the Navy men, already hard pressed to salvage what they can from earlier damage, are dwarfed by the rising pillar of flame. Note the undispersed aircraft parked close together, and therefore vulnerable to air attack.

3 It was not only military installations that suffered from the attack in Hawaii. A Japanese bomb falling in a suburb of Waikiki, a favourite resort for visitors from mainland America, caused this devastation, and the photograph of it touched a chord in the heart of America.

4 Japan announced its hostilities with the USA on December 7th, conveniently after the Pearl Harbour attack. Although a state of war clearly existed between Japan and the USA, and was now certain to come between the USA and the European dictatorships, a resolution had to be passed by Congress to formalise that decision. This was brought to President Roosevelt for signature on December 22nd 1941, and this historic picture shows him applying the signature that doomed the Axis regimes to defeat, over three years later.

5 Also on December 22nd began the first Washington Conference to determine Allied policy for the conduct of the war. To it came Winston Churchill, Lord Beaverbrook and the chiefs of the three services from Britain and the USA. At the conference, Churchill was to be seen sporting his famous 'siren suit', so called because it was a warm and convenient garment that could be donned in a hurry when air raid sirens sounded.

6 In November 1945, with the victory over Japan securely won, a bi-partisan Congressional Committee conducted an investigation into the Pearl Harbour disaster. Seated in the foreground is Lt-General Walter C. Short, commander of Army installations in Hawaii at the time of the raid, who was relieved of his command as a result of the shortcomings of security that made the attack so successful. Behind him are (left) Joseph Grew, Under-Secretary of State at the time of the enquiry, and Ambassador to Japan before Pearl Harbour, talking to Sumner Welles.

advance, he would have sent off all our forces to meet the Japanese.'

'We had not one aircraft carrier capable of opposing Admiral Nagumo's aircraft carrier formation, and the Japanese would have sunk all our ships on the High Seas. We would have lost 6,000 men and almost all our Pacific fleet.'

The greatest single effect of the Pearl Harbour incident was the almost total polarisation of world opinion that it brought about, the consequences of which were colossal. The United States formally declared war on Japan on December 8th, and on the same day Britain honoured Churchill's pledge to join the USA in war with Japan if the USA were obliged to declare it. Germany and Italy rashly declared war on the United States on December 11th, thereby signing the death warrant of the Axis in Europe. Throughout the next week, nation after nation fell into place on one side or the other; virtually all of Latin America fell in behind the United States and declared war on, or broke off diplomatic relations with, Japan. Before Christmas, thirty-eight nations of the world, representing half the population of the earth, were at war.

This more than any other factor made the attack on Pearl Harbour, while a military success, a strategic blunder. More than any other single event of the war, it mobilised opinion and diverted effort to the defeat of the Axis.

CHAPTER 14

JAPAN TAKES ALL
THE ALLIES DRIVEN FROM S.E. ASIA

In the early stages of the Pacific and Far East war, between December 7th 1941 and June 1942, the great Japanese strategy was outstandingly and, for the Allies, ruinously successful in a purely military sense, although, as we have seen, the political effect of Pearl Harbour was in no way to the advantage of Japan or of her Axis partners. The Japanese inflicted an appalling series of defeats upon the USA and Britain, and seemed unstoppable. It was not until the reverse for Japan of the Battle of Midway, in June 1942, that it seemed possible for Nipponese might to be beaten, and not until the Battle of Guadalcanal in August that the USA showed signs of achieving the miracle. But the fight back across the Pacific was to prove long, arduous and bloody.

Japan brought to her war approximately 1,400,000 men as 51 divisions, 1 million of whom (40 divisions) were in China, Korea and Manchuria. She had 2,400 aircraft of which 1,540 were earmarked for the Pacific, 11 aircraft carriers, 41 cruisers, 129 destroyers and 67 submarines. At the same time, the USA was able to field 1,643,477 men as 34 divisions, of whom 31,000 were in the Philippines; about 2,846 aircraft; 17 battleships (of which 9 were in the Pacific, and six were put out by Pearl Harbour); 6 aircraft carriers (3 in the Pacific); 37 cruisers (24 in the Pacific); 171 destroyers (80 in the Pacific) and 114 submarines (56 of which were in the Pacific).

Hostilities were not long delayed following Pearl Harbour. Later the same day, the Japanese struck at British territory for the first time by bombing Singapore and landing at Kota Bharu in Malaya. Further landings took place at two points in Thailand, Sangora and Patani, and the next day, December 8th, the Battle for Hong Kong began, as

the Japanese 38th Infantry Division attacked the 12,000 strong British, Canadian and Indian garrison. That same day, the Japanese landed on Bataan Island, South of Formosa, now Taiwan, and destroyed more than 100 American aircraft in raids on the Philippines.

Hearing the news of the Japanese landing at Singora, not far from the Malayan border, Britain's Admiral Sir Tom Phillips, recently appointed C.-in-C. of the Royal Navy's presence in Singapore, weighed anchor and sailed with *Prince of Wales* and *Repulse*, escorted by three destroyers, to try and surprise the enemy while the Japanese were landing men and supplies. Although he asked for fighters as air cover, he was told that none was available. On the 9th, the arrival of Japanese aircraft over his small force caused him (erroneously) to believe that the element of surprise was lost, and, learning that, in any event, no fighter cover could be provided for an attack at Singora, he turned for Kuantan to investigate reports of enemy landings. But, although the aircraft he had spotted had not blown his cover, a Japanese submarine had. Japan's Rear-Admiral Matsunaga despatched 11 reconnaissance planes, 52 torpedo planes and 34 bombers from Saigon to attack the squadron at sea.

The encounter came at 11am on December 10th, some 322 kilometres North-East of Singapore after Admiral Phillips had established that nothing was amiss at Kuantan and had turned back for Singapore. With no RAF aircraft to deter the aim of the Japanese pilots, the crossfire of torpedoes was unavoidable. First *Repulse*, then *Prince of Wales* was sunk, taking with them 840 officers and men, including Admiral Phillips and Captain Leach of the *Prince of Wales*.

1 The speed of the Japanese invasion machine after Pearl Harbour was breathtaking. Two areas of Thailand were invaded on the same day as the Hawaiian raid, and Singapore was bombed before December 7th was through. Next day, the island of Bataan was invaded and attacks on Hong Kong and the Philippines began. These Japanese troops were landing on an unspecified Pacific beach early in the spate of conquest.

2 The sheer pace of events during the Japanese race to take Southeast Asia, the less sophisticated attitude of the Japanese to news photography at that time by comparison with later in the war, and the scarcity of neutral nations to send correspondents, resulted in a tremendous lack of good pictures of the early weeks of Japan's campaign. But those that exist show a curiously ragged yet efficient army. Note the bicycle – a frequently-encountered feature in pictures of Japanese military transport.

Ironically, even as the rescue operation was under way to pick up the 2,081 survivors, the RAF appeared to provide the cover that might have saved the ships.

The elimination of these two formidable battleships at a stroke was of tremendous benefit to the Japanese Navy, which had the task of protecting the Japanese armies that were about to conquer the Philippines, Malaya and Singapore. Their loss by the failure to provide air cover was a major blunder.

The Philippines Invaded

The Japanese landings in the Philippines on December 10th found the Americans considerably outnumbered and outgunned. General MacArthur's forces numbered some 31,000, of whom about 19,000 were American, whereas General Homma's 14th Army totalled two divisons. MacArthur's air power numbered 350 aircraft, rapidly

3 The 32,000 ton battlecruiser HMS *Repulse* was completed in 1916, and, unlike her sister ship HMS *Renown* was never reconstructed, so went to her doom in December 1941 looking just as she did here, in a photograph taken as early as 1926. She was, by Second World War standards, inadequately armoured, with only 9" armour plating to her side. Most battleships of the time carried 13" to 15" thickness of armour plate.

4 HMS *Repulse* carried a main armament of six 15" guns, plus secondary armament of nine 4" guns (the reconstructed *Renown* carried 20 4.5" guns as secondary armament), and was capable of 30 knots. Here the 15" guns of *Repulse* fire a broadside, a deafening experience for the crew.

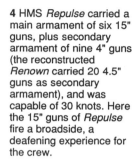

5 Wartime radio pictures were poor, but this photograph, sent from threatened Singapore, shows the scene of the actual sinking of HMS *Repulse* after being hit by five torpedoes and a bomb launched by Japanese aircraft, which were unopposed in the air in the absence of RAF fighter cover.

6 Almost as soon as the dust had settled over Pearl Harbour, the US forces in the Philippines were ready for hostilities – and they did not have to wait long. Not all the soldiers were Americans; these Moro tribesmen, a company of the 45th infantry of the Philippine Scouts, formed part of the defensive force of Mindanao island. Inspecting them is Colonel Ralph McCoy, commander of the 45th Infantry, Philippine Scouts, at Zamboanga.

reduced by the bombing of Clark Field, which eliminated almost half of the US B-17 Flying Fortress fleet of 36 aircraft based in the Philippines. The Japanese were able to put 750 aircraft in the air. In this, as in all the opening battles of the campaign, the many myths about the inferiority of Japanese aircraft and their pilots were swiftly shown to be false.

When, on December 10th, General Homma established his first beach-head at Aparri, in the North of Luzon, his plan was to keep the defenders busy while a second landing was made at the bay of Lingayen with the intention of encircling and destroying the American force. General MacArthur was not fooled, and ordered a swift and effective withdrawal in a manner that was quite unexpected by the

Singapore

The balance of forces in the Japanese attack on Singapore favoured the Japanese far less than in their other operations. General Tomoyuki Yamashita was given the task of taking Singapore before the 100th day of the campaign to capture South-East Asia — which gave him until March 16th 1942. He began with three divisions, and was later reinforced with one more, but even so his army was only slightly larger than that of the British defenders. However, the Japanese regarded Singapore as a plum target, and had given Yamashita's 25th Army both the best troops and the most up to date air cover. In the end, the effectiveness of the air cover, plus the celebrated fact that Singapore's defensive guns could not be pointed inland, were to win

1 At the same time as the sinking of HMS *Repulse*, the Royal Navy's newest battleship, the 38,000 ton *Prince of Wales*, Churchill's headquarters for his meeting with President Roosevelt for the signing of the Atlantic Charter only months before, went to the bottom after being hit by six torpedoes and a bomb. Completed less than a year previously, the *Prince of Wales*, with 15" armour and ten of the new 14" guns, was a key factor in the defence of Malaya and Singapore. Here the crew of *Prince of Wales* scramble to abandon ship as she sinks.

2 On the same day as the sinking of *Prince of Wales* and *Repulse* shocked the Allied world and shifted the balance of power in Malaya, the Japanese under Lt-General Masaharu Homma established a beach-head at Aparri in the north of Luzon. This picture was shot by a Japanese army photographer in one of the invasion craft as it drove towards the Luzon beach.

3 By the time Lt-General Homma, later to be known as 'The Butcher of Bataan', arrived in Luzon in person, on December 24th 1941, (stepping ashore, assisted by an aide), he was facing a much tougher military situation than he had expected. General MacArthur had completed a strategic retreat to a strong defensive line across the Bataan Peninsula, from which Homma's troops were unable to shift them for five months.

1

2

Japanese. For, instead of falling back, as expected, to defend Manila, the capital, MacArthur moved swiftly West to prearranged defensive positions on the peninsula of Bataan. There his army dug itself in and defended its positions bravely and well for some five months.

At the same time as Homma was discovering MacArthur to be a tougher opponent than expected in the Philippines, General Sakai and the Japanese 23rd Army were attacking Hong Kong, defended by Britain's Major-General Maltby and 12,000 men. During the night of December 9th to 10th, the Japanese attacked the mainland peninsula of Kowloon, and, after three days of fierce resistance, the British were forced to withdraw to the island of Victoria. Five days later, again at night, the Japanese crossed to the island, and General Maltby found himself hopelessly outnumbered. Nonetheless, his force held on bravely until Christmas Day 1941, when they were forced to surrender.

3

4

5

the causeway joining the island to the mainland was blown up. Now the almost total lack of defences against attack from the mainland became appallingly clear. In his 'Second World War', Winston Churchill said that 'the possibility of Singapore having no landward defences no more entered my mind than that of a battleship being launched without a bottom.'

It took only a week for Yamashita to prepare. The night of February 8th/9th saw his troops cross the Strait of Johore and establish a beach-head North-East of the city. On the 9th, the airfield at Tengah fell, and with it the reservoirs that provided Singapore with water. By the 15th General Percival had no alternative but to surrender.

The Malayan campaign cost the Japanese 3,507 dead and 6,150 wounded. The Allies lost almost 9,000 dead, and 130,000 as prisoners of war, most of whom were treated with appalling cruelty and inhumanity by their captors, who, applying Japanese traditional

6

the day for Japan. For the air attacks were so effective, and became so frequent, that the British forces were unable to regroup and counter-attack.

Yamashita, although a vicious and cruel man hanged after the war for his crimes, was a capable general and a cunning tactician. Known as 'the Rommel of the Jungle' he was every bit as wily as his namesake, as he showed when he advanced on Singapore by a series of rapid flanking attacks which kept Lieutenant-General A.E.Percival's troops constantly on the retreat. Yamashita had picked commando groups infiltrate the British lines and harry the retreating units, thereby maintaining the impression that his army was invincible and that the British were surrounded. By the end of December Yamashita's army was, if anything, ahead of schedule. He had taken Kota Bharu, half way up the East coast of the Malay Peninsula, and was well placed for the final push to take Singapore.

The problem of defending the Malay Peninsula, which fell to Lieutenant-General Percival in his role as GOC Malaya, was demanding and difficult. He had two Indian divisions and one Australian division to hold a country almost entirely covered by dense jungle. Percival deployed his troops to cover forward airfields, and to hold the few main roads of the peninsula, bringing up reinforcements as they arrived to assist in his army's plight — four brigades arrived during January. But the Japanese troops were trained to jungle conditions, were tough and well disciplined, and moved South through the jungle, constantly outflanking the British positions.

On January 1st 1942, the Japanese had reached Kuantan, roughly halfway down the East coast from Kota Bharu to Singapore. On the West side of the peninsula, Kuala Lumpur fell on the 11th, and Percival decided by the end of the month that his best chance of holding off the Japanese was to conserve his army by falling back to the supposedly impregnable 'fortress' of Singapore. On January 30th,

7

standards to their Western prisoners, regarded the Allied troops as unworthy of honourable treatment because they had chosen surrender rather than death.

The Islands, Borneo, Java, Sumatra

Meanwhile, the Japanese invasions and successes had proceeded apace all over South East Asia. As early as December 10th, the American island of Guam, isolated among other islands of the Marianas, which were legitimately Japanese following the Treaty of Versailles, surrendered when its commander found himself in a totally indefensible position. Wake Island was able to put up a better show, and the US forces there managed to inflict some psychologically important reverses upon the Japanese before the island fell. A squadron of Grumman Wildcat aircraft had arrived on Wake Island on December 4th, just before Pearl Harbour, and the

4 In Malaya, Lt-General A.E. Percival commanded two Indian divisions and one Australian division, which were continuously outflanked by General Yamashita's marginally larger army and appreciably more cunning tactics. This picture, one of the first to reach the European press of Australians in action in Southeast Asia, shows a gun crew firing on Japanese positions in the jungle.

5 The battle for Hong Kong began on December 8th, the day after Pearl Harbour, when the Japanese 38th Infantry Division, supported by artillery, attacked the 12,000 Allied troops holding the garrison. By 13th December, the Allies had been forced to withdraw to Victoria Island, and Hong Kong fell on Christmas Day 1941. This Japanese artillery crew are firing on Allied positions in Kowloon from close range.

6 The conquering Japanese sought to give their newly-won territories all the trappings of colonial empire. In February 1942, Lieutenant-General Rensuke Isogai, previously Chief of Staff of the Japanese Kwantung Army, was appointed Governor-General of Hong Kong. This picture was issued via neutral sources at the time of the appointment.

7 As the Japanese closed in on Victoria Island from the landward side of Hong Kong, British and American women and children were evacuated for their own safety, initially with the intention of going to Manila. The success of the Japanese campaign in Luzon, and General MacArthur's withdrawal from Manila, made it necessary for the evacuees' ships to be diverted, usually to Australia.
Here, curiously, it is the *Empress of Japan* that is carrying the evacuees to safety.

1 Even Darwin, on Australia's northern coast, was under threat of Japanese invasion, although it never actually came. So great was the fear of Japanese 'Blitzkrieg' that freight trains like these were pressed into service to move hundreds of civilians away from the potential battle-zone.

Japanese received a considerable surprise when they attacked, losing two destroyers and a large number of men. The garrison fought on, but the all-conquering Japanese Zero fighter, with its 332 mph maximum speed, was too much for the Wildcats which, although only slightly slower, were less manoeuvrable and not so well armed. On December 21st, the last Wildcat was shot down, and on the 23rd, with the defensive batteries bombed and destroyed, the garrison was forced to surrender.

The Celebes and the Moluccas fell in January and February 1942, and as each new island territory was added to the Japanese Empire, the Japanese Navy and air force units gained new bases, new superiority. The first landing on Borneo came on December 16th, the invasion of Sumatra on February 14th, and that of Timor on the 20th. As General Wavell, commanding the American, British, Dutch and Australian forces in South East Asia was ordered to move his headquarters to Ceylon — now Sri Lanka — on February 25th, news came of the imminent invasion by the Japanese 16th Army of Java, defended by only 30,000 troops under the Dutch General ter Poorten.

To try and head off the invasion convoy, Rear-Admiral Karel Doorman of the Royal Dutch Navy was despatched with a fleet consisting of two heavy cruisers (the British *Exeter* and the American *Houston*; three light cruisers, the Dutch *De Ruyter* and *Java* and the Australian *Perth*; and nine destroyers — three British, four American and two Dutch. Theirs was to be the disaster of the Battle of the Java Sea.

At 4.15pm on February 27th, the fleet began firing on the Japanese convoy, the stopping of which represented the Allies' only real hope of gaining control over the Japanese assault on Java. The Japanese stood off as far as possible, and conducted the battle at extreme range — 13 miles — which gave their ships the advantage because they had more 8″ guns. The Allied fleet had no air cover, and had poorly co-ordinated communications, so was unable to make effective use of its fire power. Shortly after 5pm, HMS *Exeter* was hit in her engine room and had to retreat out of range. The Dutch destroyer *Kortenaer* was hit by a torpedo, exploded and sank. The British *Electra* was set ablaze by gunfire. Later, the Allied fleet inadvertently crossed a minefield, and the British destroyer *Jupiter* was blown up. As matters

2 The Japanese coveted the oilfields of the Dutch East Indies, and the Netherlands Navy formed an important part of the Allied naval force in the Java Sea. At Surabaja, bombed for the first time on 3rd February 1942, the Dutch had a major ship repair facility, where the USS *Houston* was photographed on 15th December 1941.

became worse for the Allied fleet, the Japanese ships *Nachi* and *Haguro* moved in and sank both *De Ruyter* and *Java*, the former taking Rear-Admiral Doorman with it to the bottom.

Perth and *Houston* broke off the battle and returned to Batavia, from where they were ordered to retire Southwards through the Sunda Strait. Here they ran into another Japanese convoy and, after a fierce battle which cost the Japanese four ships, both were sunk. The final disaster came when *Exeter* and the US destroyer *Pope* were sunk trying to run the Sunda Strait on March 1st.

The defeat of the Java Sea ensured that Java would fall to Japan. On March 5th, the Dutch were obliged to evacuate Batavia, which was declared an 'open city', and on March 9th the Dutch and Allied forces in Java surrendered.

The Philippines

While all these events were causing the British, Australians and Dutch grave problems, General MacArthur and his Americans were making a determined stand against General Homma's 14th Army in the Bataan Peninsula. A demand from the Japanese for surrender on January 10th was ignored, and the fierce attack that followed made it necessary for the US forces to fall back to their secondary defensive line. From this, Homma could not budge them, and had to call for reinforcements, something no Japanese General ever did willingly.

On February 22nd, as the US troops, now getting desperately short of food and medical supplies, still held their line, MacArthur was ordered by Washington to leave for Australia. He politely declined and kept fighting. By March 10th Roosevelt was adamant,

3 The continuing stand by General King's US troops in Bataan was an irritant to the otherwise universally triumphant Japanese army. When they captured a large American gun emplacement in Bataan – in fact a relatively small advance – the event was turned into a propaganda opportunity.

4 As the Americans in the Philippines gradually but inevitably retreated in the face of the overwhelmingly reinforced Japanese invading army, they destroyed installations and military positions as they went in order to deny their benefit to the invaders. These Japanese soldiers are running forward past burning oil storage tanks.

5 In late March the Japanese advance along the Bataan peninsula became inexorable, and for the Americans the end was clearly in sight. The Japanese had brought in substantial armour to increase the pressure on the US force, but they were still suffering considerable losses of men and material at the hands of the defenders.

6 Early in April 1942, disease, semi-starvation and the hopelessness of their position was wearing down the American and Filipino defenders in Bataan. The casualties are Filipino soldiers; the Americans in the background are visibly thin as a result of the shortage of food. On April 10th, the defence force surrendered; the largest surrender numerically in American history.

7 The 12,000 US troops and 64,000 Filipinos who had survived the fighting and the dysentery to surrender in Bataan had worse to follow. With those who were later obliged to surrender in Corregidor, they were forced to march fifty-five miles from Mariveles to San Fernando, on their way to appalling camps at Capas and O'Donnell. More than 9,000 men died – here we see the captured and exhausted men being lined up before the long trek.

8 Once Bataan had fallen, Japanese pressure was turned on the 15,000 exhausted and dispirited defenders of the island of Corregidor, commanded by General Wainwright. These US Marines, only recently landed in the Philippines, were among the troops caught up in the final defence of the islands and in the inevitable surrenders.

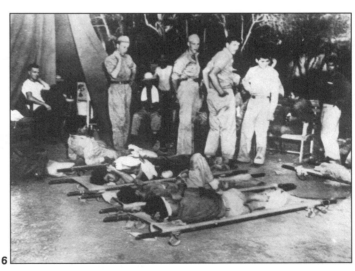

Japan Takes All

and it became clear that even General MacArthur had to do what he was told sometimes. He reluctantly handed over his command to General Wainwright, and left with his family and staff in four PT boats from the island of Corregidor. After a hazardous and eventful journey, they made it to Mindanao, from where they were flown to Australia by B-17. There General Douglas MacArthur made his most famous, and entirely accurate, pronouncement. 'I shall return!'

Meanwhile, in Bataan, General King and the US troops were in serious trouble. Lack of food, dysentery, almost exhausted medical supplies, and sheer exhaustion were telling on morale and the ability to fight. A further demand for surrender from General Homma on April 1st was ignored by Wainwright as studiedly as previous similar demands. But this time the Japanese were able to break through, and on Thursday April 9th it became clear that the end of the brave stand had come. The numerically largest surrender in US history was signed on the 10th, and 12,000 American troops and 64,000 Filipinos, including a great many civilians, were taken prisoner. Although their long battle was at an end, their sufferings were far from over.

1 On May 6th 1942, General Wainwright on Corregidor, believing that there was no other course open that could prevent unnecessary and fruitless further loss of American lives, decided to accept the Japanese demand that he surrender not only the force on Corregidor, but also all remaining Allied forces in the Philippines. Watched by a Japanese officer, he broadcast an appeal to all remaining defenders to lay down their arms.

2 Triumphant after their long campaign, the Japanese conquerors hauled down the Stars and Stripes in Corregidor. Not for almost three years would it fly again on the island.

3 The treatment meted out to American prisoners of war by the Japanese was in many cases extremely cruel and inhumane. After the fall of Corregidor, these Americans were held at bayonet point with their hands high in the air, wondering what fate would befall them. They soon learned the worst, and were forced to take part in the Death March of Bataan.

4 These men of the Japanese 15th Army are ceremonially saluting the Rising Sun flag before their advance into Burma.

5 The unreliability of press photograph captions is demonstrated by the fact that this picture appears in the files of two different libraries, in one case captioned as the British crossing the Moulmein River, in the other as the Japanese making the same crossing. The soldiers are in fact Japanese, crossing the Moulmein on January 31st 1942.

6 Between January and April 1942, the Japanese army advanced rapidly and seemingly unstoppably across Burma towards the Indian frontier. British forces were far too few to hold the increasingly reinforced Japanese 15th Army, despite the excellent leadership of Major-General Hutton, and later of General Sir Harold Alexander. This Japanese propaganda picture shows the advance being ceremonially sounded as the army approached the Indian frontier.

For, having taken their prisoners, the Japanese ruthlessly imposed upon thousands of men already ravaged by hunger, disease and exhaustion the terrible 55-mile 'Death March' from Mariveles to the railhead at San Fernando. No less than 2,330 Americans and over 7,000 Filipinos died during that ordeal, and General Homma was tried and executed after the war for the suffering he thus inflicted.

With the fall of Bataan, only the island of Corregidor and some islets nearby remained in US hands, but these last possessions were of vital importance because they controlled the approaches to Manila harbour. A tremendous assault was mounted by the Japanese at the beginning of May 1942, and a large force was landed on the island on May 4th under cover of a barrage of 16,000 shells. Wainwright was in a hopeless position, commanding 15,000 men, most of whom were not in a fit state to fight. The Japanese called for a surrender, insisting that it must encompass not only Corregidor, but also all other US forces in the Philippines archipelago — which implied their taking Mindanao and a number of islands without a fight. Both MacArthur from afar, and Wainwright's subordinates on the spot, tried to prevent him surrendering, but on May 6th, Wainwright agreed to sign and all US resistance in the Philippines came to an end.

Siam and Burma

Of all the assaults by which Japan bagan its conquest of South East Asia in December 1941, Siam — now Thailand — caused her armies the least trouble. General Iida met virtually nil resistance as his 15th Army marched through to Burma, his way smoothed at every major obstacle by a Quisling government. When his army reached the borders of Burma, important to the Japanese for its oil and natural resources, but strategically vital because it offered control of the 'Burma Road' by which US arms and supplies were reaching Chiang Kai-shek's Nationalist army, he encountered stiff resistance. The recently appointed British commander in chief, Major-General T.J.Hutton, was poorly equipped for the fight, with roughly one division of mixed British, Burmese and Indian troops, reinforced in late January with most of the 17th Indian Division. His air power was virtually non-existent; four Blenheims and 24 obsolete Brewster Buffalo fighters.

On January 18th, as the Japanese took Tavoy in the South and moved on to Moulmein, which fell on the 31st, the British were attempting to round up infiltrators, collaborators and spies, and arrested the appropriately named Prime Minister U Saw among many others. Early in February, the Japanese pushed on towards the Sittang River, held by the 17th Indian Division under Major-General J. Smyth, VC. Sadly, the Allied forces blew prematurely the bridge they planned to use while they were still on the wrong side of the river, thereby creating their own disaster. Two thirds of the division, all its guns and most of its transport was surrendered on February 22nd, and the future for Burma looked grim.

The remnants of the 17th Division fell back to defend the capital, Rangoon, and the 1st Burma Division was in action to the North. But the lack of manpower in both caused a gap to open between them, through which the Japanese were able to push. On March 5th 1942, General Sir Harold Alexander had arrived in Burma to take over from Hutton, but had rapidly realised the appalling gravity of the situation. His first view was that Rangoon must be held at all costs, but he quickly came to agree with Hutton that the Japanese were too strong, and the Allied force numerically too weak for this to be feasible. He therefore ordered a retreat to the North, and abandoned Rangoon on March 7th. At this point, as the British retreated up the Irawaddy valley, reinforcements arrived in the shape of the British 7th Armoured Brigade, infantry battalions, and more air support. The whole was regrouped under the command of Lieutenant-General William Slim.

The strategic objective now was to prevent the Japanese gaining control of the Yenangyaung oilfields. To the battle came the Chinese 5th and 6th armies under the command of American Lieutenant-General Stilwell — known as 'Vinegar Joe'. But the Japanese army had also been reinforced, and had two additional divisions and many more aircraft. The Allied line South of Mandalay proved unable to contain the pressure of the Japanese advance, and the oilfields fell in mid-April, although not before the Allies had sabotaged the oil-wells and put them out of action. On the 29th April, the Chinese were driven back over the border into China, and General Alexander was obliged to evacuate Mandalay and retreat to India via the Irawaddy and Chindwin rivers.

Thus Burma fell too, and Japan, by mid 1942, had achieved virtually all her initial objectives. But retribution was not to be long in coming.

1 The rural population of Burma let the war wash over them, taking little interest in whichever army was passing through, and simply hoping that they would do it without destroying homes or crops. These Burmese are far more interested in the activities of the Japanese cameraman than in the mounted Japanese officers advancing towards India through their village.

2 Lieutenant-General 'Vinegar Joe' Stilwell (left), the American commander of the Chinese Nationalist 5th and 6th Armies, was brought up to reinforce Alexander's last desperate attempt to hold the Burmese oilfields. At the end of April, the oilfields had to be abandoned, and Stilwell and his men literally walked back to China.

3 On April 5th 1942, ninety one Japanese carrier-borne aircraft attacked Colombo harbour, seriously damaging two ships. Later the same day, fifty three Aichi dive-bombers overwhelmed the cruisers HMS Cornwall and HMS Dorsetshire in the Indian Ocean off Colombo, and both were lost. This picture of survivors from the Dorsetshire was taken from the British destroyer that rescued a large number of them.

CHAPTER 15

ROOSEVELT AND CHURCHILL
AND THEIR WAR LEADERS

Franklin D. Roosevelt was a politician and a statesman, but never a soldier. He was a man of consistent and balanced views, with a strong sense of moral purpose and a desire to serve his people. Winston Churchill was at once a patrician and a rebel; a soldier in his youth, a politician in his prime and a statesman in his maturity. Churchill was a man of action, an inspired leader. Roosevelt was a creature of reason. That the two achieved such close understanding and coincidence of purpose was in many ways remarkable, for they were in almost every respect quite different men.

Roosevelt brought to the strategy of the Second World War exactly that quality of balance, compromise and political opportunism that was needed to steer the rocky course between Stalin and Churchill; between conflicting ideologies and viewpoints. His was a contribution that, it might be argued, no soldier could have made. For Roosevelt recognised that the great weakness of the Axis was its inability to take and follow joint decisions that were mutually beneficial and jointly acceptable.

Both Roosevelt and Churchill reasoned that the greatest potential strength of the Allies rested in true international strength and command, and both worked ceaselessly to achieve the unity and consistency of policy that, contrasting with the grotesque disharmony of the Axis commands, did so much to hasten the end of the war. Yet it was Churchill's pugnacious inability to compromise, which had brought him long periods in the political wilderness before the war, that made him unwilling to accept anything less than what he saw to be right, and which, ultimately, steered the Allies towards total victory. For much of Europe, Churchill's determination was the pivot of freedom.

Nonetheless, it fell to Roosevelt to seek the middle course that would preserve the unity of the alliance with the Soviet Union, and thus make it possible to win the war. He saw that Stalin wanted the British and Americans to open 'The Second Front' in France in 1942. He recognised that Churchill was correct in his view that the Allies were not ready—but proposed instead that the USA should join in prosecuting a new offensive in North Africa and thereby appease Stalin. He knew that there was a powerful groundswell of public opinion that demanded an all-out effort to defeat the Japanese as a higher priority than the conquering of Germany, but saw that the

4

5

6

7

Allied strategy of 'Germany first' must be preserved if world peace was to be achieved. His was a rare ability among men of politics, for he was able to compromise without being seen to deviate from an agreed policy.

These, then, were the men who led the USA and Britain to war. Whom did they choose to help steer their ships of state?

The strength of Roosevelt's team rested in men of his own kind, the civilians mainly from the Eastern states with a predominance of Harvard graduates, the military an immensely able group of commanders, each capable of seeing and valuing others' points of view. General George C. Marshall was Army Chief of Staff, a man who later demonstrated great political ability during the postwar

4 President Roosevelt, photographed at the White House during a conference with Soviet Foreign Minister Vyacheslav Molotov in 1942.

5 President Roosevelt's personal adviser and friend, Harry Hopkins, was at the time of the coming of war something of a shadowy and enigmatic figure. He rapidly emerged as an emissary extraordinary, travelling between Britain, the Soviet Union and the USA frequently, and often secretly, to negotiate arrangements between the President and the other Allied leaders, commonly in advance of their being any Congressional acceptance of the initiative. On 10th January 1941, he met British Foreign Secretary Anthony Eden at the Foreign Office in London.

6 Harry Hopkins brought, on his visit to London in January 1941, a letter from President Roosevelt to King George VI. In it Roosevelt described Hopkins as 'a very good friend of mine in whom I repose the utmost confidence'. Here he is pictured in Washington during December 1941 with his daughter Diana, Commander C.R. (Tommy) Thompson, Royal Navy, Churchill's naval aide, and Winston Churchill in his famous siren suit.

7 Outside 10 Downing Street after the crucial meeting of 10th January, Harry Hopkins and Winston Churchill shake hands for the press photographers, with Churchill's friend and confidant Brendan Bracken looking on. During the weekend party that followed, Churchill made an informal speech about the moral issues of the war. Asked what the President would say to that, Hopkins replied 'Well, Mr Prime Minister, I don't think the President will give a dam' for all that. You see, we're only interested in seeing that Goddam sonofabitch, Hitler, gets licked'. The friendship between Hopkins and Churchill never looked back.

period. Admiral Ernest J. King was Chief of Naval Operations, General Henry H. Arnold the head of the Air Corps. All were far more than just military leaders, for they were the backbone of wartime government in the USA. Alongside them worked men of the calibre of Henry L. Stimson, Secretary of War; Edward R. Stettinius, who first ran Lend Lease, then became Secretary of State in 1944, and Joseph C. Grew, who as US Ambassador in Tokyo had foreseen the risk to Pearl Harbour and Hawaii and was now senior adviser on Asian matters.

Add to these and other men of stature—Cordell Hull, Sumner Welles, Frank Knox, James Forrestal—the extraordinary Harry Hopkins, son of an Iowa harness maker—and one cannot but recognise the unique nature of the team. Hopkins was the fast-moving, fast-talking go-between who did much to fashion Roosevelt's working relationships with Churchill and Stalin and to whom Roosevelt turned more than to any other. Few actually liked him, but all respected him.

1 This was the first picture ever taken of the Joint Board meeting held every week at the War Department in Washington. Taken during November 1941, it shows, left to right: Major-General Henry H. Arnold; Major-General William Bryden; General George C. Marshall, Chief of Staff; Admiral H.R. Stark, Rear-Admiral R.E. Ingersoll; Rear-Admiral J.H. Towers and Rear-Admiral R.K. Turner.

2 Immediately following the attack on Pearl Harbour, Secretary of the Navy Frank Knox flew to Hawaii on a fact-finding visit. This picture of Knox leaving the White House on December 15th 1941 was taken after he had reported his initial findings to the President.

3 On December 26th 1941, Britain's Prime Minister Winston Churchill addressed a joint session of Congress in Washington, DC. Present in addition to Congressmen were members of the US Cabinet and the US Supreme Court. In the picture are (left to right, front row) Attorney-General Biddle; Postmaster-General Walker; Secretary of the Navy Frank Knox; Secretary of the Interior Harold Ickes; Secretary of Agriculture Wickard; Secretary of Commerce Jesse Jones.

In Britain, Churchill had assembled men whose integrity, drive, ability and determination almost matched his own. Impelled by the events of April and May 1940 and the fall of his own party leader Neville Chamberlain to create a coalition government of national unity, he turned a political situation which most party politicians would have regarded as a disaster into a source of strength. Instead of being constrained by party loyalties to appoint to great office only parliamentarians of his own Conservative party, Churchill was able to select the finest talents in the land. He began with the service ministries. From the Labour Party he drew A. V. Alexander, later first Earl of Hillsborough, to become First Lord of the Admiralty. From the Liberal Party came Sir Archibald Sinclair as Secretary of State for Air. From the Conservative Party he appointed, as Secretary of State for War, Anthony Eden, who as Foreign Secretary had resigned from Chamberlain's government because of his opposition to Chamberlain's appeasement of the dictators.

In addition to his role as Prime Minister, Churchill also created

for himself the position of Minister of Defence. He resisted immense political pressure in 1940 to remove from office as Foreign Secretary the greatly experienced Lord Halifax, and retained at that time even Neville Chamberlain in the post of Lord President of the Council, setting the value of experience above considerations of politics. Halifax was eventually replaced as Foreign Secretary in December 1940 by Anthony Eden, Viscount Halifax becoming Britain's Ambassador in Washington, and David Margesson replacing Eden as Secretary of State for War.

Continuing the all-party policy, Churchill appointed Labour's extremely able Ernest Bevin as Minister of Labour, the leader of the Labour Party, Clement Attlee, as Lord Privy Seal and Herbert

Morrison as Minister of Supply. The charismatic Canadian newspaper publisher Lord Beaverbrook became Minister of Aircraft Production, his success as a non-politician in that role providing a curious parallel to that of Germany's Albert Speer, an architect by profession and an immense success as Reich Minister for Armaments Production. Brendan Bracken, Churchill's Parliamentary Private Secretary and an unfailing support during his wilderness years, was appointed a Privy Councillor, despite initial opposition from King George VI.

Churchill's Chiefs of Staff were, like their American counterparts, both able and successful as a team. Admiral of the Fleet Sir Dudley Pound was First Sea Lord and Chief of Naval Staff until his death in

4 Three days after Pearl Harbour, senior officers of the US Army Air Force were photographed at Army headquarters in Washington 'planning war moves'. Left to right: Colonel Edgar P. Sorenson, Material and Supply Division; Lt-Colonel Harold L. George, Air War Plans Division; Brigadier-General Carl Spaatz, Chief of Air Staff; Major-General Henry H. Arnold, Chief of the Air Corps' Major Haywood Hansell, Air War Plans Division; Brigadier-General Martin F. Scanlon, Assistant Chief of Staff, Air Intelligence; and Lt-Colonel Arthur W. Vanaman, Secretary of the Air Staff.

5 Lord Halifax, who had been British Foreign Secretary in Neville Chamberlain's government at the time of the Munich Agreement and at the outbreak of war, was British Ambassador in Washington during the crucial months of 1941 before the USA entered the war. Here Halifax (left) is talking with Henry A. Wallace, Vice-President of the United States, in February 1941.

6 President Roosevelt's 'Supreme Defense Council', called in May 1941, heard from Major-General H.H. Arnold, just returned from Britain, of Britain's desperate need for a large number of American heavy bombers. At the meeting were (left to right) Secretary of the Navy Frank Knox; Rear-Admiral John H. Towers, Chief of Bureau of Aeronautics; Admiral Harold R. Stark, Chief of Naval Operations; Secretary of the Treasury Henry Morgenthau Junior; and General Arnold, Chief of the Army Air Corps.

7 This happy picture taken at Pearl Harbour shows both senior and comparatively junior officers of the US Navy with Secretary Knox after a two-week, 12,000 mile flying tour of the Pacific battle area during which the party twice became caught up in Japanese air attacks.

8 Appearing before the Senate Foreign Relations Committee in Washington on September 30th 1942, former US Ambassador to Japan Joseph C. Grew (2nd from left) explains a Pacific war incident on the map. At left is Senator Tom Connally, who was Chairman of the committee, and on the right Assistant Secretary of State Breckinridge Long.

Roosevelt and Churchill

1943, when he was succeeded by Admiral of the Fleet Andrew Cunningham, later Viscount Cunningham of Hyndhope. Chief of the Air Staff, appointed in October 1940, was Air Vice Marshal (at that time) Sir Charles Portal, and in the key role of Chief of the Imperial General Staff was General Alan Brooke, later to be Field Marshal Lord Alanbrooke, more than any other Churchill's friend and military confidant. Another vital figure, acting as principal intermediary between the Chiefs of Staff and Churchill in his role as Minister of Defence, was Major-General (later General Lord) Hastings Ismay, Secretary of the Imperial Defence Committee.

The Allies had good cause to be grateful for the immense ability of the men both Roosevelt and Churchill gathered around them. For their quality was such that, on both sides of the Atlantic, virtually no cabinet or Chief of Staff changes were necessary throughout the war other than where caused by ill health or death. Rarely in history has there been such a consistent and unanimous sense of purpose felt by the great men of nations at war.

1 In October 1942, James F. Byrnes, former Supreme Court Justice, was appointed Stabilisation Director to the Administration. In this picture he is talking with Harry Hopkins (centre) and Lewis Douglas (right), Deputy War Shipping Administrator.

2 Photographed in April 1942 on their way to a conference with President Roosevelt are the 'Big Three' of the US Navy of the time are (left to right) Admiral Ernest J. King, Commander of the US Fleet; Frank Knox, Secretary of the Navy; and Admiral Thomas C. Hart, formerly Commander of US Naval Forces in the Far East and by this time a Presidential naval adviser.

3 James V. Forrestal, later, in 1944, to succeed Frank Knox as Secretary of the Navy, had become Under-Secretary of the Navy in August 1940.

4 On the 25th July 1942, an Allied naval conference took place in the Painted Hall at Greenwich, England, hosted by Winston Churchill and the Board of Admiralty. In the front row of this group picture are (left to right): Admiral Sir Charles Little, RN; Rear-Admiral A.C. Bennett, USN; Harry Hopkins; Winston Churchill; Admiral Ernest J. King, Commander in Chief of the US Fleet and Chief of Naval Operations; A.V. Alexander, First Lord of the Admiralty; Admiral Harold R. Stark, Commander, US Naval Forces in Europe; John G. Winant, US Ambassador to Britain; Admiral of the Fleet Sir Dudley Pound, First Sea Lord and Chief of Naval Staff; and William Bullitt, Special Assistant to the Secretary of the US Navy.

CHAPTER 16

ROMMEL AND THE DESERT CAMPAIGN
THE PUSH TO EGYPT

At this point, this book must go back in time — a manoeuvre that all writers tackling a subject as vast as the Second World War seem unable to avoid. We must return to North Africa, and to March 1941. General O'Connor and his two divisions, who had on December 9th 1940 set out on what was intended as a 9-day raid, had instead advanced 560 miles across the desert to Tobruk and Benghazi, destroying nine Italian divisions, capturing 130,000 men (including 22 Generals and an Admiral), and eliminating 845 guns and 380 tanks, all for the loss of 500 dead, 1,373 wounded and 56 missing. The Italians were humiliated, Hitler was angry, and Lieutenant-General Erwin Rommel was summoned by Field Marshal Brauchitsch to take command of a new offensive.

Rommel arrived in Tripoli on February 12th, and presented himself to the Italian General Gariboldi, who had just taken over from Graziani. During the eighteen months from March 1941 to September 1942, Rommel was to prove himself one of the most able field commanders of military history; a man capable of leading an army from a major defeat at Tobruk to almost total victory at the gates of Alexandria; a man whose name and ability were respected on both sides of the battle he so nearly won. He was also to prove infuriatingly blinkered and single-minded to his army command colleagues, whose understanding and appreciation of the overall strategy of the war was usually greater than his, and who resented bitterly Rommel's purloining *Luftwaffe* resources intended for the capture of Malta and

5 On February 12th 1941, General Erwin Rommel (right in rear seat of car) arrived in Tripoli to command what was to become the *Afrika Korps* – the 15th *Panzer* Division and the 5th Light Division. He was driven through the streets of Tripoli with General Italo Gariboldi, Italian Commander-in-Chief in North Africa, to view a parade of German and Italian troops.

6 Rommel arrived in North Africa to take command of a situation that was a source of considerable Axis humiliation. In December and January 1941, General O'Connor's lightning advance had forced back the Italians and his South African Division under Major-General De Villiers had liberated the important town of Bardia. As they did so they had freed these British prisoners of war, who had been imprisoned by the Italians in this grim camp for five weeks.

5

6

7

8

the relief of the fierce Allied campaign against Italian merchant ships in the Mediterranean. First Cavallero, then Kesselring became exasperated with Rommel's insistence on ever-greater support, and with Hitler's acceptance of his arguments.

The new German offensive was to be launched by the 15th *Panzer* Division and the 5th Light Division, and advance units were sent to Tripoli from Italy during February. It was expected that the whole 5th Light Division would be ready in North Africa by mid-April, and that the last of 15th *Panzer* would have arrived by the end of May. The first attack on Agedabia was therefore scheduled by the German High Command for May, and General Wavell, in command of the Allied force, knowing that extensive German forces and armour had perforce to be shipped to North Africa, believed that no counter attack was likely before then. Thus, there was not undue concern that many of O'Connor's hard pressed tanks had to be withdrawn from Tobruk for maintenance because the speed of O'Connor's unscheduled advance had left the maintenance facilities far behind.

Rommel, who had been awarded Benghazi as his spring campaign objective, was not pleased with the conservative approach of the High Command, and sensed that the Allies were less well

7 Mussolini (pictured above during a visit to North Africa) resented deeply the independence and consequent success demonstrated by Rommel early in his North African career. Like most dictators, he did not trust anything he could not totally control.

8 According to the original German caption of this picture, these are three of six British generals captured near Derna, and flown by Junkers Ju52 to be imprisoned in Germany. In the centre is General O'Connor, on the right General Neame.

prepared for a fight than their success against the Italians suggested. He resolved to test their strength, and at dawn on March 24th, the 5th Light Division attacked El Agheila. The British defenders fell back without a fight to stronger positions at Marsa Brega, with the Gulf of Sirte on one side, and a salt marsh that tanks could not cross on the other. Rommel's orders now required that he wait for the remainder of the 15th *Panzer* Division to arrive before exploiting his initial advantage, but he was unwilling to allow the Allies time to regroup and bring up more armour. So, on March 31st he attacked again, and, despite putting up a stiff fight, the British defenders were dislodged from what would have become an excellent defensive position.

By the end of April 2nd, Rommel and his German forces, backed by two Italian divisions, had occupied the Agedabia area almost two

1 The officer to the right of the picture, wearing the Australian slouch hat, is Brigadier Horace 'Red Robbie' Robertson, with his aide, following the ceremony at which the Italian mayor of Benghazi had surrendered the city to the 19th Brigade of the Australian 6th Division on the 7th February 1941.

2 Admiral Sir Andrew Cunningham (right), who commanded the British Fleet in the Mediterranean that gave support to Tobruk from the sea, in a picture taken on board the 22,000 ton French battleship *Provence* in 1939. Then a Vice-Admiral, he is pictured with Vice-Admiral Ollive of the French Navy.

3 A German PzKpfw III battle tank being unloaded for the Afrika Korps in Libya in 1941. Note the spare tracks at the rear of the tank, and the spare bogie wheels stacked on the rear hull deck – the German army always faced maintenance problems in long-distance armoured operations, and it became standard practice for each tank to carry quite major spares into battle.

months sooner than the German High Command had envisaged. The Rommel legend was in the making. So also was trouble with High Command. For not only did nobody know what Rommel was up to, but neither General von Rintelen nor Gariboldi was able to answer Mussolini's questions as to what he would do next. They soon found out. On the night of April 3rd/4th, as Gariboldi chased after Rommel to stop his impetuous habit of winning battles, the reconnaissance unit of the 5th Light Division took Benghazi, and swept on towards Mechili. Berlin, recognising that success was at hand, whether intended or not, applauded Rommel's adventures, and Gariboldi was obliged to retire and leave Germany's one-man success story to his desert *Blitzkrieg*.

The Allies sought to reorganise their command structure before it was too late, and Wavell decided to put O'Connor, whose own

version of *Blitzkrieg* had rivalled Rommel's, in charge of a counter-attack. But O'Connor had the ill-luck to be captured by a German patrol while driving with General Neame to a staff conference. The apocryphal story goes that, on arrival at Rommel's desert Head-quarters, O'Connor barked 'Anybody here speak English?'. 'I do, sir' replied a German officer, snapping to attention. 'Well, get lost.' retorted O'Connor. It was, regrettably, his last shot in North Africa.

The *Afrika Korps* thrust onward, from Mechili to Derna and the Gulf of Bomba. Recognising the O'Connor tactic of Beda Fomm being performed in reverse, the Allies escaped the net and retreated to Tobruk. There it was decided by Wavell, Air Chief Marshal Longmore and Admiral Cunningham that the line would be held. To stop Rommel, the garrison consisted of the 9th Australian Division, a brigade of the 7th, an armoured regiment equipped with armoured cars and an anti aircraft brigade — some 36,000 men all told, commanded by the immensely tough and experienced General Leslie Morshead, who had commanded a battalion in the Great War at the age of 20.

The initial German attack on April 10th by a motorised detachment of the 15th *Panzer* Division was repulsed, with the loss of General von Prittwitz, who was killed by a shell. Three days later, a battalion of the 5th Light Division found its way through the minefield but was destroyed by the ferocious Australian defence. The Italians attacked, and were repulsed. But, while Tobruk was besieged, Rommel's units were re-taking other major positions — Halfaya, Sollum and Capuzzo — and were thus back on the Egyptian border.

Nonetheless, the continued success of the German campaign in North Africa depended on the capture of Tobruk, and General Halder and Field Marshal Brauchitsch at German Army High Command saw in the stalemate on the Tobruk perimeter complete justification for their distrust of Rommel and his methods. But Hitler remained convinced that Rommel could provide Germany with much needed victory, and, over the next two months, changed the command structure such that the North African command came under OKW (Armed Forces High Command) rather than OKH (Army High Command).

In mid-May, a beleaguered Allied convoy managed successfully to unload much needed aircraft and tanks for Wavell's army at Alexandria, and Wavell was ordered by the British War Cabinet to attack and relieve Tobruk. This was attempted as an encircling movement to Halfaya Pass, but went badly wrong, partly because

4 A German reconnaissance unit of PzKpFw II's and motorcycle combinations mobilizes during preparations for Rommel's advance on Agedabia in April 1941.

5 A squadron of Bren Gun carriers of a South African Infantry Brigade photographed among the palms of an oasis during a patrol in the Western Desert.

6 One of the keys to the success of Erwin Rommel's *Blitzkrieg* tactics in the desert was an adequate supply line and the maximum possible base support. Rommel consequently took a keen interest in ensuring that the supplies he needed were in fact sent by a Germany already hard pressed on other fronts. Here, he watches supplies being unloaded at the docks.

7 This picture was published in an Italian newspaper after Rommel, on instructions from Hitler, awarded the Iron Cross to General Bastico. The numbered figures in the picture are: 1. General Erwin Rommel, 2. General Ettore Bastico, 3. General Gambara, 4. General Count Calvi di Bergolo.

the units of the 15th *Panzer* Division at Halfaya Pass fought exceptionally well, but also because the German 88mm gun was capable of knocking out the British tanks before they had the German armour within range of their 40mm guns. The defence at Halfaya gave Rommel the time to bring his full force to bear, and the battle developed by mid-June into an ugly and expensive stalemate.

A lesser General would have breathed a sigh of relief. Rommel saw the respite as an opportunity. He went on to the attack, and fought his way rapidly South, then East, attempting to encircle the main British force, which saw the threat and managed to escape. But to do so they had to retreat. Once more, Rommel had the initiative.

The British War Cabinet now attempted to improve matters by replacing Wavell with General Sir Claude Auchinleck, known as 'The Auk'. Auchinleck infuriated Churchill by demanding three months of preparation time and three or four extra divisions before he would be ready to launch his offensive, and a protracted argument developed, with Auchinleck summoned to London to explain himself to Churchill. Meanwhile, the battle lines in the desert were comparatively quiet as the battle around Malta raged in the Mediterranean, and the Russian campaign preoccupied the German High Command. Auchinleck's offensive was first put off until September, then, to Churchill's great displeasure, until November 1st. To satisfy Australian public opinion, the Australian 9th Division in Tobruk was relieved by sea, and replaced with the British 70th Division and the Polish 1st Carpathian Division. Finally, to cap all the other delays, the late arrival in Egypt of the 22nd Armoured Brigade caused the Allied attack to be postponed once again, to November 18th.

Rommel had plans too, and, like those of the Allies, his schemes were being postponed because of military priorities elsewhere. The considerable Allied successes against Italian convoys in the Mediterranenan were preoccupying the *Luftwaffe*, and reducing the flow of supplies to the *Afrika Korps* to such an extent that Rommel's planned campaign to take Tobruk was put off again and again. Not until November 4th was he able to present his proposals to Marshal Cavallero in Rome, when he outlined his intention to attack when the moon was full, between November 20th and December 4th. He planned that, on the day before that set for the attack, the Italian *Brescia* Division would make a diversionary attack from the South-West, to lessen resistance to his own attack with the *Afrika Korps* and the Italian XXI Corps from the South-East. He and his staff officers took pains to emphasise to the Italians their 'belief' that there was no imminent Allied attack planned, and no build-up of Allied

1 A conference between the German and Italian general staffs in the field during 1941. Feelings frequently ran high between the two, the Germans disliking the ill-disciplined and emotional Italians, and the Italians the stiff and uncompromising approach to warfare shown by the Germans. The German General second from left is talking to General Bastico (in profile).

2 An interesting shot of General Bastico, wearing his Iron Cross, in Benghazi with his staff officers. Note the considerable variety of uniform among the Italians.

3 Lieutenant-General Sir Alan Cunningham, brother of Admiral Sir Andrew Cunningham, had achieved considerable fame for his lightning defeat of the Italians in Abyssinnia in March and April 1941, and became commander of the Eighth Army when it was created by Sir Claude Auchinleck in 1941. In this picture he is inspecting Free French Senegalese troops.

4 After British defeats at the hands of Rommel's *Panzergruppe Afrika* in November 1941, Major-General Neil Methuen Ritchie, until then Deputy Chief-of-Staff to Sir Claude Auchinleck, replaced Lieutenant-General Cunningham as commander of the Eighth Army.

strength, although it is now known (since Rommel's intelligence chief Major von Mellenthin's memoirs were published in 1955) that Rommel knew full well that Auchinleck was almost ready to strike. Clearly, his faith in his Italian allies was minimal.

Meanwhile, Auchinleck had created the Eight Army by combining the reinforcements he had received with the battle hardened troops that remaining from Wavell's campaign. This was under the command of Lieutenant-General Sir Alan Cunningham, brother of Admiral Sir Andrew Cunningham who commanded the fleet giving support from the seaward side of Tobruk. Because the C-in-C of the Royal Air Force in the desert was, coincidentally, Air Vice Marshal H. Coningham, the troops referred to their commanders as 'Cunningham, Cunningham and Coningham'. All told, the Allies had six divisions.

In August, Rommel had been elevated to the command of *Panzergruppe Afrika*, of which his *Afrika Korps* was but one corps, now under the command of General Cruewell. The 5th Light Division, reinforced with new armour, became the 15th *Panzer* Division, and there were other units of German armour. The Italian XX and XXI Corps completed Axis forces totalling ten divisions on paper, although the worsening supplies position and manpower shortage in the Italian formations meant that the Axis were actually appreciably less powerful than the figures suggest.

The Allies attacked on November 18th, expecting that their appearance in strength would draw Rommel's forces out to fight at Gabr Saleh. Instead, Rommel, who was preparing his own attack, decided that the Allied effort was no more than a large scale reconnaissance, and stayed put in his defensive position near the coast

5 The failure of the German *Panzer* Divisions to take Tobruk at the end of 1941, and Rommel's increasingly stretched supply lines, made strategic retreat inevitable. Here, a Horch Kfz 15, one of the *Wehrmacht's* early workhorses, leads a column of reconnaissance vehicles through the deserted streets of Benghazi.

6 The sinking of HMS *Ark Royal*, Britain's most famous aircraft carrier, on November 13th 1941 was a major propaganda triumph for Germany, whose Propaganda Minister, Dr Josef Goebbels, had 'sunk' *Ark Royal* several times previously. Her loss was a serious blow to the Mediterranean Fleet's convoy protection, for her aircraft – here, Blackburn Skua fighter-bombers – played an important role in defending the ships.

7 Taken from a destroyer that was taking off survivors from the *Ark Royal* before the great aircraft carrier sank, this picture shows the list that had developed, and gives some idea of the difficulty of such rescue operations at sea, even in comparatively calm weather.

8 The Italians were keen to demonstrate in their newspapers the important role that they wished their commanders to be seen to be playing in the war in North Africa, and pictures like this, in which General Bastico (with map) appears to be making the plans as Rommel looks on, were important to Mussolini's face-saving operation. In fact, Rommel sought actively to conceal his plans from the Italians.

1 At 4.25 p.m. on November 25th 1941, HMS *Barham* was attacked by the German submarine U331 while operating with other ships of the Mediterranean Fleet, 200 miles WNW of Alexandria. The salvo of torpedoes, fired at close range, struck *Barham* on the port side, between the funnel and the after turrets. She immediately took a heavy list to port and, when she was on her beam end, about four minutes after being hit, her magazine blew up. She sank with the loss of 859 officers and men.

2 The importance of convoy protection in the Mediterranean to the success of the Allied campaign in North Africa cannot be over-estimated, for the British and Commonwealth forces, like Rommel's army, depended totally on their supply line. The key to the success of convoy protection was the defence of Malta, which remained a British naval base despite extensive planning by the Axis of 'Hercules', the operation to take Malta and Gozo, which was abandoned by Hitler at the instigation of Rommel, and seemingly endless air raids. These Mediterranean convoy protection vessels were photographed in 1941.

3 Most of the raids on the island fortress of Malta were carried out by bombers of the Italian Air Force *(Regia Aeronautica)*, which was at the time held in scant respect by the pilots of the Royal Air Force. These aircraft unloading their bombs over the island later awarded the George Cross by King George VI are Italian Cant Z.1007 Bis Alcione (Kingfisher) trimotor bombers, which sometimes flew with a pair of 450mm torpedoes under the fuselage instead of the internal bomb load.

at Gambut. This first failure of British planning was compounded by the German capture on the 19th of the Eighth Army's operational orders, and by the failure of the 22nd Armoured Brigade to take Bir-el-Gubi. The problems mounted for the Allies as the British XXX Corps was defeated at Sidi Rezegh on November 22nd, with massive tank losses, and the 5th South African brigade was similarly devastated on the 23rd. It looked as if the Axis would annihilate XXX Corps entirely, as would certainly have happened if the initial success had been pressed home. Instead, Rommel showed his skill as a tactician by using the confusion created as an opportunity to take personal command of the 15th and 21st *Panzer* Divisions, and to set out across the desert to the Mediterranean via Sidi Omar to attack the already vulnerable Allied troops from the rear.

Auchinleck refused to be rattled, although Cunningham was clearly pessimistic about the situation. In a lightning move which restored morale and stiffened British resolve, Auchinleck replaced Cunningham on November 24th with Major-General Neil Methuen

Ritchie, and moved himself firmly into the driving seat. By November 27th, the New Zealand division had made contact with the Tobruk garrison, which had broken out at El Duda, and Rommel, now back at *Panzer* Group headquarters, was failing still to take Tobruk despite frequent attacks. On December 5th, realising that his supplies were desperately stretched with little potential for new arrivals of ammunition, food and fuel before the second half of December, Rommel began his withdrawal from Tobruk, pursued by the Allied forces under Ritchie, who reached Benghazi on Christmas Day.

The pursuit continued, but Rommel's retreat was as skilful as his advance and the British armour did not succeed in engaging the Axis formations before they reached their planned defensive position at El Agheila, 340 tanks down on the strength they had enjoyed when the Allied attack began on November 18th. On January 17th came the final act of Auchinleck's successful 'Operation Crusader', when the Italian *Savona* Division, left behind by the retreating Rommel with the thankless task of defending the Bardia/Sollum/Halfaya area, surrendered to the 2nd South African Division. In two months, the Eighth Army had taken 32,000 prisoners, for the loss of 18,000 men, variously killed, wounded or taken prisoner.

It seemed on the face of it that the Allies could now launch their long awaited Operation 'Acrobat' to advance to Morocco and Algeria. But events at sea in the Mediterranean had been going disastrously wrong for the Allies at the end of 1941 and at the turn of the year, and the balance of power at sea changed dramatically the extent to which Germany was able to re-equip and resupply Rommel's forces for their next offensive. On November 13th, the *Ark Royal*, Britain's finest aircraft carrier had been sunk by U-81. This was rapidly followed by the loss of the battleship *Barham* and the light cruiser *Galatea*. Force K, based on Malta, and the greatest hazard of all to the Axis convoys, was virtually annihilated. Hitler saw his advantage

developing, and both reinforced the *Luftwaffe* in the Mediterranean theatre by withdrawing *II Fliegerkorps* from the Eastern Front, and also changed the command structure by instituting a 'Supreme Commander South' in the person of the likeable, yet ruthlessly effective Field-Marshal Kesselring, once an artilleryman, now one of the architects of the *Luftwaffe* (and, incidentally, an accomplished pilot and aerial photographer.)

At the same time, reinforcements that had been earmarked for Auchinleck and 'Operation Acrobat', the planned 8th Army push to the frontier of Tunisia, and four squadrons of Hurricanes intended for Air Chief Marshal Tedder's Middle East Air Force were diverted to Singapore and to the new war against Japan. As the Allied strength weakened, so Rommel's was greatly enhanced by the arrival of large numbers of new tanks and vehicles, huge quantities of fuel and new

4 Despite the different tailplane by comparison with the previous picture, this Italian bomber, which had attacked the British warships left burning below in Maltese waters, is also a Cant Z.1007 Bis Alcione. The Z.1007 was decidedly unusual, and possibly unique, in being manufactured in two quite distinct types, one with single-fin, the other with twin-fin tailplane. Both versions were in service at the same time.

3

4

5

5 The saga of the three Gloster Gladiator biplanes known as Faith, Hope and Charity, which defended Malta alone during the early stages of its siege, is and was the subject of a book in its own right. The burned-out shell of one of those aircraft here stands as a memorial to the considerable heroism of their pilots.

2 So important both to the success of the Eighth Army campaign in North Africa and to national morale in Britain was the ability of the Mediterranean convoys to get their supplies through to Malta that announcements of their success in reaching Valetta were made by the Admiralty in London. This convoy, whose arrival was announced in August 1942, had been the subject of three days' air, sea and submarine attacks. The picture shows destroyers standing by the damaged tanker *Ohio*, which reached Malta safely after being torpedoed.

3 This remarkable picture taken from an Italian bomber flying over Malta shows almost the entire island. The puffs of smoke are the shell-bursts of anti-aircraft fire from the island – which helps to explain the remarkable view. For it was the considerable success of the anti-aircraft gunners on Malta which caused the Italian Air Force to begin to bomb from high altitudes. The original caption to this picture estimates the height at 20,000 ft – probably not far out.

guns of improved performance. In mid-January he decided to counter-attack, telling neither the German High Command nor the Italian of his intentions until the attack had begun on the grounds that "the Italian Headquarters cannot keep things to themselves." As a result, the Axis forces achieved almost total surprise.

Rommel's Lightning Advance

Moving against the British 1st Armoured Division, which was new to Africa and had a mere 150 tanks, the advance of the Italian Mobile Corps on the coast and the *Afrika Korps* inland was made easier by the splitting of the British Division into three separate forces, each of which was too small to be self-supporting. To make matters worse for the Allies, the experienced 4th Indian Division was stuck at Benghazi, and the 7th Armoured Division had been sent back to Tobruk. Within two days, Rommel was at Agedabia, and on the 27th January almost succeeded in cutting off the 4th Indian Division in Benghazi. Mussolini had issued orders personally to Rommel that he was to retreat back to his former positions. Rommel simply ignored the Duce. By February 3rd, the *Afrika Korps* had skirted around Derna, reached the Gulf of Bomba and ground to a halt at the British positions at Gazala. This was *Blitzkrieg* in the grand manner, and General Ritchie, having lost almost 1,400 men, 72 tanks and 80 guns was not in a strong position. Rommel had pushed 375 miles back towards Egypt in defiance of his orders, yet, despite, his insubordination was rewarded with a promotion to Colonel-General.

1 As the North African campaign ranged up and down the coast of Libya, it was frequently possible for ships of the Mediterranean Fleet to play a significant role in the course of the battle. This picture shows the main armament of a British battleship (probably *Rodney*) bombarding German positions at night.

4 It became a truism of the desert war that fighting in the desert had much in common with manoeuvring ships at sea, and there were times, as can be seen from this picture, when the visual impression was strikingly similar too.

5

The effects of the Axis advance reached well beyond North Africa. The island of Malta was still being defended against ever increasing German and Italian air attacks, and needed desperately the air support that the mainland Middle East Air Force could provide from Benghazi and Derna. With those forward positions lost, air support became impossible because Malta was out of range from Tobruk. Add to that the ability of Rommel's forces to harass the Malta convoys from Cyrenaica, and it can be seen that Admiral Cunningham's problems in attempting to supply Malta were made much greater. Only endless disputes throughout the spring of 1942 between the German and Italian High Commands, and between the individual members of those commands prevented 'Operation Hercules' to take Malta and Gozo being mounted. Kesselring believed that, if 'Hercules' had gone ahead, it would have succeeded. That belief was based on the positions of the 8th Army and the *Afrika Korps* after Rommel's advance.

Meanwhile, Auchinleck's failure to go on to the offensive against the Axis forces was galling Winston Churchill. Since February he had been demanding action, but Auchinleck and Tedder agreed that no offensive launched before June could succeed. Attempts to persuade them otherwise by sending Lieutenant-General Nye and Sir Stafford Cripps to Cairo resulted in the visitors being converted to Auchinleck's viewpoint. By mid-May there was still no British offensive, but a Churchill ultimatum to Auchinleck finally secured action and planning. By then it was too late. Rommel was ready, and

6

5 The effective use of artillery was a key factor in the desert campaign for both sides. This 105mm howitzer is in action against the besieged Allied army in Tobruk, and the large quantity of ammunition boxes and debris suggests that they had despatched a significant quantity of hardware in the direction of their enemies.

6 The moment of inevitable surrender. A British soldier emerges from his tank, out of fuel and ammunition, to face his German captors and some three years in a prisoner of war camp.

Rommel and the Desert Campaign

attacked first. Once more the Eighth Army had been caught on the wrong foot, albeit for the best of reasons. Current British tanks, aircraft and anti-tank guns available in North Africa were all outclassed by their Axis equivalents. Auchinleck was right to judge that trouble lay ahead.

The Axis forces attacked in two principal groups; on the one hand the Italian XXI and X Corps plus some German reinforcement were to launch, under General Cruewell, a frontal assault on the Eighth Army to 'keep them busy' and prevent them manoeuvring for advantage. On the other, Rommel himself took command of the mobile and armoured units — the Italian XX Corps and the divisions that made up the *Afrika Korps*, the 15th and 21st *Panzer* plus the 90th Light Division. In the evening of May 26th, Rommel moved from the positions he had held for so long to outflank his enemy by passing both North and South of Bir Hakeim, thereby putting his tanks to the rear of the Eighth Army. Thus, on May 27th, the British forces found themselves attacked on both sides, yet, after a confused battle in which both sides could claim some success, the Allies had not fared badly. The two Italian divisions of the 20th Corps, the 'Trieste' and the 'Ariete', were virtually routed, and lost many tanks. Although the 15th and 21st *Panzer* Divisions did great damage to the 4th Indian and 7th Armoured Divisions, their armour was somewhat dented, and many German tanks were badly damaged. By the end of the 27th, the Eighth Army's communications remained intact, and the Axis forces were already short of fuel — Rommel's perennial problem. Two days later, General Cruewell was captured after a forced landing behind the British lines.

Rommel was, however, not to be daunted by a few reverses. Having sent advance parties to improve communications with the Italians, and clear a narrow path through the minefield that lay between his forces and the British XIII Corps, he attacked the strongpoint at Got el Oualeb, while the Italian 10th Corps attacked

1 As in other theatres of war, the Free French were active and effective in the Western Desert. The Free French Brigade in the Middle East was made up of Foreign Legion, French Colonial troops and other Free French units under the command of General de Larminat and General Koenig. These men of the French Foreign Legion were applying French cooking techniques to British army rations.

2 Bread for the Australian troops defending Tobruk was baked in these so-called Aldershot ovens. Built of brick and sealed with mud, the ovens were primitive but effective. The dough was placed on the hearth, which had been heated by a wood fire, and the oven was sealed. The heat of the brick and stone hearth baked the bread in about an hour.

3 Rommel undoubtedly had a flair for spotting an opportunity for a propaganda picture. A photographic enthusiast himself (he used a Leica), he frequently suggested shots for the cameramen. According to the German caption, this is Rommel directing operations in the Libyan desert. In fact, it was almost certainly a posed shot.

5

6

7

tracks across the desert which led to Sidi Muftah, Gazala and Bir Hakeim. As the two British corps, which were too thinly spread across the desert with poor communications and control, fell back before the German attack, 4,000 more prisoners fell into German hands, and the 32nd Tank Brigade lost more than half its tanks.

Now Bir Hakeim was surrounded, with no hope of relief. General Koenig, commanding the 1st Free French Brigade, politely declined to surrender, and held on valiantly for eight days, falling back to the British lines only when directly ordered to do so on June 10th. By the 13th, Ritchie was in danger of being encircled and attempted to fall back to Tobruk, but his greatly depleted tank force was outflanked and cut off. The way was now open for Rommel to attack Tobruk.

Thus, at dawn on June 20th, the 15th and 21st *Panzer* Divisions and the Italian XX Corps made their final assault from the South-East, supported by Ju87 'Stuka' dive bombers. Progress was rapid. By 8am, the anti-tank ditch was breached; by nightfall the forts at Solaro and Pilastrino had fallen. The next morning, June 21st, Major-General Klopper surrendered the garrison to General Navarrini. Another 33,000 men fell into Axis hands, but the greatest windfall for Rommel was the huge quantity of gasoline and supplies that he had captured – some 2,200,000 gallons of fuel for which the German armour was desperate.

Now Rommel was set for the advance to Egypt, but the agreement between the German and Italian High Commands to embark upon 'Operation Hercules', the attack on Malta, stood in the way. Substantial sections of his *Panzerarmee* were due to be withdrawn for the assault on Malta, and Rommel knew he could not hope to advance further in North Africa without them. He appealed to Hitler to abandon 'Hercules' in favour of an advance to Egypt, and the

from the West. By June 2nd he had a victory. The British 150th Infantry Brigade and the 1st Army Tank Brigade surrendered, and 3,000 men, 124 guns and 101 armoured vehicles of all descriptions fell into Axis hands. Now Rommel was able to move reunited Axis forces through the minefield and close in around Bir Hakeim. British communications were as bad as those of the Axis forces were good. Probably because of this, General Ritchie failed to exploit any of the opportunities for counter-offensive with which the overstretched Axis forces provided him, and by the time XIII and XXX Corps attacked the German forces, the Germans had laid effective minefield defences. The Axis assault now centred on the battlefield known as 'Knightsbridge' — little more, in fact, than a convergence of sand

Rommel and the Desert Campaign

Fuehrer, probably seeing the potential for a link-up of Axis forces in the Middle East following a successful summer offensive in Russia, agreed. The assault on Malta was abandoned, and Rommel, who had just been promoted Field-Marshal on the strength of his successes, was given the authority to proceed. As always, he had not waited for permission, and was already beyond Sidi Barrani and heading for Mersa Matruh, where General Ritchie was preparing for a last ditch stand.

At this crucial point, Auchinleck took over command on the spot from Ritchie and saw the acute danger that X Corps might be trapped at Mersa Matruh. Auchinleck's speedy response to the situation enabled the Corps, and in particular Major-General Freyberg's New Zealand Division to retreat back to defensible positions at El Alamein, between the Mediterranean and the Qattara Depression, an impassable area of salt marshes. There they were joined by the

9th Australian Division brought in from Syria, and the 4th Indian Division from Cyprus.

Having advanced 644 kilometres – over 400 miles – in 36 days, Rommel was badly overstretched. His total forces facing the British positions on July 1st amounted only to 6,400 men, 41 tanks and 71 guns. He should have stopped, dug in, held his line and waited for reinforcements in strength. But an almost Messianic belief in the invincibility of speed and thrust drove him on to attack immediately. The assault, to become known as the First Battle of El Alamein, was a disaster, and by July 17th, despite having been reinforced during the preceding two weeks to a nominal strength of 30 battalions, his four armoured divisions were reduced to having only 58 tanks between them, and he could call on fewer than 5,000 infantry. Now, in a fit of depression, Rommel contemplated retreat, but, once his customary verve was restored, he recognised the situation for what it was and prepared defensive positions to await supplies, further reinforcements and developments. Meanwhile the Axis powers, anticipating that the halt in Rommel's advance represented only a temporary lull, promised Egypt, whose borders were almost in sight of Rommel's army, complete independence and national sovereignty.

There we leave North Africa and turn to the war at sea. But we shall return in Chapter 19 to the Desert and to the Allies' triumphant reversal of their position.

1 Field-Marshal Kesselring, (left) and Rommel did not always agree – in fact the always orderly and organised Kesselring, an expert in effective political manoeuvre to gain military ends legitimately, despaired of Rommel's tendency to ignore any instruction with which he disagreed. The two men were rivals for effective power in the Middle East and (later) Italy, and competed for Hitler's favour.

2 After the capture of Tobruk by the Axis forces, the Germans and Italians found that the departing British forces had destroyed much that would have been useful to them. In this street scene in Tobruk after the British had left, fires are still burning in the distance, and the disorder typical of a town that has been the centre of a battle is everywhere.

3 This German eight-wheeled SdKfz 232 armoured car was captured by the British army during one of the many tank battles of 1942 and taken back to divisional headquarters for study. The SdKfz 232 was one of the most popular armoured vehicles the *Wehrmacht* ever had, and was extensively used in the Western Desert. Its 150 hp eight-cylinder petrol engine gave it a road speed of 53 miles per hour and a range of 170 miles.

4 This British Official Photograph, released to the press in August 1942, shows a 4.5" gun being fired by a crew of the 2nd Armoured Brigade South of El Alamein, shortly after Rommel's nose had been bloodied by the First Battle of Alamein. The stiff positions of attention of the crew suggest that the gun was not being fired in anger at the time.

5 The First Battle of Alamein was a major boost to the Eighth Army's morale. Although it secured no advance, it stopped positively Rommel's push to Egypt, and proved that the Allied army could hold the *Panzerarmee Afrika*. This picture's official caption read 'The British 8th Army stands fast – then attacks. Bofors AA gunners ready for action', and reflected the new feeling of cautious optimism felt at the end of July 1942.

CHAPTER 17

THE BATTLE OF THE ATLANTIC
THE U~BOAT WAR

Once more, this book must step back a little in time, to March 1941. You may remember from Chapter 9 that, following the fall of France, Admiral Doenitz had established the headquarters of the U-Boat fleet at Lorient, and had prepared for the mighty offensive against the Atlantic sea routes that were so crucial to supplies of both food and war materials from the USA and Canada. The British success in countering the effectiveness of the magnetic mine had pinned German hopes for an Atlantic victory firmly upon the submarine fleet, to which was now added the strength of the *Luftwaffe's* latest acquisition, the 4-engined long range *Focke-Wulf* Fw200 Condor bomber, which proved very effective against merchant ships at sea.

In March 1941, Churchill established in London a Committee to meet daily and marshal the resources required to "defeat the attempt to strangle our food supplies and our connection with the United States". This group recognised the fact that *Luftwaffe* attacks on the British ports were every bit as serious a threat to the convoys across the Atlantic as the U-Boat attacks themselves, and set about strengthening the anti-aircraft defences of the principal docks and ship repair facilities around the British coast. They did not have long to wait.

As soon as March 13th and 14th, the *Luftwaffe* attacked the docks along the River Clyde in Scotland with great force, putting some of them out of action until the summer and even into the autumn. At the beginning of May, the attack hit the docks of Liverpool and the Mersey, which were pounded remorselessly for seven consecutive nights. Sixty-nine of the 144 available mooring bays were eliminated, and some 3,000 people were killed or injured. Then, just as it seemed

6

7

that a pattern of airborne offensive against the docks was becoming established, the *Luftwaffe* raids ceased as suddenly as they had begun. Churchill was of the opinion that, had the assault on the ports continued, the war might well have been lost.

Now RAF Coastal Command, whose aircraft searched the seas, reported enemy shipping movements, attacked enemy ships, laid mines and hunted surface raiders was placed under the command of the Admiralty from April 1941. The fitting of better anti-aircraft defences to merchant ships was given a high priority. Britain had, in the summer of 1941, a total of 695 vessels deployed for the defence of the Western Approaches, but of these only 248 were destroyers, of which 59 were being refitted and were out of action. There were 99 of the little corvettes that were to prove so effective against the U-Boats, and 48 sloops. The biggest trump card that Admiral Sir Percy Noble, C-in-C Western Approaches had was the presence on most of the escort vessels of radar, which effectively prevented the U-Boat fleet attacking on the surface after dark. Radar was also

8

6 A dramatic (and genuine) picture taken by a German cameraman aboard a small German warship attempting, as part of a German convoy, to break out into the Atlantic via the Channel. Unexpectedly, the searchlight of a British ship caught them, and the photographer has in turn caught the uncertainty and alarm in the crewmen's eyes. The young seaman in the foreground wears the insignia of a Seaman 2nd Class of the line.

7 RAF bombing of U-Boat facilities was largely concentrated on the yards where they were built, in Kiel and Wilhelmshaven. The extensive damage that was done to the facilities, particularly the slipways from which the U-Boats were launched, caused the Germans to build bombproof shelters over the slipways. These are the shelters in one of the yards under construction.

8 This briefing of commanders and first officers aboard a German ship before an operation or convoy is sadly lacking in information on the identity of the officers or of the ship. It does, however, give an excellent impression of the men who held executive rank in Hitler's *Kriegsmarine* and of the way they wore their uniform in 'working' conditions. Although it is difficult to be certain about rank from the picture, the officer pointing in the foreground appears to be a Captain.

The Battle of the Atlantic

gradually added to the armament of RAF Coastal Command aircraft.

Strangely, the British did not take the opportunity of destroying the U-Boat pens as they were built along the French Atlantic coast at Brest, Lorient, and Bordeaux. Had they done so, the course of the Battle of the Atlantic might have been different. Once the pens were completed, their 12 feet thick concrete walls proved capable of withstanding all the bombs then available, and many fine pilots lost their lives attempting to rescue the strategists from their earlier mistakes.

The course of the Battle of the Atlantic in 1941 can best be viewed in the light of a comparison between shipping sunk and new shipping built — which in turn highlights one of the principal reasons why the Battle swung in the Allies favour in 1942. British official records show that in 1941, shipping losses were some 340,000 tons (240 ships) higher than in 1940, with a total tonnage sunk of 4,328,558 tons, a total of 1,299 ships. Losses of Allied ships to submarines were down in 1941; losses to air attack were up. Total Allied shipbuilding in 1941 came to just over 1.5 million tons. Thus, in the year, the available shipping tonnage to bring arms and food across the Atlantic was reduced by around 2.8 million tons. By the end of 1941, the USA was officially in the war — and that brought American shipbuilding capacity of some 5 million tons per annum into the equation, which redressed the balance in the Allies' favour.

The Battle did not go entirely Germany's way in the early stages, despite the fact that her strategic objectives were being achieved.

1 The U-Boat commanders were very much the 'glamour-boys' of the German Navy, and the more successful captains achieved considerable public following. This U-Boat commander is being interviewed on the radio about the successes of his recent operations, for which he has just received the Iron Cross. He is being interviewed by a Petty Officer, and another Petty Officer in the background takes notes.

2 A Fairmile 'B' class motor launch, with her crew at action stations, off the coast of Scotland. These boats could reach a speed of only sixteen to twenty knots and were relatively lightly armed, carrying no torpedoes.

3 British operations in the Battle of the Atlantic were directed from the headquarters of Admiral Sir Percy Noble, C-in-C Western Approaches (centre with pen), based in Liverpool. This picture of Sir Percy and his staff was taken in December 1941.

Although 41 British and Allied ships totalling 243,000 tons were sunk by U-Boats in March 1941, five U-Boats were lost by the Germans, three of them commanded by 'ace' captains whom Doenitz could ill afford to lose. On March 7th, Gunther Prien, famed for his attack on the *Royal Oak* in Scapa Flow, was located by the destroyer HMS *Wolverine* using radar, and was blown up while attacking convoy OB.293. Nine days later on March 16th 1941, Captain Donald Macintyre, commanding the escort to HX.112, scored heavily after the U-Boats had claimed five ships from his convoy, with considerable loss of life. The destroyer *Vanoc* rammed and destroyed U-100, crushing to death her famous commander Joachim Schepke in the collision, and Captain Macintyre's own HMS *Walker* depth-charged U-99, capturing the far more famous Otto Kretschmer, darling of the U-Boat fleet, who had sunk a total of 44 ships.

The worst month of the campaign for the Allies was May 1941, when 58 ships were lost to the German attacks. Totalling 325,492 tons, the lost ships took to the bottom many fine sailors and thousands of tons of supplies and arms that were vital to the Allied war effort. At the same time, the adventures in the Balkans and Greece were costing many more ships, and putting the two together one sees a pattern emerging that must have been very satisfying to the German strategic planners — total Allied losses in April and May 1941 of over 1.1 million tons.

The second half of 1941 was far less damaging to the Allies. The part of the Atlantic between Iceland and Eastern Newfoundland was now in the US Security Zone announced by President Roosevelt, and this and the posting of US naval forces near Greenland and Iceland released Royal Navy vessels for escort duties in the main battle zone.

Moreover, from September 11th, US ships in the Atlantic were authorised to shoot on sight. But German policy was also working against continued success in the Battle of the Atlantic. Hitler had ordered the detachment of four U-Boats to the Arctic Ocean as soon as the attack on the USSR began, and, although they were recalled, they were deployed next to defend the Norwegian coast against British attack. Six more U-Boats were detached from the Atlantic fleet in the summer of 1941 to the Mediterranean, where they did a great deal of damage, but that was small consolation to Doenitz, who believed (probably correctly) that to win the Battle of the Atlantic before the USA entered the conflict was to win the War.

By the turn of the year, there were no less than 23 U-Boats in the Mediterranean, where they were virtually trapped, since currents through the Straits of Gibraltar prevented them leaving through the

Straits underwater, and Royal Navy defences effectively prevented their leaving on the surface. Doenitz now had 55 U-boats under his command for the continuation of the Battle of the Atlantic into 1942. Had Goering recognised the full potential of co-operation between the new Condor bombers and the U-Boats, and had the servicing of the Condors been more effective and capable of keeping more than two airworthy at a time, the utilisation of the U-Boat fleet might have been far more damaging to the Allies.

Perhaps more to the point, 60% of the German Atlantic U-Boat fleet was unserviceable at the end of 1941 because the vital maintenance resources had been diverted during the year to the prestige projects of repairing the Scharnhorst, Gneisenau and Prinz Eugen, all of which had been damaged by air attack during the middle four months of the year.

4 HMS *Ark Royal*, not long before she was lost, in company with HMS *Renown*, the 32,000 ton battleship that had been reconstructed in 1939. The aircraft being launched by *Ark Royal* appear to be Fairey Fulmars.

5 Convoys in port frequently flew kite balloons from cables attached to the ships as a deterrent to dive-bombing attacks – the cables made it difficult for pilots of attacking aircraft to fly low without their wings becoming fouled.

6 The kite balloons used to protect the convoys in port were flown at a variety of heights, again to make attack more difficult for enemy pilots. The ships in this convoy are small coastal freight vessels.

7 Once the convoy was at sea, radio silence was observed, since it was recognised that the Germans had some means, not yet understood, of directing U-Boats to the source of radio signals. Signalling was visual, by means of the Aldis lamp. Notice the gun at the stern of this merchant ship.

8 An impressive shot of oil tanks burning on the Norwegian shore, framed by the barrels of a ship's anti-aircraft guns. Norway became important to the Atlantic battle as a base for warship repair and fuelling, and the fiords were used extensively as a place of retreat for the capital ships.

However, it would be wrong to underestimate the extent to which the Royal Navy was improving in its counter-submarine measures. Larger escort forces, better radar, improved use of ASDIC and the benefit of hard-won experience were making the Navy escorts tough opponents for the U-Boat crews. A much-quoted example of this is the experience of Convoy HG.76 which conducted a running battle with a pack of U-Boats from Gibraltar to Ushant in December 1941. The escort force consisted of an escort carrier, three destroyers, four sloops and ten corvettes, which between them protected 32 merchant ships. After one of the toughest nine days of the Atlantic battle, the Royal Navy had lost the escort carrier *Audacity* and the destroyer *Stanley* plus two merchantmen. Against that, the *Kriegsmarine* had lost five of the ten submarines that took part in the battle, including U-567 commanded by Leutnant Endrass, another of Germany's U-Boat aces. These sinkings brought total U-Boat losses in 1941 to 35.

1 As 1941 wore on, the convoy escort activities of still neutral US ships in the Atlantic became progressively more on a war footing. In October 1941, the US destroyer USS *Kearny* was torpedoed while on patrol, but managed to return to port. The *Kearny* (left) is made fast to another destroyer at anchor.

2 The corvette was a small, anti-submarine vessel used for convoy escort duties (immortalised in Nicholas Monsarrat's book and film 'The Cruel Sea'). They were quickly and relatively cheaply built, and had a significant impact on the U-Boat attack. This shot shows the crew at action stations on the 4" gun.

3 A picture taken during an Italian air attack on a convoy in 1941. A plume of smoke is rising from a stricken ship in the distance (right), and a bomber flies low over the ship in the foreground.

4 A picture believed to have been taken from the stern of the 14,500 ton German heavy cruiser *Prinz Eugen* in the English Channel as Allied aircraft attacked the ship during a dash through the channel in company with the battle-cruisers *Scharnhorst* and *Gneisenau*. A bomb from one of the aircraft has just scored a near miss astern.

5 The long-distance bombing raids at sea by the Focke-Wulf Fw200 Condor four-engined bomber could have been very much more serious for the Allies had Hitler recognised the potential of the aircraft and given greater priority to it. This picture shows the extensive damage done to the *Apapa*, a merchant ship sunk by a Condor raid.

6 The actual moment of sinking of any ship is an awe-inspiring sight – this picture shows the last moments of the *Apapa* as she slid beneath the sea with her back broken. Steam rises in clouds from her hot boilers as the sea rushes over them, and the smoke of the fires started by the bombs is still billowing forth. A moment later, the fires were out for good.

of which 27 had gone in the Battle of the Atlantic. Nonetheless, Doenitz ended the year with more submarines than he had had at the beginning — no less than 198 new U-Boats had been built during 1941.

The Battleships — and the Hunt for the *Bismarck*

The preoccupation with the U-Boats, both then and now, has a way of obscuring the very important events that took place in the declining arena of surface sea power. Germany was heavily committed to major surface ships, as has been mentioned briefly in an earlier chapter, and during 1941 had also developed the concept of the armed offensive merchantman. These surface vessels between them destroyed the considerable total of 427,000 tons of Allied merchant shipping in 1941. The warships also performed the less obvious but tactically vital task of tying down Allied surface vessels that might

7 Survivors of sunken ships from the beleaguered convoys were often drifting in the open sea for days, even for weeks, before they were rescued. Many died of exposure. These men clinging to an upturned lifeboat are some of those who survived the sinking of the merchantman *Laconia* during the Battle of the Atlantic.

otherwise have been used for convoy escort duties.

The sister ship of the *Admiral Graf Spee*, the 12,000 ton pocket battleship *Admiral Scheer*, sank some 99,000 tons in the first three months of 1941 before evading the watching British warships to dock at Kiel. The 14,000 ton cruiser *Admiral Hipper* had had remarkable success in February, sinking no less than seven merchant ships in 90 minutes with her torpedoes and 8″ guns, and returning to Kiel in triumph ahead of the *Admiral Scheer*. Meanwhile, the heavily armed battle-cruisers *Scharnhorst* and *Gneisenau*, at 32,000 tons apiece, had managed to slip out of Kiel in January with orders from Admiral Raeder not to engage any ship with 15 inch guns. After failing to engage Convoy HX.106 because the venerable 29,000 ton battleship *Ramillies*, completed in 1917, was leading the escort, they sank three merchant ships and two tankers off Newfoundland, then headed South-East across the Atlantic towards the North African coast.

Off the Canary Islands they again failed to attack a convoy, this time because the even older (1916) battleship *Malaya*, again with 15 inch guns, was leading the escort, following which they headed back North-West and played havoc with a convoy from Halifax, Nova Scotia. By the time the two ships reached Brest, successfully evading the Royal Navy, they had sunk 22 ships, but had run their turbines into the ground. Repairs were scheduled to take weeks, and neither ship was ready to accompany the *Bismarck* and the *Prinz Eugen* on their marauding foray into the Atlantic, which began on May 20th 1941.

Bismarck was not hampered by the restriction on attacking capital ships that had prevented the previous squadron doing more damage.

The Battle of the Atlantic

At 41,700 tons, with eight 15″ guns in four turrets plus a new range-finding radar, the *Bismarck* was one of the finest ships afloat. Her captain and crew were similarly out of the top drawer. She was a formidable opponent. The heavy cruiser *Prinz Eugen*, although much smaller at 13,900 tons, was also brand new (1940) with eight 8″ guns and a top speed of 32 knots.

The day after the squadron put out from Kiel, they were photographed by aerial reconnaissance in Korsfjord, south of Bergen. Vice-Admiral Holland of the Royal Navy was ordered from Scapa Flow towards Norway with his squadron — the battle-cruiser *Hood*, the battleship Prince of Wales and six destroyers — and the squadron sailed taking with them some civilian workmen who were still working on the newly installed 14″ gun turrets of *Prince of Wales*. By the next day, it was apparent that the two German raiders had eluded reconnaissance and had vanished from their fjord. So Admiral Tovey sailed with the main fleet to intercept.

During the evening of May 23rd, the *Bismarck* was spotted on

1 The value of the British Royal Navy submarine service in combating the menace to merchant ships of the German armed surface raiders should not be underestimated. The presence of British submarines on patrol was a major deterrent to the German ships, and substantial German and Italian supply ship and merchant tonnage was sunk by them.

radar by the Kent class cruiser HMS *Suffolk*, who called up the cruiser *Norfolk*. Jointly they stalked *Bismarck*, reporting her position so that Holland's squadron was able to intercept early the next morning. Although Admiral Holland's initial position was ideal, and enabled him to bring virtually all his squadron's guns to bear, he turned to a less favourable position before attacking, a manoeuvre that has been the subject of debate ever since. The likely explanation is that he did it to get as close as possible as rapidly as possible, so as to get the lightly armoured and ageing 41,000 ton *Hood*, which first entered service in 1920, inside the range at which enemy shells would plunge down on the battle-cruiser's relatively thin deck, and gain the benefit of a flatter trajectory, which presented armour almost four times as thick to the enemy.

After half an hour, Holland opened fire, believing he was aimed at *Bismarck* when he was actually attacking *Prinz Eugen*. *Prince of Wales* rectified the error in part by attacking *Bismarck*. Ten minutes later, the British squadron turned, and the *Hood* prepared to fire on the *Bismarck*. A 15″ salvo from the German flagship got to *Hood* first, and in what must have been one of the mightiest non-nuclear explosions of the war, the *Hood* blew up, killing all but three of her total crew of 95 officers and 1,324 men. Without pausing, the German ships bore down on *Prince of Wales*, landing seven shells on the ship, and killing all on the bridge except Captain Leach and a signaller. Several of *Prince of Wales'* turrets were now out of action, and she broke off the battle.

2 An unusual shot of an RAF biplane used for torpedo-bombing on training flying over the Channel with a British T-Class submarine on the surface below.

3 An impressive picture of the 32,000 ton First World War vintage battleship *Malaya* ploughing through choppy seas. *Malaya* was one of five ships of the *Queen Elizabeth* class, and was reconstructed in 1929 after being completed in 1916. Her main armament consisted of eight 15″ guns. She survived the war and was scrapped in 1948.

4 The last picture taken of HMS *Hood* as she went into action against *Bismarck* when the German battleship was first contacted in the Denmark Strait. This photograph was taken from HMS *Prince of Wales*, and it is interesting to note the canvas covers over the barrels of the guns. These were blown off when the gun was fired, but served to protect the barrels from spray damage.

Although *Bismarck* had clearly achieved major success, one of *Prince of Wales'* shells had damaged a fuel bunker, and her fuel was becoming contaminated with sea water. An oil slick behind the ship was also a clear hazard to its security. So Admiral Lutjens advised his High Command that he was making for St. Nazaire. There followed a remarkable chase across a broad stretch of the Atlantic by Vice-Admiral Wake-Walker, who took under his command *Prince of Wales* and the rest of Holland's battle-cruiser squadron, and Admiral Sir John Tovey with *King George V* and the Home Fleet. An epic attack by Swordfish biplanes from HMS *Victorious* succeeded in hitting the *Bismarck* with a torpedo but did little actual

5 A County class cruiser of the Royal Navy forming part of the escort of a large convoy during the Battle of the Atlantic. This picture was released in July 1942, but was probably taken somewhat earlier.

6 The 30,000 ton British aircraft carrier HMS *Victorious* after she returned to Portsmouth from her encounter with *Bismarck* in 1941. She was at this stage a very new ship, having been completed earlier that same year. *Victorious* was able to carry fifty-four aircraft and had a speed of thirty-one knots.

7 An impressive German picture of *Prinz Eugen* in action in the Atlantic, her guns blazing across a turbulent sea. The heavy cruiser *Prinz Eugen* was completed in August 1940, and survived the war to be ignominiously sunk in 1947 during an atomic bomb test in the Pacific.

1 This picture was taken by an amateur photographer among the crew of the *Dorsetshire* as her torpedoes struck home and sank the *Bismarck*. The bow of the great ship is clear of the water, and the stern has already vanished. A moment later, one of Germany's greatest ships was gone.

2 On March 27th 1942, a British naval and commando raid on St. Nazaire put out of action the only dry dock on the Atlantic coast suitable for the repair of the *Tirpitz*, sister ship of *Bismarck*. The raid was thus a major blow to Germany's ability to terrorise the Atlantic with surface raiders. Here two of the British commandos who carried out the daring raid are marched off.

3 Later in the war, in September 1944, the *Tirpitz* was finally brought to book in a Norwegian fiord, where she was put out of action by British midget submarines. With no dry dock facilities available, and British and Soviet navy patrols constantly on watch in case the ship should attempt to leave the fiord, the *Tirpitz* was effectively stranded for the duration of the war. This is one of the actual aerial reconnaissance pictures used for the planning of the raid.

4 Before the midget submarines managed to cripple the *Tirpitz*, a daring attempt to deliver the *coup de grace* from the air had been made by Royal Navy pilots flying the new Barracuda dive-bomber and torpedo-bomber. At dawn on April 3rd 1944, they attacked the warship as she was attempting to leave her berth in Alten Fiord, hitting her and starting fires but failing to do sufficient damage to meet the main objective.

damage. Gradually, all Tovey's ships had to break off for refuelling until only *Prince of Wales* was left on the trail of the German ship — *Prinz Eugen* having been ordered to break away and continue her mission independently of *Bismarck*. Contact with the damaged German ship had been lost, but, on May 26th, a Coastal Command Catalina (PBY) spotted the ship and reported her position.

Now Force H, which had been diverted to the hunt from near Gibraltar, took a hand, and launched an attack with Swordfish biplanes from *Ark Royal*. The first attempt almost sank HMS *Sheffield* — a rather nasty case of mistaken identity — but the second attack took 15 aircraft through a wall of fire to score two hits, the second of which disabled *Bismarck's* steering gear. Admiral Lutjens knew he could not now make port, and sent a signal saying he would

fight to the last shell. Shortly after, the *Bismarck* ran into a force of five destroyers commanded by Captain Vian, who decided to attack, but achieved only two inconclusive hits because of the devastating accuracy of *Bismarck's* fire and the need for constant evasive action. Next morning, *King George V, Rodney* and *Norfolk* arrived, and sent a hail of 16″ and 14″ shells crashing on to the German ship. Although the *Bismarck's* superstructure was almost destroyed, none of these shells pierced the ship's armour, and she remained afloat. At 10.36 am, two torpedoes from the *Dorsetshire* holed and sank her. Sir John Tovey concluded in his report.

'*Bismarck* fought an extremely courageous battle against greatly superior forces; in the best tradition of the old Imperial Navy, she went down with her colours flying.'

CHAPTER 18

PACIFIC TURNING POINT
THE CORAL SEA AND THE BATTLE OF MIDWAY

In the earlier chapter of this book covering the initial Japanese conquests in South-East Asia following their surprise attack on Pearl Harbour, the Japanese strategy was defined as being first the neutralisation of the US fleet, then the rapid concurrent conquest of all key areas of South-East Asia, followed by the establishment of a defensive perimeter around those conquests. We have seen that, to a large extent, Japan succeeded in putting that strategy into effect.

Nonetheless, success was not total, and the USA and her allies survived to fight, and ultimately to win. Foremost among initial Japanese miscalculations was the belief that the attack on Pearl Harbour could be expected to immobilise the US Pacific fleet. What it actually did was to force naval warfare firmly into the 20th century. For, although the capital ships that were the pride of the US Navy were either disabled or sunk, neither the aircraft carriers nor the bulk of the Navy's destroyers were in Pearl Harbour when the attack came. Entrusted with the task of holding a line from Alaska to Midway Atoll in the Pacific, and from Midway to Australia, the newly promoted Admiral Chester Nimitz, Roosevelt's personal choice as C-in-C Pacific Fleet, had little choice but to think in terms of using air power.

Thus, as the Commander in Chief of the Imperial Japanese Navy, Admiral Yamamoto, argued with his colleagues and with Japanese High Command about the rights and wrongs of invading Oahu and taking Pearl Harbour, and of the potential for an assault on Australia to prevent its eventual use as a base for Allied counter-offensive, Nimitz was calling up reserves and reorganising the fleet for the battle he knew had to come. From the Atlantic, the 20,000 ton carrier *Yorktown* was ordered through the Panama Canal to join her sister ship *Enterprise*, already with the 33,000 ton sister carriers *Lexington* and *Saratoga*, together and the smaller 19,800 ton *Hornet* in the Pacific — although the *Saratoga* was in fact out of action until May 1942 following a contretemps with a torpedo on the 11th of January 1942. Nimitz also had, in addition to the carriers, 16 cruisers, 44 destroyers and 16 submarines.

In February, carrier groups under Vice-Admiral Halsey and Rear-Admiral Fletcher each launched raids on Japanese held positions in the Marshall Islands and the Gilbert archipelago, and Wake Island and Marcus Island were bombed at the end of the month. These comparatively minor adventures, which nonetheless brought the war to within little more than a thousand miles of Tokyo, reinforced Yamamoto's unwavering opinion that the US Pacific Fleet had to be finally and irrevocably crushed. At the beginning of April,

Yamamoto submitted his plan for an attack on the Midway Atoll, with a diversionary assault on the Aleutian Islands to draw off some of the power of the US Fleet. The ostensible reason for the attack was to gain control of the forward airfield on Midway and deny it to the US forces. The actual reason was that Yamamoto intended to smash the US Navy once and for all.

Because the arguments within Japan's High Command about strategy were still raging, Yamamoto's plan might well have been put on ice or simply turned down. But in the third week of April came the Doolittle Raid, a daring attack on the Japanese mainland that, although militarily and strategically unimportant, was extremely effective as an exercise in propaganda. Lieutenant-Colonel James H. Doolittle of the Air Corps, already 45 years old and a veteran of World War 1, had conceived the idea of launching a force of fully laden twin-engined Mitchell B-25 bombers against Tokyo from an aircraft carrier. Doubt had been expressed whether this was possible; nobody had ever flown such large or heavy aircraft from a ship before. Practising in Florida, Doolittle's pilots proved they could get

5 Senior members of the US government took a close interest in the progress of the war and made frequent tours of the operational fronts. Under-Secretary of the Navy James V. Forrestal (right), later to be Secretary of the Navy, was photographed with Admiral Nimitz during one of these tours.

6 An impressive shot of the US Navy anchorage at Ulithi in the Caroline Islands before hostilities began gives an impression of some of the United States' naval airpower that confronted the Japanese in the Coral Sea and at Midway. The five carriers from foreground to the right include the 14,700 ton *Wasp* (nearest), which was torpedoed and sunk in September 1942; the 20,000 ton *Yorktown*; her sister ship *Hornet*; and two others, possibly *Enterprise* and *Saratoga*. To the left in the background is USS *Lexington*. Ulithi Atoll encircles an anchorage that was at that time large enough to accommodate an entire fleet.

Pacific Turning Point

their lumbering B-25s off the ground in the 750 feet run that was available to them. Getting them back down again was another matter − that simply could not be done. So a plan was devised by which the aircraft would be brought within 500 miles of Tokyo aboard the carrier *Hornet*, launched on their raid, and then landed in friendly Nationalist China.

On April 18th, after the *Hornet* had unexpectedly encountered an enemy patrol while still 700 miles out from Japan, it was decided that, as secrecy could no longer be guaranteed for the force, the B-25s should be launched. All 16 aircraft made successful take-offs despite rough seas and high winds, and arrived over the Japanese cities of Tokyo, Nagoya, Osaka and Kobe, and over the Yokosuka naval base, at treetop height with almost nil warning.

The Japanese people, who had been assured that US aircraft could not reach the shores of Japan, were first terrified, then appalled. Where had the bombers come from that now climbed to 1500 feet, dropped their 500 pound bombs and then turned out to sea at wavetop height? Enjoying the discomfiture of the Japanese military enormously, Roosevelt suggested they had come from Shangri-La, the mythical mountain kingdom of Hilton's 'Lost Horizon'.

Because of their premature launch, the brave pilots of the Doolittle raid did not fare well. Doolittle himself crash-landed in China, unhurt; one aircraft was seized after landing at Vladivostock airfield; the crew of another were executed after crash-landing in Japanese-held territory. None other than the Vladivostock arrival landed normally.

The damage to the all-important Japanese self-esteem was immeasurable, and Yamamoto now had no difficulty in securing

1

2

approval for his plan to attack Midway. On May 5th the order was given for the attack to have been mounted by June 20th. Meanwhile, although the views of those in the Japanese High Command who believed that Australia should be attacked were not gaining support, the potential of Australia as an Allied base was taken seriously. The Japanese 4th Fleet, reinforced with three aircraft carriers and two heavy cruisers, was therefore despatched to take Port Moresby on the southern coast of New Guinea, and to occupy Tulagi in the Solomon Islands, as a preliminary to seizing New Caledonia and Fiji.

Earlier in the year, the US backroom boys in Washington had secured one of the most important victories of the Pacific War by breaking the Japanese Naval code. Thus Admiral Chester Nimitz knew of the 4th Fleet's orders almost as soon as they did, and was able to act on the recently concluded Anglo-American agreement by which the USA took responsibility for the Pacific defences of Australia and New Zealand. Rear-Admiral Fletcher's Task Force 17, with the carriers *Yorktown* and *Lexington* was sent to Port Moresby, and was joined en route by an Australian cruiser force under Rear-Admiral Crace. The actions that followed from May 6th to May 8th are remembered as the Battle of the Coral Sea.

There is no doubt that the Battle of the Coral Sea was something new in naval warfare. For the first time in history an entire sea battle was fought without a ship's guns being brought to bear or a single salvo fired. From start to finish, the battle was fought by carriers and aircraft. But the Battle of the Coral Sea was also a strategic milestone. Although the Battle of Midway that followed it is regarded as the great reverse for the Japanese, and is remembered as the turning point of the Pacific War, the Coral Sea was in fact the first significant failure of the Japanese Navy, and the first occasion when a Japanese force was obliged to retreat. For, although the action resulted in the sad

4

1 The massive US naval build-up that began in 1941 and 1942 produced several new classes of aircraft carrier, notably the *Essex* class (twenty-four ships) and the *Independence* class (nine ships). The leading ship in this picture of part of the US Third Fleet is USS *Independence*, 11,000 tons and capable of carrying forty-five aircraft.

2 An interesting aerial shot of USS *Houston*, sister ship of the USS *Augusta*, in which President Roosevelt travelled for the signing of the Atlantic Charter. *Houston* was completed in 1930 with a standard tonnage of 9,200 tons. Armed with nine eight inch guns and twelve five inch guns, she was sunk on 28th February 1942 with HMAS *Perth* after sinking four Japanese transport ships.

3 A view from the superstructure of the Australian Navy's cruiser HMAS *Perth*, which, with USS *Houston* took a prominent role in the battle of the Sunda Straits, off Java. Attempting to escape southwards through the straits after the Battle of the Java Sea, the two cruisers encountered the Japanese cruiser *Mogami* and several destroyers, which were covering the unloading of Japanese transport ships. *Mogami*, *Mikuma* and several other ships quickly sank both the Allied cruisers after they had destroyed four of the fifty-six Japanese transport ships.

loss of the US carrier *Lexington*, and of an oiler mistaken by the Japanese for another carrier, the Japanese themselves lost the elderly 7,500 ton light carrier *Shoho*, a destroyer, a minelayer and three minesweepers, and, more important, were left with the new 26,000 ton carrier *Shokaku* severely damaged and her sister carrier *Zuikaku* virtually without aircraft. Because of the severely depleted carrier force, Admiral Inouye gave up the idea of landing at Port Moresby, and New Guinea was spared the pleasure of his company. Moreover, the task forces charged with the assaults on Midway and the Aleutians found themselves significantly depleted.

The Battle of Midway

The plan with which Admiral Yamamoto approached the set piece Battle of Midway made sweeping assumptions which were not realised on the day. The first was that the diversionary attack on the

5

6

7

8

Aleutian Islands would cause Admiral Nimitz to split up the US Fleet and weaken his defences. The second was that the intended bombardment of Midway Atoll on June 4th would cause Nimitz to commit his fleet to a major sea battle on June 7th or 8th, giving Yamamoto time to reassemble his five separate task forces into one cohesive battle group. The third was that the Japanese submarine force which, since the Twenties had been built and trained on the assumption that the right and proper function of a submarine was scouting and reconnaissance, would be able to detect all US movements to the Midway area as they developed.

Yamamoto did not know, of course, that the US Fleet was well aware of his intentions and battle plan, and had even proved to its own satisfaction that the target was Midway by planting some false information for Japanese listening posts to report back to High Command. He did not know that Nimitz had the *Yorktown* —

Japanese intelligence had assured him, quite erroneously, that an 800lb bomb that had hit the carrier during the Battle of the Coral Sea had sent her to the bottom. He assumed, with dangerously cavalier arrogance, that his carriers would be enough and that he could keep his other ships in reserve — in the event, the nine battleships, 11 cruisers and 32 destroyers that Yamamoto had available were not allowed near the battle, and did not fire a single shot. On Midway Atoll itself, the small (and understandably nervous) US garrison had been built up to more than 3,000 men and 115 aircraft, and was bristling with anti-aircraft guns.

When Yamamoto's submarines reached their stations to report the expected movements of US ships after the 'surprise' attack, the birds had already flown. Yamamoto thus had no information on the size and disposition of the US forces, and could do little else but rely upon his already dangerously inaccurate intelligence. On June 3rd,

4 The success of the exceptionally close collaboration that was maintained throughout the Pacific war between the senior US commanders was a major factor in the eventual defeat of the Japanese. In this picture, Admiral Chester W. Nimitz (right), Commander-in-Chief of the US Pacific Fleet, discusses future strategic policy with General Douglas MacArthur, US Commander-in-Chief of the Southwest Pacific Area. This was the first meeting between the two commanders since the outbreak of the Japanese war.

5 An interesting shot of the Captain of HMAS *Perth* and his officers on the bridge during a patrol in temperate waters. *Perth* was a 7,000 ton cruiser armed with eight six inch and eight four inch guns, originally completed in 1936 as HMS *Amphion* and subsequently transferred to the Royal Australian Navy.

6 A prewar shot of the American carrier USS *Lexington* when she was still operating biplanes. Note the twin eight inch/203mm turret, two of which were fitted to the carrier when originally built, but which were removed just before the outbreak of war.

7 Launching a carrier's aircraft in the days before modern electronic aids required considerable individual skill and teamwork by the flight-deck crew, as well as great skill on the part of the pilots. Here, the deck crew of *Lexington* have just put another of their aircraft into the air.

8 A wartime view from the after machine gun platform of the 33,000 ton aircraft carrier USS *Lexington* as one of the vessel's ninety aircraft landed on the flight deck after a reconnaissance sortie. It is an interesting reflection on changing values that *Lexington*, when converted from an existing battle-cruiser in 1927, had cost a total of $45 million including her full complement of aircraft!

1 Pacific convoys to the United States, while less threatened than the Atlantic convoys to Britain and Russia, were nonetheless crucial, and there was a considerable investment in their protection by warships against submarine attack. This picture, filed in October 1942, shows a Pacific convoy as dawn broke.

2 On May 8th 1942, USS *Lexington* was crippled by Japanese dive-bomber attack during the Battle of the Coral Sea. Rescue launches from accompanying cruisers and destroyers were packed with survivors as they hastened to complete the rescue of the crew of the burning carrier.

3 Douglas Dauntless dive-bombers of the US Navy on patrol from their carrier in the Pacific theatre. These aircraft had a 1,200 hp Wright Cyclone radial engine, which gave them a maximum speed of 252 mph and an operating ceiling of 24,300 ft.

4 Visual deck control of landing aircraft was vital to carrier-borne aircraft, and the responsibility resting on the shoulders of 'Bats' was great in any navy. On board a Royal Navy carrier, this officer shows the strain and concentration that inevitably went with the job, especially when damaged aircraft had somehow to be landed.

5 Boeing B17 'Flying Fortress' bombers, which were used in the opening phase of the Battle of Midway. The B17 first flew in 1935, and roughly 12,000 B17 bombers had been built for the Allied air forces by the end of the Second World War. Most of those operating in the Pacific War were of the B17E type, which had a tail turret to eliminate the blind spot in the earlier marques' armament.

6 The 20,000 ton USS *Hornet*, from which the Doolittle raid's B25 bombers had been launched, played an important role in the success of the Battle of Midway, but lasted only fifty-three weeks from her completion in 1941. In October 1942 she was attacked by Japanese aircraft off the Santa Cruz islands, and this picture shows her as a dead hulk before a Japanese destroyer attacked her again and finished her off with four large torpedoes. A US destroyer is standing by taking off survivors.

a US Navy Catalina spotted the invasion fleet approaching, and called up a force of B-17 four engined bombers to attack the Japanese. By dawn on the 4th, the Japanese fleet was 280 miles off Midway, and launched 108 aircraft to the attack. The fighters put up by the US defenders on Midway had a bad day against the greatly superior Japanese Zeros, and 17 of the 26 aircraft that took off to meet the first assault were shot down. Despite this, the Japanese, acting on ill-considered advice from the commander of the Japanese air attack, launched a largely unnecessary second wave of fighters against Midway, with the result that, when the US Fleet was spotted only 240 miles away and approaching rapidly, Admiral Nagumo had no fighters available to cover his dive bombers if they were sent to attack the US ships. He therefore waited for the fighters' return.

Meanwhile the approaching US force under Admirals Fletcher and Spruance had decided to launch their attack at the earliest possible moment, and by sheer good fortune caught the carriers *Akagi* and *Kaga* at their most vulnerable, just as the fighters returned. The first two waves of US torpedo bombers were TBD Devastators from USS *Hornet*, an obsolescent slow type of aircraft quite incapable of defending itself against the Zero, which, with the British Spitfire was one of the world's two finest fighter aircraft. The returning Zeros made mincemeat of them, destroying all fifteen of the first wave, with a loss of 29 of the 30 crewmen, and 20 of the

26 of the second wave. But the Zeros were so busy demolishing the Devastators and their luckless crews that they failed to notice the arrival of a squadron of Douglas Dauntlesses, the latest and fastest US dive-bomber, capable of carrying a 1,000lb bomb at a maximum speed of over 250mph. The Dauntlesses attacked the Japanese carriers from just short of 20,000 feet, and, in moments, the 36,500 ton *Akagi* was holed and burning. The 38,200 ton *Kaga* had also been hit and was burning fiercely with immense loss of life. The older 18,800 ton *Soryu* had lost her rudder and engines to the Dauntlesses, and was unable to manoeuvre. Only the 20,000 ton *Hiryu* remained in action, and she despatched an attack to wreak vengeance upon the US carrier *Yorktown*. American fighters despatched 12 of the 18 Japanese attackers, but the *Yorktown* was hit, first with bombs, then with torpedoes, and had to be abandoned because of the danger of capsizing. That evening, Admiral Spruance had his revenge. Twenty four Dauntlesses under Lieutenant-Commander Clarence W. McClusky hit *Hiryu* with four bombs and disabled her. The next day Yamamoto ordered his fleet to finish off *Hiryu* and *Akagi* with torpedoes. The entire Japanese carrier force had been lost.

Admiral Nimitz's policy of concentrating his defence and attacking forces early had caught Yamamoto's forces still widely scattered. On June 5th, there was nothing Yamamoto could do to

5

6

7

7 The USS *Yorktown* was damaged during the Battle of the Coral Sea in May 1942, but was patched up sufficiently for her to be able to play a part in the Battle of Midway the following month. She was abandoned prematurely after being severely damaged by Japanese carrier aircraft, and salvage operations had only just resumed when she was torpedoed and sunk by the Japanese submarine I 168.

8 Although the Battle of Midway was Japan's first defeat, they had succeeded in occupying the Aleutian Islands while the USA's back was turned. In October 1942, US Army and Navy forces succeeded in establishing new bases in the Aleutians without Japanese opposition, and from there attacked Japanese bases only 200 miles away. Shrouded in fog, this US transport ship is landing men and supplies during the re-invasion of the Aleutians.

8

recover the situation, and he ordered the abandonment of the assault on Midway. But his fleet's troubles were not yet over. Two of his cruisers collided with each other during the night; the *Mogami*, badly damaged, was unable to defend herself properly against air attack, and was so badly damaged as to be out of action until mid-1943. The other cruiser, *Mikuma*, sank on June 6th.

The Americans, too, had their problems. Later the same day a Japanese submarine came upon the disabled *Yorktown*, under tow for Pearl Harbour, and sank both her and the destroyer *Hammann*.

The final tally for the Battle of Midway was the loss by the Americans of 1 carrier, 307 men and 147 aircraft. The Japanese lost 4 carriers, 3,500 men and 332 aircraft. The battle proved that the Japanese could be beaten, and gave the Allies hope that they would be vanquished. The sole ray of brightness for the Japanese was their success in the Aleutians. They had expected the USA to defend them heavily — instead, because Nimitz concentrated on Midway, the Aleutians were undefended. The Japanese occupied them on June 6th and 7th.

CHAPTER 19

MONTGOMERY AND THE DESERT FOX
ALAMEIN AND THE ALLIED RECOVERY

We left the British Eighth Army and Rommel's much-depleted *Panzerarmee Afrika* in mid-July 1942 facing each other at El Alamein, 60 miles from Alexandria. Rommel was badly over-stretched; short of men, supplies, equipment and fuel. The Eighth Army had been severely demoralised by Rommel's lightning advance after the fall of Tobruk in June, had been heartened by their comparative success in the first Battle of Alamein, and now awaited badly needed reinforcements and some more positive leadership than that provided thus far by General Auchinleck and Lieutenant-General Ritchie.

On hearing of the fall of Tobruk, President Roosevelt and General Marshall had arranged, almost without asking Churchill, to re-equip the Eighth Army with the new 30 ton M4 Sherman tank, whose superior turret, 75mm gun and greater off-road speed than the M3 Grant made it approximately the equal of the German PzKpfw IV. The USA also supplied 100 self-propelled guns, and the combination of the American guns and tanks potentially changed the balance of power in North Africa. But the most potent of weapons is inadequate without the inspiration of great commanders, and Churchill, impetuous as always, yet understanding of the psychological need of an army to taste success, grew increasingly impatient of Auchinleck's failure to capitalise on his recent success against Rommel's attempt to push on to Egypt.

Anglo-American planning was already well-advanced for the Operation Torch, the Allied landings in French North Africa, scheduled for November 1942, and General Sir Harold Alexander

1

2

3

1 In August 1942, Winston Churchill visited the Middle East to discover for himself the reasons for the lack of morale and success that plagued the British Eighth Army. His presence alone did much to improve morale, and his subsequent appointment of General Sir Harold Alexander to succeed General Sir Claude Auchinleck as Commander-in-Chief raised great hopes. Winston Churchill managed to maintain his cigar supply even at the darkest hours of the war, and his trademark was in considerable evidence even among the sands of the desert. Churchill was no stranger to the Middle East, having fought in the Sudan at the end of the last century. Before he died, he had the honour of being the last surviving officer of the charge of Omdurman.

2 The American M3 Grant medium tank was an important mainstay of the Allied army in North Africa. Although indisputably slower than the German PzKpfw IV, the Grant was unusual in having both a sponson-mounted 75mm gun capable of firing HE, and also a turret-mounted 37mm anti-tank gun. Late versions also sported a .30" machine gun above the 37mm gun. To train the British crews, these American sergeant instructors were sent to the Western Desert.

3 General Sir Harold Alexander was asked on the evening of August 6th 1942 to become C-in-C Middle East, on the recommendation of the Chief of the Imperial General Staff, General Sir Alan Brooke. He arrived by air to replace General Sir Claude Auchinleck, and is pictured here (right) with his pilot.

4 This remarkable picture of a German Ju87 Stuka dive-bomber crashing was shot at the moment of impact on July 23rd 1942 in the North African desert. The aircraft was shot down by British anti-aircraft gunfire; the German pilot baled out and was taken prisoner by the British unit.

4

5

7

5 The total surprise that General Montgomery's plan achieved at Alamein in October 1942 caught the Axis armies off balance. Even Rommel was away from his command, and had to hurry back, arriving to confer with his commanders on October 26th, two days after his deputy General Stumme had died of a heart attack. After conferences like the one illustrated here, during that fateful week, Rommel attempted to smash through the Allied army by concentrating his armour, but failed, mainly because of the greatly increased strength of the Desert Air Force.

6 It was not only modern tanks that the USA supplied to the British Army struggling to reassert themselves in the desert. A large number of 155mm US howitzers, built to a design that had originated in France, were shipped to the Eighth Army before Alamein, and were manned by troops of the Medium Regiment, Royal Artillery.

6

7 To replace General Corbett as Chief of Staff in the Middle East, the popular Lieutenant-General R. McCreery was appointed to serve under General Alexander. Of McCreery, Alexander wrote 'He is one of those officers who is as successful at HQ as at the head of his troops'. Later knighted, General McCreery was to become commander of the 5th Army 10th Corps under the by then Field-Marshal Alexander in Italy.

had been appointed as General Eisenhower's deputy for that operation, in command of the British 1st Army.

Churchill decided, at the beginning of August 1942, to see for himself the Eighth Army, its command structure and the position in which it found itself, and on August 4th arrived in Cairo. He found that the Cairo GHQ favoured a wait at least until September for an attack on Rommel's positions, in order to assemble reinforcements, regroup and plan its offensive. He was not pleased, and on August 6th asked the Chief of the Imperial General Staff, General Sir Alan Brooke (later Field-Marshal Lord Alanbrooke) to assume command in the Middle East, with General Auchinleck taking only the Iraq and Iran theatres. Brooke felt that he was of more service in his existing role, and tactfully refused, whereupon Churchill asked the Americans to accept that General Alexander be released from his responsibilities to Operation Torch to take over in the Western Desert. For the command of the Eighth Army, Alexander and Churchill

Montgomery and the Desert Fox

initially selected Lieutenant-General W.H.E. Gott, but he was killed in an air crash days afterwards. Their choice then fell on General Bernard Law Montgomery, who had been intended as Alexander's replacement as commander of the British 1st Army for 'Torch', and now moved to the desert, leaving Eisenhower wondering why Churchill kept taking his deputies away from him. The arrival of Montgomery in Cairo was historic. Arrogant, less than totally lovable, yet an inspiration to all who served with and under him, he was destined to become one of the best known figures of the Second World War. His was the fire that was to drive the Eighth Army forward and the *Afrika Korps* back, not only to Rommel's starting point, but far beyond to Tripoli, in less than a year.

There was much to do. Montgomery launched himself upon the task of strengthening the defences of the El Alamein position and, knowing that the *Panzerarmee Afrika* was now heavily reinforced, made the assumption that it could not be long before Rommel attacked. The presence and virtual impassability of the Qattara depression, the height of the Alam el Halfa ridge, and the proximity of the sea made it unlikely that Rommel could execute one of the outflanking manoeuvres that he had made peculiarly his own. Montgomery therefore decided that Rommel would attack where he was least expected, and would try to 'tease' out the tanks of the Eighth Army to be destroyed by the superior German anti-tank guns. Acting on this hunch, the British commander ordered the 44th Division and two brigades of the 10th Armoured to reinforce the defences of the Alam el Halfa ridge, and ordered the tanks to dig in and act defensively rather than adopt a mobile offensive role.

The German attack expected at full moon on August 26th did not materialise. The British generals (Horrocks and de Guingand), under

Montgomery's direction, used the interlude to indulge in a little deception which had almost the qualities of comic opera, but which was nonetheless effective in misleading the Germans and giving the British army the edge in the battle that followed. They produced a map which gave a highly inaccurate yet detailed picture of the Allied minefields and the natural hazards of the desert, and then arranged for it to be abandoned after an armoured car 'broke down' in no-man's land. The Germans took the bait. When the attack finally came in the early hours of August 31st, the progress of the 15th and 21st *Panzer* Divisions was slow; they were hampered by unexpected minefields and by an enemy who seemed to know exactly where to shell and attack from the air. In the melee, the commanders of both

1 The intensity of the Allied bombardment at Alamein, and the ferocity of the fighting during the advance that followed, prevented the German and Italian troops from reasserting their former initiative. These Italian troops are under fire and are clearly (and very sensibly) keeping their heads well down.

2 To believe that the Western Desert is all sand dunes is a sad misconception. Much of the terrain over which the Axis and Allied armies fought is rocky and covered with loose stones. These British soldiers are moving forward to attack a German position.

3 The numbers of dead and wounded were far greater on the Axis side at Alamein than in the Allied armies, but British casualties should not be treated lightly. The Axis armies lost 25,000 dead and wounded and 30,000 prisoners of war. The Allies lost 13,560 dead and wounded. These men are soldiers of the 51st Highland Division being treated by RAMC orderlies in a field hospital.

4 A soberly reflective Field Marshal Erwin Rommel listens to the increasingly bad news about the progress of the Axis armies after Alamein. This picture was filed on 16th November 1942 in London, so was probably taken a week or so previous to that date, when the German army had failed to re-establish its line.

5 The strength of the Desert Air Force under Air Chief Marshal Sir Arthur Tedder, and the relative weakness of the *Luftwaffe* in Africa, resulted in a seemingly endless succession of bombing raids which prevented the Axis armies regrouping and reorganising. These Italian soldiers are running for cover as yet another British air raid sends bombs raining down upon them.

6 A 'Lorraine Schlepper' self-propelled gun, captured intact, with only 1,000km on the clock, by the British during the Battle of Alamein. These machines were German conversions of French tank chassis, and carried a 150mm howitzer.

7 The lifting of the Axis siege on Malta, which ended in July 1942, improved the Allied supply position, and also greaty reduced the ability of Germany and Italy to supply *Panzerarmee Afrika* by sea, since the Allied navies once again had the use of Malta's important bases from which to conduct anti-shipping operations. This fine picture shows British ships patrolling in the Mediterranean.

Panzer Divisions were put out of the action — Major-General von Bismarck of the 21st, killed by a mine, and Lieutenant-General Nehring of the 15th, severely injured by air attack.

Air power and a defensive use of artillery were, in fact, the deciding factors in the Battle of Alam el Halfa. The Germans and Italians were repulsed at every turn, and were losing men and armour to little effect. The enormously long line of supply back to Benghazi began to tell once more, and, on September 3rd, Rommel called off the attack.

Alexander and Montgomery, despite this considerable success, decided still to remain on the defensive until such time as they had been reinforced to a level of men and equipment that they knew could and would defeat their enemy. Shortly after the Battle of Alam el Halfa, in the early part of September, President Roosevelt's gift of 300 Sherman tanks and 100 self-propelled guns began to arrive in Egypt, and the improvement in Allied sea and air power in the Mediterranean (British submarines were able to use Malta again from July) was ensuring an ever greater volume of supplies for the Allies. The reverse was, for the same reason, true for the Axis, and the German and Italian forces now experienced a considerable reduction in supplies of fuel and arms to reinforce the *Panzerarmee Afrika*.

Allied air power was built up impressively. The lessons of Hitler's *Blitzkrieg* had been well learnt, and long-range bombers became an important part of the tactical planning for the coming desert offensive. The crews of newly arrived American B-25 Mitchells and British Wellingtons began training in desert conditions, and a full-scale ground training programme initiated British crews into the mysteries of the Sherman tank.

8 This picture, taken from an Italian ship in the Mediterranean, shows vividly the shell bursts of a Royal Navy attack on the Italian convoy, which was attempting to get vital supplies of fuel and ammunition through to Rommel's armies.

Montgomery and the Desert Fox

Deception began once more to take a hand in the planning of the great Battle of Alamein, which was such a mighty undertaking that it was not to come until October's full moon. Montgomery made the assumption that Rommel would expect him to follow, as had previous commanders of the Eighth Army, the established British approach to tactical planning. Given that assumption, Montgomery reasoned, Rommel would expect him to attack from the South and try to drive the Axis forces into the sea, and to attack the armour first, expecting to mop up the German and Italian infantry later. The British plan was therefore based upon exactly the opposite procedure — an assault from the seabound North; a massive artillery barrage being followed by an infantry advance, the objective being to cut off the German armour, separate it from its supporting infantry and eliminate it piecemeal.

If Rommel was not to learn of this plan, the massive movements of British troops northward from the southern positions had to be

1 Shortly before Alamein, the RAF had sent four long-range fighters to attack the Italian seaplane base at Bomba, on the Libyan coast. This impressive picture was shot from the cockpit of one of the aircraft as it banked across the Italian base. The same four fighters also attacked a parade of Italian troops at Gazala, killing some fifty of the Italian soldiers.

2 After bombing an Italian supply column, this RAF sergeant pilot was shot down by anti-aircraft fire and captured by the Italian soldiers he had been bombing. Held by two Italian guards, the right-hand of whom seems to find the situation entertaining, the sergeant, still holding his parachute harness, is looking up to watch his colleagues continue the attack.

3 By December 1942, the RAF were bombing Axis positions in Tunis from their advance bases in Libya. This crew have just returned from a raid in their Blenheim twin-engined bomber, an aircraft with a maximum speed of 266 mph and a range of 1,950 miles.

concealed. Montgomery's mastermind of 'Operation Bertram' was Major Charles Richardson, who hit upon the idea of replacing every vehicle that stole away in the night with an inflatable rubber replica, realistic enough to fool aerial reconnaissance and long distance observers. A fake pipeline was built, and was deliberately constructed slowly so that the Germans would believe the attack to be scheduled for November rather than October. False radio traffic was used to make the Axis listening posts believe that a third Armoured Division was in position to the South, between the Qattara Depression and Ruweisat Ridge. Camouflage assumed a new importance as the vast dumps of fuel and stores near the coast were concealed from prying Axis eyes.

Meanwhile the 7th Armoured Division and XXX Corps had new commanders — Major-General Harding and Lieutenant-General Sir Oliver Leese respectively — and a far tougher training programme than they had previously experienced. A third Corps — X Corps — had been formed under Lieutenant-General Lumsden with the specific brief to pursue the enemy once the artillery and infantry had created a breach in the line. By mid-October, the Allies were ready. But what of Rommel?

He had in fact left the front because of poor health, and handed over command of *Panzerarmee Afrika* to General Georg Stumme, albeit with strict instructions to his successor to follow the agreed plan of campaign without undue display of initiative. The Axis had not been idle during the previous six weeks, and almost half a million German mines now lay between the Allied attackers and their enemy. The German and Italian Armoured Divisions had been withdrawn to the rear, and six divisions of infantry, including one Airborne, held the line. The 21st *Panzer* and the Italian 'Ariete' Division were in the northern sector. The 15th *Panzer* and the 'Littorio' Tank Division were stationed in the South.

4 Towards the end of November 1942, the Allied advance and Rommel's retreat were gaining momentum. The Axis army was losing men and equipment fast – these British soldiers are seen using an abandoned German PzKpfw III Battle Tank as cover as they advance upon their objective – a picture from a newsreel of the time shown in British and American cinemas.

5 In an effort to bolster flagging *Luftwaffe* morale, Field-Marshal Albert Kesselring toured operational Axis fighter units in North Africa and awarded decorations to his successful pilots.

6 The original print of this picture is captioned to the effect that the German sentry is standing guard over aircraft just returned damaged from a mission over Libya – in fact, the Dorniers in the background look like relatively long-term inhabitants of the scrap heaps that were proliferating all over the desert, and the picture was probably posed for the benefit of the sentry.

The Greatest Bombardment in History

When Montgomery's surprise attack came at 9.40 in the evening of October 23rd 1942, the Axis were totally unprepared for its force, and had no inkling of the appointed date or hour. Rommel was still away from his command, and two of the Italian commanders were on leave in Italy. A total of 592 Allied guns opened up simultaneously along a front from the Mediterranean to the Qattara Depression, the vast bulk of them — 456 — in the northern sector. For 15 minutes this enormous fire power hammered at the Axis positions, cutting communications, detonating many mines, disorientating the German and Italian defenders. As soon as the barrage ended, sappers with mine detectors — new devices at the time — and specially adapted tanks called 'Scorpions' with flails to detonate mines advanced into the minefields, with the infantry close behind. In the southern sector General Horrocks' XIII Corps staged a successful but costly diversion which succeeded in its objective of preventing the 'Ariete' Division reinforcing the armour to the north.

Although the British divisions made considerable progress, they had by the 26th, when Rommel returned to his command, two days after his deputy Stumme had died of a heart attack in the field, failed to punch their way through to the Axis' rear, as Montgomery's plan demanded. The British armour was therefore held up and relatively

7 Major-General B.C. Freyberg V.C. (centre) commanded the New Zealand Division during the 'Supercharge' operation which drove the Axis front back to Tunisia, and was promoted Lieutenant-General in 1943. Freyberg was a man of detail, and is here briefing two of his brigadiers.

Montgomery and the Desert Fox

ineffectual, although in fact the Axis forces had taken heavy losses, and had few tanks, widely dispersed. Rommel's first move was to concentrate the armour and, as always, lead from the front, taking a powerful tank force to attack Montgomery's forward positions. But he reckoned without the formidably increased air power of Tedder's Desert Air Force, which now had a total of 1,200 aircraft, several times the available *Luftwaffe* resources.

The RAF bombers killed large numbers of troops and disabled tanks by the score, as did the new 6-pounder anti-tank gun that was newly arrived in North Africa. As Rommel fell back, the Allied armoured formations began to cut through their opponents' positions and fan out. By the 31st of October, Rommel was in a desperate position but was holding the line by bringing up his last reserves. There had in fact been a reduction in the ferocity of Montgomery's assault, and a withdrawal of Allied troops into reserve. This tactic reportedly

1 South African troops played an important role in the reconquest of Cyrenaica. This picture dates from January 1943, and shows a South African armoured car passing Sikh troops of the Indian Division who were about to occupy Giovanni.

2 The Crusader III tank was lightly armoured and still comparatively lightly armed, although this version had a 6-pounder gun instead of the previous marks' ludicrous 2-pounder. The Crusader could, however, be persuaded, to compensate for this, to travel considerably faster than its official top speed of 27 mph.

3 As the last phase of the desert war drew near, there were many casualties to be cared for in the forward field hospitals. These New Zealand nursing sisters and their charges were photographed in January 1943.

4 Despite the reverses suffered by *Panzerarmee Afrika*, Field-Marshal Rommel managed to retain the favour of Adolf Hitler until 1944, when his connection with the Stauffenberg bomb plot finally broke the bond and brought about Rommel's death by suicide. This picture dates from September 1942, and was taken at a rally in the *Sportpalast* in Berlin. The figure between Hitler and Rommel is Dr Robert Ley, leader of the *Arbeitsfront*. Ley cheated the Nuremberg tribunal by hanging himself in his cell before his trial began.

caused Churchill much disquiet, and he had to be calmed by the ever-present Sir Alan Brooke. In fact, Montgomery was setting up the final assault that would set the Eighth Army on the road to Tunis — 'Operation Supercharge'.

On November 2nd, Major-General Freyberg's New Zealand Division led 'Supercharge' and encountered some of the closest in-fighting of the war — tank battles at ranges of only 20 and 30 yards were reported. Despite enormous Allied losses, the attack gradually wore down the *Afrika Korps*, which by November 3rd had only some 35 tanks left. On the 4th, the German line was breached, and X Corps almost wiped out the 'Ariete' Division and captured General von Thoma, the commander of the *Afrika Korps*.

The remains of *Panzerarmee Afrika* was now in full retreat westward, but much of the Italian infantry strength was surrounded and captured. The Battle of Alamein was over. Montgomery and Tedder had shown that Rommel was not invincible, but the cost had been considerable. The Allies had lost 13,560 men, of whom 4,610 were killed or missing. The Axis had fared far worse — they had lost 25,000 killed and wounded, and 30,000 prisoners including nine Generals.

Rommel was never again to hold the initiative or win a major victory in North Africa. His path to Tunis and defeat was clear. Despite orders from 'Commando Supremo', he made no attempt to stand and counter attack at El Agheila. He had met his match.

CHAPTER 20

OPERATION TORCH
THE U.S.A. STEPS INTO AFRICA

The invasion of French North Africa by an Allied force in November 1942 had as its objective the seizure of Morocco, Algeria and Tunisia, and the creation, with the British and Empire armies in the Western Desert, of a giant pincer within which to crush the Axis forces under Rommel. Militarily desirable as the operation was, it nonetheless had a firm basis in politics. This is not, however, to restate the old and inaccurate claim that Roosevelt set up Operation Torch to corner a greater Democratic vote in the 1944 Presidential election. The politics were of a higher order.

In January 1942, the so-called 'Arcadia' conference between Churchill and Roosevelt, immediately following America's entry into the war, had confirmed the policy of 'Germany First' that had been tacitly agreed long before the USA had been officially part of the conflict. As the Russians fought back after their appalling 1941 losses, Stalin put great pressure upon both Roosevelt and Churchill to open a second front against Germany — by which Stalin meant an invasion of France. Churchill knew that there was no way in which such an invasion could be possible before 1943 at the earliest, with or without the complicity of America, but there was substantial, and

slightly naive, pressure from both public and military opinion in the USA for an invasion of the European mainland in 1942. Among the generals wanting to hit Germany where it hurt was Dwight D. Eisenhower. He and other generals outlined a proposal to build up US forces and arms in Britain — a plan which became known as 'Bolero' — prior to a limited attack on France in 1943 to seize a bridgehead in the area of Cherbourg. This latter operation was to be known as 'Sledgehammer'. This in turn was to be followed by a full-scale invasion across the Channel, also in 1943, to be known as 'Roundup'.

Roosevelt doubted the short term practicality of this scheme, whatever its emotional desirability, since the USA had the potential for little more than three combat divisions ready for action in 1942. He therefore sent Harry Hopkins, his adviser and confidant, and General Marshall to London to discuss the whole issue with Churchill and his military staff. The outcome of this meeting was that 'Bolero' was agreed for initial action, with Eisenhower as its commander, but the second front remained a matter of contention. Marshall wanted the 'Sledgehammer' plan agreed as a means of

5 Dieppe saw the first use in action of Britain's new Churchill tank. Thirty Canadian Churchills took part and, of these, twenty-seven reached the shore, fifteen struggled to the esplanade, and only three got into the town. By the end of the day, all had been lost. This is a Mark II. Note the raised exhaust pipe, intended to assist deep wading.

5

6

7

6 The devastation on the Dieppe beaches by the afternoon after the raid, intended to test the practicality of a cross-Channel invasion, was horrific. Beached and burning landing craft, knocked-out Churchill tanks and dead soldiers were everywhere.

7 Over 6000 Canadian and British Troops took part in the raid, which lasted for nine hours. Of 4,963 Canadians who fought at Dieppe, 3,363 were killed, wounded, captured or declared missing. The full report on the raid was not released for thirty years.

1 Despite the appalling perils of the beaches, significant numbers of Allied soldiers made it into the town, but many were killed or captured in the fierce fighting that followed. Next morning, the battle over, these German troops cleared up stragglers, leaving the dead British sergeant for the burial party.

2 One of the few Churchill tanks that got into Dieppe town, 'Bert' is a Mark III of the Canadian Calgary Regiment. The Mark III was fitted with a six pounder gun, and was powered by a twelve cylinder 350hp petrol engine.

reducing military pressure upon and political pressure from the USSR. Churchill wanted an operation in North Africa to provide evidence of political will to the USSR and evidence of active US involvement in the 'European' war, without the peril of an invasion of Europe that was ill-prepared.

Eventually, following Churchill's visit to Washington in June, and a further visit by the American team to London in July, all prospect of a full-scale invasion of Europe being launched in 1942 was vetoed by Churchill, but it was agreed that the experimental 'mini-invasion' at Dieppe, which had been in the detailed planning stage for months, should go ahead under the recently (November 1941) appointed Chief of Combined Operations, Rear-Admiral Lord Louis Mountbatten. It was intended that this landing, which took place on August 19th 1942, should test on a small scale whether it was realistically possible to mount a cross-Channel invasion on the scale necessary to open the Second Front in Europe. In the event, the raid was a disaster, not least because the defending Germans were aware that it was coming. The Canadian 2nd Division lost 882 killed of the 4,963 men who took part, with 597 wounded. The British Commandos of Nos 3 and 4 Commando lost 275 killed, wounded or taken prisoner. But the raid nonetheless proved that a cross-Channel invasion was feasible, and pointed the way to the training and equipment requirements that needed to be met if the eventual invasion of France was to be successful.

However, to the Soviet leaders, operations like the Dieppe Raid were a sideshow, and to maintain credibility with the USSR 'Operation Torch', the invasion of North Africa, was agreed upon. Because of French susceptibilities following the events of 1940, it was felt to be advisable that, although 'Operation Torch' was to be demonstrably a joint Allied operation, with, in fact, more British troops than American, the actual invasion force should appear to be almost entirely American, and should have an American ground commander. This job fell to the colourful, aggressive and World War I experienced Major-General George C. Patton. As Deputy Commander-in-Chief, Eisenhower chose Major-General Mark Clark, who was to prove an able commander in his own right. The British troops who were to land soon after the Americans were to be commanded by Lieutenant-General Kenneth Anderson.

After much discussion based upon fears of Axis countermeasures from nearby Sicily, a plan for 'Torch' was agreed upon which called for three separate US landings, two on the Mediterranean coast of North Africa, at Oran and near Algiers, and one on the Atlantic coast at Casablanca. Once the American landings were established, the British 1st Army was to go ashore at Algiers and, having established a bridgehead, turn East for an attack on Tunis. 'Torch', at 60,000 men, was the largest combat force ever to have been shipped from the United States, and Norfolk, Virginia, its embarkation point, was absurdly stretched to cope. Training was at

3 General Sir Harold Alexander (left), General Eisenhower (centre) and Lieutenant-General George Patton. Alexander had originally been appointed as Eisenhower's deputy for Operation Torch, but was instead appointed British commander in the Middle East. Eisenhower, in overall command of 'Torch', chose Major-General Mark Clark as his deputy, and had Patton to command his US land forces. Later, when the Eighth Army reached Tunisia, General Alexander found himself working alongside Eisenhower after all.

a frantic pace, command structures were fragile because of constant changes of personnel, and many of Patton's officers despaired of ever getting the force together as a cohesive whole.

In Britain, from where the Centre and Eastern Taskforces were to begin their voyage, similar stresses prevailed and confusion reigned. The US Army had not attempted any feat of organisation quite so large before, and problems arising from inexperience and mismanagement were everywhere. Despite it all, the US 1st Armoured Division, and the 1st and 34th Infantry Divisions were embarked in Liverpool and Glasgow late in September and headed in convoy for the Straits of Gibraltar and the Mediterranean, traversing the Straits on the night of November 5th to 6th.

The Western Taskforce of the invasion, consisting of more than 100 ships also managed to arrive off the coast of Morocco on schedule after a rendezvous at sea and an encounter with a U-Boat

on the way across the Atlantic. On the night of November 7th 1942, the Western Taskforce split into three attack groups and, early in the morning of the 8th, went ashore by landing craft. Their initial objective was to capture the heavily defended city of Casablanca and its airport. The group given the airport landed at Mehdia, the others either side of the city at Safi and Fedala.

The Mehdia landing group under Major-General Lucien Truscott, which consisted of some 9,000 men from the 2nd Armoured and 9th Divisions, ran into heavy resistance from the Vichy French defending forces, and, having had reinforcements delayed by French shelling of the fleet, was in a decidedly tricky position by the evening of the 8th. The arrival of reinforcements from the fleet on the 9th enabled them to fight on and capture the airport on the 10th, but not before 79 Americans had been killed and many more injured.

At Safi, to the South of Casablanca, Major-General Ernest Harmon, commander of the 2nd Armoured Division took 6,500 men of the 2nd Armoured and 9th Divisions ashore, again encountering tough opposition, and established the necessary beach-head. On the 9th November, Harmon's force encountered a French infantry force at Bou Guedra, and the resulting battle held up their advance until the next day when he was once again able to advance towards Casablanca. Harmon took Mazagan on the morning of the 11th and was on the road to Casablanca when he, like the other commanders, heard news of a ceasefire arranged with the complicity of Admiral Darlan, second in command to Marshal Petain in Vichy France, who was coincidentally in North Africa when the invasion took place.

The northernmost landing group of the Western Taskforce landed against similarly stiff opposition at Fedala under Major-General Jonathan Anderson, who had the largest force of the three — 16,500 men, mainly of General Anderson's own 3rd Division. They had almost reached Casablanca, and were about to turn their artillery loose on the city when news of the ceasefire reached them.

4 The French Navy in Morocco, like the French Army in Tunisia, was in the understandable position of not knowing for whom to fight when the Allies landed. Under orders from collaborationist Vichy France to oppose the landings, most of the commanders were in sympathy with the Allies, but obeyed orders and fought a brisk battle. In this picture, two French destroyers and a light cruiser (background), have been beached after heavy damage had been inflicted upon them.

5 Once the port of Casablanca had been secured, the Allied Expeditionary Force was heavily reinforced with thousands of additional men who poured in aboard troop transports like this one. Notice the large number of additional life rafts that have been strung along the sides of the ship – troopships were normally loaded with as many as four times the number of passengers for which the ship had been designed, and the available lifeboats were always woefully inadequate in case of trouble.

6 The fortuitous presence of Admiral Darlan in Algiers (he was visiting his sick son, who was in hospital in the city) when the Allied landings took place made it possible for an impromptu peace conference to be arranged. After Major-General Mark Clark arrived on November 9th, a meeting on the 10th concluded a ceasefire for the whole of North Africa. At that meeting are (left to right) Britain's Admiral Cunningham, General Clark, Admiral Darlan and General Eisenhower. On November 13th, Darlan was recognised as French Commander-in-Chief in North Africa by the Allies. Six weeks later, on Christmas Eve, he was assassinated by a French fanatic in Algiers.

7 Once the ceasefire with the French had been agreed, the British entered Tunisia (on November 15th) and American troops and equipment were poured into Morocco and Algeria and went into action against the German and Italian army which had been landed in force at Bizerta and Tunis, in north Tunisia. Much of the landscape of that part of North Africa is arid desert and semi-desert, and American troops like these had quickly to learn the principles of survival in desert warfare.

Operation Torch

The Centre Taskforce, whose objective was the capture of Oran in Algeria, was the only one of the three taskforces to be able to claim a concluded military victory. The 22,000 men of the force attacked at several points, the 1st Infantry Division being allotted the task of encircling the city from East and West, and the 1st Armoured the job of pushing inland to come back upon the city from the South. Initial resistance was weaker than expected because the attack came as an almost total surprise to the defenders, but November 9th brought heavy fighting. On the 10th a US armoured thrust penetrated the city, and the French authorities surrendered at mid-day. The fighting in Oran cost the American force some 600 killed or wounded.

By far the most crucial job fell to the Eastern Taskforce, whose assault was upon Algiers, the centre of all French government in

1 The US advance across Algeria was rapid and effective, for the Allies had learned much from the earlier British experiences at the hands of Rommel and his motorised columns. These American troops were on their way to tackle the Axis army that had been landed in Tunisia.

2 Close on the heels of the American Army in Northwest Africa came the establishment of major air bases to bomb the Axis forces in Tunisia. From this time on, Rommel's army was doomed to a gigantic pincer operation, with Montgomery's Eighth Army chasing *Panzerarmee Afrika* from the east, the British First Army on the north coast and the weight of Eisenhower's forces pressing in from the east. In this picture, three American Generals are watching the arrival of an armada of allied aircraft. Right to left: Brigadier-General James Doolittle, Commander of the Allied Air Forces in North Africa, Major-General Mark Clark and Major-General Lloyd R. Fredendall, Commander of the American Central Task Force.

3 Monday November 30th saw the British 36th Brigade, which was advancing towards Bizerta, bogged down in a pitched battle with German paratroops on Djebel Azzag (Green Hill) and Djebel Agred (Bald Hill). This British six-pounder anti-tank gun, photographed during the action, is of the type that saw extensive service during the Tunisian campaign. This crew have been busy – notice the spent cases scattered about the gun.

North Africa and the jumping-off point for the planned assault on Tunis. Landings on both sides of the city by three separate parts of the taskforce met comparatively little resistance — the westernmost landing party at Castiglione found that the local French defenders claimed to have been ordered not to resist at all. Only a small assault group of 650 Americans, plus some British officers in American uniforms, ran into heavy resistance when they attempted a frontal assault on the harbour at Algiers, a bold venture that enabled them to capture their initial objectives only to be forced to surrender when their position became hopeless.

In the afternoon of the 8th, Admiral Darlan recognised that the French position was hopeless, and that he had a choice between surrender without further bloodshed and defeat with a great deal of bloodletting on both sides. After consultations by radio with Petain, Darlan and General Juin agreed to a ceasefire in Algiers, but not, at this stage, elsewhere in North Africa. On the 9th November,

General Mark Clark arrived in Algiers to negotiate a ceasefire for the whole of French North Africa, and agreement was reached late the following day.

Meanwhile, General Anderson's British 1st Army was on its way over rocky roads to Tunisia, almost 400 miles to the East. Prompted by the Allied invasion, German and Italian troops were already arriving at Bizerta and Tunis by sea and air to secure Tunisia and the rear of *Panzerarmee Afrika*, and the French forces between the newly arrived Germans and the advancing Allies lacked the orders or the clear moral guidance that was necessary if they were to resist the Axis landings – quite simply, they were not sure for whom they were supposed to be fighting. Thus the German and Italian invaders rapidly established defensive positions in Tunisia, which were contained by French troops from mid-November once the French

5

6

7

4 British infantry advancing alongside M3 Stuart tanks in Tunisia during the actions at the end of November 1942. This picture was billed at the time of its arrival in November 1942 as 'one of the first actual pictures of British troops on the Tunisian front'.

5 German infantry photographed moving up for the battle of Tebourba at the end of November. The Axis were in firm control of Bizerta and Tunis, the great Mediterranean ports of north Tunisia, yet the new *5th Panzerarmee* under Colonel-General Hans-Jurgen von Arnim, made up of divisions brought from Europe to resist the new assault on the rear of *Panzerarmee Afrika* consisted only of 47,000 Germans and 18,000 Italians. This picture is taken from an issue of *Munchner Illustrierte Presse* at the time.

6 The British armoured assault on German positions at Tebourba-Djedeida, on Sunday November 29th 1942, proved a tough initiation into Tunisian battle conditions for the German paratroops newly arrived from Italy. These men are gaining what cover they can from the sparse landscape to shelter from shell bursts. The man on the far right is carrying a flamethrower.

7 At the end of 1942, on December 14th, came Anglo-French agreement on Madagascar. The Japanese advance into the Indian Ocean, in the spring of 1942, and Laval's return to power in the Vichy French government, had raised Allied fears that Madagascar might be handed over to the Japanese, complete with its important naval base of Diego-Suarez, which controlled the Mozambique channel. Allied landings (Operation 'Ironclad') on May 5th 1942, and again in mid-September, finally resulted in the surrender of Vichy forces on November 6th and the Anglo-French agreement the following month. Here, a Fairey Fulmar fighter of Britain's Royal Navy lands back on its carrier after operations supporting the Madagascar landings.

had clear guidance as to which side they were on. Although Anderson made contact with his enemy on November 20th, the momentum had gone, the Axis forces were too strong to be shifted quickly, and no amount of reinforcements and fighting could alter the position of stalemate. On Christmas Eve, as Darlan was assassinated by a young French monarchist, Eisenhower had reluctantly to abandon the idea of a swift capture of Tunis and Bizerta. Roughly 110,000 troops had taken part in 'Torch' which, as improvisations go, was outstandingly successful, and laid the ground for the final defeat of the Axis in North Africa.

Although American soldiers had experienced battle in the 'Torch' landings, they had yet to discover just how tough a foe the Germans could be. The bitter experience of the Battle of Kasserine Pass in 1943 would teach them that. Thus far, the US land forces had fought only the Vichy French army, whose loyalties were in any case divided, and who had been relatively easily overcome. The US Navy and the

British Royal Navy had, however, not had quite such an easy time off North Africa.

The Vichy French Navy had joined battle in earnest with the escort vessels of the US taskforces, and had sustained heavy losses, including the cruiser *Primauguet*, 10 destroyers and 13 submarines. At Casablanca, the USS *Massachusetts* fought a brisk battle with the still incomplete French battleship *Jean Bart* and was fired upon from the shore. Attempts to send British naval sloops into Algiers harbour early in the battle for the French seat of North African government had resulted in the *Walney*, the *Hartland* and the *Broke* being lost, and the *Malcolm* making a hair's breadth escape.

Nonetheless, the overall picture was one of Allied success, not only in the objective of strategically occupying French North Africa, but also in its being the first large-scale Allied combined operation, and the first major Allied amphibious invasion. It was the taste of things to come.

CHAPTER 21

THE EASTERN SUMMER OFFENSIVE
STALINGRAD, AND THE BEGINNING OF THE END

For Germany, and for Hitler in particular, the Eastern front was of dominating importance during 1941 and 1942. The sheer scale of the task that the Third Reich had undertaken in attempting to overrun Russia, and the overwhelming proportion of the German armed forces that were committed to the task, made it inevitable that its successful completion should be at the forefront of Hitler's thinking.

The winter of 1941/42 had, as we have seen, inflicted appalling suffering upon an ill-prepared German army that lacked proper winter clothing, and which was subjected to a ferocious counter-attack by Zhukov's Russian forces in December. Morale had reached a desperately low state. Generals had asked for and had been refused permission to retreat. Yet, somehow, the superbly trained and

1 As the Russian counter-attack before Moscow proved that the mighty German army could, after all, be stopped and even put into retreat, morale reasserted itself, and Russian soldiers became determined and grimly effective. Propaganda picture this may be, but the expression of resolve on the face of the Red Army soldier loading his heavy anti-aircraft gun in the defence of Moscow sums up the new spirit of the Soviet troops.

2 Soviet artillery and heavy armour improved greatly from the beginning of 1942 onwards as huge and relatively safe armaments production facilities were established in the Soviet hinterland, far from the German offensives. These young Soviet soldiers are preparing shells for a large calibre howitzer during the spring of 1942.

3 A German soldier takes a closer look at a knocked-out Soviet KV-1 heavy tank, of which almost 1,400 had been built by the time of the Battle of Moscow. The KV-1 was slow (22 mph) and inadequately armoured, and was later replaced by the much superior JS Josef Stalin series. A dead Red Army soldier, presumably one of the tank crew, lies on the ground unnoticed on the right.

experienced German army had held its line despite the hardships inflicted upon it. The Hitler magic was still there. The decay of the conquering spirit of the Third Reich had not yet eaten into the fabric of the world's greatest fighting machine.

Thus, by April, when Hitler issued his Directive No.41 for the 1942 summer offensive and beyond on the Eastern Front, the Fuehrer was able to claim with some truth that "Thanks to the extraordinary bravery and spirit of sacrifice displayed by our troops, the defensive battle on the Eastern Front is proving a most striking success for German arms. The Directive went on to define the objectives for the *Wehrmacht* in Russia, and the means by which it was to achieve them. In summary, the objectives were to capture or destroy the remaining Russian armed forces" Hitler believed on the basis of faulty intelligence that the Russian army was so depleted as to be near defeat — and to capture the rich sources of raw materials that the southern USSR had to offer.

To achieve this, Hitler directed, the entire force of the *Wehrmacht* on the Eastern Front, with the exception of those engaged in the siege of Leningrad, was to be concentrated in the southern sector in a drive to the Don, and to the oilfields and mountains of the Caucasus. Beyond the Caucasus lay Turkey and the Middle East — and Hitler confidently expected that 1942 would also see the Axis conquest of Egypt and an assault on the British protected territories beyond, making it theoretically possible for the Axis forces to link in a mighty circle from Libya almost to the Arctic. While there is no firm evidence that Hitler actually planned such a vast operation, there is written proof that it was discussed (and rejected) by his generals, notably by Halder. On a more limited canvas, the generals were, in any case, less than enthusiastic about Hitler's planned offensive, believing that there was more than a danger of the Russians having

4 Mussolini, as always, sought to demonstrate that he remained (as he had never been in fact) Hitler's right hand man, and visited the Eastern Front headquarters with the *Fuehrer*. Behind Hitler is Field-Marshal Wilhelm Keitel, one of the survivors of Nazi German military politics.

5 A study of German troops in the snows of early 1942 as the Russians continued to press home the successes of the winter. An officer named by the contemporary caption as Colonel von der Goltz is issuing final orders to his unit before an attack.

6 On March 5th 1942, Red Army troops entered and occupied the small town of Yukhnov in pursuit of the retreating German army. This scout company was the first into the town, devastated by the shelling that had driven the Germans from it. Wearing white camouflage suits – for where there was not recently fallen rubble there was still snow on the ground – the men in the foreground are being covered by those kneeling watchfully to the rear.

7 In the midst of the pace and action of *Blitzkrieg* and the world's first mechanised conflict, it is easy to forget that the Red Army still had large numbers of cavalry units in action during the early part of the Second World War. The German army also had cavalry units, which they employed most effectively in savage, anti-partisan actions through the vast forests of the Soviet Union.

1&2 These pictures tell the sad story of 17 year-old Zoya Kosmodemyanskaya, a Russian girl hanged by the German invaders for insubordination. The contemporary caption to these pictures reports that 'fiercely, with her bruised and beaten body, she fought the hangman who finally managed to slip the noose around her slender neck. She was not afraid of death, but wanted time to shout her last words, "Farewell comrades; Stalin is with us; Stalin will come". A minute later and her limp body was swaying in the air as the rope choked her further shouts.' Reputedly, the pictures were found in the pocket of a German officer killed in action, but this source is frequently quoted in propaganda captions for pictures of German atrocities in Russia and must be viewed with caution. There is, however, no doubt of the horror of these pictures, nor of the fact that the Soviet Union's enduring lack of trust in the Western powers owes something to the treachery of Nazi Germany.

3 The weather of the summer and autumn of 1942 provided the German army with many problems, although on the southern front Field-Marshal von Bock had the benefit of long spells of warm, dry conditions. This picture of men of the German Engineers dates from the early autumn of 1942 and shows them crossing a river swollen by the rains to carry out repair work on bridges.

4 Amidst all the ebb and flow of warfare across the vastness of the Soviet Union, the vicious siege of Leningrad, far to the north, went on. Here, at the approaches to Leningrad, sappers of the Red Army lay anti-personnel mines in preparation for the assault on the city which they expected at any time.

5 This is yet another picture reputedly found in the pockets of a German prisoner captured by the Russians. Published extensively at the time as evidence of German atrocities against prisoners (which undoubtedly took place in huge numbers), the picture itself may not be genuine, since it is not inconceivable that Russians dressed in captured uniforms posed for the picture. Even if false, the picture did no more than represent the sad truth.

greater reserves than German intelligence indicated, and that the commitment of greater resources to the Russian adventure would further weaken the ability of Germany to sustain its position on other fronts.

To the final defeat of what Hitler believed was a severely depleted Russian enemy, the *Wehrmacht* brought 18 more infantry divisions than had been available in Russia in 1941, but virtually no increase in the available armoured and motorised divisions — a factor that was to prove important to the coming campaign. On paper, the equivalent of 215 German divisions were massed against Russia for the summer offensive, of which 31 were 'Satellite' (Rumanian, Hungarian and Slovak) divisions. These in fact numbered 46, but were marked down in value by a third by cautious German planners doubtful of their actual capability in the field.

The assault by the augmented Army Group South was code-

5

6 Hitler's order that the Russians were to be treated as sub-human, and the interpretation of this that prisoners were not to be taken unnecessarily, resulted in many thousands of executions both of civilians and soldiers. Women searched among the rotting corpses for their menfolk, and all too often found them. Those that did not usually never heard what had happened to those they loved. The tightly-held noses of the men and women in this picture give an indication of the awfulness of the scene.

7 Red Army soldiers mount an anti-tank rifle against a Panzer III. Note the smoke from the region of the tank's bogies, which seems to indicate a hit.

6

named 'Operation Blue', and was to be preceded by attacks designed to retake the positions around Izyum captured by the Russians during their December offensive, and to mop up the remaining Russian defence of the Crimea. Beginning on May 8th 1942, 9 Axis divisions, three of them Rumanian, attacked 17 Russian divisions. The German formations, despite their numerical inferiority, made rapid progress, largely because of their superiority in the air. Colonel-General Lohr's *Luftflotte IV* provided constant dive-bombing and strafing support, and reduced the effectiveness of the Soviet Air Force in harrying the advancing German columns. By May 9th, the day after the attack began, the Germans had broken through the Russian lines and were fanning out. By May 11th, 8 Russian divisions had been driven back to the Sea of Azov; on May 20th what was left of the Russian forces in the northern part of the Crimea retreated across the narrow Strait between the Black Sea and the Sea of Azov, losing in the process

7

The Eastern Summer Offensive

170,000 prisoners, 258 tanks and 1,138 guns.

On the Izyum salient, things did not go so easily for the Germans. Bock had decided to attack on the 18th May, but the Russians attacked first, advancing on General Paulus' Sixth Army around Kharkov with great ferocity. As if from nowhere, the Russians under Marshal Timoshenko produced a major force of some 36 divisions with plenty of modern armour, advancing as a two-pronged attack. The northern attack was checked comparatively quickly, and held by the Germans, but in the South the Russians advanced inexorably until the 16th, virtually routing a Hungarian division and a German 'Security' Division. The German commanders, somewhat rattled, revised their plan intended for the 18th, and launched their armoured assault under Kleist on the 17th, whose *Panzergruppe* advanced rapidly with *Luftwaffe* support to the Donets.

At this point Timoshenko appealed to Stalin to allow a retreat from Kharkov, but was ordered to hold his position, vulnerable as it was to encirclement. He did not have to wait long. General Mackensen's 3rd *Panzerkorps* moved swiftly up the right bank of the Donets river, pushed the rear positions of the Russian army aside, and made contact with General von Seydlitz-Kurzbach's Corps, thereby sealing off the Russians in the Izyum pocket. Fight as they might, the Russian forces could not break out, and by the 28th, when the end came, the German Sixth Army had crushed the Russian army, which lost 1,246 tanks, 2,026 guns and an incredible 214,000 prisoners. General Gorodnyansky was killed in the closing stages of the fighting.

1 Around the perimeter of the besieged and endlessly bombed city of Leningrad were Soviet anti-aircraft gun emplacements, manned constantly by their crews, dug in and camouflaged to provide some measure of protection against shellfire and bomb blast.

2 Dramatically silhouetted against the skyline, these Soviet riflemen are taking part in the battle for Kharkov.

3 A dramatic picture which shows German soldiers dashing to safety as an oil installation in the Caucasus is blown up by Russians to save it from being captured by the Germans. This picture was taken after the fall of Krasnodar.

4 The battle for Rostov was fierce and bloody. The Russian resistance turned every successive street into a stronghold that the German attackers had to overcome before they could move on to the next. These German infantry are being brought up as reinforcements under cover of street barricades amid tremendous devastation.

5 Heinrich Himmler (left), Hitler's *Reichsfuhrer-SS*, who numbered among his responsibilities command of the *Einsatzgruppen* murder squads which had wrought such dreadful atrocities throughout the Soviet Union, visited Russia in the belief that his presence would lift troop morale. In fact he was cordially loathed by most German soldiers.

5

6

6 By the summer of 1942, the German advance was approaching the North Caucasus oilfields that Germany desperately needed to resolve the *Wehrmacht's* fuel problems, and the ill-fated Paulus had been delegated to take Stalingrad. Here Field-Marshal von Bock, shortly before being relieved of his short-lived command on July 13th 1942, is being brought up to date on the state of operations by General Fritz Lindemann.

8

7

9

7 Two German N.C.O's examine a disabled Russian T28 heavy tank. Such obsolescent machines were used as defensive strongpoints by the Russians, as they were far too slow, and therefore vulnerable, to be effective in an attacking role.

8 Soviet soldiers equipped with the older pattern rifle with which they began the defence of Russia running across a pontoon bridge under fire, with smoke billowing around them.

9 The caption to the original print of this picture says that 'Germany has sent many workers to help their soldier comrades in Russia. These workers belong to the *Reichsarbeitsdienst* organisation and work in uniforms'. The *Reichsarbeitsdienst*, or National Labour Service, enabled the state to regulate all work, and registration was compulsory. Those that did not find themselves in the armed services were obliged to work where they were told – and for some, like these young men, that meant delivering bread in Russia.

By failing to allow Timoshenko to pull Gorodnyansky's army back, Stalin had temporarily lost much of his ability to restrain the German advance in that part of Russia. Paulus was quick to seize the advantage that this offered, and the German Sixth Army pushed onward and eastward to the River Volga, meeting comparatively little resistance by comparison with its recent experiences.

Meanwhile, in the South of the Crimea, Colonel-General Erich von Manstein, probably Germany's greatest military strategist of the war, was preparing to take Sebastopol. With the Russians gone from the North of the peninsula, he was able to devote all his forces to the attack on the besieged Russians, which began on June 7th. Reinforced with massive siege artillery and large numbers of the comparatively new *Nebelwerfer* rocket launchers, and supported as ever by the strafing and dive-bombing attacks of the *Luftwaffe*, against which the Russians had no effective remedy, Manstein's task looked straightforward. That it was not, and became a protracted and bloody battle, was entirely due to the tactical skill and bravery of the Russian commander, General Petrov, and of his 8 divisions plus 3 brigades

of Marines. Not until July 9th, five days after Hitler promoted von Manstein Field-Marshal, did the last defenders of Sebastopol surrender. Even then, their capitulation was due only to total exhaustion of their ammunition and water supplies. For the loss of just over 24,000 German dead, the invaders had captured 95,000 prisoners and 467 guns.

The Push to the Caucasus and Stalingrad

Throughout June and the first half of July, the 1st and 4th *Panzerarmee* under Colonel-Generals von Kleist and Hoth respectively maintained their advance towards the Caucasus, and General von Paulus' Sixth Army continued towards Stalingrad, as set out in Hitler's Directive for the summer offensive. But, in late July, Hitler's Directive No.45 meddled with the original plan, and, against the judgment of Halder, Hoth and Kleist, swung the *Panzer* armies South-East, away from their eastward course. General Paulus and his Sixth Army continued, in accordance with the original plan, towards Stalingrad, but without the support of the *Panzer* armies.

The Eastern Summer Offensive

This made his position progressively weaker as his supply line became more extended and his rear more vulnerable. By 15th August, four weeks later, after a slow advance hampered by lack of fuel and poor supplies of food, ammunition and medical supplies, General Paulus was close enough to Stalingrad to issue his orders for an attack upon the city.

The German assault on 15th August was in two waves. The 14th *Panzer* Division attacked the North of the city, defended by General Gordov, and by the 22nd of August was ensconced in the northern suburbs. On August 23rd, the 79th *Panzergrenadier* Regiment announced by radio that it was in the suburb of Spartanovka, on the Volga, commanding a view South over the southern suburbs. Stalin was not pleased, and for the next few crucial days took tactical command of operations himself, drawing to do so on his detailed personal knowledge of the city. When the Germans failed to make rapid progress in the southern part of Stalingrad, the *Luftwaffe* was called up to deliver a demoralising blow to the defenders, and *Luftflotte VIII* bombed both residential and commercial areas with a devastating rain of high explosive.

Once more, defective German intelligence hampered German planning and assisted the Russian defenders. The sheer size of Stalingrad had not been appreciated by the Germans, and their tactical plans had not taken account of the fact that the city extended 20 miles along the banks of the Volga. Perhaps more to the point,

1 Nurses displayed great heroism with the Allied armies, and the Russian women were no exception, although they were often very much younger than their British and American counterparts, and took a more direct role in the fighting. This is a young Red Army nurse named Sacha Sekolova, pictured in a front line trench after going under fire to collect a wounded man and his sub-machine gun.

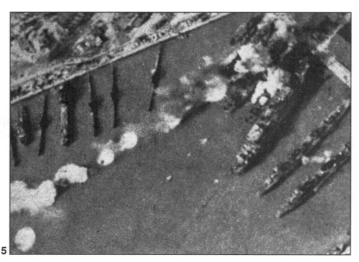

2 The more mountainous topography of the Caucasus helped to slow down the advance of the German army, and it was here that the advance was finally contained, never to go further. This Red Army trench mortar crew has positioned itself on a ridge and is pounding a German column below.

the assumption was made that the Russians were a demoralised and almost beaten enemy. In fact, Stalin was as determined to prevent Hitler taking Stalingrad as Hitler was determined to capture it, and massive reinforcements were poured in as the battle for the South of the city wore on. Everywhere, the Soviet troops displayed a toughness and a skill in street fighting that was quite unexpected by the Germans. The battle for Stalingrad stretched on through September and the Autumn and into the Winter, and by its nature deprived the Germans of their principal strengths — air support and skill in tank warfare. Reduced to street by street clearance of the Russian troops, the Germans found the Soviet army difficult to beat.

To the South, Army Group A's advance on the Caucasus had begun to peter out after the fall of Rostov, and Hitler had become enraged at the failure to make the rapid, searing progress that he had envisaged for the assault. After sending General Jodl to check on Field Marshal List's plans and strategy, and receiving a report from Jodl that he agreed entirely with what List was doing and planning, Hitler dismissed Field Marshal List and, extraordinarily, took command for himself of Army Group A, in addition to his roles as Commander in Chief of OKW (Armed Forces High Command) and Commander in Chief of OKH (Army High Command). Hitler was now personally directing the attack on the Caucasus, and, to cap his other changes, dismissed General Halder from his position as Chief of Staff at OKW and appointed in his place the relatively inex-

perienced General Kurt Zeitzler, whose principal qualification for the task was that he could be relied upon not to disagree with the Fuehrer.

Defending the southern areas of Stalingrad, General Chuikov made the maximum use of the resistance to artillery fire offered by modern concrete commercial buildings, of which there were many in the city, and of the guerilla tactics of sniper fire and Molotov cocktails. More than 1,000 armed workers fought alongside the Russian troops in the defence of the city. At the end of August, on the 27th, Stalin reinforced the Russian armies around Stalingrad by sending Zhukov and the 24th, 66th and 1st Guards Armies to attack the Germans to the North of the City. After some initial failures, Zhukov launched a fierce offensive, supported by heavy bombing by General Golovanov's heavy bombers, but had to report to Stalin that he could not make sufficient headway against the 14th *Panzer* Division to be able to link up with the Russian defenders in the South of the city.

General Paulus' army was taking severe losses, but Hitler was determined to have Stalingrad. On September 12th, 3 *Panzer* Divisions and 11 infantry divisions were added to the German strength in the South of the city. Colonel-General Hoth's *panzers* had penetrated the southern suburb of Kuporosnoye, (thereby dividing the Russian armies) and had taken the high Mamaya Kurgan which provided a commanding view of the city, but lost it again to the

3 It seems possible that the German despatch rider so totally bogged down in the mud was shouting to the photographer to put his camera down and help. The extent of the quagmire in some areas of the Russian front during the autumn of 1942 had to be seen to be believed, and this picture is graphic evidence that there actually was mud that came up to men's knees.

4 If you think the German infantryman has problems, marooned in his foxhole watching the Russian tank advance towards him across the grassland, consider the position of the photographer. Not an occasion to shout 'Hold it!' one suspects. The outcome of the encounter is not recorded, but the photographer survived to bring back this remarkable picture.

5 As the Germans struggled unsuccessfully to reach the Caucasian oilfields, they took the opportunity of launching frequent air attacks on the Soviet Black Sea fleet. This picture, taken by the crew of a German bomber, shows a string of near misses on a row of Soviet submarines in a Black Sea port.

6 The harsh terrain encountered by the German army in Caucasian Russia can be seen clearly in this action picture of part of a German infantry platoon advancing quickly with their heads down across a hilly wasteland.

6

7

8

7 A dramatic picture of one of the first German machine gun crews to be established in the outskirts of Stalingrad, at the beginning of what was to become first one of the most protracted battles for a city of the whole war, and then the greatest and most humiliating defeat the Third Reich ever suffered.

8 The Red Army used aircraft to considerable effect in the mountains of the Caucasus for reconnaissance and artillery spotting. This USSR official photograph of October 1942 shows an improvised Soviet airfield, with two spotter biplanes and their ground crews on the ground in the foreground.

Russian 13th Guards in fierce hand to hand fighting on the 14th. Every day throughout September the Stukas dive-bombed, the shelling continued, and the bloodiest battles ebbed and flowed through the streets of Stalingrad.

At the beginning of October 1942, Paulus was ordered to take the city at any cost, and was supplied with five battalions of sappers to reinforce his efforts. Even this was not enough to ensure results, for the Russian forces continued to be reinforced nightly, as they had been in September, via ferry boats from the other side of the broad River Volga. For every new German that appeared at Stalingrad, there were several new Russians.

The suffering on both sides during the Battle of Stalingrad was appalling. Bombing attacks reduced large areas of the city to rubble.

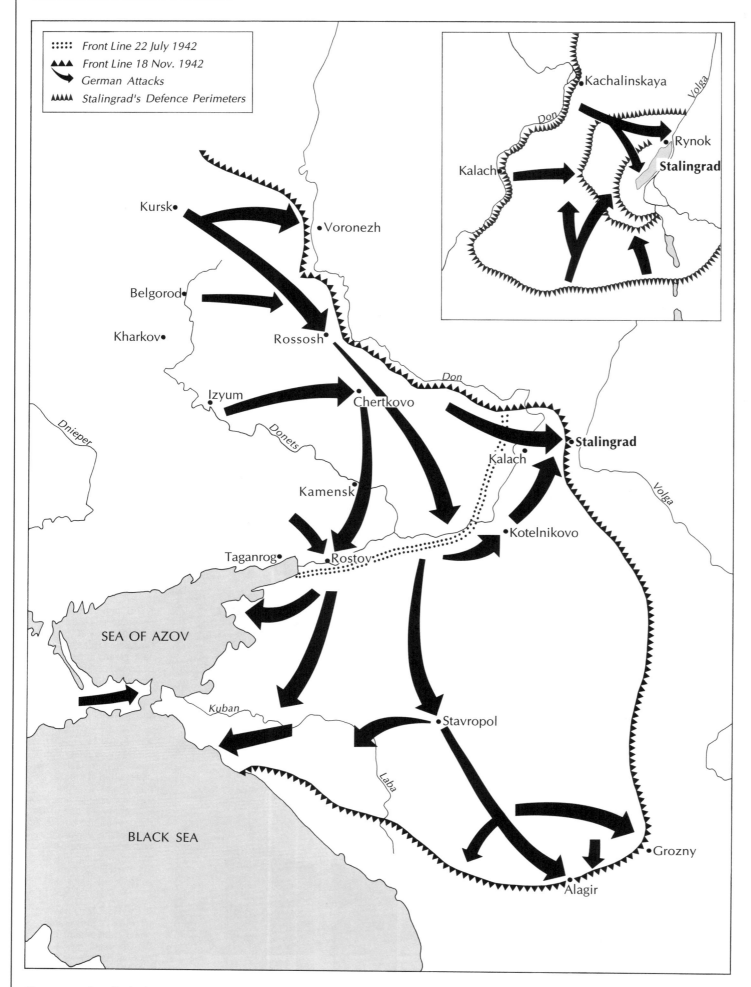

Legend

:::: Front Line 22 July 1942
▲▲▲ Front Line 18 Nov. 1942
➤ German Attacks
▲▲▲▲ Stalingrad's Defence Perimeters

Kursk

Voronezh

Belgorod

Kharkov

Rossosh

Izyum

Donets

Chertkovo

Dnieper

Kamensk

Kalach

Stalingrad

Volga

Taganrog

Rostov

Kotelnikovo

SEA OF AZOV

Kuban

Stavropol

Laba

Grozny

BLACK SEA

Alagir

Kachalinskaya

Volga

Don

Kalach

Rynok

Stalingrad

1 The street fighting for Stalingrad was a no-holds-barred contest with tanks and artillery used freely among the buildings. This German artillery crew was shelling a factory used by the Russian defenders as a base: when issued by the Germans, the picture was captioned 'This is a fight for smoking ruins. Street by street must be cleared of the stubbornly fighting enemy. Our artillery must beat off their bitter counter attacks'.

German tanks climbed over that rubble to the attack and, not infrequently fell victim to snipers with anti-tank rifles, able to get a good shot while the tank was relatively immobile. Civilians had either left and become homeless refugees on the other side of the Volga, or were being killed and maimed in the fighting. The Russian soldiers were being bombed, strafed, shot at and beleaguered from all sides. Yet still they held on.

Both sides planned massive attacks for 7th October. In the event the German assault started first, with two divisions attacking Chuikov's forces on Paulus' direct orders. They stood little chance of success and the attack resulted in enormous slaughter of German troops — almost four battalions were killed and dozens of tanks were destroyed. It has been said that this and other suicidal missions ordered by Paulus had their origin in Paulus' personal ambition to be promoted Field-Marshal once successful at Stalingrad, but it seems more likely that the Germans continued to underestimate the strength of the Russian forces, and their superiority in a street fighting environment.

On October 14th, a massive German push by two *Panzer* Divisions — the 14th and 24th — and two infantry divisions wrought appalling damage on the two major industrial areas of Stalingrad, known as 'Barricades' and 'Dzerzinsky', but, despite inflicting crushing damage, failed to make much headway. Not until a month later did the Germans succeed in penetrating the area of 'Barricades', and cutting off its defenders from the rest of the Russian 62nd Army. But even then, on November 11th, they were unable to press home the final force of their attack. For their men and machines were in a sad state − the two *Panzer* Divisions had fewer than 200 tanks between them, and the German infantry were at less than half strength. Every man was exhausted, most had minor wounds. All were hungry.

Stalingrad's Russian defenders were in a similarly poor state, but the German attacks of November 11th proved to be the last, and Chuikov at last had time to breathe again, albeit for a very short time. Winter was setting in, the ice was forming on the Volga, and once again the Russians planned a winter counter-offensive to take advantage of the Germans' poorer winter equipment and ability to withstand the cold. General Chuikov had only to hold his ground for a little longer.

Away from Stalingrad, Colonel-General von Kleist's 1st *Panzerarmee* had been ground to a halt only some 50 miles from the Groznyy oilfields, and had been unable to reach them. The German forces in the foothills of the Caucasus had been unable to complete the encircling movement that Hitler's Directive required of them. The German advance had come to an end.

The Sixth Army Forced to Surrender

On October 14th, Hitler had issued a Directive ordering all *Wehrmacht* Eastern Front offensives other than in Stalingrad and the Caucasus, to cease. The German forces in Russia were ordered to prepare for winter defence, and it was announced that the Red Army would be destroyed in 1943. He and Zeitzler had decided, again apparently on the basis of intelligence that the Soviet armies had little in reserve, that no Russian offensive would be possible this winter. All the *Wehrmacht* had to do was wait for spring.

In fact, Stalin and Zhukov had spent a large part of October planning alternative versions of a major offensive. The offensive in the North, on the River Don, was to be very similar in concept to that which in August 1942, Hitler had himself warned could occur − foresight which he seemed to have abandoned by November. Codenamed 'Saturn', the northern offensive was to break through the German line and retake a line from Rostov to Milerovo. The alternative plan for a southerly offensive, known as Uranus, sought to break through at two points simultaneously North and South of

2 The close-proximity fighting that ranged for months on end around the city of Stalingrad made the mortar an effective and much-used weapon. This Soviet trench mortar crew is moving under cover of smoke to a new position, since staying in one place for too long with a mortar is likely to attract unhealthy interest.

3 As the battle developed, Stalingrad became more and more derelict, yet still the inhabitants and the Russian army fought on. Street fighting is a terrifying form of warfare − observe the tension in the figures of these German soldiers as they run through alien streets, never sure from where the next shot will come.

4 The battle for Stalingrad was, of course, fought across many miles of open country around the city as well as in the city itself, and Soviet counter-attacks sought from the beginning the objective that they eventually achieved − that of encircling and trapping the German Sixth Army.

the German Sixth Army some sixty miles West of Stalingrad, and encircle the much weakened German forces in the battle-torn city.

Stalin, Vasilievsky and Zhukov opted for 'Uranus', and, on 19th November, ten days after the 'Torch' landings in North Africa, the carefully planned offensive was launched after weeks of personal briefings by Zhukov and his colleagues of all the commanders in the field. To the operation, the Russians brought 1,000,500 men, 13,541 guns, 894 tanks and 1,115 aircraft. Bad weather hampered routine German reconnaissance, and the Germans had little or no idea of what was about to hit them. It has been suggested that 'Uranus' was the greatest surprise the *Wehrmacht* ever received.

The initial attack was to the North of Stalingrad. After an artillery barrage through freezing fog, Russian infantry poured down upon Rumanian Axis troops, who fought vigorously to defend their positions. Unclear as to exactly what was happening, Hitler sent orders from his HQ at Vinnitsa that General Heim's 48th *Panzerkorps* should attack towards Kletskaya. This did not work because the enemy was somewhere else, and the unfortunate Heim lost valuable time and tactical advantage. Instead he found himself facing General Romanenko's 5th Tank Army in the snow, which caused panic among the Rumanian infantry. The 1st Rumanian Armoured Division was virtually annihilated, and the breakthrough in the North was achieved. Late on the 19th, Hitler ordered Paulus to deal with the gap in his defences to the North, not knowing that the next morning would see even bigger events to the South of the line.

Next morning, General Eremenko's southern offensive began with an artillery barrage at 10am, again in freezing fog. The Rumanian 6th Corps surrendered, and what was left of the 4th *Panzerarmee* had to withdraw at considerable speed to avoid being encircled and trapped. Two days later, General Volsky's advance over-ran the positions of the German headquarters, and by November

1 An example of the Soviet BT-7 fast tank, an already obsolescent type when the Germans invaded, but one which continued to be used until the end of 1942. The BT-7 was a derivative of the American Christie design that was also the basis of the British cruiser tanks – notably the Crusader – and had a maximum road speed on tracks of thirty-three mph. However, like the American tanks, it could be converted in less than half an hour by its crew to run on road wheels at speeds of up to 46 mph.

2 The battle for the industrial areas of Stalingrad was fierce and long-lasting, and took a huge toll of lives and property. When it was over, the German soldiers found nothing but ruins. What the fighting had not destroyed, the Russians had sabotaged to ensure that the Germans could not make use of it.

23rd, the Russian forces of the northern and southern attacks had met at the village of Sovetsky to complete the encirclement of the Axis forces in Stalingrad.

To the utter amazement of the unfortunate General Paulus, Hitler sent a telegram commanding him to 'adopt a hedgehog position' and await relief 'when it was convenient'. Paulus swiftly sent a signal back to Hitler telling him that the situation was desperate, that ammunition and petrol supplies were running out, and that the only available course of action was to break out by delivering a knockout blow to the encircling Russians. Colonel-General Weichs, who was still in contact with Paulus, supported this view. He told Hitler that it would be impossible to supply an army of 22 divisions from the air, and that an offensive to relieve Stalingrad could not possibly be launched until December 10th, by which time the 6th Army's position would be desperate in the extreme. Hitler replied, after some hours, with a new order to Paulus to hold Stalingrad at all costs, apparently based on boastful and groundless assurances from Hermann Goering that

500 tons of supplies per day would be dropped to the besieged army by the *Luftwaffe*.

In fact, as winter set in, and the much improved Soviet Air Force took its toll of *Luftwaffe* supply aircraft, the average drop of supplies reaching Stalingrad from December 1st to 12th was only 97.3 tons per day. In the second half of December the figure rose to just over 135 tons per day, then it fell again as the winter weather and the worsening military position made the airlift more difficult. The deficiency of supplies by comparison with Goering's estimate was 81% over the whole 70 days of the airlift, and the Germans lost 488 aircraft, including 266 valuable Ju52 transports.

Besieged within the city and immediately around it, Paulus had 278,000 men and their equipment. The task of relieving the city and making possible the rescue of the 6th Army was given to Field Marshal Erich von Manstein, who had just been given the command, in the third week of November, of a new Army Group, to be called 'Army Group Don'. On November 27th, his command was reinforced

3 This terrified old woman was discovered in her underground hideout in Stalingrad by *Luftwaffe* field troops. Judging by their expressions, they did not intend her much harm, and found the situation mildly amusing – perhaps because of the presence of the German army cameraman who took the picture.

4 By the time the Germans had established themselves with tanks and full equipment in the centre of Stalingrad, the city was little more than a ruin – some token ruins are still preserved in the city, now named Volgagrad, as a memorial. These tanks are providing transport for the infantry as they move into the centre of the city during a comparatively quiet period of the battle.

5 The Germans in Stalingrad had learned not to trust any ruin, however deserted it seemed. Soldiers who advanced too confidently across an apparently deserted area of devastation often paid with their lives for their self-assurance. These infantrymen are obviously taking things very carefully.

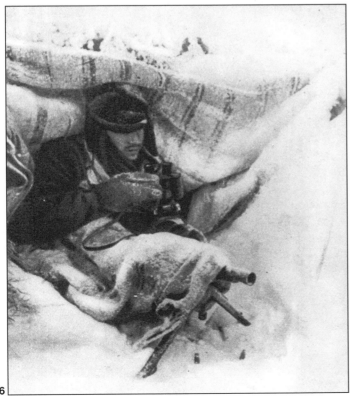

6 By late January, the position in the German lines was very bad. The Russians were putting heavy pressure on the German defences, and the weather was excruciatingly cold. This unfortunate German machine gunner has an unenviable task.

7 The German army had learned much from the terrible experiences of the 1941/42 winter, and were much better equipped with warm, white camouflage clothing. They hoped to sit out the 1942/43 winter in defensive positions, but the Soviet army, also better equipped than the previous year, launched a massive counter-attack. This picture shows the well-prepared trenches that the Germans had dug for the winter.

by the arrival of the first units of the 6th *Panzer* Division, assigned to him from France. Once the whole division had arrived, it added 160 tanks, 42 self-propelled guns and a battalion of half-tracks to his much depleted strength — by now the 4th *Panzerarmee* amounted to little more than one Corps. The 23rd *Panzer* Division, imported from the Caucasus, had only 20 tanks, and the 17th had only 30.

On December 12th-13th, the Germans succeeded in crossing the Aksai River, and, by December 16th, were within 30 miles of Stalingrad after battling 50 miles in eight days. But they were not to succeed, for the Russians launched an attack under Zhukov to destroy the Rumanian 3rd Army and the Italian 8th Army, and thereby open the way for an advance to Rostov. Manstein's plan to bring the 48th *Panzer* Corps across the Don to reinforce the advance on Stalingrad had to be abandoned, and that in turn made it necessary to call the 6th *Panzer* Division back across the Don to counter the Russian offensive. The attempt to relieve Stalingrad was effectively over.

As the New Year came and went, the situation of the Sixth Army became more desperate, and the extent of the criminal disregard of reality by Hitler and Goering in asserting that they could be supplied from the air became clearer. As the Russians advanced towards Rostov, the *Luftwaffe* was obliged to retreat to new bases, which lengthened its flights to the besieged city. General Paulus and his men were starving, virtually without fuel and ammunition, victims of Hitler's megalomaniacal zeal for unattainable victory. On January 8th, the Russians offered Paulus surrender terms under flag of truce. Paulus made no reply. Two days later, the Russians attacked the half-starved German army around Stalingrad with 7,000 guns and mortars. Gradually, the Russians closed in, capturing on January 17th the airfield at Gumrak, the last at which German aircraft could land to bring supplies to Paulus' army. On January 26th, after Hitler had ignored Paulus' appeal to be allowed to surrender, the Russians drove a wedge between two halves of the 6th Army, separating the 71st, 113th, 297th and Rumanian 20th Divisions from Paulus' command. All were obliged to surrender. Finally, on the 31st January 1943, Paulus, newly and cynically promoted Field-Marshal by Hitler, apparently on grounds of superstition because Hitler had noted that no German Field-Marshal had ever surrendered, decided that the end had come. Honourably and with dignity, he surrendered to the Russian General Shumilov. But even that was not the end of the Stalingrad tragedy. General Strecker, commanding the northern pocket of the besieged army, held out until February 2nd. He and his men were the last of the betrayed to surrender.

1 The saddened face of Field-Marshal Paulus after the surrender at Stalingrad, listening to his Soviet interrogator. At his throat is his Knight's Cross. The surrender at Stalingrad marked finally the end of Hitler's *Blitzkrieg* and the beginning of his total defeat. It was Germany's greatest humiliation.

2 This picture, captioned at the time as 'German generals captured after the surrender of Stalingrad' certainly shows senior German officers being marched by Russians through the snow, but it is difficult to identify either their rank or their faces.

3 The final image of Stalingrad must be of the German prisoners, whose army had brought destruction to Stalingrad, being marched away to captivity and, for many of them, a miserable end far from home. Thousands of men, many of them unwilling soldiers, snatched from their lives by the maniacal acts of a dictator and awarded a share of the guilt for oppression and mayhem on a scale the world has rarely seen.

STALEMATE IN BURMA
WINGATE, THE CHINDITS, AND THE BURMA ROAD

An earlier chapter has described, as a part of the story of Japan's whirlwind conquest of South East Asia, the series of events that culminated in the Japanese occupation of Burma, and the Allies' departure to India. As a prelude to subsequent events in this theatre of the war, it is worth taking a look at the reasons why Japan bothered to capture Burma in the first place, and at why she did not then go on to attack India.

The events of 1942 to 1945 in Burma had their origins in Japan's struggle with China, which had begun with the Japanese occupation of Manchuria in 1931 following a faked bomb outrage against Japanese possessions, and their creation of the puppet state of Manchukuo. The League of Nations, to which China had protested, had ineffectually urged Japan to desist from her occupation of Chinese territory, and had been totally ignored. Since, as was always the case, no member of the League was prepared to do more than

4 After Japan's 1931 seizure of Manchuria, and its renaming by them as Manchukuo, new warships were built under Japanese control to form the Manchukuo Navy. This picture shows some of those ships during manoeuvres at the junction of the Sungari and Amur Rivers, at the border of Manchukuo and Siberia.

5 The fierce and bloody Sino-Japanese war, which began in 1937, provided the Japanese armed forces, particularly the air force, with battle training prior to the Second World War, just as the Spanish Civil War did for Germany's pilots. These Japanese troops are parading in Nanking after taking the city at the end of 1937.

6 The Sino-Japanese war even provided the Japanese Marines with experience of amphibious landings, for China's rivers are in many cases so wide that they simulate closely a seaborne landing. These marines are landing from the Yangtse through barbed wire barricades during the successful assault upon Kiukiang in 1938.

express displeasure, however grave the crime, it seemed that there was no country prepared to stand up to Japan.

The United States, a neutral and an isolationist power, was not a member of the League of Nations, had a close relationship with China, and was disturbed that another major Pacific power was acting aggressively, so warned Japan that their sovereignty over territory seized by force would not be recognised. Although this achieved little at the time, the gesture strengthened the ties between the USA and China, and created permanent US distrust of Japanese intentions. By 1937, when Japan invaded the Chinese mainland in force, Japan had signed the Anti-Comintern Pact with Hitler, had made her belief in the destiny of Japan to rule South East Asia clear to those who would listen, and was becoming a formidable military power. By 1939, after a protracted and bloody war, the North and the Eastern coastal strip of China were largely occupied by Japan, but the West and South-West were held by Chinese troops under General Chiang Kai-shek, who continued to fight bravely and well and to contain further Japanese advances. But Chiang Kai-shek had an enemy within as well as the enemy without. Mao Tse-Tung and his Communist revolution sought to dislodge Chiang's hold on China for other reasons, and the USSR, then as now, had every reason to

Stalemate in Burma

support the revolution that might enable a Communist government to seize power.

Thus a complex situation existed in which the Russians were concerned lest the Japanese should capture China, inhibit Mao's revolution and knock at the Eastern door of the Soviet Union; the USA was worried lest the Japanese should over-run their Chinese friends, and the British were concerned that a Japanese victory would position an aggressive Japan just North and East of British possessions. The key to the exercise, Britain and America agreed, rested in maintaining supplies to Chiang Kai-shek via the Burma Road, which ran through the mountains from Lashio, in northern Burma to Chungking, Chiang Kai-shek's capital, and along which vital supplies of arms, fuel and food could be convoyed through incredibly rugged terrain.

When France fell to Germany in June 1940, and Britain was hard-pressed at home, the Japanese applied pressure to Britain to close the road, implying that not to do so would result in severe Japanese reprisals. In the circumstances Britain could do little else but accept the situation, and cut off supplies to Chiang. So, in October 1940, Chiang asked the USA for a fleet of aircraft and pilots to fly his supplies over what became known as the 'hump' — the Eastern Himalayas — from Assam to China. Roosevelt agreed, and in November 1941 the American Volunteer Group was formed with 100

aircraft and pilots under Colonel Claire Chennault, a former US Army Air Force officer. US Lend Lease was now supplying war materials to the Allies in considerable quantities, so far larger supplies of arms began to be flown to Chiang Kai-shek than had been envisaged originally — and there was always the nagging doubt in American minds that Chiang was using the arms more to hold back Mao's Chinese communists than to fight the Japanese. Therefore, Roosevelt sent General Stilwell to act as Chiang's military adviser, and mastermind the training of the Chinese to give the Japanese a hard time.

By April 1942 the Japanese had taken Burma, primarily to close the Burma Road and remove the possibility of Chiang being supplied by road. Because the existing Burma Road started so far to the North-East, at Lashio, Stilwell and Britain's General Wavell, now Commander in Chief in India following his replacement in the Middle East decided they would set as their objective the recapture

1 A picture, taken in 1938, of a scene that was soon to become depressingly familiar throughout South Eastern Asia — columns of straggling Japanese troops on the move, apparently ill-disciplined but in fact totally committed and immensely effective in action.

2 Led by an officer brandishing the sword that every Japanese officer held as almost sacred, these troops were photographed by a Japanese war photographer as they rushed the burning camp of Nationalist Chinese soldiers at Vhangaha.

3 Many of China's Eastern cities were heavily bombed and strafed during the Sino-Japanese war — the destruction in Shanghai was immense. These Japanese fighter biplanes are flying above the Chinese city of Tientsin.

of central Burma and the building of a new road, from Ledo to Kunming. Stilwell therefore began the task of training and re-equipping as many Chinese divisions as he could, and Wavell seized upon a brilliant idea originally conceived by the highly individualistic, academically inclined and even slightly eccentric Brigadier-General Orde Wingate. The idea was the formation of a long-range penetration group, to prove Wingate's belief that victory in South-East Asia could be achieved only by an army prepared to fight in the jungle, away from the confines of the few vulnerable roads and rivers, and willing to accept the hazards of being supplied from the air when necessary. His group became known as the Chindits.

The Chindits were a small force of highly-trained, immensely fit, lightly equipped guerilla marauders who were dropped from the air far behind Japanese lines to harass and disorientate the Japanese troops in the jungle. They were supplied entirely from the air, and

6

7

8

4 Support of Chiang Kai-Shek's Nationalist Chinese army by the USA began more than a year before America was brought into the war, and rapidly grew after the attack on Pearl Harbour. Initially, American aircraft did no more than fly supplies to the army. By 1942, American fighter aircraft like these Curtis P40 Warhawks were being assembled in Burma, then flown to China for the Chinese Air Force. Chinese ground crews were trained in the maintenance of the aircraft in Burma by American training squadrons.

5 The denseness and comparative impassability to vehicles of the Burmese jungle, the mountainous terrain of much of the country and the small number of roads that existed between major strategic locations, made every road important to both sides in Burma. This aerial picture of the winding Imphal-Tiddam road, snaking around the hills, was taken in 1944.

6 This picture is something of a curiosity, showing clearly, or perhaps by its lack of clarity, just how much radio transmission of photographs has improved since 1942. It shows two Japanese platoons advancing on their stomachs during the fighting for the Yenangyaung oilfields in Burma.

7 The Japanese advance through Burma was frequently frustrated by the use of 'scorched earth' techniques, just as was that of the Germans during their advance through Russia, but not every picture is what it seems. This picture was captioned at the time in Britain as showing an example of that policy – it was claimed to be a shot of Japanese troops turning back after encountering burning houses. It is, however, far more likely that they were going on their way after starting the fire.

8 Chinese infantrymen of Chiang Kai-Shek's army positioned in a front-line trench in the central sector of the Salween front in 1943. The smoke in the background is from a Chinese shell bursting close to Japanese positions.

their support team was equipped with a remarkable American short take-off and landing aircraft known as the L1, which enabled them to get Chindit wounded out to base hospitals from relatively small clearings and narrow river banks. The attitude of the Chindits was summarised by Wingate's famous telegram — 'The impossible we do in a day. Miracles take a little longer.'

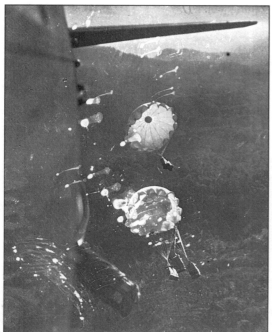

In February 1943, 3,000 Chindits embarked on their first operation, a four-month excursion into Burma to attack the Japanese from behind. In several senses, the operation was a success. It proved conclusively that Wingate's basic contention, backed by General Wavell, was correct. A small, highly mobile force could survive for months in the jungle, doing a great deal of damage to its enemy, while being totally dependent on radio communication and supply from the air. The operation showed that well-trained guerilla troops could cross the heavily defended River Chindwin, despite the all-conquering Japanese presence. It demonstrated to the Japanese that they could not expect the land war to go their way for ever.

Nonetheless, the first Chindit operation cost many lives. Of the 3,000 men who went in by glider and on foot, only 2,200 returned to be the nucleus of the second and far more ambitious Chindit raid. This did not take place until the beginning of 1944, when, over five days from March 5th, a considerable fleet of Allied aircraft transported 9,000 of the Long Range Penetration Group to air strips that had been prepared earlier by smaller Chindit groups, 161 kilometres behind the Japanese lines at Indaw. Later that same month, Orde Wingate, now a Major-General, was killed at the age of 41 in an air crash in Burma. His loss was a sad blow to the Allies.

During the long period from mid 1942, when the Japanese were consolidating their hold on Burma, to the winter of 1943/44, the

1 After being replaced in his Middle Eastern command, General Sir Archibald Wavell (right) became Commander in Chief in India. In April 1942 he flew to Burma to acquaint himself with the situation on that front, and was met by General Hutton, seen here on the left.

2 The enigmatic Brigadier-General Orde Wingate, in a characteristically thoughtful attitude, discussing tactics with his officers at their rudimentary transit camp on the borders of Burma and Assam.

3 Some of Wingate's officers were almost as colourful after their own fashion as he was. This jocular, bemonocled figure is Major Bernard Fergusson of the Black Watch who, despite his benign appearance, had commanded one of of the Chindit columns in the first raid carried out by the Jungle Penetration Force.

4 The key to the success of the Chindit forces was their total reliance upon support from the air – and the reliability of the air force personnel who ran enormous risks to get their supplies to them and ferry out their wounded. This picture was taken by one of the crew of an RAF supply aircraft as it dropped vital supplies to Wingate's men in the jungle below.

5 As the Chindit forces operated against the Japanese covertly, the Nationalist Chinese continued their conventional operations, trained and supported by ever-greater United States investment in maintaining the integrity of Chiang Kai-Shek's position. These Chinese soldiers, photographed late in 1943, had just completed a year's stiff training in jungle fighting and were about to go into action for the first time.

6 In July 1943, two of Wingate's Chindits were rescued from a jungle clearing by an RAF aircraft that made a hazardous landing in minimal space to pick them up. Photographed by an RAF photographer on their return to their rescuer's base, Sergeant Jack Berry of Salford and Sergeant Edward Whittaker of Ashton under Lyne are seen discussing the finer points of a hand grenade which, according to the original (slightly suspect) caption to the picture, they had defused on the flight back.

7 Brigadier-General Wingate, and his colleague Colonel Phil Cochrane, who commanded a unit of 'Air Commandos', (left), were known as 'The Wing and the Beard'. After Wingate, who was by then a Major-General, was killed in an air crash, Cochrane carried on in command until Wingate could be formally replaced, and was successful throughout 1944 in cutting Japanese supply lines which might otherwise have made the opposition to General Stilwell's forces in the North much tougher. With Colonel Cochrane in this picture is Captain John Birkett (centre, with pipe) and an unidentified officer.

8 Successor to General Orde Wingate in command of the Jungle Penetration Group was Major-General Walter D.A. Lentaigne.

9 Short take-off and landing aircraft like this L4 Cub were crucial to the success of the Chindits' operations. This L4 is part of a US Army Air Forces Liaison Squadron which specialised in the evacuation of wounded from improbable landing strips, and is seen here making use of the Ledo road while it was still under construction.

10 Admiral Lord Louis Mountbatten, (foreground), with General Stilwell, commander of the US and Chinese forces in Northern Burma when Mountbatten, as Supreme Allied Commander in South-East Asia, returned from a London conference to meet his commanders in Ceylon, now Sri Lanka.

Burma front was almost entirely stalemated. The Japanese, having cut the Burma Road, seemed disinclined to devote more effort to the capture of territory in the Indian sub-continent, and the Allies lacked the resources to do more than contain the Japanese in their current positions. General Wavell's attempt in the Spring of 1943 to recapture Akyab, on the west coast of the Arakan peninsula, failed for lack of amphibious support from the sea — the landing craft had been appropriated for operations against the Vichy French in Madagascar — and achieved little. But during the 1943/44 winter, both sides began to brew some action for early 1944. The Japanese had recognised that, although the Burma Road was not available for Chiang Kai-shek's supply line, the US Air Force were achieving significant successes with their airlift of supplies over the 'hump', and resolved to close the air route. To do this, they decided to attack and cut the Bengal-Assam railway, which connected the port of Calcutta with the Indian railhead used for Chiang's supplies.

The Allies meanwhile, by now under the command of Admiral Lord Louis Mountbatten with Stilwell as his deputy, had resolved to launch attacks by General Stilwell's by now well-trained Chinese forces towards Myitkyina, by the British 14th Army towards Indaw, and by Chiang Kai-shek's army westward across the Salween River from China. The 14th Army was also to take Akyab.

In the event, the Japanese offensive began first, and in the early stages made strong progress through the Arakan hills to outflank the forward units of the 14th Army. But the commander of the 14th Army was one of the truly remarkable Generals of the Second World War — General (later Field Marshal) Sir William Slim. Keeping cool, and assessing that the principal strength of the Japanese lay in their skill in jungle warfare, and that their main weakness was in open battle, Slim withdrew to two highly defensible positions at Imphal and Kohima. There he made his stand, and wrought a defeat that was the beginning of the end for the Japanese in Burma.

CHAPTER 23

U.S. COUNTER~ATTACK
DRAMA IN THE PACIFIC ~ GUADALCANAL

The Battle of Midway had brought harsh realisation to Japan that they had not wrought at Pearl Harbour the devastation of the US Pacific Fleet that they had intended, even believed, and that they now had little hope of bringing about the destruction of the fleet at sea. The easternmost line of the Japanese Empire seemed stationary at the point where Midway had stopped it — from the Aleutians in the North, past Wake Island to the Gilbert Islands.

In the West, Japan had wisely decided not to emulate Hitler's Napoleonic dreams of conquering Russia, and had advanced no further than her prewar positions along the coastal strip of eastern China and in Manchuria. In Burma, Japan had stopped short of pushing South into India. There was only one place left into which Japan might profitably and with some prospect of success attempt to expand — the southern part of New Guinea and the southern Solomon Islands. From airfields there, the Japanese would be able to bomb and disrupt the vital Allied shipping routes between the USA and Australia, where General MacArthur was building the Allied forces for a counter-attack. Despite the Allied policy of defeating Germany first, a large proportion of the Allied reinforcements that were available for all theatres were being diverted to Australia — for every American soldier sent to Europe in the first half of 1942, four were sent to the Pacific theatre, and Australian units in the Middle East were withdrawn to defend the homeland.

In July 1942, US Intelligence became aware that the Japanese were building an air base on the island of Guadalcanal, at almost the extreme southern tip of the Solomon Islands. The threat was clear and immediate. A plan that had already been agreed and briefed to senior commanders for an amphibious invasion in the Solomon Islands was put into effect. At dawn on August 7th, eight months to the day after the Japanese attack on Pearl harbour, a massive bombardment from the sea heralded the arrival of the first major seaborne invasion fleet of the Second World War off Guadalcanal and its nearby smaller islands, all of them heavily defended by the Japanese.

Three hours after the Navy's bombardment began, the gunfire ceased and the US Marines under Major-General Vandegrift landed with an initial deceptive lack of opposition. They captured the airfield that was still under construction, fought out a few short sharp engagements on the surrounding islands, and then paused, wondering when the trouble would start. They were not left wondering for long. Two days after the initial landings, a Japanese Navy force struck suddenly at the US Navy off Guadalcanal and sank four ships, one of them Australian, before disappearing as suddenly as it had come without attacking the many vulnerable transport vessels that were sitting duck targets.

Over the next two months, with periodic harassment from the

1 Operation Watchtower, the American assault to take the Pacific island of Guadalcanal, at the southern tip of the Solomons, began on August 7th 1942. It was the first of many seaborne landings carried out by the US Marines during the Second World War, and one can sense from this picture of the Marines embarking on their invasion barges for the final run to the beach the tension that must have prevailed.

2 The shelling of Guadalcanal before the Marines went in raised a pall of thick smoke from the island, on the horizon in this picture of the landing craft making their way to shore over a choppy sea.

3 The worst moment of any seaborne invasion, and one where, frequently, many men are lost, is the first sprint from the landing craft on to the beach and to whatever cover is available. Although there was, in fact, little opposition to the initial landing on Guadalcanal, the photographer who took this shot must have been wondering who was watching his back.

4 Some idea of the conditions under which the US Marines sought and fought well-entrenched and suicidally-inclined Japanese troops can be gained from this picture of a US patrol in the jungle on Guadalcanal. Local hazards of poisonous reptiles and insects, and the constant problem of dysentery and other diseases were at times almost as unnerving as the snipers.

5 High on a grassy hill some four miles west of Henderson Field, American troops dig in to await developments.

6 Although this picture is not of high quality, it does convey some idea of the remarkably effective camouflage that the Japanese army was able to assume. These troops blend into the landscape around them and would easily pass unnoticed from an observation point or low-level aerial reconnaissance.

7 One of the high spots for the Americans of a series of naval engagements off Guadalcanal was the night-time sinking of seven and the damaging of the remaining four of a fleet of Japanese transport ships sent to bring supplies to the Japanese army on the island. On the morning after that battle, an SBD-5 Dauntless is silhouetted against the morning sun as Japanese ships burn on the shoreline.

8 This picture, shot during one of many Japanese airborne torpedo attacks on the transport fleet supplying the US Marines on Guadalcanal, shows the intensity of the anti-aircraft fire that the US ships and shore emplacements could muster. The Japanese pilots are flying almost at wavetop height to avoid the lethal shellbursts.

Japanese, the US Marines built up their presence on the island until more than 17,000 troops were on the exposed area around the airfield. Japanese naval vessels bombarded the US troops and their supply ships at increasingly short intervals, and detachments of Japanese troops were sent by sea from Rabaul. Two and a half months after the original August landings, in late October, the Japanese chanced their arm on a major carrier sea battle, sending a task force that included four of their aircraft carriers to the area of the Pacific North of the island. Two US Navy aircraft carrier forces went out to meet them, one led by the *Hornet*, the other by the *Enterprise*, the whole operation being under the command of Admiral Thomas Kinkaid.

The fierce naval gunnery and air battle that followed, known as the Battle of the Santa Cruz Islands, resulted in the Japanese losing two destroyers, and having two carriers and two battleships badly damaged. Japanese dive bombers inflicted severe damage of the USS *Hornet*, which was subsequently sunk by Japanese naval gunfire with considerable loss of life. But the battle did nothing to conclude the matter of Guadalcanal. Just over two weeks later, the Japanese Navy once again attempted to re-establish its dominance on Guadalcanal and repel the American invasion. A large Imperial Navy task force carrying troops to reinforce the Japanese forces still on Guadalcanal arrived during the night of November 13th, and the two battleships

U.S. Counter-Attack

and many smaller warships of the Japanese fleet began furiously to shell the American fleet. In the darkness a considerable melee developed, and the Japanese, in what can only be described as the naval equivalent of close hand to hand fighting, lost a battleship. The US Navy lost two cruisers, one of them, the *Juneau*, with 700 men aboard, including a family of five brothers named Sullivan. Two other US ships were damaged, but the US emerged from the first night of the Naval Battle of Guadalcanal bloody but unbowed.

The next night aircraft from the USS *Enterprise* did severe damage to another smaller Japanese squadron, but the major turning point came when US aircraft from the captured airfield on Guadalcanal, now known as Henderson Field, scored a major victory by sinking seven and damaging the remaining four of a force of eleven transport vessels bringing Japanese troops to the island. Now the Japanese gathered up their remaining naval resources in the area for a last try at getting a significant force of reinforcements ashore. A battleship and four cruisers approached Guadalcanal at high speed along the infamous channel between the islands known as 'The Slot'. As they came from one direction, Admiral Willis A. Lee and a US Navy flotilla approached from the other. Lee hurled his force precipitately but effectively into the battle, and claimed another battleship sunk and two more cruisers damaged. By the next day, the Japanese knew they had lost another round, and with it the naval battle of Guadalcanal, for they simply did not have sufficient naval forces remaining in the area to pursue the attack.

Now the Japanese land forces in the densely overgrown jungle

1 Improvisation is the name of the game in jungle warfare, and the engineers with the US Marines on Guadalcanal were not short of ideas. Here they have used amphibian tractors (visible on the left of the picture) to provide the foundations for a bridge over a stream.

2 The commander of the US Marines on Guadalcanal, Major-General Alexander A. Vandegrift (left) with Colonel Gerald Thomas (centre) and Colonel Merritt Edson after they and their men had driven the Japanese from positions on the Matanikau River.

3 The Japanese army made considerable use of flame throwers during the war in the Pacific. During the Battle of Tenaru, part of the campaign to recapture Guadalcanal, this flame thrower was captured by the US Marines, and was subsequently demonstrated to the press by a Marine to show just how inhuman a weapon it was.

4 Among the few Japanese taken alive during the Guadalcanal campaign – some 12,000 soldiers were evacuated by the Japanese Navy – were these members of a Labour Battalion, who, lacking the strict code of honour of the soldier which regarded capture as deeply shaming, allowed themselves to be captured by the Marines and put into a barbed wire compound.

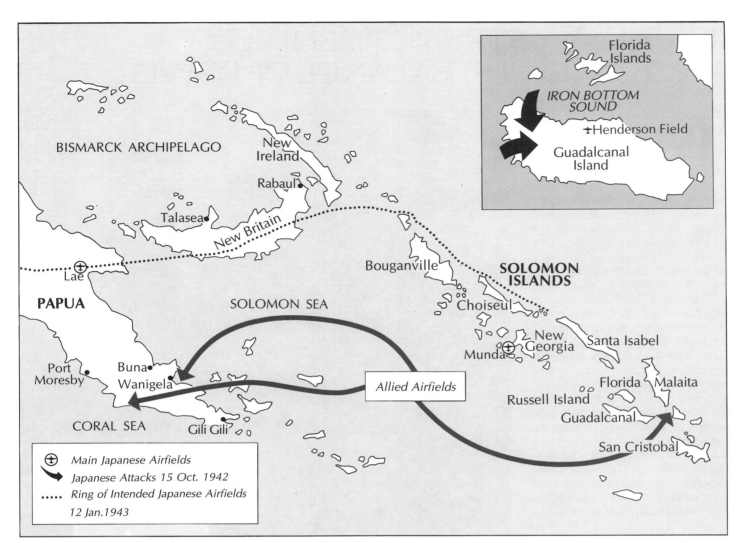

5 Helped by American troops, these emaciated Japanese prisoners, captured at Kokumbun on Guadalcanal Island, were taken to the beach, put aboard barges and ferried to prison camps. Their poor condition is the result of near starvation after they were cut off from all sources of supply but continued to hold out and fight.

of Guadalcanal were on their own without potential for reinforcement, and the young and, until now, almost entirely inexperienced US Marines began the task of flushing out skilled Japanese jungle-trained troops from what was virtually their natural environment. Tackling this task amid heat, discomfort, decomposing vegetation and the risks of poisonous reptiles and insects, often racked with dysentery, malaria and a host of minor ills, the Marines, whose average age was only nineteen years, had also to face the even greater risk of encountering suicidally motivated Japanese snipers. Despite these privations, they methodically fought their way across the island, winkling out pockets of Japanese soldiers from caves and dugouts as they went.

During the first week of February 1943, the Japanese decided that they had little chance of success on Guadalcanal, and sent in the Imperial Navy at night to evacuate the remaining Japanese troops, some 12,000 of them, from Cape Esperance on the north-western

corner of the island. Their evacuation was almost totally successful. At last, Guadalcanal was in American hands, the Japanese had been defeated on land for the first time, and American morale shot sky-high. Now the Marine Corps, having earned a brief respite, built and equipped a rest and retraining centre among the palm trees of Guadalcanal. In the months that followed it was to be sorely needed, for Tokyo, the ultimate goal of the US island hopping campaign across the Pacific, was still 3,000 miles away.

The US forces had lost 1,600 dead during the campaign for Guadalcanal, with just over 4,700 wounded. The Japanese losses were astronomical. No less than 24,000 Japanese soldiers died. The Japanese Navy lost 1 aircraft carrier, 2 battleships, 4 cruisers, 11 destroyers, 6 submarines (including their semi-experimental giant I-1 sub) and 16 transport vessels. The US Navy lost 2 carriers, 8 cruisers, 17 destroyers, 6 MTBs and 4 transports. It had been an expensive but, from the Allies' standpoint, necessary campaign.

6 Each of the battles fought during the Guadalcanal campaign, and, indeed, during most of the Pacific war, ended with Japanese dead piled high in grisly heaps, victims of their own code of honour and willingness to die in suicidal *banzai* attacks. Here, US Marines are examining the crop of death and mutilation wrought by their latest action.

CHAPTER 24

CASABLANCA ~ STRENGTHENING OF THE ALLIANCE AND THE BALANCE OF POWER

After a year of America's participation in the war, the extent of the political manoeuvre and counter-manoeuvre between the Allied leaders seemed to be increasing rather than decreasing as 1943 began. The previous year had seen endless discussion between Roosevelt and Churchill and their respective political advisers and generals on the strategic objectives that the Allies should adopt. 'Bolero', the building and training of a potential invasion force for the opening of a second front on continental Europe, had been agreed as a policy early in 1942, and put into effect. 'Sledgehammer', the creation of a limited bridgehead in Europe, was still in the discussion stage. 'Roundup', the full scale invasion of Europe from the United Kingdom, for which General Dwight D. Eisenhower had been campaigning, had been abandoned as a short term objective in July/August 1942, much to the displeasure of Josef Stalin, who raged at Churchill and accused Britain of cowardice when Britain's Prime Minister went to Moscow to discuss strategy in August. Instead of 'Roundup', which Churchill knew was far beyond the Allies' state of preparedness in 1942, Operation Torch had been mounted against French North Africa, and had been successful.

The second Battle of Alamein had changed the character of the war in North Africa, and it was clear that the days of domination of the Western Desert by the Axis were past. In the Pacific, the year that had begun so catastrophically with Japan's sweep through the islands; with Corregidor; with Singapore; had suddenly become the year of Midway and Guadalcanal and the dawning of the realisation that the Japanese could be and would be defeated. The year had ended with the Germans encircled at Stalingrad, and faltering on their drive to the Caucasus. There were undoubtedly more successes to the Allies' credit than they might have dared to hope just a few months

earlier. As Winston Churchill said in a speech at the Mansion House in the City of London; 'This must not be taken as the end; it may possibly be the beginning of the end; but it is certainly the end of the beginning'.

The political discussions at the end of 1942 had extended even to lengthy arguments about who should be allowed to take part in the discussions. Roosevelt and Churchill agreed that a conference was necessary to determine future policy, but Churchill, who showed a frank dislike and mistrust of Stalin, wanted to meet Roosevelt and agree a common strategic policy for the future conduct of the war with which jointly to confront Stalin. Roosevelt disagreed, believing that to be seen to conspire against Stalin would be intensely damaging to the future of the alliance with Russia. In the event, Stalin resolved that particular conundrum by pointedly declining to attend the Casablanca conference on the grounds that his army was busy defeating Germany at Stalingrad, and he had better things to do.

Thus the conference that assembled in two luxurious rented villas high in the hills behind Casablanca between January 14th and 23rd 1943 consisted only of Roosevelt and Churchill and their chiefs of staff, with their entourages and aides housed in a nearby hotel. Essentially, the conference was faced with deciding two major, fundamental and interdependent issues. The first was the balance of war resources to be allotted to the European war on the one hand, and to the Pacific war on the other. The second was the question of whether the Allied invasion of Europe should be from the Mediter-

ranean during 1943, or across the Channel from Britain, probably rather later.

The British team, often subsequently accused of railroading the US delegation to accepting their viewpoint, certainly came better equipped with a closely argued case than did their US counterparts. The fact that Churchill was now Britain's Minister of Defence as well as her Prime Minister, and his effective role as Commander in Chief and pivot of all policy, ensured that the facts and figures presented in support of the British contention that Europe should be invaded from the Mediterranean were almost incontrovertible. Churchill had in fact argued strongly before the conference for the original 'Round-up' plan for a cross-channel invasion during 1943 following the success of Operation Torch, but had eventually been dissuaded by his service chiefs on the basis of the sheer weight of evidence that showed such a plan not to be practical. That the Allies agreed that the defeat of Germany must be given a higher priority than the humbling of Japan was already settled – the only question was one of degree.

General George C. Marshall and the US military staff argued strongly that the resources allocated to the Pacific should be sufficient to permit offensive action against the Japanese and to prevent them being able to choose their times and places for battle. The US planners proposed Pacific offensives from the Solomons and New Guinea to New Britain and Rabaul, through the Gilbert, the Marshall and the Caroline Islands to the Japanese naval base at Truk, and against

1 At the Casablanca Conference in two villas high above the city, President Roosevelt and Britain's Prime Minister Winston Churchill, with their aides and staff, conferred in strict secrecy on the whole spectrum of the war, and did not hold a press conference until the morning of January 24th 1943. Then, according to Churchill in his memoirs, 'When the Press reporters saw us both they could scarcely believe their eyes or, when they were told we had been there for nearly a fortnight, their ears'.

2 The one that stayed away – Josef Stalin (centre), with Vyacheslav Molotov, the Soviet Foreign Minister (left) and Marshal Semyon Timoshenko, who commanded the Soviet 61st and 62nd Armies of the Stalingrad Front against Field-Marshal von Weichs' Army Group Centre. Stalin made it clear that he regarded discussion of the reasons why the Western Allies could not open a Second Front in Europe as less important than actually fighting the crucial battles of the Eastern Front, and it is difficult not to concede his point.

3 The Casablanca Conference brought together an impressive collection of British and American political and military 'brass'. In this picture are (front row) President Roosevelt and Winston Churchill; (standing, left to right) Lieutenant-General Henry H. Arnold, Chief of the US Army Air Forces; Admiral Ernest J. King, Commander-in-Chief, US Navy; General George C. Marshall, US Chief of Staff; Admiral Sir Dudley Pound, Chief of Naval Staff (Britain); General Sir Alan Brooke, Chief of the Imperial General Staff; and Air Chief Marshal Sir Charles Portal.

4 The French were represented at Casablanca by General Giraud (far left) and by General Charles de Gaulle, who had rapidly become the best-known and most unpredictable Frenchman since Napoleon. Both Frenchmen had an interest close to home in the talks, for they discussed at length how, when and where the Allies should re-invade their homeland.

Casablanca

Japanese positions in the Aleutians to regain the islands of Kiska and Agattu. In Burma, the Americans postulated, the time had come for a land based offensive to reopen the Burma Road, and for a seaborne invasion of Burma, both with the objective of making Chiang Kai-shek's forces better supplied and more available as an effective ally — an asset of whose value the British were by now somewhat doubtful. The American viewpoint on the European invasion remained, as it had been a year earlier, strongly in favour of a head-on cross-channel confrontation with the German Army. The US military staff believed that the war would and could be shortened by a cross-channel invasion in 1943.

The British position was more circumspect in its approach. In the first place, great stress was laid upon the necessity of winning the Battle of the Atlantic and defeating the U-Boat menace. If the convoys did not get through from the USA to Europe and from Britain to the USSR, the war with Germany might well be lost. The British military staff, with memories of the huge and bloody stalemate of the trenches of 1914-18, did not believe in the advisability of a full-scale confrontation with the German Army until the Allied armies were stronger, and the German armies were weaker. Since the scale of the German defeat at Stalingrad, and the probability of further major disasters for Germany in the East, suggested that time would certainly weaken the might of the Third Reich, Britain favoured a waiting game. Nevertheless, to hasten the weakening of Germany's resources, Britain proposed an increased bombing offensive to damage further German armaments production and her ability to supply her armies and air force, and an invasion of Italy from the Mediterranean. In the Pacific, the British position was that no more than the offensives from the Solomons and New Guinea, and limited operations in Burma to open road communication to Chiang Kai-shek and, possibly, to recapture Akyab, were desirable or feasible in 1943 given the available budget.

Not suprisingly, after four days of wearisome conference

1

2

discussion, the two sides were poles apart in their proposals. General Sir Alan Brooke, the British Chief of the Imperial General Staff, argued for many hours with General Marshall over the issue of the cross-channel invasion, making the point that Germany could, in 1943, mass 44 divisions in France without withdrawing any from Russia, and that it was strategically sounder to invade Italy and force Italy out of the war. This, he argued, would oblige Germany to find troops to replace the Italian garrisons in the Balkans, would deprive Germany of the Italian troops currently fighting in Russia, and would improve the Allies' position in North Africa if that were still a problem at the time of the Italians' defeat.

Gradually, Marshall's colleagues were forced to recognise the merits of other aspects of the British case. It was agreed that an invasion of Italy would disperse German air power, and make effective bombing of German industry more possible. Admiral King came to support a landing in Sicily. Eventually General Marshall came round to accepting the Mediterranean concept, and a Memorandum on the Conduct of the War in 1943 was drawn up for signature. Essentially this allocated the greater part of Allied resources to the defeat of Germany in 1943, but allocated 'adequate forces . . . to the Pacific and Far Eastern theatres'. A 'full scale offensive against Japan by the United Nations' was promised 'as soon

1 General Henri Giraud (left) had, following the successful Allied invasions of North Africa two months previously and the subsequent assassination of Admiral Darlan, become High Commissioner of French North Africa. He and de Gaulle were implacably opposed because of Giraud's former association with the Vichy Government, and de Gaulle had initially refused to attend the conference. According to Churchill 'de Gaulle and Giraud were made to sit in a row of chairs, alternating with the President and me, and we forced them to shake hands in public. ...They did so, and the pictures of this event cannot be viewed even in the setting of these tragic times without a laugh'.

2 A fascinating picture of the press call on January 24th 1943, held on the lawn in front of Villa No.2, which marked the end of the Casablanca Conference. It is of particular interest to those who, like the author, are interested in photography and the history of cameras, for it shows clearly the different approaches of the US war photographer, who, like most of his kind, continued to rely on a 5"x 4" Speed Graphic plate camera, and of the British war correspondent who is using a Zeiss Super Ikonta folding rollfilm camera and a Rolleiflex – both, it shuld be noted, good German cameras! The WAAC stenographer on the right is Captain Louise Anderson of Denver, Colorado, who had the distinction of being the only woman present at the Casablanca Conference.

3 President Roosevelt making the famous speech in which, without Allied agreement to an announcement, he referred to the decision to exact 'unconditional surrender' from the Axis powers. Churchill wrote that 'It was with some feeling of surprise' that he heard these words, and his expression in this picture certainly bears this out. The 'unconditional surrender' statement, with which Churchill spontaneously concurred in his subsequent speech at the conference, was greatly criticised by many analysts as having lengthened the war by reducing the possibility of a compromise to end hostilities, but Churchill disagreed with this viewpoint.

as Germany is defeated'. The Mediterranean was to be the principal area of Allied effort, and Sicily the first target. The 'defeat of the U-boats remains first charge on resources' the Memorandum stated, and it went on that 'Russia must be sustained by greatest volume of supplies . . . without prohibitive cost in shipping'.

Having reached agreement on policy, the Casablanca conference now tackled the task of planning how to achieve the agreed objectives. The conference agreed that the bombing of the yards where U-boats were built and maintained should be stepped up; that the shortage of escort vessels for Atlantic convoys must be rectified. The strategic bombing offensive against German industry was agreed in detail, including what proved to be the immensely costly and relatively ineffective US precision daylight bombing by unescorted formations. The invasion of Sicily — Operation Husky — was scheduled for the end of August, and it was agreed that the build-up of US forces in Britain for the eventual cross-Channel invasion should be continued.

Perhaps the most significant outcome of the Casablanca conference was the decision to accept nothing less than total surrender from Germany and Japan — the so-called 'total surrender

policy'. Although arguably a propaganda-inspired decision to appease Stalin's scathing view of his (as he saw it) weak-kneed allies, a view that could be expected to become still more disparaging when he learned that there was to be no cross-Channel invasion early in 1943, the 'total surrender policy' was also a reflection of the realisation that much of the cause of the Second World War lay in the inconclusive ending of the first. Germany had been left with a feeling of 'unfinished business' as well as her sense of betrayal at the terms of Versailles. The Allies did not intend that the Second World War should end with an undefeated Germany or Japan hungering for a chance to start the third.

The Casablanca conference was one of the most significant meetings of the war, and represented the point at which the US and British conflicts of viewpoint were finally reconciled into a cohesive joint policy that was followed by both sides of the alliance. Had the nations of the Axis been as successful in meeting, reconciling their opposing viewpoints and putting common policies into action, the war may have followed a different course. Rarely in history has unity been such a source of strength.

CHAPTER 25

TUNISIA AND THE END OF THE AFRIKA KORPS

The autumn of 1942 had brought major Allied successes in North Africa. Having been roundly defeated by the British 8th Army at El Alamein, Field Marshal Rommel was, during November, retreating as fast as he could to Tunisia, in the hope that he would be able to inflict there a crushing defeat on the recently arrived American and British forces under General Eisenhower. Because the agreed plan for Operation Torch had precluded any landing where fighter air cover was not available, there had been no Allied landings East of Algiers, some 400 miles from Tunis. Rommel knew that, if he could get to Tunis soon enough, the potential was there for inflicting considerable damage on the British 1st Army formation under Lieutenant-General Anderson.

The German and Italian High Commands, not for the first time, saw things rather differently. Hitler ordered Rommel to hold and defend the position at Marsa el Brega, which General Montgomery and the Eighth Army approached on December 13th 1942. The Italians had earlier ordered him to hold the Sollum — Halfaya line, a patent impossibility given the great superiority of equipment that Montgomery's army had after Alamein, and Rommel had treated the Italian command with the contempt it deserved. However, the Fuehrer's order to hold Marsa el Brega, on the extreme western edge of Cyrenaica, was not entirely without merit. Field Marshal

1 The immensely tough French troops commanded by General Leclerc, later to become beloved of all Frenchmen for his precipitate arrival to liberate Paris, played an important part in the Tunisian campaign. These French soldiers were typical of Leclerc's army, which made one of the greatest treks in military history.

2 The remarkable General Leclerc was the stuff that heroes are made of. Wounded during the fall of France, and unable to leave France before occupation, he escaped in civilian clothes by borrowing a bicycle from a German soldier and pedalling to freedom. He rapidly became one of the greatest field commanders in French military history. In 1943 he led the great march from Chad, and is seen here (right) with two of his soldiers in Tunisia.

Im Kampfgelände von Tebourda

Das erste größere Zusammentreffen der Achsen-
streitkräfte mit den anglo-amerikanischen Verbän-
den in Tunesien, die zwischen Tunis und Bizerta
durchstoßen sollten, um von hier aus die deutschen
Stellungen aufzurollen, hat mit einem eindeutigen
Sieg der deutsch-italienischen Kräfte geendet.
Unsere Aufnahmen zeigen deutsche Grenadiere, die
im Gelände von Tebourda unseren vorstoßenden
Panzern folgen. Darunter: Panzerschützen beim
„Stellungswechsel nach vorn"

Tebourda

Links:
Schwere Flak geht im Kampfgelände von Tebourda
in Stellung

PK-Aufnahmen · Kriegsberichter Arere (Seh)

3 The German success at Tebourba-Djedeida against the British 'Blade Force' was one of the few opportunities afforded the German propagandists for exultation during the Tunisian campaign. These German PzKpfw III medium tanks were photographed driving into Tebourba itself.

4 An example of contemporary German magazine editorial on the successes of the German army at Tebourba (the spelling varies according to language). The crew of the 88mm gun are Grenadiers, holding positions in the vicinity of Tebourba.

5 British Crusader III cruiser tanks, photographed in Tunisia in January 1943. This late marque of the Crusader, introduced in time for Alamein, had the much improved six-pounder gun, and significantly greater reliability than earlier Crusaders, but was nonetheless outdated by this late stage of the North African campaign, being relatively lightly-armoured. More Crusaders fell into Axis hands because of mechanical failure than were knocked out in battle.

6 Field-Marshal Erwin Rommel meets Lieutenant-General Walther Nehring for discussion of tactics during the Tunisian campaign. This is the Rommel of the popular imagination of the time – sand-goggles, binoculars with eyepiece cap, informal scarf. Nehring was later to have commands on the Eastern Front during bitter fighting as the Russians advanced upon Germany.

7 A powerful picture of a group of German parachute troops, apparently sizing up some Allied activity in the distance. Extensive use was made of motor-cycle and sidecar combinations by the German Armed Forces.

8 Rommel fought his last battle in Africa at Medenine against the British Eighth Army on March 6th 1943, knowing that he could not win, and sustaining heavy losses to British anti-tank guns. Three days later he left Africa for the last time. This picture is the classic study of a fine soldier and one of the greatest field commanders of the century.

Kesselring, no mean tactician, believed that Montgomery's advance could have been delayed for weeks or even months if he had been made to fight for the 700 miles between Marsa el Brega and Gabes, a town in Tunisia on the western side of the great gulf that forms the Libyan coast. Rommel nonetheless resolved to retreat from Libya as rapidly as possible, believing that if the remains of *Panzerarmee Afrika* made a stand, it would achieve little, and that by strategic withdrawal to Tunis and Bizerta, the veterans of the *Afrika Korps* could first take part in the battle in Tunisia, and then, if that went badly, as Rommel believed it would, be repatriated safely to Europe to continue the war.

In fact, although by his retreat he envisaged lending the weight of his army to the Axis defence of Tunisia, he also assisted the Allied assault on Tunisia by bringing Montgomery's 8th Army to bear on the South-East of the country as Eisenhower's forces, including the British 1st Army under General Anderson, attacked in the North-West. Throughout the latter part of November and December, the build-up of German forces in Tunisia under Colonel-General Hans-Jurgen von Arnim had continued. After December 8th, these were known as the 5th *Panzerarmee*, and by December 31st, von Arnim was in command of 47,000 German troops and more than 17,000 Italians, a battalion of Tiger tanks and the 10th *Panzer* Division,

Tunisia

brought in from a comparatively peaceful existence in France. The *Luftwaffe* in North Africa, under the energetic overseeing eye of Kesselring, had been extensively re-equipped and had during December regained effective control of Tunisian airspace, thereby limiting drastically the availability of photo-reconnaissance information to the Allies, and wreaking destruction on Allied supply convoys and troop movements.

Since the negotiated armistice with the French forces in North Africa following Operation Torch in November, substantial French formations had become available to Eisenhower, and the resourceful Frenchmen had miraculously 'rediscovered' large stocks of pre-war vintage arms that had been concealed from the Armistice Commission after the fall of France in June 1940. The French 19th Corps in particular was well dug into defensive positions on the Eastern Dorsale, a mountainous area overlooking the coastal plain of Tunisia, in the vicinity of the holy city of Kairouan and the coastal ports of Sousse and Sfax, and the Barre Group was similarly dug in along the Medjerda River. Their task was to cover the US forces entering the front line between Gafsa and the Mediterranean, along the western edge of Tunisia.

On January 18th 1943, a German force of infantry and tanks attacked and surprised the Barre Group, completely outclassing their outdated French guns with the latest Tiger tanks. Von Arnim followed up this success at the Medjerda River with a push south, but was repulsed by a counter attack by the US Army II Corps. The inability of the French troops, equipped as they were, to fight the German formations on equal terms lent support to changes in the command

1 A last look at Africa, eyes screwed up against the sun, memories crowding in of great victories and proud times, now gone in defeat. Erwin Rommel goes home to Europe; beyond his gaze a German U-Boat also puts to sea, bent on destruction in the Mediterranean.

2 Before the crucial battle for the fortified Mareth Line on the border between Libya and southeast Tunisia, a British Eighth Army tank C.O. briefs his tank crews under the desert sun.

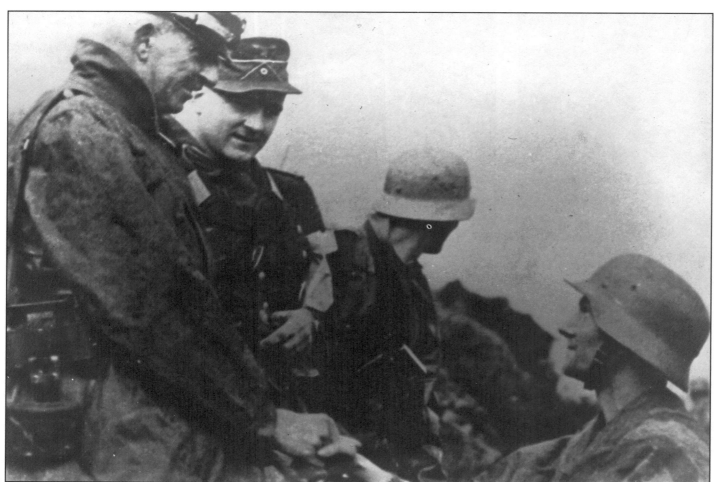

3 On the American front, north and west of Tunisia, the armoured divisions were well equipped and, because they had seen relatively little action, their tanks and armoured vehicles were in good fighting condition. This impressive picture is of an M10 tank destroyer – sometimes called the Wolverine – which, with the 0.5" M2 anti-aircraft machine gun visible in the picture, a 3" M7 anti-tank gun at the forward end, five crew and a road-speed of thirty mph was a formidable weapon. M10 vehicles delivered to the British army had their 3" gun removed and a 17-pounder installed instead. This version, known as the 'Achilles' was a far more effective tank-destroyer, and was one of the best anti-tank weapons of the war.

4 After Rommel's departure from Africa on March 9th 1943, his command was assumed by Colonel-General Hans-Jurgen von Arnim (left), here seen shortly before his promotion to a post virtually certain to lead to his death or capture

structure brought about by the Casablanca conference, which took place in Morocco at the same time as these events were occurring. From the beginning of 1943, the French troops were absorbed directly into the British 1st Army. General Juin, who had commanded the French forces in North Africa, was given the task of creating and training the French Expeditionary Corps, later to play an important part in the battle of Monte Cassino.

At the end of January, Rommel finally withdrew from Tripoli and into Tunisia, and viewed with some scepticism the arrival in Tunisia of General Giovanni Messe to command the new Italian 1st Army,

5 The success of Lieutenant-General George S. Patton's command of land forces during the 'Operation Torch' landings in French North Africa rapidly earned him a reputation as a superlative battle commander, in addition to that for personal toughness and irascibility. On March 6th 1943, after the American II Corps had lost 7,000 men and 235 tanks under General Fredendall, he took over the command of II Corps and led it throughout the remainder of the Tunisian campaign.

6 While the battles for Tunisia were fought during the early months of 1943, the defence of the Straits of Gibraltar remained a key factor, both to the North African war and to the final stages of the Battle of the Atlantic. A tight watch on the Straits was the key to preventing U-Boats entering or leaving the Mediterranean, and to ensuring that the Axis army in North Africa had to be supplied from Italy, under the constant eye of the Royal Navy based in Malta. This slightly quaint and typically British picture shows a machine gun post, insignificant in itself, that was one of many scattered about the rock amidst major land gun emplacements, naval guns and many anti-aircraft batteries. Visiting raiders were guaranteed a warm reception.

7 The Americans rapidly developed the technique, already well-established by the British and Commonwealth troops during the desert war, of turning enemy weapons against their former owners whenever possible. This Italian 75mm cannon was captured by the American soldiers in the picture, who, after a little study and practice, used the gun (according to the original caption) to knock out a German PzKpfw III tank.

8 Brought by the ubiquitous trimotor Junkers Ju-52 transport aircraft, these troops were reported in the UK press at the time (March 1943) to be reinforcements arriving for the beleaguered 5th *Panzerarmee*. The same caption stated that the picture showed that the Germans 'have converted many of their big bombers into transport planes', which was not the case. All the aircraft in the picture are Ju-52s.

made up of the German and Italian Axis forces pulled back from Tripoli. Rommel's view of Italian military achievement was never enthusiastic, and the idea of handing over his command to an Italian General did not appeal to him at all. However, since he was organising the defences along the Mareth line, and had not been recalled as expected by OKW, Rommel decided to make use of the unexpectedly long time that Montgomery was taking to move up to the attack. He embarked upon an assault against the US Army II Corps, which was comparatively close to his forces, in the mountainous area to the West of his positions. Rommel knew that, by virtue of his own position between Montgomery and the Americans, there was little likelihood of the British 8th Army being able to assist their Allies, and reinforcements for his army were arriving steadily, although he was still very short of tanks and artillery. Leaving two Italian Corps and the German 90th and 164th

Tunisia

Light Divisions at the Mareth line to keep Montgomery busy, he pulled together at Sfax the 10th and 21st *Panzer* Divisions under Lieutenant-General Ziegler, and the Italian 'Centauro' Armoured Division and his own *Afrika Korps* under his own command. Ziegler's formation was given the task of a surprise attack against Major-General Orlando Ward's 1st US Armoured Division at Faid Pass, while Rommel's force was to head South-West to Gafsa. Once they had succeeded in their initial objectives, the two formations were to join at Sbeitla and attack the Allied position in the Grande Dorsale.

Ziegler's surprise attack at Faid on February 14th was entirely successful, and disorganised the thinly-spread American defending force so much that II Corps withdrew entirely into the Grande Dorsale. Next day Rommel, in the confusion, took Gafsa without a shot being fired, and the two German columns merged for their assault upon the Grande Dorsale. At this point, Rommel, whose position thus far in the command structure had been somewhat vague, was belatedly appointed to the command of a new 'Army

1 Colonel-General von Arnim was well-known and liked for keeping in close personal touch with his divisional commanders and their staffs. Here he is at a forward divisional headquarters in the mountains of central Tunisia, studying maps and discussing tactics with one of his divisional commanders and his officers.

2 A fine action picture of German PzKpfw III tanks moving up to the front in Tunisia. Note the spare tracks which are fixed across the front armour of the tank to provide additional protection against Allied anti-tank guns, which the German crews had by now come to respect. This practice had developed initially in Russia, where it was found that the added thickness of metal provided by the tracks was frequently the difference between penetration by the shell from a T-34 tank and deflection.

3 Despite the discernibly shaky fortunes of the Axis war effort on several fronts in January 1943, as Stalingrad fell in the east, Tunisia looked likely to fall in the south, and US forces were clearly on their long journey to Japan in the Pacific theatre of war, Dr. Josef Goebbels felt able, as always, to speak optimistically of Germany's prospects of victory. On January 30th 1943, the tenth anniversary of Hitler's coming to power, Goebbels demanded in this speech at the Berlin *Sportpalast* that the German people have full confidence in their *Fuehrer*.

Group Africa', perhaps to try and bring him under control. Undeterred by his regained authority, Rommel pressed on, and, after an initial reverse when the French 19th Corps repulsed the 21st *Panzer* Division at Shiba Pass, the 19th *Panzer* Division broke through the Kasserine Pass and headed for Tebessa over the Algerian border, an important supply centre for the Allies. Rommel wanted to push on quickly, as he had done so often before, and take not only Tebessa but also Bone, thereby cutting the British 1st Army's communications and greatly delaying the expected Allied offensive.

Rommel's success rattled the command structures of both the Allies and the Axis. The Allies saw the probability of Rommel attacking Tebessa and argued about the steps to take if he did. The Axis split three ways — von Arnim wanting to hold the assault at Kasserine, Kesselring supporting Rommel's plan and the Italian *Comando Supremo* overriding all of them with an order to turn North-West and attack along a line from Thala to Le Kef, right into the positions of the greatest Allied strength. Rommel was appalled at the order — but did as he was told, meeting fierce and well-organised resistance from the British 6th Armoured Division. Not suprisingly, with his supplies running low, Rommel's attack failed. But the ten days of actions had cost the Americans over 4,000 prisoners, almost 3,000 dead and substantial losses of equipment.

Now Rommel turned South again with his 10th and 21st *Panzer* Divisions to join Messe and Ziegler in tackling Montgomery's

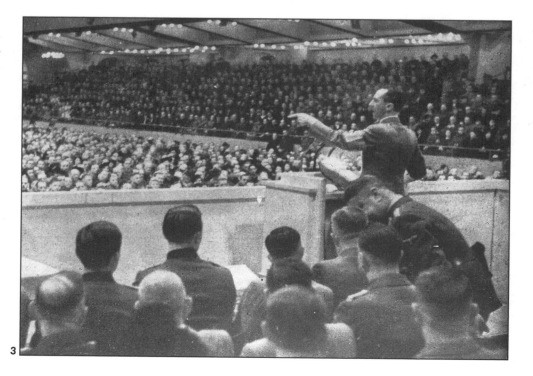

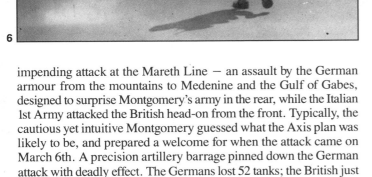

4 Cooperation between American and British soldiers and technical units increased rapidly as the commanders of the two nations' armies became accustomed to the new fighting alliance. Here a unit of American Army Engineers attached to the British Eighth Army are being briefed by a British officer.

5 As the war progressed, the use of mine detectors became more widespread, and saved many lives by enabling sappers to find and defuse anti-personnel mines. These American engineers are demonstrating mine detection technique, possibly for the benefit of the cameras, since the American at right at the back of the group is holding a Leica camera and looks as if he knows how to use it.

6 American infantrymen of II Corps entering the abandoned Axis stronghold of Gafsa on March 17th 1943. Gafsa had been lost by II Corps in mid-February, largely as a result of disastrous miscalculation by General Fredendall which enabled Rommel to sweep down in the manner of the wolf on the fold. It was a source of great satisfaction in II Corps when, under Patton's leadership, they recaptured the town.

7 The capture of Gafsa produced a substantial bag of some 5,000 Axis prisoners, many of them Italian. These Italians seem reasonably relaxed about their relatively troublefree exit from active operations as they troop off to the prisoner of war cage.

8 At the end of April 1943, the remarkable Lieutenant-General George S. Patton, having revitalised the morale of US II Corps, was given the job of organising the forthcoming Allied landings in Sicily. The command of II Corps fell to another name shortly to become internationally renowned – General Omar Bradley. According to General Eisenhower in his *Crusade in Europe*, Bradley was 'a keen judge of men and their capabilities, and was absolutely fair and just with them … he possessed a grasp of larger issues that clearly marked him for high office'.

impending attack at the Mareth Line — an assault by the German armour from the mountains to Medenine and the Gulf of Gabes, designed to surprise Montgomery's army in the rear, while the Italian 1st Army attacked the British head-on from the front. Typically, the cautious yet intuitive Montgomery guessed what the Axis plan was likely to be, and prepared a welcome for when the attack came on March 6th. A precision artillery barrage pinned down the German attack with deadly effect. The Germans lost 52 tanks; the British just one Sherman.

This misguided offensive, which Rommel knew could not succeed, was the last of Rommel's battles in Africa. He received orders to return to Germany, and Colonel-General von Arnim became the commander of Army Group Africa. But von Arnim faced an impossible task. His supply lines were being harassed on land, and the shipping that brought his reinforcements, his fuel and his replacement vehicles was being decimated by the ever more effective Allied Mediterranean fleet. Knowing that the Axis forces were gradually being hemmed in, the Allied commanders formulated a plan to bring the Tunisian campaign to a successful end in time for the landings in Sicily to go ahead in July, as decided at the Casablanca conference.

On March 20th, the 8th Army's final push northwards from Mareth to Tunis began. The initial frontal assault by Montgomery's artillery was followed by an attack by XXX Corps on the coast, and the plan called for a dash for the Gabes gap and the plain beyond, but appalling weather, swollen rivers and effective resistance bogged down the assault. Not until March 26th did the attack finally break out at El Hamma, assisted by fierce and constant air support from the Desert Air Force. The bulk of the Italian defending army was able to withdraw to Wadi Akarit, but the Allied advance was at last under way. On April 5th/6th the XXX Corps again attacked Messe's positions and, after initial reverses, the British force found its enemy in retreat. It later proved that Messe had wanted to hold his position, but that von Arnim, knowing that the fearsome General Patton was approaching the Italian Army's right, had decided to pull Messe's force back to regroup for what promised to be a major battle.

The tough, uncompromising General Patton had in fact been having a successful few weeks after revitalising the morale of II Corps, and had taken Gafsa on March 17th, and El Guettar, Maknassy and Sbeitla before the end of March. Now he was ready to join up with the British 8th Army, which he did on April 8th, a link which created a unified arc of Allied forces from the US II Corps to the British 1st Army, through the French 19th Corps to the 8th Army. The scene was almost set for the final Allied victory in Africa.

To meet the requirements of General Alexander's plan finally to push the Axis forces back to Tunis and Bizerta, the US II Corps was moved the following week to the right of the 1st Army, to the centre of the attack, and, as this was taking place, lost their charismatic commander. General Patton had a new task — the organisation of the US participation in the forthcoming landings in Sicily. The task

of taking the US Army to Bizerta fell to General Omar Bradley, Patton's second in command.

Through the last week of April and the first of May, the attack spearheaded by the British 1st Army under Lieutenant-General Anderson, and the US II Corps under General Bradley went ahead, advancing slowly, losing some of its encounters but winning most. On May 5th, General Bradley's masterly grasp of tactics enabled his 1st Armoured Division to descend from the high ground it had been holding above Mateur and seize the vital Tunis to Bizerta railway line, which the Axis was using for supplies. Gradually the armies closed in, and on May 7th the first units of the British 7th Armoured

1 The German PzKpfw VI 'Tiger' heavy battle tank, which was equipped with the famed 88mm anti-aircraft gun in its massive turret, and 3.94" thick frontal armour that no existing battlefield weapons could penetrate, rapidly gained the reputation of being the most formidable armoured fighting vehicle in the world after its introduction in 1942. In fact, the Tiger was relatively slow (twenty-four mph on the road; only twelve mph cross country) and, at 55,000 kg operational weight, decidedly cumbersome.

2 Infantry lore has it that there is no future in advancing over a bare skyline, but in the Tunisian semi-desert there was often little available alternative. These American troops have only the minimal cover of smoke created by air strikes on their target ahead.

3 On Friday May 7th 1943, the British occupied Tunis, and the Americans captured the great port of Bizerta, removing all realistic possibility of further reinforcement of the Axis armies. Over 50,000 prisoners were taken during the capture of the area around the capital – these are just some of them, crowded together with nothing to do and nowhere to go, but glad to be alive.

4 On Wednesday May 12th 1943 came the effective end of all Axis resistance in Tunisia. Here the Italian commander, General Costa, raises his hand to return a salute as he leaves Allied Air Force headquarters after signing the surrender of his troops.

Division entered Tunis, the US 9th Division reached Bizerta, and the 1st Armoured Division linked up with the 7th. On May 9th, the commander of the Axis troops in the northern part of Tunisia, General Vaerst, asked for an armistice.

On May 12th, the southern forces were surrounded and forced to surrender, General von Arnim being among the men captured after fierce fighting. Virtually the entire Axis army was captured; only a few hundred escaped to Italy to continue their war. Almost a quarter of a million prisoners were taken.

Thus ended the battle for North Africa, the reign of the Desert Fox, and one of the fastest moving campaigns of the Second World War. Almost 50,000 Allied soldiers were killed or wounded in the seven months' campaign for Tunisia. Eisenhower's, Alexander's, Montgomery's and Patton's success was not without price, but final victory could not have been achieved without it.

5 One of the most interesting aspects of this picture, which clearly shows a German general and one of his staff officers being driven to captivity after the fall of the Axis in Tunis, is why the photograph, having been passed 'by the appropriate US authority' for publication, was also marked 'not for use in Western Hemisphere'. Just what was the security risk?

6 On June 12th 1943, His Majesty King George VI arrived in Morocco, and made an extensive tour of the American armed forces units. The King was shown demonstrations of street fighting techniques, and took the salute at a parade. Here, the King is riding in an American staff car through lines of tanks.

7 At the beginning of June 1943, aware that the greatest test of Italian political and military stability must inevitably come if the Allies invaded Italy, Mussolini dismissed his only recently-appointed Chief of the Italian Staff, General Ezion, and replaced him with the tough and uncompromising General Mario Roatta. It was not to prove effective in sustaining his regime.

8 King George VI was immensely popular, both with British soldiers and with the civilian population at home. His visit to North Africa raised morale even higher than it had already become as a result of the Tunisian victory, a valuable preparation for the privations of the invasion of Sicily that was only brief months ahead.

CHAPTER 26

TOEHOLD IN EUROPE
THE ASSAULT ON ITALY

The defeat of the Axis in North Africa made possible the next stage of the strategy agreed at Casablanca, and reinforced by a meeting between Churchill, Generals Marshall, Eisenhower, Alexander and Ismay, Air Chief Marshal Tedder and Admiral Cunningham in Algeria in May 1943. At this meeting it was agreed that the first objective should be the securing of the Mediterranean sea lanes by the conquest of Sicily. If that went well, the next was to be the increase of pressure on Germany by an invasion of Italy, the elimination of Italy as a combatant, and the establishment of the first Allied permanent presence in mainland Europe since 1940.

Italy had suffered huge losses of men and equipment since her entry into Germany's war, and Mussolini had compounded those losses by his unnecessary and ill-conceived adventures in Albania, North Africa and, more recently, Russia. Of the 95 divisions that the Italians had had at, or had raised since, the start of the war, a third had been annihilated by death or capture, more than another third were distributed about the Axis Empire doing Hitler's bidding, and the remainder, nominally 30 divisions but in fact rather less, were available for the defence of the homeland. With a victorious, battle-hardened and ever better-equipped Allied army poised just across the Mediterranean, it was clear that that defence was about to be necessary.

The Italian Air Force and Navy were in no less difficulty. The Italian fleet had lost approaching a half of its strength, and those vessels that remained, particularly the overworked destroyers and escort vessels, were becoming ill-maintained and unreliable. The air force lacked aircraft that were in any way a match for the latest Allied fighters and bombers, and was extremely vulnerable to losses in combat. To add to all these problems, all three services were desperately short of fuel, a situation which seemed likely only to become worse.

Recognising the inability of the Italian forces effectively to resist invasion, Mussolini appealed to Hitler for more assistance, particularly with aircraft and anti-aircraft defences. It was in some ways an unrealistic appeal, for already the *Luftwaffe* was in severe difficulties. Losses of aircraft and crews in Russia were mounting, the fuel shortage was every bit as desperate for the Germans as it was for the Italians, and the demands of Hitler's over-extended position in the Soviet Union were becoming greater every day. Nonetheless, Hitler and Kesselring had maintained considerable land forces in Italy, on the premise that they were better off defending Germany in Italy than defending Germany in Germany, and had allocated two German divisions – the 15th *Panzergrenadier* and the 'Hermann Goering' *Panzer* Divisions – to the defence of Sicily, albeit with greatly

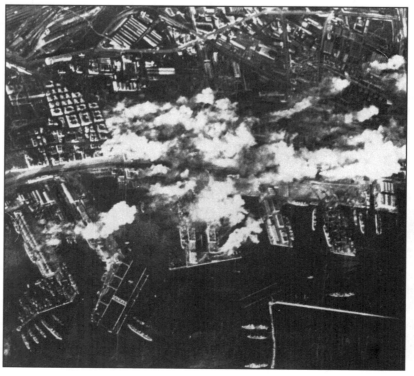

1 The 14,500 ton Italian heavy cruisers (left to right) *Fiume, Pola* and *Zara* were three of a class of four ships known as the *Zara* class, completed in 1931. Designed for the Mediterranean, with emphasis on armour rather than speed or range, they were lost more by poor seamanship and a lack of radar than by faulty design. *Zara* and *Fiume* were both caught unsuspecting with their guns trained fore and aft by British battleships at Matapan, and were sunk by point blank fire without reply. *Pola* was hit on 28th March 1941 by a torpedo from a Royal Navy aircraft carrier, and finished off by a second torpedo from a destroyer.

2 June 1943 opened with this massive air attack on the island of Pantelleria, half way between Tunisia and Sicily, which took place on June 1st. On June 8th, leaflets were dropped on the island calling for the unconditional surrender of the Italian garrison. When there was no response, the island was bombed again on June 9th, and on June 11th the Italians on the island surrendered. In this picture, two Douglas DB7-B Boston twin-engined bombers of the South African Air Force are seen attacking the airfield. At the far end of the airfield, beyond the smoke from oil fires, can be seen the entrances to underground hangars and workshops in the side of the hill.

3 So as to maintain a state of uncertainty about Allied intentions, there had been a continuing programme of Allied air raids on military targets in mainland Italy for months before the invasion of Sicily. This picture of an attack on Naples Harbour by the United States Army Air Force was issued in March 1943. Fuel tanks are burning briskly, and several ships have been hit.

reduced armament, and considerably under strength. They joined the Italian 6th Army under General Guzzoni, which had some 230,000 men and 1,500 guns, few motor vehicles, and quite impossibly large areas of Sicily to defend.

It was, however, by no means accepted in the Axis High Commands that Sicily would be the initial target. A substantial body of opinion that the first invasion would occur in Greece had been created by British Naval Intelligence, who had on 30th April 1943 planted in the sea to drift ashore in Spain the body of a man who had died of pneumonia (and therefore had fluid in his lungs not unlike that expected of someone who had drowned). Dressed in the uniform of a Royal Marines officer, the body, 'Major Martin', carried letters from the Imperial General Staff to Generals Eisenhower and Alexander and to Admiral Cunningham, which referred to 'the imminent landings in Greece'. While treated with reserve, the ruse was taken seriously enough for immense efforts to be spent mining the waters around Greece, and for a *Panzer* Division to be diverted from France to Greece.

Nonetheless, both Hitler and Italy's Marshal Ambrosio were confident that the first landings would be in Sardinia, and were later certain that the Allies had failed to take full advantage of their position by invading Sicily. They believed that an invasion of Sardinia would have enabled the Allies to sever the Axis forces in the South from those in the North — and in fact feared just this eventuality as the Allied build-up to the landings continued.

For these and other reasons, Italy was not in a happy condition. Most of those who had formerly been close to Mussolini now believed not only that Italy had lost the war, but that Germany would

4 Sicily was, until allocated the 15th *Panzergrenadier* and 'Hermann Goering' *Panzer* Divisions, very lightly defended – Italian troops had amounted to only forty men per mile of coastline. Coastal gun emplacements like this were few and German prognoses for the defence of Sicily against the expected Allied invasion were not optimistic.

5 German reinforcements improved the anti-aircraft defences of the airfields on Sicily – this gun crew arrived at an airfield near Messina in spring 1943. In this picture they are apparently being entertained by the local children.

6 A British Sherman tank leaves an LCT on the Sicily beaches. The crew are clearly not under fire, and the fact that the officer in the turret is wearing his peaked cap rather than a helmet suggests that this picture was taken during the period of reinforcement after the initial invasion was over.

7 On July 17th 1943, the Eighth Army was held up at Catania in its attempt to advance to Messina, and General Montgomery called on the Royal Navy for support. Tons of shells were fired at German positions from this battleship at ranges varying between 15,000 and 11,000 yards, and destroyers engaged the shore batteries at close range. The ships were attacked during the bombardment by *Luftwaffe* Fw-190 fighter-bombers, but sustained little damage.

never be able to win it. A powerful group led by Count Ciano and two other ministers, and by Marshals Badoglio and Caviglia, was pressing either for Mussolini to break with Hitler and sue for peace, or for the arrest of Mussolini so that others could end Italy's association with Germany.

Against this background, Eisenhower and Alexander planned 'Operation Husky', with broadly the same command structure as had so recently been successful in Tunisia. The American 7th Army under General Patton was made up of II Corps, commanded by General Omar Bradley, and the autonomous 3rd Division under the command of the immensely tough General Truscott. Their role was to establish a beach-head in the Gulf of Gela, between Licata and Scoglitti, west of Sicily's southernmost tip, and then penetrate inland to the North. The British 8th Army under General Montgomery, consisting of XIII Corps under Lieutenant-General Miles Dempsey and XXX Corps commanded by Lieutenant-General Oliver Leese had the task of taking the coastline to the East of that Southernmost point, between Pachino and Avola.

1 A total of 1,500 Allied naval vessels and 40,000 naval officers and men took part in the invasion of Sicily. This picture, taken from an American cruiser, shows Licata burning on the horizon.

2 During the bombardment from the sea of German positions beyond the Eighth Army at Catania, a German submarine attempted an attack on the Royal Navy vessels shelling the shore. British destroyers located the submarine and attempted to disable it with depth charges, without result. Here, British depth charges are seen exploding astern of a destroyer steaming at speed.

3 One of the more colourful features of the British Army's approach to battle which the Germans always found difficult to understand was the Scottish habit of advancing to the music of the bagpipes – the sound was, reputedly, more effective for terrifying sentries than a Bren gun, although it was usually less lethal. Here a Scottish regiment advances to the sound of the pipes on the road to Catania, in Sicily. The intended destination of the Jeep that is pointing the other way is not clear.

As an essential first step, the Allies began on June 1st a major bombing offensive against Italian targets, starting with a round the clock bombardment from the air of the island of Pantelleria, midway between Tunisia and Sicily. This tremendous air attack on the island, which brought down some 6,500 tons of bombs on the 12,000 defenders (and the 10,000 civilians they were supposed to be defending), culminated in a landing on June 11th, and surrender by the Italian commander Admiral Pavesi on June 12th. On the same day, a hapless Sergeant pilot in the Royal Air Force, Sergeant Cohen, earned his place in history by capturing an enemy garrison single-handed. He made a forced landing on Lampedusa, a small island off Sicily, and the Italian defenders, seeing the arrival of the dreaded Allies of whom they had heard so much, surrendered without enquiring the reason for his visit.

All through June, Allied aircraft attacked Italian airfields, Italian ships at anchor and military installations both in Sicily and throughout mainland Italy. By dawn on 10th July, when the Allied invasion of Sicily began, the Axis air defences in the area had been virtually destroyed. Tedder's 4,000 aircraft found they had only 200 Italian and 320 German aircraft with which to contend. The invasion itself, planned by Admiral Ramsay, who had masterminded the evacuation of Dunkirk, went extremely well. For the first time, new LST (Landing Ship, Tank) and LCT (Landing Craft, Tank) vessels were used to put armour ashore with the first wave of infantry, and the invaders were rapidly established, capturing the coastline and driving inland. Eight divisions landed from a thousand ships along a front some 100 miles long. By evening on the 11th July, 80,000 troops and 8,000 vehicles were ashore, Montgomery's 8th Army had occupied the ports of Syracuse and Augusta without a shot being fired, the garrisons having taken themselves elsewhere, and the *Hermann Goering Panzer* division had been badly mauled by US Navy fire from the cruisers *Boise* and *Savannah* when they attempted to take the US 1st Division to task on the coast near Niscemi. This was probably the first occasion when sea power decided a tank battle.

Both the American and the British Armies were heading for Messina at the northern tip of Sicily, and nurtured hopes that they might get there before the German army, so preventing an evacuation of Axis troops to the mainland. Field Marshal Kesselring, one of whose considerable talents was a mastery of organisation, was too clever to allow that to happen. By a minor miracle of improvisation, Kesselring transported on to the island from mainland Italy two paratroop regiments and the 29th *Panzergrenadier* Division, and put General Hube of XIV *Panzer* Corps in command of all German fighting troops in Sicily. From that point onward, the standard of Axis resistance to the Allied advance on both sides of Mount Etna became

very much tougher. Nonetheless, General Patton made the rapid progress that was soon to become his trademark. The 7th Army established contact with the British 8th Army on July 14th, and then, despite appallingly rough terrain in the West of Sicily, launched one division upon the major task of taking Palermo, in the North-West of the island, and two others under General Bradley on the problem of fighting directly northwards to the North coast. Incredibly, Patton arrived in Palermo, to the cheers of a mightily relieved populace, only a week later, on the 22nd July, having overcome the Italian 'Assietta' Division on the way. From Palermo Eastward to Messina was not so easy.

Montgomery, meanwhile, had been having a difficult time on the Eastern plains of Sicily. Having captured Syracuse and Augusta by default, the 8th Army faced the problem of attacking across an open coastal plain towards the larger port of Catania, and of taking the town, before the entirely different problem of the assault through the foothills of Etna to Messina could be overcome. Montgomery encountered fierce resistance all the way to Catania, and was not able to take the town until August 5th. Before that, however, he had detached the 1st Canadian Division to attack to the West of Mount Etna (which displeased the US Army), and had hemmed in General Hube's forces ever closer to the North-East of the island.

Substantial Allied reinforcements were arriving via Palermo and Syracuse in the shape of the US 9th Division in the North-West, and

5

6

7

the British 78th Division in the South-East, and the US and British forces now had an enormous numerical advantage over Hube's German defence force. A massive German withdrawal to the mainland began, and on 17th August, shortly after Hube had left on the final assault craft for Calabria, Patton arrived in Messina, a few hours ahead of the furious Montgomery, who had in his own view reserved the right to take the key northern city.

The Allies now found that they had captured 132,000 prisoners, 260 tanks and 520 guns. Approximately 8,600 German and Italian troops have known graves on Sicily, and almost 8,400 Allied soldiers were killed or posted missing, with nearly 14,500 wounded.

Italy's Turning Point

While these events had been taking place in Sicily, the politics of the Axis had been reaching crisis point in Italy. The King, under pressure to remove Mussolini, in fact sought to remove the entire Fascist party from power. The Fascists, at a meeting in Feltre with Hitler and Keitel, had sought far greater military support from the Germans, which, to some extent, Hitler said he was prepared to give, on condition that Mussolini mobilised Italy's manhood to greater effort and restored flagging Italian morale. Mussolini, urged by Ambrosio and his colleagues to break with Hitler and broadcast to the Allies for terms of surrender, could not bring himself to accept defeat, and to believe that Hitler's boasts of new reprisal weapons capable of destroying London by the Autumn were exaggerated. The meeting broke up inconclusively, with Mussolini still relying upon his faith in Hitler, and the Fascist ministers and High Command fuming.

A Fascist Grand Council on July 24th, called by Mussolini to discuss the situation, became the scene of a plot to oust the Duce. A motion put by Count Grandi, by which the Council required Mussolini to hand over authority over the Italian armed forces to the

4 A fine picture of a British Sherman tank, crewed, according to the original caption, by Scottish soldiers, advancing south of Catania at the end of July 1943.

5 During the brief respite between the end of the campaign for Sicily on August 17th 1943, and the landings by XIII Corps of the Eighth Army in Calabria on September 3rd, General Dwight Eisenhower, Commander in Chief Allied Forces in North Africa, visited American units and the newly-arrived Canadian troops in Sicily. Eisenhower is on the left – the Royal Navy Captain in white with the huge binoculars is Captain J.E.Moore.

6 An unusual photograph of General Montgomery in shorts – he was watching the advance of his troops at Augusta during the conquest of Sicily, at the end of July 1943.

7 In April 1943, Mussolini and Guiseppe Bastianini, his Foreign Minister, had visited Hitler to plead for air support and fuel for the impending Allied invasion of Italy. Here accompanied by Hermann Goering (right), who knew only too well the impossibility of meeting Mussolini's needs, *Il Duce* had left with only vague promises of a secure future guaranteed by Hitler's secret weapons.

Toehold in Europe

King, was carried by a large majority. The motion also authorised the monarch to remove Mussolini from power. At 5pm on the 25th, the King informed Mussolini that he was accepting his (unsubmitted) resignation, and that Marshal Badoglio was to be appointed Head of the Government in his place. Mussolini was driven ignominiously in an ambulance to a military police barracks, and the Fascist conspirators were denied all complicity in the new government. Count Ciano left for Germany lured by an invitation to a non-existent meeting, a trap which was ultimately to cost him his life.

Badoglio issued as his first act a proclamation that 'the war goes on'. But Hitler was not enthusiastic about the intentions of the new Italian government, and decided to take action to ensure that Italy was not snatched from the Germans' grasp by a defection to the Allies. Field Marshal Rommel was given command of 'Operation Alarich', and instructions to move Army Group B to Bologna by mid-August. By the time the Allies' conquest of Sicily was complete, eight divisions of crack German troops including the 24th *Panzer* Division and the *Leibstandarte Adolf Hitler Waffen SS* 1st Panzer Division were in position North of the Appenines. Kesselring, still the supreme commander in the field in the Mediterranean theatre, was reinforced with the 2nd Parachute Division.

On August 15th, General Jodl and Field Marshal Rommel met General Roatta, the Italian Army Chief of Staff in Bologna, and attempted to assure themselves that the Italian Government was not in the process of seeking an armistice with the Allies. Three days previously, Generals Castellano and Montenari had secretly met Eisenhower's Chief of Staff in Lisbon and had discussed the text of an armistice, but the Italians succeeded in lying their way out of their meetings with the Germans. On August 27th, the Generals returned to Rome with secret radio equipment capable of contacting the Allies, and with the text of the surrender. After extensive and intensive negotiations by which the Italians sought to gain the maximum protection from German reprisals against the Italian population and cities, the armistice was signed at 5.15pm on September 3rd. On the 8th, the Armistice was announced by Badoglio to the Italian people.

The German reaction was immediate, devastating and brutal. Whole divisions of Italian troops serving alongside those of Germany in Italy were taken prisoner and given scant comfort as prisoners of war. In the small hours of September 9th, the morning after the announcement of the armistice, a convoy of Italian warships heading for Malta to surrender was bombed by the Germans, and the battleship *Roma* was sunk with the loss of more than 1,500 lives. Away from the Mediterranean theatre, the Italian troops fared no better. In the Balkans, 29 divisions were attacked and surprised by the German army and disarmed. Two divisions (the 'Acqui' and the 'Bergamo') that put up a fight were besieged into surrender — and

1 On July 25th 1943, Mussolini was deposed and King Victor Emmanuel III, aged seventy-four, appointed Marshal Badoglio as head of the Italian government.

2 Despite Kesselring's overall authority in the Mediterranean theatre of war, it was to Rommel that Hitler gave the task of moving Army Group B to Bologna after the removal of Mussolini posed the threat of an Italian accommodation with the Allies and the loss of Italy to the Axis. These PzKpfw IV medium tanks are of the *1st SS Panzer Division Leibstandarte Adolf Hitler*, and are causing quite a stir in the streets of Bologna.

3 The Axis Commander-in-Chief in Italy during the Allied invasions of Sicily and the Italian mainland was Field-Marshal Albert Kesselring (second from left), former artilleryman, one of the architects of the *Luftwaffe*, and himself a skilled pilot. In this picture he is talking with two *Luftwaffe* pilots. Reputedly, Kesselring played a significant part in the planning of the daring and successful Skorzeny raid to liberate Mussolini, who had been imprisoned by the Badoglio government.

5

6

7

4 Although it was Marshal Badoglio who made the radio announcement of the Italian Armistice on September 8th, the document itself was signed by General Castellano. Here, at the actual signing ceremony, Castellano (centre) shakes hands with General Eisenhower. On the left is General Wedell Smith.

5 On Friday September 10th 1943, huge crowds assembled at Grand Harbour, Valetta, to watch the arrival of the surrendered Italian fleet, led in by the British battleships *Warspite*, *Valiant* and *King George V*. General Eisenhower congratulated Admiral Sir Andrew Cunningham, saying 'My congratulations to you and all the forces under your command on the happy and conclusive ending of your three years' campaign against the Italian Navy'. This picture, sent by radio from New York to Britain, shows General Eisenhower with Admiral Cunningham on the bridge of a British warship as the Italian warships sail in.

6 Following the success of the 'Man Who Never Was' deception, when the body of a 'Royal Marine', in fact a civilian, was floated ashore in Spain bearing forged orders, Germany fortified many of her Mediterranean coastal installations in areas not scheduled for Allied invasion. This team of Germans appear to be installing new equipment and camouflage in a shore emplacement.

7 Lieutenant-General George S. Patton Jnr, who had a well-earned reputation for strong language and was impatient of moderation in anything, also knew how to command respect and loyalty from his men. After the completion of the Sicilian campaign, he gathered his men together in a vast assembly and thanked them for a job well done.

8 September 3rd, the fourth anniversary of the outbreak of war between Britain and Germany, was the date set for the British and Canadian landings in Calabria, just across the Straits of Messina. In the anxious time just before the invasion, Generals Montgomery (left) and Eisenhower stand on a high vantage point in Messina and study the opposite coast.

then thousand of soldiers were murdered after they had capitulated. Those that escaped joined the partisans and fought Germany from the hills.

Mussolini was sent to a remote residence in the *Gran Sasso*, high in the mountains. Hitler, determined to hold the brotherhood of fascist dictatorship high, sent a daring commando unit under Otto Skorzeny to rescue him from his captors. They succeeded brilliantly, landing in the mountains with several light aircraft, and bearing him back to a Hitler who felt that honour had thus been satisfied. Under pressure from the Fuehrer, Mussolini proclaimed on September 18th the 'Italian Social Republic', but it was an empty gesture recognised only by the puppet Axis governments and Japan.

On 12th September, as confusion continued to reign in the former Axis, the Free French embarked on the liberation of Corsica, and by October 4th the Allies had gained an additional valuable base by Italy's side door. Despite tremendous efforts by the French and Moroccan troops of the invasion force, the Germans kept their escape route open, and were able to evacuate 28,000 valuable battle-trained troops to the mainland.

Salerno — the Allied Success that Almost Wasn't

Having taken Sicily and achieved a considerable victory, and then secured the capitulation of the Italian state, the Allied High Command planned hastily — perhaps too hastily — to capitalise on the advantage thus created by establishing a presence on the Italian mainland.

The plan for the Salerno invasion was a two-part exercise. A Corps of the British 8th Army was first to launch an attack across

8

the Straits of Messina with the objective of drawing the German army into battle. This, it was hoped, would divert attention away from the major landing — the second phase, which was to bring the US 5th Army commanded by General Mark Clark ashore in the Gulf of Salerno. When the British force — XIII Corps under General Dempsey — made its landing on September 3rd, the fourth anniversary of the outbreak of Hitler's war, it met very little

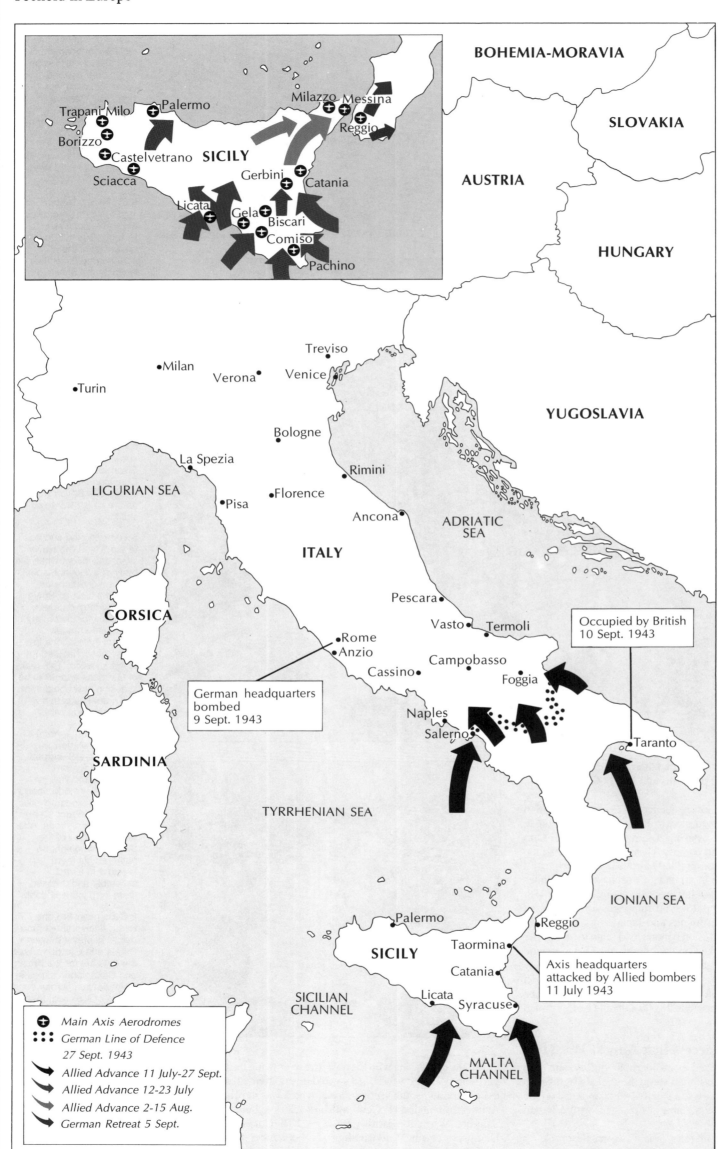

Left the invasion of Italy.

1 Thousands of troops board landing craft at Catania, Sicily, for the short crossing to the battlefield of Calabria. Within a week of these landings in the toe of Italy, the political manoeuvres of the Italian armistice following the fall of Mussolini had ensured that Calabria was almost entirely in Allied hands.

2 As the Allied army that had landed in the Gulf of Salerno battled to avoid defeat against unexpectedly well-prepared and reinforced German armoured opposition, the RAF flew bombing raids against German columns which were advancing to the area to further strengthen the German defence. These RAF Baltimore twin-engined bombers — note the aircraft close to the camera at top right — are bombing German formations moving up the valleys to the coast.

3 Anxious to be out of Germany's war, the pilot of this Italian four-engined Piaggio P.108 bomber flew South to Calabria and landed at an airfield already occupied by the Allies.

4 The mountainous terrain of much of Southern Italy is not ideal for the movement of artillery, and the crews of guns had their task made more difficult by the broken state of the war-torn roads. This 4·5 inch gun of a Medium Regiment, Royal Artillery, was photographed in the outskirts of Ravello, in the mountains southwest of Salerno. The brush fire in the distance was started by German mortars.

On the map:

German headquarters bombed 9 Sept. 1943

Occupied by British 10 Sept. 1943

Axis headquarters attacked by Allied bombers 11 July 1943

Legend:
- ✠ Main Axis Aerodromes
- ⠿ German Line of Defence 27 Sept. 1943
- Allied Advance 11 July–27 Sept.
- Allied Advance 12–23 July
- Allied Advance 2–15 Aug.
- German Retreat 5 Sept.

resistance. Kesselring, expecting a diversionary attack before a main landing (which he thought would be further North, near Rome), had instructed the German 76th *Panzer* Corps not to become involved in battle unless it was unavoidable. Dempsey was able to advance some miles inland and await developments, a situation for which the Allied plan of attack did not provide. Ready withdrawal to strong defensive positions in the MacArthur mould was not expected of the German army.

'Operation Avalanche' began in earnest on September 9th, when the US VI Corps and the British X Corps landed in the Gulf of Salerno between Paestum and Maiori along a front of 25 miles. Initially, the invasion went well, and by the end of the first day the US 36th Division had made 5 miles progress inland, and the British X Corps, although held up in and around Salerno, was established, and seemed likely not to be thrown back into the sea. But Kesselring had a surprise in store. For a start, Hitler had long regarded Salerno as potentially important, and had allocated the crack 16th *Panzer* Division to its defence. Secondly, having captured Rome following

1 Many Italian airfields were captured intact by the advancing Allies, and those that were not were, in the main, quickly repaired. Once operational they became the bases for maintaining the Allied Air Forces' by now almost total superiority in the air over Italy, providing forward bombing and fighter cover for advancing troops. This RAF Spitfire is being refuelled on an airfield near Taranto.

2 U.S. Rangers took a vital role in the establishment of the US 5th Army in Italy after the Salerno landings. Put ashore at Maiori, a small town northwest of Salerno, the Rangers had the task of clearing German forces from the hills overlooking the Plain of Naples, and then holding the mountain passes leading to the plain. This 105mm howitzer was in action supporting the Rangers in the hills.

3 General Eisenhower was never far from the action in Italy, and frequently toured the front line to see the enemy positions for himself. As the Italian front opened up and stabilised for the long drag of the 1944 campaign, Eisenhower travelled more and worked hard to encourage commanders to sustain the morale of their men. In this picture, taken in November 1943, 'Ike' is with his British aide, Lieutenant-Colonel J.F. Gault.

the Italian government's armistice with the Allies, Kesselring was able to divert from the area around the capital the 3rd *Panzergrenadier* Division, and by September 12th General von Vietinghoff's 10th Army was able to field four and a half divisions against the Allies' three. Over the next three days, the situation was touch and go. The Germans almost succeeded in surrounding the American 45th Division, which had advanced farther than the British 56th that should have been alongside it, and only desperate measures by the stubborn and determined General Mark Clark saved the day at the Battle of Ponte Bruciato. The story has it that Clark armed as infantry two artillery battalions, the regimental band, all the HQ orderlies and the cooks. In any event, the effort succeeded in stopping the German advance some five miles from the beach-head, where the tactic of using naval gunfire in support of the land army, so effective in Sicily, was used again with considerable success.

Now General Alexander called Montgomery's 8th Army in to attack the German forces from the side. Montgomery's 5th Division reached Agropoli on September 16th, just as the US 5th Army, at terrible expense of life, was beating back the attack. Later that day, faced with the additional strength of Montgomery's troops in a battle that was already lost, Kesselring pulled back the 10th Army, and admitted that the Allies had won the Battle of Salerno. Speedily, the British army occupied the important Italian ports of Brindisi and Taranto.

It is arguable that the Germans would not have lost the battle for Salerno had Rommel and Kesselring not been in violent disagreement on the strategy for the defence of Italy. Rommel thought Germany should abandon Rome and pull back to the North. Kesselring, in theory the senior commander, resolved to defend the

German Southern positions, but could not, because of Hitler's ambiguous orders and duplicated command structure, pull enough weight to force Rommel to release his best *Panzer* troops for the battle in the South.

Now began the arduous and extremely wet advance up the southern part of Italy to Rome during which the heavy armour of the British and American troops, unable to leave the roads because of the sea of mud on either side, became vulnerable and slow. At Termoli in early October, at Sangro at the end of November, at Monte Cassino — again and again General von Vietinghoff turned the bad weather and the confusion it caused to the maximum advantage, turning and making a determined, even heroic stand at every opportunity. It was clear that neither Kesselring nor his commanders had any intention of giving up Italy lightly — and that Hitler was firmly behind this policy was made clear by the recall of Rommel on November 21st. Kesselring was now in total charge in Italy.

How Kesselring tackled the subsequent stages of the Battle for Italy will be discussed in a later chapter. At this point this narrative must return to the war at sea.

CHAPTER 27

THE U-BOAT BEATEN
ALLIED SUCCESSES AT SEA

The winning of the Battle of the Atlantic was seen in 1941 and 1942, by Allies and Axis alike, as vital to their winning of the war. Churchill and Roosevelt knew that, if there was one major hinge upon which defeat might swing, it was the ability of Germany to prevent both the convoys from USA reaching Britain, and the convoys from Britain and the USA reaching the USSR. Hitler, Grand-Admiral Raeder and Admiral Doenitz believed that, given the much-vaunted *Luftwaffe's* demonstrated inability to subjugate Britain, their principal hope of final victory over their one enemy left in the West was to win the submarine war before the USA came officially into the conflict.

By 1942, America, whose ships had already been on active convoy protection duty for months while the USA was still neutral, had been brought into the war by Japan — an event that was as much a surprise for Hitler as it was for the United States. The Royal Navy's anti-submarine radar and Asdic techniques were improving dramatically, and despite the successes of the German U-Boat

building programme, the balance was shifting perceptibly in the favour of the Allies. Nonetheless, the U-Boat remained throughout 1942 and into 1943 one of the major threats to the Allies' hopes of winning the war. An important reason for this was the continued ability of Admiral Doenitz's codebreakers to read the signals of British Western Approaches Command to the convoys. For some unknown reason, British Naval Intelligence never realised that this was happening, or, if they did, never did anything to improve their coding practices. As a result, the U-Boat controllers were able not only to establish the positions of the convoys from the signals sent by the ships, but also to decode the information on supposed U-Boat positions sent to the convoys, and the instructions for avoiding the 'Wolf Packs' that were given by Western Approaches Command.

By 1943, although the *Kriegsmarine* was becoming short of skilled U-Boat crews, and was having to keep U-boats in port at Lorient or La Pallice (and later at Brest, St. Nazaire and Bordeaux)

4 The sight of a U-Boat sinking became more and more common as the tide turned against the *Kriegsmarine* in the middle of 1943. This particular U-Boat is a Type VII, of which 705 of various sub-types were built between 1936 and 1944. The Type VII carried a crew of forty-four men at a surface speed of seventeen knots and a submerged speed of eight knots, and had a range of 6,500 miles at twelve knots. This picture was taken after a US Navy Grumman Avenger from an escort carrier had successfully depth-charged the U-Boat. Note the group of survivors huddled by the conning tower.

5 The U-Boats that made it back to base — and 781 U-Boats and more than 32,000 German officers and men in them were lost during World War II — were serviced, refuelled and rearmed in these gigantic concrete pens at strategic points along the Atlantic coast of France. This battle-scarred boat has just returned from patrol.

6 A picture taken in July 1942 by one of the crew of an RAF Catalina (PBY) when it spotted and attacked a U-Boat that was patrolling on the surface. The splashes of the aircraft's machine gun fire can be clearly seen. The U-Boat was, according to the original caption, sunk as a result of the attack.

for longer between operational trips than hitherto, those boats that were at sea were hunting in larger packs with deadly efficiency. Although U-Boat losses were mounting, German production figures reached an average of between 23 and 24 submarines a month in 1943, despite heavy Allied bombing of the shipyards in which they were built. There seemed to Doenitz every prospect of sustaining the Battle almost indefinitely − in fact, at the beginning of 1943, Germany had the formidable total of 212 operational submarines, more than double the number of a year previously.

Until 1943, the U-Boat arm of the *Kriegsmarine* had been largely spared the phenomenon of Hitler as Commander in Chief and tactician. But at the beginning of January 1943, a battle took place in the Barents Sea between the Royal Navy escort of Convoy JW 51B, commanded by Captain Robert St.Vincent Sherbrooke (who was awarded the Victoria Cross for his outstanding bravery and devotion to duty) and a German force of surface raiders and submarines. This engagement, which involved *Hipper*, *Lutzow* and U-354 provoked a crisis between Hitler and the German Navy because Vice-Admiral Kummitz, in command of the German flotilla, broke off the engagement, which he might conceivably have won, before it was concluded. He did this because he was aware of Hitler's contradictory orders that Germany's prestige surface ships should not take unnecessary risks, and because, just as he knew that he might win the battle, he was also acutely aware that he might lose it.

Although it was because of his orders that the incident occurred, Hitler was furious, and vented his ire on Grand-Admiral Raeder, who promptly resigned. Doenitz, until now the Admiral that could do no

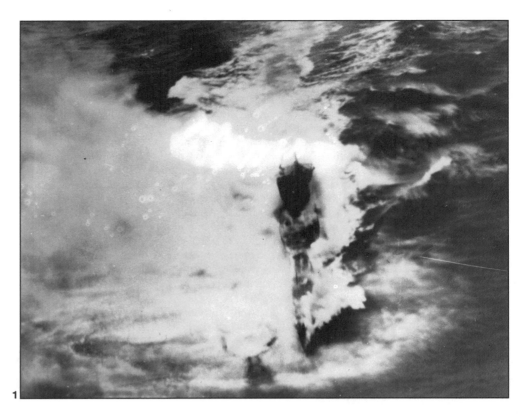

1

2

3

4

1 Another daring piece of U-Boat photography, whose less than perfect photographic quality can be excused by the fact that the Liberator bomber of the Royal Canadian Air Force from which the picture was taken was flying low, fast and under fire when the shutter was tripped. According to the contemporary caption, Flight Lieutenant Robert Fisher of Vancouver returned the Liberator to base successfully despite a damaged wingtip from the submarine's guns. The submarine sank shortly after the picture was taken.

2 The outlook for survivors in the freezing Atlantic during winter was not good, and many died of exposure or wounds before they could be picked up. The risk of being torpedoed by another U-Boat of the same pack while hove-to to collect survivors made Allied commanders reluctant to spend long on missions of mercy, but a majority of German submarine survivors were rescued.

3 In 1941, the U-570, a Type VII U-Boat, was caught and disabled on the surface by a Hudson aircraft, which then called in the Royal Navy, who captured the boat and its crew intact. This picture shows the boat after it had been brought back to Britain, where it was decided that it should be refitted to serve with the Royal Navy.

wrong, was promoted Grand-Admiral in Raeder's place − but never again commanded without the baleful eye of Adolf Hitler on his every move. Thus the U-boats entered 1943 with a new commander, Rear-Admiral Godt, and without the moral support of the surface raiders, which were effectively retired from active service for the time being as a result of Hitler's outburst.

The year also saw the eclipse of the *Luftwaffe* as an effective strike and defensive force at sea, which enabled the Allied air forces to become ever more effective at anti-submarine operations. During 1943, the RAF sank 41 U-boats in the Bay of Biscay without significant response from the *Luftwaffe*, and the production of escort carriers, mainly in United States shipyards, was stepped up to provide much wider airborne protection for convoys at sea. By the end of 1943, aircraft from escort carriers had destroyed no fewer than 26 U-boats. Typically, these mass-produced American ships of around 10,000 to 12,000 tons were built from scratch in less than a year. Like the other rapidly produced products of the American shipyards, notably the 'Liberty' ships, they made a very significant contribution to the Allied war effort.

Losses of merchant ships from the convoys were also reduced by the application of research into the history of convoy losses. It was found that, contrary to popular belief, large convoys were safer than small ones. Although easier to find, the large convoys, it was observed, lost only the same number of ships as a smaller convoy,

4 Depth charges, looking, as this does, deceptively like an oil-drum, were the staple weapon of the convoy escorts. According to the original caption, this picture was shot aboard a destroyer on patrol, although it seems more likely to have been a posed shot for propaganda purposes. The cap-band of the sailor on the right is just readable in the original print as HMS *Wakeful*.

5 The size and bulk of the near-bombproof exterior doors of the huge U-Boat pens can be judged from this picture of German workers – probably of the *Organisation Todt* – working on somewhat rudimentary ladders during their construction.

6 On convoy duty in the Atlantic, a United States destroyer, from which the picture was taken, has just fired a line to the US Coast Guard cutter in the centre of the picture prior to an exchange of orders. The ships of the convoy of whose screen the destroyer is part are spread as far as the eye can see.

7 Both in the Atlantic and in the Mediterranean, air observation was an increasingly important aspect of the anti-submarine war. Here, a Walrus floatplane is being catapulted from HMS *Warspite*, probably in this case in the Mediterranean just before the Salerno landings, since the carrier in the background appears to be HMS *Illustrious*, with both biplane and monoplane aircraft – probably Hurricanes, although positive identification is not possible – on deck.

given constant numbers of attacking submarines. In other words, six submarines could be expected statistically to pick off roughly the same number of 'kills' from any convoy, almost regardless of its size. Since a large convoy required a smaller number of escort vessels as a proportion of the total number of ships in the convoy to achieve the same degree of safety, it followed that more large convoys could be escorted by the same number of warships with fewer losses overall.

All these developments tended to decrease Allied shipping losses and increase the sinkings of German submarines. But of the four decisive advances that turned the Battle of the Atlantic and gave the Allies the upper hand, two were electronic and two were major advances in maritime weapons systems.

The first was the advent of centimetric radar. Installed on board the convoy escort vessels, this form of short-wave radar could not be spotted by the U-boats' detection equipment, which was designed for the much lower frequencies until then in use. The U-Boats had come to rely extensively on their ability to track convoys and find them at night by the detection of their radar emissions. Suddenly this facility was denied them.

The second electronic development was 'Huff Duff', otherwise and more correctly known as H/F D/F or High Frequency Direction Finder. This goniometric radio equipment was able to provide a fix on any U-Boat transmitting radio signals. With this equipment installed, the convoy could be steered away from the U-Boat packs, and the 'Hunter-killer' Allied submarines could be directed on to their kill.

The first of the weapons systems that helped to end the Battle of the Atlantic was the 'Hedgehog', a projector in the bows of an escort vessel capable of firing a pattern of 24 contact-fused bombs for 250 yards ahead. By making it unnecessary for the escort to pass directly over its target before succeeding with depth charges, and by providing a larger spread of fire and less chance for the submarine to detect the presence and position of the escort, the 'Hedgehog' greatly increased the success rate of escorts against U-boats.

The fourth contributor was the airborne rocket. Increasingly being brought into use as a tank-busting weapon by the Allies, the rocket was shown to be every bit as effective against submarines on the surface, and speedily contributed to U-Boat sinkings from the end of May 1943 onwards.

The U-Boat Beaten

With all these new found advantages, the Allies turned the tide of the Atlantic war dramatically. The decisive year began, in January 1943, with a relatively quiet month in the North Atlantic because of appalling weather — only 50 Allied merchant vessels were sunk — but Doenitz achieved a major success off North Africa by sinking seven of a convoy of nine tankers carrying vital fuel to the Allied armies closing in on General von Arnim's army in Tunisia. In the next month the weather improved and so also did the German score. A total of 73 ships went to the bottom. But so also did 19 U-boats, and the much greater success of the escorts in defending the convoys, as well as in sinking the submarines, was causing great concern at *Kriegsmarine* headquarters.

March seemed almost to reverse the situation. The carnage of Allied ships was awe-inspiring. In the first twenty days of the month no less than 97 Allied ships were sunk, almost two-thirds of them

1 The US Navy operated many escort vessels in the Atlantic on convoy protection duties, and many merchant seamen owed their lives to the skill of the crews of US Navy subchasers. This picture shows a depth charge being fired from the rear of an American escort vessel on patrol, after it had made contact with a submerged Axis submarine.

2 Part of the control centre in the engine room of a captured German U-Boat, which was put on exhibition during 1945, at the end of the war, on the Thames near London's Westminster Pier. The cramped conditions in which German — and most other — submariners lived, worked, fought and often died can be readily appreciated.

3 Not all the submarines operating in the Atlantic Ocean were German, although there were times when it must have seemed so to many merchant seamen. British submarines of the Royal Navy were active in each of the naval theatres of war, but whereas Britain started the war with 57 submarines, built 176 during the war, and lost a total of 74, Germany started with 56, built 1,093 and lost 785. Thus, at any one time, particularly in 1942 and 1943, the chances were that a submarine seen in the Atlantic was German. This picture shows a British 'S' class boat of 670 tons, of which 62 were built in all.

in properly escorted convoys. By the end of the month the total had passed 100 and settled at 102. Only 15 German submarines were destroyed during the month. For a moment it seemed to the Allied seamen that all was lost. But their commanders knew of the new weapons; were certain the battle was about to turn. April saw only half the Allied losses for a further 15 U-boats sunk. May brought 47 U-Boat losses for fewer Allied ships sunk than in April. Doenitz recognised defeat when he saw it.

On May 24th, Doenitz withdrew the U-Boat fleet from the Atlantic for modification and improvement. In July, the German submarine fleet reappeared in the Atlantic fitted with quadruple cannon on the conning towers. But this expedient proved useless

against the Allied aircraft with their rockets, bombs and depth-charges. During the month of July, 37 more U-boats went to the bottom. In August a further 23 were destroyed.

By December 31st 1943, despite the intensive construction rate of U-boats throughout the year, the German submarine fleet was down to 168 operational vessels, as compared with 212 a year earlier. U-boats were no longer able to attack, or even operate, on the surface, and were forced to observe radio silence or be detected. Gone were the days of German superiority in radio communications. Gone was Doenitz' ability to direct his wolf-packs on their target without also calling in the Allies to their kill. Germany had lost the Battle of the Atlantic.

CHAPTER 28

THE CARDS STACK UP AGAINST JAPAN
NEW GUINEA AND THE SOLOMONS

After Japan's lightning success of the first two months of 1942, there had been a strong body of opinion in the Japanese High Command, particularly in the Navy, that Japan should press on and take Australia, partly for the resources it offered and the prestige of its capture, but more as a means of preventing its becoming the base for an Allied counter-attack. Those who disagreed with the idea of conquering Australia did so largely on the grounds that its sheer size would make it impossibly expensive to hold and garrison. That view, as we know, prevailed.

Nonetheless, it was agreed that New Guinea — the second largest island in the world — should be taken for its strategic position. During May 1942, Japan's planned capture of Port Moresby in New Guinea from the sea had been thwarted by the Battle of the Coral Sea, but on July 21st Major-General Tomataro Horii's South Seas Detachment had landed east of Gona with the intention of taking Port Moresby from the landward side, across the Owen Stanley mountains, via the village of Kokoda. To US and European military planners, this would have seemed an impossible task, but the training and native skills of the Japanese soldiers made them as capable of marching through jungle and apparently impenetrable vegetation as the western armies were of marching along a highway. In fact, the Japanese believed from

aerial reconnaissance that there was a road over the mountains; only later did they discover it to be a two feet wide path known as the Kokoda Track.

By July 28th, the advance party had taken all the initial territory between their beach-head and Kokoda with virtually nil resistance, and had captured Kokoda itself with surprising ease, largely because the Allies had not so far taken the Japanese attack as a serious threat to New Guinea as a whole, or to Port Moresby in particular. On August 24th, General Horii arrived in Kokoda at the head of 8,500 troops that had been put ashore in the wake of the initial landing. He found that a force of Australians — some of them relatively raw militiamen, the rest battle veterans recently returned from North Africa — was putting up a determined stand in the mountains at Isurava. His bombardment of their positions marked the beginning of a bitter struggle; not only did the Australians hold that position for three hard days, inflicting massive casualties on the Japanese, but they made Horii's army fight for every inch of that mountain trail.

The Owen Stanley Mountains are a series of steep, jungle-clad ridges rising to 7,000 feet and more, interspersed with deep valleys. Rivers, disease, the local wildlife and the damp all contributed to making the battle a miserable one for the Australians. Although they fought tenaciously and well, Japanese skill in jungle warfare enabled Horii's infantry to advance inexorably through the raw jungle by a series of the same outflanking movements that had defeated the British Army in Malaya earlier in the year. By mid-September, the Japanese were within thirty-two miles of their objective, Port Moresby, and Horii called a halt on Ioribaiwa Ridge because his supply lines were getting stretched and because, in any event, he had orders not to attempt to take Port Moresby until he was reinforced from the sea via nearby Milne Bay.

Japanese attempts to land those reinforcements went badly. First, the army units assigned to the landing were diverted to Guadalcanal

4 General Douglas MacArthur, Supreme Commander in the Southwest Pacific, striding purposefully from his headquarters in Australia from which he directed operations in New Guinea and the Solomons when not touring the theatre of war that he made peculiarly his. A remarkable, if controversial, figure, Douglas MacArthur proved to be an example of that rare blend of successful soldier and astute politician.

5 Japanese intentions in New Guinea were never in doubt – it was only the means by which they would seek to realise their aims that came as a surprise to the Australians. Here, Brigadier-General Martin F. 'Mike' Scanlon (right) and two Australian officers survey the wreckage of an American aircraft hit by a Japanese bomb during one of the many air raids on Port Moresby.

6 A cigarette for a wounded Australian, hit during the fighting around Kokoda. The grim conditions in which the soldiers of both sides fought during the New Guinea campaign is readily apparent from pictures such as these. Disease and hardship were almost as potent an enemy as the opposing army.

7 High in the mountains of New Guinea, an Australian observation post watches for signs of Japanese troop movement.

1 This Australian army unit pursuing the Japanese has stopped for a break and a conference in a village in the foothills of the Owen Stanley mountains after the recapture of Kokoda. The local inhabitants seem quite relaxed about the regular changes of tenure, although it is noticeable that there is not a single woman in the picture.

2 Lieutenant-General S. Rowell commanded the Allied forces which successfully resisted the Japanese attempt to take Port Moresby from the landward side via the Kokoda track, and subsequently played a major part in the pursuit and humiliation of the Japanese in their retreat over the Owen Stanley mountains.

3 M3 light tanks sheltering in a coconut grove on Cape Endaiadere, New Guinea, during the campaign for Buna. The men in front of the tank on the left wear the familiar slouch hats of the Australian army – it is not clear from the visible markings on the tank to which unit they belong.

4 A striking study of some of the Australians who did so much to make the eventual victory in New Guinea possible – a picture actually taken in Papua at the beginning of 1943, as the Australians mopped up the last pockets of resistance from Japanese remaining in the southwest of New Guinea.

5 General MacArthur was a frequent visitor to his soldiers in the front line, and always wanted to know the hard facts, rather than a laundered version of the truth supplied by staff officers. In this shot he was taking a break during a visit to Australians facing the Japanese at Buna, in the closing months of 1942.

6 The tasks faced and the difficulties overcome by the engineers of the combined Australian-American force in New Guinea were formidable, for moving men, equipment and supplies through a jungle on a mountainside in great heat and humidity taxes the strongest character. These men are bridging a stream using local materials, for there was no means of bringing in prefabricated bridges as was done in Europe when rivers had to be crossed.

because of the US Marine Corps landings there. Then, because the Japanese discovered that the Allies were building an airfield overlooking Milne Bay, the site for the landing was switched to a nearby obscure coconut growing area called Gili-Gili, which not even the Japanese knew well. When the landings took place on August 25th, most things that could go wrong did. One detachment of the Japanese Marines was attacked by Allied aircraft and stranded without its invasion barges miles from its proper landing place. Another Marine unit landed miles from its target and was faced with a long march over densely vegetated hills to rejoin the fight. But this second group, under Commander Hayashi, was made of tough stuff. Fighting only at night, and advancing with a psychologically devastating flame thrower, Hayashi advanced to the airfield that the US Engineers were building between Rabi and Gili-Gili. There he called up reinforcements and, once they had arrived, launched a ferocious

attack on August 31st. To Hayashi's considerable surprise, the Japanese encountered effective, indeed, devastating resistance, and by morning were forced to withdraw, with the Australian defenders in hot pursuit. During the retreat, Hayashi lost his life and his deputy was wounded. Over 600 Japanese soldiers were killed, another 300 were wounded. The Japanese force asked for and were sent an evacuation force, and by September 6th all the survivors were on their way back to Rabaul. The attempt to reinforce Horii's Port Moresby assault had failed, after the great success of the most hazardous part of the endeavour — the actual crossing of the mountains. Only thirty miles or so from Port Moresby, the assault had seemed certain to succeed. What had gone wrong?

The simple answer was — Japanese Intelligence. Between the end of June and the end of August, 4,500 Australian infantry, 3,000 Australian engineers and 1,300 American engineers had been brought into the Milne Bay area. This the Japanese did not know, and did not calculate for, so based all their tactics on the assumption that their opposition was of less than half the strength they actually encountered on the day of the invasion. They were not usually so careless. Now Horii was obliged to pay the cost of that carelessness.

With studied calm, the Allied troops waited. The attack that Horii and the Japanese troops expected did not come, for the Australians knew that his army's supplies were running out and that sooner or later Horii would be obliged to retreat with a hungry army. Desperate attempts by the Japanese to get supplies in from the other side of the mountains failed. On September 24th, the Japanese High Command ordered Horii to withdraw back across the mountains to the coast at

7 The remarkable Lieutenant-General Robert Eichelberger, already known, before General Eisenhower became as famous as he was later to be, as 'Uncle Ike', had been, prior to his command in New Guinea, Commandant of the United States Military Academy at West Point.

8 These heavily-laden assault boats, part of 'Operation Landcrab', are shown making for a beachhead in the Aleutian Islands, on May 11th 1943. The American Marines landed at Holtz Bay, on Attu, in appalling weather, bombarded by fire from Japanese snipers, and fought their way inland over extremely rough terrain.

Buna. The order was a shattering, unimaginable blow to the pride not only of the officers of Horii's army, but also to the ordinary soldiers. They had been brought up to believe that under no conditions could a Japanese soldier retreat. When they were ordered to do so, the psychological blow was such that their morale evaporated. Hungry and ashamed, they ran for their lives.

Two days after the retreat began, the Australians counter-attacked. In hot pursuit, they were stopped on October 21st in the mountains by a rearguard unit positioned by Horii to hold out as long as possible and delay the Australian advance. With suicidal intensity, this small Japanese force did its job well. Despite almost equal determination, the Australians did not manage to break through until October 28th, which gave Horii sufficient time to evacuate Kokoda and set up his final defensive positions at Oivi and Gorari, below the mountains near the Kumusi River.

9 Several British Royal Navy aircraft carriers saw extensive service in the Pacific. This is HMS *Victorious*, a 30,000 ton carrier, completed in 1941, her decks lined with US Navy fighters and torpedo bombers.

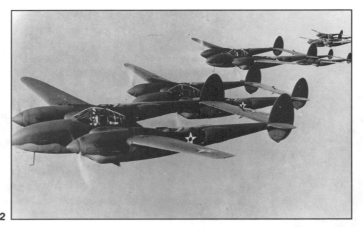

1 The role of the United States submarine service in the Pacific war should not be underestimated, since sinkings of Japanese cargo and military transport ships made an important contribution to Japan's defeat. This small cargo vessel is well ablaze after being torpedoed by an American submarine.

2 The long-range operation to shoot down the plane carrying Admiral Yamamoto to Bougainville was carried out by a squadron of Lockheed P-38 Lightnings like these, flying to the very limit of their fuel capacity. The Lightning was the most successful long-range tactical fighter of the Second World War.

3 Extensive training in the techniques and problems of amphibious landings was undertaken before the series of invasions that recaptured the Solomon Islands. These American invasion barges are driving towards a southwest Pacific island beach laden with steel-helmeted Marines during one of many training exercises.

The Australians reached Oivi first, on November 5th 1942, and heavy fighting ensued, with the attackers making little headway against well-organised Japanese defence. Five days later, Australian troops attacked Gorari, and quickly overcame resistance. Now the defenders of Oivi risked being cut off if they did not head for the sea. They retreated again, along the river towards the coast. In small units, the South Seas Detachment crossed the Kumusi and headed for Buna. When they reached the coast, those that survived were in appalling condition. Starvation, Allied bombing, malaria and infected wounds wrought havoc with Horii's army. Horii had himself been killed attempting to cross the Kumusi on a raft to rejoin his soldiers. But, somehow, having completed the retreat, and thereby discharged their orders under grave adversity, the surviving Japanese soldiers' morale

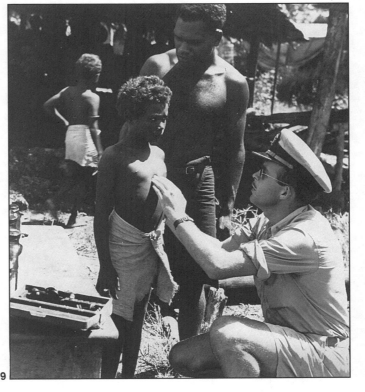

recovered, and they set about a spirited defence of their position at Buna. Japanese reinforcements arrived from Rabaul, in New Britain, their Australian attackers themselves became bogged down by the same problems of disease as had afflicted the Japanese, and by the end of November, no further Allied progress was being made at Buna.

General Douglas MacArthur responded to this situation from his base in Australia by sending US General Robert L. Eichelberger and 15,000 fresh troops to take Buna. His orders to Eichelberger were direct and to the point. 'Take Buna, or don't come back alive'.

Eichelberger was one of those remarkable Generals — Rommel was another — who genuinely and without affectation lead from the front because they know no other way. He wore badges of rank within view of snipers despite the common practice of not doing so. He operated from command posts only yards from his enemy. His example revitalised the Australian troops' morale and determination and brought great spirit and bravery from the Americans. Early in December, a remarkable exploit by one Sergeant Bottcher and his platoon of eighteen US soldiers had resulted in the capture and holding of a vital position on the beach between the two halves of the Japanese force. This gave the subsequent major assault on December 18th, when tanks and infantry advanced on 150 Japanese

4 Admiral Halsey, who commanded the US forces in the campaign to retake the Solomon Islands, showed himself to be an expert tactician and an excellent commander in the relatively new military discipline of combined operations. Here Halsey (right) is shown with two officers of his staff, Colonel W.E. Riley, US Marine Corps (left), and Lieutenant W.J. Kitchell, US Navy.

5 The real thing, as seen from the air. American invasion barges full of crouching Marines snake in across a sparkling sea to an apparently innocuous sandy beach. Behind almost every palm lies the threat of death as waiting Japanese defenders, expecting to hold the island to the last, prepare for the invaders.

6 On the beaches of Mono Island, in the Treasury group of the Central Solomons, American soldiers lie dead at the water's edge, shot by snipers in the dense undergrowth that seem to ring every beach in the Pacific. In the background, crouching US troops move forward cautiously, watching for every movement that might betray the position of the Japanese marksmen.

7 An aerial view of the fire-swept island of Tanamboga after an American carrier-based air attack had competed a raid on Japanese gun emplacements and anti-aircraft batteries. In the upper left of the picture is Gavutu Island, which was also attacked from the air and then invaded.

8 As the Americans recaptured islands that had been taken early in 1942 by the Japanese, the often poorly-fed population were examined by US Navy doctors and treated at improvised clinics. Treatment, particularly for infectious diseases, was as much a preventative measure against epidemics among American troops as a humanitarian gesture towards the local population.

9 This clinic was on the island of New Georgia, where the Americans had landed on June 21st 1943. The small boy looks none too sure of the good intentions of the Navy doctor who is examining him. The lad's father is there to reassure him – doubtless he too had been examined.

The Cards Stack up Against Japan

bunkers in the face of deadly fire, a real chance of success. Despite enormous casualties — something like half the Australians taking part were killed or wounded — the Allied force established itself in strength along the coast. Gradually the battle went the way of the Allies, but losses both to Japanese arms and to malaria and other diseases remained very high. Incredibly, General Eichelberger managed to go through the whole campaign without injury or illness, and, at the end of January, was able to report to General MacArthur that Buna was once more in the possession of the Allies.

For two more years, almost to the end of the Pacific war, the battle for New Guinea was to continue, as the American and Australian troops pushed the Japanese ever further northward in an endless battle of pocket and foxhole, sniper and ambush. The fight for New Guinea was hard on both sides. It was, in a sense, a microcosm of the Pacific war — yet it was unique. It was the island to end all islands in a war to reclaim islands.

The Solomons

The battle for Guadalcanal, which was taking place at the same time as the events in New Guinea, ended after a hard and bloody campaign with total victory for the US Marines in February 1943. Japanese and American commentators alike were to reflect with hindsight that Guadalcanal was the beginning of the end for Japan. After that first battle for the Solomons, Japan was never to achieve another advance. For the next two and a half years, she was to be in retreat.

For the time being, however, there was no sign of defeatism in the Japanese approach to their problems in the Solomon Islands.

1 The Battle of the Bismarck Sea, which started on February 28th 1943, had been a major disaster for the Japanese army in New Guinea. Eight troop transports and five escorting destroyers were, over a period of almost four days, destroyed by aerial bombardment directed by Major-General Kenney. The original caption to this aerial picture of the Japanese fleet, taken by one of the bomber crewmen, claimed that every one of the twenty-two ships visible in the original print was sunk. This exaggeration was designed to lift morale.

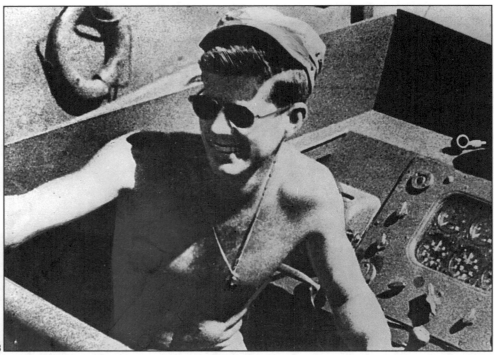

2 Japanese camouflage techniques were often extremely clever, but on other occasions were downright bizarre. This Japanese transport ship had been covered overall in palm leaves and tropical foliage so that it could pass between islands without being spotted. However, in the open sea it was a trifle obvious. and, as US fighter-bomber crews found, burned rather better than usual following a hit.

3 Lieutenant John F. Kennedy at the controls of his PT Boat in the Solomon Islands in 1943. Second son of Ambassador Joseph Kennedy, who had raised a furore in London in 1940 by his apparently pro-Axis views, JFK and his elder brother Joe, who was killed in slightly mysterious circumstances while flying a Liberator bomber, more than compensated for any lingering doubts about the family's patriotism.

4 Some of the tough and battle-hardened New Zealand troops in the Pacific theatre took over the garrisoning of islands taken by the US Marines in the Solomons. This was no easy option, for the Japanese were given to attempts to re-invade territories that they had lost in order to salvage their honour, however unrealistic in practice such an invasion attempt might be.

5 The town of Lae, in the Huon Gulf in the east of New Guinea, was the scene in September 1943 of the first Allied airborne invasion in the Pacific theatre of war. General MacArthur was unable to resist the temptation to go along and watch the drop from the air, and saw American paratroops descend on the Markham Valley, west of Lae, to block the escape of 20,000 Japanese troops who were facing Australian troops who had landed east of Lae. The aircraft is, of course, the familiar Douglas DC3 Dakota.

6 A remarkable picture of American paratroops descending on New Guinea, taken from the open door of the aircraft. As the leading soldier's parachute begins to open (bottom right) the next man puts his head down and dives out of the door, his spade flying at his side.

7 A dramatic aerial picture of the drop-zone at Lae as the American paras spread out behind a smokescreen laid to conceal the action from the Japanese troops on the other side of the river. The Lae drop was carried out from a lower altitude than had ever before been attempted in battle.

8 An Australian infantryman (left) shakes hands with a US paratrooper after the successful drop in the Markham Valley near Lae, New Guinea, had made possible a successful pincer operation to encircle Japanese garrisons at Lae and Salamaua.

9 Back in the Solomons, on August 15th 1943, invasion craft loaded with men of the 25th US Division made a relatively unopposed landing on Vella Lavella. This was the scene at dawn on that day as the apprehensive soldiers, who had no way of knowing that their landing was to prove uneventful, made their way ashore across a choppy sea.

The Cards Stack up Against Japan

They were, quite simply, determined to hold on to them at all costs, and to surrender nothing without a major battle. Fresh Japanese infantry, aircraft and ships were rushed to the Solomons after the debacle of Guadalcanal, and a major air offensive was launched in April 1943 against Allied bases in the Solomon Islands and New Guinea, although it did not achieve anything very significant. Admiral Yamamoto, who had planned and executed the attack on Pearl Harbour, decided to visit the area in May for a factfinding and morale-boosting tour, and had coded messages sent to local commanders so that they knew when he was coming. Unfortunately for him, he still did not know that the American Navy was able to decode virtually all Japanese naval transmissions. The news of Yamamoto's travel arrangements was communicated to Admiral Halsey, and he in turn set up a reception committee.

Yamamoto was due to arrive on Bougainville, in the Northern Solomons, at 9.30am on April 18th. With split second timing, an American squadron of eighteen P-38 Lightnings that had flown at the very limit of their range from Henderson Field on Guadalcanal pounced on his aircraft as it landed, shot it up on the runway, and killed Japan's greatest leader. As a psychological blow, following the Japanese reverses in New Guinea and Guadalcanal, the killing of Yamamoto was unparallelled during Japan's war until the nuclear attacks on Hiroshima and Nagasaki.

The Allied campaign in the Solomon Islands was one half of the strategy agreed by the Allies in the summer of 1943 by which the attack that the Japanese were expecting on their heavily defended southern Pacific base at Rabaul should be abandoned. Instead, the Allies put General Douglas MacArthur in command of a two

1 A dramatic picture of bombardment by United States naval guns during the hours immediately before dawn on the day that one of the many amphibious invasions of the Solomons campaign went ashore. Extended periods of shelling, often lasting days and usually culminating in a final, morale-breaking bombardment immediately before the assault, were found significantly to reduce American losses on the beaches.

2 A striking portrait of Lieutenant-General Alexander Vandegrift, taken in 1944 when he had become Commandant of the US Marine Corps. In 1942 he had commanded the Marines on Guadalcanal, and on November 1st 1943, as a Major-General, he led the US Marines at the Empress Augusta Bay landings to retake Bougainville.

3 The Second World War was a major opportunity for engineers of an inventive turn of mind to exercise their skills to the full, and the development of new and ever more sophisticated landing craft made a major contribution to the success of the Allied war effort. This is an LVT-1 of the US Navy, photographed off the island of Bougainville in the Solomon Islands during US operations to recapture it from the Japanese. The LVT-1, often known as the 'Alligator' because of its being derived from a civil amphibian used in the Florida Everglades, had a 120 hp engine and no armour. From it was developed the LVT-2 'Water Buffalo' which saw service in all the major amphibious operations of the second half of the war.

pronged pincer movement around the base in New Britain which would both recapture the Solomon Islands in the North-East and New Guinea to the South-West, while at the same time cutting off from reinforcement and supplies the Japanese forces in Rabaul. Thus the battles in New Guinea as the US forces fought their way slowly North-West after the capture of Buna from the Japanese, and the island-hopping forays along the chain of the Solomons were part of one and the same campaign. Admiral Halsey, who commanded the US forces in the Solomons, was therefore under the overall command of General MacArthur. His objective was Bougainville, the north-ernmost island of the archipelago, but there was little chance of attacking Bougainville without first gaining the islands between as bases to provide fighter cover for the landings.

Halsey began with an assault on New Georgia, which offered an

4 The hand-to-hand fighting on Bougainville is illustrated by this picture and the story behind it. The M2 light tank was that of the unit commander, Lieutenant Leon A. Stanley of Anniston, Alabama. As the tank approached the body of a marine, who had been killed by the Japanese and deliberately left in the centre of the track, it struck a trip wire which set off a mine, disabling the tank. Armed with carbines, the crew climbed out of the tank and were met with Japanese fire, which killed Lieutenant Stanley, whose body can be seen in front of the tank. In the foreground, Private First Class Robert E. Lansley (second from left) is drawing Japanese fire to reveal the enemy positions. The Japanese mounting the ambush were all killed by the Americans in the end.

5 The amphibious LVT vehicles used for the landings in the Solomons were used by the Marines, once ashore, as an effective means of traversing the swampy ground that was one of the hazards of Pacific island warfare. These marines were taking a break during the reconquest of Bougainville.

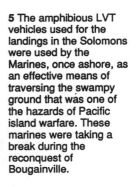

6 A dramatic picture of US soldiers of the 37th Division during mopping-up operations on Bougainville. Remaining Japanese soldiers were launching themselves in *Banzai* attacks on US positions in the Empress Augusta beachhead area, and these infantrymen were going forward under cover of a tank. The picture was taken as the soldier nearest spotted a hidden Japanese soldier and fired.

7 Clearing Pacific islands of Japanese soldiers whose code permitted no consideration of retreat, and for whom death was an honour to be sought, required searching every thicket, every knot of trees. These Marines are cautiously searching some undergrowth in the belief that Japanese snipers may be hidden there. They are totally exposed should an enemy open fire – but what option had they but to accept that risk?

8 A speech of thanks from Major-General Allen H. Turnage of the US Marine Corps to the battle-weary men under his command, after they had defeated the Japanese totally at the Battle of Cape Torokina on Bougainville.

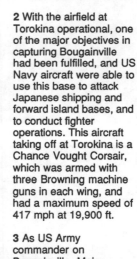

1 After the capture of Torokina, a major building operation was mounted to construct a fully operational military airfield there for the onward thrust towards Japan. The airfield was opened on December 10th 1943, and early in 1944, Marine Major-General Roy S. Geiger, Commanding General of the first Marine Amphibious Corps (right) greeted Major-General Oscar W. Griswold, XIV Army Corps Commanding General.

2 With the airfield at Torokina operational, one of the major objectives in capturing Bougainville had been fulfilled, and US Navy aircraft were able to use this base to attack Japanese shipping and forward island bases, and to conduct fighter operations. This aircraft taking off at Torokina is a Chance Vought Corsair, which was armed with three Browning machine guns in each wing, and had a maximum speed of 417 mph at 19,900 ft.

3 As US Army commander on Bougainville, Major-General Oscar Griswold (left, in peaked cap), was under the overall command of Lieutenant-General Millard F. Harmon, (right, holding map), Commander-in-Chief of US Army Forces in the South Pacific area. Together they were a formidable team.

ideal base for fighters at Munda airfield, but which was almost unassailable by conventional amphibious landing techniques because of the coral reefs around the island and the narrowness of the channels through which landing craft would have to pass. Halsey therefore planned a preliminary series of landings on neighbouring islands from which to attack from the air before putting his ground forces at risk. After a few small unopposed landings at the southern end of New Georgia itself and on nearby Vangunu Island, 6,000 men of the US 43rd Infantry Division landed on the night of 29/30 June on Rendova Island, South-West of New Georgia and, without too many problems, secured the island. Two days later, the rest of Major-General John Hester's 43rd Infantry Division landed successfully at Zanana on the southern coast of New Georgia, and another smaller force landed on the northern coast.

Their joint attempt to capture Munda did not go well. The Japanese defenders were determined, well dug-in, armed to the teeth and well supplied. The heat and the jungle terrain were devastating to inexperienced troops. Despite reinforcements, the advance slowed to a halt within five days. Encouraged, the Japanese commander called up reinforcements from Rabaul. Despite a series of 'Tokyo Express' naval battles North of New Georgia as the US Navy attempted to stop the troop transports — a situation reminiscent of the earlier battles around Guadalcanal — some 2,000 Japanese soldiers were successfully put ashore to join Major-General Sasaki's defenders. The inexperienced American troops soon learned of the Japanese predilection for night attacks, and of their skill in jungle warfare. US losses were high, and their successes minimal.

Six weeks after the initial landing, the American forces were only half way to their first objective at Munda, despite reinforcements.

To inject new resolve into the campaign, Major-General Oscar Griswold, commander of XIV Corps, decided to take over in New Georgia and get some results. A major attack with additional artillery began on July 25th, but progress remained slow. Griswold reacted by replacing General Hester with Major-General John Hodge, who had been at Guadalcanal, and gradually the campaign gathered momentum. On August 4th, the 43rd finally took Munda, although at enormous cost, and Halsey had got his first island airfield North of Henderson Field. By August 14th it was in operation. By the end of August, all remaining Japanese troops on New Georgia had been flushed out.

The next target in the Solomon Islands was Kolombangara, which also had a useful airstrip, and therefore a force of Japanese defenders, commanded by that same General Sasaki who had recently been ejected from New Georgia. Sasaki had, in fact, 10,000 troops under his command, and was planning his counter-attack on New Georgia to assuage the dishonour of his recent defeat. Reinforcements were being brought in from Rabaul to take part in this attack, and the transports and their escorts bringing them were being attacked by US PT boats from Rendova. One of those PT boats was commanded by Lieutenant John F. Kennedy. After his boat was run down by a Japanese destroyer, he managed first to get himself ashore, and then to carry out a one-man seaborne rescue operation which saved most of his crew. He swam miles despite injuries to his back. The future President was tough as well as charismatic.

Five days later three of a force of four Japanese warships attempting to reinforce Sasaki's army were torpedoed by American destroyers, and took to the bottom almost two whole battalions of Japanese soldiers. Nonetheless, some got through, and Admiral Halsey began to like less and less the idea of another grinding offensive against an even more suicidally determined Sasaki. So he

4 As 1943 drew to a close and 1944 began, fighting continued in New Guinea, and new landings were planned and put into effect. This wounded Australian was being carried back from the forward area of the Australian attack on Sattelberg, in November 1943.

5 In this dramatic action picture shot during the full fury of the Australian attack at the Battle of Sattelberg, New Guinea, the uncertainty and tension of fighting amid jungle undergrowth against an enemy who is adept at jungle warfare comes over vividly. The soldier on the right has a large field dressing around his head but is still fighting.

6 On December 15th 1943, substantial American forces landed at Arawe, on the island of New Britain, whose major seaport Rabaul had been the principal Japanese base in the Southwest Pacific. This LST (landing ship – tank) is crammed with troops and supplies as it noses into the beach at Arawe.

7 The extraordinary scene on the beach at Arawe as the rows of LST craft disgorged men, tanks, bulldozers and transport vehicles – a scene that was to repeated many times in both the European and Pacific theatres of war during 1944.

8 Further US landings in New Britain took place at Cape Gloucester, a former Japanese stronghold on the island. As the Americans captured the majority of the island, the Japanese withdrew to defensive positions on the Gazelle Peninsula in the northeast, and Cape Gloucester became a major supply base for the giant LST landing craft. The size of these vessels can be judged from this picture of the deck of such a craft, loaded with jeeps, trucks, fuel, food supplies and weapons.

decided instead to go around Kolombangara and take Vella Lavella, just North-West of his original target. There, he reasoned, he could build an airfield from scratch, then isolate Sasaki and bring him down gradually. Moreover, Vella Lavella was that much closer to Bougainville, the ultimate objective in the Solomons.

On August 15th, part of the 25th Division landed on Vella Lavella against some resistance from the air but comparatively little on the ground. This proved to be because there were few Japanese on the island. As military historian Lieutenant-Colonel Bauer put it The Americans had more trouble finding them than defeating them. By the end of September, Vella Lavella was securely in Allied hands, and a detachment of New Zealanders had taken over its custody from the American troops that had captured it. At about the same time, General Sasaki was ordered to evacuate Kolombangara, and early in October some 9,000 Japanese troops were succesfully pulled back to Bougainville despite the energetic efforts of the US Navy to stop them. Now there were some 40,000 Japanese troops on Bougainville, under the overall command of General Hyakutake, late of Guadalcanal, plus a further 20,000 Japanese Navy men. A tough nut for Halsey to crack.

He decided to employ again the strategy of bypassing the objective in order to isolate it, and resolved to attempt an amphibious landing at the relatively lightly defended Empress Augusta Bay region in the centre of the Western coast of Bougainville, where he could establish airfields and attack the supply convoys from Rabaul bringing reinforcements to the Japanese forces in the North and South of the island. To confuse the Japanese as to his objectives, two small diversionary landings were staged, on 27th October in the Treasury Islands to the South (by New Zealand troops) and later the same day on Choiseul to the East (US Marines). For a week, these assaults caused a lot of noise and confusion, and diverted attention from the Empress Augusta Bay landing, which, when it took place on November 1st, met very little opposition. The Japanese had believed that nobody would be mad enough to land on such open marshy land.

The commander of the Marines landing at Empress Augusta Bay was the formidable General Vandegrift who had led the conquest of Guadalcanal. He quickly captured a substantial beach-head and organised effective defences against air attack. The Japanese attempted to counter-attack against the beach-head both by air and by sea, but in both cases encountered stiff opposition and suffered severe

losses — although the US Navy fared almost as badly as the Japanese in the Battle of Empress Augusta Bay overnight on August 1st/2nd. Halsey struck back with two carrier borne air strikes against the Japanese bases at Rabaul on November 5th and 11th, which pushed the Japanese Navy back to safer bases further North, and thereby reduced the pressure on Bougainville and the other Solomon Islands.

On November 8th, the 37th Infantry Division landed to reinforce Vandegrift's force, and he began to enlarge his beach-head. He never looked back. Gradually the Japanese were pushed further and further from the beach-head, although with no major American assault. In March 1944, Hyatuke made his last attempt to push the Americans off Bougainville but achieved nothing more than the loss of 6,000 troops. He had lost the battle, and never again attacked in force.

1 At Aitape on the Northern New Guinea coast, on April 22nd 1944, US landing craft made successful landings and established large beachheads. In all, it was estimated that the various landings in Northern New Guinea late in April 1944 faced opposition from about 60,000 Japanese troops.

2 Mountain peaks silhouetted against the early morning sky make a striking picture as an LST manned by US Coastguardsmen shoves forward at the head of its task force unit into Tanahmerah Bay during the invasion of Hollandia. The landing craft is packed tightly with men and equipment.

3 A very different landing craft from the huge LST was the LCI – (landing craft – infantry). During the landings on the north coast of New Guinea, these US infantry were brought ashore by this LCI, and charged down the twin ramps with their rifles ready for action.

4 The effectiveness of the US Army Air Force in the reconquest of New Guinea should not be underestimated. These Japanese aircraft on what had been Wewak airfield have been destroyed by bombing by the 15th US Army Air Force. In the centre background, parachute bombs are still falling to complete the destruction of the formerly powerful Japanese base.

5 A further ever-present hazard of tropical jungle warfare is the rain and the resulting mud. In this powerful picture, the torrential tropical rain on New Britain has almost hidden a 75mm howitzer crew whose commander has his arm raised to give the command to fire

During the first half of 1944, the US troops on Bougainville were replaced with Australians, and the Americans moved on to capture more islands on their relentless journey to Tokyo. Rabaul had, by the two successes of the campaigns in the Solomons and in New Guinea, been successfully isolated from the rest of the Japanese war effort, and could be disregarded as an effective war base.

Almost as important was the huge drain on Japanese human and arms resources caused by their losses in the twin campaigns of New Guinea and the Solomons. Their army, navy and air force could never recover from the slaughter, and their ability to counter-attack was relentlessly reduced as each successive island campaign was won. The seal had been affixed to Japan's eventual defeat. It was a matter of time – and determination.

6 In July 1944, another major American parachute drop was made in support of amphibious landings on Noemfoor Island off the north coast of New Guinea. About 100 miles west of Biak Island, and 800 miles from the Philippines, Noemfoor Island had three important, strategic Japanese-built airstrips, which were captured by the Allied soldiers during a five-day campaign. Note the men and vehicles already ashore from the amphibious landing as the parachutists descend.

7 As the parachutists descended to do battle inland on Noemfoor, US Army troops stormed ashore from landing craft to the beaches, quickly seizing three airfields and silencing Japanese resistance within four days of their arrival. The seizure of Noemfoor was particularly important since the island's airfields were within bombing range of the Philippines for the American aircraft of the time.

CHAPTER 29

THE POLITICS OF WAR
QUEBEC, CAIRO AND TEHERAN

By mid 1943 it was clear to the leaders of the three senior Allied powers, indeed to most of the world, that Germany and Japan would lose the war, and that the combined forces of the Allies would win it. Each of those leaders — Roosevelt, Churchill and Stalin — began to speculate on the attitudes of the others to the postwar world. Each was prey to the prejudices about and fears of the others that had until now been suppressed in the common cause.

Roosevelt and the US advisers began once more to think as an isolationist government — and yet to see the potential for world power that the USA's coming of age in international politics had brought. Roosevelt had an underlying belief in seeking and finding good in everyone, even a Communist tyrant who had been liquidating his opponents since before Roosevelt was President. He did not see in the USSR's fearsome accumulation of armed might the threat to the future of Europe that Churchill had come to believe was inevitable.

With General Marshall, the keystone of Washington strategic planning, Roosevelt shared a deep mistrust of the extent to which Britain was committed to an invasion of Europe across the English

1 On the other side of the Atlantic, in Britain, some of the greatest decisions of the war were taken in this room, the underground headquarters of the British War Cabinet and Chiefs of Staff in Marsham Street, Westminster. Situated fifty feet below ground, the headquarters had 150 rooms, and could provide work and accommodation space for 270 people, who could eat, sleep and work without surfacing for weeks on end.

2 It is easy to think of the policy of the Allied war effort as being entirely in the hands of the great Western leaders. In fact, scores of important leaders, military and political, many of them little remembered except by historians, played major roles in the planning and execution of Second World War strategy. In this picture, President Roosevelt is being shown a model of the newly-designed escort carriers by Henry J. Kaiser (second from left), the miracle ship-builder whose drive and leadership resulted in fifty escort carriers being constructed in just one year.

3 Winston Churchill is met in Washington by President Franklin D. Roosevelt when he arrived for talks in May 1943.

4 The Washington Conference of May 1943 was in itself a significant gathering of the US and British Chiefs of Staff. In this group picture are (left to right) Field Marshal John Dill, Lieutenant-General Hastings Ismay, Air Marshal Sir Charles Portal, General Sir Alan Brooke, Admiral Sir Dudley Pound, Admiral Leahy, General George C. Marshall, Admiral King and Lieutenant-General McNarney.

5 The Cairo Conference in November 1943 was dominated, against Churchill's wishes, by the aspirations of the Chinese Nationalists. Here the issue of who should sit in the central chair for the photograph has become the subject of a friendly argument, Roosevelt and Chiang Kai-shek (in peaked cap, behind) each insisting that the other should take the place of honour. Dr Hollington Tong, Vice Minister of the Chinese Ministry of Information, is in earnest discussion with the President on this important point.

6 This picture of the three leaders at Cairo was presented by the news media at the time as 'the three men who drew up the plans for the shrinkage of the Japanese Empire into the confines that bound it fifty years ago'. In fact, the Cairo Conference did little to achieve that particular objective. With (left to right) Generalissimo Chiang Kai-shek, Roosevelt and Churchill is the popular Madame Chiang, who acted as her husband's interpreter, and was known as 'Missimo'.

7 Surely the picture that the big three (particularly Churchill) intended should be taken. Resolute determination and confidence shines forth from all three leaders.

Channel — to the operation that had been called 'Roundup' and was now rechristened 'Overlord'. Twice already, Britain had deferred a major landing in northern Europe when the USA was eager to fight Germany in France. Now, Roosevelt feared, Churchill and his adviser Sir Alan Brooke would do it again, and would seek to involve the USA in Southern Europe, bringing America into the Mediterranean theatre even more deeply than she was already. The American President and his advisers believed that the memory of Dunkirk, of Flanders, of the Somme and Passchendaele was too vivid for Britain's military leaders to commit themselves wholly to France. Therefore, they reasoned, 'Overlord' must have an American commander. In fact they went further, and sought to gain acceptance from Churchill of a US Supreme Commander for all operations against Germany.

Britain's military planners, for their part, had never lost their mistrust of US military methods; of what they regarded as slapdash planning, brash arrogance and an insensitive attitude to European needs. To them, as to Britain's mothers guarding their daughters, the US forces were 'oversexed, overpaid and over here'. Churchill, despite his close personal relationship with Franklin D. Roosevelt, was aware of Roosevelt's leaning to acceptance of his military advisers' views, and he did not like it. Churchill and Brooke were doubtful of the wisdom of Roosevelt's continuing faith in and desire

to help Chiang Kai-shek in China, and had no confidence in American acceptance in principle of demands by Chiang for greatly increased commitment of US troops and aircraft that were desperately needed to win the war against Germany. Churchill believed deeply in the strategy of 'Germany First', and was (probably wrongly) doubtful of the extent of the Pentagon's belief in the strategy agreed and reaffirmed at each Allied conference.

Perhaps more important, Churchill saw clearly Stalin's intention that the USSR should dominate Europe after the war, but was obliged nonetheless, in order to preserve the alliance and the relationship with Roosevelt, to participate in strategic planning which pivoted on the basic and inaccurate assumption that the USSR was honest, trustworthy and prepared to honour its pledges. To Churchill, Roosevelt's trust of Stalin, and the ailing President's courtship of the tyrannical Soviet leader, were deeply disturbing.

Stalin, for his part, believed that Russia had been fighting the Germans virtually single-handed since June 1941 — a view to which statistics alone would lend credence. His perpetual impatience, rising to blazing anger, at the failure of Britain to support US plans for an invasion of Northern Europe in 1942, then again in 1943, caused him to accuse Churchill and the British people of cowardice, an unwillingness to fight and a lack of fellow feeling for Britain's allies. The probability is that he had hoped for a premature invasion of

The Politics of War

France so that the British and Americans would become bogged down in a stalemate battle that they could not win, and thereby weaken Germany in the East by causing her to fight on two major fronts. That weakening would have enabled Stalin to realise to an even greater degree than he eventually did his true objective — the subjugation of Europe. Had Churchill not held out against a cross-Channel invasion until the Allies could push the German Army back where it came from, West Germany as we know it today would not exist.

Quebec

All these conflicts, undercurrents, fears and doubts came to the surface when Churchill heard from Averill Harriman that Roosevelt was planning a US-Soviet meeting without Britain. Swiftly, Churchill proposed an alternative summit meeting in Canada, which Roosevelt accepted. On August 14th, after a sedate crossing of the Atlantic in the *Queen Mary*, the Allied Chiefs of Staff met in one place, while Churchill and Roosevelt met in private elsewhere. It soon became apparent that these and the subsequent meetings at Quebec turned on the fundamental issue of 'Overlord' versus the Mediterranean theatre — a disagreement that had already been settled once at Casablanca. The American planners were convinced (with some justice in the light of postwar evidence) that Churchill was still seeking either greater commitment in the Mediterranean, or an invasion in Norway, or an assault in the Balkans — anything rather than a head-on confrontation in France. The facts were that, although Churchill had been energetically pursuing alternatives in the belief that 'Overlord' was an intensely risky undertaking, he had been convinced by the immensely upright Sir Alan Brooke that the commitment to 'Overlord' was right, and must stand.

Nonetheless, the British position at the Quebec conference was that a full-scale invasion in Italy to capitalise on the confusion following Mussolini's departure was vital as a prelude to an invasion of France. Only by having bases in northern Italy, the British argued, could the Allies have the means to strike at vital aircraft and arms manufacture in Southern Germany. This view, subject to an acceptance by Britain that 'Overlord' should have over-riding priority, was accepted reluctantly by the US President and the Chiefs of Staff, but the slowness of the campaign in Italy was to show that General Marshall may well have been right, and Brooke and Churchill wrong. During its discussions of European strategy, the Quebec conference also concluded that the bombing offensive on Germany should be intensified, again as a necessary preliminary to an invasion of France.

When the conference discussed the Far Eastern war, it was the turn of the British to express doubts about American objectives and policies. Yet here there was an illogical and unrealistic contradiction in the British position, perhaps because Churchill knew that it was the intention of the US delegation to suggest and promote at a later date a large scale landing in Burma with the objective of reopening the Burma Road. On the face of it, all the Americans were proposing for the Far East at Quebec was a nebulous British commitment to a greater effort in Burma, possibly because they feared that Britain did not intend doing much to advance the defeat of Japan in the forseeable future. The British Chiefs of Staff, resenting the implication of inaction and unwillingness to do battle, were nonetheless unprepared to agree to a Burma commitment because they knew such a strategy would inevitably mean amphibious landings, which would drain the available resources of landing craft and support vessels needed for 'Overlord'.

The contradiction was that, despite this rejection of positive plans for Burma, Churchill was enthusiastic about the plans propounded by Brigadier Orde Wingate, who was also at Quebec, for Chindit operations on a huge scale as a means of retaking Burma. In alarm, it was pointed out that such a plan would cause an even greater drain on 'Overlord' than an amphibious landing.

Ater days of muddled discussion on the Far East issue, one of the few positive, far-reaching and successful decisions reached was the creation of an Allied South-East Asia Command, and the appointment to its command of Vice-Admiral Lord Louis Mountbatten, with General Stilwell as his deputy. In addition, the conference endorsed the decision, already being acted upon, to advance in New Guinea and the Solomons as a two-prong pincer movement to bypass and isolate Rabaul, and set a target date for the defeat of Japan as twelve months after the defeat of Germany.

1 A less formal group at the Cairo Conference is interesting for its inclusion of two subsequent British Prime Ministers – Mr Anthony Eden, standing, second from left, who was Britain's Secretary of State for Foreign Affairs at the time, and Mr Harold Macmillan (back row, right). In the dark suit on Eden's left is Mr John Winant, US Ambassador to Britain.

2 At the Teheran Conference that followed the Cairo meeting in November 1943, Winston Churchill presented to Josef Stalin on behalf of the people of Britain the Sword of Stalingrad. This fine sword, which had been specially forged in Britain, commemorated the hard-fought Soviet victory at Stalingrad which had turned the tide of war in Russia. Here, President Roosevelt holds the sword aloft.

3 Following the presentation of the Sword of Stalingrad, Prime Minister Winston Churchill stands in salute with Foreign Secretary Anthony Eden beside him during the playing of the Russian National Anthem. Marshal Stalin is flanked by Marshal Voroshilov on his right and Soviet Foreign Minister Molotov on his left.

4 Winston Churchill was not usually as cheerful as this when confronted by Josef Stalin, of whom he was not overly fond.

Cairo and Teheran

In November 1943, after Roosevelt had refused to meet Churchill privately in Malta for a preliminary discussion before a summit conference at which Stalin and Chiang Kai-shek (the latter at Roosevelt's insistence) were to be present, Churchill sailed for Cairo in the battlecruiser *Renown*. The two linked conferences at Cairo and Teheran that were to last three weeks through the second half of November and the first week of December would clearly decide Allied strategy for the conduct of the remainder of the Second World War, and Churchill was far from happy — and, incidentally, far from well, with a severe sore throat and the effects of his inoculations for the trip keeping him in bed for days.

The Cairo conference took place in the shadow of the Sphinx at Giza, with Chiang Kai-shek present, but without Stalin. Mountbatten and Stilwell, the latter still Chiang's Chief of Staff despite his additional appointment as Deputy Supreme Commander South-East Asia, were also there. To Churchill's intense irritation, South-East Asia strategic issues were moved to second place on the agenda, and the continuing debate about the relationship between 'Overlord' and the Mediterranean war was relegated to third spot on the bill. Chiang was determined to get more than his fair share of conference time, and, if he could, more than a sensible slice of Allied resources, with the result that the detailed debate about Europe that Churchill wanted in plenary session before the encounter with Stalin in Teheran was late coming, and limited in scope. Despite this, separate meetings on Europe and Asia took place between the Chiefs of Staff each day, and there was considerable overlap between the two groups. Chiang fought hard for an impossibly large airlift of supplies over 'The Hump' to China, and in fact gained a commitment to 8,900 tons of supplies per month for the next two months. He also pushed hard

5 The inevitable press conference at the end of the Teheran Conference resulted in this interesting glimpse of the scramble by photographers and newsreel cameramen of the various service film units, as Josef Stalin, President Roosevelt and Winston Churchill sit at the top of the steps. Note the senior staff officers waiting 'in the wings'.

6 Far away from the conferences in Cairo and Teheran, Secretary of State Cordell Hull (left) was becoming ill, and would be obliged to resign in November 1944 because of his ill-health. Succeeding him would be his deputy, Under Secretary of State Edward R. Stettinius Junior (right), who thereby became the second youngest Secretary of State in US history – the youngest was Edmond Randolph, appointed at the age of 41 by President George Washington in 1794. Stettinius became, as its administrator, a major factor in the success of the lend-lease programme.

7 The US candidates for the European Supreme Command photographed together – General George C. Marshall (forage cap) and General Dwight D. Eisenhower (peaked cap). Churchill, if he had to accept an American commander for 'Overlord', wanted Marshall. Roosevelt said Marshall was too valuable to lose from Washington – and Eisenhower got the top job.

8 A fine picture of Sir Alan Brooke, Churchill's Chief of the Imperial General Staff, and the man Britain's Premier wanted to command the Normandy invasion, as he was at the end of the war, when he had been promoted Field Marshal. He is talking to Major General Skliarov of the Red Army.

for an invasion of the Andaman Islands (Operation 'Buccaneer') as an essential precursor to driving the Japanese northwards across Burma and reopening the Burma Road, and had the support of Roosevelt and the American Chiefs of Staff for this plan. The British demurred, wanting the overall strategy in South East Asia agreed before detailed individual operations were planned, and presented their proposals for further operations in the Mediterranean.

The British proposal was neatly summed up by Churchill as "Rome in January, Rhodes in February, supplies to the Yugoslavs, a settlement of the command arrangements and the opening of the Aegean, subject to the outcome of an approach to Turkey; all preparations for Overlord to go ahead full steam within the framework of the foregoing policy for the Mediterranean." The American Chiefs of Staff saw in this plan some confirmation of their worst fears, but Roosevelt, with some reluctance, accepted it as the basis for discussion with Stalin.

On November 28th, the British and American leaders and their staffs having moved to Teheran to meet Josef Stalin, the first plenary session with all three Allied leaders present took place. From the outset, Stalin surprised the other delegations by leading the debate, and announcing quite unexpectedly that, once Germany was defeated, the USSR would join her two allies in defeating Japan. When Churchill put the British strategic proposals for 'Overlord' backed by the capture of bases in Italy, Stalin cross-examined him remorselessly on the proportion of the British and American commitment that would be devoted to the French and Italian campaigns, and on the size and nature of the force that Churchill envisaged for the Balkans assault. Having got his answers on these points, Stalin announced that he did not agree with the proposed Balkans campaign (presumably because it would have muddied the Eastern European position for his intended postwar colonisation), and that the major effort for 1944 should be devoted to 'Overlord'. All this was music to the ears of Roosevelt and the US Chiefs of Staff.

Next day, General Sir Alan Brooke was subjected by the Russians — by Marshal Voroshilov in particular — to the kind of mistrustful interrogation on Britain's belief in and commitment to the 'Overlord' concept that he had previously experienced at the hands of the Americans. Progressively, and ever more determinedly, Stalin and his staff pushed for greater and more definite agreement on the invasion of Europe across the Channel. Churchill in turn pushed Roosevelt to abandon the 'Buccaneer' operation in South-East Asia, without apparent effect. When finally the Conference minute of agreement was drawn up, it was with the unanimous approval of those taking part. The Allies had agreed their strategy for the remainder of the European War as follows:

'(a) That we should continue to advance in Italy to the Pisa-Rimini line. (This means that the 68 LSTs which are due to be sent from the Mediterranean to the United Kingdom for Overlord must be kept in the Mediterranean until 15th January).

(b) That an operation shall be mounted against the South of France on as big a scale as landing craft will permit. For planning purposes, D-Day to be the same as Overlord D-Day.

(c) That we will launch Overlord in May, in conjunction with a supporting operation against the South of France.'

On December 2nd 1943, Churchill and Roosevelt arrived back

1 Throughout the war, Winston Churchill remained in close and cordial touch with Jan Christian Smuts, (front left) the South African premier, whose sympathy with Churchill's objectives had been the principal motivation behind South Africa's large-scale commitment to the Allied cause. During the Boer War, Smuts had commanded the Boer forces in Cape Colony against the British, yet, by 1941 his loyalty to the Crown had resulted in his promotion to Field Marshal. This would seem to make him the only enemy commander ever to have become a Field Marshal in the Armies of the British Empire (as it then was). Behind Smuts and Winston Churchill are (left) Sir Arthur Tedder and Sir Alan Brooke.

2 Leaping forward in time to September 1944, we find the Allied leaders again meeting in Quebec for their eleventh war strategy conference of the war. The conference laid plans for the final victory in Europe, and for the final offensive against Japan. In the front row are (left to right) General George C. Marshall, US Army Chief of Staff; Admiral William D. Leahy, Chief of Staff to the President; President Roosevelt; Winston Churchill; Field Marshal Sir Alan Brooke, Chief of the Imperial General Staff and Field Marshall Sir John Dill, by this time Head of the British Joint Staff Mission in the USA. In the back row (left to right) are Major-General Leslie Hollis; Lieutenant-General Sir Hastings Ismay, Deputy Secretary to the British War Cabinet; Admiral Ernest J. King, Commander in Chief of the US Fleet; Air Chief Marshal Sir Charles Portal; General H.H. Arnold, Commander of the US Army Air Forces and Admiral Sir Andrew Cunningham.

in Cairo. There they tackled the tactical considerations that the strategic decisions raised, and conferred with their Chiefs of Staff on the logistics of two major simultaneous landings in France. For three days, amid the detailed discussions, Churchill and the British delegation urged Roosevelt and his Chiefs of Staff to forget 'Buccaneer', the operation to invade the Andaman Islands, and the drain on resources that it would bring. The US Generals stood firm on their commitment to Chiang Kai-shek. But on December 5th Roosevelt overruled them and told Churchill that Buccaneer was off. Now only the vexed question of the choice between an American and a British commander for the 'Overlord' invasion remained.

Churchill had long held that the preponderance of British and Empire troops in the fight against Germany made a British

commander obligatory, and had an informal understanding with General Sir Alan Brooke that he (Brooke) would have the command. But the US President stood firm on the necessity for an American commander. Given that they were obliged to accept an American general, the British wanted General Marshall. However, Roosevelt demurred, feeling — probably rightly — that Marshall's presence in Washington was too important to the successful prosecution of the war for him to be given another task, even one as important as this. In looking for an alternative there was, to Roosevelt, only one candidate — General Dwight D. Eisenhower. Thus it was that Eisenhower gained the most prestigious command of the Second World War, and with it the awesome responsibility of bringing to reality the long-awaited Allied assault on Europe.

CHAPTER 30

SOVIET ADVANCES KURSK, THE COUNTER-ATTACK AND THE UKRAINE

On the Eastern Front, the colossal build-up of Soviet armed might had continued following the defeat of the German 6th Army at Stalingrad. In this chapter, we deal with the events of Summer and Autumn 1943, and the only major German offensive of that year, but as background to the story it is worth noting just how greatly the Soviet Union had succeeded in mobilising its manhood to war. Between mid-1941, when Germany launched its ill-fated invasion of Russia, and the end of 1943, Russia's total infantry forces had been increased from 175 divisions to 513 divisions; her armoured and mechanised brigades had risen in number from 78 to 290, and even her somewhat anachronistic cavalry forces (which were, despite their quaint appearance, magnificent in the mud) had been expanded from 30 to 41 divisions. Some differences in the way the Russians worked out their brigade and divisional strengths make the apparent

superiority of these figures over the comparable German numbers exaggerated, but nothing can alter the fact that Russian military strength had tripled in the two and a half year period, despite the enormous Soviet losses of men and armaments during the first German advance to the perimeter of Moscow.

Similarly, German commanders on the Eastern Front were surprised not only by the apparently endless supply of human reinforcements that the Russians could conjure as if from nowhere, but also by the number and superiority of the new Russian weapons that were appearing. Perhaps most significant of these was the latest version of the famed T-34 tank, the T-34/85, which mounted an 85mm gun capable of knocking out any German tank at any likely range, and which was so effective a weapon that it stayed in production until 1958. But the emergence of the Soviet SU-152 self-

3 The cold of the Russian winter had exacted a heavy toll of German morale all along the Eastern Front during the winter of 1942/43, and the defeat at Stalingrad had prepared many German soldiers psychologically for nothing more than retreat. This German gun crew is making the best of the late winter cold of early 1943.

propelled gun also proved important, countering as it did the German 'Ferdinand' self-propelled gun, which proved to have a major disadvantage in having no forward firing machine gun.

Finally, the perseverance and suffering of the British and American sailors who operated the North Atlantic convoys despite the threat of the U-Boats was paying off in the form of a considerable arsenal of Western Allied weapons and aircraft in Soviet hands. Britain supplied Russia with over 4,000 tanks, more than 4,000 anti-aircraft guns and almost 6,000 guns under Lend Lease; the USA provided almost 4,000 tanks and over 6,000 aircraft; Canada supplied over 1,000 tanks. Nevertheless, Stalin's propaganda machine attempted to belittle the Allied contribution. However much it stressed victory over Nazism in the East as the totally Soviet creation that Russians still believe it to have been, the fact remains that the USSR would have found it impossible to have turned the tide against Germany without Allied support on a massive scale.

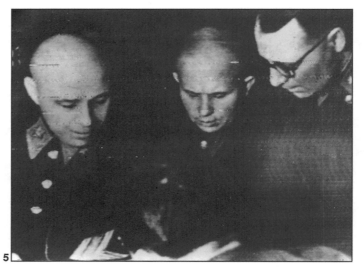

1 Far to the north, the German 18th Army, commanded by Colonel-General Lindemann, had suffered defeat beside Lake Ladoga, and the siege of Leningrad had been lifted. Here, Colonel-General Lindemann (left, with stick) makes use of the local forms of transport to cope with the snow.

2 German troops during the retreat to Rostov at the end of 1942 had been obliged to fall back in some disorder, so rapid was the Russian advance. These specially equipped German troops are pulling back after the Soviet Army had captured Kamensk.

We have already seen in an earlier chapter how badly 1943 had begun for the Germans at Stalingrad and in the Caucasus. In the North, the Army Groups Centre and North had fared little better. In January, first the German defenders of Velikiye-Luki had been besieged for a fortnight before being defeated by the Russians under Marshal Voroshilov. Then the German 18th Army commanded by Colonel-General Lindemann had been defeated on the shores of Lake Ladoga, following which the 17 month siege of Leningrad had at last been lifted. Railway communications between the city of the Winter Palace and the world from which it had been cut off for so long were restored on February 6th.

In the face of these defeats, Hitler permitted at long last the withdrawals to more defensible positions for which his generals had been pressing, and 30 divisions of the 4th and 9th Armies were withdrawn approximately 100 miles over a period of some three weeks without undue losses of men or equipment. This strategic retreat straightened the line that the Germans held, reducing its length by half to 230 miles and releasing 14 divisions for other tasks.

3 In many respects, the great German retreat had, during its winter periods in 1942/43 and 1943/44, many similarities to Napoleon's ignominious retreat back to Western Europe, 130 years before. Not least among these was the sorry plight of the horses used for carrying supplies across appalling terrain in parts of the northern front.

In April, it became clear what 'other tasks' Hitler had in mind. His Operational Order No.16 set out his plan for 'Operation *Zitadelle*', an offensive designed to surround and annihilate the Soviet forces holding Kursk. The tone of the Operational Order makes it quite clear that Hitler saw this offensive as the means by which the world was to be jolted into realising that the force of German arms was not yet spent. His generals saw it in a somewhat different light, their opinions varying from the open and positive support for the plan on military grounds offered by Kluge, to the open opposition of Colonel-General Heinz Guderian, Inspector-General of Armoured Troops, who believed that the tanks that would be lost in the attack would certainly be needed during 1944 to repel an Allied invasion in Northern Europe.

In the event, Hitler's plan was acted upon, but not until July 1943, when the first units of the new PzKpfw V (Panther) tanks had arrived on active service. No less than 41 German divisions were thrown into the attack on July 5th, including 18 armoured *Panzer* and *Panzergrenadier* Divisions with a total of about 1,000 tanks and 376 self propelled guns. Air support was provided by *Luftflotte IV*. Against this German strength, the Soviet armies in the Kursk salient numbered about 75 divisions and 3,600 tanks, plus an amazing figure of 20,000 guns, howitzers and mortars, including 6,000 anti-tank guns and almost a thousand rocket launchers. The Russians had amassed, as a deliberate policy, sufficient artillery to form specific Artillery Divisions, something no other army had attempted, and the policy was to pay off handsomely during the advance on Germany.

Almost as important as the Russians' superiority of sheer firepower was her intelligence success in gathering up-to-date and accurate information on the German troop dispositions and strengths, and the sheer luck of having on July 4th, the day before the German offensive began, a Czech *Wehrmacht* deserter come over to the Soviet side and give exact details of the timing of the attack. As a result of

4 This cover of the German propaganda magazine *Berlin Illustrierte Zeitung* dates from the summer of 1941, and the heyday of the German advance as the all-conquering *Wehrmacht* swept across the River Don. Exactly similar scenes of destruction were now afflicting the great front in Russia two years later, as Germans, this time heading westward, picked their way through wreckage that their war had created.

5 Political commissars were a fact of life for Soviet generals, and even the greatest among Russia's military men were not immune from their attentions. Some political commissars were later to become even better known than the generals whose decisions they closely watched – this is Nikita Kruschev (centre) advising Marshal Semyon Timoshenko (left) and his aide Colonel Cherevichenko.

6 German soldiers captured by the Russians were subject to the full, pent-up fury of a Soviet people who had been subjected to appalling brutality and hardship. Although many German prisoners survived the war, a great many more did not, and most of those that eventually returned home did not do so until long after the end of the war.

6

7

8

7 Colonel-General Hoth, who commanded the 4th *Panzerarmee* during the German counterattack in July 1943, Operation *Zitadelle*, observes enemy positions through a periscope in the front line. Hoth's troops were among the most successful of those taking part in the German advance, taking many prisoners, but were thrown back by the Soviet 5th Guards Tank Army.

8 The Germans had tried numerous ideas to help cope with the problems of transport caused by the enormous distances and near-impossible weather conditions which they found to prevail on the Eastern Front. This armoured train was one of them. It was not spectacularly successful, because it was easily blown off the rails, and thereby blocked the passage of everything behind it.

this good fortune, the Red Army was able to deliver a formidable psychological stroke against the German 9th Army when, only twenty minutes before zero hour for the attack to begin, a massive Soviet artillery barrage hit the German positions with pinpoint accuracy, throwing the units keyed up for a surprise attack into considerable confusion. Although the German formations quickly recovered themselves, and launched their assault on time, the 9th Army advanced only six miles against the Soviet 13th during that hard-fought first day. In the next two days, the leading German units advanced only another six miles. On July 7th, the 9th Army's advance stopped, outgunned and outnumbered.

Further South, the German 4th Army did better, but not well enough. Strong air support enabled them to make initial advances more or less to plan, and by July 11th two defensive lines had been broken and the advance units were in a position to breach Russian supply lines. The 2nd *Waffen SS Panzer* Corps had played a major part in Manstein's being able to report on July 13th that the 4th *Panzerarmee* had taken 24,000 prisoners. But trouble had by then been brewing for the Germans for days. Aware that the two German armies that were seeking to establish a pincer movement and cut off the Russian forces were still 75 miles apart, the Russian General Vatutin, in command of the Voronezh Front, decided to counter-

1 A picture that somehow says it all about the Soviet spirit of the Great Patriotic War – and which was and has been used to exemplify the joy of the people at serving Mother Russia. Sergeant Korneiko, the best armourer of a Soviet Naval Air Unit, loads a bomb inscribed 'A present for Hitler' into a Russian naval bomber.

2 Field-Marshal Erich von Manstein, in command of forty-two German divisions in the south of the front, faced 120 Soviet divisions at the time of his loss of Kharkov in August 1943, and many more only two months later. One of Hitler's ablest generals, he could not contain an advance made by so crushingly superior a force.

3 This graphic picture shows clearly in the faces of these *Waffen SS* troopers the desperate state of exhaustion which many had reached by August 1943. The picture was taken after the capture by the Soviet Army of Karachev, the last major outpost before Briansk on the road to White Russia.

4 The unseasonally late winter conditions in the Orel salient made the tension among the Germans there even greater as they waited for the expected assault that they knew would come with the thaw. This German soldier is lookout on an 88mm defensive gun emplacement.

attack. From July 10th, he brought up the crack 5th Guards Tank Army (the 'Guards' title was awarded for achievement in the Red Army) and the 1st Tank Army, and on the 12th launched the greatest tank battle of the Second World War against the Germans defending the over-extended positions of the Orel Salient. Well over 5,000 armoured vehicles took part in the Battle of Kursk, the might of the new Russian armour being pitched against German *Panzer* Divisions that were greatly weakened both by losses of men (20,000 during the previous week alone) and by mechanical wear and unreliability after months or years of campaigning in often appalling conditions with only rudimentary field maintenance to keep them going.

The main assault by the Russians on Orel, with 3,000 guns and 400 rocket launchers, made rapid progress, covering 15 miles in the first 48 hours. All along the complex front, other Russian formations breached the German defences and pushed infantry and artillery through the gaps to harry the Germans and break up their command structures. By July 15th, the German armies were clearly getting the worst of the situation around them; by the 20th the Germans had no alternative but to throw large numbers of precious aircraft into the desperate struggle to hold their positions against the mighty tank and artillery assault. On July 29th, the German evacuation of the Orel Salient, approved by Hitler, began.

Field-Marshal Kluge had been gloomy in his prognosis when he had, the previous week, reported events to Hitler. The Fuehrer was, in any event, already plunged into depression by the Allied successes in Sicily and the Italians' manifest failure to defend their territory. Faced with the need to withdraw resources from Russia to defend the Italian mainland against imminent invasion, Hitler did exactly what Roosevelt and the American Generals had said he would not do — he gave the order to withdraw and abandon Operation *Zitadelle*, and thereby demonstrated that the Allied invasion in the Mediterranean had succeeded after all in taking the pressure off the Eastern Front.

As the German armies retreated they destroyed everything in their path, leaving local populations without food and shelter. To the South of the retreating 9th and 4th Armies, Manstein's 42 German divisions faced some 120 Russian divisions, and even these numbers were being rapidly increased — by September, he was outnumbered eight to one. On August 3rd 1943, Colonel-General Vatutin and his colleague Colonel-General Konev advanced a wedge into Manstein's army, dividing the 4th *Panzerarmee* from the *Gruppe* 'Kempf' and thereby breaking the front. Now the Russians were swiftly able to liberate Belgorod and Bogodukhov, and, crashing on through the Ukraine, recaptured the city of Kharkov, which the Germans lost on

5

6

7

5 This picture, taken during the German defence of their positions in the Crimea, shows a *Panzerhaubitze* 18 'Hummel' (bumble-bee) self-propelled gun. This powerful combination of the ubiquitous PzKpfw IV chassis with a 180mm howitzer, was used by most of the Panzer divisions from 1943 onwards.

6 Each of the cities for whose recapture the Red Army fought suffered dreadfully from the effects of shelling and bombing, often for the second or third time since the German invasion of June 1941. Here a bomb explodes and demolishes a building during an air raid, with hundreds of people exposed to the effects of the blast on the streets nearby.

7 A German machine gun post blazes away at Russian positions, apparently in the building which looks on the point of collapse. According to the original caption, the Germans were defending a railway line against a Soviet Army counter-attack.

Soviet Advances

August 22nd. By September 7th, Manstein's army was reduced to 257 tanks and 220 assault guns. Clearly, he had little alternative but to withdraw.

Hitler, realising at last that he was about to lose the great mineral resources of the Donets basin, and that the 'divisions' he still moved on his map were no longer the full strength *Blitzkrieg* units of June 1941, decided to visit Manstein at Zaporozhye on the Dnieper. From September 9th to the 16th they argued about the situation that faced them, Manstein putting clearly the impossible position in which the German armies found themselves. Finally, Hitler agreed to the withdrawal. On the night of September 15/16th it began with the evacuation of the Taman peninsula, a huge amphibious operation under Vice-Admiral Schurlen bringing over 200,000 troops and 15,000 vehicles, to say nothing of over 54,000 horses and 1,200 guns, across the Kerch Strait on the Sea of Azov. Manstein's forces to the North of the Sea of Azov (the 1st and 4th *Panzerarmee* and the 8th Army) were brought back across the Dnieper between Zaporozhye to the South and Kiev to the North, destroying crops and villages as they went.

1 In the extreme south of the front, heavy fighting took place along the northern shore of the Sea of Azov. This picture was taken in the town of Mariupol as German armour was driven back, causing something of a traffic jam in the narrow streets. The self-propelled gun struggling against the traffic is a *Panzerjaeger* 47mm PaK (t), and the assault gun in the foreground is a 75mm *Sturmgeschutz* III Ausf. G., of the *1st SS Panzer Division Leibstandarte Adolf Hitler*. Because assault guns were easier and cheaper to produce than tanks, they were issued increasingly as replacements as the war ground on.

2 The gloom and exhaustion of a retreating army is the same the world over. Nobody could doubt that these weary German soldiers resting by the roadside in Russia wanted no more than to go home – although, at the time, home was none too attractive, since the Allied bombing attacks on Germany were reaching their peak. Note the bicycles on the cart towed by the tractor in the background.

3 The fighting in the Crimea as the Germans retreated was every bit as fierce as it had been when they arrived two years previously. Here, amid the ruins of Sevastopol, German defenders are flushed out of their last positions by Soviet troops. It was estimated that 110,000 German soldiers were killed or captured in the Crimea alone.

If the Germans believed that getting to the Western bank of the Dnieper would earn them a chance to regroup, they were disappointed. The Russians rapidly crossed the river and established bridgeheads to secure their support positions from artillery and tank attack. This time they were West of the Dnieper for good. By the beginning of November, the German 17th Army had been trapped in the Crimea by the headlong advance of the Russian armies, although, after taking Zaporozhye on October 14th, the Russians had been checked on most fronts for a week or two by determined German defensive fighting. At Krivoi Rog, particularly, the XL *Panzer* Corps, reinforced by the 24th *Panzer* Division, had on October 28th pushed General Rotmistrov's 5th Guards Tank Army back some 15 miles, with Russian losses of 10,000 dead and 5,000 taken prisoner. This check on the Russian advance gave Manstein the chance to retreat from the Dniepropetrovsk salient that had developed, but the comparative peace did not last long.

On November 3rd, Colonel-General Vatutin attacked the German VII Corps defending Kiev, the capital of the Ukraine. With 30 infantry divisions and 1,500 tanks levelled against them, the German defenders could do little. On November 6th, the Russians were once more in possession of a city that had become a symbol of eventual German defeat on Russian soil. Manstein, however, did not take such humiliation lightly, and fought back vigorously, coming during December within 25 miles of recapturing Kiev. But to do so he had

drawn on the resources of the German 8th Army, which, thus weakened, lost Cherkassy to Colonel-General Konev.

Thus 1943 ended with the Germans in full retreat all along the Eastern Front, with severely depleted formations, and with a massively reinforced Red Army flushed with success pursuing it relentlessly towards Berlin. The Russians had a long way to go. But their objective was never in doubt.

4 Safe again – a Russian child is lifted like a jack-in-the-box by Soviet soldiers from her underground hiding place in a Ukrainian city where she had been hidden with her parents.

5 German armaments designers, encouraged by Hitler, had a talent for the development of mildly fantastic super-weapons that might – just might – be the secret panacea that the *Fuehrer* sought. This huge mortar was used by the German army in the Crimea, but was immensely cumbersome and quite unsuitable for a mobile war.

6 Although the Soviet Army was to a large extent re-equipped with modern weapons by the autumn of 1943, many of their earlier armoured vehicles and guns had survived the first impact of the German invasion to fight on as the German army retreated. This self-propelled anti-tank gun was already obsolescent, but was still in service.

7 As the Soviet Army consolidated its hold in the Ukraine, and eliminated the Kiev 'bulge' in December 1943, the shape of the line for the spring advance in 1944 began to take shape. These German grenadiers are cautiously approaching a brewed-up T34, wary of any further explosions, or surviving crew members.

8 Flushed with the success of their advances during the summer of 1943, the Soviet Army developed their own form of the high-speed armoured advance that had initially brought the Germans so much success. Russian armoured vehicles were fast and highly manoeuvrable; the Germans were never to regain the initiative against the overwhelming superiority of numbers of the Soviet armies. These Soviet tanks and guns are crossing a river during the advance towards Lvov.

CHAPTER 31

THE BATTLES FOR THE ISLANDS
THE GILBERTS, MARSHALLS AND PHILIPPINE SEA

By September 1943, the Japanese were under severe pressure — indeed, it can be argued that they were already beaten. Although Tojo, Japan's warlike and dictatorial Premier, was talking of and planning for the great offensive that would win the Pacific war for Japan, the High Command knew that they were in trouble. Shipping losses to US submarines were mounting because of inadequate convoys and worse convoy protection. Vital raw materials and supplies were going down with the ships. Terrible losses of pilots were being met only by cutting the training programmes of the pilots that replaced them, which inevitably produced still higher losses of both aircraft and crews. New aircraft types were just not materialising, with the result that Allied aircraft design and technology had overtaken the once all-conquering speed and firepower of the Zero fighter and Mitsubishi bomber. Perhaps most important, the USA was building and putting into action not only faster and better aircraft carriers, but also faster and more manoeuvrable longer-range and better-armed aircraft to fly from them.

To face this threat, the Japanese established in September 1943 a 'New Operational Policy' by which the Japanese garrisons holding a defensive line from Timor through western New Guinea, Biak Island, the Caroline Islands and the Marianas were to be immoveable. To them fell the honour of fighting to the death. To the US Marines fell most of the task of providing that glorious end. The first target was, after some initial debate between Admiral Nimitz on the one hand, and Admiral King and General Marshall on the other, settled as the Gilbert Islands, sixteen tiny atolls in the Central Pacific lying astride the Equator. In particular, the tiny yet colossally defended Tarawa Atoll was singled out as the most important target, because of its potential as a Japanese base to combat the necessary US conquest of the Marshall Islands.

The US attack on Tarawa Atoll, and most notably on the fortress-like two-mile by 900 yard island of Betio, was launched on November 20th 1943, and was to prove disastrous for the force that undertook it, yet entirely successful in its objectives. Over 4,500 Japanese were on the little island; virtually every palm tree, every fold in the beach concealed an arsenal. In sand-covered concrete bunkers, the defenders survived a barrage of 3,000 tons of shells from three battleships, nine destroyers and four cruisers of the US Navy plus bombing from the air, an assault which set virtually the entire island afire. When the first of 16,798 Marines attempted to land, they were met by a hail of fire such as few had ever imagined. Tricky tides, about which the invasion force had been warned, caused the landing craft to run aground on the reef, well short of the beach, and as the Marines waded ashore they were gunned down by the hundred.

1 Something of the ferocity of the initial barrage on Tarawa, and of the battle that followed, can be judged from this picture of US Marines, bent low and doubling from cover to cover, during the early stages of the three-day battle.

2 As the ferocious battle pounded on in the equatorial heat of Tarawa, the fighting was almst hand-to-hand. This Marine has raised his head from his sandbagged machine-gun post for just long enough to hurl his grenade — and for just long enough to be killed, if a sharp-eyed enemy has his sights on the emplacement. Almost 6,000 Marines were killed or captured in the campaigns on Tarawa, Makin and Abemama Islands.

3 Amid devastation and the smoking ruins of a Japanese pillbox, triumphant US Marines scale a hill that had been their objective for several bloody hours during the assault on Tarawa. Small objectives assume major importance when your friends have died to achieve them.

Despite calling up his reserve forces on the afternoon of the first day, Major-General Julian C. Smith finished his first day ashore less than 200 yards from the waterline.

Over the next two days, every inch of the tiny island had to be fought for with flame throwers, grenades and small arms against an opponent who was determined to die. And die he did. By the end of the battle on Betio Island, 5,500 men had met their end, including more than a thousand US Marines. Over 2,000 Marines were wounded. Of the Japanese, all were slain except for one officer, 16 other ranks and a party of Korean labourers.

Nobody, least of all Admiral Nimitz, had expected such murderous resistance from such a small and apparently insignificant target. The appalling US death toll on Tarawa served as a warning for future invasions in the island-hopping campaign that was to lead ultimately to Tokyo, and the complete rethink of the pre-invasion barrage technique that resulted from it undoubtedly saved many lives in subsequent operations.

4 As in all mopping-up operations during the Pacific war, there were many US casualties in the Gilbert Island campaigns caused by suicidally-inclined Japanese defenders with no thought for their own skins. Here, on Tarawa, US Marines cautiously approach a Japanese bombproof shelter. When the Japanese refused to come out, the Marines tossed in a hand grenade. In such cases, US soldiers had to kill or be killed.

5 A significant number of Japanese aircraft were lost during the campaign for the Gilbert Islands, against a background of greatly-increased losses throughout the Pacific war. This Japanese plane was shot down by US carrier-borne fighters during the landing on Tarawa, and is here examined by Marines after the island had been secured.

6 This American landing craft, wrecked during the initial landings on Tarawa, was occupied by a Japanese machine-gun crew during the night, and used to strafe the Americans on the beach. The Japanese could not have expected to survive, and the US Marines moved in and killed them. Their bodies can be seen still in the barge.

7 US soldiers who died during the battles for the Gilbert Islands were buried where they fell – these thirty-four graves were on Suricki Island. The natives of the islands, who hold the dead in great reverence, marked out the graves initially with bottles and rough crosses, so that the US Marine Corps could later erect these properly marked crosses.

Elsewhere in the Gilbert Islands, the pattern was variable and less dramatic. To take the Makin Atoll to the North-West of Tarawa, Major-General Ralph C. Smith's 27th Division lost 64 men killed and 150 wounded, a considerably higher death toll than he had been led to expect, whereas the Abemama Atoll was taken with no problem at all by just a company of US Marines. The next target was the Marshall Islands, a bigger problem altogether, and one for which the US 5th Fleet was greatly reinforced. Newly-commanded by Rear-Admiral Mitscher, the fleet's Task Force 58 embarked upon the Marshalls operation with no less than 12 aircraft carriers, bearing 715 fighters, dive-bombers and torpedo-bombers. Rear-Admiral Turner's amphibious force was made up of 300 warships and transport ships.

1 This dramatic picture was shot during the landings on Namur beach, Kwajalein, Marshall Islands, as the Marines began to dig in and establish their beachhead. Silhouetted against a sea crowded with US craft, a stretcher party bears away a Marine wounded in the landing.

2 A US signals post on Roi Island, at the northern tip of Kwajalein Atoll in the Marshall Islands. Roi was one of the first islands in the Kwajalein chain to be secured. By the time the whole of Kwajalein had been taken, 8,122 Japanese troops had been killed and 264 taken prisoner during a single week.

Against all advice, Admiral Nimitz decided to make the obvious principal target of Kwajalein the main objective for an amphibious landing. The other two targets that were to be overcome, Maloelap and Wotje, were presented as objectives to Task Force 58. The Japanese, correctly anticipating that Nimitz would be advised, after Tarawa, to land on the easier targets first, cunningly diverted a significant part of their defence force away from Kwajalein to the other islands − and thereby contributed unwittingly to the success of Nimitz' bold stroke. With the lessons of Tarawa ever in mind, the air offensive against Kwajalein, Maloelap and Wotje, launched between the end of January 1944 and February 11th, was heavy and unrelenting. Over 6,000 missions were flown and more than 1,100 tons of bombs were dropped. In the midst of the holocaust the US 5th Amphibious Force, including the newly arrived 4th Marine Division, which had never been in action before, went ashore on Kwajalein in force and without major losses. Some 42,000 men landed, and this time only 372 were killed. The Japanese lost almost 8,000 men − but, to a man, they preferred death to surrender.

On February 17th came the next assault, against Eniwetok, which was again successful with relatively small losses. Once again the Japanese defenders preferred death — of 2,741 on the island, 2,677 were killed. Viewing the success of the operations in the Gilbert and Marshall Islands, Nimitz decided once again, as he had before in the Solomon Islands, not to bother with invading targets that, although held by the Japanese, were tactically unimportant once they were isolated from their brethren. The proposed assaults on Wotje and Maloelap, and the possible invasions of other small Japanese held groups, were cancelled. The Japanese that held them were left to consider their positions until the war was over. Similarly, the great Japanese naval base at Truk in the Caroline Islands was attacked fiercely and successfully from the air from February 17th to 20th with the loss of 33 ships and 250 Japanese aircraft — and was then left to its own devices for the remainder of the war. Interestingly, the sunken ships in Truk lagoon have, since the war, become a major site for marine biological research. Before the attack on the Japanese fleet, the sandy floor of the lagoon had suggested little marine life, and biologists are able to measure exactly the development of marine life in a controlled environment with a known timescale.

However, marine biological research was far in the future as Nimitz and MacArthur, the latter having fought his way almost to the tip of New Guinea, looked to their next target — the islands of Saipan, Tinian and Guam in the Philippine Sea, and ultimately the reconquest of the Philippines. Not for nothing had Douglas MacArthur vowed that he would return.

3 A dramatic moment in a shell hole on Namur Island as a Marine platoon commander motions his men to keep low and listen. Much of the battle consisted for the Marines of sprints from shell-hole to shell-hole, dodging the Japanese fire as they went, and coping with snipers as they made their presence known, for the island was covered with craters after the ferocious pre-invasion bombardment.

4 When the initial assault on Namur Island was over, the island was littered with blasted trees, wrecked armoured vehicles and weapons and dead soldiers, most of them Japanese. The dead Japanese soldiers in this picture are naked only because their clothes were torn from their bodies by the blast of the shells that killed them during the bombardment before the landing began.

5 Old Glory flies above the debris of a Japanese gun emplacement on Kwajalein, reduced to rubble by the US Navy bombardment that preceded the landing. This picture was taken by a US Coastguard photographer who took part in the invasion.

6 This picture, taken from a position among US Marines returning sniper fire on Roi Island beach, shows the plume of smoke on nearby Namur Island as American engineers blow up Japanese installations. Getting pictures like this was a hazardous business, for snipers were not averse to shooting a photographer who raised his head to take a picture.

7 After a series of threats to dynamite his dugout, this Japanese soldier surrendered and was pulled out by US Marines. The watchful expressions were because another, wounded, Japanese soldier had told the Americans that there were two in the dugout. This incident took place on Namur Island, Kwajalein Atoll.

8 One of the less-pleasant weapons of the Second World War was the flame-thrower. This US Marine, with his flame-thrower at the ready, is inspecting the bodies of two of his Japanese victims, scorched by the searing heat of the chemically fuelled flame. The Japanese pillbox behind has been hit by a shell.

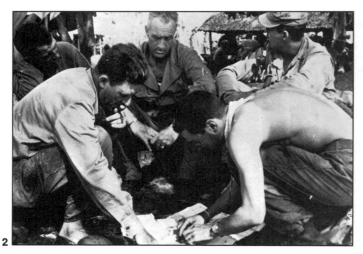

2 An island-hopping campaign placed great responsibility for command on individual commanding officers. Most of the decisions were taken at hurried conferences on the beach, like this one on Makin Island.

3 As the original heartfelt caption to this 1944 news picture points out, going after an enemy with cold steel requires one type of courage, but the task of identifying and burying one's own army's dead requires quite another. Here, John Darraugh (left), and George A. Schwille, both of New York, fingerprint an unidentified dead American soldier.

The Philippine Sea

A rapid and successful island-hopping exercise carried out by MacArthur's troops up the coast of New Guinea between May and July 1944 gave the Allies the islands of Wakde, Biak, and Numfoor and positioned MacArthur's troops by the end of July in the region of the 'Vogelkop' at the tip of New Guinea. Landings in April 1944 by the US 24th Division (Tanahmerah Bay) and the 41st Division (Hollandia and Aitape) to take General Adachi and the Japanese 18th Army by surprise were successful and, although the Japanese counter-attacked and fought fiercely through July, by the end of the month the pincer movement of the two American forces had over 120,000 Japanese neatly trapped in appalling tropical conditions.

Meanwhile, the plan to take the islands of Guam, Saipan and Tinian, which were to become the air bases from which the assault on the Philippines and, eventually, the nuclear attacks on mainland Japan were launched, had been put into action on June 11th when the first of a long series of devastating bombing raids took off for the Marianas. Vice-Admiral Ozawa of the Japanese Navy, as soon as the bombing began, was ordered to take his 1st Mobile Fleet into the attack, since simply to await developments, now that the US Navy had twice the carrier-borne air power of the Japanese, was certain to result ultimately in US recapture of the Philippines. The Japanese High Command believed by this time that they had little to lose by attempting the near-impossible, and on June 15th Ozawa's fleet came through the San Bernadino Strait and into the Philippine Sea, there

linking up with Ugaki's Attack Division. On the same day, the 2nd and 4th US Marine Divisions landed on Saipan against ferocious defence by 32,000 Japanese soldiers, and by evening V Amphibious Corps had 20,000 Americans on Saipan.

As Ozawa's fleet approached to do battle, Admiral Spruance recalled his carriers and their aircraft, redeployed his fleet, and awaited events. He could not sail out to meet the enemy in the classic manner, for to do so would have exposed the Marines on Saipan to attack. So he just waited. He did not have to wait for long, and was, in any event, well briefed by US Intelligence, who continued to be able to decode and read in full Japanese Navy signals.

On June 19th two Japanese naval forces approached. The first was a decoy fleet under Vice-Admiral Kurita whose role was to attract Admiral Spruance's aircraft into battle. This was followed at a respectful distance of over 100 miles by a much larger force that was intended to pick off the American aircraft carriers while their aircraft were away attacking Kurita's ships.

4 The end of the battle for Roi Island, and, as the Stars and Stripes flutters from one of the few trees left standing, weary American soldiers take time out to relax just a little before the next landing and the next island.

5 A dead Japanese soldier – the Marine ordered him out of his foxhole; the Japanese refused, so the US Marine did the only thing he could. He shot him. That this was happening many times a day is obvious from the casual glance of the other US Marine in the picture.

6 Two horrific pictures of a Japanese Imperial Marine who was caught by an American flame-thrower as he crawled from his foxhole during the US campaign on Engebi, one of the islands of Eniwetok Atoll, in the Marshall Islands. Few pictures demonstrate more effectively the instant death caused by the flame-thrower.

On the face of it, this was an excellent plan. It failed because of the massive superiority of US aircraft, crews and training. The Japanese lost 243 aircraft in the operation, two thirds of those that took part, and achieved almost nothing – minor damage to American ships, and 30 US aircraft shot down. The Japanese ships fared little better. Admiral Ozawa's flagship, the 29,300 ton aircraft carrier *Taiho*, was torpedoed and sunk during the morning, and a few hours later, in the afternoon, the 25,675 ton carrier *Shokaku*, completed only in 1941, met the same fate. Vice-Admiral Lockwood's submarines had had a good day.

Ozawa had survived the loss of his ship, and was now commanding his fleet from *Haguro*, a 13,400 ton heavy cruiser. During the late afternoon of 20th June, another battle took place in fading light, some 200 miles from the first. Amid fierce aerial combat, the Japanese lost another carrier, the 24,000 ton *Hiyo*, and a further 40 aircraft. The American fleet lost a total of 49 planes, more than half of which crashed while trying to land on the carriers after dark –

7 Evacuating the wounded is a major logistical problem on any battlefield; it becomes a significantly larger problem when the battlefield is a small island surrounded by empty sea. These US Coast Guard and Navy medics are preparing to evacuate Marine casualties after the first wave of landings on Eniwetok Atoll in the Marshall Islands.

albeit with the benefit of full landing lights that Spruance had had switched on despite the submarine risk. This decision saved many lives and enabled the rescue crews to find ditched pilots in the water around the carriers.

Following this second Battle of the Philippine Sea, Ozawa had only 35 aircraft left of the 473 with which he embarked upon his attack. The battles marked the end of effective Japanese carrier borne operations, and also the end of Tojo's reign of terror at the head of Japan's government. Desperately seeking someone to blame for the disaster, governmental opinion in Japan rounded upon Tojo, who resigned. He was succeeded by General Kuniaki Koiso.

Meanwhile, on Saipan the 27th Infantry Division and the 2nd and 4th Marine Divisions had been fighting a gruelling campaign across rocky and mountainous terrain in which small pockets of Japanese soldiers were able to dig themselves in using caves and rocky defiles for cover. As each unit of Japanese infantry was pinned down and surrounded, its remaining soldiers would suddenly launch a last

1 On Kwajalein, US infantry were provided with substantial armoured support, and advanced, as in this picture, with a tank to provide fire power and cover when needed.

2 February 22nd 1944, and a picture that says everything. A US Marine lies dead on the shore of Parry Island, Eniwetok Atoll, his hand still grasping the rifle he doubtless hoped would be his salvation. In the foreground, another rifle stuck muzzle-down in the sand marks a shallow temporary grave.

3 US Naval strength in the Pacific grew dramatically during 1944, as the ability of the Imperial Japanese Navy to fight back was reduced by massive losses. This picture, dating from the beginning of 1945, shows USS *Lexington*, photographed above the port bow. Grumman Hellcats are visible on the foredeck, and an Avenger is landing over the stern.

4 Propaganda picture it may be, but there is no disguising the triumph with which these US Coastguardsmen and Marines display a captured bullet-torn Japanese flag as they return to their transport offshore after the capture of Eniwetok. The scrambling net was the only way up to the waiting ship – one had to be athletic to serve with the Marines.

desperate suicidal *Banzai* attack, taking with them as many of the US troops as they could. Despite this wearying and grisly way of taking an island inch by inch, the Marines made progress, and by July 1st the battle was entering its final stage. Almost a week later, on the 7th, the last 2,500 or so Japanese defenders swept down upon the Americans in a final suicide attack and were annihilated. Admiral Nagumo shot himself, and General Saito, rather more colourfully, ceremonially slit his own stomach with his sword, then had his adjutant shoot him in the head. Who shot the adjutant is not clear.

Guam

While the Japanese Navy had been losing its aircraft in the Philippine Sea and the US 2nd and 4th Marines plus the 27th Infantry Division had been clearing Saipan, the 3rd Amphibious Corps (the same troops that had taken Bougainville, but under a different organisational title) had embarked upon the recapture of the 28 mile long narrow island of Guam. This important base for future operations was held by 18,500 Japanese army and navy personnel, a large proportion of whom were clustered around the airfield at Orote, close to the main town of Agana. With the massacre at Tarawa still fresh in their minds, and rather more experience of Japanese techniques of war since, the US commanders took no risks. The bombardment of Guam that preceded the landing began on July 2nd, almost three weeks before the actual invasion on July 21st.

The landing, close to and south of Agana, went well, and the US forces advanced rapidly, despite fierce fighting, towards the airfield and the high ground beyond. Then, on 25th July, the Japanese counter-attacked, and there was a night of ferocious battle during

5 The growing success rate of the US submarines resulted in many death-plunges of Japanese merchant ships, like this one, photographed through the periscope of an American submarine. The vertical black bars across the picture are the range indications on the optics of the periscope.

6 Carrier flying is a hazardous business, even in peacetime, and in war there were many losses as a result of the problems of landing damaged aircraft. In this picture, crewmen of the carrier are hosing burning gasoline over the side of the ship after a Corsair F40 lost its belly tank during landing. The pilot died in the resulting blaze.

7&9 Not all landings with damaged aircraft ended in tragedy. This sequence of two pictures shows the successful landing of a US Navy torpedo-bomber with one leg of its undercarriage shot away. The pilot was Lt. J.C. Huggins of Columbia, South Carolina.

8 Admiral Jisaburo Ozawa, photographed after he had survived the war and had become a member of the Japanese postwar defence agency.

which the Japanese troops all but overwhelmed the US headquarters on the island, taking as they did so quite appalling losses. By morning their losses were such that they could do nothing but fall back, and the battle for Guam was almost over. Yet it was not until August 10th that General Obata and his troops had been pushed to the sea, and not until the 11th that he too killed himself as the battle finally came to an end.

The battle for Guam cost the Japanese 17,300 dead at the time, and quite a few later as Japanese soldiers surfaced from hideouts determined to have their own last stand, some of them months after the battle was over. The Americans lost just under 2,000 soldiers on the island.

Tinian

The last of Nimitz's three Mariana targets was Tinian, a smaller island only 12 miles long but, unlike the others, almost entirely flat and capable of providing an easily constructed airfield for operation of the new Boeing B29 Superfortress long range bomber. Less than three miles from Saipan, it was, as soon as Saipan had been invaded, within gunnery range of land batteries. On July 24th 1944, the 24th and 25th Marines went ashore across narrow beaches after heavy gunfire both from the sea and from Saipan had reduced the level of resistance, and managed to establish a sound beach-head by nightfall. The battle lasted for a little over a week, and followed a similar pattern to that of the other islands — stubborn resistance by small groups of Japanese, followed by *Banzai* attacks when it was clear that Japanese arms could not prevail.

By July 31st, the Marines had taken Tinian town, the principal objective on the island. On August 1st the last militarily organised Japanese action ended, but once again it took until August 12th to round up all the remaining soldiers and hostile civilians. A further 6,000 Japanese soldiers died on Tinian. Only 235 prisoners were taken. A total of 290 US Marines died in the assault.

Thus ended the conquest of the Marianas, a necessary prelude to the reconquest of the Philippines. All told, the Japanese deathroll amounted to about 40,000 men, with just over 2,000 Japanese taken prisoner. The Americans lost 4,596 dead, with 19,323 wounded or missing.

1 A dramatic picture of a Japanese airfield during a raid which destroyed more than fifty aircraft on the ground. The parachutes are attached to bombs intended for the machine gun emplacements that are clearly visible in this remarkable shot taken by a member of the crew of one of the aircraft of the US Fifth Air Force carrying out the attack.

2 The US Army made increasing use of artillery spotter aircraft during 1944. This Cub aircraft is being unloaded from an LST landing craft at Saidor, New Guinea, at the beginning of 1944.

3 It was not only the heat and the Japanese which caused US troops problems in the Pacific. This picture gives an impression of the monumental scale of the mud which bogged down the US troops in New Britain in early 1944. PFC Paul Van Dyk, of Wallington New Jersey, is seen doing his bit to try and ungum a field gun near Cape Gloucester.

4 By May 1944 the Americans were ashore in the St Mathias group of islands, a landing which provided the Allies with a potential base less than 600 miles from Truk, the great Japanese base in a vast natural lagoon in the Caroline Islands.

CHAPTER 32

THE ADVANCE ON ROME ANZIO, KESSELRING AND THE STRUGGLE IN ITALY

The advance from the toe of Italy after the landings at Salerno had been slow and beset by unseasonably cold and wet weather. By the late autumn of 1943, it had developed into a sluggish near-stalemate from which neither side was making significant progress. The topography of Italy's boot is mountainous and difficult for all but the best mountain troops. Field-Marshal Kesselring, having stabilised the military situation following Italy's surrender to the Allies and the blood-letting that followed, was defending positions along the Gustav Line to the South and West of Rome with divisions that were severely under-strength and short of artillery ammunition, but whose morale, given the worldwide decline in Axis fortunes, was surprisingly good. Every day, the Germans shelled from their vantage points in the hills Allied positions that were little more than a welter of mud. Modern weapons became useless and unmoveable with a choice only between the morass of the valley or the rocky heights of the hills. The Second World War in Europe, for the whole of that miserable winter, became an echo of the mud of Flanders.

5

6

7

8

The stalemate, and the underlying Allied conviction that Rome was the psychologically important target in Italy for both sides, brought forward a number of Allied proposals, but Winston Churchill's idea for 'Operation Shingle' emerged by the end of 1943 as the plan that Roosevelt and Stalin had both accepted. A major attack in the South by Lieutenant-General Mark Clark's US 5th Army and Britain's 8th Army would draw Germany's depleted forces away from the areas around Rome, and from the Colli Laziali (or Alban Hills) between Rome and the coast. This was to make possible a surprise landing by the US VI Corps under Major-General John P. Lucas in the Anzio/Nettuno area, and a rapid advance into the Alban Hills to cut German communications and 'threaten the rear of the XIV German Corps'.

Clearly, the fundamental principle of the plan depended on speed at Anzio, since it was realised that a breakout towards Rome through

9

5 In the autumn of 1943, General Mark Clark's US 5th Army, after weeks of shelling amid a welter of mud, needed all the morale boosters it could get. This is US Under-Secretary of the Navy, James V. Forrestal, firing a 240mm howitzer during a tour of the 5th Army front.

6 In January 1944, the Adriatic seaport of Ortona was captured by Canadian troops of the 8th Army, who drove the German Army from the town building by building in fierce street fighting. This RAF aerial reconnaissance picture of the harbour and railway shows how badly the town had suffered during the battle.

7 Each side attempted during the war in Italy to capitalise on what it portrayed as the vandalism of the other directed against the ancient buildings of Italy. This is the venerable cathedral of St Thomas in Ortona, which was ruined during the battle for the town in January 1944. Allied sources captioned this picture as the cathedral 'demolished by the Germans in an attempt to block a street'. In fact, the demolition was partly the result of Allied shellfire.

8 Much of the terrain in which the US 5th Army and the British 8th Army were holding positions and endeavouring to advance during the autumn of 1943 was extremely mountainous. These British troops are manhandling supplies to forward positions 2,200 feet up hills near Rochetta.

9 Old jokes about generals not getting mud on their boots were given the lie on the Italian front. Here (left to right) Lieutenant-General C.W. Allfrey and General Sir Alan Brooke are seen squelching towards 8th Army headquarters, a photograph released on 7th January 1944.

the Alban Hills was unlikely to be realistically possible unless Kesselring had diverted a substantial part of the German forces defending Rome to the South and South-West. It was also clear that, once he was aware that a beach-head had been created at Anzio, Kesselring, a master organiser, would not be slow in plugging the gap in his defences.

When the plan was put into action, in January 1944, things did not go as Churchill and Roosevelt had hoped, although the reasons were less than simple. Journalists at the time, and some historians, have tended to place all the odium for the failure of the breakout from Anzio on Major-General Lucas, but, while there is no doubt that his

approach to the problems that faced him was not the fire-eating 'go gettem' approach of a General Patton, some of the blame must be ascribed to Lieutenant-General Mark Clark. For it is established that, instead of passing on Alexander's orders simply to seize the beach-head, and then cut the enemy's communications, Clark ordered Lucas to seize *and secure* the beach-head then advance on the Colli Laziali. In other words, Clark's order implied that, until the beach-head was secure, the breakout was not to be attempted. Furthermore, even when the breakout began, it was in order to 'advance' on the Alban Hills, not to rush them and cut the enemy off from Kesselring's main forces as the original plan had envisaged.

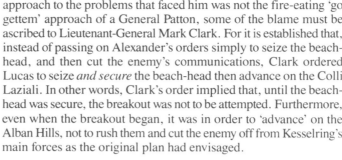

1 Troops of the US 5th Army race ashore from a Higgins Boat to create the Allied beachhead near Nettuno, southwest of Rome. The initial landing met with surprisingly little resistance, but the slowness of the breakout from the beachhead gave the Germans time to move several divisions into the line to resist the drive to Italy's capital.

2 The scene on the British sector of the beaches at Anzio as landing craft disgorged men and equipment for the assault on Rome. The DUKW that is being unloaded from the landing craft is carrying a cargo of six-pounder anti-tank guns.

3 A near miss as a German shell sends a geyser of water high in the air close to US Army amphibians near the beach at Anzio during the reinforcement phase of bringing supplies to the beachhead. After the initially almost unopposed landing, heavy enemy resistance made operations at the beach hazardous for many weeks.

4 The build-up of armour on the beaches before the breakout order was given was tremendous, due to General Lucas obeying orders to the letter and 'securing' the beach-head. These British Army Bren gun carriers have just been disembarked to join the force waiting to go into action against General von Mackensen's divisions, hastily moved into the area to counter the invasion.

5 With the invasion fleet in the background, a Sherman tank of the US 5th Army rolls uphill to join the advance on Rome. Another Sherman is lurking in the undergrowth to the left in the foreground of the picture, and a further tank is following the first (partially hidden by the head of the commander of the leading tank).

6 Extremely rough weather – not uncommon West of Italy in January and February – hampered the bringing ashore of men and equipment at Anzio on some of the all-important build-up days. This view from a British DUKW amphibious truck gives an impression of the difficulties and miseries of landing supplies under such conditions.

7 The transition from seagoing to land vehicle was not always easy for a DUKW, since it was a wheeled rather than a tracked amphibian, and finding a wheel purchase while there was still water available for the screw to push the vehicle forward could be difficult. As a result, drivers who found a trouble-free way ashore in poor conditions were followed by other drivers who had no wish to get stuck, and traffic jams like this developed.

Anzio

On January 16th 1944, General Clark's 5th Army once more attacked the German positions on and around Monte Cassino. This hill – or mountain – topped by a beautiful 14th century Benedictine monastery filled with priceless art treasures had already become symbolic of the Italian stalemate. Over the next four months it was to renew fears of apparent Nazi invincibility, and to become the focus of allegations of Allied vandalism that roll on into the Eighties.

Now, just before the amphibious landing at Anzio that was to come just under a week later, Monte Cassino was defended by General von Vietinghoff-Scheel's XIV *Panzer* Corps of the German 10th Army. The assault on the Cassino defile was to be carried out by the US II Corps under Major-General Geoffrey Keyes, supported on its right by General Juin's French Expeditionary Corps, which included Moroccan and Algerian troops who were to distinguish themselves many times during the ensuing months, and on the left by Lieutenant-General Sir Richard McCreery's British X Corps. The intention was to get across the Rapido, some five miles South of Cassino, and bypass the mountains along the Liri Valley towards Anzio. However, the plan took insufficient account of the terrain. Although X Corps got across the river – at that point the Garigliano, formed by the confluence of the Liri and the Rapido – they could

8 An interesting view of Allied forces assembling in the square of a small Italian town just inland from the Anzio beachhead. The picture appears to have been taken from the turret of a tank or othered armoured vehicle – as well as the substantial gun there are two machine guns, one on each side. However, the author has been unable to identify the vehicle from the shape of the superstructure beneath the gun.

The Advance on Rome

advance little further and were badly mauled. The US 36th Division, which started North of the Rapido, was even thrown back across it, with terrible casualties. Only the French, who, because of their colonial mountain troops, had been given the task of taking the high ground, had any measure of success. But even they, having captured the mountains above the Rapido, did not have the necessary strength to descend to the valley behind the German defenders.

Nonetheless, although the operation seemed to achieve little militarily, it did succeed in part in its primary objective. General von Vietinghoff called for reinforcements, and Kesselring transferred the

29th and 90th *Panzergrenadier* Divisions from Rome.

At 2am on January 22nd, General Lucas's US VI Corps began landing at Anzio and Nettuno, and by midnight the same day had put ashore over 36,000 men, more than 3,000 vehicles and virtually all the guns that were to take part in the operation. The Corps in fact included, in addition to the US 3rd Division, the British 1st Division, a regiment and a battalion of paratroops, a brigade of commandos and three battalions of US Rangers. The two battalions of Germans that were the only German forces in the area were quickly wiped out, and, on the face of it, Rome was 37 miles away, and there was virtually nobody in the way of a speedy advance to the objective. Had General Patton been in command, he would undoubtedly have set off at high speed to the Eternal City, revolvers gleaming and eyes glinting. But would he have been right? And would he have succeeded?

General Truscott, the commander of the US 3rd Division, who was something of a fire-eater himself, thought not, and defended his then superior, General Lucas, for following the orders General Clark had given him and 'securing the beach-head'. In his view, Kesselring would have pulled back to the area between Rome and Anzio within days regardless of how far VI Corps had pushed on to Rome, and would probably have been able to cut the communications of the over-extended Allied advance while at the same time shelling the under-defended beach-head and inhibiting the landing of reinforcements and supplies. Nonetheless, Churchill was furious that Lucas stayed put at Anzio landing the remainder of his Corps, building up an immense stock of vehicles — one report quoted 17,000 vehicles for 70,000 men — and preparing his armour, while Hitler was issuing his Directive for the Battle of Rome, and Kesselring was organising LXXVI *Panzer*

Corps for a counter attack. In a famous comment, Churchill said 'I expected to see a wildcat roaring into the mountains — and what do I find? A whale wallowing on the beaches!'

In fact, on the day after the Anzio landing, General von Mackensen arrived to take command of the already prepared German plan for tackling the problem, but had at that stage only a small detachment of the *Hermann Goering Panzer* Division and a few guns. By the 28th, he had three divisions in the defensive line. By the 31st he had eight, and the landing was effectively, for the time being at least, contained.

Hitler was, however, not content with containing the situation. He had ordered a counter-attack that was to drive the Allies back into the sea, and had altered the plan by which LXXVI Corps was to carry out the attack so that the luckless *Panzer* Corps was to attack on a front only 4 miles wide without adequate air cover — for Field-Marshal von Richthofen's *Luftflotte II* simply did not have the aircraft, the pilots or, most important of all, the fuel for a sustained aerial assault and cover operation.

The German attack on February 16th ran into trouble almost as soon as it began. The initial barrage was, because of lack of ammunition, simply not enough to deter effective resistance to the first advance, and the Allied air attacks were pressed home effectively against tanks which could not leave the roads because of the softness of the Pontine marshes on either side. Air strikes also limited the quantity of supplies that the Germans could bring forward; nonetheless Mackensen's Corps had by the end of the first day advanced a third of the twelve miles to the Anzio beaches. On the second and third days, the German troops fought hard to pursue their initial advantage, but the Allied artillery and air power was too great for any significant progress to be possible. The Allied commanders reinforced the beach-head by bringing in the British 5th and the US 34th Divisions, and a new stalemate developed. The German artillery in the Alban Hills maintained constant harassment on the Allied position, and the Allies' guns and aircraft responded in kind. Nonetheless, the initiative had gone, and Rome had not been taken. Now the emphasis had to be returned to the route via Cassino.

The Battles of Monte Cassino

The failure of the Anzio landing to secure an immediate advance on Rome became the reason for some of the fiercest fighting of the war as the 5th Army struggled to take Monte Cassino from a remarkably tenacious German Army. The French Expeditionary Corps under General Juin had as early as January 23rd/24th been given the ultra-hazardous task of attempting to go round Cassino via Monte Belvedere and Colle Abate, with the objective of surrounding their enemy and attacking them from all sides, and, although the encirclement had not been achieved, they had succeeded brilliantly in diverting two thirds of the German defenders to the job of holding

1

2

3

4

down the Algerians and Tunisians. Not for nothing did Kesselring feel uneasy whenever the French Expeditionary Corps was thrown in against his armies. Juin's force held their mountaintop positions, but the US 34th Division was bogged down in its beach-head on the Cassino side of the River Rapido.

To give new impetus, Alexander provided General Clark with General Freyberg's New Zealand Corps — but Freyberg, believing that the historic abbey of Monte Cassino was being used as a German headquarters and stronghold, demanded its destruction by bombing to give his force a chance in the forthcoming battle. Clark opposed this bombing, partly because he was far from sure it was necessary, partly because it was to him an act of vandalism. But Freyberg's view

1 During the protracted campaign to take Monte Cassino, the Allied armies were up against the German 1st Parachute Division, an elite division commanded by the redoubtable Lieutenant-General Richard Heidrich (left). Here he is conferring with his Commander-in-Chief, Field Marshal Albert Kesselring.

2 The ancient monastery of Monte Cassino after the Allied bombing attack of February 15th 1944, when over 450 tons of explosive rained down on the ancient building to eliminate a supposed German garrison when it was, in fact, inhabited only by its monks. With hindsight this seems an error of judgment or intelligence, and at the time the Germans made much of the act of 'Allied vandalism'.

3 The eighty-three-year-old Nicola Clemente, Abbot Bishop of the Benedictine Monastery of Monte Cassino, was, in fact, well-treated by the Germans, who endeavoured to avoid incursion of soldiers and arms into the monastery until after the Allied bombing raid. This picture of the Abbot was radioed to New York via Stockholm on February 29th 1944, but was taken before the raid.

4 To overcome the problems of artillery observation in the mountains of Italy, the British and New Zealand artillery units used Auster light reconnaissance aircraft loaned by the RAF as airborne observation posts. They were flown by specially-trained artillery officers.

5 The almost total destruction of the small town of Cassino wrought by the intensive air attack of March 15th 1944, carried out by 775 aircraft, was awe-inspiring. The near-total failure of the raid to achieve any clear tactical advantage for the Allies made the local population's loss of life and property even more poignant. This picture was taken from a USAAF reconnaisance aircraft a few minutes after the last of the bombers had left.

won the day. On February 15th, 229 Allied bombers in three waves dropped 453 tons of high explosive on the venerable building and reduced it to total ruin.

In fact, before the attack, there were no Germans in the monastery other than two military police whose sole function was to protect it from incursion by troops. The only occupants were the abbot and his monks. But, once the damage had been done, the Germans moved into the ruin in force, and used the magnificent vantage point it provided to drive back first the 4th Indian Division and then the 2nd New Zealand Division as they attempted to storm the mountain top. Worse was to follow. On March 15th, the Allied commanders attempted once again to use the same tactics to dislodge the Germans from Cassino by heavy bombing. A total of 775 aircraft dropped 1,250 tons of bombs on the town of Cassino and the country immediately around it. As the Allied troops attempted to capitalise on the effect of the bombing and take the town, the extent of the destruction and cratering made it impossible for the tanks to enter the town. The infantry were on their own, and the ferocity of the fighting was

5

6 An Allied medical team searches the wreckage of the devastated town of Cassino for survivors following the great Allied air raid of March 1944. The genuine concern and compassion of the army doctors and nurses was poor recompense to the people of Cassino for a largely pointless destruction of their homes and way of life.

6

7

8

7 In the debris of Cassino, men of the German 1st Parachute Division take up positions to await the arrival of Allied troops. The principal effect of the enormous quantity of rubble created by the bombing was to slow the advance of Allied armoured columns and make them more susceptible to anti-tank weapons. In some cases, the debris was piled so high that tanks were unable to force a way through.

8 The mighty flash of an 8-inch howitzer of the Allied 5th Army lights up the American crew of the gun clearly as they fire on German positions in the mountains during a night barrage. Notice how the nearest tree to the right of the flash has bent to the blast.

The Advance on Rome

appalling. Anti-personnel mines inflicted terrible casualties, and little progress was made against the crack German parachute troops defending Cassino and the area around it.

An equal lack of success was experienced on the hill below the monastery. It was like Verdun all over again — mud, blood and frustration. On March 23rd, Freyberg recognised the obvious and called off the attack. The losses of the attempts to take Cassino were frighteningly high. Over 22,000 Americans, more than 22,000 British, almost 8,000 French and nearly 400 Italians were killed, wounded or missing for virtually no gain. Alexander now decided to reorganise his forces. The British X Corps passed from the 5th Army to the British 8th Army, which had been since December 23rd under the command of General Sir Oliver Leese following Montgomery's recall to Britain for his part in 'Overlord'. Leese was given the sector of the Italian front between the Abruzzi heights and the Liri valley. Clark's 5th Army was responsible now only for the Anzio beach-head and the area between the Liri and the Tyrrhenian Sea.

Alexander's objective remained the smashing of the German 10th Army, and on May 11th he launched his newly reformed forces into the Battle of the Gustav Line. After a night of bombardment and surprise Allied attacks along a 25 mile front, neither the British nor the Americans had made significant progress, and even General Anders' fearless Polish II Corps had been repulsed on the slopes of Monte Cassino. But, after enduring heavy attack, minefields, flame throwers and just about everything the German Army had, General Juin's tough French Expeditionary Corps took Monte Majo on May 13th, and then went on to capture Monte Petrella on the 15th. On the 17th, the Poles finally made it to the ruined monastery on Monte

1

2

3

4

1 German reinforcements continued to be brought into the line for the defence of Rome, but these men were already veterans of the battle. In the background is a StuG III Assault Gun, a PzKpfw III tank chassis with a 75mm short-barrelled gun mounted in it, which was an effective, mobile and well-protected self-propelled gun with a road speed of twenty-five mph. Some 10,500 had been built by the end of the war.

2 It was not only Cassino that suffered almost total destruction from bombardment, both from the air and from the ground. This is Cisterna, as it was when it was captured by General Truscott's VI Corps on May 25th 1944. An Allied column of American military vehicles is making its way up the road to the right of the picture.

3 The co-belligerent Italian Army, fighting now alongside the Allies against the Germans, brought some useful weapons to the fray. This 194mm railway gun, manned by an armoured regiment of the Italian Army, is firing on German positions 16·5 kilometres (over 10 miles) from the gunners, during March 1944.

4 Two Royal Air Force Baltimore twin-engined bombers fly over picturesquely snow-covered peaks in Italy during March 1944 on their way to a target. Picturesque it may have been, but terrain like this is what every military pilot dislikes most, since forced landings are virtually impossible, and baling out is likely to lead to death from exposure.

5 On the morning of 28th May 1944, the so-called 'tobacco factory' at Carroceto, scene of much bitter fighting, fell to British troops. In this picture, Sergeant E. Newbury of Melbourne, Derbyshire, and Lieutenant E.L. Strauss of Brakpan, Transvaal, South Africa, are searching the cellars under a block of flats in the area.

Cassino, only to find it deserted. By May 23rd, the US II Corps was approaching Terracina, and Kesselring, to stop the advance, took reinforcements from Colonel-General von Mackensen's forces that were restraining the US VI Corps at Anzio. As a result, VI Corps, now under the command of General Truscott, broke out, captured Cisterna and, on May 25th, II Corps and VI Corps joined forces.

The Advance on Rome

Now the Allied air offensive against the regrouping German 10th and 14th Armies was stepped up, and Churchill began sending signals urging Alexander to cut off as many of the German divisions from retreat as possible. There is no doubt that General Clark had a magnificent opportunity to capture much of Kesselring's army in a pocket — but instead of turning North to Valmontone to achieve this, Clark headed for Rome, sending only a small detachment towards Valmontone. Kesselring meanwhile was endeavouring to hold a line from the Alban Hills to Monti Lepini, and looked like succeeding until May 31st, when the US VI Corps pierced the German defences, scaled the Alban Hills, and started to advance on Rome. Kesselring had little option but to withdraw and proclaim Rome an open city, to avoid its bombardment and the destruction of its ancient buildings and historic treasures. On June 4th, the American 88th Division was the first Allied force to enter the Eternal City, for which so many had fought for so long.

This was by no means the end of the war in Italy — it had almost a year yet to run before the Italian people could begin to clear up the turmoil into which Mussolini's Fascists had let them fall. But the attention of the world now switched to 'Overlord', the great amphibious invasion of Normandy, which began only two days after the entry into Rome. We too shall look at 'Overlord' — but let us first take a look at the great bomber offensive; the war in the air.

6 On June 5th, the day after the city fell, General Mark W. Clark was able to ride in his three-star Jeep through the streets of Rome. With St Peter's Basilica in the background, General Clark is driven by Technical Sergeant Holden with rear seat passengers Major-General A.M. Gruenther, his Chief of Staff, (on left) and Major-General Geoffrey Keyes, Commanding General of II Corps.

CHAPTER 33

BOMBER OFFENSIVE
THE ASSAULT FROM THE AIR

In earlier chapters of this book the bombing of Warsaw, the London Blitz, the devastating German air raids on Coventry, Clydebank, Plymouth and other targets have been described in the context of their tactical use as part of campaigns to capture Poland and Britain. The Allies took a different view of air power from that adopted by the *Luftwaffe* in general, and by Goering and Hitler in particular. To the Allies, air power was a strategic weapon aimed almost totally at the destruction of the means of production on the one hand, and of enemy towns, cities and morale on the other.

From the beginning, the *Luftwaffe* was designed as a weapon to achieve massive conquest in the shortest possible time — it was a *Blitzkrieg* weapon. Hitler's burgeoning ambition and proliferation of active fighting fronts stretched the *Luftwaffe* badly, as did its severe losses in the Battle of Britain, with the result that, after the initial successes in Russia in 1941, German air power began to wane. One of Hitler's least far-sighted directives had, in 1940, ordered the abandonment of work on all new aircraft types that could not be in service by 1942 on the grounds that 'they would not be needed after the war', and, as a result, development of new aircraft types was 'too little and too late'.

The British had quite early in the war — in August 1940 in fact — proved false Goering's notorious boast that Berlin would never be bombed, and throughout 1941 had maintained constant harassment of Germany by night, albeit on a relatively small scale by comparison with later raids. By spring 1942, the British build-up of bombers, and the development of longer range aircraft, had reached the point where large scale raids could be mounted, and on May 30th 1942, the RAF delivered its first '1,000 bomber raid' on Cologne. In fact, although there were actually just over 1,000 aircraft, many of them were obsolete, and losses were quite high. Cologne was left ablaze and the propaganda effect on the populations of both Britain and Germany was substantial. There followed a rapid series of night carpet bombing raids against the major strategic cities of the Reich — Essen, Dortmund, Leipzig, Hamburg, Berlin — in which civilian populations were hit as hard as German industry. But the assault was not against cities alone.

As longer range four engined aircraft such as the Stirling, the Halifax and the Lancaster became available, more ambitious heavy raids on specifically industrial targets were undertaken. Important centres of production like the steelworks of the Ruhr were hit

1 The bomber offensive in the early part of the war relied upon twin-engined bombers that were rapidly to become obsolete as the pace of wartime progress accelerated the development of the heavy bomber. This 1941 photograph of the crew of an RAF Blenheim shows last-minute preparations before a raid on port installations at Le Havre, France. Note the small size of the aircraft by comparison with the heavy, four-engined bombers illustrated later in this chapter.

2 Fighter sweeps to keep German aircraft occupied at the time of an Allied bombing raid, and fighter escort duty, were integral parts of early daylight bombing operations. This fine picture shows one of the many American pilots who flew with the RAF on fighter sweeps over Europe before the USA came into the war. He is standing on the wing of his Spitfire after returning from an operation.

3 There were many inspiring stories that emerged from the saga of fighter operations over Europe, but few more demanding of respect than those of the legless fighter pilots. The first was Wing-Commander Douglas Bader, later Group Captain Sir Douglas Bader, whose flying career was abruptly curtailed when he was obliged to bale out (minus one of his artificial legs) and became a prisoner of war. Then came Colin Hodgkinson, a Sub-Lieutenant in the Royal Navy Fleet Air Arm, who was granted a transfer to fly on fighter operations with the RAF. This picture of Hodgkinson, aged 21, in the cockpit of a Spitfire, was released in October 1942.

4 The Westland Whirlwind was a fast (360 mph at 15,000ft) twin-engined fighter of advanced design that was very manoeuvrable and fought well. Unfortunately, it was designed around the ill-fated Rolls-Royce Peregrine engine, which was late into production, never attained full reliability or performance, and was abandoned as an engine in January 1942, when only one hundred and sixteen Whirlwinds had been built.

5 The first of the Royal Air Force's heavy bombers was the Stirling, illustrated here in flight. With four Bristol Hercules radial engines, the Mark III version in production by 1940 had a maximum speed of 270 mph at 14,500ft, and was capable of carrying a 3,500 lb bomb load over 2,000 miles, although the fact that it could carry no one bomb larger than 2,000 lb was a significant disadvantage.

6 A fine picture of the Lockheed Hudson in flight in 1941. The Hudson was the first American-built bomber to see action in the Second World War when, on 8th October 1939, a Hudson disposed of the first German aircraft to fall to RAF guns. Later, a Hudson of the US Navy became the first US-built aircraft to destroy a German submarine.

7 A gunner's eye view of a raid by the Royal Air Force on the Fortuna factory installations in Germany during 1941. The out-of-focus machine-gun projecting from the aircraft turret can be seen, as can the black, billowing smoke from the bomb bursts as the plane climbs away after its low-level bombing run.

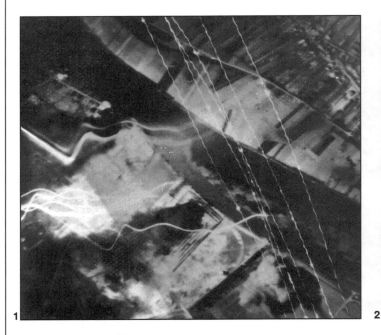

1

2

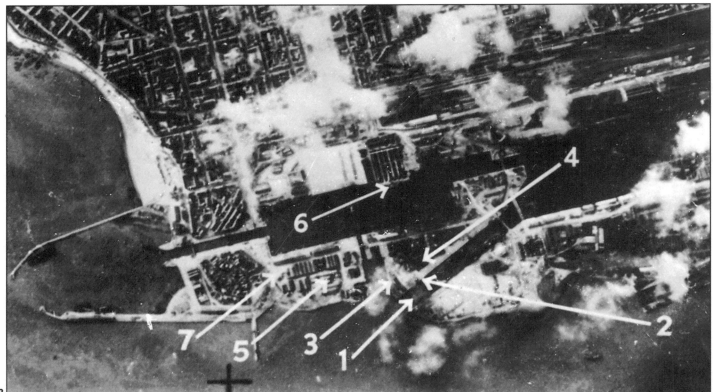

3

4

5

GUIDE PRINT ONLY

1 The photographs produced by bomber aircraft during night raids became progressively better as techniques improved during the war. This picture shows a truck factory at Poissy, France, ablaze during a raid by RAF Bomber Command on the night of April 2nd 1942. The factory was producing 600 lorries a month plus parts for a further 400 per month before the raid.

2 Pictures shot during a raid were extensively analysed by RAF scientists in an effort to determine the true effectiveness of raids on German installations. This picture, also taken during the April 1942 raids on Poissy, is marked up for analysis: A: main building B: smaller buildings, with tracks of fires across them C: smoke drifting away from the works. D: tracks of tracer shells fired at the aircraft by ground defenders. E: burst of bomb or bombs which had overshot the main building.

3 After bombing raids, fast high-flying aerial reconnaissance aircraft – usually under considerable pressure from German fighters – photographed the target in daylight to enable experts to determine the extent of the damage that had been inflicted upon the enemy. The principle was extended to obtain evidence of the success of combined operations, and this picture was taken of the harbour installations at St Nazaire, France, after the daring raid (Operation Chariot) carried out by British Commandos on March 27th 1942, when HMS *Campbeltown* (formerly the USS *Buchanan*) deliberately rammed and blew up the dock gates. The picture showed that the main objective of the raid – the destruction of the outer lock gate of the dock – had been accomplished and that dock buildings and installations had been destroyed. 1: missing outer gate. 2: dock pump house. 3: dock machine house. 4: two small sheds of pump house, destroyed. 5: fire-bay building with roof missing. 6: damage to submarine pens under construction. 7: south end of multi-bay building damaged.

4 In May 1942, the shipyards of Rouen in Normandy were attacked in daylight by Boston twin-engined bombers of the RAF. This photograph, taken during the course of the attack, shows bombs bursting on the quays and installations.

repeatedly, and in May 1943, Barnes Wallis' famous bouncing bomb was used effectively against the Moehne, Eder and Sorpe dams by 617 Squadron RAF led by Wing Commander Guy Gibson – the raid portrayed by the British motion picture 'The Dam Busters', made early in the 1950s.

Once the USA was into the war, an argument developed between the US 8th Air Force, formed and led in Britain by General Carl Spaatz, and RAF Bomber Command, under the command of Air Chief Marshal Sir Arthur (Bomber) Harris. The US aerial bombardment strategy was based upon the assumption that heavy bombers carrying sufficient guns could defend themselves against

attacking fighters in daylight, and that daylight bombing with pinpoint accuracy was therefore possible. If this were correct, there was obviously much to commend the US approach, as it would reduce to a minimum the impact upon civilian populations and increase the effectiveness of every bomb. Spaatz also rejected Harris's contention that carpet bombing of German cities would break German morale; he argued that if German bombing had failed to bring London to its knees, there was no justification for assuming that Berlin or Hamburg would give in any more easily.

Sir Arthur Harris believed that there was no way in which heavy, relatively slow and largely unmanoeuvrable bombers could defend

5 In August 1942, RAF Boston bombers took part in the ill-fated Dieppe raid. Early in the attack, these Bostons dropped modest bomb loads on the defences at Dieppe, but failed to inflict damage sufficient to avert the disaster that followed.

6 By late 1942, the B17 Flying Fortress was becoming a familiar sight in the skies of Britain and Europe, though it was more welcome in the former than the latter. The reason for this can be seen pouring from the bomb bays of this B17 as it flies on a daylight raid over Germany. Bombing from heights approaching 30,000ft and with a maximum speed of around 300 mph, the B17 was armed with eight or nine machine guns plus a 0·30in gun in the nose.

7 Losses of B17 bombers before long-range Mustangs were available were high, and many crew were lost. This remarkable picture shows a B17 over Germany with its entire tail assembly shot away spiralling helplessly towards the earth. Above it, the rest of the bomber force, contrails streaming, heads on towards its target.

8 Throughout 1942, the number of American soldiers and airmen in Britain increased rapidly, as the build-up for the eventual invasion of Europe began and the daylight raids by the USAAF on Germany were stepped up. The comparatively wealthy (by British standards) and fun-loving American troops caused some civilian resentment, and some troops were, therefore, given introductory training on how to approach being in Britain. These soldiers are being shown London and its bomb damage, with St Paul's cathedral in the background.

9 Parties for British war orphans were organised by American troops – this occasion was a Thanksgiving party for fifty children from London's poor East End at the Red Cross Club in London's Hans Crescent. The American soldier had, according to the contemporary caption to the picture, been saving his candy for weeks for the occasion.

10 Christmas itself produced parties for children at US forces establishments up and down Britain – this picture shows a party at which fifty US soldiers played host to 400 London children at Paddington Town Hall.

themselves effectively without fighter cover – a point which to British eyes had been substantially proved by the *Luftwaffe's* failure in daylight raids over Britain – and that, since no fighters existed with long enough range to fly to Germany and back, the only practical approach to strategic bombing was large scale carpet bombing at night of the areas in which large production and military installations were known to exist. He was also confident that bombing of the cities would result in the civilian population of Germany bringing massive pressure to bear on Hitler for an end to the war.

Since neither side wanted to give, and because there was no way of knowing for sure who was right without testing the hypothesis, a compromise was reached in September 1942 by which the US 8th Air Force attacked by day, and the RAF flew by night.

The American crews flew B-17 Flying Fortresses and B-24 Liberators – each bristling with pairs of 0.5 calibre Browning machine guns from hydraulically controlled turrets pointing in almost every direction. The B-17, originally designed in 1934 and first flown

in 1935, operated during the Second World War in three principal versions, the B-17E, the B-17F and the B-17G. The majority of operational aircraft by mid 1944 were of the last type, distinguished by its unusual 'chin' gun turret, of which 8,680 were built. The B-17 typically carried a crew of nine, could carry a 10,500lb bomb load, and was fitted with the remarkably accurate Norden bombsight. If it got through to the target, which a significant proportion did, it was able to do tremendous damage with its pinpoint bombing. But, in the early days of the daylight bombing offensive, before suitable fighters were available to provide long range escort, German Messerchmitt 109 and Focke-Wulf 190 fighters were able to shoot down large

Bomber Offensive

numbers of the close formations of American bombers. In 1943, the *Luftwaffe* fighters even used successfully the tactic of bombing the formations from above.

In August 1943, the US Eighth Air Force began the process of attacking the *Luftwaffe* production lines as a means of reducing the available German air power to combat 'Overlord' when it came. On August 17th, 376 Eighth Air Force aircraft bombed the aircraft factory at Regensburg and the massive ball-bearing production plant at Schweinfurt. Ball-bearing production was key to the entire war production programme, and Albert Speer, Germany's Minister of Armaments Production, was quoted after the war as saying that if the pressure on ball-bearing production had been maintained, the war production machine would have ground to a halt in only four months. But the raid on Schweinfurt was very expensive indeed in both men and machines. Sixty bombers did not return to their bases in England, and that meant that over five hundred highly-skilled aircrew were lost to the war, either killed or taken prisoner. Not until long-range Mustangs with drop-tanks were available could the massive raids on

1 The oilfield and its installations at Ploesti in Rumania were relied upon almost totally by the German regime for its supplies of oil and aviation fuel. Without the oilfields, the *Luftwaffe* would soon be unable to fly.

2 The raid on the oilfield at Ploesti in August 1943 was a triumph both of organisation and courage, and determination, for it was an extremely dangerous mission. This remarkable picture shot from a low-flying Liberator shows the oil installations ablaze.

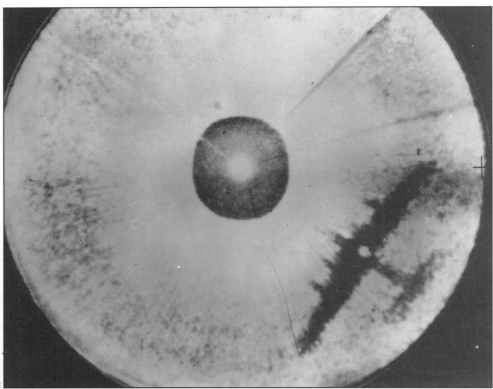

3 This picture was taken during the war as a demonstration of trailer-mounted radar used to direct anti-aircraft guns onto their target.

4 The image of bombers departing, pregnant with bombs, into the sunset, is powerful yet sinister, for their purpose was indiscriminate death. Nonetheless, this picture of Lancasters taxiing into the setting sun is strangely beautiful.

5 By contrast with the precisely-aimed American tactical daylight raids on Germany, the Royal Air Force bombed strategically at night. One of the most famous of the RAF bomber pilots was Wing Commander Guy Gibson who, in addition to his D.S.O. and bar and D.F.C. and bar, won the Victoria Cross for his leadership of the raid on the Möhne, Eder and Sorpe dams in May 1943. This picture was taken four months earlier when Gibson (with pipe) and his crew had just returned from bombing Berlin.

the more distant parts of Germany continue. In fact, in October 1943, the loss of 153 US bombers in one week caused the cancellation of all raids without fighter escort.

The US raids were not all based in England. Just over two weeks before the raid on Schweinfurt, a force of 178 Consolidated B-24 Liberators took off from Libya to raid the Rumanian oilfields at Ploesti, the principal source of *Wehrmacht* fuel. This raid was enormously hazardous, stretching the range of the Liberator to the absolute limit, and requiring the crews to fly most of the 1,500 mile mission over German occupied territory beset by attacking fighters. Many of the force did not reach their target, but those that did caused great damage to the German war effort. Of the 1,733 men who flew the mission, 446 were killed. Only 33 of the original 178 aircraft flew in action again — many of those that managed to get back to North Africa were not economically repairable.

After the end of 1943, the invention of drop tanks made long range escort of the US bomber formations by the new Mustang fighter entirely routine, and bomber losses fell sharply as the damage

6 The bomb capacity of the incredible Lancaster bomber was something of a legend in its own time. Designed originally to carry bombs of up to 4,000lb, the aircraft was given a succession of modifications to its bomb-bay which enabled it first to carry 8,000lb, then 12,000lb, and finally Barnes Wallis' extraordinary 22,000lb 'Grand Slam' armour piercing bomb.

7 Incredibly, over 12,000 B17 Flying Fortress bombers of all types were built, 8,680 of them being of the final B17G model.

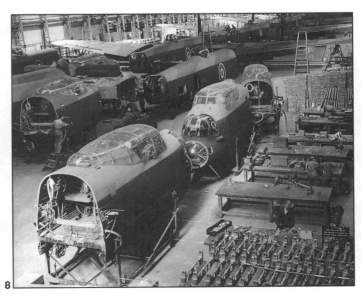

8 The Avro Lancaster, Britain's most successful heavy bomber, was a direct descendant of the unsuccessful Manchester twin-engined bomber, which was seriously underpowered. Its first bombing raid was flown against Essen in March 1942, and 3,440 of the Lancaster Mark I were built by various British manufacturers, including Avro themselves. Almost 4,000 more Lancasters of later marks were built subsequently, although the differences between types were mainly concerned with the power plant.

Bomber Offensive

inflicted on the *Luftwaffe* by the Mustangs rose. The Mustang, with a range of 850 miles, was the longest-range fighter of World War Two, and performed many roles successfully — Group Captain Leonard Cheshire, VC, of the RAF even using one in his pioneering of pathfinder marking of night targets for the RAF bomber forces.

The biggest problem that had afflicted RAF night bombing in the early part of the war was the difficulty of finding the target. In 1940, investigations had shown that two-thirds of the RAF crews on a raid had not bombed within five miles of the target. This was solved to a large extent first by a guidance device known as 'Gee', then, from March 5th 1943, by a more sophisticated radar installation codenamed 'Oboe'. A Pathfinder Force was formed of crack crews, usually flying Lancasters, which were fitted with an even more effective radar known as 'H2S'. Their task was to precede the main force to the target and bomb it accurately with coloured flares to show the bomb-aimers of later aircraft where to target their bombloads.

The techniques of carpet bombing by night became gradually more effective, and all pretence of seeking military targets alone was abandoned after the Casablanca conference sanctioned the use of all-out strategic bombing of Germany. The RAF, in four nights between July 24th and August 3rd 1943, killed an estimated 33,000 people in Hamburg by creating a firestorm, a phenomenon previously known

1 With so many aircraft flying such a large number of missions, bombing up before a raid became a major task for the armourers of squadrons all over the eastern counties of England. In this case the aircraft is a B17 Flying Fortress.

2 In November 1943, the RAF launched what became known as 'The Battle of Berlin', designed, in Air Marshal Harris' words, to 'wreck Berlin from end to end'. Over a period of five months, the RAF dropped 25,000 tons of bombs in thirty-two attacks, destroying nine square kilometres of the city, damaging 315 factories, and leaving 6,166 people dead, 18,431 badly injured and 1·5 million homeless. The Royal Air Force lost 1,047 aircraft during the course of the battle. This crew had just returned from the first raid of the campaign.

3 American bombers were designed for larger crews than the British aircraft. This is the nine-man crew of a B24 Liberator in 1942.

5

6

7

8

9

4 The four Rolls-Royce Merlin XX engines of the Lancaster I gave it a maximum speed of 287 mph at 11,500 ft, and a range of 1,730 miles with a bomb load of 12,000lb. This picture of Lancasters both on the ground and in flight shows clearly that, although the aircraft was graceless at rest, it had a majesty all its own once airborne.

5 The USAAF had established training squadrons in Britain, not only for crews, but also for the ground crews and maintenance teams. This US airman is at work on the belly turret of a B17.

6 As the RAF prepared to set off at sunset, so the survivors of the day's raids would reappear above the USAAF stations and peel off to land. These B17 bombers had just returned from a raid over Germany.

7 Constant anti-aircraft fire and frequent fighter attacks greeted the B17s on their daylight raids. Every black puff of smoke around this Flying Fortress is a bursting flak shell.

8 Frequently, returning US bombers made it to the British coast, but had to force land well short of their home base. In these cases, the Mobile Machine Shop travelled to the damaged aircraft and either dismantled it for land transportation, or repaired it to take off again. In this case, after repairs to the aircraft's radial engines, a temporary airstrip was built, and the Fortress was flown out of the field on the South Coast where it had landed.

9 During the period immediately before the Normandy invasion, the bombing of important targets was stepped up. On May 1st 1944, the entire works of the *Pouderie Nationale* (explosives plant) at Toulouse was destroyed by RAF Bomber Command. This reconnaissance picture shows how throughly the devastation had been carried out.

only in theory. Most of the dead were suffocated by the lack of oxygen resulting from the colossal and unimaginably intense fires that engulfed the city. Known to the German population, understandably, as *Die Katastrophe*, the raids on Hamburg stirred fierce resentment against the RAF, whose crews were known as *terrorflieger* and were treated roughly by North German townspeople if they were forced to bale out over the cities. In the first eight months of 1943, 11,000 tons of bombs were dropped by the RAF on Hamburg, 8,000 tons on Essen, 6,000 tons each on Duisburg and Berlin, and 5,000 tons each on Dusseldorf and Nuremberg.

Against these raids, the Germans developed a guidance system for its night-fighters which was known as the *Wurzberg*, a radar which enabled the night fighter controller to talk his squadrons on to the British formations, and a low-frequency radar called *Freya*, which acted as an early warning system. To combat these radar devices, which were becoming progressively more effective, British scientists came up with a delightfully simple idea codenamed 'Window' —

nothing more than thousands of strips of metal foil dropped from the formations of aircraft, which, as it fluttered thousands of feet towards the ground provided the German controllers with thousands of false echoes and obscured the real ones that represented the aircraft. By pursuing a non-committal course until after the 'Window' was dropped, the bomber formations were able to conceal their real target from the night fighters and flak gunners until ground reports of the attack gave their positions away.

As 1944, the year of 'Overlord' approached, the Allied air offensive was stepped up, partly to maintain the pressure on armaments production and civilian morale, more to cause the *Luftwaffe* to pull back such reserves as it had from the Atlantic Wall and the defence of the Channel coast to Germany and the defence of the cities. Between January 1st and June 5th 1944, the day before D-Day, the US daylight marauders and the RAF night bombers between them delivered 102 major attacks on German cities. Berlin was almost destroyed by 17 fierce raids; Braunschweig was next in the league of

Bomber Offensive

destruction with 13 raids; Frankfurt received 8 raids and Hanover 5. Many other cities were attacked – Leipzig, Magdeburg, Duisburg, Essen, the other cities of the Ruhr and North Germany. Even Vienna was raided in March.

By the spring of 1944, the *Luftwaffe* was severely depleted, its means of production were being attacked almost daily, and, most important of all, its fuel supplies were reaching crisis point. Much of the credit for this acute shortage of fuel was due to the success of a campaign launched at the beginning of April 1944 by General Spaatz against Germany's sources not only of natural fuels, but also of the synthetic fuels that her scientists had learned to manufacture. We have already described the previous year's assault by Liberators on the oilfield at Ploesti in Rumania. By April 1944, the US Army Air Force was established in Italy, at Foggia, and was in a much stronger position to attack the oil-producing area at shorter range and with far greater chances of success.

On April 4th, a raid from Foggia on Ploesti by 230 bombers did far more damage to oil-field installations than had the previous raid, and the US airmen followed it up with attacks on refineries and storage depots in Bucharest, Budapest and Vienna, and with raids on the Danube ports and on the convoys of barges that transported fuel along the Danube. Between February 1944 and the end of June 1944, the amount of Rumanian oil and refined petroleum reaching Germany was reduced by 80%, from 200,000 tons a month to 40,000 tons per month.

1 At 9th Air Force headquarters, Major-General Lewis H. Brereton, Commanding General of the US 9th Air Force, Lieutenant-General Carl Spaatz, Head of US Strategic Air Forces and General Dwight D. Eisenhower work together on plans for the role of the Air Force in the imminent Normandy invasion.

2 Liberators as far as the eye can see. In the original print, it is possible to count sixty bombers in this picture (not counting the aircraft from which it was taken), and that was probably a small part of the total formation.

3 When the invasion day came, on June 6th 1944, the US Army Air Force was there in force. These B24 Liberators are returning after attacking German positions beyond the beaches, flying over, as they return, some of the vast fleet of ships that brought the Allied armies and their equipment to Normandy.

German synthetic fuel sources were hit even harder. On May 12th 1944, just under 1,000 US bombers attacked synthetic fuel plants at five separate targets – Brux, Lutzkendorf, Zeitz, Bohlen and Leuna. Just over two weeks later, on May 28th and 29th, those same targets were attacked again, and, in addition, the US Army Air Force destroyed the vital coal hydrogenation plants at Politz in Pomerania. The effect was devastating to the German war effort. From producing 181,000 tons of aviation fuel in March 1944, slightly more than the severely rationed *Luftwaffe* actually used, the Germans were down to a production of 10,000 tons in September, when they used 60,000 tons, and never again managed to get fuel production up either above 49,000 tons in a month, or up to the rate of consumption. The attacks on the fuel supplies were the death knell of the *Luftwaffe*.

Thus, when General Eisenhower was briefing his troops for 'Overlord', the long-awaited Allied invasion of Normandy, he was able to tell them, with some truth, that if they saw a warplane overhead, they could regard it as friendly. That this was so was due to a large extent to the success of the air offensive.

CHAPTER 34

OVERLORD THE ATLANTIC WALL AND D~DAY

Since 1940, on Rommel's evidence, Hitler had predicted that an Anglo-American invasion of the Channel coast of France would one day come. Since he had failed, before tackling Russia in the East, to conquer Britain in the West, his forecast did not require great perception. But by the end of 1943 and the beginning of 1944, as the Allied bombing offensive bit deep into German sources of production, as the Allies advanced slowly but inexorably in Italy, it was clear that the landings could not long be delayed. For years, Hitler had stubbornly, in considering where the Allies would strike, favoured the beaches of Normandy. His subordinates, particularly Field-Marshal Gerd von Rundstedt, now his Supreme Commander in the West, were convinced that he was wrong, and that the Allied attack would be made across the narrowest part of the English Channel to the Pas de Calais. Only in the summer of 1944 did Hitler change his mind, and come round to believing in the invasion via the Straits of Dover.

His change of heart was in part due to some inventive Allied deceptions. An Army Pay Corps Lt. who in civilian life was an actor, Clifton James, who looked remarkably like Bernard Law Montgomery, was sent to make a much publicised tour of the Mediterranean theatre to direct German attention to the possibility of increased activity in the South. A bogus British Army was deployed with rubber tanks around the South-East corner of England to give German reconnaissance aircraft evidence of a build up around the Straits of Dover. Fake radio traffic was assiduously inserted into the normal transmissions for German monitors to hear. It all pointed to the Pas de Calais, and while it would exaggerate the effect of these devices to claim that the Germans were totally deceived, they were sufficiently unsure of the Allies' intentions to maintain a significant part of their forces in the Calais area, far from the Normandy beaches where the assault would actually come.

To guard against the expected invasion, wherever it was launched,

4 Field Marshal Rommel embarked upon his task of inspecting and improving Germany's Atlantic Wall defences with his usual thoroughness and pace. This picture was shot aboard a German patrol boat near the border of Holland and Belgium.

5 Germany had few commanders as capable of Rommel in the assessment of defences, and he knew that concrete gun emplacements and bunkers alone could not hold the Channel coast against an invasion. It was greatly to the Allies' advantage that his advice to use the *Panzer* divisions as weapons of first resort was ignored.

4

5

6 It was to the Organisation *Todt*, Germany's mainly slave labour constructional force, that the task of strengthening the Atlantic Wall fell. *Reichsminister* Albert Speer, head of the Organisation *Todt*, inspected the defences in the Pas de Calais area to acquaint himself with the task before him.

6

Overlord

Germany had during her years of occupation of France and the Low Countries progressively built and armed fortifications along the coast which were known, somewhat inaccurately, as the 'Atlantic Wall'. These fortifications, which extended from Holland to the Bay of Biscay, were for most of their length only well-protected gun emplacements with quite modest armament — 3-inch guns were typical. But in the vicinity of the Pas de Calais the guns were bigger and the defences more formidable. The British coastal towns of Dover, Deal and Ramsgate knew to their cost the range and power of the fourteen guns of calibres from 16-inch to 11-inch at Cap Gris Nez. During the spring of 1944, the state of readiness of these and the other armaments along the Atlantic Wall was to be increased sharply, but von Rundstedt had little faith in the capacity of the Wall to contain an Allied invasion, and believed that his Army Groups 'A' and 'B', held with their armour to the rear of the front line, would have the task of destroying the beach-head. As ever in the German High Command, there was sharp disagreement as to the use and dispersal of forces.

Field-Marshal Erwin Rommel, now in command of Army Group 'B', had been given by Hitler at the end of 1943 the task of inspecting and improving the defences of the Atlantic Wall, and had not been impressed by what he found. Under his direction, half a million men

1 All the German services and military organisations were caught up in Rommel's review of the Atlantic Wall defences – here he confers with officers of the Army and Navy on the disposition of defensive positions along the shoreline.

2 On the French coast near Cap Gris Nez, a German soldier stands by a sandbagged anti-tank gun, scanning the horizon for signs of the approaching Allies. There were many isolated emplacements like this which were not supported by massive concrete blockhouses, and this gave the lie to German assertions of the existence of a concrete wall extending from the Baltic to the Atlantic.

3 More formidable were the fully-defended emplacements like this one, surrounded by defensive ironwork, barbed wire and earthworks. Many men and women of the *Todt* organisation died during the forced-labour construction programme that built the concrete structures into which these guns and their magazines were installed.

262

of the *Todt* Organisation were put to work on a massive programme of improvement and additional fortification. Rommel, while agreeing with von Rundstedt that the invasion would not be repulsed by static defences alone, believed strongly that the combined effect of the Wall and a mobile *Panzer* force immediately behind it could destroy the invasion force during what he saw as the critical first twenty-four hours.

As Army Group B commander, Rommel had the 7th and 15th Armies plus LXXXVIII Corps at his disposal, and put to Hitler his conviction based on successful experience of tank warfare that the only potential for victory over an Allied landing lay in the swift and effective deployment of mobile armour to destroy the British, American and Canadian troops on the beaches before they had had the opportunity to develop and strengthen their beach-head. Impressed by this argument, Hitler had on March 20th given Rommel command of *Panzergruppe* West, which consisted of I *Waffen SS Panzer* Corps, plus six other *Panzer* Divisions including the *Leibstandarte Adolf Hitler*. But despite gaining this tactical command, Rommel remained subject to the strategic decisions of von Rundstedt, who still favoured the outmoded concept of holding *Panzer* divisions back to the rear as a means of containing the

attempts of the Allies to break out from their beach-head. Thus, although Rommel pushed hard to have the tanks ready to conduct lightning attacks on the Allied soldiers as they landed, wherever that might prove to be, he was not to have his way. In the event, this proved a major factor in the Allies' success on D-Day.

Allied preparations for the greatest amphibious invasion of all time had been in the melting pot for years. But, by the beginning of 1944, the approximate date had been set, General Dwight D. Eisenhower had been appointed to Supreme Command of the operation, General Montgomery had been recalled from Italy to command Allied land forces in Normandy, and S.H.A.E.F. – Supreme Headquarters Allied Expeditionary Forces – had established the team that would see the invasion through to success.

The technological problems set by the landings and by the logistics of supplying the vast army that was to break out from the beach-head and liberate France and the Low Countries before advancing on Germany were quite unprecedented. They inspired scientific invention on a scale that had never before been seen in such a short span of time, and brought forth from the Allied scientists called upon by a British planning group under Lieutenant-General Sir Frederick Morgan, and taken over by S.H.A.E.F., an abundance

4 The Japanese interest in German defensive techniques was considerable, since the frequency with which they were having to defend themselves against seaborne invasion in the Pacific was becoming greater by the month. This delegation of Japanese officers was brought to inspect the anti-aircraft batteries along the Atlantic Wall.

5 Training of the Allied armies in Britain was intense and realistic. Whole areas of coastline were sealed from the public, villages were evacuated, and the chaos of the beaches was realistically simulated with live ammunition and explosives. All training was based on the assumption that 'The first thousand yards will be the worst'.

6 By May 1944, the whole south and southeast of England was a vast, armed camp, with military vehicles parked wherever there was space. In suburban side streets like this, in town after town, behind pubs and around factories, camouflaged trucks and armoured vehicles awaited the day when they would go to France.

7 In Britain, General Eisenhower, as Supreme Commander for the invasion, had worked since the beginning of 1944 with his generals to perfect the plans for the greatest invasion man had ever known. His map, in this picture, released before the invasion, was deliberately large to show the whole of France, and his gesture would seem to indicate an airborne landing between Tours and Bordeaux!

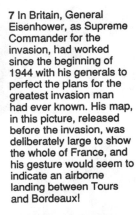

of ideas, some of which seemed to border on fantasy.

The Normandy coastline is rich in sandy beaches that are often pounded by surf, but has few ports capable of berthing ships of any size or in any numbers. Some means of docking and unloading ships over a period of weeks, maybe months, had to be found. The answer was towed across the Channel with the invasion fleet − prefabricated concrete 'Mulberry' harbours that were sunk into position and used with complete success. Their hulks can still be seen off the Normandy coast today.

The fuel requirements of the Allied armies were recognised as being too large to be supplied entirely by sea. Again the scientists came up with an answer, this time known as PLUTO − pipeline under the ocean. Revolutionary at the time, the trans-channel pipeline worked well and overcame the problem. 'Crabs', developed versions of the tanks equipped with flails to clear mines − similar to the Scorpions which had earlier assisted the Eighth Army in the Western Desert − were deployed in far larger numbers, and proved invaluable during the invasion to combat the large minefields that Rommel had had laid along the coast. Innovation and inventiveness were as much weapons of the Allied assault as tanks and guns.

During the months immediately preceding D-Day, the build-up

1 The 505th Regiment of the US 82nd Airborne Division accorded to Sainte Mere-Eglise the distinction of being the first village in France to be retaken by the Allies, when Lt. Col. Krause raised the stars and stripes over the town hall in the early hours of June 6th, after a costly parachute attack in which many Americans died. German snipers were everywhere, and these American paratroops fired a precautionary volley into the church tower, which the Germans had used as an observation post.

2 Rifle at the ready, Private Elmer Habbs of Delaware takes a few moments of relaxation after the capture of St. Mere-Eglise and the link up with the US 4th Division, which landed on Utah Beach.

3 The moment of truth that no man in his right mind would envy − American soldiers approach one of the heavily-defended Normandy beaches aboard a landing craft. Ahead is that first thousand yards of mined and bullet-raked sand that every soldier in the first wave of the invasion had to face.

4 Once across that first beach − and thousands failed to make it on Omaha beach alone − the struggle to hold and establish the beachhead began. This American mortar crew are beginning the task of harassing the German positions that must be taken before the break-out from the beachhead can begin.

of Allied troops and equipment in the South of England was colossal, and the whole area South of London and East of Lyme Regis became one vast army camp. Airfield resources were strained to breaking point as the mighty force of aircraft was crammed as close to France as possible for the attack. Close on 3 million men were under arms in Southern England as the day approached. Amidst this organised chaos, the Generals finalised their plans.

Despite occasional friction between the British and American commanders, the principle suggested by Montgomery of landings on a broad front by separate US, Canadian and British forces on separate beaches had been accepted early in the planning process. Montgomery was convinced — rightly — that funnelling too many men through too small a front was an invitation to disaster. His plan to disperse the landings ensured that relatively few successive waves of troops would land over any one area of beach on the first and second days, and thereby limited the risk to men and materials until the beach-head was secured and the danger of large-scale enemy attack on the beaches had been reduced. Once that beach-head was firmly in Allied hands, Montgomery's plan called for a massive feint by the British and Canadian troops eastwards towards Caen to draw the German defenders into battle on the East of the beach-head, while

General Omar Bradley and the US 1st Army made the actual breakout in a Southerly direction from the West, followed by a swing Eastward, and an advance up the Seine to Paris. By cutting between the beach-head and the German rearguard, the American army would thus cut off the troops on the coast from their supply-line, and also, assisted by the damage already wrought from the air against bridges, prevent reinforcements arriving to hinder further Allied landings.

The sheer scale of the invasion plan agreed by S.H.A.E.F. required a transport fleet of 4,126 vessels manned by almost 200,000 sailors. The fleet included no less than 1,173 ships of all sizes carrying tanks and other armoured vehicles — vital to the initial assault on the Atlantic Wall if the infantry was to survive the initial attack. The assault fleet itself was made up of a further 1,213 ships, including 300 warships, of which 79 were detailed to attack the German batteries between Villerville and Barfleur Cape, under the direction of RAF Spitfires acting as airborne observation posts.

Going ashore on D-Day from the sea were 57,500 American and over 75,000 British and Canadian troops, plus 900 armoured vehicles and 600 guns. A remarkable total of 13,743 aircraft took part, including those that landed the 27,000 airborne troops on the night of June 5th/6th by parachute and in the force of 867 towed gliders.

5 After the first wave came thousands more troops and their equipment, pouring ashore for weeks on end to reinforce those already ashore and replace the dead and injured in the advancing line. Vehicles and men alike followed pathways cleared through the minefields on the beaches and in the grass and woddland just beyond.

6 Units landed to reinforce the invasion army assembled and got their kit together at the head of the beach before moving inland to join the battle. These American soldiers seem relieved to be ashore in one piece.

7 On the second day – D-Day plus one – the American assault troops continued to pour ashore to reinforce the army massed in the beachhead. Wading ashore from their landing craft, these US soldiers had a tough battle ahead of them, and some would not survive.

Overlord

The first attack was to be by these three airborne divisions, landing from midnight onwards just inland from the coast to the West of the main landing area, and securing vital bridges and positions prior to the amphibious assault. From 6.30am onwards, the landings were scheduled for five major beaches – the US 1st Army on Utah and Omaha Beaches, West and East of the Vire estuary; the British 2nd Army on Gold Beach at Arromanches, and on Sword Beach between Lion-sur-Mer and Ouistrehem; and the Canadians, also part of the British 2nd Army, on Juno Beach between Bernieres and St Aubin.

As June 5th, the scheduled day for the invasion, approached, the weather began to look worse by the hour. On June 4th, confident that not even the British would be mad enough to launch themselves upon their greatest adventure in gales and torrential rain, Rommel left France and went to visit his family in Ulm. On the next day, the fleet was actually at sea in appalling conditions when it was ordered back.

1 Assembling, identifying and burying the dead was a major task in the initial days after the invasion. Necessarily, the early burials were somewhat rudimentary, but US medical orderlies like these men tackled their sad task bravely and efficiently.

2 This dramatic picture was taken at dawn on June 6th aboard the Captain class Frigate HMS *Holmes*, which formed part of the escort to the Royal Navy's capital ships which bombarded German positions along the invasion coastline. Above, the airborne armada can be seen streaming towards Normandy.

3 The sixteen inch guns of the British battleship HMS *Rodney* pounded the German positions beyond Juno and Sword beaches from dawn on the sixth and were successful in creating a number of breaches in the Atlantic Wall defences. Capital ships played a significant role in the protection both of the invasion fleet at sea, and of the troops as they landed.

Finally, despite continuing bad weather, Eisenhower, quite literally, decided to chance going ahead. So much organisational and logistic effort had gone into getting the fleet to sea that to delay longer meant an almost greater risk than launching the invasion in unfavourable conditions. D-Day was on.

That Longest Day

As the invasion fleet massed in the Channel during the night of June 5th/6th 1944, the US 82nd and 101st Airborne Divisions were landed North of the Vire. Their task was to secure the right bank of the River Merderet and provide cover for the westmost force of those landing on Utah Beach – VII Corps, commanded by Lieutenant-General Collins. In the bad weather, the airborne divisions' gliders and parachutists were blown off course and scattered, and relatively few units of the two divisions were able to carry out their prescribed tasks. Only one regiment of the 82nd achieved success — and made Sainte Mere-Eglise, on the main road from Cherbourg to Carentan (and the rest of France) the first French town to be liberated by the Allies. Despite considerable losses, the US troops managed to hold the town and link up with the US 4th Division after its landing on Utah Beach in the morning.

As dawn broke, the invasion force came out of the mist over the sea, to the frank disbelief of virtually everybody the German troops along the Atlantic Wall tried to tell. The German commanders were so convinced both that any landing would come in the Pas de Calais, and that the weather was too bad even for the English to cross the Channel, that the state of readiness was universally low. At 6.30 am, the US 4th, 9th, 79th and 90th Infantry Divisions began to stream from their landing craft on to Utah beach, and were supported by a

tremendous naval bombardment which was deadly, accurate and effective. The shellfire and rockets from the fleet – which in the American Sector (Utah and Omaha) was commanded by Rear-Admiral A.G. Kirk, US Navy – destroyed minefields, pulverised bunkers and eliminated many of the German defensive positions before they had had a chance to do much damage. The Allied fire power was overwhelmingly superior to anything the Germans could lay down.

As a result, the Utah Beach forces had a rapid and successful landing, with very few men killed. On Omaha Beach, the story was sadly different. Most things that could go wrong did, and the beach became known as 'Bloody Omaha' with good reason. The air strike that was intended to eliminate the German defensive positions before the American divisions came ashore missed its target and left the defenders largely unscathed. Unknown to the combat troops of the

4 As the American forces consolidated their beachhead to the west of the invasion area, and began their planned breakout, they encountered stiff resistance. These infantrymen are inching forward flat on their bellies to keep out of sight of known snipers in the damaged buildings ahead.

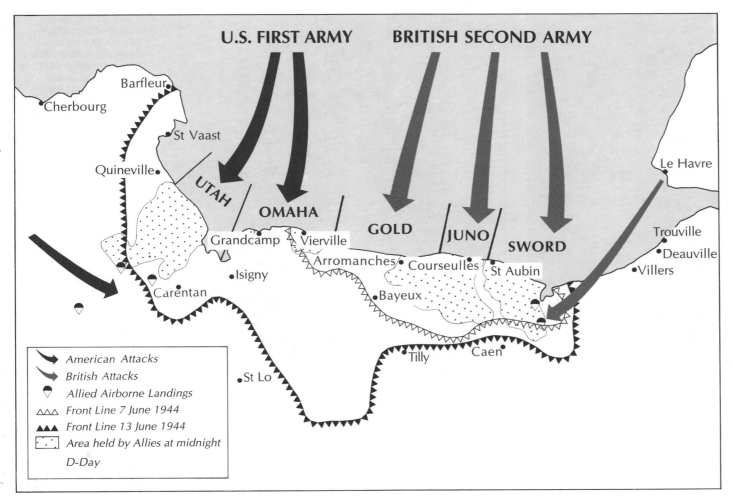

U.S. FIRST ARMY **BRITISH SECOND ARMY**

Cherbourg
Barfleur
St Vaast
Quineville
UTAH
OMAHA
Grandcamp
Vierville
GOLD
JUNO
SWORD
Le Havre
Trouville
Deauville
Villers
Arromanches
Courseulles
St Aubin
Isigny
Bayeux
Carentan
Tilly
Caen
St Lo

→ *American Attacks*
↘ *British Attacks*
☟ *Allied Airborne Landings*
△△△ *Front Line 7 June 1944*
▲▲▲ *Front Line 13 June 1944*
⬚ *Area held by Allies at midnight D-Day*

5 Normandy is a countryside of wooded lanes and thickly-hedged rural roads, and was not easy for the infantry, since there was a sniper behind practically every hedge and barn. This American soldier, probably an avid movie-goer, has raised his helmet on his rifle to draw any fire that may be around, and thus reveal the enemy's position. The German machine gun abandoned by the side of the road shows how recently the German troops had vacated this position.

US 2nd, 29th and 1st Infantry Divisions as they streamed ashore, their beach was defended by a newly arrived and very tough German division — the 352nd. The landing craft were shelled by expertly handled artillery as they lumbered to the beach. Many of the Americans' amphibious tanks sank in the rough water. Those of the 1st Infantry Division that managed to get ashore and run up the beach to the sea wall (and many did not get even that far) were pinned down by accurate and well-directed small-arms fire. The US demolition teams had suffered severe casualties and had lost much of their equipment, so were slow to smash openings in the wall. The situation was desperate.

Once again, the Navy came to the rescue. Admiral Kirk brought the guns of his destroyers to bear on the German 352nd Division's positions, and shelled them remorselessly. By 1pm, the Germans' lack of *materiel* was making itself felt, as the defending artillery began to run out of ammunition. During the afternoon, the US divisions were able to get off the beach, capture the coastal defence positions, and get their armour past the anti-tank obstacles. By comparison with Utah Beach, where 197 men had died, Omaha was frighteningly expensive. 3,881 men were dead, missing or wounded at the end of the day.

6 The dying of both sides were tended by the medical teams and the padres. Wearing his stole over his field jacket, this US chaplain is administering the last sacrament to a dying German soldier.

1 The German troops defending positions in Normandy were in a thankless position, with little armoured support, no air cover and limited ammunition and fuel. These German paratroops are keeping their heads down behind a wall in the face of mounting pressure from the advancing Allied armies.

2 The grimy reality of war, and particularly of street fighting, shows in the faces and the uniforms of these Canadian soldiers, who had just repulsed a German attempt to dislodge them from the ruined French house in which they are photographed, and were now considering their next move — how to advance and yet stay alive.

3 The commanders in the field — General Montgomery (left), Commanding Allied Land Forces; General Eisenhower, Supreme Commander; and Air Marshal Tedder (with pipe), Deputy Supreme Commander.

4 One of the major organisational implications of establishing the Allied Air Forces in Europe was the necessity for mobile repair units capable of moving forward as the squadrons advanced. The problems of the RAF and US Air Forces were compounded by the weather, for the summer of 1944 brought a great deal of rain, and the temporary airfields on which the repair units operated became seas of mud. The aircraft (appropriately, with so much water around) is a Seafire.

On Gold, Juno and Sword Beaches, the British 2nd Army, commanded by General Dempsey, was assigned a formidable programme of operations and objectives. They were to capture Bayeux, Caen and Troarn and to extend its reconnaissance to Villers-Bocage and Evrecy — some 18 miles of Calvados coastline. In the light of later events, that the British Army did not quite succeed in all those objectives is less surprising than that they almost achieved most of them. The British sector, like the American, also had its crucial Airborne Division landings, which were blessed with better luck and appreciably greater success than those of the US Airborne Divisions. The objectives of the British 6th Airborne Division, who were, like the Americans to the West, entrusted with protecting their Army's flank, were:

1. To capture intact the bridges across the Orne and its canal between Benouville and Ranville.

2. To destroy the German coastal battery at Merville, close to the mouth of the Orne.

3. To destroy the Dives bridges between Troarn and the coast.

Only half an hour after midnight, the British Airborne had taken the Benouville bridges and by 4am the Merville guns had been silenced at considerable cost of life. As dawn came up, the British invasion swept ashore, their zero hour an hour later than that on the American beaches to the West. At 7.30am, as the British began to wade ashore from their landing craft, the Germans were no longer surprised and were only too well aware of what was going on. Here, as on Utah Beach, the role played by the fleet offshore in subduing the defences and lessening the casualties inflicted on the invaders was incalculable. Rear-Admiral Vian's British warships began shelling the Atlantic Wall defences in the British Sector at dawn, and succeeded in breaching the defences in several places.

5 The only Victoria Cross awarded during the Normandy landings was won by Company Sergeant Major Stanley Elton Hollis of the Green Howards. He won the award for a succession of gallant deeds which effectively prevented British units in his section of the British beaches being held up by enemy action.

6 The RAF's highly successful twin-engined Mosquito was a fast, versatile aircraft that served in all theatres and virtually all roles. Designed as a light bomber, it became a very successful radar-equipped night fighter, flew as a fighter-bomber in Normandy, and carried out many precision bombing raids where speed was essential – the famous attack on Gestapo headquarters in Copenhagen was an example. This Mosquito crew were photographed in Normandy – note the invasion stripes just visible on the wing.

5

The British troops had better luck with their amphibious tanks, being able to put them into the water nearer the beach with fewer underwater obstructions. Few were lost, and most were able to break out from the beach within the first hour or two of landing. The inventive flair of the British again proved useful – not only were the 'Crabs' able to detonate mines without harming personnel, but a new device called the A.V.R.E. carried a 9-inch mortar on an armoured tank chassis into close encounters with concrete gun emplacements and proved effective in dealing with them. Also in evidence on the British beaches was 'Crocodile', a tank with a long-range flame-thrower built into it and towing its own fuel tanker behind it.

Despite these wondrous devices, good generalship and the remarkably adept support of the Royal Navy, the British 2nd Army did not and could not meet its objectives. However, by the end of that first day, Major-General Rennie's British 3rd Division had got off

6

1 At a 9th Air Force bomber base back in England, a B26 Marauder is bombed up for a further sortie over the German defences in Normandy. Crossing the Channel, the B26 crews are reported as saying that they saw destroyers, battleships and landing craft, and the red flashes of fire from the guns of the destroyers. One returning Marauder crewman said 'I saw the flashes all around. It was a grand seat at the biggest show the world has ever had'.

2 Allied air supremacy over the Normandy beaches was one of the crucial factors in securing the success of the invasion. Virtually all the food, arms and ammunition, and much of the fuel, needed to supply the invasion force, was brought in by sea and unloaded in exposed conditions. Imagine the effectiveness of an air attack on operations to unload these 500lb and 1000lb bombs from the hold of a beached ship into a DUKW.

3 A powerful picture of one of the American soldiers who worked ceaselessly to unload the incoming supplies upon which the invasion depended. He is at the controls of a DUKW amphibian.

4 Many of the smaller ships bringing supplies to the Normandy beaches were beached for unloading. This is the Norwegian ship SS *Heien* (left of the two) on the American sector of the beaches, with another Norwegian ship beached a little further away. The wheel tracks show the intense unloading activity by trucks at low tide.

Sword Beach, had joined up with the 6th Airborne, had crossed the Benouville bridges and had reached a point only 3 miles from Caen after a brisk battle with the German 21st *Panzer* Division. The Canadian 3rd Division had had a more difficult time on Juno Beach, again because of natural obstacles and sheer bad luck, but had overcome its problems sufficiently to be close to taking the Carpiquet airfield. Major-General Graham's 50th Division, which had landed on Gold Beach, was almost at Bayeux. All this had been achieved with the loss of less than 3,000 men killed, wounded or missing.

The comparative slowness of the German response to this substantial success on the first day of the Allies' long-awaited Second Front was due in part to their sheer surprise that an invasion could be mounted in such terrible weather, and rather more to the fact that the German armour was not near the coast (although the effects of sea-power on tanks had been demonstrated convincingly at Anzio, and might have been demonstrated again if Rommel had had his way). A major factor in slowing the German chain of command was the simple fact that Hitler was asleep when the invasion started and nobody dared to wake him. But by far the largest influence upon German ability to react to the threat was Allied air supremacy.

Throughout the day, the Allied Air Forces gave support to every movement that the ground forces made to break out from their beaches, and attacked German columns, tanks, defensive gun emplacements, every obstacle that the Armies encountered. Some 4,600 air sorties were flown by Allied aircraft during that first day, most of them in the ground-attack role. The recently introduced Hawker Typhoon, resplendent, like other Allied aircraft over Normandy, in its black and white striped invasion markings, demonstrated convincingly with the eight 60-pounder rockets that it carried beneath its wings that it was the heir to the Stuka in its ability to destroy equipment on the ground. The American P-47 Thunderbolts, with their ten 5-inch anti-tank rockets did tremendous damage to German armour. And the Mustangs, Hurricanes, Spitfires and Mosquitoes were everywhere.

Perhaps the greatest superiority of the Allies over the German forces on D-Day, apart from the sheer fire-power that they could muster, was the success of the integrated Allied command structure. There was no one commander other than Hitler himself who could co-ordinate the activities of the German Army, the *Luftwaffe* and the *Waffen-SS*. Jealousies and duplicated command structures meant that few senior commanders in the German services had a clear idea of who could and who could not tell him what to do next. Everybody was afraid to act. Hence effective orders came only from the top, and delays were inevitable. In contrast, the careful planning of S.H.A.E.F., and the detailed briefing of every fighting man in the Allied forces resulted in complete harmony and cohesion of action at virtually every level in the Allied land, sea and air forces. Not for the first time did the Allied commanders reflect on how differently the war might have gone if the three Axis powers had co-operated as effectively from 1941 onwards.

5 Ships carrying cargo to Normandy to supply the beachhead also carried troops. These are men of the Royal Engineers, relaxing on the deck of the Norwegian ship *Vestmanrod*, on its way to France.

The Week After D-Day

Having been caught with the entire eighteen divisions of their 15th Army in the Pas de Calais, the Germans might have been expected to move the lot southwestwards to Normandy as soon as the invasion had landed. But Hitler, incredibly, persisted in his belief that the Normandy attack was a diversionary exercise for another landing in the Pas de Calais, even after the Allied battle orders had been captured. He seemed to have convinced himself even that the orders captured from an abandoned American battle barge were forged and designed to mislead him. Rommel was therefore forbidden to use the reinforcements of the 15th Army to contain the Allied beach-head, and was thereby constantly at a greater disadvantage than was actually necessary

The German counter-attacks began on the day following the initial invasion, as the Allied 'floating reserves' were beginning to land to build up the size of the Allied Armies for the breakout into Normandy. On June 7th and 8th, the formidable 12th *SS Hitlerjugend Panzer* Division, aided and abetted by the *Panzer Lehr* Division, attacked the British 2nd Army formations near Caen with the avowed intention of thrusting them back into the sea. Despite severe Canadian casualties, the Allied line held.

6 On the 14th June 1944, the Supreme Commander and his US Army and Navy Chiefs paid their first visit to the beachhead battle zone. Left to right: General Henry H. Arnold, Chief of the Army Air Forces; Admiral Ernest King, Commander-in-Chief of the United States Fleet; General Eisenhower, Supreme Comander; and General George C. Marshall, United States Army Chief of Staff.

Overlord

On D-Day+2, June 8th, the US 1st Army and the British 2nd Army linked up at Bayeux. The German 7th Army, constantly harried by Allied air attacks, was set to counter-attack when its commander, General Geyr von Schweppenburg, was seriously injured in an air attack on his headquarters, and the attack was called off by his successor, General Sepp Dietrich. Four days later, on the 12th, now reinforced by the arrival of the 2nd *Panzer* Division, Dietrich successfully contained an attempt by XXX Corps to break out, but on the American front, the US 29th Division and the 101st Airborne jointly took Carentan. Thus, by the 12th, the Allied front extended from the Dives to Saint Marcouf. During the six days since the initial landing, five more infantry and three more airborne divisions had joined the Allied armies from the sea. The Germans — mainly because Hitler had refused to use the 15th Army — had on paper brought up seven divisions, but all were under strength, and there was no doubt on either side that the Allies were succeeding in bringing up reinforcements more quickly and more effectively than were the Germans.

Now the world waited for the breakout from the beach-head — and the beginning of the true liberation of France.

1 Most of the photographs in this book, and the newsreel films that thrilled audiences in America, Germany and Britain, were shot at considerable risk by brave men armed only with cameras, yet who were rarely given credit for the daring they displayed in getting their pictures.

2 On June 14th, General de Gaulle returned to France as the leader of the Free French, four years after leaving his homeland. The next few weeks were to be memorable for him. He is surrounded by French officers and one officer of a Scottish regiment.

3 By mid-July 1944, the mighty supply organisation that the Allied planners had envisaged was a reality, and the scene was set for the breakout from the beachhead. This picture dates from the 14th July, and shows the mass of American transport vessels and landing craft disgorging reinforcements and supplies.

CHAPTER 35

THE BREAKOUT FROM NORMANDY
AND THE LIBERATION OF FRANCE

Everything that Rommel had tried with his beleaguered and depleted 7th Army during the week following the landings to contain the Allied beach-head and drive the invasion back to the sea had failed. The superiority of Allied air power was overwhelming. Everything that moved, it seemed, was attacked by the rockets and bombs of the Typhoons and Thunderbolts of the RAF and the US Army Air Force. Experienced field commander that he was, Rommel knew he was beaten; that Germany had little prospect of anything but defeat. Covertly, he was deep in the ill-destined plot to overthrow Hitler that was to cost him, Count von Stauffenberg and many other prominent Germans their lives — but still he knew his duty and his job, and fought tenaciously and well for the country he had served so brilliantly. The appalling mortality of senior German commanders in Normandy was already making itself felt — General Marcks of LXXXIV Panzer Corps had been killed, and more were soon to

follow — and the German troops desperately needed success to boost their morale.

That success, albeit on a limited scale, almost came as Lieutenant-General Collins' VII Corps began its attempt to take first the West coast of the Cotentin, and then the port of Cherbourg. Montgomery's whole strategy for the initial battle of Normandy was aimed at drawing the firepower and the strength of Rommel's force to the Eastern sector of the beach-head, around Caen, so as to reduce the German defences in the West and give VII Corps an opportunity to take the vital port facilities that the Allies needed to control if the Allied armies were to be supplied. The much criticised failure of the British 2nd Army to take Caen quickly achieved this secret objective fully, although the world's press did not realise the fact, and levelled many harsh words at Montgomery. Despite the weakening of German strength along the Western side of the beach-head, the first

4 The early weeks of the breakout in Normandy were immensely costly in American lives. This picture of American soldiers braving a crest upon which some will almost certainly be hit is reminiscent of pictures of the First World War trenches.

5 Amid the litter of war, US soldiers stoop low as they advance between hedgerows, watching always for snipers hidden in the trees.

6 Thousands of soldiers of all the Allied armies were hit by sniper fire during those first months in Normandy. Near Carentan, an American doctor attends to a wounded man, as another soldier stands watch.

attempt by a US division to break out was unsuccessful. The 90th Division failed to get across the River Douve in the face of fierce opposition, and had to be withdrawn.

But now one of those rare commanders of vision and spirit made his appearance — Major-General Eddy, in command of the US 9th Division. Starting on June 14th, he led his division in a remarkable advance that earned him praise at all levels of the Allied armies, sweeping across the Cotentin in less than 24 hours, cutting off the remnants of three Divisions of General von Choltitz' LXXXIV Corps and wheeling smartly round to join the other two divisions of VII Corps in the attack on Cherbourg. As reinforcements poured in via the beaches before the great 4-day storm that began on June 19th wrecked the Mulberry harbour on Omaha Beach, the American XIX and V Corps joined the front facing General Schlieben's Cherbourg defence. Nonetheless, a combination of spirited defence and prevarication about surrender ensured that it was not until July 3rd that the port fell to the American troops. The capture of Cherbourg provided the landfall, in August, for PLUTO, the undersea pipeline that was to supply a quarter of a million gallons of fuel per day to the Allied armies.

Now General Bradley, in command of the US 1st Army, who had

1

2

3

1 An enterprising news photographer took this picture during the capture of Cherbourg, as two American Major-Generals climbed on a woodshed to get a better view of the lie of the battle. Their names are not recorded, but their agility will be with us for all time.

2 A nicely posed shot, illustrating how powerful the Panther tank looks from close-up, even when knocked out. The Panzer divisions lost more tanks in Normandy through Allied domination of the skies than they did through direct ground combat, and according to the original caption, this Panther was the victim of a rocket-firing RAF Typhoon.

3 The Americans did not have things all their own way, although many Americans captured during the Normandy campaign were recaptured by the Allies during the lightning advance across France. War correspondent Koll of the *Propaganda Kompanie* took this picture at the beginning of July, presumably while looking for some good news to send back home.

4 This dramatic picture was taken during the fall of Cherbourg. US troops of the US 9th Division had encountered spirited opposition from a German pillbox, which knocked out an American tank before being forced to surrender by a second US tank. As US soldiers, wary of traps, watch from doorways, the German soldiers come out under a flag of truce, carrying their wounded.

4

arrived in Normandy on June 12th, regrouped his forces rapidly for an all-out attack on the German 7th Army between Coutances and St Lo, which began on June 24th. Appallingly wet weather had made the marshy ground soft and almost impassable to tanks, and the Normandy woodlands provided in any case a natural obstacle, so the armour had little option but to use the roads. This made the Churchill and Sherman tanks easy targets for the redoubtable German 88mm gun, and for the mighty 52 ton Mark VI Tiger tank, whose gun, also of 88mm, was capable of 'brewing up' a Sherman almost instantaneously. In one remarkable incident at Villers-Bocage in the British sector, *SS-Obersturmfuhrer* Wittman destroyed the whole of a column of 25 assorted tanks and armoured vehicles with his one Tiger tank. Not surprisingly, US Army progress was slow and fearsomely expensive of life. During the four weeks between June 19th and July 22nd, American casualties went from 3,012 dead since D-Day to 10,641, and from 15,362 wounded to 51,387.

Meanwhile, in the East of the beach-head, Dempsey's British 2nd Army had been fighting against mounting German odds to take Caen. On June 25th, General Sir Richard O'Connor, back from captivity after the Italian armistice, took his new command, VIII Corps, into action and by the 27th had captured a bridge over the

5 As Cherbourg was finally taken and in Allied hands, the victorious Allies made the position clear by hoisting, amid general celebrations, the Stars and Stripes, the Union Jack and the French Tricolour.

6 When British Prime Minister Winston Churchill toured the Normandy battlefront, he took great interest in a V1 flying-bomb launching site which had been captured before it could be completed for use against Britain. In typical stance amid the massiveness of the steel and concrete structure, Churchill asked detailed questions of the officers accompanying him.

River Odon on his way to positions near Villers Bocage, South of Caen. But there he was held, under increasing pressure, while the Battle for Caen raged on. Not until July 9th were the ancient town (now virtually in ruins), and the nearby Carpiquet airfield, finally taken.

To keep the German *Panzer* Divisions busy for a little longer until Bradley's great thrust to break out of the beach-head was ready to go, the British 2nd Army was now given the task of fighting their way out of Caen southwards towards Falaise against German opposition that was well prepared and ready to fight for every inch. Initial progress on July 18th was rapid, aided by an effective bombardment of the German 21st *Panzer* Division's positions from the air, but by the afternoon of the 18th the advance had slowed to a stop, and the British 11th Armoured Division was badly hit by a late night counter-attack. The real success came the next day, not militarily, for O'Connor's force remained (literally) bogged down, but strategically, as Montgomery's main objective was realised. Believing that the British were about to take Falaise, Field Marshal von Kluge, who had just taken over from von Rundstedt, ordered the 2nd *Panzer* Division from St. Lo in the West, to the area of Caen

in the East, and committed (at long last) the German 15th Army to the fight against the British. Getting this far had cost the British 2nd Army 34,700 wounded, killed and missing. But there were now three times as many tanks defending Falaise against the British as there were facing the Americans.

On the German side, the casualties were mounting and, unlike the Allies, they were unable to bring up reinforcements at a rate sufficient to maintain strength. In the six weeks after D-Day, the German Army had lost 97,000 men killed, wounded or missing, including 28 Generals and the remarkable figure of 354 Lieutenant-Generals. Perhaps most portentous of all, Field-Marshal Rommel had been seriously injured when his car was strafed on July 17th, and had left the front for what was to prove to be the last time.

The US Army Breaks Out

On July 24th, the German LXXXIV Corps to the west of the Normandy beach-head experienced Allied air power at its most formidable, as 4,000 tons of bombs were dropped on its positions. Next morning, 2,410 aircraft poured more than 4,000 more tons of high explosive and napalm on to the German positions along the

7 Ten-year-old Jean-Louis and his father were injured by a German grenade outside St Sauveur. An American First Aid station treated his crushed hand and leg injuries, and the leg injuries sustained by his father. Between coping with heavy battle casualties, the Allied medical teams devoted considerable care to the hard-pressed civilian population whose towns and villages were being devastated by the fighting.

1 Roads and fields alike had frequently been heavily mined, and many tanks, vehicles and men were lost to German mines during the advance into France. This Sherman tank has been held up by the discovery of a mine just in front of it, and sappers are endeavouring to deal with it and clear the road for advance.

2 The bazooka earned its fearsome reputation among the narrow lanes and fields of Normandy. Here, a team from the US 1st Army score a direct hit on a German Panther.

3 As the smoke begins to clear, the US troops move in to ensure that the crew of the Panther tank are either dead or captured. The French houses behind the tank, like so many other homes across France in the summer of 1944, have been virtually destroyed.

4 Most small children in Occupied Europe had never seen a chocolate bar or any of the good things that children usually enjoy. This small French boy has just had some candy presented to him by an American soldier, and is making the most of it.

5 Captured German weapons were increasingly put to use against their former owners, since, by mid-1944, Germany had the world's leading anti-aircraft/anti-tank gun and the world's most deadly tank (the PzKpfw VI Tiger). This gun, captured by the Americans, together with a substantial quantity of ammunition, was rapidly serviced, greased, and put back into action. Captured equipment was also a major source of intelligence on the capability of the German army – Tiger tanks were put through extensive trials by the Allies.

River Vire, opposite the US VII Corps – although some of that explosive was dropped on the Allied positions by mistake, and killed 111 men including a Lieutenant-General. The carnage on the German side was horrifying; all along the front up to half the men and much of the equipment of the defending units were put out of action. As a 'softening-up' exercise, the attacks were both successful and thorough. On July 26th, General Collins was able to break through the German line, and advance to Marigny and Saint Gilles.

Now Field Marshal von Kluge began to realise what Montgomery had succeeded in doing around Caen and Falaise. Hastily, he attempted to withdraw two *Panzer* Divisions back to the west, but they were two days getting to the Marigny area, and by then the breach in the line was permanent. General von Choltitz, in command of LXXXIV Corps could do nothing but pull back and

try to keep his battle-scarred forces together and in fighting order. The US VIII Corps under General Middleton was making the retreat more difficult for von Choltitz in the region of Periers, and Field Marshal von Kluge issued, against von Choltitz' wishes, the order to withdraw in a south-easterly direction rather than to the South-West. Unwillingly, von Choltitz did just that, and thereby provided the Allies with the opportunity to send the US VIII Corps into Brittany, which, as we shall see, was captured in less than a week.

July 28th had seen the US 4th Armoured Division take Coutance and, only one day later, the 6th Armoured Division captured Avranches. The pace of the advance threw the German army into confusion, and von Kluge demanded reinforcements from Hitler, who reluctantly decided at long last that the invasion in Normandy was the real thing, and that there was not to be a further bigger

6 His Majesty King George VI, who, like his father King George V at the outbreak of the First World War, had wanted to play an active role in the war against Germany, lost little time in touring the Normandy battlefront once the breakout was established. Here he is with Lieutenant-General Sir Miles Dempsey.

7 The British commanders confer in Normandy — (right to left) General Montgomery, Lieutenant-General Sir Miles Dempsey, whose appointment as commander of the British 2nd Army was announced on June 28th, the day the 2nd Army crossed the River Odon, South-West of Caen, and Lieutenant-General Sir Richard O'Connor, commander of VIII Corps, who had been repatriated following the Italian armistice in 1943 after more than two years in a prisoner-of-war camp.

8 The Normandy command was Field-Marshal Rommel's last, for on July 17th his car was strafed by RAF Typhoons and he was seriously injured. His complicity in the Stauffenberg bomb plot to assassinate Hitler, which failed three days later on July 20th, resulted in his being encouraged to commit suicide rather than stand trial. This picture was taken in Caen a month earlier, as Allied pressure on the city mounted.

landing in the Pas de Calais. Too late to achieve any real effect, a Corps and two divisions were ordered from the 15th Army to von Kluge's line, and a further Corps and two divisions were ordered up from the South of France to join the 7th Army. But large scale troop and tank movements take time. The US VIII Corps was now commanded by General George C. Patton, and on July 31st, hearing that the US 4th Armoured Division was at Pontaubault and had captured a bridge intact, he decided to push ahead and break out of Normandy once and for all.

Two US divisions, the 6th Armoured and the 79th Infantry set out across Brittany for the port of Brest, and two more made for Rennes. Patton, who had once had General Omar Bradley under his command in Italy, was now subordinate to Bradley, who had recently been confirmed in his appointment as C.in C. 12th Army Group.

That this arrangement worked well most of the time is a tribute to both men. Nonetheless, during the first week of August, as Patton thrust on towards Brest, and Bradley issued orders to hold the advance until intermediate objectives were taken, there were moments of considerable discord and confusion. By August 5th, the 6th Armoured Division was tackling the German 265th defending Lorient, the 4th Armoured was attempting to flush the German 2nd Parachute Division out of Brest — and Patton was eyeing with interest a 65 mile gap in the line between Rennes and Nantes caused by the rapid advance of the US armour. When Eisenhower ordered that Brittany should not be allowed to occupy more than the minimum Allied forces, Patton seized his chance for a lightning advance which excited the world.

With three Corps, Patton headed South and South-East. By

The Breakout from Normandy

August 7th, XII Corps had liberated Nantes and Angers, and XV Corps had taken Chateau-Gontier and Laval. Now Patton was all set to drive South and East with his newly constituted US 3rd Army from Laval to take Le Mans, a move which would create the potential for a pincer movement carried out with the British 2nd Army, now almost due North of the Americans, to encircle von Kluge's German Army Group B, part of which was positioned between them.

Unknown to the Allied commanders, a substantial disagreement had been taking place between von Kluge and Hitler following von Kluge's request a week earlier to be allowed to withdraw and regroup in better defensive positions. Hitler had, after initially agreeing with Colonel-General Jodl that von Kluge should be permitted to retreat, changed his mind and issued an order for a counter-attack that was sheer fantasy. Von Kluge was ordered to advance on Avranches and cut off the American troops in Brittany as a prelude to advancing on St. Lo, overthrowing the US 1st Army and throwing the Allies back to the sea. To do this he was to use the *Panzer* units of the 7th Army. In vain, von Kluge pointed out that the *Panzer* Divisions were now desperately under strength, that his losses of troops were into six figures with almost nil reinforcements, and that those German soldiers who were nominally still fit to fight were exhausted. The attack was set for August 7th.

Thus, as Patton was taking Chateau-Gontier and Laval, and beginning his push to Le Mans, heading Eastwards, the German 7th Army to its North began its thrust Westwards towards Avranche, increasing its danger of being encircled as it went. The counter-attack was mounted by four *Panzer* divisions — the 2nd and 116th, plus two SS divisions, the 1st *Leibstandarte* and the 2nd *Das Reich*. Their

1 Waiting for the order to attack Caen are Sherman tanks of the British 2nd Army. On June 28th, the British 2nd Army crossed the River Odon, southwest of Caen, and on Tuesday July 4th, Carpiquet, west of Caen, fell to the advancing armour and infantry under General Dempsey.

2 The pilots of the RAF and USAAF were in almost constant action in ground attack and interceptor roles. Here, the pilots of an RAF Spitfire squadron in Normandy listen to an impromptu briefing on an airfield. Some of their aircraft are parked in the background.

3 An armoured column of the British 2nd Army in Lisieux, west of Caen, shows how the devastation had miraculously passed by the beautiful and recently-built Basilica of St Therese on the hill. The mud which plagued the advancing Allied army is also much in evidence.

4 When Caen finally fell, on July 9th, much of the old city was in a state of ruin. Hardly a building was left untouched by the shelling, and many of the civilian population had died. That the French continued to welcome the Allied liberation despite the destruction wrought by it is an indication of the extent of their loathing of German occupation.

5 To reinforce Allied defensive positions in France, 3·7" anti-aircraft guns, which had been used during the Battle of Britain and in the defence of Dover, were taken to France shortly after D-Day. Since Allied air supremacy was almost absolute, the ack-ack guns were used in a new role, firing bursts over German positions in support of infantry attacks.

6 The town of Vire, formerly the capital of Lower Normandy, at the base of the Cherbourg Peninsula, was liberated by the Allies after fierce enemy resistance on August 7th 1944. Heavy Allied air attack had played an important part in defeating the German defence of the town, and the Allied soldiers found that severe damage had been done to the railway and its rolling stock by the bombing.

7 The destruction of Caen and the suffering of the people within the city struck a chord in the hearts of the Allied troops, who did all they could to improve the lot of those who could do little to help themselves. His rifle to one side, this British soldier has been brewing soup for himself and the little girl, whose bandaged leg is evidence of her recent troubles.

thrust, which went well for the first eight hours, was countered by the US VII Corps (Major-General Collins) and the US 30th Division (Major-General Hobbs), both of which stood their ground well. As the weather and visibility improved after mid-day, the RAF Typhoons launched rocket attacks against the *Panzer* units, unhindered by the *Luftwaffe* aircraft that had been promised as air support because these had been attacked by Allied aircraft as they left their bases.

Once more, von Kluge recommended retreat. Once more it was refused, and, despite the obvious risk of the British 2nd Army attacking southwards from Caen, von Kluge was ordered to reinforce the attack on Avranches at the expense of the defence of Falaise. As General Bittrich' II SS *Panzer* Corps was detached from Falaise, Montgomery attacked from the North at midnight with two infantry and two armoured divisions. By morning, the headquarters of I SS *Panzer* Corps had been over-run, the 89th *Panzer* Division was in desperate trouble, and the 272nd was clearly losing ground. But, not for the first time, the redoubtable Brigadefuhrer Kurt Meyer and his 12th SS *Hitlerjugend Panzer* Division fought the attack to a standstill. Two days after it had begun, and only ten miles from Falaise, the Anglo-Canadian offensive ground to a halt. On the same day, Patton arrived in Le Mans and turned North towards the British 2nd Army, hoping to join up with them and encircle Kluge's Army Group as it tried to attack Westwards.

By August 13th, the US XV Corps was only 15 miles from Falaise, and seemed likely to get to the British and Canadian forces before the German Army, now beginning to retreat, could escape through the Falaise gap. But Bradley, on still-controversial orders from Eisenhower, ordered Patton to stop, and not to close the gap.

The Breakout from Normandy

whereupon the German Army Group, whether Hitler liked it or not (which he did not), went into headlong retreat in an attempt to escape the pocket. SS General Sepp Dietrich, now C. in C. 5th *Panzerarmee* succeeded in extracting what was left of I SS *Panzer* Corps, and, adding to it a motley collection of German troops of every imaginable unit, broke through to the East of the gap, just as the Canadians took Falaise and joined up with the US V Corps to close the ring on August 17th.

For those German troops left within the pocket, the next few days were hell. A US 90th Division artillery barrage killed thousands. In full-scale panic, thousands more deserted their equipment and attempted to break out on foot. In the Argentan/Chambois area the Allies took 50,000 prisoners and buried 10,000 German dead. The 90th Armoured Division captured 380 armoured vehicles, 700 guns and 5,000 trucks. The French 2nd Armoured Division took a further 100 guns and 700 vehicles.

Von Kluge, dismissed and disgraced by Hitler, replaced by Field Marshal Model and totally disillusioned, took cyanide on August 18th. Model had taken over a chaotic situation on August 17th, with rampant Allied advances in Normandy all set to head for Paris, and his depleted Army Group B being ordered to withdraw to positions along the Seine by the same Commander in Chief who had so recently forbidden Kluge the withdrawal that would have saved half

Legend:
▲▲▲ Siegfried Line
Allied Attacks 3 Aug.-28 Aug. 1944
Allied Attacks 4 Sept.-20 Sept 1944

*August 1944
Attack from North Africa
and Naples*

Above the liberation of France.

1 Many of the more committed German officers found capture by the advancing Americans a matter for humiliation – having been educated to believe that the German army was invincible, they found their own capture difficult to accept. This officer, a major, is being led away for questioning.

2 As General Patton's armoured columns sped towards Brest, the world held its breath, not for the first, nor the last time, at the sheer pace that the impulsive US commander seemed to be able to inspire and demand from his men. Patton was the Allies' answer to *Blitzkrieg*; the living proof that high-speed armoured advance was not an exclusively German talent. Here, US tanks of US VIII Corps are pushing on through the devastated town of Lambezellec.

3

4

5

3 As French towns were freed, not only of their German occupiers, but also of the curfews and fear that had been the inevitable consequences of occupation, resentment against those who had collaborated with the hated German invaders rose to boiling point. The next few months would see scenes like this repeated throughout France and Belgium, as collaborators were mobbed, brutalised and ridiculed. This picture was taken in Chartres, as two women, one with a baby born to her by a German father, were led back to their homes after having their heads shaved.

4 Captured German officers and NCOs, watched over by a US military policeman, await questioning by American intelligence officers. They are a mixed group. The original caption tells us that the *SS* officers are members of the *17th SS Panzer Grenadier Division* 'Goetz von Berlichingen'.

an army. Two days before, on August 15th, the overall situation in France had been further confused for the Germans by the Allies' embarking on their long-projected landing in the South of France. This was the next step in the elimination of the German occupation, and another nail in the coffin of the Third Reich.

Operation Dragoon, Nee Anvil

At successive Allied conferences, Roosevelt and Churchill had discussed at length the potential value and the risks of a landing on the Mediterranean coast of France either simultaneously with or shortly after the 'Overlord' landing in Normandy. As a result, 'Operation Anvil' had been a part of Allied strategy since the Casablanca conference, but, as late as August 6th 1944, Churchill was expressing doubts about the validity of the operation and propounding his oft-asserted belief in the potential benefit of an invasion in the Balkans. By now, the Mediterranean invasion was known as 'Operation Dragoon', and the Americans, correctly, believed that it could in part provide the coup de grace against German occupation in France.

The third major amphibious landing in Europe of 1944 took place on August 15th between St Raphael and le Lavandou, close to Monaco and the Italian border on the French Riviera. A fleet of a thousand ships and landing vessels, including five battleships, nine escort carriers with 216 aircraft, and 146 other warships brought the US 7th Army under the command of Lieutenant-General Patch to land under the guns of the German 19th Army, part of Colonel-General von Blaskowitz' Army Group G. The 19th Army, after losing

6

5 As it became clear that the fall of Brest was inevitable, the German Command ordered the crack parachute troops and front-line defenders to withdraw from the city for action elsewhere, leaving the port defended by a mixed bag of troops, port employees and naval personnel. This Army officer surrendered with ninety men who had been under his command, most of whom were seamen.

6 On 18th July, newspapers carried this picture of a Sherman tank of the British 2nd Army crossing the Orne at 'London Bridge'. Theirs was to be the challenge of Falaise.

1 A fine picture of the British armoured column's Sherman tanks, heading eastward from the Orne in the morning light at the beginning of the month-long campaign that was to culminate in the near-entrapment of Field-Marshal von Kluge's Army Group in the Falaise Pocket.

2 Issued on August 16th 1944, this Canadian official photograph shows heavy 5·5" guns of the Royal Artillery pushing forward on roads leding south and east from Normandy towards Paris.

3 As the campaign along the Orne advanced, the residents of the villages and towns fled before the ferocity of the battle. By the time this anti-tank gun was in position in Amaye-sur-Orne, the village was deserted. Around the corner of the road to the right was the River Orne, covered by German machine-gun fire.

some of its strength to the Normandy battles, consisted of six divisions — three each side of the Rhone, commanded by General Neuling.

Before the landing itself, following what was by now the established practice, the Allies launched on August 13th and 14th an air offensive all along the Mediterranean coastline from Genoa in the East to Port Vendre in the West, attacking communications, gun emplacements and coastal defences. On the day of the landing, the fleet, under the command of Admiral H. Kent Hewitt, fired some 50,000 shells in a prolonged barrage on enemy positions, while the Air Forces flew a total of 4,250 sorties opposed by only a token appearance by the once-powerful *Luftwaffe*. As the US VI Corps landed, supported by part of the French 1st Armoured Division, they met relatively little resistance by comparison with that of the Normandy beaches. By the end of the first day, the Allies had safely put ashore 60,000 men, 6,000 vehicles and 50,000 tons of supplies for the loss of 320 men.

4 When Falaise was taken, it too was in virtual ruins. This picture was taken by photographer W.H. Dewhirst of the *Yorkshire Post*, and shows British armour passing through Falaise to forward positions. RAF bombing had wrought terrible damage during the final phases of the battle.

5 American troops moved inland rapidly after the relatively little-opposed landing in the South of France. These troops are marching past an eight-foot thick wall running the length of the beach, part of the German defensive system, in which a large breach was blasted by assault engineers. In nine days, 20,000 Germans surrendered in this sector, and the Allies had liberated Marseille, advanced to Grenoble, 140 miles north of the coast, and were closing in on the port of Toulon.

6 The success of the Allied landing in the South of France meant that Germany now faced Allied advances across the length and breadth of France. This American M10 tank destroyer, its crew watching for aircraft, was photographed near Le Colunvier.

7 Scenes like this were commonplace in country districts as the Allies advanced across France. An American platoon has just finished off a German sniper who was hiding in the loft of the barn.

Progress from the beach-head was rapid. Just twenty-four hours after the first toehold, the Americans had taken Le Luc (and with it the German commander, General Neuling), Draguignan and Frejus, and had spread out along the coast on a broad front. The second wave arrived on the 16th, and brought four divisions of French colonial troops, whom the Germans had learned in Italy to dread, plus the French 1st Armoured Division, all under the command of the immensely capable and much respected General de Lattre de Tassigny. The German *Panzer* units who were to do battle with the French 1st Armoured were to discover just how effective and spirited the French commanders were, and to comment many times after the war that these were some of the finest soldiers of the Second World War.

Enthusiastically, the Frenchmen set about liberating their homeland, taking in rapid succession Salerne, Brignoles and Cuers. The US VI Corps, followed by the US 36th Division, set off from Digne, in the Basses Alpes, towards Sisteron, intending to cut off

the German 19th Army at Montelimar, the US 45th Division set out for Aix en Provence, and the Germans decided that the time had come to fall back. In fact, Hitler had issued the initial order for the evacuation of South and South-East France on the day after the landing, August 16th, and it was decided that Army Group G would retreat to join up with Model's similarly retreating Army Group B at or near Sens. The ports of Toulon and Marseille were, however, to be defended to the last, and the 11th *Panzer* Division was ordered to cover the retreat.

As the Germans fell back from the South, hotly pursued by the Americans and French, Hitler issued a new directive on August 20th instructing Field-Marshal Model's Army Group B to hold a line around Paris and South to Switzerland — but it was already, like so many of Hitler's directives in the last year of the war, far too late. General Patton was already almost at Sens and Montereau, and was about to order XV Corps across the Seine at Mantes. The US XX Corps had reached Chartres as early as August 16th, 20 days ahead

1 The British advance in the north continued along roads strewn with German dead and the rubble of war. This makeshift German grave, marked by a shrapnel-torn helmet and a rough wooden cross, is surrounded by the dust of the advancing British column.

2 The extraordinary rapidity of the advance across France to the borders of Germany by Lieutenant-General Patton made him the star of the European campaign as far as the media were concerned, to the intense chagrin of General Montgomery. This picture shows how much Patton enjoyed his starring role, as he advances from his tent to meet the press.

of schedule. The *Wehrmacht* in France had lost almost 300,000 officers and men since June 6th, and much of its equipment. To stop the headlong advance of Patton's US 3rd Army and the hardly more sedate push of Bradley's and Montgomery's troops further North was simply impracticable.

General de Gaulle had arrived back in France on August 21st, and made representations to Eisenhower about the liberation of Paris. Eisenhower had intended simply to go around the French capital, but de Gaulle was aware of the grave risk of Communist uprising in Paris, fuelled by the acute lack of food in the capital for the population. Since August 16th, the Paris police had been on strike, and the danger was imminent. Reluctantly, Eisenhower agreed to allow the French troops to launch themselves upon the liberation of the city. General von Choltitz, who had since August 7th been Military Governor of Paris, had received on August 21st instructions from Hitler (whom he now regarded, according to his memoirs, as being mad) to defend Paris as a bridgehead against the approaching Americans. The order ended with the instruction "Paris must only fall into enemy hands as a heap of rubble".

Von Choltitz was both a realistic and a reasonable man. He saw no virtue in destroying a fine city in a spirit of revenge, so conducted clandestine negotiations with the Swedish Consul-General Raoul

3 A remarkable example of wartime aerial photography shows a column of Allied tanks moving up west of Falaise, with an RAF Mustang like that from which the picture was taken in a tight turn in formation with the photographic aircraft. Later Mustangs had a very different outline, with a plastic bubble cockpit which gave all-round visibility.

4 On August 19th 1944, left-wing elements of the Resistance began the long-awaited uprising in Paris, based on resentment at the food shortage. De Gaulle was alarmed at the potential that the uprising suggested for a postwar Communist government in France, and therefore insisted on the Allied Liberation of Paris. But the uprising served to provide bargaining power by which General von Choltitz agreed to the surrender of Paris without its destruction. Barricades like this appeared in main streets throughout the centre of the city.

5 General von Choltitz, a reasonable man who considered Hitler mad, signed the surrender of Paris, ignoring Hitler's order that the Allies should not capture the city with a building intact. More than anybody else, it was he who saved one of the world's loveliest cities. Unglamorously, he signed the surrender document in the left-luggage office of the Gare Montparnasse. The date was August 25th 1944.

6 Despite the German surrender, some German snipers barricaded themselves into buildings and fought on, even after the Allies were in the city. In this picture, Americans and Frenchmen are taking cover behind a Sherman tank and are returning sniper fire, while two of the French Resistance have also realised that the fire is coming from their right.

Nordling and the potential leaders of the uprising in Paris. He gained agreement to a compromise by which, if the uprising did not take place, the Germans would not destroy the city. Thus, the French 2nd Armoured Division was able to fight its way towards the city in two Combat Commands, losing over 300 men and more than 40 tanks to the German anti-tank guns as they went. By morning of August 25th, the French tanks were in the suburbs of Paris. On the 26th, amid considerable rejoicing, Paris was freed. Hitler, in a bloodthirsty rage, ordered that the city be destroyed by the German Army's huge siege mortars. To his everlasting credit, General Speidel ignored the order, and Paris survived.

Meanwhile, in the South of France, General de Lattre de Tassigny had launched his French divisions on the daunting task of taking the fortresses of Toulon and Marseilles, the German defenders of both of which had been ordered to defend their positions to the last, an instruction taken literally in both cases. The fighting for Toulon on August 21st and 22nd was so fierce, so unrelenting, that heroes and acts of outstanding bravery were commonplace. The French commandos of Colonel Bouvet's famous unit distinguished themselves by climbing into Fort Coudon on ropes in the best Beau Geste fashion and hunting down the German occupants one by one, and on the 22nd earned equal distinction in the battle for the Toulon

magazine from which few emerged alive. Toulon finally fell on August 27th after some of the bloodiest fighting of the European war. Over 2,700 French soldiers died, but they took more than 17,000 prisoners.

While the Battle for Toulon was raging, General de Lattre de Tassigny had ordered the French 1st Armoured Division with the 3rd Algerian Division and the Moroccan mountain troops into Marseilles. The battle was almost as fierce as that in Toulon, and culminated on the same day. On August 27th, the German commander asked for terms to end the fighting, and on the 28th an armistice was signed. Although the equipment and installations of the ports at Toulon and Marseilles were blown up by the Germans before their capitulation, the success of the French troops can be measured by the fact that their ending of the war in Provence and the South was a full month ahead of the Allies' schedule, and by the fact that the two ports, once brought into use, were key factors in the landing of Allied supplies for the remainder of the war.

In the northern sector of the battle for France, town after town fell to the remorseless advance of the American, Canadian and British troops until, on September 10th, only the three coastal bastions of Boulogne, Calais and Dunkirk remained substantially defended by German troops, and the British and American troops

1 Under guard of men of the FFI, the largely-Communist Resistance, German officers and their men are marched through the streets of Paris after the liberation.

2 As the German garrison surrendered, General de Gaulle entered Paris to almost universal jubilation. Amid cheering crowds he marched the length of the Champs Elysees.

had advanced into Belgium and Luxembourg. Field-Marshal Montgomery (as he now was) had occupied Antwerp, Bruges and Ghent, and the US 12th Army Group was in Liege, Bastogne and Luxembourg. By the 15th September, further South, General Patton had taken Nancy and could see the way ahead into Germany, through Metz, if only he had the fuel. Desperately he appealed to Eisenhower who remained unmoved. Patton must advance at the more considered pace of his colleagues in arms.

The logistic crisis brought about by the sensationally fast advance through France to Belgium was in fact now affecting all Allied land forces decisions. It was to be the underlying cause of the much-publicised dispute between Montgomery and Patton as to who was to assault Germany and how. It was to make the next phase of the European war just a little less dazzling than the past three months. For France, give or take the coastal fortresses and a few isolated pockets of German resistance, was free of the German invader for the first time since May 1940. It had been a long four and a half years for the French.

3 The arrival of General de Gaulle at Notre Dame for the service of thanksgiving for the liberation of Paris was punctuated by a hail of sniper fire which the General, an undeniably brave as well as a somewhat mystical figure, simply ignored. Here he is seen leaving Notre Dame after the service.

CHAPTER 36

RUSSIA'S INDOMITABLE ADVANCE
POLAND AND THE APPROACH TO GERMANY

June 1944 saw not only the Allied assault on Normandy and successes for the Americans in the Far East, but also the resumption of the war between Finland and Russia. Following breakdown of negotiations to settle the position resulting from the Winter War of 1940, some 20 divisions of Russian troops attacked the Finns and made rapid progress, taking Viipuri on June 20th. By mid-July, the Soviet Army had retaken the Karelian Isthmus and its advance had slowed to a stop. The Finns had little option but to accept the situation imposed on them, although their counter-attacks went on for months.

For the Russians had weightier matters afoot. Three years to the day after Hitler had launched 'Barbarossa' against an unsuspecting

Soviet Union, the Red Army and Air Force began on June 22nd 1944 the summer offensive that was to end all summer offensives, at least in this war. The objective was the annihilation of the German Army Group Centre, which was in a dangerously exposed salient in Belorussia following the retreats during the winter of Army Groups North and South, and which had recently been deprived of six infantry divisions and two *Panzer* Divisions by the need to reinforce Field-Marshal Model's Army Group B in France. Army Group Centre, commanded by Field-Marshal Busch, thus had only 37 divisions, all of which were well below strength and none of which stood any real chance of being reinforced.

Against these German forces were hurled 166 Soviet divisions, each of 10,000 men, and a total of 4,500 tanks against which the Germans could muster only some 400 tanks. The ratios of Soviet to German guns and aircraft were little different. The Germans were outgunned and outnumbered, but were nonetheless as willing as ever to fight bravely for their country. They were, however, fighting not one enemy but two. Like the armies in Normandy, the men of Army

4

5

4 By 1944 the Red Army was a formidable fighting machine. Much of its strength came from equipment supplied by the USA and Great Britain under the lend-lease agreements. This picture shows an M3A1 armoured car of American origin in use on the Eastern Front.

5 Cavalry, traditionally one of the most successful arms of the Russian army, played a major role in the early stages of the Russian war, and continued to be a significant factor even after the massive build-up of Soviet armoured might that characterised the Russian war effort in 1943 and 1944.

6 The German armies' ability to resist effectively the colossal attacks from east and west of the summer of 1944 was much reduced by Hitler's purge of his generals and staff that followed the attempt on the *Fuehrer's* life, known as the Stauffenberg plot, in July 1944. This picture was taken immediately after the bomb at the Rastenburg 'Wolf's Lair' had failed to kill Hitler, and was issued to prove that he was indeed still alive. Behind Hitler is Martin Bormann; to his left, with his head bandaged, is General Alfred Jodl, and at the extreme lower right is Captain Bauer, Hitler's pilot.

6

Russia's Indomitable Advance

Group Centre were given by Hitler impossible orders based on erroneous hunches and irrational assessments. The obligation to carry out Hitler's Directive of the moment was almost a greater obstacle than the might of the Red Army.

Hitler had decided, on the basis of his own assumption that the Russians would seek next to take the Rumanian oilfields, that the Summer offensive would be directed against Army Group South. Despite compelling and ever growing intelligence based on factual reconnaissance that Soviet troop movements in early and mid-June were all directed at the area between Pripet and the Dvina, Hitler obstinately dismissed the possibility of an attack in Belorussia and a subsequent advance into Poland. He refused totally to consider moving troops to the threatened area from Army Group South, or to go back on an earlier and equally irrational decision to make certain important German strongholds 'fortified areas' in which the defenders would fight to the last after deliberately allowing themselves to become encircled. In vain did the experienced and senior Generals of Army Group Centre remonstrate about the loss of men, weapons and supplies. Hitler was beginning to apply his Gothic Wagnerian fantasy of the nobility of war to every decision.

The attack, when it came on 22nd June, was directed at Army Group Centre on a front totalling some 435 miles, with a primary first objective of encircling and taking the prestige target of Vitebsk, one of the cities that Hitler had nominated a fortified area. In only 48 hours, the German 3rd *Panzerarmee* was overrun on either side

1 Hitler seemed crumpled and demoralised after the Stauffenberg bomb attack, and looked suddenly much older. Here he confers with Dr Josef Goebbels, the Nazi Propaganda Minister, outside his Rastenburg headquarters, while they were planning the counter-measures and trial that followed the assassination attempt.

of the city, and the circle began to close. Colonel-General Reinhardt, in command of the 3rd Army, whose LIII Corps held Vitebsk, appealed to be allowed to withdraw, knowing from experience and from the evidence of his commanders in the field that there was no hope of holding the city. Hitler's reply, through his Chief of Staff, Zeitzler, was that Vitebsk 'would be held'. Five hours later he countermanded his instruction and gave Reinhardt's LIII Corps permission to withdraw leaving only a token defending force. But it was already too late, and the Russians virtually annihilated the retreating force, which surrendered on June 27th leaving a gap nearly thirty miles wide in the German line.

The same story was repeated all along the line at each of the 'fortified areas'. Not until June 28th did Hitler accept that the attack in Belorussia was the actual assault rather than a feint. By then the brilliant and resourceful General Chernyakhovsy and his commanders had pushed forward and broken the line at countless points, destroying German communications and tactical command. As he did so, General Rokossovsky and his 1st Belorussian Front had

bypassed the fortified areas, and had thrust through gaps to encircle the German forces beyond. By June 29th, he had destroyed two German Corps, had taken 16,000 prisoners and had killed 18,000 more.

All through July, the Soviet armies pushed relentlessly forward on six major fronts towards Poland and East Prussia, taking Vilnyus on the 13th, Pinsk on the 14th, Grodno on the 15th. July 18th saw Rokossovsky cross the arbitrary Russo-Polish frontier that had been fixed at the Teheran conference; without a backward glance he pushed on to Lublin by the 23rd, Brest-Litovsk by the 28th and Praga, in the suburbs of Warsaw, by the 31st. An idea of the pace of the advance can be gained by looking at the distance between Brest-Litovsk and Warsaw — 120 miles in less than three days. Vast Russian reinforcements had been brought into the battle during the month, and the ratio of fire-power and manpower against the German Army became ever more disadvantageous. So headlong was the German retreat at times that experienced and able commanders took desperate risks. The 8th *Panzer* Division was caught by Russian aircraft on the

2 The scene in the courtroom of the 'People's Court' as the conspirators of the July plot were tried for their lives. Few survived.

3 One of the defendants stands before the judges of the 'People's Court', on trial for his life for conspiracy to murder Hitler. According to the original news agency caption, this is General Maase.

move in broad daylight along the main road to Brody, breaking every rule of tank warfare, and paid dearly with the total destruction of a large proportion of its tanks in one attack. In the same area, General Hauffe and 17,000 men of XIII Corps were taken prisoner. Another 30,000, either the lucky or the unlucky ones, depending on your view of Russian prison camps, were killed.

Having crossed the Vistula and reached Praga, within a few miles of the centre of Warsaw, Rokossovsky's Soviet advance came to a sudden and exhausted halt. That his troops were greatly fatigued, and that his lines of supply were extended and not at their best is beyond doubt. Nonetheless there was a strong political motive for the halt. Knowing that the Russians were close, an uprising of the non-Communist Polish Home Army, sparked by a broadcast by

5

6

7

8

4 Reprinted from a German report on the heroes of the *Wehrmacht* who had been awarded the Oak Leaves to their Knights Crosses, this picture provides an interesting portrait gallery of German commanders. Second from right is Field-Marshal Ernst Busch, the Commander of the depleted Army Group Centre which was destroyed by the massive Soviet summer offensive of June 1944. In the centre is Field-Marshal Georg Kuchler, who was Commander in Chief of Army Group North in 1944 until succeeded by Colonel-General Lindemann (extreme right). Colonel-General Otto Rendulic (left) was the Commander of the German 20th Army in Lapland from June 1944 after its previous commander, Colonel-General Dietl, died accidentally.

5 This picture, dated on the original caption as 21st January 1944, was taken while riding on the back of a Soviet SU 152 self-propelled gun with an ML-20S gun of 152mm calibre, and shows another SU 152 gun in the middle distance. The SU 152 had a road speed of twenty-three mph, and entered service in 1943.

6 Desperate for effective means of combating the ever-greater superiority of the Soviet armoured forces, the *Luftwaffe* ordered some specially-adapted ground-attack Junkers 88 fighter-bombers, known as the Ju 88P. These were equipped with either a 75mm cannon (Ju 88P-1) or two 37mm cannon (Ju 88P-2), mounted below the nose of the aircraft. This picture shows the massive 75mm cannon of a newly-arrived Ju 88P-1.

7 A remarkable picture taken through the commander's viewing port of a Soviet tank as it attacked a German PzKpfW III medium tank. The *Panzer III* has been hit, apparently amidships, and the Russian tank is closing in for the kill.

8 The beginning of a Soviet attack on a German fortified position. A Russian T34/76 in the foreground on the right is providing covering fire while infantry who have been brought up on the hull of another T34 tank (left) bend low as they leap from the tank and rush forward to storm the German position.

Russia's Indomitable Advance

Radio Moscow, was under way in Warsaw. Stalin had every reason for wanting as many non-Communist Poles as possible to be killed before his Communist 'Polish Army' 'liberated' their homeland. He knew that the Germans were massing what force they could to retake Praga, and that they would put down any insurrection, whatever its motives, without a thought. Throughout the first two weeks of August 1944, Stalin studiously ignored Churchill's calls either for Russian help for the Warsaw insurgents against the Germans, or for permission to land and refuel on Soviet-held territory Allied aircraft airlifting supplies to the beleaguered city.

The Germans counter-attacked the Russians and drove them back from Praga — then turned their tanks and guns on the lightly armed Poles who held the centre of the city of Warsaw. A motley collection of ex-convicts and Russian prisoners in German uniforms under *Waffen-SS* control were turned loose on the gallant Polish patriots under General Bor-Komorowski, who were gradually hemmed in

1 A Soviet machine-gun crew, whose somewhat stiff demeanour and suspiciously clean gun makes this almost certainly a posed, propaganda picture. Nonetheless, it is interesting for showing in some detail the deflection sights fitted to the gun.

2 Leaving a German anti-tank gun and its dead crew behind them, a Soviet T-34 tank and its attendant infantry continue their advance towards Germany.

3 The rains of the summer of 1944 added to the problems of the retreating German Army. According to the contemporary news agency caption, this picture shows a flooded German defensive position, being evacuated by dinghy.

4 Each town and city in the path of the sweeping Soviet advance had to be fought for, street by street, building by building. The tension of street fighting is somehow captured in this picture of Soviet troops of the First Ukrainian Front clearing German snipers from a recently-occupied town.

5 German armaments designers, encouraged by Hitler's desire for all-conquering secret weapons, seemed on occasion to suffer from Wagnerian fantasies similar to those of the *Fuehrer* himself. Here, four members of the Soviet Supreme Command study a colossal siege mortar, probably of either 240mm or 305mm calibre, that had been captured from the retreating Germans. Left to right are: Admiral Kuznetzov, Marshal Voronov, Marshal Zhukov and Marshal Voroshilov.

and either killed or captured. Appalling atrocities were committed in the name of order in the city before Bor-Komorowski finally surrendered on October 2nd, with 22,000 of his 40,000 fighters dead. Estimates put civilian deaths in the capital as high as 200,000.

By the end of September, the whole of the vast Russian front had caught up with the high-speed advance that had singled out Rokossovsky's advance on Warsaw, and the front stabilised along the line of the Rivers Narew and Vistula. The Russians had now advanced almost 400 miles since June 23rd, and had virtually annihilated 25 of the 37 divisions of the German Army Group Centre. As winter came on, the pace quietened, and the Red Army in Poland and on the border of East Prussia prepared its supply lines, brought up its new tanks and equipment, and trained yet more reinforcements for the final push that would clearly bring to Germany the peril it had dreaded more than any other — the Bolshevik invasion.

In Germany, the immense losses of men and equipment brought desperate measures. On October 5th it was announced that all 16-year old youths were to be conscripted for military service and that all hospitals were to be under military control. The *Volkssturm* or People's Militia was formed to defend the homeland, and all night clubs that had remained open after the disaster of Stalingrad, together with other places of entertainment were closed. To add to the gloom, Goebbels announced that Erwin Rommel had 'died of his wounds'. In fact, he had committed suicide, aged 52, when it was made plain to him that this was the only permitted alternative to trial, humiliation and execution for his part in the July 20th plot. Thus did Hitler serve those of ability.

The anguish of the German civilian population could only get worse, and get worse it assuredly did as the Allied air offensive maintained the pressure on German cities and sources of production, and the armies of the USA, Britain and Canada advanced on Germany's cities from the West. But it was in the East that terror lay, and the vast exodus of German refugees Westward caused by the Russian advance early in 1945 was to see no equal in the West. The Germans had had their fill of tyranny, and had no wish to exchange one tyrant for another.

6 This German news picture was issued by the Reich Propaganda Ministry to show how responsibly German troops were battling with the uprising in Warsaw in August 1944 — when in fact SS units were killing indiscriminately all over the city. Apparently taken on August 30th, it shows the familiar German eight-wheeled scout car fitted with radio direction-finding aerials, and an SS officer leading his men off on patrol, presumably to find and eliminate a rebel radio transmitter.

7 As the Polish patriots' positions were overrun in Warsaw, the Germans were merciless in executing those who had taken part in the uprising. This immensely sad picture was taken by a German photographer as Polish women were led away to be executed for no greater crime than that they were Poles and had supported their menfolk in resisting tyranny.

6

7

8

8 Once the Russians arrived in Warsaw, the tables were turned on the few Germans who were left in the city — incendiarists detailed to remain behind and set the city ablaze.

CHAPTER 37

BACK IN THE PHILIPPINES
AMERICA'S TRIUMPH WON WITH BLOOD

As the Allies in Europe advanced on Germany, the Americans in the Pacific were torn between General MacArthur's sworn intention to liberate the Philippines at the earliest possible opportunity, and the preference of the Admirals for bypassing the Philippines to take Formosa. By the end of September 1944, after some powerful argument by MacArthur, they had made their decision in the favour of the Philippines, and had set a date for an invasion of the island of Leyte in the Central Philippines by the combined forces of Nimitz' and MacArthur's until now separate offensives. The date was October 20th.

Meanwhile, Admiral Halsey had successfully landed the US 1st Marine Division on the island of Peleliu in mid-September, an action that was to continue, with reinforcement by the US 85th Infantry Division, until November 25th before the last of the Japanese under Lieutenant-General Inouye had surrendered. MacArthur captured the island of Morotai to isolate the Japanese bases in the Moluccas, and at the beginning of October, Admiral Halsey's Task Force 38 attacked Japanese positions on the Ryukyu Islands to prevent them being used as bases for attacks on the forthcoming invasion of Leyte. Rear-Admiral Marc Mitscher's 1,100 carrier-borne fighters and

fighter-bombers engaged almost as many Japanese aircraft during the attack on the Ryukyus, and scored a clear victory by destroying more than 500 of them for the loss of only 110 US aircraft, although two US cruisers were also torpedoed.

Leyte and the Battle of Leyte Gulf

With the Japanese ability to respond to a landing in the Philippines thus reduced, Vice-Admiral Thomas Kinkaid's 7th Fleet arrived in the Gulf of Leyte on October 17th with 174,000 men of the US 6th Army, and began a two day bombardment of the island to 'soften up' the defence, which consisted of just one Japanese division under Lieutenant-General Makino. The Japanese had in fact realised the extent to which the island was under-defended, and General Yamashita, the Japanese C.in C. in the Philippines had been ordered to reinforce Leyte with another of his seven divisions. Fortunately for the Americans, the US Army got there first.

All through the day on October 20th the US 6th Army poured men and equipment ashore on the island and by evening a substantial bridgehead had been established on a seventeen mile front. MacArthur had himself landed during the day — Yamashita later said

1 In the confusing conditions of jungle warfare, the specially adapted armoured vehicles designed to clear former enemy positions often themselves came under heavy fire. This US Marine tank-dozer has been fired upon by a Japanese machine-gun post on the hill above the clearing in which it is working, and those of the crew working outside have taken cover behind the vehicle while the gunner returns the fire.

2 Men of a US Marine Corps unit attack a Japanese jungle position on Peleliu, one of the Central Pacific Palau Islands, invaded on September 14th 1944. The Marines found from experience that improvised 'Molotov Cocktails' were often more effective than conventional weapons in close jungle conditions, and in this picture the Marine standing in the centre is throwing one of these deadly gasoline bombs after lighting it from a torch stuck in the undergrowth.

that he would have launched a suicide attack against the island if he had known that the hated MacArthur was there in person. As the bridgehead was strengthened and supplied the Japanese were not idle, and put into action a complex plan which was potentially brilliant in the short term if it succeeded, and failed almost as completely to provide for the long term if it failed.

The greatest single shortage from which the Japanese suffered was that of aircraft and the trained crews to fly them. We noted in an earlier chapter the failure of Japanese aircraft design and

technology to keep pace with that of the Americans, and the consequent progressively greater outclassing of Japanese aircraft in combat. This had led by 1943 to the disproportionate losses of Japanese aircraft by comparison with US planes that characterised every battle from the Solomon Islands onwards — and, because virtually all these aerial engagments were fought over the sea, the loss of an aircraft usually meant the loss of a pilot.

Thus, by the time the Japanese came to respond to the invasion of Leyte Gulf in 1944, they were desperately short of aircraft and crews, and had aircraft carriers at sea that were down to less than half strength. The Japanese plan for the Battle of Leyte Gulf used this fact alongside the concept, alien to Western cultures, of willing acceptance of suicide as a glorious death for a warrior. Vice-Admiral Ozawa was ordered to take his task force of carriers, only four of which actually had operational aircraft, supported by two battleship-carriers, three light cruisers and eight destroyers, to the East of Luzon as a gigantic decoy. This, it was planned, would lure Vice-Admiral Mitscher's aircraft carrier force out to a battle that was virtually certain to result in the destruction of Ozawa's fleet, but which would cause the invasion force on Leyte to be virtually unprotected. Then, the plan went, Vice-Admirals Kurita and Nishimura would launch a pincer attack against Leyte with their fleets from North-East and South-West.

In the event, although it resulted in the greatest naval battle the world has ever seen, the Japanese scheme did not go entirely to plan. Kurita's 1st Striking Force, the more northerly of the two, ran into

3 Once Peleliu had been cleared of Japanese, a task which took the US Marine Corps two weeks, the guns of the tanks were turned towards the smaller islands of the group, and landings were carried out successfully on September 28th. Once these remaining Japanese positions had been taken, the US forces had captured nine strategically important bases in two weeks.

4 The wreckage of defeat was everywhere on Peleliu — in the foreground is a wrecked Japanese Type 95 Ha-Go light tank, a relatively poorly-armoured vehicle which was armed with one 37mm gun and a single 6·5mm machine gun, and which was by this time an obsolescent weapon, having first entered service in 1935. The aircraft which has been destroyed in the background is less easy to identify, but may be a Mitsubishi G4M bomber.

5 A Japanese destroyer is outlined against the setting sun over Palau after taking a fatal hit amidships. Losses sustained by the Japanese Navy during September, October and November 1944 were on a scale never seen before in the history of naval warfare.

two American submarines, *Dace* and *Darter*, on October 23rd. In a short sharp engagement, Kurita lost the 13,200 ton heavy cruiser *Maya*, which blew up, her sister ship *Takao*, which had to retire from the operation for repairs, and his own flagship, also a 13,200 ton sister ship of *Maya* called the *Atago*, which sank. Nonetheless, bloody but unbowed, Kurita arrived off Mindoro, a Philippine island North-West of Leyte, on the 24th. On hearing of the exploits of the two submarines, Admiral Halsey, who had been tracking the movements of Rear-Admiral Shima's force coming from the North, and of Nishimura's fleet South-West of Leyte, decided that he could leave Vice-Admiral Kinkaid to cope with anything that Shima and Nishimura might offer, and set out with Task Force 38 to deal with Kurita.

During the afternoon of October 24th, Admiral Halsey's aircraft flew more than 250 sorties against Kurita's force, sinking the 64,000 ton battleship *Musashi* and damaging several other smaller warships against heavy anti-aircraft fire, but without significant opposition from Japanese aircraft which were elsewhere attacking the US 3rd Fleet, resulting in the loss on that same day of the 11,000 ton light carrier USS *Princeton*. Believing that he had effectively removed the danger from Kurita's fleet, and still under the impression that Admiral Kinkaid could handle any Japanese activity around Leyte, Halsey now did exactly what the Japanese High Command had hoped he would do — he set off Northwards to intercept what seemed on the face of it to be the main Japanese fleet. This was in fact Admiral Ozawa's half-empty fleet of carriers.

By sailing North, Halsey left the San Bernadino Strait unguarded — apparently because he over-estimated appreciably the extent to which his force had neutralised the potential for attack of Vice-

1

2

3

1 A fine portrait of General Douglas MacArthur, taken in the USA at the end of the war in 1945, which shows something of the spirit and dogged determination which carried him and those under his command through from defeat to victory in the Pacific war.

2 US Navy PT boats add their firepower to that of other US craft to fight off a Japanese air strike at Leyte Gulf during the US invasion of Leyte. Bombs exploding in the water have thrown up geysers of spray in the middle background as the anti-aircraft shells detonate in black puffs of smoke overhead. The Liberty ship in the background was subsequently hit by the bombs, according to the original newsagency caption.

Admiral Kurita's fleet. Although he knew soon afterwards that Kurita had turned back East, he pushed on, believing that Ozawa's fleet represented the more important objective. Vice-Admiral Kinkaid was therefore on his own with his fleet of 42 ships, divided as two Attack Groups, when he first encountered Nishimura's fleet on October 25th. This initial engagement went well for the Americans, the Japanese losing in rapid succession a battleship and three destroyers, and suffering severe damage to the 1917 vintage 35,000 ton battleship *Yamashiro* that was Nishimura's flagship. Despite this setback, *Yamashiro* pushed on with the 12,500 ton cruiser *Mogami* into Leyte Gulf. There they met Rear-Admiral Weyler's six battleships, which sank *Yamashiro*, killing Admiral Nishimura.

Vice-Admiral Shima's force, which had been a few miles behind Nishimura, ran into the same US Navy trap, and was attacked relentlessly by the torpedos of the PT boats and the aircraft of Kinkaid's carriers. By dawn on October 25th, only 2 of his 19 ships had survived.

On the face of it, the Americans had achieved at Surigao overnight a major victory, but they had reckoned without the presence of Kurita and the absence of Halsey. For Kurita was now hell bent on the destruction of the US Navy in Leyte Gulf, and by 7am that same morning Kurita's modern, fast and heavily armed fleet was off Samar Island shelling the nearest ships of the much slower and more lightly-armed American fleet in Leyte Gulf — Rear-Admiral Sprague's Task Force 77.4. Despite the Americans' situation being apparently hopeless, the US Navy fought hard and well against an adversary which, fortunately for them, seemed to lack a cohesive plan of attack or any direction. The American commanders created

as much confusion as possible by laying smoke, and thereby heightened the misdirection of effort of the Japanese fleet. Nonetheless, the Japanese advantage was colossal, and the escort carrier *Gambier Bay*, the destroyer *Samuel B. Roberts*, the *Johnston* and the *Hoel* were lost. Remarkably, however, the Japanese did not have it all their own way, for they lost the cruisers *Chokai* and *Chikuma* and the *Kumano*. But it seemed that the Japanese could not fail to defeat the US Task Force in the end, so severely outnumbered were the US ships.

Then, at almost 9.30am, the Japanese ships turned tail and retreated, apparently because they were sufficiently confused to believe that they were in battle with Halsey's Task Force 38 after all. Whether they were actually confused, or whether there were other reasons that have never come to light we shall probably never know, but by retreating from the Battle of Leyte Gulf, Vice-Admiral Kurita cost the Japanese their best chance of a victory in 1944. Later that same day, October 25th, Admiral Kinkaid's fleet had to contend with a new menace — the infamous *Kamikaze* attacks. Fanatical pilots flew suicide missions in aircraft loaded with explosive and converted, in effect, into piloted bombs. Dived directly at the deck and superstructure of an Allied ship, the *Kamikaze* aircraft was a formidable weapon. During the 25th, one such attack hit and sank the escort carrier *Saint Lo*, and five other suicide attacks caused substantial damage to a further five ships. *Kamikaze*, incidentally, literally translated as 'Divine Wind', was the name given in the Middle Ages to a storm that saved Japan from invasion by blowing away enemy ships. The symbolism was apposite.

The battle off Samar Island cost the US Navy 5 ships, 23 aircraft

3 An armada of landing ships (LSTs) pouring army equipment ashore at Tacloban airstrip on Leyte Island during the invasion.

4 This dramatic picture was shot as a Japanese suicide pilot attempted to fly his *Zeke* (Zero) fighter, packed with high explosive, into the deck structures of an American warship, blowing the gun emplacement and himself to pieces. Experience showed that this was a surprisingly difficult feat, because of the speed at which the aircraft was obliged to fly, and this pilot, like many others, missed, crashing and exploding his aircraft in the sea. Nonetheless, a great many hits were scored by the so-called 'kamikaze' aircraft, and, in April 1945, a kamikaze strike on the US hospital ship *Comfort* caused the deaths of twenty-nine people with thirty-three injured.

4

5

and 2,043 men killed or wounded. Far to the North, Admiral Halsey was about to do battle with what was left of Ozawa's fleet, and early in the morning on October 26th the first of six attacks totalling 527 sorties took off. By mid-day, the Japanese fleet had lost 4 carriers either sunk or put out of commission, including the 25,675 ton *Zuikaku*, completed in 1941, the last remaining carrier of those that had launched the attack on Pearl Harbour. During the afternoon another Japanese carrier went to the bottom.

Taking all the engagements of the Battle of Leyte Gulf together, it was undoubtedly the greatest naval battle in history by tonnage (just over 2 million tons of warship employed), although the Battle of Jutland brought together ten more ships than the 244 at Leyte Gulf. The Japanese lost an incredible 306,000 tons to the US Navy's losses of 37,000 tons. The way to the final re-conquest of the Philippines was open.

6

5 Following the loss of the USS *Lexington* during the Battle of the Coral Sea in May 1942, a new *Essex* Class carrier was given the name *Lexington*. Luckier than her predecessor, she survived a torpedo in the stern during the Marshalls campaign, and here is seen, in a remarkable pair of pictures, being hit by a Japanese kamikaze attack. The top picture shows (albeit indistinctly) the suicide aircraft nearing the end of its dive on to the ship's deck; in the lower, a column of smoke rises from the ship's island after the hit.

6 The Japanese sent reinforcements to Ormoc, and this transport ship was part of a supplies convoy, on its way to the Japanese stronghold, which was attacked by American B-25 aircraft. The American aircraft sank three transports and six escort vessels and damaged several more.

MacArthur's Promise Finally Fulfilled

The efforts of the US Navy in Leyte Gulf had ensured that the Japanese fleet's original objective of being able to attack the US invasion of Leyte in force could not be fulfilled. As a result, the initial American landing was successful, the Marines' stores and vehicles were put ashore without serious losses, and the beach-head was established on a broad front by nightfall on the first day ashore. General MacArthur made a (justifiably) emotional broadcast to the people of the Philippines announcing his return, and asked the population of the islands to rise against the Japanese and assist the Americans with the reconquest of their homeland.

General Makino's 16th Division was ordered by General Yamashita to hold the airfields at all costs so that two more divisions and a brigade could be flown in from Luzon, to the North. Makino's orders were to hold a line well back from the coast and, by November 2nd, MacArthur's 6th Army of 183,000 men had advanced well inland and had captured all of the available coastal airstrips. During November, heavy USAAF and US Navy attacks on Japanese convoys

1 Its flight deck packed with US Navy fighters and fighter-bombers, one of the US *Essex* Class carriers moves forward to the next engagement as part of a carrier task force in 1944. On the deck are Grumman Hellcats, Curtis Helldivers, and Grumman-designed but General Motors-built Avengers. Other carriers are visible in the background – another *Essex* Class carrier in the lead, and light carriers following.

2 Aboard a US aircraft carrier hit by bombs from Japanese aircraft, fire-fighters struggle to control the flames from blazing aircraft during the battle for the Philippines. This shot is a still from a US Navy documentary film, *Brought to Action*.

3 Despite the inevitable damage brought about by the retaking of the Philippines, the population were undoubtedly pleased to see the return of the Americans after years of occupation by Japan. Here, a column of American amphibious carriers and their crews pause along a road in Binmaley, Luzon, and mingle with the local people.

bringing men and equipment to Leyte succeeded in reducing the effectiveness of the Japanese High Command's attempt to reinforce the island, but did not prevent them quadrupling the number of defenders to 60,000 — still less than a third of the strength of the US 6th Army. Yamashita decided to counter-attack, and to launch his assault by destroying the airfields that the Americans were using to supply the army.

A series of misadventures made several attempts by army demolition engineers and parachutists to land and destroy the installations almost farcical, and not until December 7th did the Japanese Army manage to put down a paratroop attack in any force. Even that fizzled out after two nights of fighting. The situation began to look like a stalemate, and with MacArthur's original optimistic date of December 20th for the invasion of Luzon already deferred, delay could not be tolerated. General Walter Krueger, commanding the 6th Army, decided to make a second landing at Ormoc with the objective of dividing the enemy force and weakening its resistance. When the US 77th Division came ashore on December 7th they met virtually no resistance, and by December 10th they had taken Ormoc, the principal Japanese base on Leyte, before General Suzuki could reach and reinforce it from his former position opposing the original landing.

By December 20th the two American forces had joined up, and on December 25th they took Palompon, the last significant port on the island. Although organised Japanese army resistance was over, Yamashita had ordered his countrymen to fight to the death while he concentrated on the defence of Luzon. Thus isolated skirmishes continued on Leyte until the end of March. The capture of the island had cost the US Army over 15,500 casualties, including more than 3,500 killed.

The Assault on Luzon

On December 15th, while the battles on Leyte were still being fought to their close, the small US 'Western Visayan Task Force' under Brigadier-General Dunckel had landed on and taken unopposed the small island of Mindoro to build two airstrips for the assault on Luzon. By Christmas, they were in use, building up the aircraft that were to support the January landing on the principal island of the Philippines.

On Luzon itself, General Yamashita had 250,000 men of the 14th Area Army, but only 150 aircraft. Although his force seemed adequate for the defence of the island at first sight, it must be remembered that the great damage inflicted upon the Japanese fleet during the recent Battle of Leyte Gulf and in earlier encounters had removed virtually all possibility of reinforcement from the sea. Like Hitler's Germany, thousands of miles away in Europe, Japan was, and was looking, a spent force. Nonetheless, MacArthur's army faced the prospect of defeating a quarter of a million Japanese soldiers

4 Smoke rises from the *Casablanca* Class Escort Carrier USS *Ommaney Bay* after she was attacked and disabled by Japanese gunfire off the Philippines during the battles to retake the islands. The *Casablanca* Class were the first vessels to be built as escort carriers from the keel up – earlier escorts had been essentially conversions of existing designs. USS *Ommaney Bay* was scuttled on 4th January 1945.

whose culture and commander alike demanded that they die for their country rather than surrender.

To achieve that defeat, the US 6th Army under General Walter Krueger had almost 200,000 men with plenty in reserve, and the resources of Admiral Kinkaid's 7th Fleet of over 850 ships. The plan for the invasion required that the 6th Army land on the broad open beaches of Lingayen Gulf and then establish rapidly a large beachhead on the central plain of Luzon. This opens immediately beyond the beaches, and leads directly to Manila, the capital of the Philippines. General Yamashita, a veteran of amphibious landings, decided not to attempt to repel the Americans on the beaches, but to position his entire army in the high ground surrounding the central plain of the island, and thereby fence the invaders into their beachhead. He also issued orders that the new *Kamikaze* weapon was to be used to the greatest possible extent against the US Fleet that brought the invasion.

Thus, when Vice-Admiral Jessie Oldendorf's battle-fleet sailed for Luzon on January 2nd to begin the bombardment prior to the landing, the *Kamikaze* attacks were vicious, frequent and damaging. On January 4th, the escort carrier *Ommaney Bay* was lost. On the 5th, eleven American and Australian ships including two escort carriers, two cruisers and two destroyers were hit and damaged. On the 6th, as Oldendorf's ships reached Lingayen, the *Kamikaze* attacks reached a shattering climax as two battleships, three cruisers, three destroyers and several other ships were damaged. Fortunately the next day saw successful attacks by Halsey's carrier-borne aircraft against the airfields of Luzon, which were so badly hit that all the Japanese aircraft left on the island were withdrawn.

Now Oldendorf's bombardment, for which the men of his fleet had endured so much, could begin. For three days the guns roared and the bombs dropped on the invasion zone. On January 9th the troops of the 6th Army went in expecting their toughest reception yet — but, because Yamashita had chosen not to fight on the beaches,

there was not a Japanese in sight. Quickly, the army capitalised on its good fortune, got its supplies ashore and established its beachhead. By nightfall the 6th Army had secured an area seventeen miles wide and, in some places, four miles deep. General MacArthur had landed too — this was one day he had no intention of missing.

Now the 6th Army was to fight as two Corps, one (I Corps) under Major-General Swift with the task of securing the left flank of the proposed path of advance, the other under Major-General Griswold to advance to and take Manila. Krueger's orders to Griswold were to bide his time until Swift had tackled the immediate opposition in the high hinterland beyond the plain — the 'Shobu' Group, made up of 152,000 of Yamashita's men well dug-in along a 25 mile line. Swift found the battle tough going, but made gradual progress, and by the end of January had pushed Yamashita's troops back into the mountains, had cut across the island to the Eastern shore, and had

5 Most of them barefoot, some carrying young children, women pick their way through the wreckage of North Manila after escaping from the centre of the city, where the battle still raged, and reaching the comparative safety of the American-held side of the Pasig River. The women are accompanied by a Catholic sister from an Inthamuros convent, who carries a motherless infant born less than three days before.

6 Back in the Bataan Peninsula after three hard-fought years, General Douglas MacArthur is surrounded by battle-hardened troops as he looks reflectively at the dead representatives of the empire that brought so much pain to his beloved Philippines.

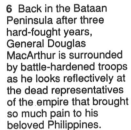

297

thereby cut Yamashita's communications with a large part of his army. Meanwhile, Griswold had begun to advance in the wake of Swift's gradual success, with little trouble or opposition in the early stages.

The Liberation of Manila

By January 17th MacArthur was pressing for faster progress towards Manila, partly to be able to take over and use Clark Field for air operations, partly to liberate the ill-treated prisoners of the Japanese. As Griswold attempted to comply he ran into another smaller group of Yamashita's troops, the 'Kembu' Group, made up of 30,000 men, whose task was specifically to prevent the Americans gaining access to Clark Field. The fighting was bitter, but by January 31st the 'Kembu' Group was beaten back into the mountains, American troops were cleaning up Clark Field, and Griswold had resumed his drive on Manila.

Meanwhile more troops had landed on Luzon at fresh invasion points — XI Corps on the West coast above Bataan Peninsula, part of the 11th Airborne at Nasugbu Bay, 50 miles South-West of Manila,

and the rest of the 11th Airborne on February 3rd at Tagaytay Ridge, well inland and South-West of the capital. As the combined strengths of the American forces now on the island converged on the capital the Japanese resistance strengthened to the point where it was all the Americans could do not to retreat. No further progress was being made from the southerly side of the city.

Realising the position even before it had fully developed, MacArthur had therefore given the 37th US Infantry and the 1st US Cavalry the unenviable task of taking Manila from the North. By February 3rd, real progress was being made, as the 1st Cavalry liberated the Santo Tomas civilian internment camp, and the 37th Infantry opened up another prison and freed 1,300 civilians and prisoners of war. But at that point progress stopped. Detachments of naval troops had been ordered to defend Manila to the last, regardless of the damage this would do to its ancient buildings, and, after a week's reluctance to embark on shelling and street fighting, the Americans began what was to prove to be the only street battle of the Pacific War.

1 With the words, reported all over the world 'Well; I'm home again', General MacArthur visited the rubble of what had been his home on Corregidor until the Japanese invasion of 1942. This picture was taken during his first visit to the island after it was recaptured in mid-February 1945.

2 General MacArthur had the gifts, unusual among successful soldiers, of being also an adroit politician, an excellent administrator and a man to whom most of those with whom he dealt warmed and became friendly. In this picture he greets Sergio Osmena, President of the Philippines, at the capitol building in Tacloban, before the liberation of Manila.

The fighting was fierce and bloody, and took a terrible toll of civilians, whom the Japanese refused to allow to leave the city. Not until March 3rd was Manila finally taken, and by then it was a city in ruins, with over 100,000 of its civilian population dead. Over 6,500 Americans were killed or wounded to take the city. Virtually every one of the 17,000 Japanese Navy men defending it died.

By the third week of March 1945, the Bataan Peninsula had been cleared of Japanese troops, the Japanese defenders on the island of Corregidor having capitulated on the 28th of February after two weeks of bitter fighting. Not until mid-April was the centre of Luzon and Manila Bay officially clear of enemy influence, but even then there were still almost 200,000 Japanese troops on the island, still commanded by Yamashita, and holding the North and South-East of Luzon.

General Krueger's first target was the 'Shimbu' Group, which had given General Swift so much trouble, and which was now dug in East of Manila. The battle to dislodge General Yokohama's 80,000 troops was to prove long and arduous. By the end of March, General Griswold's troops had managed to penetrate Yokohama's army and divide it into two groups, but not until the end of May was the 'Shimbu' Group finally annihilated. During the same period, three other Groups of Japanese had been wearisomely attacked, worn down and defeated, and the South of Luzon was clear by the end of May. But still there remained the largest and most fearsome Group of all — that commanded by Yamashita himself, and consisting of 110,000 dedicated troops in the North of the island. After a month of unremitting fighting through June, an Airborne Division landing and many men's lives lost, Yamashita still had 65,000 men under his command in his mountain stronghold. There they stayed for the remaining weeks of the war, the only Japanese to succeed in holding any part of the Philippines until their Emperor bade them leave.

CHAPTER 38

THE GERMAN RETREAT
FROM THE BALTIC AND THE BALKANS

The last four months of 1944 in Eastern Europe were increasingly disastrous for the Third Reich and its armies, as Russian fire and air power became progressively more dominant over a diminished, tired and ill-equipped German *Wehrmacht*, and as Hitler's orders, directives and responses to events became ever more irrational, dangerous and bizarre. In telling the story of such a confused period affecting the futures of several countries and millions of people, one must inevitably generalise, but to retain some measure of clarity the text of this chapter is divided into sections, with one section per country.

Finland

The passionately fought Winter War of 1940, in which Finland had faced the Russian aggressor with such determination and had then been obliged to accept armistice terms requiring the loss of a significant part of her country to Russia, had left the Finns with little option but to accept German overtures to ally themselves with Germany for the assault on Russia. The alliance was shaky and incomplete, and the Finns flatly refused to take part in the Siege of Leningrad and other punitive operations. As

the Soviet forces gained the upper hand over the *Wehrmacht* and drove it back Westwards, Finland looked likely once more to be the subject of the unwelcome attentions of the Soviet Union.

During the summer of 1944, war came once more to the Isthmus of Karelia, and once again the Finns put up fierce resistance to Russian incursion. In an effort to acquire the arms to sustain the fight against the Soviet Union, President Ryti allowed himself to be blackmailed by Ribbentrop into signing a document confirming Finland's unconditional alliance with Germany. By the end of July it was clear that Finland's best hope lay in the betrayal of this document, which had in any case been signed under duress, and President Ryti was replaced by the 77-year-old Marshal Mannerheim, who negotiated an armistice with the Soviet Union. The ceasefire came on September 5th.

One of the conditions of the armistice was the removal of all *Wehrmacht* troops from Finland by September 14th, or their internment by Finland thereafter. Because General Vogel's XXXVI Mountain Corps, part of Colonel-General Rendulic's 20th Army, was over 600 miles from the nearest Finnish border, it was clearly not possible to get them out of Finland by the deadline. As Mannerheim

3 In the Baltic States, the Soviet Army had been making progress against the German Army Group North throughout the winter of 1943/44 – here an advance patrol of the Red Army on the Estonian border in February 1944 is advancing cautiously against German positions. By autumn 1944, the Germans in Latvia and Estonia were cut off and could not escape defeat.

4 As winter 1944/45 set in, the Russians of the 3rd Belorussian Front were advancing into Poland from Lithuania to the northeast, as their compatriots of the 1st and 2nd Belorussian Fronts pushed westwards into Poland further South. This wounded Soviet soldier was given first aid in his foxhole as other troops continued firing on the border of Lithuania and Poland.

3

4

sought means of interning them, Hitler, true to form, ordered the *Kriegsmarine* to attack the Finnish island of Sur Sari in the Gulf of Finland in an attempt to provide a temporary haven for German troops. The assault took place on September 14th and 15th, and was a disaster for the Germans. Over 300 men were killed or wounded, and 1,000 were forced to surrender.

Over the next month, there was fierce fighting in several parts of Finland. Mannerheim's troops attempted to prevent the Germans escaping from the area around the Gulf of Bothnia into occupied Norway, but eventually had to allow them to retreat into safety in mid-October, leaving a trail of devastated villages and destroyed bridges behind them. In Finnish Lapland, Colonel-General Rendulic attempted to retain the base at Petsamo and the nickel mines at Kolosjoki for Germany, but was attacked on October 7th by the Russian Karelian Front under General Meretskov. By October 15th, the Russians had captured Petsamo, and had also carried on into Norway and captured Lyngenfjord. By the armistice between

The German Retreat

Finland and Russia, signed on 19th September, and by the force of subsequent events, Finland had now lost her access to the Atlantic, via Petsamo, and the valuable nickel mines of the region.

Lithuania and Estonia

The advance of the Soviet armies towards East Prussia during the summer of 1944 had cut off from Germany and her other armies the unfortunate Colonel-General Schorner and his Army Group North, now retreated to the Baltic States that had been occupied by Germany immediately before the war. In mid-August, Colonel-General Raus and the 3rd *Panzerarmee* managed to counter-attack from the South of General Bagramyan's 1st Baltic Front, and re-established contact with Army Group North near Tukums. Desperately, Colonel-General Guderian, in his recently acquired role of Chief of Staff at OKH, tried to persuade Hitler to permit a withdrawal by Schorner's army while there was a gap through which they could retreat. Hitler refused, his grounds being that a retreat might cause Finland to withdraw from alliance with Germany! Since this had virtually happened anyway, the Fuehrer's reason made little sense.

A month later, on September 24th, Marshal Govarov had captured almost the whole of Estonia, and launched six divisions in an amphibious invasion of the islands of the Gulf of Riga, held by two German divisions. After a spirited and hopelessly outnumbered defence lasting almost two months, the German divisions were successfully evacuated by the *Kriegsmarine* under cover of fire from the *Lutzow*, *Scheer* and several cruisers. Six weeks earlier, soldiers of General Eremenko's 3rd Baltic Front had taken Riga, the capital of Latvia, on October 13th. As long before as August 21st, Guderian had instructed Schorner to reinforce the port of Memel because he

of crack German troops busy for almost two months until the insurgents were driven into the Low Tatra mountains in October.

On September 8th, following a declaration of war against Bulgaria on September 5th, the Russians entered Bulgaria and took the port of Varna. On the same day, the 8th, the Bulgarian government declared war on Germany in an effort to counter the Russian attack, and launched its 5th Army, commanded by General Stanchev, against Germany. This army was well equipped with German weapons, including the 88mm anti-aircraft and anti-tank gun, and had 88 German PzKpfw 4 tanks. It became the left wing of Marshal Tolbukhin's army, and was given the task of cutting the retreat of the German army as it made its way from the Balkans.

Rumania

But the major interest in this area of the Balkans centred on Rumania. After Russia's defeat of German troops at Stalingrad, the Rumanian opposition forces had secretly contacted Great Britain and the United States, and a revolutionary plan had been formulated against the day when it could be put into effect. Now, as Marshal Antonescu, who had taken Rumania into active participation in the Axis war, organised with Hitler's staff the defence of Rumania against the Russian advance, King Michael I of Rumania and the leader of the National Peasants' Party, Julius Maniu, planned to unseat Antonescu and turn the tide of Rumanian action against Germany.

This was potentially much more significant for Germany's ability to resist the Soviet advance than similar events in other Balkan countries simply because of the level of commitment and integration of Rumanian troops into the German armies. Of the four Armies making up the two sections of the German Army Group South

was certain that the Russians would attempt to take it and isolate Army Group North again. Schorner did not accept Guderian's reasoning, and disobeyed the order. On October 5th, he had cause to regret it.

General Bagramyan attacked the weak defences along the road to Memel with 500 tanks and, meeting inadequate resistance, averaged 15 miles per day to reach the Baltic at Palanga in just six days. The 26 Divisions of Army Group North were largely cut off from German supplies and were isolated. Defeat was inevitable.

Hungary, Bulgaria and Czechoslovakia

Throughout the second half of 1944, Soviet troops of the 2nd and 3rd Ukrainian Fronts fought their way through the Balkan states. From August 20th, when the 2nd Ukrainian front attacked Iasi, capital of Moldavia, through to the siege of Budapest at Christmas, the German Army was gradually pushed back. As the Russian conquests moved Westwards, the Bulgarian government announced on August 26th that it was withdrawing from the war, and set about disarming German garrisons. On August 29th, a German move to take over the puppet state of Slovakia to prevent similar action sparked off a Slovak national uprising that kept significant numbers

Ukraine and defending Rumania, two were Rumanian, and had sworn an oath to their king. Although it might be argued that for some considerable time they had not been discharging that oath effectively, King Michael was confident that loyalty of the Rumanian rank and file to Germany was less than their loyalty to him.

So, on August 23nd, Michael called Antonescu and his Minister for Foreign Affairs to his palace and ordered them to conclude an immediate armistice with the Allies. They did not agree, and were immediately arrested. That evening, Radio Bucharest broadcast an order to all Rumanian troops to cease fire, which caused Colonel-General Friessner, in command of Army Group South Ukraine, to telephone Generals Dumitrescu and Steflea, who commanded the two Rumanian Armies in the German line. Both refused to disobey their king's orders.

Because of this turn of events, Hitler took characteristically rash and ill-considered action, and ordered the bombing of Bucharest. This gave the new Prime Minister of Rumania, General Sanatescu, good reason to declare war on Germany, which he did on August 25th. Rumanian troops occupied the bridges over the Danube, the Prut and the Siretul and opened them to the advancing Russians, who speedily cut off the German 6th Army in a gigantic pincer movement.

1 The German preoccupation with unconventional weapons produced, among other things, a variety of multi-barrelled rocket launchers to fire solid-fuel rockets, usually of 15cm calibre. These 10-barrelled self-propelled launchers are a late development – earlier in the war a simpler 6-barrelled launcher with the 15cm tubes arranged in a circle on a light trailer was known as the *Nebelwerfer*, because the troops manning the secret weapon had been code-named *Nebeltruppen*, or smoke troops, to disguise the fact that they were equipped with rockets. The rocket itself was a masterpiece of German ingenuity, having the propulsion motor in the nose and the explosive charge at the rear end, with a ring of venturi around the middle of the rocket to provide for the blast of the motor.

2 A Red Army anti-tank gun crew of the Second Ukrainian Front under Senior Sergeant A. Orel in action on the outskirts of the village of Brissuleny, near Falticeni in Rumania. The Rumanian declaration of war on Germany on August 25th following the bombing of Bucharest greatly increased the speed of the Soviet advance because so many 'German' troops in Rumania were in fact Rumanian.

Fourteen German divisions were annihilated, and only two of the divisional commanders escaped without being killed or captured. The German 8th Army fared little better, for its IV Corps was forced to surrender. Colonel-General Friessner had lost 16 of his 24 divisions in just two weeks.

Albania and Greece

The change of loyalties of the Rumanian Army brought a speedy order to Army Group E in Greece at the end of August to begin an evacuation of the Aegean and Ionian islands and of the mainland, but Bulgaria's declaration of war on Germany early in September caused a further change of plan. Now Hitler's instruction to Colonel-General Lohr was to retreat to what had in 1939 been the frontier between Bulgaria and Yugoslavia. There he was to join up with General de Angelis' 2nd *Panzerarmee* and the tail of Army Group F to protect a corridor through which German troops could retreat, and by which the Danube plain could be defended against the Bulgarian 5th Army, now on the attack.

Some 40,000 of the 60,000 German soldiers on the Greek islands were evacuated, the remainder staying in considerable comfort until the war was over. The unlucky ones were pulled back first to Athens, which was handed over to its Mayor on October 4th, and then to

Yugoslavia. The smooth and relatively untroubled nature of the withdrawal was helped by an undercover agreement between the Germans and the ELAS Communist partisans, by which ELAS undertook not to obstruct the retreat if the Germans left them large quantities of weapons and ammunition.

Back in Greece itself, a British Airborne force had, on October 4th, helped Greek patriots to liberate Patras, and on October 14th a naval squadron made up of both Greek and British ships and commanded by Rear-Admiral Troubridge arrived in Piraeus. There it disembarked Lieutenant-General Scobie and III Corps of the British Army, with specific instructions from the British Government to prevent the overthrow of the Greek regime by communist insurrection. In fact, Scobie was unable to prevent a revolution that was, after an initial success that brought near-peace in February 1945, to drag on for almost four years. Even as he arrived in Greece, the Communist ELAS was straggling across country into Athens bearing the arms that they had so recently acquired by their deal with the Germans. The best that Scobie's British troops could do was to overcome the initial surge to arms, then provide a policing presence – a procedure to which the British Army was to become accustomed during the coming decades.

Yugoslavia

In Yugoslavia, unlike the other Balkan countries, war against the occupying Axis army had been conducted with considerable success for more than three years by Tito and his Partisan Army, despite the British government's politically expedient but misguided belief in, and support of, Mihailović' much smaller and virtually inactive non-communist Četnik army until early in 1944. Tito's Partisan Army had withstood seven major offensives by vastly better equipped and numerically superior German forces, and had aroused the admiration of the world. Nonetheless, Britain, committed to support of the Royal Yugoslav government in exile under King Peter, could not support fully Tito's fight against the Axis until there was some form of agreement between Tito and the government in exile on the form of government in postwar Yugoslavia.

In June 1944, Tito somewhat unwillingly met the leader of the government in exile at the Partisan Army's new headquarters on the island of Vis, off the Dalmatian coast. The government in exile agreed to full support of the Partisan Army, and both agreed to allow the Yugoslav people to determine the question of whether there should continue to be a monarchy after the war. Mihailović was dismissed from his nominal post as Minister for War in the Royalist government,

3 A Soviet T-34 tank of the 2nd Ukrainian Front, heading west through the mountainous region of Transylvania, the historic plateau bounded by the Carpathian Mountains in central Rumania, passes a peasant cart heading away from the unpleasantness of war.

4 In the heady days of 1941, the German occupiers of Czechoslovakia had been able to parade their 'Free Slovak' sympathisers in front of the National Slovak Theatre to celebrate the second anniversary of 'Slovak Liberation'. As the Russians swept into Czechoslovakia, there was little evidence of the Free Slovak movement.

5 A German convoy in the Balkans demonstrates considerable ingenuity in the face of the need to retreat quickly, employing an unlikely combination of vehicles and motive power. Alongside the trucks and battered motor-cycle is a small but heavily-loaded peasant cart, drawn by a horse (partly out of the picture) and a mule in tandem. Beyond the group of soldiers following the cart are more mules.

6 Allied airborne troops landed in Greece on October 4th 1944. A few days before, RAF Spitfires of the Balkan Air Force had landed on the Greek mainland, and in this picture some of the RAF fighter pilots are meeting British Army officers, surrounded by interested spectators from the local population.

and the way was open for Churchill to meet Tito and provide full support for the closing stages of the Partisan campaign. The meeting took place on 12th August in Naples, to which Tito was flown by the RAF. Two weeks later, as the Red Army entered Rumania, Tito suggested that he should visit Stalin, and on 21st September he was flown in a Soviet aircraft to Moscow, where he startled the Soviet leader, not for the last time, by making it quite clear that Yugoslavia was not to become simply a Soviet satellite state, as Stalin expected, and that the Red Army had only the right to fight through Yugoslavia, if need be, not the right of occupation.

As we have seen, General von Löhr's Army Group E, retreating from Greece, sought to establish a defensive line north of Yugoslavia to prevent encirclement by the advancing Red Army. Von Löhr's withdrawal started at the beginning of September 1944, and the Partisan Army, supported by the RAF and the United States Air Force, launched attacks against Axis communications. The Bulgarian army, now fighting against the Axis, had taken Nis, and had thereby barred the German columns' most practical route to the Danube, so the Germans had little choice but to retreat through the length of Yugoslavia. By the end of September, Partisan armies were converging on Belgrade under two of Tito's most successful commanders, Popovic and Dapćević, and two strong Red Army forces advanced from other directions, joining with the Partisans as they approached the city. Desperate to retain their communications southwards until the German retreat was complete, the Germans reinforced the Belgrade garrison with every soldier available, and the battle that followed was as savage as any in Eastern Europe. Not until 20th October did Tito's First Proletarian Division, the elite formation of the Partisan Army, finally drive the Germans from their capital city so that Tito could enter in triumph as his country's liberator.

From Belgrade, the Germans continued their withdrawal as best they could, and within only a few weeks most of the country was free of the Axis presence. Tito's National Committee ruled in Belgrade as the effective government, soon to be ratified as the official government by the Allies and, in March 1945, by King Peter. What remained of the German army of occupation was trapped in Croatia and Slovenia until the German capitulation, and lost almost 100,000 killed and 200,00 wounded during the last two months of the war under furious attacks from the Partisans. On 7th May 1945, General von Löhr was forced to surrender to the Partisans. He expected death at their hands, and was duly executed.

Hungary

The battle to push the German Army Group South out of Hungary rolled on throughout the autumn and winter of 1944 and into the New Year. Once again the unique brand of bizarre incompetence that Hitler had espoused as his own was to play a major part in events, and from the actions he took to defend Budapest were to spring the successes of the Soviet Army in East Prussia and Eastern Germany. When, on October 6th, Marshal Malinovsky's 2nd Ukrainian Front launched its offensive westwards into Hungary, it was opposing 9 corps and 26 divisions of Army Group South. But 14 of those divisions were Hungarian, and Colonel-General Friessner, commanding Army Group South, had grave reservations about their battle-worthiness, doubts that were fully to be realised when they went into action.

Manoeuvring on the vast Hungarian plain, the *Panzer* corps of Friessner's Group were able to use their North African desert experience to the full, and did in fact frequently outmanoeuvre the Russian armour. But so outnumbered were the German troops that no amount of skill could produce a victory. By October 20th, Malinovsky had taken Debrecen. Ten days later, the German High Command announced, with some exaggeration, that Malinovsky had lost over 18,500 men killed or captured, 1,000 tanks and over 900 guns, as a result of an excursion by General Pliev into the Tokay vineyards along the River Tisza and a successful pincer trap pulled on his force. Victory for the German 6th Army though this was, it had been won at an enormous price, for the 6th Army now had only 67 tanks. Nonetheless, it had saved the German 8th Army from being trapped by the Russians.

Now the weight of the offensive shifted away from the German 6th and 8th Armies to the Hungarian 3rd Army, which stood in the way of Malinovsky's 6th Guards Tank Army's approach to Budapest. The offensive began on October 29th, and rapidly overcame the Hungarian Axis defenders. Within days, they were within 40 miles of Budapest itself. The German defence rapidly regrouped, but were desperately short of men and equipment. Hitler decided to reinforce Army Group South for the defence of Budapest, and sent three new *Panzer* divisions and three additional battalions of tanks. But the Soviet Army was also able to call up major reinforcements in the

shape of the 3rd Ukrainian Front following the fall of Belgrade. On November 27th, the Russians went on the offensive again.

From both sides of Budapest, the two Russian Armies, the 2nd and 3rd Ukrainian Fronts, converged on the capital. Throughout the first three weeks of December, the German armies were pushed remorselessly back on two fronts. Just before Christmas, the Germans lost 12,000 dead, over 5,000 prisoners, over 300 tanks and almost 250 guns in a last ditch defence of the small town of Szekesfehervar. Three days later, on December 27th, the two Russian armies met and joined for the final assault that would finally clear the Germans from Hungary. Four days earlier, Colonel-General Friessner and his colleague General Fretter-Pico had been dismissed and disgraced for allowing the Russian armies to triumph, and Friessner was replaced by General Woehler. On Christmas Day, Hitler issued a fateful order that was to have grave consequences for his defence of East Prussia. Because he had designated Budapest a 'fortress', and it could not therefore be allowed to be lost, he transferred two *Panzer* Divsions and a *Panzer* Corps from Army Group Centre's defence of East Prussia, and brought them South to Hungary. In vain did his Generals protest at the danger this presented to Germany. To delay the inevitable in Budapest for just a few weeks, Hitler opened the way for the Russians into the Fatherland.

1 The liberation of Greece was completed by the Allies in just one month, and by November 4th the country was free of German soldiers. On Christmas Day 1944, Britain's Prime Minister, Winston Churchill, and Foreign Secretary, Anthony Eden, flew to Athens to mediate in the Civil War, and on December 30th, Archbishop Damaskinos was appointed Regent. This picture was taken at the peace conference that followed, at which no heat or light was available, so overcoats and hurricane lamps were *de rigeur*. At the right of the table are Eden, Churchill, Damaskinos, and Field Marshal Harold Alexander, C-in-C Mediterranean Theatre.

2 Bitter fighting had taken place between the Yugoslavian partisans and the Germans throughout the troubled occupation of the mountainous country east of the Adriatic. As the partisans sensed victory, their attacks became fiercer – this picture was taken in a mountain village in Dalmatia as a German armoured unit attempted to flush out partisan units who had long since taken to the hills.

CHAPTER 39

REVENGE HITLER'S V-WEAPON TURNED ON BRITAIN

From 1942 onwards, Hitler frequently told those who dared to express doubt in the eventual German victory that the war would be decided by Germany's secret weapons, against which there would be no defence. In fact, among his Staff, the constant assertions about secret weapons that never seemed to materialise became something of a joke. Yet, in strictest secrecy, research was well advanced, and the German Minister for Armaments, Albert Speer, recalled after the war in his book 'Inside the Third Reich' that the first experimental firing of a V2 rocket had taken place on June 13th 1942 — and had almost killed him and the armaments chiefs of all three armed forces in one fell swoop when it went out of control and crashed back to earth half a mile from where they stood. On October 14th 1942, Speer told Hitler that the second test firing had gone perfectly, and on December 22nd 1942, Hitler signed an order for their mass production.

Rumours and fragments of information about German research into new and terrible means of creating death and destruction were, by the beginning of 1943, reaching Allied intelligence through Resistance and espionage sources so frequently that it was clear that something was afoot. In the spring of 1943, the Polish Home Army obtained information about a secret establishment at Peenemunde,

on an island named Usedom at the mouth of the River Oder. A Polish engineer studied the evidence and decided that it could mean only that Germany was experimenting with rockets and techniques of jet propulsion. The Poles, at enormous risk to themselves, sent the information through to London. At about the same time, British Intelligence received from occupied Denmark a photograph taken by a Danish officer of a small pilotless monoplane with what seemed to be a jet engine mounted above the fuselage — the shape that was to become known to millions of long-suffering British and Belgian civilians as the flying bomb, nicknamed by Londoners the doodle-bug, and correctly designated the V1.

The V1 that had crashed without exploding on the island of Bornholm had been photographed, and the picture provided British Intelligence with confirmation that the Poles were on to something. A hazardous reconnaissance sortie photographed the Peenemunde site from the air, and the results made it clear that action was needed. On 17th July 1943, 600 bombers launched a major raid on Peenemunde, doing damage that postwar evidence confirmed had set back German rocket development substantially. Later that summer, an experimental launching ramp for the V1 was built in Poland near Blizna, and test launchings of the V1 went ahead in

3 The sinister silhouette that Londoners, and later the inhabitants of Antwerp and Brussels, came to dread – a V1 Flying Bomb, the hated 'doodlebug' pilotless aircraft, burbling its way towards an almost random target anywhere within a 15-mile radius of Tower Bridge. Note the flame from the ram-jet engine above the fuselage.

4 The most successful of various designs for civilian air raid shelters in Britain was the Anderson shelter. It was usually based on a crude concrete platform with a well in the centre, sunk into a suburban back garden with the level of the platform below ground level, although some were simply erected over a pit. An arch of corrugated iron was erected over the well, as the workmen in the far garden are doing, and a face plate with a rectangular entrance was fitted to it. Earth was heaped over the whole shelter to bury it and provide protection against blast, and a mound of earth was usually built in front of the doorway to protect against frontal blast and shrapnel. Bunks were installed along the walls inside. Whole families spent every night for months in Anderson shelters like these – the author remembers lying in a bunk in one as a child listening to bombs exploding.

5 An anti-aircraft battery in England, positioned just south of London, photographed during its nightly duel with Hitler's pilotless weapons during July 1944. The gun is silhouetted against the intense fire caused by the explosion of a V1 Flying Bomb that it has shot down with shellfire.

3

4

5

profusion. The ever-vigilant Polish Resistance rapidly discovered the site, and by studying it and the missile launchings guessed that the device could have a range of some 200 miles. The Home Army collected fragments of flying bombs that had exploded, and were able to determine where they had been built — information which was passed to London and became the basis for targetting raids of the mounting Allied bomber offensive. But the Poles' greatest coup came when an unexploded V1 settled in the mud of the River Bug.

At enormous risk, the intrepid Poles removed its wings (which had been showing above the water) so that the Germans could not find their lost secret weapon. At a suitable moment, Polish engineers recovered most of the bomb (although sadly not the warhead) and smuggled it in small pieces to Warsaw, from where the results of detailed examination were sent to the Polish government in exile in London. This excited the British and American scientists enough for them to decide to collect the prize from occupied Poland. In an extraordinarily risky and yet successful operation, a Douglas DC3 'Dakota' was flown from Italy and landed in a muddy Polish field. Several days later, the crew and the Polish resistance men together managed to ungum the Dakota from the mud, and Germany's secret weapon was flown to England.

As a result of this acquisition, the Allied scientists and defence chiefs knew with considerable accuracy, by the time the Flying Bombs came to be used in earnest, what the weapon could do and how it worked. They knew its range. But they did not know Hitler's plans, or when the weapon would be ready.

The Battle of London

A combination of Allied raids on the 96 original V1 launching ramps and the natural delays that all new technologies are heir to had made Hitler's new revenge weapons late. Not until a week after the D-Day invasion in Normandy were the first V1 Flying Bombs launched against London. On June 13th 1944, three V1 weapons reached Britain's capital. One landed in the East London area of Bethnal Green, killing six and injuring nine people. The other two, by sheer good fortune, caused no casualties. But this was no more than a foretaste. Two days later, on June 15th, the Germans began their second great campaign to smash London and the Londoners' morale — christened some weeks later 'The Battle of London'. No less than 244 V1 Flying Bombs were launched in that one twenty-four hour period, of which 144 crossed the English coast and 72 exploded in Greater London.

1 The semi-detached and terraced houses of London's suburbs were no match for the considerable power of nearly a ton of high explosive carried by the V1 bombs. A direct hit would normally bring total destruction to at least two houses, and often wrecked as many as six, with considerable damage to others for hundreds of yards around. Many suburban areas had more broken windows than whole ones.

2 General Sir Frederick Pile, General Officer Commanding Anti-Aircraft Command in Britain, photographed beside a new 'rocket gun' during March 1944. The corporal on the gun is a member of the Home Guard, the UK part-time home army of men who were unfit for military service, or who were in reserved occupations vital to the war effort.

3 Atop a huge pile of rubble that had been, until the night before, a London block of apartments, rescue workers tackle the colossal task of digging for the victims of the attack. At the time this picture was taken there were still many dead beneath the debris.

The Commander of 12 Group RAF, Air Marshal Roderic Hill, now faced a major task, quite unlike any that Fighter Command RAF had faced previously. He put into action Operation Overlord/Diver, an extensively planned defence exercise designed to combat pilotless bombs with RAF fighter aircraft in close co-operation with Anti-Aircraft Command and Balloon Command. Eight day-fighter squadrons — flying Spitfires, Tempests and Typhoons — and four Mosquito night fighter squadrons were allotted to that task of destroying the Flying Bombs. To them, in August 1944, would be added the first of the Gloster Meteor I jet fighters, the Allies' first operational jet aircraft.

On Sunday June 18th, a V1 scored a direct hit on the Guards Chapel at Wellington Barracks, close to Buckingham Palace, Westminster Abbey and the Houses of Parliament. Nearly two hundred Guardsmen and many civilians were killed or wounded. As the weeks of June wore on, every part of London was hit, but the areas South of the Thames and in direct line between the German launch ramps in the Pas de Calais and Tower Bridge, upon which all the bombs were theoretically aimed, took the brunt of the attack. The aiming of the V1 was inherently crude, and a fifteen mile radius of error was normal, with undershooting of the target more common

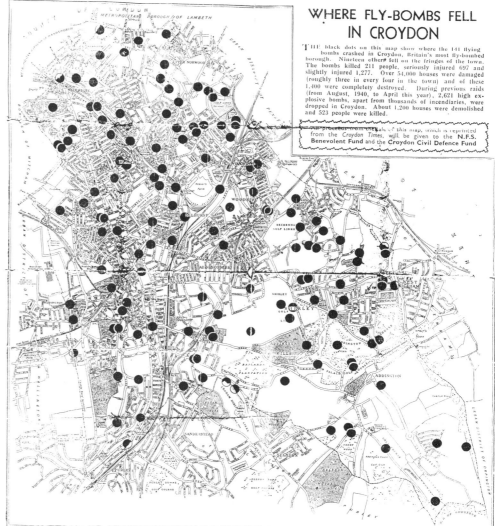

WHERE FLY-BOMBS FELL IN CROYDON

THE black dots on this map show where the 141 flying bombs crashed in Croydon, Britain's most fly-bombed borough. Nineteen others fell on the fringes of the town. The bombs killed 211 people, seriously injured 697 and slightly injured 1,277. Over 54,000 houses were damaged (roughly three in every four in the town) and of these 1,400 were completely destroyed. During previous raids (from August, 1940, to April this year), 2,621 high explosive bombs, apart from thousands of incendiaries, were dropped in Croydon. About 1,200 houses were demolished and 523 people were killed.

All proceeds from the sale of this map, which is reprinted from the *Croydon Times*, will be given to the N.F.S. Benevolent Fund and the Croydon Civil Defence Fund

than overshooting. Thus the suburban boroughs within 10 miles or so of the river to the South were badly hit.

Worst hit of all was Croydon, some twelve miles from central London, where the author lived as a child at the time. Some idea of the concentration of the attack can be gained from the map of the Croydon area — 141 fell on the borough, destroying totally 1,400 houses, and damaging 54,000 more (75% of all the houses in the borough). Most explosions killed or maimed a considerable number of civilians; in Croydon, 211 people were killed, 697 were seriously injured and 1,277 slightly injured by V1 attacks.

London's anti-aircraft defences fought back strongly, but shooting a bomb down over London merely served to fulfil German inten-

tions, so other means were sought. It was soon found that the V1, with a speed of slightly more than 400mph, outpaced all available fighter aircraft except the newly introduced Hawker Tempest V, which, with its 2,180hp Napier Sabre engine had a maximum speed in level flight of 436mph. Roderic Hill's 12 Group, which attempted initially to attack the V1 Bombs with Spitfires and Typhoons as well as the Tempest, found that attempting to shoot down the V1 was both unreliable and hazardous — at 400yds the V1, with a wingspan of only 17.5 feet, presented too small a target; at 200 yds the attacking aircraft was likely to be destroyed along with its target as the 1,870 lb of high explosive in the V1 blew up. Nonetheless, many were detonated in the air by cannon fire. However, the RAF pilots devised

4 The horrifying extent of the casualties of the V1 Flying Bomb attack during the Battle of London brought rapid action in the form of the opening to the public of five deep shelters with sleeping accommodation for a total of 40,000 people. These were in existing service tunnels running beneath the underground railway lines. Into the tunnels went medical posts, canteens and control rooms, plus the inevitable radio sets and gramophones, which provided the music for the unquenchable cheerfulness of Londoners under pressure.

5 The rapid progress of the Allied armies across Northern France after the Normandy invasion brought an end to the worst of the V1 attacks in September 1944, when the principal launching areas in the Pas de Calais were captured. For most readers of British and American newspapers, pictures like these were the first that had been seen of more or less intact V1s on the ground. This particular V1 had crashed after launching. The circular, football-like object is one of the fuel tanks that were contained in the rear part of the fuselage.

1

2

3

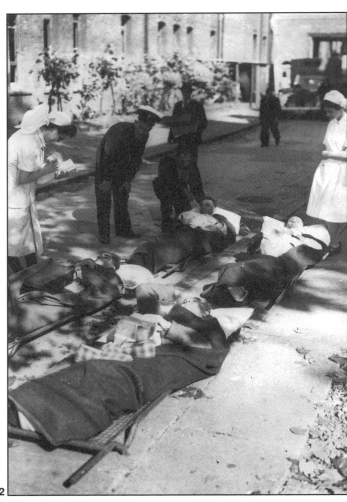

4

1 Many of the buildings partly destroyed by Hitler's bombs in London had subsequently to be demolished because there was no way of making the old structure safe. Many women worked on the demolition squads – here one of the brave ladies of London takes a drink while working to improve the city's landscape.

2 During July 1944, several London hospitals were hit due to the near-random targetting of the V1 bombs. This picture was released on 6th July and shows uninjured but sick patients who had been evacuated from the damaged hospitals awaiting collection by ambulances.

3 Far to the South, as General Patton's Third Army swept into Germany, these American soldiers had the opportunity of inspecting an underground Flying Bomb factory at Thil, near Metz. The factory was located in an iron ore mine, and had been in full-scale production for four months until it was captured. The soldiers are looking at nosecone sections, stacked awaiting assembly.

4 This picture was taken in December 1944, a few minutes after a Flying Bomb struck the outskirts of a Dutch town – the original caption did not specify which town for censorship reasons.

a precision flying technique by which the airflow over the upper surface of a Tempest's wing, positioned only inches below the wing of the Flying Bomb, disturbed the aerodynamic performance of the VI's wings sufficiently to tip the bomb over and send it crashing into the sea. In one way or the other, RAF fighters, mainly Tempests, accounted for more than a third of the VIs that were destroyed before they reached London and its suburbs.

But before that technique could be developed, urgent means had to be found to reduce the number of VIs reaching their London targets. Allied bombers were remorselessly bombing the underground storage caverns in Northern France in which the bombs were kept until launching, and were achieving significant reductions in the number launched. Nonetheless, large numbers were still crossing the Channel. By June 21st, all the central London anti-aircraft defences had been moved to the North Downs, some twenty miles South of the capital. Barrage balloons floated over the Southern edges of London, and succeeded in trapping 232 VIs during the course of the Battle. By July 6th, Winston Churchill was reporting to Parliament that 2,754 bombs had so far been launched against London, that "a very large proportion of these have either failed to cross the Channel or have been shot down and destroyed by various methods" and that 2,752 fatal casualties had been sustained.

In mid-July, it was clear that something more was needed. Duncan Sandys, Winston Churchill's son-in-law, had been given the task of co-ordinating defences against the V-bomb attack, and his 'Crossbow' committee recommended the bold step of moving the anti-aircraft defences to the coast, where the newly available American proximity-fused shells could safely be used against Flying Bombs approaching from the sea. These shells exploded only if close to their target, so fell back to earth unexploded if badly aimed. As a result, they could not safely be used over land. In only four days, four hundred heavy anti-aircraft guns and six hundred Bofors guns were moved and re-sited. Three thousand miles of telephone cable were laid, and 23,000 personnel were relocated.

By the end of August only one VI in seven was getting through to London, and on August 28th ninety of ninety-four bombs crossing the Channel were destroyed. Of those, the coastal guns shot down sixty-five. In the first week of September, the rapid advance of the Allied armies Eastwards through France reached the launch sites, and the V1 attack came virtually to an end, although isolated long-range versions of the weapon continued to be launched from Holland almost until the end of the war, the last arriving over London in March 1945. A total of 6,184 civilians had been killed, 17,981 had been seriously injured, and countless people had sustained minor injuries without hospital treatment. The total number of Flying Bombs launched against the southern part of England is not clear − in his "The Second World War", Winston Churchill quoted a grand total of 8,564 Flying Bombs launched, of which 1,006 crashed soon after launching and never crossed the Channel. Other writers since have quoted varying figures, their information differing according to its source. The highest figure the author has seen is one of 10,492 launched against England, with 3,000 not getting across the Channel − which, in terms of Flying Bombs arriving in England, more or less agrees with Churchill's figure.

The V2 Rockets

While wrestling with the problems of the V1 attack, the British scientists and defence planners were also faced with a potentially more serious threat from the V2 rocket, the brainchild of Wernher von Braun, later to achieve further fame at NASA. By late July 1944, as a result of a remarkable error on June 13th, gleefully reported by Winston Churchill in his 'The Second World War', the Allied scientists had sufficient fragments of a V2 that had exploded in neutral Sweden after a test flight to know most of its specification and performance. What they had learned was not encouraging. The V2 weighed about 12 tons, carried a ton of high explosive − slightly more than the V1 − and had a range of approximately 200 miles.

6

5

7

5 The V2 rocket, more correctly known by its German developmental designation A4, was a bi-fuel rocket carrying sufficient liquid oxygen and alcohol to provide a burning time of 70 seconds. Weighing 13·6 tons at launch, it carried a warhead containing one ton of amatol, a mixture of TNT and ammonium nitrate. The use of more powerful explosives was tried, but failed because of premature detonation due to skin friction during flight.

6 Dr Wernher von Braun, the inventor of the V2 rocket, was a scientific prodigy who became, at the age of twenty-five in 1937, the technical director of the German Army's rocket research centre. The son of the Minister of Agriculture in von Papen's government before Hitler came to power, von Braun surrendered himself and all his papers to the Americans at the end of the war, and went on to work on the development of NASA's rockets which ultimately took men to the moon. He died in 1977.

This distance it traversed in a huge parabola at speeds of up to 4,000 mph, completing its journey from launch to detonation in only three to four minutes, and giving the recipients of its destruction no warning whatever.

By May 1944 (postwar captured records showed), the Germans were manufacturing 300 of these formidable weapons per month, and had a stockpile of some 1,800. Between September 1944 and March 1945, they were building an average of 618 per month. Massive German resistance to Allied attempts to capture the V2 launch sites around The Hague in Holland lasted until March 1945, and until then rocket attacks were a regular feature of life not only in London but also in Antwerp, attacked once it had been taken by the Allies because of its crucial importance as a source of supply to the advancing Allied armies.

The first two V2 rockets to land in London arrived within sixteen seconds of each other, the first in Chiswick, to the West of London, the second in Epping, just North of the capital. A total of 1,359 rockets were fired against London during the ensuing autumn and winter, of which 1,190 actually succeeded in leaving the launch pad. More than half of those fell short of England's capital, but the five hundred that did get to London killed 2,724 people and injured 6,476 more.

By comparison, Antwerp received 8,696 V1 Flying Bombs and 1,610 V2 rockets, of which 5,960 of the combined total fell within eight miles of the city centre. Another 3,141 flying bombs were launched against Liege, and a further 151 V2 rockets against Brussels. The attacks on Antwerp alone killed 3,470 Belgian civilians and 682 Allied servicemen.

7 The original news agency caption on this picture states that it shows a V2 being fired at Cuxhaven, but examination of the picture suggests that it was in fact photographed at the Peenemunde research establishment on the Baltic coast of Germany. It was there that the V2 made its first successful flight on 3rd October 1942. In all, some 10,000 V2 rockets were produced.

An Even Bigger Bang

But for the successful Allied Commando raids earlier in the war on the German heavy water plant in Norway, Germany would probably have succeeded in having available a nuclear bomb before the date of the actual end of the war. Since this weapon would have become available in the very last stages of the conflict, when Hitler's decisions were irrational and unbalanced, the effects of his having had the nuclear bomb available are almost unimaginable.

Nearer to actual realisation was his V3 revenge weapon, which was horrific on paper, but which simply failed to work in practice. A fifty-barrelled long-range gun installation was buried in a fortified emplacement near the village of Mimoyecques in the Pas de Calais. Each of the smooth-bored barrels was about four hundred feet long, and had successive small explosive charges in side-tubes at frequent intervals along the barrel. These charges were fired in rapid succession as a shell of approximately six inches diameter with fins at the back end passed up the barrel. The idea was that the fins would stabilise the shell, and that the range would be sufficient for the device to hit London continuously at a rate of one shell every few minutes. In the event, the shells from the weapon simply toppled in the air, and turned end over end, thereby losing speed and range. London, when it heard about that particular failure, was suitably grateful.

In truth, Hitler's revenge weapons were less than successful. Although they killed many people, they did little to alter the course of the war against Germany and used huge resources that could have turned out thousands of tanks and fighters which would have directly contributed to Germany's success against the Allies. The Normandy invasion might not have succeeded at all if the *Luftwaffe* had been as strong in 1944 as it had been in 1941. In his lust for revenge, and in his misdirection of resources to unattainable objectives, Hitler made yet another of his personal contributions to the loss of a war that Germany might just have won.

1 As the US First Army advanced into Germany, one of its units discovered a train, lying in sidings at Bromskirchen, which was made up of thirteen wagons, each loaded with a V2 rocket on its way to be launched. This was the first time that Allied soldiers had captured examples of the rocket intact, and some initial investigation on the spot was followed by extensive scientific study of the design. In this shot, American engineers are measuring and examining the control mechanism which established the trajectory of the rocket after its fuel had been expended.

2 An excellent visual impression of the size of the V2 rocket can be gained from this picture. Quite small by the standards of space rocketry, the V2 stood for launch on its four fins, clearly visible in the picture. The shape of the rocket had reputedly been derived from that of the German Army's standard rifle bullet.

3 As his army advanced through Belgium, Field-Marshal Montgomery had the opportunity to take a look at the remains of a V2 rocket which had been directed at Antwerp, but which fell and exploded in a Belgian field.

4 In a sense, a postscript to the tribulations of Londoners at the hands of Hitler's revenge weapon designers, this picture was taken when a V2 rocket was brought to London in the autumn of 1945 and put on display in Trafalgar Square as part of the National Savings week campaign.

CHAPTER 40

ARNHEM
THE AUTUMN OF 1944 IN THE WEST

Like the Normandy invasion that preceded it, and the Battle of the Bulge in the Ardennes that was to follow it, the Arnhem adventure has been made part of British and American folk history by the books that have been written and the films that have been made about it. The Arnhem airborne landing had and has all the ingredients of a ripping yarn — daring, risk, imagination, the secret enemy that nobody allowed for in the planning, even commanders on the same side in disagreement with each other. And yet it was so much more than a film scenario in the making. Given a great deal of good luck, which the plan almost presupposed, it could have worked. Given a

5 Following the breakout from Normandy, and the high-speed liberation of France, the American, British and Canadian troops pushed on into Belgium. This picture dates from mid-September 1944, and shows a Sherman tank preparing to cross the Moselle on a pontoon bridge built by US Army engineers.

6 Almost the last redoubt of the German Army in Northern France was the garrison in Calais. On 24th September 1944, the Germans there were bombed for the fifth day running by a force of British heavy bombers, which dropped almost 1,300 tons of explosives. Shot from one of the Lancaster bombers taking part in the raid, this picture shows another of the RAF Lancasters outlined against the smoke of the bomb blasts below.

7 Aboard one of the aircraft that carried the US Airborne Divisions into Holland for the ill-fated Arnhem operation, an air gunner keeps a watchful eye open for German fighters. All around are Douglas DC3 'Dakota' transports, the principal Allied military transport aircraft of the day.

great deal more good luck in the couple of months immediately following its successful conclusion, it could have brought an end to the war in 1944. And that in turn would have called a halt to Russian advances outside East Germany, and might have changed the face of postwar politics.

However, the plain fact is that Operation Market Garden, as it was curiously named, was a sad failure that nonetheless inspired the Dutch people and earned for Britain a lasting tie of friendship in that part of Holland. The scheme was conceived by Field-Marshal Montgomery, who, like General Patton, was frustrated. He had come so far through France and into Belgium so quickly since D-Day, and

yet was unable to push on through Holland and into Germany. The sluggishness that had overcome the campaign was due to the appalling weather, to the acute shortage of fuel and ammunition from which the Allied army was suffering, and to the fact that the Allies were now facing the first thoroughly prepared defensive positions that they had encountered since Normandy. Everything was having to be brought from Normandy by road along the 'Red Ball Highways' until the vital Belgian port of Antwerp could be put to use to supply the Allied armies. Until then, there was not enough fuel for an advance on a broad front. General Eisenhower, who had always favoured the broad front concept, with each of the armies advancing

1

2

3

1 British gliders, piloted by the intrepid men of the Glider Pilot Regiment, head for their landing points. Without power to correct a faulty approach, or to 'go round again' if a chosen field looked unfavourable when seen close to, glider pilots had to think and act quickly and be very skilful in handling their aircraft. That so few of their landings were unsuccessful is a tribute to their skill.

2 A dramatic picture of American paratroops of the Airborne Divisions heading for the ground beneath their canopies of silk. Although not taken during the Arnhem landing, but at the conclusion of the paratroopers' training course, this picture somehow sums up the vulnerability of the airborne soldier, and the beauty of his fall to earth into the midst of battle.

3 The German troops and armour that the Allies had assumed would not be available to fight move up to the attack through the streets of Arnhem.

at roughly the same pace, had earlier ordered Field-Marshal Montgomery to concentrate first on the capture of Antwerp itself (which was achieved on September 4th), and then on the positions along the Scheldt estuary that would enable the Allies to open and use the port. Despite these orders, Montgomery argued persuasively that the Germans had a long front to defend, had few fixed defences at the northern end of their front in Holland, and that a concentrated thrust on the left of the front would cause those relatively light defences to crumble. If, he reasoned, an airborne landing in the vicinity of Arnhem could capture roads and bridges to form a 'carpet' along which an armoured thrust could advance quickly around the northern end of the Siegfried Line and into Germany's industrial heartland in the Ruhr, the Reich's armaments production programme would be strangled, and the war could be brought to an early end. Eisenhower was persuaded by the sheer imaginativeness of the Arnhem scheme, and gave it his approval.

General Bradley was amazed, not only that the 'pious teetotalling Montgomery', known for the caution of his actions, should have come up with what he regarded as a harebrained plan, but also that his commander, Dwight Eisenhower, should have allowed it to go ahead. Nonetheless, he conceded after the war the potential of the idea, and regretted deeply its failure.

Eisenhower gave Montgomery for the Arnhem operation the 1st Airborne Army, commanded by the US Lieutenant-General Brereton. The brunt of the airborne assault was to be borne by Lieutenant-General 'Boy' Browning's I Airborne Corps, made up of the US 82nd Airborne Division, the US 101st Airborne Division and the British 1st Airborne Division. Of these, the British 1st Airborne under Major-General Urquhart was to take the bridges over

4

4 Men of Major-General Urquhart's British 1st Airborne Division fight in the streets of Arnhem under constant mortar and machine-gun fire. The leading soldier holds a Sten gun, the rudimentary yet effective sub-machine gun originally developed for airborne and subversive operations.

5 As each of the second and third waves of airborne reinforcements were dropped, delayed by bad weather, supplies were dropped in to the landing areas outside the immediate battle area. Here, as a supplies canister drifts landward, British troops move out towards the battle in Jeeps.

the Neder Rijn at Arnhem, establish a bridge-head around the town, and await reinforcement by the Polish 1st Parachute Brigade and the British 52nd (Airportable) Division. The US 101st Airborne was to surprise the garrison at Eindhoven and capture the bridges over the Wilhelmina Canal, the Dommel and the Willems Canal. The US 82nd Airborne was given the task of taking the Grave bridge over the Maas and the bridge over the Waal at Nijmegen.

To land these three divisions, General Browning had available only 2,800 aircraft and 1,600 gliders, clearly not enough to land the entire force in the first wave. Three waves were therefore required, which introduced the first major hazard to the plan — the need for accuracy to ensure that the second and third waves were dropped in such a position as to be able to reinforce the first wave.

The first wave of the British 1st Airborne had a less auspicious start. The plan decreed that, because of stiff anti-aircraft defences around Arnhem, their landing would take place in open scrubland over seven miles from the bridges that were their principal objective. Soon after their arrival, as they began to advance on Arnhem, the British division's radio communications proved unsuitable for the terrain and conditions, and General Urquhart found himself completely unable to control his division. He therefore went up to the front line himself, which in the event made his communications problem worse rather than better. By evening, the 2nd Battalion of the 1st Parachute Brigade under Lt.Col John Frost had reached the Arnhem road bridge, but was pinned down and virtually surrounded.

Montgomery's plan had envisaged General Horrocks and XXX

6 German sniper activity was intense in Arnhem and the other Dutch towns into which the Airborne Divisions fought their way. These American airborne troops are moving fast and low to give the German snipers as small a target as possible as they skirt a burnt-out truck.

7 Part of the huge column that made up the thrust of XXX Corps, commanded by Lieutenant-General Sir Brian Horrocks and led by the Guards Armoured Division, stretched out along the narrow road that led into Holland and on to Arnhem. The narrowness and vulnerability of the road to attack was a major factor in slowing the advance of the column that was to link up with the Airborne Divisions in Arnhem.

5

6

7

8

9

The three Airborne Divisions, by meeting their objectives, would open up a corridor along which General Horrocks' XXX Corps, made up of the Guards Armoured Division, the 50th Division and the 43rd Division, could advance swiftly to Arnhem, then on to the Zuider Zee, 37 miles further towards towards Germany.

The airborne landing took place on schedule on Sunday September 17th 1944, under the cover of 1,200 Allied fighter aircraft. The initial landings by the American Divisions achieved a considerable degree of surprise. The 82nd Airborne successfully took the Grave bridge, only to be baulked at their first attempt on the bridge at Nijmegen several hours after they had landed, the Germans having by this time recovered from the initial shock of unexpected company. The 101st Airborne achieved their initial objectives with the exception of taking the Son bridge over the Wilhelmina Canal which was blown before they reached it.

8 Not every bridge was captured intact during the advance of XXX Corps – this one across the Albert Canal was blown up by the Germans as they retreated.

9 According to the original caption – which may have benefited slightly from propagandist's licence – these two young Dutch Resistance fighters were the first Dutchmen the British column encountered during their drive into Holland. The Resistance men have sleeve patches representing the Dutch flag, and are talking to a British Bren gun crew.

1 An impressive shot of a British mortar crew operating from a trench near Arnhem in the thick of the battle. Note the strain that is visible on the soldier's face as he shouts to another of his unit.

2 When the battle in Arnhem was over, and the remaining British troops had been obliged to withdraw back across the river, many dead British Paratroopers were left in the streets of the town they had sought to liberate. Across the street is a German patrol. This picture is from an original radio print, which, to reach London newspapers early in October 1944, had been radioed from Germany to Stockholm, in neutral Sweden, and from there to New York.

3 Some idea of the ferocity of the fighting in Nijmegen can be gained from this view of the town and bridge after it had been bombarded by shellfire from both sides at various stages in the battle.

4 After capturing Lt. Col. Frost and his men on Arnhem Bridge, the German propagandists broadcast that they had taken 'the leader of the British forces in Arnhem'. To counter this inaccurate claim, British sources issued this picture of Major-General Urquhart arriving back in England. He is talking with four pilots of the Glider Pilot Regiment, (left to right) Staff Sgt. J. Bonome, Staff Sgt. David Hattey, Sgt. John Woodword, and Staff Sgt. H. Counter.

6

7

8

5 Despite the failure of the bold airborne assault on Arnhem, the Allied advance went on — these are tanks of the Polish Army crossing the frontier into Holland.

6 A blast ring flaring from its muzzle as the shell speeds on its way, a 155mm 'Long Tom' self-propelled gun, mounted on a Sherman tank chassis, fires on German positions along the Moselle in Belgium during October 1944. As the gunner yanks the firing lanyard, the soldier in the foreground has clapped his hands over his ears to avoid damage to his ear drums.

7 As the land forces advanced across Europe, the ground attack and air defence units of the Royal Air Force and the US Air Forces moved with them, taking their maintenance facilities wherever they went. In this picture, mechanics of the Ninth Air Force are changing the engines of a P-38 Lightning fighter-bomber in Belgium.

8 The grim instruments of war in a scene of peace and tranquillity — Sherman tanks of the Polish Army rest awhile in Dutch woodland as the morning sun streams through the trees around them.

Corps being at Arnhem within two days. Lieutenant-General Browning had guessed that the forward units of his 1st Airborne would with luck be able to hold the bridges, if necessary, for four days. Nonetheless, he observed to Montgomery, as though providing the title for a film, that he thought they might be going 'a bridge too far'. What neither he nor General Horrocks had been told by Field-Marshal Montgomery was that there were two *Panzer* Divisions resting and refitting just North of Arnhem, one of them the crack 10th SS *Frundsberg Panzer* Division. Montgomery had evidently discounted these divisions from his calculations because they were out of service, but this was to prove a sad error of judgement. By coincidence, Field Marshal Model and his headquarters staff of Army Group B were just along the road at Oosterbeck when the landing began. Having watched the British troops land, Model moved smartly back to avoid capture, set General Bittrich's II SS *Panzer* Corps on the alert, and despatched the two *Panzer* divisions towards Arnhem, one on each side of the river.

Thus, as XXX Corps began its armoured thrust at 2.35pm on the 17th, preceded by the rocket firing Typhoon fighter-bombers of Air Marshal Broadhurst's 83 group, TAF, its approach up the narrow corridor was awaited by a far stiffer force of defenders than Montgomery's planners had envisaged. To make matters worse, the entire Allied plan for the whole Market-Garden operation had been captured from an American troop carrying glider that had been shot down over German held territory. General Kurt Student, Germany's leading expert on airborne operations, was already co-ordinating

defence operations based on exact knowledge of Allied intentions by the evening of the first day.

By the end of the 17th, the column had reached Valkenswaard. By the 19th, the Guards Armoured Division had reached, repaired and crossed the Son bridge. That evening, having joined up with the 82nd Airborne Division, XXX Corps reached Nijmegen with the Americans, but it took another day of fierce fighting to get across the Waal. By now, Colonel Frost and his stalwarts of the Paras had held the bridge at Arnhem for three days. On the 21st, Urquhart was forced to pull back from Arnhem to Oosterbeck, leaving Frost and his men defending the bridge alone. That evening, Colonel Frost was seriously wounded. He had only 100 men left, and they were overrun and captured.

Too late, having been delayed for days by the terrible weather, Major-General Sosabowski's fearsome Polish 1st Parachute Brigade landed opposite Oosterbeck to reinforce the British 1st Airborne. The Guards Armoured Division and the 43rd Division, battling to cover the ten miles to Arnhem from the Waal, were trapped by the 10th SS *Panzer* Division and could not advance further. It seemed certain that the Allied armoured column of XXX Corps would be divided and encircled at any time. Accepting the inevitable, Browning ordered the survivors of the British 1st Airborne to retreat back across the Neder Rijn. Of the almost 9,000 officers and men, plus 1,100 glider pilots, that had been holding the II SS *Panzer* Corps at bay for almost ten days, only 2,163 got back across the river on September 26th.

Over 3,700 American Airborne personnel and a total of around 11,000 men of all units were killed, wounded or posted missing at Arnhem. It was one of those operations which brought out the best among soldiers.

Antwerp and the Scheldt Estuary

The capture of the vital Belgian city of Antwerp on September 4th had been achieved relatively painlessly by British tanks largely because of the guile and planning of a lone Belgian resistance worker named Vekemans who was also an engineer with experience of demolitions before the Belgian surrender in 1940. Vekemans had reconnoitred the German positions along the Scheldt South of the port, and had used his specialised knowledge as an engineer to assess the size, number and positions of demolition charges on the bridges. On the 4th September, Vekemans waited beside the road for the advancing British tanks and succeeded both in flagging down the first squadron to come along and in convincing its commander to accept his plan. Taking a small lane off the main road, and skirting around the German defences, Vekemans enabled the tank squadron not only to cross the Scheldt without having to fight for the privilege, but also to capture the bridges intact.

The frustrating sequel to this story was that, although the city and port of Antwerp was in British hands, the estuary, and with it the vital access to the North Sea, was not. In this vital strategic point lay the reason for General Omar Bradley's opposition to Montgomery's plan to take Arnhem and its bridges. If the same Allied effort that was devoted to Arnhem had been applied to the

1 A fine picture of the ubiquitous British Bren Gun in action in Holland. Private Baker of Wimbledon, London, is about to take part in an attack on German positions at Meijel, twenty miles southeast of Eindhoven, on 6th November 1944.

2 Landing craft carrying British Commandos, Royal Marines and other troops approach Westakapelle, the fiercely-defended westernmost point of the island of Walcheren in the estuary of the Scheldt on November 1st 1944. Allies losses were high – in one spot, twenty out of twenty-five landing craft were sunk before hitting the beaches.

3 Commandos run their landing craft ashore at Westkapelle. By dusk on November 1st, the town had been captured, and a 3,000 yard beachhead had been established. From these positions the Commandos pushed north and south on November 2nd, along the dyke beside the sea, knocking out German positions as they went.

4 Another scene during the landings at Westkapelle on the island of Walcheren. As smoke rises from the battle ahead, more Royal Marines go ashore.

capture of the Scheldt estuary in September, the Germans would have been overcome, and the port of Antwerp opened, within the month. With Antwerp open at the beginning of October 1944, the war would have been shortened by at least a month or two. As it was, by the time the Arnhem adventure was over, and the more mundane operations to capture the islands and positions along the Scheldt estuary had begun, the German 15th Army had had plenty of time to take up strong defensive positions.

The first three weeks of October 1944 were spent by the British I Corps and the Canadian II Corps in fighting their way slowly northwards from the city, and in eliminating pockets of German resistance from the area around Antwerp. The one German 64th Division put up a brave and effective defence against the three British and Canadian divisions, and it was not until October 22nd that Breskens was captured. Between the 22nd and the 31st, the British and Canadians fought a successful pincer operation, so that, by November 1st, General Eberding, commanding the German 64th Division, had been captured and Zuid-Beveland had been taken by the Allies.

Now began the fight to take the island of Walcheren. The sea-dyke around the island had been breached by bombing, so that the centre of the island, which lay below sea level, was flooded. The German 70th Division under Lieutenant-General Daser was therefore obliged to defend the narrow perimeter. On November 1st, under covering fire from three warships, a brigade of Royal Marines went ashore on the island at Westkapelle, and were joined by the British 52nd Division crossing from Breskens (opposite Flushing across the estuary). Fierce fighting lasted until November 3rd, and the mopping-up operations went on until the 9th, when General Daser was captured.

Thus, by mid-November, Antwerp was open and, after the clearance of mines laid by the Germans, in use to provide the Allies with the vital port facilities that were needed to keep supplied the 60 divisions that Eisenhower had in Europe. Clearing the estuary had cost almost 13,000 Allied casualties, the majority Canadian, and had resulted in the taking of over 40,000 German prisoners.

The Assault on the *Westwall*

References to the Autumn 1944 battle for the *Westwall*, or Siegfried Line, Germany's fortified defensive line along her western border, are usually limited to General Bradley's US 1st Army assault along a five-mile front of the Dutch/German frontier near Maastricht, which began on October 8th, and undoubtedly faced the most heavily defended section of the wall, guarding as it did the natural approach to the Ruhr. The US XIX Corps under Major-General Corlett advanced slowly and painfully with the support of almost 400 fighter-bombers and with frequent attacks by 4-engined bombers on the railway marshalling yards at Cologne, Kassell and Hamm that were the basis of the German supply line. In five days, Corlett advanced five miles, but as he did so his colleague General Hodges was able to encircle Aachen by October 17th and take it on the 21st — the first German city to be captured by the Allies.

Meanwhile, the endlessly frustrated General Patton fumed with his stationary US 3rd Army at Metz, starved of fuel by the shortages,

5 Fishing boats requisitioned by the Germans at Breskens to enable them to evacuate their troops across the Scheldt to Flushing were methodically bombed by the Allied air forces, thereby cutting off the German forces' retreat. Here, Canadian soldiers inspect the wrecked vessels after the capture of Breskens.

6 British troops in the streets of Flushing cross the road junction fast and low to avoid the fire of German snipers who were still everywhere in the town.

7 Once the islands of the Scheldt and the major strategic points along the estuary had been captured, it became possible to open the port of Antwerp – after the mines in the shipping channel had been cleared. In this picture, the Royal Navy explodes mines blocking access to Europe's third largest port, crucial to the supply of Eisenhower's advancing armies.

1 In front of the much-vaunted Siegfried Line along the frontier of Germany, a battery of American 155mm self-propelled guns mounted on Sherman tank chassis fire on German positions. They opened this particular barrage with twenty-one rounds of high explosive shells, each weighing approximately 100 pounds.

2 The fighting along the Westwall, as winter set in, was fierce and uncompromising. A dead German soldier has been blown from his tank by the force of the explosion of the shell that killed the rest of his crew. They are still inside the tank.

3 During the figting for Aachen, an infantryman uses the comforting solidity of a Sherman tank on one side and a substantial building on the other to protect him while he fires on German positions across the street.

and by Eisenhower's decision to give the 1st Army priority. A top-level command conference at Montgomery's Brussels headquarters in late October decided that the next offensive should be a two-pronged attack to break the *Westwall* and thrust into Germany. The US 9th Army was to advance on Cologne, the US 3rd Army further South was to advance on Mannheim and Frankfurt.

The 9th Army's Northern attack began on November 16th, and made slow progress against the 5th *Panzerarmee*, but by December 10th, the Americans were within 25 miles of Cologne, albeit with the considerable problem of the capture of the dams on the Roer to be overcome before they could safely advance further. Patton's 3rd Army was not ready to launch its advance to strike at the *Westwall* until November 8th, when the Americans were able to field 250,000 men against approximately 90,000 German defenders in Lorraine. The extremely wet weather of the second half of 1944 continued, and the terrain was so sodden that the German defenders believed an attack was impossible. Thus, when Patton's army went over to the offensive despite the rain, the surprise was a significant factor in Patton's success, and the 90th Infantry Division reached the German frontier on November 20th. On December 3rd, General Walker's XX Corps took a bridge over the River Saar near Saarlouis, securing the right bank, and by the 18th, joined by the 5th and 90th Infantry Divisions, the 3rd Army had a substantial bridgehead in the Saar.

All down the line of the *Westwall* and the German frontier to Switzerland, the Allied forces wore down the defences of the once-great German nation, yet the morale of the German troops remained high, and the *Wehrmacht* formations and garrisons continued to fight bravely. The French Generals — de Lattre de Tassigny and Leclerc

— fought magnificent actions in the Vosges, on the Swiss border, and throughout the Southern sector. General Leclerc succeeded by a series of daring attacks in capturing Strasbourg, and in securing the surrender of Lieutenant-General Vaterrodt and his defending force. In Alsace, General Patch and the US 7th Army fought hard against considerable frustrations, and by December was attacking the *Westwall* with his VI and XV Corps in support of the 3rd Army.

His objective was to break through between the Rhine and the Saar. Then, a SHAEF order removed his objectives and gave them instead to the French 1st Army, leaving Patch frustrated once more. Such are the political hazards of command. But the French went on to advance on the German border and thrust one more finger of defeat in the direction of Hitler's Thousand Year Reich.

It seemed that the Allies were about to eliminate Germany as a military power for ever. Then, just as over-confidence might have begun to establish itself at SHAEF, Hitler sprang the last great offensive of his career, a brilliantly executed counter-attack that set the Allies reeling. This was the Battle of the Bulge — and it is the subject of the next chapter of this book.

4 The American Army made extensive use of tanks during the street fighting in Aachen, following the Soviet example of using the tanks as cover for an infantry advance.

5 Two American lieutenants, accompanied by a private carrying a makeshift white flag, carry a surrender ultimatum to the German commander in Aachen. The Germans blindfolded them and took them to their commander, who refused the ultimatum and returned the Americans to their lines. The battle then continued.

6 Much of the city of Aachen was devastated by the fighting before it was finally taken, as this picture of an American M10 tank destroyer in action clearly shows.

7 Lieutenant-General George S. Patton (left) and Lieutenant-General Omar L. Bradley, aboard a C47 transport aircraft in which they visited various fighting areas.

8 The French troops to the south of the line were at their best fighting in arduous conditions, and tackled seemingly impossible tasks in the snows of winter. This is a patrol of the French First Army holding a position in the mountains from which to observe German troop movements.

CHAPTER 41

THE BATTLE OF THE BULGE
HITLER'S LAST OFFENSIVE

As Christmas 1944 approached, it seemed that Germany's final collapse could only be a matter of time and continued Allied determination. The Allies had been on the offensive, with varying degrees of success, for so long that the notion of the German High Command having the will, the equipment or the manpower to achieve a new offensive in any strength seemed absurd. To Eisenhower, to Bradley and even to Montgomery, by now perpetually at odds with his American colleagues in arms, the only questions to be answered were where, when and how the assault on the Rhine was to be launched.

They reckoned without the last flush of Adolf Hitler's considerable talent for major strategic vision and tactical bravura. For Hitler, always one to be mindful of historical precedent, had observed that history was repeating itself, and saw in that phenomenon an opportunity. Four years earlier, a plan that had itself seen its origins in a First World War strategy had enabled General Guderian to surprise the French and British armies with a lightning advance to the Meuse through Belgium's Ardennes forests which had, to traditional military eyes, seemed impassable to tanks, and were therefore only lightly defended. Despite that salutary lesson in *Blitzkrieg*, the Allies had once again made the assumption, Hitler observed, that an offensive through the Ardennes forest was not a practical option for either side. Like General Gamelin in 1940, Bradley had not allowed for the possibility of an armoured thrust. Only four divisions of General Middleton's VIII Corps were holding a front of fully eighty miles.

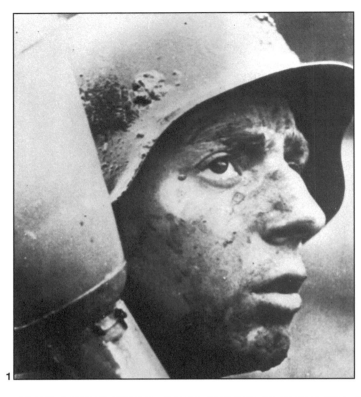

Because the German armies had now been pushed back almost to Germany, and were in some areas already fighting on German soil, major troop movements and concentrations of armour necessarily took place in Germany. Thus the Allies had now lost the important intelligence advantage of constantly updated information on troop movements that the French and Belgian Resistance had provided. As a result, Hitler was able to assemble the twenty-one divisions for which his plan called without the Allied commanders knowing anything of it from a hostile civilian population. Nonetheless, it has never been explained satisfactorily why Allied intelligence ignored information from captured German soldiers almost two weeks before the German push began which clearly indicated a major build-up.

Although the plan for the Ardennes offensive has often been credited to Field-Marshal von Rundstedt, now reappointed at the age of seventy to be Commander-in-Chief in the West, Rundstedt in fact

1 Hitler's master plan for the Ardennes offensive was almost successful, and would probably have achieved most that the *Fuehrer* envisaged had the resources that he imagined to be at von Manteuffel's disposal actually been available. The Allies did not realise the extent to which men like this *Panzer Grenadier* could still be rallied to fight fiercely to the death.

2 The *Nashorn* or 'Rhinoceros' was one of the most powerful of Germany's self-propelled anti-tank guns, but its high sides and comparatively light armour made it extremely vulnerable to side attack. Mounted on a PzKpfw IV tank chassis, the *Nashorn* was equipped with the formidable 88mm gun.

opposed the whole concept bitterly. The entire plan was the work of Hitler and his immediate staff, prepared in total secrecy without even von Rundstedt's or Model's assistance. The orders to Army Group B for the attack were complete down to the last detail. Attempts by Field-Marshal Model and the youthful General Hasso von Manteuffel, who at 47 had been put in command of the 5th *Panzerarmee*, to impose alterations met only with limited success, and changed only the times of attack and the sequence of events during the initial assault. The plan itself, declared Hitler, was irrevocable.

The scheme was magnificent in its simplicity, and, had Germany in fact had the equipment, the men and the resources of fuel and supplies that Hitler's plan required for success, it could have succeeded and given Germany a major victory in the West. Nothing less would satisfy the Fuehrer. Three armies were to take part in the offensive, the newly-formed 6th SS *Panzerarmee* under Colonel-General Sepp Dietrich, the 5th *Panzerarmee* commanded by General von Manteuffel, and the 7th Army under General Brandenburger.

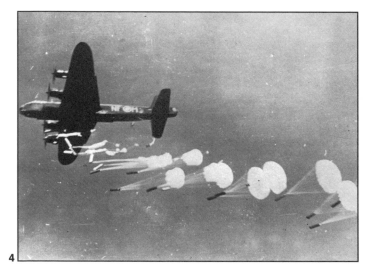

4

5

6

7

The 5th and 6th were to push in one massive breakout through the Ardennes forests to the Meuse, and were given by the plan just 48 hours to reach their goal. There they would fan out, Dietrich's 6th crossing the Meuse North of Liege and driving forward to re-capture Antwerp, and von Manteuffel's 5th heading for Namur and Brussels. To the 7th Army fell the task of covering the whole exercise against outside Allied interference from the South. Once the 5th and 6th reached Brussels and Antwerp, the communications and supply lines of the entire Allied 21st Army Group and most of the Allied 12th Army Group could be attacked from two sides and put out of action. More than half of Eisenhower's army would be destroyed.

3 As the Allies advanced into territory formerly held by the Germans, many examples of films and propaganda material were captured. This photograph is said by the original news agency caption to have been taken from such a film, and the handsome young *Waffen SS* soldier is certainly armed to the teeth and ready for anything. Note the knife, trenching tool and belt of machine-gun ammunition.

4 During the occupation of Belgium, the resistance organisation *L'Armee Blanche* had been a valuable source of information on German troop movements and build-up, and had been supplied by air with arms, ammunition, communications equipment and supplies in canisters like those being dropped here by an RAF Stirling heavy bomber. As the Allies pushed the Germans back to German soil, they lost the benefit of Resistance information, and this loss was a major factor in making the German surprise attack in the Ardennes possible.

5 German resistance grew fiercer as British and American troops penetrated the westernmost villages and towns of Germany late in 1944, and this feeling of violation of the fatherland was played upon by Hitler in securing the determination necessary for the great winter offensive. These Americans are diving for cover in a trench near Alsdorf as mortar shells come in from German positions just 100 yards away over the parapet.

6 In mid-November 1944, these men of the US 9th Army entered Geilenkirchen through the ubiquitous mud that characterised Europe that autumn, accompanied by British armoured units equipped with Sherman tanks. With so much Allied strength gathering along Germany's borders, Hitler believed that he had little to lose and everything to gain by his grand offensive.

7 According to the original caption to this picture, the medical orderly on the ground, extreme left, went to help some wounded American soldiers, among whom there was a wounded German. When the cameraman got nearer, the caption claims, the German had gone, and the medic was dead.

The Battle of the Bulge

Fortunately for the Allies, Hitler's fantasising about the manpower, the availability of equipment and the logistics of his armies had reached an advanced stage, and his plan took no account either of the fact that the three German *Panzer* Divisions of 5th *Panzerarmee* were already down to roughly 100 tanks per division, roughly half the divisional strength of the American armoured divisions, nor of their desperate shortage of fuel, despite Albert Speer's Armaments Ministry's considerable success in maintaining production throughout the Allied bomber offensive. Only the four divisions of Sepp Dietrich's 6th *Waffen SS Panzerarmee* had been brought up to full strength with a total of 640 tanks.

At 5.30 in the morning on December 16th 1944, Hitler's greatest gamble began. With the benefit of fog and cloud which kept the Allied air forces on the ground, twenty-one German divisions attacked the American line between Monschau and Echternach along a 90-mile front, with high morale but minimal fuel. The 6th *Panzerarmee* launched their assault between Saint Vith and Malmedy· in the Northern sector; the 5th under von Manteuffel pushed straight into the Ardennes forests in the direction of Celles and Dinant — the point on the Meuse where the German victory of 1940 had been accomplished. To the South of the 5th *Panzerarmee*, and North of Trier, General Brandenberger's 7th Army guarded the flank of von Manteuffel's thrust against the expected move Northward by General Patton's US 3rd Army.

A feature of the attack was the activities of the so-called 150th *Panzer* Brigade, a unit of some 2,000 English-speaking German commandos who knew American service slang and customs. Under Colonel Otto Skorzeny, using captured American Jeeps, and wearing American combat jackets over their German uniforms, the Germans advanced far ahead of the main force, cutting telephone wires,

1 Stavelot was taken by the Germans on December 17th and retaken by the Americans on December 19th, although the battle ebbed and flowed locally through the town during those two days. In Stavelot, American troops accustomed to the horrors of war were shocked by the evidence they found of atrocities against civilians.
In this picture, an American soldier looks sadly at the body of a small Belgian boy of some six years. Beyond are the huddled bodies of other Belgian civilians, all of whom had been hustled out of a cellar where they had been hiding, to be machine-gunned to their deaths. According to the original caption of this picture, the Americans were only a short distance away from the scene of the massacre, and heard the screams but could do nothing.

2 Atrocities against American prisoners of war in Belgium were also extensively reported at the time. According to the original caption to this picture, the GI was 'looking at the corpses of American soldiers killed in cold blood by fire from a German tank after they had been captured on December 17th'.

3 The fierceness of the fighting during the German Ardennes offensive — adjudged by those who took part to have been some of the hardest of the European war — is apparent from the many pictures of devastation and death that exist, all taken within a few miles of each other, and all within a few days. This picture of a knocked-out German PzKpfw V *Panther* tank of Lieutenant-General Heinz Lammerding's 2nd *SS-Panzer Division Das Reich* and its dead crew was taken in Manhay after Christmas 1944. Lammerding took the town on Christmas Eve amidst the chaos of an American planned withdrawal that went wrong, and lost it again to Brigadier-General Hasbrouck and the 7th Armoured on December 26th.

4 At St Vith, scene of much heavy fighting during the Ardennes offensive, seven GIs were shot in the face with their hands up after having been captured. Their frozen bodies were recovered from a ditch. In this picture, their identity discs are being checked so that relatives might be informed and records maintained.

turning signposts, setting up false red minefield indicators and creating as much confusion as possible. Each was under orders, if captured, to tell their captors that thousands of Germans were loose in American uniforms, driving Jeeps. The success of the first group was outstanding — forty Jeeps got through the American lines to commit their sabotage, and all but eight got back again. Those that were captured duly carried out their orders and spread rumours of a vast force of Germans in US uniform — with the result that huge traffic jams developed on the narrow roads through the forest as Jeeps were stopped and checked. Hundreds of American soldiers who failed to prove their American origin by answering check questions correctly were arrested. Many a GI had cause to reflect in the cooler that a little more attention to schoolday lessons about the height of the Empire State Building and the content of the Gettysburg Address might have saved him a lot of bother.

Later groups of Skorzeny's saboteurs were less successful, although one man captured on the 19th launched a fresh rumour of an attempt on Eisenhower's life which caused a rash of extra security precautions that did much to slow the Supreme Commander's progress for days. Since the activities of the 150th *Panzer* Brigade were entirely contrary to the Geneva Convention, the Americans began summarily to try and shoot the men captured in US uniform, and this ended their incursions. The whole idea had been Hitler's — unbalanced he may have been, but a measure of originality still characterised his military solutions.

Less palatable were the appalling and unnecessary atrocities committed by the leading column of the elite 1st SS *Panzer* Division, known as 'Battle Group Peiper', after its commander *SS Standartenfuhrer Peiper*. This unit captured the important communications centre of Stavelot (only to lose it again later the same day), but in the meantime discovered a group of civilians, mainly women and children, huddled in a cellar. Despite the fact that there was no evidence whatever of their complicity in any military activity, they were all taken out and shot in cold blood, with exception of one woman and her two children. Unarmed American prisoners were

also murdered in contravention of the Geneva Convention.

The 'Battle Group Peiper' was the first thrust of the 6th *Panzerarmee* in the northern sector, which encountered far stronger resistance than it had expected at the hands of the US 99th Infantry Division, the southernmost of General Gerow's V Corps. The men of V Corps held their positions until reinforcements arrived, and prevented Peiper from proceeding towards his objectives. Incredibly, while Peiper was held up at Stavelot he was within a mile of a vast and lightly guarded US fuel dump containing over 2.5 million gallons of gasoline — but he did not know it was there, and made no attempt to capture fuel which might have transformed the offensive for Hitler. By contrast, von Manteuffel's 5th broke through strongly in the Schnee Eifel sector (just to the South of Dietrich's positions) against the newly arrived US 106th Division and the 14th Cavalry Group. By the following day, the 17th December, the 5th *Panzerarmee* had surrounded the 106th and forced the surrender of some 7,000 men — the worst reverse suffered by the American Army during the whole of 1944 and 1945 in Europe.

Further South again in von Manteuffel's sector, the 58th and 47th *Panzer* Corps made strong progress. The 58th crossed the River Our

Above the Battle of the Bulge.

5 Just five miles from the besieged town of Bastogne, scene of the heroic stand of the 101st Airborne Division, an American infantryman, with bayonet fixed, crawls under barbed wire during an advance on German positions. What he said to the cameraman, who was under the wire first, and had his back to the Germans, is not recorded.

GERMANY

• Jülich

NETH.

Maastricht •

Düren •

BELGIUM

• Aachen

Liège •

Eupen •

Meuse

Huy •

Amblève   Spa •

○ Malmedy   Monschau

Werbomont   ○ Stavelot

Ourthe   • Losheim

Dinant

• Celles   • Manhay   St Vith

• Houffalize

• Bastogne   Echternach

Sûre

LUXEMBOURG

Luxembourg

FRANCE

German Attacks 16-20 Dec. 1944
German Attacks 21-25 Dec. 1944
△△△ *German Front Line 16 Dec. 1944*
▲▲▲ *German Front Line 25 Dec. 1944*
●●●● *Extent of "Battlegroup Peiper" penetration*
○ *U.S. Petrol Dumps*

Moselle

1 Allied and German armies alike suffered the extreme cold of the winter of 1944 in the Belgian forests. The soldiers of the US 82nd Airborne Division are anything but airborne, trudging through the snow as they follow a tank in a heavy blizzard.

2 Another knocked out Panther tank of the 2nd *SS Panzer Division Das Reich*, in the streets of Manhay. For the Panzer divisions, already weak and weary, the Ardennes campaign dealt the final blow.

3 Getting supplies to the front under fire is never easy even in good weather, but the combined effects of heavy snow and a substantial part of the remaining German *Panzer* strength in the West made the problems of those manning American supply vehicles in Belgium considerably greater than usual. This picture was taken by a photographer named Vandivert from a Taylor Cub aircraft as trucks delivered ammunition and food to a unit based in a barn. Note the shell holes in the snow near the trucks.

and pushed on towards Houffalize to attempt to secure a bridgehead over the Meuse between Ardenne and Namur. The 47th was to cross the Our and capture Bastogne, a key town positioned at the junction of vital roads. By the night of the 17th December, both Corps were close to their objectives at Houffalize and Bastogne.

Only now did the Allied High Command take the offensive seriously and realise just how vigorously the German High Command was bidding for an eleventh hour victory. The 6th *Panzerarmee* had come perilously close to the US First Army HQ at Spa, which had been pulled hastily back. By December 18th, the US 7th Armoured Division had been equally hastily moved to counter German pressure on the important road centre of St. Vith, but were failing to hold the assault of the 6th *Panzerarmee*, which was outflanking St. Vith on both sides. So hard pressed were they that no help could be detached for the trapped regiments of the 106th Division at Bastogne. As the German 47th *Panzer* Corps closed in, combat command and engineer reinforcements from the US 9th Armoured Division reached Bastogne and slowed the German advance. This was crucial, since, on the 19th, the US 101st Airborne Division arrived at Bastogne (after delays caused by being sent to the wrong place), just before the town was bypassed by von Manteuffel's tanks and cut off from all other American forces on the 20th.

4 Two American paratroopers cover a German prisoner as he emerges from a barn in Henumont. One of four German soldiers captured when US soldiers searched the barn, he is so muffled against the intense cold in his greatcoat and scarves that no badges of rank or unit are visible.

On the 19th December, General Bradley ordered the 10th Armoured Division to move North to reinforce the American line against the advancing *Panzers*. This brought 60,000 more US troops into the endangered area; a further 180,000 would be moved up over the next eight days. The US 30th Division was sent to Malmedy from rest positions near Aachen, and was then moved further West to push *SS Standartenführer* Peiper's Battle Group out of Stavelot with the help of fighter-bomber attacks. Peiper was now himself cut off from the rest of the 6th *Panzerarmee*, and was running desperately short of fuel. By the 24th he had no gasoline at all, and his Group abandoned their tanks and walked back through the forest.

Further South, von Manteuffel had forced the US defending troops out of St Vith, and was pressing hard against the US 7th Armoured and 106th Divisions, which were obliged to retreat to safer positions. The Allied line was now burst wide open, and Eisenhower decided that rapid action was needed. In a major change of the command structure, he put Montgomery in charge of all land forces North of the breach, and Bradley in command of those South of it. Montgomery insisted of having Major-General J. Lawton Collins, commander of the US 7th Corps, for the task of commanding the two armoured and two infantry divisions that were to be given the task of stopping von Manteuffel reaching the Meuse. To 'Lightning Joe' Collins were given the 2nd and 3rd Armoured Divisions and the 75th and 84th Infantry Divisions. His orders were to mount a counter-attack.

South of the breach, General Bradley gave General Patton the formidable task of wheeling and repositioning two Corps (III and XII) from the Saar front to the counter-attack to relieve Bastogne, where the position was, and remained for days, critical. The commander at Bastogne was Brigadier-General McAuliffe, who earned

5 The essence of street fighting is to move fast and keep out of sight – but try moving quickly when winkling out snipers with snow up to your knees. This is PFC D.C. Cox of Amerillo, Texas, looking for trouble in shell-damaged houses in Muringen, early in 1945.

6 On Saturday afternoon, January 23rd 1945, the US 7th Armoured Division attacked and retook St Vith. General Hasbrouck awarded the privilege of being first to enter the town to the combat command that had heroically defended St Vith when the German Army had taken it just one month before – Brigadier-General Bruce C. Clarke's Combat Command B. Here, American soldiers line the road into St Vith after its recapture.

7 During the period between Christmas 1944 and the successful link-up of the 7th Army and General Patton's 3rd Army at Houffalize on January 16th, the Germans had utilised twenty divisions, and had lost 24,000 men killed, 16,000 as prisoners and over 63,000 wounded. These graves of German dead were at Forge-a-la-Plez.

The Battle of the Bulge

his place in history not only with his inspirational leadership of the defenders of the town, but also by his one-word answer to General Luttwitz' offer of surrender terms. McAuliffe instructed his staff officer to tell the German white flag party 'Nuts!'. The Germans, with Teutonic thoroughness, queried the meaning of this answer. The young American officer thought for a moment then offered the translation 'Go to Hell!'. The Germans went, although their final destination is unrecorded.

December 23rd at last brought a break in the unremitting low cloud and bad weather of the previous week, and the Allied Air Forces were unleashed in earnest, flying 2,000 sorties on the 23rd, and a total of 15,000 over the next three days. More American reinforcements were moved up to the Southern side of the German bulge, and von Rundstedt renewed his requests to Hitler that the whole offensive should be called off. Once more, Hitler refused. By the 24th, Christmas Eve, the defenders of Bastogne were nearer than ever before to being defeated, but still they held on with great heroism. On Christmas Day, the German tanks made an all-out effort to break into the town, but, remarkably, General McAuliffe's defenders still held out. At 4.45pm on the 26th, their persistence and bravery was at last rewarded. The US 4th Armoured Division under Major-General Gaffey broke through and made contact with the beleaguered and exhausted garrison of Bastogne.

By the 24th, Patton's advance from the South was pushing back the German 7th Army, and was coming closer to von Manteuffel's flank as the 5th *Panzerarmee* continued its push for the Meuse despite heightened Allied opposition. Hitler had now released from reserve the 9th *Panzer* and 15th *Panzergrenadier* Divisions to reinforce von Manteuffel's army, but General Collins' relentless push was too strong even for the reinforced *Panzer* force, and on Christmas Day, he re-took Celles, just five miles from the Meuse. This marked the turning point of the Battle of the Bulge. Hitler's dream was to come no closer to the Meuse than this.

1 The Battle of the Bulge over, the hills and woods of the Ardennes were littered with the abandoned and snow-covered equipment of several armies, much of it German. This German field gun, photographed in January 1945, covered the valley near Sainlex.

2 With the German *Panzer* forces irreparably damaged by Hitler's last great show of strength, the British, American and French armies pushed on into Germany. In January 1945, the caption to this picture of British soldiers watching for snipers in the German village of Stein was able to claim that British infantry had captured twelve German villages since the start of the year.

3 Many Americans also saw in the New Year of 1945 in Germany for the first time. This US Army M10 Tank Destroyer is covering the main road of Schiebenhardt, which is also covered by German outposts about 800 yards away. Mst. Sgt. George J. Harrington of East Braintree, Massachusetts, is crouching by the fence with the binoculars, while T/S Morris W. James of Trenton, New York, covers the road with his 0·30 calibre machine gun. The M10 mounted the three inch M7 gun, which was already an obsolete weapon, and M10 vehicles supplied to the British Army had their three inch gun replaced with the 17 pounder anti-tank gun. This more effective combination was known as the 'Achilles'.

By the 26th December, the 5th *Panzerarmee* was beginning to retreat, and von Manteuffel was fuming at the fact that only now was he given the reinforcements he needed — but without the fuel to use them. The Battle of the Bulge was over, and Germany's last great offensive had failed. The losses had been serious on both sides, but whereas the Allies could replace arms and equipment destroyed, the Germans could not. All told, the Americans lost 76,890 killed and wounded, the Germans 81,834. Over 700 US tanks were destroyed to 324 German, over 590 aircraft to just 320 German. However, it should be remembered that these losses were approximately equal as proportions of the total of each type of equipment employed in the battle by each side.

Incredibly, Hitler now began to fantasise about a great offensive to destroy the Allies in Alsace and Lorraine, apparently oblivious to the tremendous Soviet build-up on the Vistula which heralded Stalin's final push to destroy the Reich and dominate Eastern Europe. His Generals were in despair. It was now clear that Germany as they knew it had but months to live.

CHAPTER 42

THE BATTLE FOR THE RHINE
THE LAND WAR REACHES GERMANY IN THE WEST

Although the German armies had been conclusively beaten in the Ardennes, and began 1945 at great disadvantage both psychologically and logistically, Hitler did not see the German situation in that light. As always, he viewed any notion of strategic withdrawal as an admission of failure and defeat, and therefore, against all advice, ordered that Germany should stand and fight West of the Rhine rather than follow the course of withdrawal and regrouping to its East that common sense and most of his General Staff urged upon him.

Recognising that continued German resistance without withdrawal was to characterise the next part of the drive to crush Germany in the West, General Eisenhower planned the final phase of the Allied assault that had brought him from Normandy to Germany in three stages. Always in favour of the 'broad front' approach to Allied planning, he ordered that, as phase one, the Allied armies must first destroy the German hold on all positions West of the Rhine, and then (and only then) launch phase two by crossing the river to establish bridgeheads. Phase three was to consist of two simultaneous thrusts. The first, by Field Marshal Montgomery's 21st

Army Group, which now, it should be remembered, included the US 9th Army, would drive North from Duisberg to skirt North of the Ruhr industrial region and capture the North German plain. This was to be the principal assault, and would occupy 35 of the available 85 divisions. The second thrust, using the 25 divisions of Bradley's 12th Army Group, was to push South of the Ruhr from the Mainz/Frankfurt area North-East to Kassel. The overall objective was to effect 'a massive double envelopment of the Ruhr to be followed by a great thrust to join up with the Russians'. The remaining 25 divisions of the Allied western armies were to hold the Southern Karlsruhe/Basle and Bonn/Bingen areas of the Rhine which offered minimal opportunities for large scale assault crossings.

There was considerable British disagreement with this plan, despite the fact that it gave Montgomery and the British and Canadian Armies the major opportunity to shine, and relegated Bradley's command to that of supporting the success of a commander whom he had come to loathe. The British General Staff believed that Eisenhower did not have the strength to mount more than one

4 As the Germans launched their final massive offensive in the Ardennes in December 1944, the British 2nd Army was holding a winter line along the banks of the Maas in Holland. For several weeks, the battle was almost static in this sector, German patrols making forays by night and early morning and being repelled by British defensive positions. This is a British Bren gun post near Geljesteren.

5 It is all too easy to think of war only in terms of attack and defence, defeat and victory, forgetting the vital support roles of those who bring the supplies and evacuate the wounded. This snowplough was clearing an airfield in Holland during the blizzards of December 1944 so that DC3 Dakota aircraft like that in the background could fly the wounded out to hospitals in Britain.

6 Against the background of a typical Dutch windmill, a British Vickers machine gun post fires on German positions, covering the advance of Allied infantry.

successful and crushing attack across the Rhine, and contended that that assault should properly be in the North and against the Ruhr. Perhaps, when Brooke had floated this criticism at the end of 1944, it was justified, but by the time the dispute came to be decided, in January 1945, events had proved Eisenhower to be right. The Russians were about to advance to the River Oder; Hitler, believing that he had 'regained the initiative' in the Ardennes, and could afford to relax a little in the West, had transferred the ten divisions of the 6th *Panzerarmee* to the Hungarian front; and the desperate fuel shortage that afflicted every aspect of German planning had virtually grounded the *Luftwaffe*. The defences on the Rhine were a pale shadow of what they had formerly been.

The Colmar Pocket

While this argument was being fought out, and the 21st and 12th Army Groups were almost stationary, mopping up the last vestiges of the Ardennes offensive, counting the cost and preparing for the next stage of the battle. The 6th Army Group, made up of the 1st French Army and the US 7th Army, was far to the south and was fighting fiercely to eliminate a German push to recapture Strasbourg and the plain of Alsace. Overnight on New Year's Eve, Heinrich Himmler, as commander of Army Group *'Oberrhein'* had made his bid for military fame by launching Operation *Nordwind* with the objective of reaching the Saverne Gap and cutting General Patch's US 7th Army

1

2

3

1 Germans holding positions in Holland resorted to the blowing up of dykes to hinder the Allied advance. Canadian troops attacked a dyke across open water, captured it and pushed on over dry land to a village a little further on. During the night, the village was flooded as a result of the retreating Germans blowing another dyke, and the troops had to be rescued by 'Buffalo' amphibious tanks and DUKW amphibians.

2 In February 1945, Field-Marshal Montgomery launched his offensive towards the Rhine in Holland. These British soldiers are approaching the northern part of the Siegfried Line South-East of Nijmegen. The sergeant in the foreground carries a Lee-Enfield No. 4 rifle with bayonet fixed; the soldier behind is armed with a Bren light machine gun.

3 The role of the RAF Typhoon fighter-bombers and the American Thunderbolts in ground attack had been crucial ever since they had proved their immense worth during the breakout from the Normandy beachhead. Now, as 1944 ended and 1945 began, the Typhoons were operating in Holland from bases recently abandoned by the *Luftwaffe* to provide air-cover for the Allied advance to the Rhine. Many German bomb dumps were found and disposed of by Bomb Disposal units, and the RAF had to clear the wreckage of German aircraft and equipment before they could use the airfields. In this shot of an RAF Typhoon being pushed out ready for action, taken from inside a hangar virtually destroyed by departing German troops, the fabric is that of tattered tarpaulins hanging from the roof.

4 The Siegfried Line, once believed by Hitler to be impenetrable and a total defence for Germany against land attack, was fast proving almost as vulnerable as the Maginot Line had been – although the Allies did not, as the Germans had, have the option of simply going round the obstacle. These German machine gunners are at their post within the Siegfried Line defences.

5 An American M7 self-propelled howitzer, nicknamed the 'Priest' because of the pulpit-like mounting of the 0·5" machine gun, maintains a steady bombardment of German positions in the Rhine valley, far below its dominating hilltop position.

6 ' For you the war is over' ... a column of German prisoners captured during the Allied advance across Holland is marched back westwards away from the front. The leading men are *Luftwaffe* NCOs; it is not easy to identify the service or units of those further back. Note how the Allied censor has crudely obliterated the flashes and other identifying marks of the British uniforms to prevent the picture being of use to the Germans.

7 Breda, the last important Dutch city before the mouth of the Rhine, was liberated by the ever-determined Poles, shown here making a brief halt in the centre of the city before pushing on after the retreating German army.

in two. Patch was in a difficult position, having been obliged in December to extend his line to cover the gap caused by General Patton having to head North for the Ardennes. When the German attack came, the 7th Army had only its seven divisions to defend a 90 mile front against eight German divisions including the 21st *Panzer* and an *SS Panzergrenadier* Division. SHAEF was inclined to order strategic withdrawal, abandoning Strasbourg and the Alsace plain until General Devers 6th Army Group could be adequately reinforced for a counter-attack. But General Juin, and General de Lattre de Tassigny of the French 1st Army, thought otherwise. They refused to contemplate a French Army withdrawing under any conditions to surrender newly liberated French territory back to the Germans, and earned the support of General de Gaulle for their stand.

On the night of January 2nd/3rd, General de Lattre moved his redoubtable 3rd Algerian Division up to hold Strasbourg. On the 6th, the German 19th Army suddenly launched an offensive from the Colmar bridgehead that they had stubbornly held on the West bank of the Rhine, and pushed to within 13 miles of Strasbourg on the Erstein Heights. The battle around Strasbourg raged for two weeks in a series of largely fruitless attacks and counter-attacks that served to prove only the determination of the French Army and the inability of Himmler to control operations from the far side of the Rhine. By January 26th, the German Army had accepted that it had failed to re-take Strasbourg; General Wiese was relieved of his command,

thereby 'carrying the can' for the incompetence of his superior, who had earlier failed even as a chicken farmer, and Himmler's disaster was rewarded in true Hitlerian style with a promotion for the *Reichsführer SS* to command the crucial Army Group *'Vistula'*.

In the latter days of the battle around Strasbourg, the French had set about the literal interpretation of General de Lattre's order of January 15th by which he had instructed his army to 'Leave the Germans no chance of escape.... Free Colmar undamaged ... strangle the pocket alongside the Rhine where it receives its supplies ... around Brisach.' Substantial reinforcements were provided by SHAEF for the French operation to strangle the Colmar pocket. In addition to the US 3rd Division, the French were given the US 28th Division and the US 12th Armoured Division, plus the French 2nd Armoured Division under General Leclerc which was also moved down from Strasbourg for the operation. All these reinforcements brought General de Lattre's command up to twelve strong, well-equipped divisions, of which the 3rd Algerian, being fully occupied around Strasbourg, was to take no part in the Colmar action. Thus the Allied forces at Colmar actually amounted to eleven divisions.

Facing them were seven German divisions of the 19th Army, stretched along a bridgehead of 100 miles West of the Rhine. But they were divisions in little more than name, with between 4,500 and 7,000 men per division, and a serious shortage of ammunition. The Germans did, however, have superior armour, and much greater artillery firepower, being blessed with the formidable 88mm anti-tank gun. The weather was also on the side of static defence — first it snowed, then it thawed, and the Allied forces were obliged to advance first in bitterly cold conditions, then through a quagmire of mud.

From January 20th, when the attack began, until January 27th, when the US 3rd Division finally reached the Colmar Canal, the offensive was one of the slowest and most bitterly fought of the European campaign. On the 27th, General Rasp, commanding the 19th Army, was authorised by OKW to pull his badly battered army back over the Rhine, but, newly reinforced again with the US 75th Division and US XXI Corps (whose commander, Major-General Milburn, now took command of all US troops engaged in the Colmar offensive) the French 1st Army set about occupying Colmar itself and encircling the German defenders in the pocket. On February 5th, the French and American troops joined up, and by so doing trapped approximately a quarter of the 19th Army. When on February 9th, the 19th escaped back across the Rhine, they left behind over 22,000 prisoners, 80 guns and 70 tanks. Nonetheless, although more than a quarter of his manpower was left in Allied hands, General Rasp had managed to take back to the Fatherland 1,500 guns, 60 armoured troop carriers and tanks and 7,000 other motor vehicles, in itself a considerable military achievement.

1 French troops, many of them Algerian or Tunisian, advance with their tanks on Strasbourg. The extremely wet conditions caused tanks to leave ruts behind them, and infantry were able to use these for cover.

2 General de Lattre de Tassigny explains the situation in the French sector of the line to General Eisenhower. The French general proved himself to be of exceptional talent, and to have troops whose tenacity, and unwillingness to withdraw, was a major asset to the Allies in their advance upon the Rhine.

3 A mortar crew of General Patch's 7th Army fires on German positions 200 yards away in the Bienewald Forest, near Schreibenhardt, just over the Lauter River, which forms the German border with France at this point. In this area, the battle ranged back and forth for some time, with repeated attacks and counter-attacks over the same ground.

4 After the humiliations of 1940, it was a major occasion for French troops to cross the border from France into Germany to the south of the front early in 1945. These Tunisian soldiers of the French Army had fought their way across the Lauter River into Schreibenhardt and were pushing on through the mud into Germany. The man standing third from right is carrying a German MP43 assault rifle — a highly-prized weapon and the forerunner of today's assault rifles.

The February Offensive

With the Colmar pocket cleared, the political hot potato of Strasbourg safely removed from the German oven, and the Allied front as tidy as could be expected, even by Eisenhower, the stage was set for the great advance from the *Westwall* — the Siegfried Line — to and beyond the Rhine. Although the German frontier had been crossed already by the Allies at several points, it remained broadly true that, at the beginning of February 1945 the Allied armies were ranged along the Reich's borders with (from North to South) Holland, Belgium, Luxembourg and France. Only in the vicinity of Aachen (Aix-la-Chappelle) had the *Westwall* been significantly and permanently breached.

Early in the morning of February 8th 1945, before first light, the offensive opened in the North of the line with a bombardment by 1,400 guns of the Canadian 1st Army. On the receiving end of this crippling fire was the German 84th Division, which had been reassured repeatedly by General von Blaskowitz, the commander of Army Group H, that the Allies in general, and the reputedly cautious Montgomery in particular, would not be foolhardy enough to attack in this sector. Both von Blaskowitz and OKH, reputedly all the way up to Hitler himself, had decided that Montgomery would decline to fight across marshy ground, between a flood on one side and the Reichswald Forest on the other. Just how wrong they were was proved

4

5

6

7

5 The 'dragon's teeth' of the Siegfried Line fortifications were to have protected Hitler's Thousand Year Reich from all attack, but they seemed curiously archaic and ineffective when seen as a background to a column of war-weary German prisoners being marched westwards to a prisoner-of-war compound. However they may have felt at the time, these Germans were the lucky ones – they were alive, out of the war, and out of the reach of the approaching Red Army.

6 A derisive song that was popular in Britain and among the troops early in the war claimed, at a time when it seemed all-too-likely that Nazi troops would soon be in London, 'We will hang out our washing on the Siegfried Line'. As the end of the war approached, it was inevitable that press photographers would make the promise come true – thus, this picture of an aircraftsman of the Royal Air Force festooning Germany's defences with his RAF issue shirt.

7 As the Allied armies in the various sectors reached the west bank of the Rhine, they consolidated their positions and maintained pressure on German positions across the river with shell and mortar fire, while the Allied air forces systematically bombed German communications – roads, railway marshalling yards, bridges and viaducts. Here, men of a mortar unit of the US 7th Army have established a position on a railway line across the Rhine from the German town of Kehl. They have clearly been busy for some time.

at 10.30 am, when, on a front of only seven miles between the Maas and the Waal, near the Dutch/German border, the augmented British XXX Corps attacked. Lieutenant-General Brian Horrocks put five divisions into the first wave of the attack and retained two, including the Guards Armoured Division, in reserve. By the end of the first day, the Germans had lost 1,300 men captured and were collapsing.

By February 13th, after days of fierce and bloody fighting, the Canadian 1st Army had moved on to Kleve, on the German side of the border, having finished the mopping up of the Reichswald. At Gennep, as reinforcements for the Canadians arrived in the form of the British 52nd Division and the 11th Armoured Division, General Schlemm, the commander of the German 1st Parachute Army, stepped up German resistance to the developing Allied pressure. He moved two infantry divisions and a *Panzer* division from further South, thereby balancing the Allied reinforcements. The advance came almost to a stop, some 15 miles from its jumping-off point.

It would, however, be quite wrong to assume that it had in any way failed. For Montgomery had once again played the card that had been so successful in Normandy, when the British 2nd Army at Caen had

1 In the north, Field-Marshal Montgomery's 21st Army Group was shaping up for the crossing of the Rhine. Montgomery had only just managed to retain his job after his clash with General Eisenhower following the Battle of the Ardennes. Montgomery claimed that his success in pulling the Ardennes battle round in the northern sector (at a much-publicised press conference he virtually ignored the successes of Bradley and Patton in the Southern Ardennes) proved that he, Montgomery, should have control of operations. Only after a letter of apology from Montgomery, and a speech by Churchill in the House of Commons praising the American role in the Ardennes, did Eisenhower allow him to retain his command. Bradley had insisted that he would prefer to be recalled to the USA rather than serve under Montgomery. Here, Montgomery (centre, in beret) briefs his liaison officers before their daily newsgathering tour of the units of 21st Army Group.

2 The Germans were greatly assisted during their retreat back across the Rhine by the extent to which the extremely wet weather of the winter of 1944/45 slowed down the Allied advance. These British Churchill tanks are making very heavy going in the mud. Note the censor's crude obliteration of the cap badges of the two men in the turret of the leading tank.

3 An impressive night-time picture of a 155mm 'Long Tom' firing on German positions during the 9th Army's advance on the Rhine. This shot, datelined, 11th March 1945, was taken by the light of the gun-flash.

4 On March 2nd 1945, British troops fighting their way southeastwards between the Maas and the Rhine fought their way through a forest, crossed the River Niers in assault craft and then entered the German town of Weeze. Here British troops are seen clearing the streets of Weeze of remaining German soldiers before pushing on southwards to Kewalaer.

drawn the enemy's reinforcements in advance of the American attack on the western side of the beach-head. By forcing Schlemm to concentrate the German forces against the Canadians, he had reduced the resistance to Operation "Grenade", the attack by which the US 9th Army would cross the Roer and advance to the Rhine at Dusseldorf. "Grenade" was now due for February 23rd after being postponed from February 10th because of the massive flooding of the Eifel area caused by the German engineers opening the valves on the Roer dams as they retreated. On February 22nd, as a prelude to the American attack, one of the largest air bombing offensives ever mounted was launched against Germany's communications network to reduce the German army's ability to bring up supplies and reinforcements, and to increase the confusion that was already evident in the German command structure.

Operation 'Grenade'

Next day, in the small hours of the morning, the US artillery opened its bombardment of the German positions on the Roer, defended by the German 15th Army. Quickly, the Americans took Duren and

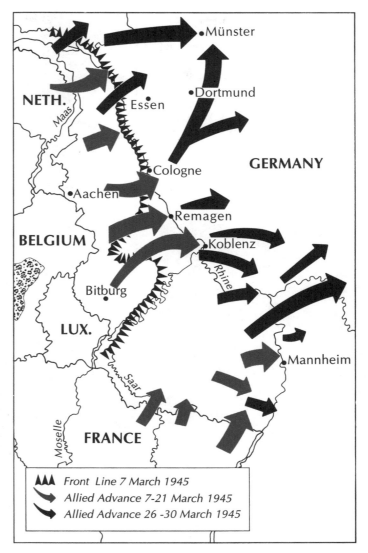

Left crossing the Rhine.

5 A rare gun-camera picture of a German Me-262 jet fighter, one of the world's first jet aircraft to see service, before it was shot down by an American Mustang fighter over Germany in 1945. The first Me-262 to be shot down was credited to a Soviet pilot, Colonel Ivan Kojedub, who was the highest-scoring Allied fighter pilot, with sixty-two victories. He first despatched an Me-262 over Berlin on 24th February 1945.

6 Constant air bombardment was a major factor in preventing the German Army from being able to regroup and reinforce its beleaguered front-line units. In this picture, German anti-aircraft gun crews run to their rail-mounted anti-aircraft guns, which were withdrawn into Germany as the Allies advanced.

Front Line 7 March 1945
Allied Advance 7-21 March 1945
Allied Advance 26 -30 March 1945

Julich, and, despite frantic German movement of the reinforcements just sent to Schlemm back southwards, the US push continued indomitably to positions near Erkolenz on February 27th, and to Rheydt on March 1st. On the US 9th Army's left, Major-General Anderson's XVI Corps made similarly rapid advances towards Roermond and Venlo, and on the right XIX Corps approached Neuss, just across the Rhine from Dusseldorf. The pressure on General Schlemm was tremendous, and he was ordered by OKH to pull back across the Rhine — itself no mean feat in the circumstances. It is a tribute to his skill and generalship that he managed successfully to set up rearguard actions at Xanten and Rheinberg which caused

sufficient delay to enable his engineers to demolish the bridges after most of his army had crossed the river.

Now the US 9th Army and the Canadian 1st Army were able to turn North and South respectively, to link up at Wesel and form a continuous front along the Rhine. The whole operation since February 8th in the 21st Army Group sector had lost the Germans 53,000 prisoners, but the Canadians and British alone had in the same time suffered losses of over 15,500 killed and wounded. The Americans fared rather better.

On March 6th came another major landmark in the defeat of Hitler's Germany as the US VII Corps entered Cologne, thereby

The Battle for the Rhine

completing the Allied chain from Nijmegen in Holland to Cologne, some 100 miles further upstream. South of Cologne, the German 5th *Panzerarmee* was facing both the US 1st and the US 3rd Armies, and was losing ground fast. General Patton's presence in the battle had not been intended by SHAEF, and was due entirely to Patton's own hotheaded and impetuous way of defeating enemies before he had been told to — he had pushed forward contrary to orders during January and February. Nonetheless, his presence hastened the defeat of Colonel-General Harpe's *Panzerarmee* significantly.

Having taken Cologne, the US Army did not rest on its laurels, for the successes against the German 15th Army made it possible for some more rapid advances to be snatched before the German army regrouped, insofar as it was now able so to do. From Cologne on

1 A fine picture of a US Army mortar crew. In the foreground, the officer in charge of the position checks his ranging with a forward observation post. Beyond, in the mortar dugout, the No. 2 ducks out of the way as another mortar bomb makes its way towards the German positions under attack. This picture dates from February 1945, and is an official US Army Signal Corps photograph.

2 A picture of an extremely brave soldier – Lt. John Battenfield Mitchell, of Brentwood, Pittsburgh, who went onto the Ludendorff Bridge at Remagen, found the explosive charges which had failed to go off after they had been placed by the German engineers, and disconnected the detonators. He had been sent to Europe for the first time only in August 1944, and was attached to an armoured engineering battalion.

3 The venting of Hitler's wrath following the Americans' capture intact of the Ludendorff Bridge and the establishment of the first Allied bridgehead east of the Rhine produced a quite disproportionately powerful offensive from the air and by tanks and artillery on the ground. The bridge was finally brought down on March 17th following repeated raids by Germany's latest Arado 234 jet bombers, and many US engineers were killed when it collapsed.

332

4 Datelined March 3rd 1945, this picture was shot in Neuss as men of the 83rd Division, US 9th Army, cleared the town of the retreating German defenders. On the wall above the soldiers are the words 'Long live the Fuehrer. Long live Adolf Hitler'.

5 The reality of war, revealed by a cameraman who, for once, had his head down every bit as much as the soldiers under attack around him. A soldier of the 78th Division, US 1st Army, is cautiously approaching knocked out German tanks and troop carriers, which are burning fiercely after rocket attacks. Among the debris are German troops returning his fire. And the photographer had only his camera.

6 The end of the war for seven German soldiers, surrendering to the US 9th Army with the help of a Red Cross flag outside Geilenkirchen. The soldier on the stretcher seems to have served some time on the Eastern Front, for he has a balalaika on the blanket by his feet.

7 This dramatic scene occurred at the moment when US tanks reached a narrow street leading to Cologne Cathedral, and was photographed by a war photographer waiting for the capture of the famous landmark. A German shell hits one of the American tanks, and one of the crew of the tank, incredibly, is blown out through the turret with one of his legs missing – the man can just be discerned on the after-hull of the tank. Prompt medical attention saved his life, but all others in the tank were killed.

8 A picture that says much about the noise and dirt of the infantry war as the American armies battled their way into Germany. As another mortar bomb makes its way to German positions close by, everyone on the crew has their fingers to their ears except the officer on the left, who is phoning his forward observation post to try and establish whether his shots are falling short of or beyond his target.

March 7th, VII Corps set off to take Bonn, and III Corps set out to capture the crossings over the Ahr. At noon on that day, the intrepid Brigadier-General Hoge, commanding Combat Group B of the US 9th Armoured Division within III Corps, heard the remarkable news that the Ludendorff Bridge over the Rhine at Remagen had not been blown. Recognising the enormous opportunity that capturing this bridge intact would present to the Allies, he went against his orders, and raced to Remagen. At 4pm that day, as his US troops attempted to cross the bridge, the German defenders attempted to explode the charges that were set along it, but failed. The Americans were across the Rhine, and Sergeant Alex Drabik became the first US serviceman to set foot East of the river. The German Major who had been supposed to blow the bridge, and two of his subordinates, were shot on Hitler's personal orders.

The Americans were more forgiving of General Hoge's temporary insubordination, and within twenty-four hours had capitalised on his magnificent stroke by putting 8,000 US troops into the bridge-head East of the Rhine. Hitler vented his wrath by launching air attacks, sending the 11th *Panzer* Division from Bonn, ordering artillery bombardments and even by commanding that a V2 rocket strike be launched against the bridge, but did not manage to knock it down until March 17th, by which time the Americans had

The Battle for the Rhine

not only built another bridge nearby, but had also got four divisions including one armoured division dug in on the eastern side. The 11th *Panzer* had been unable to rectify the situation mainly because it had only 60 tanks, 5,000 men, 30 guns and almost no gasoline.

Further South, General Patton's 3rd Army, having lost III Corps by its transfer to the US 1st Army, was still made up of 12 divisions (three of them armoured) organised as three Corps. By the end of February, these forces had eliminated most of the centre of the Siegried line, and had moved forward to take Saarburg against the extremely determined resistance of the German 7th Army of General Brandenberger, which, on March 1st, collapsed for lack of supplies. Two days later on the 3rd, the 5th Division reached Kyllburg and crossed the River Kyll. This enabled the 4th Division, on March 4th, to rush forward to Daun, and finding the route relatively lightly defended, to push on to reach the Rhine near Koblenz on March 6th. On March 11th, the US 11th Armoured Division became the first unit of the US 3rd Army to join up with the US 1st Army on the Rhine. Patton's 3rd Army had once more reinforced its reputation for speed, and had achieved its additional kudos with losses of only 3,650 killed

1 A fine picture of General Patton (left) in an informal pose with one of his commanders, on his knees studying aerial reconnaissance pictures of his Army's positions in Germany.

2 When fighting an urban war, anything goes – even local perambulators – which in this case came to be used by two infantrymen of the US 3rd Army as materials for a barricade to block a road leading to German-occupied Dillingen. Covering them behind the tree is a third soldier with his rifle at the ready.

3 It takes a cool kind of courage to check out an enemy pillbox after a grenade had been lobbed into it. Although this soldier could reasonably expect that nobody inside would be left alive, he was taking no chances as he approached the hatchway, from which the smoke of the grenade explosion is still curling.

4 So courageous and persistent were the German soldiers in defence of their homeland that there was frequently a long period of time between the date when the Allied propaganda would announce that Allied troops had entered a town, and the date when all fighting in that town was finally over. This is Saarlautern, entered on December 17th 1944, but not finally cleared of German defenders until February 17th – two months of bloody fighting for one town.

5

6

7

8

and 1,374 missing between January 29th and March 12th.

During the following week the action shifted to the US XII Corps under Major-General Eddy and to XX Corps commanded by Major-General Walker. On March 14th, the 4th and 11th Armoured Divisions of XII Corps were set on their way from Treis towards the Rhine, the 4th advancing 32 miles in its first 48 hours and becoming involved in a major pitched battle with the 2nd *Panzer* Division. After some reinforcement, Major-General Gaffey overcame that problem, and by March 19th was between Mainz and Worms. On the 21st, the 4th occupied Worms, the 90th Division had taken Mainz and XX Corps was pushing headlong for Ludwigshafen.

Further South, the US 7th Army faced an uphill struggle against the German 1st Army. Between March 15th when their assault began, and March 19th, progress was slow, and Major-General Brooks, commanding VI Corps had great difficulty in breaking through a remorselessly defended part of the *Westwall*. On March 18th the French General de Monsabert was given command of a task force to head for and take Speyer. By March 24th he had reached Maximiliansau, across the Rhine from Karlsruhe, and General Patch had taken Landau.

Two nights previously, General Patton, this time with General Bradley's full approval, had crossed the Rhine near Oppenheim during the night of March 22/23rd, and by daybreak had almost 5,000 men on the East bank of the Rhine for the loss of only 8 men killed. To Bradley's immense satisfaction, the Americans were, after all, across the Rhine before Montgomery's British and Canadian troops, but Montgomery was not to be far behind, and, when he crossed, he crossed in style.

That great crossing of the Rhine, under the eye of Winston Churchill, will in this book be the prologue to the last act of the German tragedy. Until then, we must leave the Rhine and return to the Eastern Front.

CHAPTER 43

THE RUSSIANS SWEEP INTO GERMANY
THE STRIKE AT THE THIRD REICH'S HEART

On the colossal and complex front to the East of the Third Reich, the Soviet armies had been since the end of their massive drive into Poland regrouping, refitting and improving their formidably long supply lines. In December, Major-General Gehlen, in command of German Military Intelligence on the Eastern Front, had warned OKH in general, and Hitler in particular, of the tremendous build-up of Russian strength, particularly on the Vistula, which threatened East Prussia and, through it, Prussia, Berlin and the heart of the Reich.

Gehlen was a reliable and experienced staff officer, not given (as the postwar facts proved) to exaggeration. Colonel-General Heinz Guderian, OKH Chief of Staff, supported Gehlen's conclusions that the greatest threat to the security of Germany lay in the might of the 1st, 2nd and 3rd Belorussian Fronts, and 1st and 4th Ukrainian Fronts, the five great Soviet armies poised to sweep West from Poland into Germany. Hitler disagreed, believing against all the evidence that the Soviet build-up was no more than mere propaganda, and that his armies had regained the initiative in the West as a result of the Ardennes offensive. As we have seen in an earlier chapter, Hitler even detached without reference to Guderian the IV SS *Panzer* Corps from German Army Group Centre for what was essentially a hopeless errand to relieve Budapest. By so doing he reduced the strength of the Group's reserves from 14 to 12 divisions.

The colossal foolhardiness of this action can be appreciated only by comparing the enormous strength of the Russian forces massed ready for the attack with those of the German defending armies. On paper, OKH could muster 164 divisions to defend a front extending from Hungary to Lithuania, of which 99 were effectively in the area that mattered to Prussia — Army Groups A and Centre. But all those divisions were grossly undermanned and most were seriously underequipped. All were short of fuel and some lacked normal supplies of ammunition. Against them, according to Gehlen's calculations, were massed at least 231 infantry divisions, 22 tank corps, 29 independent tank brigades and 3 cavalry corps, to say nothing of a mighty and effective air force. All these units were well-equipped and to a greater or lesser extent fully-manned.

Russian sources calculated that the Soviet/German ratios were 5.5:1 in men, 7.8:1 in guns, 5.7:1 in armour and a massive 17.7:1 in aircraft. The Russians had no fewer than 13,400 armoured vehicles, mainly tanks and self-propelled assault guns, and some 5,300,000 men on the Eastern Front. In addition to the famous T-34 tank, the Soviet army now had the JS-3, the best-armed tank of the war with its 122mm gun, a top speed of 25mph (despite its 45 tons weight), and a range of 120 miles. Russian aircraft had improved enormously, as had the quality of the Soviet pilots' training.

1

2

1 A picture dating from the time of the Stauffenberg bomb plot of July 1944 shows Hitler talking to Colonel-General Heinz Guderian. Between them are Field Marshal Keitel and Field Marshal von Bock (right). Note how Hitler holds his left hand with his right to conceal the lack of use in his left arm. As the Russians began the advance into Germany, Hitler countermanded the orders of Guderian and hastened the end of his Third Reich.

2 Described by contemporary reports as the toughest German bridgehead of the whole war on the Eastern Front, the pocket around the Baltic port of Koeningsberg was gradually worn down by a mighty Russian concentric drive on several fronts. These Soviet troops are marching through a German village on the approach to Koeningsberg.

Despite his earlier rebuff from Hitler when the subject of Soviet strength and the imminent danger of a Russian attack was mentioned, Guderian broached to Hitler on January 9th a detailed plan for a structured withdrawal to more defensible positions, and for transfer of a significant number of divisions from the western front to the East. Hitler responded with a furious rage, once again refusing to accept the possibility of a threat from a race whom he had regarded as sub-human. In his fury, he demanded Gehlen's committal to a lunatic asylum, which Guderian countered by saying that if Gehlen went, he went too. It seemed to the desperate Guderian, one of the most successful soldiers of the Second World War, that nothing could be done to forestall the military disaster that was about to befall the once-proud German Army.

The Soviet High Command, *Stavka*, had planned its new offensive for January 20th, along a 750 mile front extending from Tilsit on the Niemen, on the borders of Lithuania and close to the Baltic, southwards to Baranow on the Lower Vistula. Because of urgent appeals from Churchill to Stalin to launch an offensive in the East as soon as possible to take the heat off the western front, the Russians' first attack was brought forward to January 12th, and was

3 Soviet T-34 tanks rumble along a snow-covered highway in Poland on the approach to the eastern borders of Germany during the last hard winter of the Second World War.

4 By the winter of 1944/45, the German troops in the East were intensely weary and many felt thoroughly demoralised. The more intelligent among them knew their defeat was only a matter of time, and yet their training and spirit was, in most cases, sufficient to keep them fighting bravely and honourably. These German troops were retreating, using the tanks as transport to get as many infantry as possible away from the advancing Russians.

5 Soviet troops riding on the backs of massive SU 152 self-propelled guns. These powerful machines were manufactured at 'Tankograd' near Chelabinsk, and they carried a 152mm howitzer on the chassis of the earlier KV 1 heavy tank.

6 As the Soviet troops of the 1st Ukrainian Army poured into Gleiwitz in German Silesia, the fighting was fierce, and great destruction was caused by the shelling. These Soviet soldiers are clearing buildings of German snipers amidst the rubble of war.

The Russians Sweep into Germany

far to the South of the line. It came from the 1st Ukrainian Front, which was facing the German XLVIII Corps of the 4th *Panzerarmee* across the lower Vistula at Baranow. The German Corps was thinly spread along its front, with only three weak infantry divisions, each of which was down to six battalions. At Hitler's insistence, and against all advice from Colonel-General Harpe, the reserves were only 12 miles to the rear. Despite firm evidence of new Soviet high-speed tanks whose armament and armour made them virtually unstoppable, Hitler refused to believe that a Russian armoured column would be capable of covering 12 miles in one day. Furthermore, Hitler issued a firm order that the reserves were not to be thrown into action without his express permission – but nonetheless continued to lie abed until 11am.

The attack began at 3am with an artillery barrage, followed by a brief diversionary attack to cause the *Panzer* units to reveal their positions in the darkness. The Soviet army, commanded by Marshal Konev, swiftly demonstrated what Major-General Gehlen had meant by superiority of fire power. Along the line of attack at Baranow, Konev launched against the German defences no less than 34 infantry divisions and 1000 tanks, and hammered the German positions with guns 320 to the mile – virtually wheel to wheel. In one day on January 12th, the 1st Ukrainian Front completely overran the 4th *Panzerarmee* and advanced up to 15 miles; so rapid was the advance

Grossdeutschland Panzer Corps was in the sector it had attacked, and the experienced and skilful German tank commanders made the most of foggy conditions and the surprise their presence had created. On January 14th, the German *Panzer* units, despite their numerical disadvantage, had launched 37 counter-attacks in one day.

Clearly, the *Grossdeutschland Panzer* Corps had become a key factor in keeping the Soviet 3rd Army at bay. Hitler therefore made, and obstinately refused to alter despite the obvious facts and the outspoken criticism of his Chief of Staff, a decision that even he rarely exceeded in its sheer madness. He ordered that the *Grossdeutschland Panzer* Corps should be immediately transferred from its present location in Army Group Centre to Army Group A, where it was to attack the Russian forces advancing on Poznan, despite the fact that it would almost certainly be too late arriving there to be any use, and that its removal from its current location would assuredly cause the collapse of the German line.

The *Grossdeutschland* Corps was duly pulled out of the line, and, on the 16th of January, the Soviet armies began to break through the greatly weakened German 2nd Army. By the 20th January, Marshal Rokossovsky had reached the border of East Prussia and had crossed it, launching his 5th Tank Army towards Elbing. Meanwhile the *Grossdeutschland Panzer* Corps arrived at Lodz just in time to retreat under heavy fire in an impossible situation and only just made cover

1 General Dietrich von Saucken, who commanded the *Gross Deutschland Panzer Korps* so ineptly transferred by Hitler at the moment it was most needed. Von Saucken's *Panzers* had shown in January 1945 that they were the principal obstacle to the advance of the 2nd and 3rd Belorussian Fronts into Germany – but Hitler refused to accept this, transferred them to the north, and allowed the Soviet Army to sweep into Germany.

2 The Red Army had learned much from its bitter experiences of 1941, and had become much better trained and equipped. Soviet troops had learned the techniques of stealth and fieldcraft that enabled them effectively to out-soldier the German infantry at least some of the time. These Russian troops are stealing up on a German machine-gun post.

3 As the Soviet troops took town after town, the civilian population of Germany came to fear their depredations, for they were little more respectful of German homes and womenfolk than the Germans had been of theirs.

that by the time Hitler was available to make decisions about the reserves, the decisions were no longer necessary. As darkness fell, the Russians pushed right on without stopping.

On January 14th, the next Soviet army to the North, Marshal Zhukov's 1st Belorussian Front, broke out of the Pulawy and Magnuszew bridgeheads on the Vistula and, more by chance than planning, encountered German *Panzer* formations that were well separated from each other and thereby incapable of putting up a united front. General Berzarin's 5th Shock Army and Chuikov's 8th Guards Army virtually annihilated three German divisions that were absurdly outnumbered, and the Soviet 33rd and 69th Armies overran two luckless German divisions whose soldiers must have wondered what hit them. The tidal wave of Russian power almost destroyed the German 9th Army, sweeping across the Vistula and carrying all before it.

Further North again, the Russians encountered firmer German resistance. On January 13th and 14th, the 2nd and 3rd Belorussian Fronts and their respective Air Armies went into action against German Army Group Centre and achieved little headway until January 16th, despite outnumbering the German defenders locally by at least 3:1. Soviet intelligence had failed to note that the crack in Prussia without being encircled. Hitler's decision precipitated the destruction of no less than 28 German divisions.

To the North, the 3rd Belorussian Front under Chernyakhovsky had pressed forward, overcoming and destroying the 3rd *Panzerarmee* and approaching, as January drew to a close, within 30 miles of Konigsberg. Colonel-General Reinhardt's 4th Army had, on January 17th, been in what was clearly a dangerously exposed position, and liable to encirclement as the 2nd Belorussian Front pushed forward. Despite urgent appeals from Reinhardt, Hitler refused permission to withdraw. The inevitable happened. On January 21st, 350,000 men of the German 4th Army were encircled and trapped at Lotzen. With considerable ingenuity and great bravery, General Hossbach broke out Southwards and attempted by forced marches over five days through biting snowstorms to get to Elbing before the 5th Guards Tank Army. He failed. The Russian tanks had reached Elbing on January 27th.

Further South, Marshals Zhukov and Konev crashed on towards

4 As the war came closer to home for the Germans, boys and older men were pressed into action. These middle-aged men were troops of the *Volkssturm*, captured by the Russians in the town of Schneidemuel in Brandenburg.

4

5

their goal. The German 2nd Army was shattered and unable to do anything constructive to stop the Russian advance. Between January 19th and January 23rd, Marshal Konev fought 90 miles towards Berlin in just three days. Colonel-General Schoerner, who had replaced Harpe following the latter's disgrace at Hitler's hands following the collapse of Army Group Centre, was a competent general, and a capable administrator, but there was nothing he could do to slow the Russian advance. By the end of January the forward troops of the 1st Ukrainian Front had reached the River Oder above Oppeln and either side of Breslau. At two points they were on the West bank of the Oder. Further South, Zhukov's tank armies had, by the end of the first week of February, reached Frankfurt on Oder, and were only some 50 miles from Hitler's bunker.

At the end of January, Hitler made his last disastrous attempt at reorganising the smashed German armies into some semblance of resistance to the Russian onslaught. Instead of giving the experienced Colonel-General Weichs command of the new Army Group Vistula,

as Guderian had wanted, Hitler gave it to his uniquely incompetent and twisted *Reichsfuhrer SS* Heinrich Himmler, who had already proved with Operation *Nordwind* the massive extent of his inability to achieve military success. Himmler compounded Hitler's stupidity by appointing his commanders on a basis of party purity rather than military competence. The scene was set for total and unmitigated disaster.

After February 6th, when the Soviet front line extended almost to the border of Prussia, the Soviet advance slowed. Throughout February 1945 and into March, the Russian armies continued the task of isolating and annihilating Germany's remaining forces in Silesia and East Prussia. By mid-April, East Prussia had been taken, and the Soviet line extended from Stettin on the Baltic coast, southwards to Frankfurt on Oder, Forst and Bunzlau, then South-Eastwards around the borders of Czechoslovakia. The victory was almost, but not quite complete. The final act remained to be played, in the West as in the East.

5 The scenes that greeted troops liberating German concentration camps, whether on the Eastern or Western Fronts as the Allies closed in on Germany, were horrifying on a scale that had not been imagined by most of the men who had fought against Hitler's Germany. In the camps, American, Soviet, Canadian and British soldiers discovered what they had been fighting for all those years.

CHAPTER 44

DIVIDING THE SPOILS THE ALLIES CONFER AT QUEBEC, MOSCOW AND YALTA

As the purely military aspects of the war became increasingly clear cut following the Allied successes in 1944, the political considerations of victory began to have increasing significance in the minds of the Allied leaders. Roosevelt had become increasingly trustful and admiring of Marshal Stalin, a trait that Winston Churchill did not find to his liking but which may have had some of its origins in the pro-Soviet sympathies of the President's long-time confidant and adviser Harry Hopkins. Churchill, for his part, was deeply worried about Stalin's intentions in Eastern Europe, and, while confident of a successful and friendly relationship with the Russian leader for as long as Hitler's Germany remained their common enemy, was aware that divergent interests would almost certainly prevail once Germany was defeated.

A further factor in the equation was the imminence of the US Presidential elections of November 1944, and the President's failing health. Despite his obviously being sick and in a state of decline, President Roosevelt clearly felt it to be his duty to see America through the closing stages of the war he had done so much to bring to a succesful conclusion for the Allies. He therefore ran for a fourth term of office, and, no doubt feeling that a lame horse was better than an unknown mount at this crucial stage of the war, the American people duly elected him for a further term on November 7th 1944. However, there is no doubt that his faculties were less acute than they had been, particularly by the time of the all-important Yalta Conference in the Crimea in February 1945, and that Stalin used this factor to his own and Russia's advantage, and to the disadvantage of the whole of Eastern Europe.

The development of the Allied agreements on the partition of Europe that emerged from the series of three conferences began when Churchill and Roosevelt met in Quebec on September 11th 1944. Called principally to discuss the role of Britain's armed forces in the defeat of Japan after the victory in Germany had been concluded, the Quebec conference tackled the partition of Europe almost as an afterthought – but the discussions were crucial. On the Japanese war, the decisions reached were all made on the assumption, then current in US Staff circles, that the defeat of Japan would take a further eighteen months after Germany had been conquered. The US Chiefs of Staff had hoped that substantial elements of the British Army would be sent as reinforcements to the Australian and New Zealand troops that had long been under General MacArthur's command, but Churchill was opposed to this. In a lengthy minute quoted in full in 'Triumph and Tragedy', Volume 6 of his 'The Second World War', Churchill pronounced himself in favour of 'British diversionary exercises on a major scale calculated to wear down the enemy forces by land and air, and also to regain British possessions conquered by the Japanese'. He proposed to the Quebec Conference '. . . a direct thrust across the Bay of Bengal aimed at "Dracula" (Rangoon), "Culverin" (Sumatra) or other attainable preliminary objectives'.

According to Churchill, the British delegation at Quebec carried the Americans with it on the Rangoon plan, which he saw as having many advantages as a strategy. Churchill pointed out that six months' fighting in the hills and jungles of Burma and on the frontier of India was estimated to have cost the British and Empire forces 288,000 losses from sickness alone, but that a seaborne stroke against Rangoon and a northward advance would cut the enemy's communications and divide his forces at minimum cost. Churchill in fact went so far as to suggest that the USA might care to lend Britain a couple of divisions to fight in Burma, but his suggestion was, he says, 'not adopted'.

Thus the final verdict at Quebec on the Far Eastern War was that Britain should 'give naval assistance on the largest scale to the main American operations' but should 'keep our own thrust for Rangoon as a preliminary operation . . . to a major attack upon Singapore'.

The Morgenthau Plan

The strangest and most controversial decision taken at Quebec was the adoption of the infamous Morgenthau Plan as Allied policy. With hindsight, it seems incredible that such a plan should have been suggested, let alone supported by Roosevelt and accepted by Churchill. That it was thus accepted, and that we find its acceptance so strange, is a measure of the extent to which attitudes to Germany and the German wars, and thought on issues of the rights of nations and peoples have changed in almost forty-five years.

Henry Morgenthau Junior was the Secretary of the Treasury in

Roosevelt's administration. He became aware in August 1944 that there was discussion between General Eisenhower and the US War Department to formulate policies for the treatment of Germany and its population, industry and institutions once Germany had been defeated. Being in the President's confidence, he formulated his own proposals for the Allied treatment of Germany, and took them, behind the War Department's back, to Roosevelt. Roosevelt concurred in Morgenthau's proposals, despite the opposition of Henry Stimson, the Secretary of War, and the Morgenthau Plan therefore went to Quebec as a firm American proposal.

The Plan proposed that Germany would not only have all factories, steel production plants and industrial enterprises destroyed, but would also be forbidden the production of industrial raw materials. The coal and iron mines were to be flooded and destroyed, and the entire population was to be forced to return to an entirely agricultural and peasant way of life, dependent totally on the growing of crops and the breeding of animals.

Nobody seems to have made at the time the point that seems so obvious now – that the plan was, in all but the crucial aspect of mass murder, not unlike the SS ideals of the manipulation of populations and racial supremacy. The plan was both impractical and inhuman.

1 The American military commanders who took part in the Quebec Conference of September 1944, photographed as they left the Chateau Frontenac Hotel in Quebec to attend a state dinner during the conference. (Left to right) Admiral Ernest J. King, Commander-in-Chief of the US Fleet; General H.H. Arnold, Commanding General of the US Army Air Forces and General George C. Marshall, US Chief of Staff.

2 The Quebec Conference of September 1944 was the tenth occasion during the Second World War that President Roosevelt and British Prime Minister Winston Churchill had met to discuss the policy of the war and its aftermath. Here Roosevelt (left) looks thinner and more drawn than in earlier pictures, but Churchill (centre) shows little sign of the persistent health problems that dogged him at the time. On the right is Canadian Prime Minister W. Mackenzie King.

3 Churchill's distaste for his trips to Moscow almost equalled his mistrust for those whom he met there. Here he is with Soviet Foreign Minister Molotov during the talks of October 1944.

4 Despite President Roosevelt's obviously declining health, White House press handouts tried hard to sustain optimism about his condition. The contemporary caption to this picture says 'FDR IS LOOKING UP' – which is clearly accurate in one sense – and goes on to say that 'President Roosevelt is the picture of joviality as he enjoys a hearty laugh during a ceremony in which he received a model of the inaugural medal'. The date was 18th January 1945.

5 Contrast the appearance of President Roosevelt in this picture taken at the Yalta Conference at the beginning of February 1945 with the full cheeks and buoyant smile of pictures apparently taken only a week or two before – Churchill, shown here with the President, declared himself shocked at the appearance of his friend at this meeting.

On September 13th, Churchill is reported by his doctor, Lord Moran, as having said at a dinner in Quebec 'I'm all for disarming Germany, but we ought not to prevent her living decently. There are bonds between the working classes of all countries, and the English people will not stand for the policy you are advocating'. Yet by September 15th he had apparently been convinced by Professor Lindemann (Lord Cherwell) that the plan had the advantage of eliminating a postwar trade competitor, and should therefore be adopted. In all events, Churchill signed. Anthony Eden, then Britain's Foreign Secretary, remarked in his memoirs that its proposals for the Ruhr were like deciding to turn the Black Country into Devonshire.

Resistance to the Morgenthau Plan mounted once it was known that it had been signed. To Henry Stimson's side came Secretary of State Cordell Hull, Deputy Secretary of War John McCloy and General Eisenhower. Finally Harry Hopkins joined the protest movement – and at that point Roosevelt convinced Morgenthau that the plan must be shelved. It never saw the light of day again.

The Moscow Meeting
Churchill now turned his attention to his increasing fears that Stalin's political motives underlying the massive Soviet war effort were not

entirely unblemished. It was by now clear that the Soviet Union had every intention of sweeping Europe on a massive front from the Baltic in the North, and (apparently) to the Adriatic in the South. Although Churchill was not over concerned about Rumania and Hungary, he was deeply interested to see that Poland and Austria were treated justly, and to ensure that Greece was not enslaved unwillingly (or even willingly) to Communism.

At the end of September 1944, Churchill therefore broached to Stalin the idea of a meeting in Moscow, and flew to see the Russian leader on October 9th. Roosevelt had declined to attend the conference on the grounds that the Presidential elections were close at hand, and delegated Averell Harriman as his observer, but with no power to negotiate on behalf of the United States. Furthermore, to Churchill's considerable chagrin, Roosevelt made it quite clear in a letter to Stalin that he would not be bound by any decision taken at Moscow, and that he regarded any discussions merely as a preliminary to a further conference of all three leaders. Churchill took this (correctly) as a lack of trust on Roosevelt's part in the conservatism of his (Churchill's) strategic thinking, but coming so soon after the Morgenthau episode, one might be forgiven for thinking that Roosevelt was being high-handed, to say the least.

Dividing the Spoils

Late in the evening of October 9th, immediately after their tiring trip to Moscow, Churchill and Eden met Stalin and the Soviet Foreign Minister, Molotov, for initial discussions. Harriman had yet to arrive, so there was no US presence. As if from a hat, Churchill produced immediately proposals for the possible division of Europe into spheres of influence after the end of the war. While the translators were explaining to Stalin and Molotov the Churchill plans, Churchill wrote down on a scrap of paper the world-changing proposal that influence in the Balkans and Eastern Europe should be apportioned as:

Rumania.
Russia 90%
The others 10%

Greece
Great Britain
(in accord with USA) 90%
Russia 10%

Yugoslavia 50-50%

Hungary 50-50%

Bulgaria
Russia 75%
The others 25%

According to Eden, Stalin simply ticked the piece of paper and returned it to Churchill, who subsequently wrote 'it was all settled in no more time than it takes to write down'.

The scene is unmistakably redolent of the meeting between Chamberlain and Hitler in 1938 when Hitler almost absent-mindedly signed Chamberlain's scrap of paper. Churchill was not sufficiently naive to claim 'peace in our time' — but subsequent experience showed that his fundamental instincts about Stalin and the Soviet government were correct and that the Soviet Union had no intention of honouring any agreement in respect of Eastern Europe unless it operated to its advantage.

On October 13th, delegates of the Polish government in exile, who were naturally deeply concerned at the existence of a Russian-backed

1 Marshal Josef Stalin (centre) has the easy appearance of a man who knows he has matters comfortably in hand in this picture taken at the Yalta Conference in February 1945. Churchill appears to be seeking a little relaxation with one of his famous cigars.

2 A general view of the conference table at Yalta, in the Crimea, in February 1945. Marshal Stalin is on the left, flanked by various aides, and President Roosevelt is on the extreme right, with Admiral William D. Leahy on his right, and General Marshall next to Admiral Leahy. At left in the foreground, with his back to the camera, is Winston Churchill.

communist Lublin 'National Committee', met Stalin, Molotov, Churchill, Eden and Harriman. Their mission was to discuss two issues — the formation of a unified Polish government after the ejection of Germany from their country, and the troubled question of the postwar Polish eastern frontier. The unfortunate Poles, led by their Prime Minister Stanislas Mikolajczyk, discovered for the first time at this meeting that the Allies had already decided at Teheran that the Curzon Line was to become their postwar frontier — which meant the loss to Russia of 48% of the territory Poland had had in 1939, including the cities of Lvov and Vilnyus. Expecting support from the British delegation against this plan — after all, Britain had gone to war in 1939 over a much smaller part of Poland — the Polish government team found that Churchill was vehement in his support for it. In this, Churchill was doing no more than recognising the inevitable, but to the Poles it looked like, and possibly was, a sell-out.

And so to Yalta

During the winter of 1944/45, much occurred which altered the world stage and the dispositions of the politicians upon it. Roosevelt, re-elected on November 7th, had a new and effective Vice-President to replace the professional nonentity, Henry Wallace, who had been his understudy almost since America's war had begun. Harry S. Truman, though inexperienced in government, rose well to the occasion when catapulted into one of the most powerful positions on earth in April 1945, and was an able and worthy man.

During that same winter, the President had become visibly more frail and ill, and Lord Moran, when he saw him in February at Yalta, diagnosed at a distance advanced atherosclerosis and gave as his unofficial opinion that he had only months to live. On the military

front, as we have seen, the Ardennes offensive had come and gone, and the Allies in the West were poised for the assault on the Rhine. In Eastern Europe, the Russians had swept into Poland and were about to stabilise their front on the Oder. Germany was demonstrably defeated. The matter of final decisions on territorial rights and the administration of Germany after the war had become urgent.

On February 2nd 1945, Roosevelt and Churchill arrived in Malta to confer with the Combined Chiefs of Staff Committee, who had been finalising over the previous few days the plans for the final sweep into the centre of Germany from the West. Having agreed the plans, the two leaders flew to the Crimea for the Yalta Conference, the first meeting of which took place on the following day, February 4th. From the start, Stalin had the conference under control. He proposed that the ailing Roosevelt should be in the chair, and thereby effectively reduced the influence of Churchill's ally in the discussions. Of the other US delegates to whom Churchill might have turned, Harry Hopkins was very pro-Russian and, by now, somewhat out of favour with Roosevelt, and the US team even included a diplomat called Alger Hiss, who in 1950 was convicted in the USA for perjury in respect of his communist party membership. Clearly, the pro-socialist camp was in the ascendant.

3 An unusually intimate and informal picture of deep discussion between the two men who had done more than anyone else to steer the course of the Allied effort in the Second World War. Over the coffee cups, President Roosevelt and Winston Churchill, cigar in hand, discuss the future of Europe.

The troubled conference came to final decisions on three major areas of concern – Poland, Germany and the Far East. Let us look at the conclusions on each in turn.

Poland It was agreed that the Oder and the Neisse were to become the Western boundary of Poland, although Stalin took the opportunity to claim that he had referred all along to the Western Neisse, when everybody else had been referring to the Eastern Neisse, which actually passes through the town of Neisse. Stalin's winning of this point meant the uprooting of 8 million Germans. The Soviet leader made some modest concessions on the location of the Eastern frontier, but they were of relatively little significance. The Polish Government was to be created from both the communist Lublin Committee and from the London government in exile, but nobody specified how many members of the government were to be allotted from each. Since Molotov was to chair the steering commission, the outcome was never in doubt.

Germany After some difficulty, the British delegation persuaded Stalin to accept that France should be a member of the Allied Control Commission that would administer Germany after the surrender. The borders of the Allied occupation zones were decided, and the principle of dividing Germany permanently was agreed, although without any detailed proposals being settled. Instead, a commission was set up under the chairmanship of Britain's Anthony Eden to study the problem. Roosevelt and Stalin agreed between them that Germany should pay '20,000 million dollars in reparations, half of it to be paid in kind to the Soviet Union by the transfer of industrial equipment, annual deliveries of goods and the use of German manpower'.

The Far East In return for the return to the USSR of the Southern part of the island of Sakhalin, the port of Dairen, the Manchuria Railway and its lease on Port Arthur, all lost to Japan after the war of 1905, plus the Kurile Islands, Russia undertook in a secret agreement to lend forces to the defeat of Japan after the defeat of Germany.

Thus did a tyrant, a dying President, and a great Prime Minister with few cards to play settle the fate of a large part of Europe and the Far East in the space of a few days. Meanwhile, far from their remote meeting-place in the Crimea the war raged on.

4 This is the picture of Yalta, and of the frailty of the dying President Roosevelt, that everybody remembers. Taken by the British official photographer at the press photocall that followed the conclusion of the conference, it expresses clearly the position as it then was – Stalin, sure of himself and protected from the opposition of Churchill by the conference chairmanship of the President and by the pro-Soviet views of the President's political and diplomatic aides.

5 On the 1st March 1945, President Roosevelt reported to Congress on the outcome of the Yalta Conference. Seated on a red plush chair, he told a cheering audience that 'We shall have to take the responsibility for world collaboration, or we shall have to bear the responsibility for another world conflict'. Six weeks later, on April 12th, he died.

6 Field-Marshal Lord Alanbrooke (right), previously Sir Alan Brooke, was Churchill's principal military adviser throughout the war, and played a major part in averting problems that might otherwise have been caused by Churchill's occasional excesses of enthusiasm for a less-than-fully-researched idea. This picture, taken in 1946, shows Field Marshal Viscount Alanbrooke, Chief of the Imperial General Staff, talking to General Sir Claude Auchinleck, then Commander-in-Chief in India.

CHAPTER 45

THE END IN ITALY
THE NET CLOSES

The late summer and autumn of 1944 in Italy had seen a protracted defensive campaign by a somewhat heterogeneous German army, supported by large concentrations of forced labour units of the Todt Organisation. The German defence had been masterfully organised by Field-Marshal Kesselring to delay and hold General (later Field-Marshal) Alexander's attempts to cross the Appenines and advance to a line running from Venice to Brescia, and also to fend off an amphibious invasion that the Germans were (wrongly) convinced would come from the Bay of Venice. Such an invasion was in fact almost impossible because of the sandbanks offshore, but Kesselring appeared not to be aware of this, a fact that worked appreciably to the Allies' advantage by keeping six German divisions tied down to the defence of the coastline.

Hitler was of course aware that a successful advance to the Alps would present the Allies with not only the option of an assault on Austria and Germany from the South, but also a greatly-improved ability to bomb the Rumanian oilfields and the important aircraft factories in the South of Germany. He had made substantial resources available to Kesselring for the fortification of the 'Gothic Line', a defensive position running coast to coast across the mountains for 200 miles from a point near La Spezia on the Gulf of Genoa to Pesaro on the Adriatic. Every mountain route that Alexander and General Mark Clark could reasonably take to the Po valley was protected by heavily defended strongpoints, and when the battle for the Gothic Line began in earnest in August 1944, the Germans had installed 2,376 machine gun nests, 479 anti-tank and assault gun positions and four of the formidable 75mm Panther gun turrets. Had Alexander waited longer before attacking, there would have been 30 of these Panther installations, and the course of the battle would have been harder for the Allies.

In August, Kesselring had been able to field 26 divisions, including six armoured *Panzer* and *Panzergrenadier* divisions and six Italian divisions loyal to Mussolini's German-supported 'government in exile'. The Allies had only 20 divisions, following Alexander's having to give up seven divisions for 'Dragoon', the Allied amphibious landing in the South of France, but, as in every other theatre by this stage of the war, Allied air superiority was total. Alexander was able to call on the services of no less than 75 bomber and fighter-bomber squadrons, plus plenty of air transport and supply aircraft. Kesselring had only 170 aircraft of all types. Given that Kesselring had detached substantial forces to defend the Bay of Venice, the balance of power was in the Allies' favour, but not to a sufficient degree to make a rapid victory likely or predictable. In this context it should not be forgotten that the Italian partisans were now constantly and effectively active against the German army's depots and military installations behind German lines, and were directly beneficial to the Allies.

The Allies' originally-planned direct frontal assault against the Gothic Line in the mountains was re-planned early in August as a

1

2

1 Air communications were key contributions to Allied successes in the mountainous terrain of Italy, for without air transport, large formations operating in remote areas could not be kept supplied with food, equipment, fuel and ammunition. This is a Douglas DC3 Dakota, taking off past airfield defences to fly north.

2 The highly developed skill of the engineers in the construction of Bailey bridges was extremely important to the Allied troops as they advanced northwards. There are many rivers in Italy, and most had to be bridged after retreating German troops had blown existing ones. These are South African soldiers aboard a Sherman tank used as an artillery observation post.

3 Canadian troops on the move in the autumn of 1944, crossing a Bailey Bridge over the River Sieve.

4 The magnificent work of the medical units is given far too little recognition in most books and films devoted to the Second World War. Here, a British medical orderly carries in a wounded soldier in Italy. Because of the rugged nature of the Italian terrain, the wounded frequently had to travel further before receiving medical aid than was the case in some other theatres of the war.

'two-handed punch' towards both Ravenna and Bologna. The bulk of the British 8th Army under General Sir Oliver Leese — two Corps — was to attack towards Ravenna along the East coast via Route 16, and through the nearby hills to Route 9, the only available routes that did not cross the mountains. The other British Corps, XIII Corps, was to join II Corps of the US 5th Army for the assault on Bologna, and two more US Corps, plus the 6th South African Armoured Division, were to hold the remainder of the 5th Army line while the assault took place.

The snag, early in August, was that the entire 8th Army was in the mountains, positioned for the attack as originally planned. A massive secret operation was mounted to move the two Corps to the plain without the Germans finding out, and it succeeded brilliantly. When the attack on the coast came on August 25th, Kesselring did not take it seriously, believing that all the Allies' strength was far away in the mountains. By the time he discovered the truth it was too late, and the Polish, Canadian and British troops of the 8th Army were through the Gothic Line on a narrow front. By August 31st they held the heavily defended town of Montegridolfo, and on September 1st took Tavoleto. The Canadians suffered a great many casualties in fierce fighting, but succeeded in getting across the River Conca and establishing a bridgehead.

5 A radio picture dating from October 1944, showing Field Marshal Albert Kesselring ('Smiling Albert' to the Allied troops), the German Commander-in-Chief in Italy and the Mediterranean, visiting Marshal Graziani, who functioned in the largely titular post of Minister of War in Mussolini's 'puppet' government. This was established by Hitler after Mussolini's rescue from the mountains by German troops under Otto Skorzeny as a counter to the armistice signed with the Allies by the Badoglio government in September 1943, and that government's declaration of war against Germany in October 1943.

6 A fine and well-known picture of General Alexander in his jeep, photographed when visiting Allied 5th Army positions in Italy. Alexander was one of the most-liked Generals of the war, and his charm, tact and professionalism made him successful both in his role as a field commander and in that of a military politician and diplomat. He was also one of the few Allied commanders who could claim to have led German troops — in 1919-20 he had led a brigade of Baltic German volunteers to free Latvia from Communist rule, a deliverance that was sadly not to last.

7 There were many major examples of the large-scale German theft of art treasures from the great cities of Europe. This picture was taken in Florence as the Germans withdrew from the city, taking pictures from the Uffizi with them, and was radioed from neutral Stockholm.

The End in Italy

In the mountains, the 5th Army found the assault far more difficult and costly. Rough mountainous terrain made the advance slow, and gave the advantage to the defenders. Kesselring managed to get substantial reinforcements up to the front, and, during the first week of September, the Italian autumn once more provided the unremitting rain that had bedevilled the Allied campaign of a year before. The Air Forces could no longer guarantee the all-important 'aerial artillery' function, and the Allied advance ground to a halt. General Clark reviewed the situation, and regrouped for a set-piece attack against the German positions at their most vulnerable positions. On September 12th, with better weather permitting air support once more, the attack began again, this time with two corps on a narrow front against the Gothic Line fortifications near the Il Giogo pass. By September 18th, Clark's army held seven miles of the Gothic Line defences, and the Americans began to fight their way towards Route 9 at Imola, where it was hoped that they would join up with the 8th Army.

Kesselring threw in almost all the reinforcements he had available in the area to prevent the US 88th Division reaching Imola, and although on September 27th the US troops were ten miles from the town, they were still no closer a week later after fierce fighting against

four entire German divisions. The weather was now closing in, and the worsening conditions favoured the defenders. So General Clark abandoned his attempt on Imola for the time being, and pursued his major objective of reaching Bologna. On the plains of the Romagna, near the Adriatic coast to the East, the New Zealand, Greek and Canadian troops of the 8th Army had pushed both North and towards Route 9 from the other side, but the New Zealanders had become bogged down by the heavy rain on the banks of the River Fiumicino.

Clark's progress through the mountains towards Bologna was punctuated with heavy casualties in terrible conditions. Kesselring had reinforced the German 10th Army with five additional divisions, including the redoubtable 16th SS *Panzer* Division, and the Americans had to fight for every inch of the rocky terrain. Monte Grande fell to the US 88th Division on October 20th, but by the 25th conditins were so bad, and so little progress was being made that General Clark gave the order to dig in. Both in the mountains and on the plain the intensity of the deluge was so great that bridges were swept away and rapid advances were virtually impossible. Not until just before Christmas could the offensive be resumed, and then it was only for a matter of days before Field-Marshal Alexander gave the order to return to the defensive as the bitterly cold winter weather closed in on the armies of both sides.

1 The war of attrition by which the Allies slowly advanced against German troops determined – and ordered – not to give an inch was colossally expensive of both men and equipment. This Sherman tank of the British 8th Army is passing a knocked-out German PzKpfw V *Panther* battle tank.

2 An American 155mm 'Long Tom' crosses a Bailey bridge over a river in the central sector of the 8th Army front in Italy, watched by Indian troops. Large guns such as this had a significant role in the fierce bombardment of German positions prior to infantry assaults.

3 As the Allied advance grew more rapid, the Germans often did not have time to take their wounded with them – and may also have felt that injured Germans stood a better chance with the Allies because of their much superior medical supplies position. Thus, Allied medical teams frequently brought in wounded Germans for treatment. These are orderlies of the Royal Army Medical Corps, near Casaglia.

The Last Push into 1945 and Victory

During the lull of the winter, the Allied armies in Italy were substantially reinforced with new weapons; new better-armed tanks, armoured vehicles with wider tracks to cope with the soft ground, and tracked landing vehicles for use in the marshy areas around Lake Comacchio. Alexander had been appointed Supreme Commander in the Mediterranean in succession to Maitland Wilson, and as the winter began to recede, Allied morale was high. The Germans set to work with their huge forced labour organisation building yet more defences on every river line in the path of the Allied advance, and remorselessly trained the heavily reinforced 10th Army, now commanded by General Herr, for the struggle to come. Kesselring's Armies were now probably the best equipped facing the Allies anywhere in the European war, and the 10th Army, defending the Eastern (Adriatic) sector had had a whole Parachute Corps of 30,000 men under General Heidrich newly added to it. General Senger, commanding the German 14th Army in the Western sector, defending the approach to Bologna, had the 51st Mountain Corps holding the line towards Genoa and the Mediterranean, and the 14th *Panzer* Corps providing the defence of Bologna itself.

By comparison, the strength of the Allied 15th Army had been reduced, it having lost three divisions to the quelling of civil war in Greece, and the Canadian I Corps to the Allied push in Holland. Alexander was down to 17 divisions in the field, but remained totally in command of the air, and with it, in the end, the battle. Between February and April 1945, the strategic bombing force in Italy was progressively increased, and by the time the April offensive began, there were some 4,000 Allied aircraft taking part. As early as February 6th the bombers had begun attacking the German supply routes through the Brenner Pass, and the all-important German fuel dumps. By April, every railway line North of the River Po had been cut in several places, and the German armies were doing battle with their supply problems to an increasing degree every day. As the weather improved, the Allied bombing intensified and the Germans became more aware that the date of the new Allied offensive could not be far off, Field Marshal Kesselring was suddenly recalled to Germany on March 8th to become Commander-in-Chief in the West, in succession to Field Marshal Gerd von Rundstedt, and Colonel-General Heinrich von Vietinghoff-Scheel was appointed to succeed him as German Commander-in-Chief in the Mediterranean.

The plan for the Allied spring offensive was again based upon Alexander's favoured approach of the two-fisted thrust, but this time

4 A picturesque and typically Italian village in a beautiful valley – with a Bailey Bridge and a British armoured car in the foreground to bring the viewer back to the harsh realities of the war in Italy. The village is, according to the original news agency caption, Bifforoe.

5 Their faces lined with the concentration of a hard-fought, protracted and usually uncomfortable campaign, US 5th Army Commander, General Mark Clark (left), studies the map with Lieutenant-General Geoffrey Keyes, commander of II Corps, which was made up of the US 34th, 85th, 88th and 91st Divisions.

6 The early moments after entering a town recently deserted by a retreating enemy are tense and frankly alarming, for the Germans rarely failed to leave snipers and booby-traps to kill the unwary. These American infantrymen are advancing cautiously through Caiazzo, an Italian town in which elements of the occupying German forces had committed atrocities against civilians.

1 Every town liberated by the Allied columns gave the troops a rapturous welcome. These Italian civilians crowding onto and around a Sherman tank and its South African crew were in Florence, but similar scenes were repeated virtually everywhere. Note the bottle of Chianti held aloft by one of the South African soldiers on the turret of the tank.

2 An American 240mm howitzer, manned by a British crew, is positioned in an Italian village to fire on a German fuel dump. These howitzers had a range of many miles, and in mountainous terrain often worked with an aircraft which acted as an airborne artillery observation post. A 240mm shell can be seen on the ramming tray, ready to be loaded into the breech.

3 Taken during the final training for the advance on the Senio in April 1945, this picture shows WASPS (flame-throwing vehicles) going into action ahead of British infantry. The farthest pair of men in this picture are a Bren gun team, and their light machine gun can be seen perched on its bipod on the edge of the trench.

4 In January 1945, the US Congressional Medal of Honour, America's highest decoration, was fastened around the neck of Private First Class Lloyd C. Hawks, an army medic who was decorated for saving the lives of three comrades while under heavy fire near Carano, Italy, although seriously wounded himself. The medal was presented by President Roosevelt, and was fastened by the hero's niece, Phyllis Hawks, a member of the US Navy Women's Reserve (WAVES). In the background are Private Hawks' brothers.

with two twists. A diversionary (and yet nonetheless necessary) attack was mounted by the Commandos before the main offensive to clear the nearer shore and the islands of Lake Comacchio of German troops. The actual objective of this operation was to clear the way for the main advance by the 8th Army, almost the whole of which had been moved secretly to a position just North of Route 9, but the intention was that it should also deceive the German commanders into believing that the expected major landing in the vicinity of Venice was at last imminent. The second twist was to follow as the 5th Army began its attack towards Bologna, when elements of the 8th Army, instead of pushing ahead on the Eastern sector front, would cross Lake Comacchio in 'Fantail' tracked amphibious landing vehicles (the 56th Division) and break out from the newly-won Santerno bridgeheads (78th Division) in a push to take Bastia. This, it was hoped, would cut the German line of withdrawal to the East.

But, between the two twists, it was necessary to win the Santerno bridge-heads. To do that, the 8th Army would first have to cross the Senio river, fight its way North-West to the Santerno, then cross that river in turn. In the evening of April 9th, after three hours of ceaseless

bombing by Allied aircraft (one account says that 125,000 fragmentation bombs were dropped on German defenders along the Senio that afternoon), followed by four hours of mortar bombardment, the two divisions of V Corps, the 2nd New Zealand and the 8th Indian, plus the Polish II Corps, crossed the first river. That night, under fearsome conditions of fire, and under constant flame thrower attack, the Allied engineers built the bridges upon which the Allied armour was to cross. On the 10th, the Allied air assault began again, with 1,600 heavy bombers dropping thousands more bombs on the German positions, and opening the way to the Santerno. The carnage was appalling, and the Allied army began to win the battle by sheer attrition of manpower. The next day, on the 11th April, the New Zealanders crossed the Santerno, thereby gaining their bridge-head, and more than 2,000 German prisoners.

Bad weather grounded the Allied aircraft temporarily, and delayed the next stage of the attack, but by the 14th April conditions were again good enough for the campaign to be resumed in earnest. On that day, the Poles took the heavily-defended town of Imola, the New Zealand Division pushed forward over the River Sillaro and the

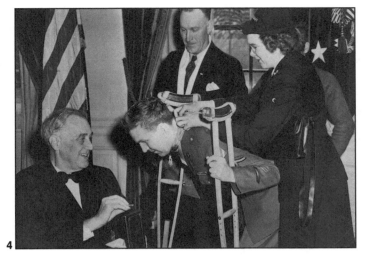

5

6

army, as the 5th Army wheeled around him to the South-West, and the 8th Army did the same from the North-East. Unless he could retreat beyond the jaws of the pincer, his army was trapped. On April 20th, von Vietinghoff, in total defiance of Hitler, ordered a retreat to the already prepared defensive positions along the River Po, but his order was already too late. Argenta had been taken by the Allies, and the British 6th Armoured Division was moving at high speed towards Ferrara. The bridges across the Po were all either destroyed by the Allied air attacks, or totally blocked by burning or burnt-out German vehicles. German positions defended by Heidrich's I Parachute Corps in Bologna, heavily threatened by the US 34th Division from the South, and by the Poles from the East, fell on the 21st April. The 5th Army, preceded by tactical air strikes every mile of the way, advanced amid the increasing ruins of the German armies towards the Po, and by the 23rd the first US soldiers were over the river — the 10th US Mountain Division claiming the honour of being first on the other side.

Now the right flank of the 5th Army, the 6th South African Division, was able to join up with the left flank of the 8th Army, and the pincer was complete. Behind them were 67,000 German casualties and 35,000 German prisoners. General von Senger succeeded, as did many of his troops, in retreating across the Po, but there was little left to fight for, even less to fight with, and overwhelming Allied superiority in every aspect of the battle. On April 25th, an Allied signal to the Italina partisans brought forth a major rising against the remaining German defenders, now little organised and unable to fight in a coherent way. Individual garrisons began to surrender — Churchill tells of the surrender of the 4,000 men of the Genoa garrison to one British liaison officer. On the 27th April, the 8th Army crossed the Adige on its way to Venice, and the 5th, which had already captured Verona, headed for Vicenza and Trento.

The Allied victory in Italy was complete. On May 2nd, recognising the situation and the many individual surrenders that had already taken place, the remaining German and Italian troops of Army Group C surrendered unconditionally. Almost a million men joined the ranks of the prisoners in Allied care.

7

5 Although the Royal Engineers were able to cope with most of the problems their human enemies threw at them, the weather was less easy to cope with. In January 1945, the first thaw after the heavy snows turned the River Santerno into a torrent, and this pontoon bridge, laboriously built by the Royal Engineers, was swept away. Floating blocks of ice ripped the canvas of the floating pontoons.

6 A British anti-tank gun position in the Sillaro valley, between Imola and Bologna, looks out over German occupied ground prior to an assault in the US 5th Army sector of the front.

7 With the war nearly over, British infantry and M10 tank destroyers push on in the spring sunshine of April 1945 along the road to Ferrara, on the Eighth Army front. These men must have been wondering how soon it would be before they could finally say that they had survived the war.

78th Division, which had been steadily moving towards Bastia managed to take the bridge in the town, join up with the 56th Division and mount a joint attack on the road to the crucial gap in the terrain at Argenta.

Now General Truscott, who, since General Clark's promotion to command the 15th Army Group, was the commander of the 5th Army, launched his army into the attack in the Western sector from positions West of the road from Pistoia to Bologna. During the next four days, the Allied air forces flew more than 4,000 sorties in support of the assault, and it was reported that during the first half-hour of the attack more than 75,000 shells fell on the German mountain positions. Despite this intensity of fire-power, the 5th Army advanced scarcely more than two miles in three days, and it took a week of tough fighting before they managed to break out, by-passing Bologna to the West, as had been agreed under Alexander's plan, and advancing North.

General von Vietinghoff was now acutely aware that Hitler's standard form of order to any defensive force, by which he had been forbidden under any conditions to retreat, was about to cost him his

8

8 Despite the imminence of the German surrender, there was no lack of rubble or destruction in the final stages of the Italian campaign. This is Portomaggiore, North of Argenta and between Lake Comacchio and Route 16, which was taken by the 8th Army on April 19th 1945. With a Sherman tank beside them, stretcher bearers move up to recover the wounded.

CHAPTER 46

VICTORY IN EUROPE
THE END OF HITLER'S GERMANY

As we noted in the previous chapter, Field-Marshal Kesselring had been recalled by Hitler early in March to take over as Commander-in-Chief in the West, and found himself heir to a situation in which Hitler and the commanders of OKW had devoted most of the remaining strength of the *Wehrmacht* to the defence of the Eastern frontier of Greater Germany, and to the fortification of Berlin. With some measure of credibility, although nonetheless with tremendous optimism, Hitler and Guderian hoped to hold and defeat the Soviet armies on the Oder, and thereby to be able in time to transfer reinforcements from the East to the West. Kesselring's task, he was assured by Hitler, was to stabilise the present position, mop up the

Allied bridgehead at Remagen, and then, when the reinforcements were available, to launch a counter-offensive to repel the invaders from the Reich.

Kesselring was nothing if not a realist, and soon realised that Hitler's requirement of him to hold the position along the Rhine was simply not practicable unless entirely unforeseen circumstances worked in his favour. The total complement of the *Wehrmacht* armies in the West amounted to 55 divisions, all of which were seriously under strength, and most of which were 'padded' with troops who were inadequately trained. Although the concentration of the German troops in and around Germany had largely resolved the supplies problem, and there was sufficient ammunition for defensive operations, the ammunition stocks were nowhere near enough for the scale of offensive that would be required to recapture the bridge-head at Remagen. There was also a desperate shortage of fuel which made reliance upon armoured strength risky in the extreme. With only some 63 armed fighting men per mile of the long Western Front, Kesselring was facing 85 Allied Divisions, all at full strength, all with plenty of fuel and all with high morale.

Yet, despite this depressing situation, Kesselring remained loyal to his leader to the extent of refusing to conspire against him. When the *Waffen SS* officer, Karl Wolff, who had been secretly negotiating

with Allen Dulles of the O.S.S. (Office of Strategic Services) for an armistice in Italy, approached Kesselring in March suggesting that the whole German Western Front should be included in the offer of a surrender, Kesselring refused – but he nonetheless approved of Wolff's efforts to secure the end to fighting in Italy. When, on March 19th, Hitler issued his notorious Order instructing the German armies to destroy everything in their path as they retreated across Germany, regardless of the needs of the German population, Kesselring secretly connived at Albert Speer's plan to frustrate the transmission and execution of this order, a sensible disloyalty that was made easier for the ever-correct Kesselring to justify to himself by the sheer speed of the Allied advance, and hence of the German retreat, and by the acute lack of explosives to destroy anything in their path.

Montgomery Crosses the Rhine

Although, when Kesselring took over his new command, the Americans were already well established in some force East of the Rhine in the Remagen bridge-head, Montgomery's 21st Army Group, made up from North to South of the Canadian 1st Army, the British 2nd Army and the US 9th Army, was still on the West bank. Field-Marshal Montgomery, its commander, was engrossed in what seemed to the less detail-conscious Americans the apparently endless

5

preparations for his crossing in force. By the third week of March, all was prepared. A Royal Navy detachment under Vice-Admiral Sir Harold Burrough had ferried 45 landing craft and a formation of Buffalo amphibious tanks from Antwerp through the canals of Belgium, Holland and Germany to the ten crossing areas along the 21st Army Group's 20-mile Rhine front, where the river is almost a quarter of a mile wide. Between March 20th and 22nd, RAF Bomber Command and the US 8th and 9th Air Forces flew some 16,000 sorties over the area selected for the assault and the supply lines beyond it, dropping almost 50,000 tons of bombs. Huge quantities of ammunition and fuel had been accumulated in dumps before the attack — the quantities gave the US generals cause for derision, although it should be pointed out that Montgomery's assaults rarely ran short of supplies, whereas those of the US forces were more troubled. For the mammoth bridge-building tasks that lay ahead once the river had been crossed, 30,000 tons of bridge-building equipment and almost 60,000 engineers had been moved up to the assault zone. Finally, before the initial assault of 80,000 men made the first crossing and opened the way for almost a million more, a smoke-screen was laid along 75 miles of the Rhine from dawn on March 21st until early evening on the 23rd to conceal troop movements and final preparations.

5 A key factor in the success of the operation to establish Allied forces east of the Rhine and begin the final push into Hitler's Germany was the disruption of German communications and supply routes by the Allied Air Forces. This 'box' of six RAF Mitchell bombers is shown attacking the rail marshalling yards at Dorsten.

6 To cover the final preparations along the east bank of the Rhine from the view of the German troops across the river, the largest smoke screen laid during the Second World War was put down along a seventy-five-mile front.

6

7

8

7 Under the cover of the mighty smoke screen, the crossing of the Rhine began on the night of 23rd/24th March. By the cold light of a smoky dawn, troops of the US 9th Army set out in Alligators from the western bank of the river for the battle that awaits them.

8 'I drew an assault boat to cross in – just my luck' one of the men in this boat was quoted as saying after the operation was over. 'We all tried to crawl under each other because the lead was flying around like hail'. This US Signal Corps photograph taken during the crossing of the Rhine speaks dramatically of the terrifying minutes under devastating fire that each man had to endure without being able to find new cover or fire back. Consider, too, the courage of the cameraman, who was not able to stay flat while taking this picture.

Through the night of March 23rd/24th, the formidable artillery resources of the British 2nd Army and the US 9th Army pounded the German positions across the river with over 3,000 guns, as the British 15th and 51st Divisions and the US 30th and 79th poured across the river in the Buffalo swimming tanks. By dawn, the Allied armies had bridge-heads and were expanding them, and the 1st British Commando Brigade was in Wesel clearing the German defenders. Under the watching eye of Winston Churchill in a command post on the Allied side of the river, the next stage of the drama unfolded as an armada of more than 2,000 aircraft including the fighter escort carried the British 6th Airborne Division and the US 17th Airborne Division to a parachute and glider attack around Hamminkeln, only some five miles inland from the river bank. More than 1,300 gliders

took part in this landing, which was a considerable success and enabled the Allied army to silence the German artillery that might otherwise have greatly slowed the vital bridge building operations on the Rhine. By evening on the 24th, the 17th Airborne had made contact with the British XII Corps, and had also taken intact vital bridges over the Ijssel which helped to make possible the subsequent rapid expansion of the bridge-head. The German 84th Division, caught between the Airborne troops in the rear, and the infantry in the front, had been virtually wiped out, with almost 4,000 prisoners being taken by the Allies. The heaviest resistance to the crossing was encountered at Rees, where a battalion of German parachutists held out bravely for three days before being forced to surrender.

1 Watched by no less a spectator than Winston Churchill, the greatest airborne invasion ever filled the sky above Wesel and Rees, spilling 40,000 paratroops from more than 1,500 troop-carrying aircraft into a sky blackened by the smoke of bursting anti-aircraft shells. These paratroops, with glider-borne infantry, spearheaded the British 2nd Army crossing. This picture was taken by Sergeant F.F. Quandt of San Francisco, from a B-17 photographic reconnaissance aircraft which was shot down minutes after the picture was taken.

2 Many of the Allied gliders were damaged as they landed, either by a rough landing site (there was, after all, no chance to 'go round again'), or by enemy fire. Some troops were killed or wounded before they had the chance to join battle in earnest, but most, like this man, rushed from their glider in one piece despite the landing.

3 A crucial factor in the success of paratroop operations is fast regrouping after the drop. These men, landed in the flat, open country near Wesel, are getting organised and locating their sections before moving forward.

4 Armoured vehicles were ferried across the river on Bailey rafts powered by small outboard power units, as shown here. This picture shows the width of the river, and gives an impression of how exposed the men crossing the river in the initial phase must have felt.

Advances into Germany

By March 26th, in an incredible feat of engineering and endurance, the engineers of the 21st Army Group had opened seven 40-ton bridges to traffic across the Rhine. The German 1st Parachute Army was cut off by US and British troops advancing on both banks of the River Lippe, a tributary of the Rhine, and by the 28th March the 8th Armoured Division was 25 miles East of the Rhine, the Guards Armoured Division was approaching Munster, and the Canadian II Corps with XXX Corps reached the Dutch frontier. Now, as the US 3rd Armoured approached the 8th Armoured, it became clear that their throwing back on to German Army Group B of the five threadbare *Panzer* divisions that had opposed their advance could mean the encirclement of the whole of Army Group B. On April 2nd, the two Allied Armoured Divisions joined up. The remains of the 5th *Panzerarmee*, plus the 19 divisions of the German 15th Army were encircled in what Hitler quickly and opportunistically named the 'Fortified Area of the Ruhr'.

General Bradley allotted the task of reducing and destroying the German 15th Army, and of capturing the Ruhr, to a new 15th Army under the command of Lieutenant-General Grerow, consisting of 18 divisions taken from the US 9th and 1st Armies and organised as five corps. By April 12th, after attacking South across the Ruhr and West across the Sieg, Grerow had occupied the entire coal-producing area, and by the 14th the two converging US forces had cut the German defences in two. By now, Field Marshal Model, who was nominally in command of Army Group B had vanished, and Colonel-General Harpe, the commander of the 5th *Panzerarmee* assumed command and ordered the whole of German Army Group B to cease fire. His surrender added a further 325,000 prisoners, including 29 Generals, to the Allied bag. Field Marshal Model committed suicide on April 21st.

5 Once the Rhine had been crossed, and the Allied forces were established east of the river, the advance began in earnest. These British Churchill tanks are carrying a mixed cargo of British and American infantry.

6 On April 5th 1945, Allied forces crossed the River Weser, and eighteen US divisions began the mighty task of clearing the Ruhr pocket of the German defenders entrapped there. These tanks of the US 2nd Armoured Division, known as 'Hell on Wheels' are crossing the Weser near Hamelin, famous in an earlier age for the story of the Pied Piper.

7 The damp and stark desolation of war on a wet day in winter comes over strongly from this picture of unsmiling GIs of the US 9th Army crossing the bridge into Duisburg, at that time the largest inland port in Europe, after the city fell to the Allies.

8 The dramatic scene as displaced persons of many nationalities picked their way hazardously across the fallen bridge over the Elbe at Tangemunde, blown up by the retreating Germans but still hanging precariously by one or two bolts. Thousands of refugees, many of them families with children, escaped the approaching Russians by this road and rail bridge before it finally fell.

1 On a shell-damaged bridge over the River Elbe at Torgau, the soldiers of the US 1st Army met Soviet troops of the Red Army. Staged pictures like this – which nonetheless were essentially re-enactments of what had actually happened only hours before – were an important element in Allied propaganda at the time.

2 As the Allies advanced, many Germans were glad of the opportunity to surrender to Western forces rather than to the Soviet armies. On Wednesday, 25th April, General Kurt Dittmar, famous as a *Wehrmacht* radio voice, crossed the Elbe at Magdeburg and entered US 30th Division lines under a Red Cross flag carried by his sixteen-year old son, apparently to intercede for the civilian wounded. He surrendered, and stayed in the West. The American officer on the right is Lieutenant-Colonel S.T. McDowell.

Advances into Germany on the Western front continued apace, and the average number of prisoners taken per day rose by mid April to an incredible 50,000. The US 9th Army took Hanover on April 10th and reached the Elbe on April 13th, crossing to take Barby and establish the first Allied bridge-head East of the river. Now the US Army was only 75 miles from Berlin, and advancing at such a pace that, had Eisenhower been prepared to recognise the political desirability, as urged upon him by Churchill repeatedly over the preceding months, of reaching Berlin either ahead of or at the same time as the Russians, the history of Europe, despite the decisions of Yalta, might have been dramatically altered. Eisenhower, however, chose to view his task only in military terms, and saw, quite correctly, that the Soviet armies were better able to capture Berlin than those of the Allies. He continued to take the view that to advance to Berlin would cost the Allies unnecessary casualties, and that the occupation of Southern Germany was also of pressing importance. In this his conviction was fuelled by the Intelligence Department of SHAEF who had convinced him that Hitler and the central figures of the Nazi regime intended to take themselves and several crack SS divisions into the mountains of Southern Germany and create there a remote 'Southern Redoubt' which could be defended almost indefinitely. Postwar evidence showed conclusively that such a plan simply did

not exist, and that the Nazi hierarchy were by this time far too fragmented for the plan ever to have been practicable. This raises the interesting possibility, for which, as far as is known, there is no shred of evidence, that the whole 'Last Redoubt' notion was planted at SHAEF by Russian agents intent on ensuring that the US Army turned South, and left Berlin to the Russians.

The US 1st Army crossed the Weser at Munden on April 8th, and pushed on at high speed across Thuringia, covering some 75 miles in five days. Its left flank joined up with the right of the US 9th Army, and thereby cut off the German 11th Army in the Harz Mountains. The *'Clausewitz' Panzer* Division, sent to rescue the 11th Army, was encircled before it arrived, and both it and the 11th Army were wiped out. On April 14th, the US VII Corps took Halle and Leipzig, joining at Leipzig the 9th Armoured Division from General Patton's 3rd Army.

General Patton had, since March 30th, pushed eastwards to Jena and on to Muhlhausen. By the 21st, his XX Corps had reached Chemnitz in Saxony, and XII Corps had moved South-East to Bavaria and was well beyond Bayreuth. By the day of the final German surrender, Patton's troops were in Linz, where Hitler had gone to school, and his 13th Armoured Division had, on May 2nd, crossed the River Inn at Braunau, where Hitler had been born. Once again,

3 During the American attack on the town of Hulirich, US infantry dash across a field under German small arms fire. In the background, the town is burning as a result of shells from American tanks, fired before the infantry went in.

4

5

6

4&5 During the American advance into Leipzig, a war correspondent captured these dramatic pictures as a sergeant manning a machine gun overlooking the street down which the infantry was advancing was shot in the head, and died instantly. As a pool of blood spread from the dead sergeant's body **4** another soldier crawled to see if anything could be done for him, and then **5** took over his gun on the balcony.

6 All over Germany, the arrival of the Allies spelt freedom for Allied soldiers, airmen and sailors imprisoned in German POW camps. Here in Kitzingen, the US 7th Army liberated over 300 French soldiers in a Stalag. Many of these men, here seen shouting and waving as the first jeeps arrived, had been in prison for five years.

7 In the increasing confusion that engulfed Germany, many men and women were arrested and tried as spies. Richard Jarczyk, an *Obergefreiter* in the 36th *Volksgrenadier* Division, has been left in plain clothes behind the US 7th Army lines as his unit retreated, with orders to sabotage US equipment and supplies, kill American soldiers and carry out espionage. After claiming he was a Pole, and offering his services to the American Military Government in Bruckweiler, claiming that the *Bürgermeister* knew him well, Jarczyk was arrested after the said *Bürgermeister* disclaimed knowledge of him. Under questioning, Jarczyk confessed that he was a spy for the *Wehrmacht*, and he was therefore put before a firing squad. This picture shows the moment of his death.

Eisenhower's misplaced trust in the Russians played Europe false. Patton was all set to push on and take Prague, but after some argument, Eisenhower ordered him on May 6th not to do so. The outcome we know.

The North German Plain and Holland

In the North, Montgomery's 21st Army Group faced the task of cutting across the North German plain to Lubeck, thereby securing the entrance to the Baltic and cutting off the German armies in Denmark and Norway. Montgomery, being more politically inclined than Eisenhower, also saw his manoeuvre in terms of preventing the Soviet armies from adding Denmark to their gains in Europe. The 16 divisions of the British 2nd Army and the Canadian 1st Army, of which six were armoured, faced the German 25th Army under General von Blumentritt plus the remnants of the 1st Parachute Army, the whole German force being under Field-Marshal Busch, who was responsible for the 'Northern Defence Zone' made up of the Netherlands, Denmark, Norway and North-West Germany.

By April 29th, the British VIII Corps of the 2nd Army, reinforced at Montgomery's request by the XVIII Airborne Corps (five divisions) had reached the Elbe on its way to Lubeck. Over two days, reinforced by the formidable support of the newly operational British Gloster Meteor jet fighters, Montgomery's force fought its way across the Elbe and by May 2nd the spearhead of VIII Corps was in Lubeck. Just 28 miles further East, on May 2nd, the 6th Airborne Division entered and took Wismar only six hours before Marshal Rokossovsy's troops arrived.

7

Bremen had fallen on April 26th to General Sir Brian Horrocks and XXX Corps, and on May 2nd, Hamburg was surrendered to the Allies by Lieutenant-General Wolz. On the 4th, the 7th Armoured Division took intact a bridge over the Kiel Canal, and on the same day the Guards Armoured Division took Cuxhaven. Thus did the Baltic coast and the great German naval base at Kiel fall into British rather than Russian hands.

In Holland, General Crerar had begun April with the dual tasks of driving up between the Weser and the Zuider Zee alongside XXX Corps in the general direction of Wilhelmshaven and Emden, and also of freeing those areas of Holland that were still occupied by German troops. The push to Wilhelmshaven and Emden was allotted to the Canadian II Corps, and progress through Holland towards Germany was brisk, Zutphen and Almelo falling to the Canadians on April 6th, and Groningen and Leeuwarden on April 10th. Once in Germany, the

defenders' resistance was extremely fierce, and Lieutenant-General Simonds, in command of II Corps, called for reinforcements to deal with the German II Parachute Corps. With the help of the Canadian 5th Armoured Division, the Polish 1st Armoured Division and the British 3rd Division, General Straube's parachutists were pushed back. By the time the German army surrendered in the North, the Canadians were almost in Emden, and the Poles were a few miles short of Wilhelmshaven.

In Holland, Arnhem had been captured by the Canadian I Corps, who then pushed on to the Zuider Zee at Harderwijk. The Germans, as the Allied armies approached, opened the sea dykes and thereby threatened the lowlands of the reclaimed areas with flooding that would have cost thousands of civilian lives and great damage to property and homes. To prevent this disaster in Holland, General Crerar agreed to a cease-fire with General Blumentritt provided that

1 Even at this late stage of the war, German snipers were claiming the lives of many American soldiers, and just before this picture was taken in Oberdorla, the US soldier in the foreground had been shot dead. The others of his unit across the street are looking for the sniper, and one GI is running across the street in front of the knocked-out tank in the background to gain cover in the buildings opposite.

2 Field-Marshal Montgomery was popular with his troops, and frequently addressed small gatherings, explaining the progress of the war and the reasons behind current tactics. This picture was taken on April 3rd 1945, as 'Monty' addressed men of the British 6th Airborne Division near Coesfeld.

Allied aircraft bringing supplies of food and medicines to the Dutch civilian population were not molested. This arrangement worked well for the remaining few days of the war.

Southern Germany and Austria

In yet another change of command in the closing days of the war, Field-Marshal Kesselring was obliged, in addition to his role as C-in-C West, to undertake the direct command of the 'Southern Defence Zone', the counterpart in the South of Field-Marshal Busch's command in North Germany and Holland. Thus, Kesselring found himself once more in command of a motley assortment of German formations of varying degrees of competence, facing General Devers' 6th Army Group.

On March 26th, the American 7th Army had crossed the Rhine at Gernsheim, and had gone on rapidly to take Mannheim and Heidelberg on March 30th. Despite quite firm resistance from the German defenders, Wurzburg fell on April 5th, and General Patch, commanding the 7th Army, launched a determined thrust to capture the heavily defended areas of Schweinfurt and Nuremberg. The American troops met determined resistance, but by the end of April were across the Danube, had captured Munich and had taken the remains of the German XIII Corps as prisoners. On May 4th, the French 2nd Armoured Division captured Hitler's mountain retreat, the Berghof, on the Obersalzberg mountain.

Meanwhile, the French II Corps had been fighting hard throughout April after an improvised but brilliantly successful crossing of the Rhine at Speyer. Against powerful and effective resistance from the German 19th Army, the French took Karlsruhe on April 4th and, in a constantly changing battle reminiscent of greater days of the German army, captured Pforzheim on April 8th.

3 British and Canadian troops sweeping across North Germany encountered fierce resistance similar to that met by their American allies further south. On 26th April 1945, the caption to this picture was able to proclaim that 'the city and port of Bremen is now virtually in British possession. About 5,000 prisoners have been taken in Bremen so far, including two Major-Generals'. These are, according to the original caption, men of the Royal Ulster Rifles, although the censor's obliteration of badges in the picture makes verification of this impossible.

4 A vast crowd of German prisoners of war assembled under the eye of an American machine gun at a former German military academy. One of the hazards of taking prisoners in large numbers is the logistical problem of feeding them and maintaining health. It was estimated that there were 20,000 Germans held in this particular cage.

5 Men of the King's Own Scottish Borderers move at the double under fire as they advance on Uelzen on April 17th 1945. The town was cleared on April 19th. Note the Bren gun over the shoulder of the rearmost soldier, and the Sten gun carried by the man in front of him.

6 On May 7th 1945, when Hitler was already dead, the port of Bremerhaven was occupied by units of the 51st Highland Division and 8th Armoured Brigade, and by tanks of the 4th Dragoon Guards, led into the town by a German officer anxious to avoid further unnecessary bloodshed. Here, Royal Marine Commando F. Hogarth of Coventry disarms the German guard of a prison ship, which proved to have 1,871 Soviet prisoners on board.

7 Kiel, on the Baltic coast of Germany, had been the principal base of the German navies in two world wars. As the Second came to an end in Europe, Kiel was in a sorry state. Here, in a heavily-bombed dry dock, two U-Boats await their end. Sifting through the mass of technical information made available by the capture of major military installations was a colossal task for military intelligence experts.

4

5

6

7

Victory in Europe

On April 20th, again after fierce battles, the French captured Tubingen and took 28,000 prisoners. Five days later, General de Lattre's formidable French Colonial Army took another 40,000 German prisoners when General Keppler's XVIII SS Corps was cut off and encircled on the Swiss border.

At the end of April, General de Lattre ordered his I Corps to attack the German 24th Army, whose defined role was to prevent the French entering Austria. They lost no time. On April 30th, the 4th Moroccan Mountain Division and the French 5th Armoured Division took Bregenz, and from there on made a flower-decked progress through Austria as the populace welcomed them as liberators. On May 7th Kesselring capitulated to General Devers and a cease-fire was declared in Austria, thus preventing any further damage to a beautiful country.

1 The bombs rain down on Hitler's mountain retreat at Berchtesgaden, in the mountains of Bavaria, indicated by the black arrow on the picture. Below and to the right of the arrow, a large cloud of smoke indicates a near miss.

2 Many Allied soldiers visited Berchtesgaden after the area had been taken, but, as the original caption to this picture stated 'so great was the devastation that souvenirs were hard to find'. Here, American and French soldiers stand in the gap left by the great window, from which Hitler used to gaze at his beloved mountains.

3 Although, for obvious reasons, most of the international publicity was concentrated upon the surrenders and capture of the major figures of the Nazi and *Wehrmacht* hierarchy, there were equally dramatic moments of surrender all over Germany as the German war machine collapsed. This was the scene as a German delegation dejectedly left the Thorak Estate, near Haar, after formally surrendering German Army Group G to the 6th Army Group under General Devers. On the right is Lieutenant-General Foertch, commander of the German 1st Army, who negotiated the surrender.

4 Some idea of the colossal amount of scrap which had to be cleared by the Allies after the end of the war can be gained from this picture of just one of many aircraft scrapyards, where the remains of crashed aircraft had accumulated during the last year or so of the war. This immense pile of aircraft remains, some of them British and American, was discovered at Grevenbroich, in the yard of a German aluminium works.

5 The great U-Boat pens near Hamburg had taken four years work by 1,700 slave labourers to build, and had cost twenty-one million Reichsmarks. They took just two seconds to destroy when thiry-two tons of *Luftwaffe* explosive was detonated inside them.

6

The Soviet Advance to Berlin

To reinforce Eisenhower's known disposition not to advance on Berlin, and to allow the Soviet armies to handle the assault on the German capital, Stalin had sent him a telegram assuring him that only 'secondary forces' were being sent against the capital. Those secondary forces proved to consist of 20 armies, 6,300 tanks, 41,000 mortars and almost 8,500 aircraft. The Russian leaders were clearly determined that their final assault on Hitler's citadel, which began early in the morning of April 16th 1945, should succeed.

The southernmost of the three Fronts of Army Groups attacking the German defenders was the Marshal Konev's 1st Ukrainian Front, with seven armies plus an Air Army. He was to advance across the Neisse and towards Dresden, wheeling towards Berlin if Marshal Zhukov's 1st Belorussian proved to need his support. Zhukov's Front was in the centre, facing the German 9th Army, and had ten armies and an Air Army. His task was to encircle and capture Berlin. To Zhukov's North was the 2nd Belorussian Front of Marshal Rokossovsky, with five armies and an Air Army. The Russians had on the Eastern front, as the British, French and Americans had on the Western, total air superiority, and used it to the full.

Initially, the attacks along the Oder were repelled by the German defenders, although Marshal Konev's forces made some slow progress. Counter-attacks followed every attack, and, had the Germans had the reinforcements to match their losses, which the Russians clearly did, the battle would have gone on for far longer.

6 In the east, the Soviet armies had crushed the German resistance by sheer force of arms and determination. These remarkably brave Red Army sappers were advancing under fire towards a building which was being used as a German defensive position. On their backs are explosives – it would have taken only the graze of a bullet to create an enormous explosion. According to the original caption to this news agency picture, the men reached and destroyed their objective.

7 Above the devastation that had been Berlin – a devastation not unlike that which the Germans had not long before wrought upon Stalingrad and many other cities of the Soviet Union – a Soviet soldier raises the hammer and sickle on the ruins of the Reichstag, where almost 3,000 last-ditch defenders of the capital were captured.

8 Martin Bormann, Hitler's secretary, was clearly realistic about the military situation at the end of April 1945. This letter from him to Grand-Admiral Doenitz, which enclosed a copy of Hitler's political testament reads:

The Secretary to the Fuehrer,
Reichsleiter Martin Bormann.

The Fuehrer's Headquarters,
Postal address München 33 Fuehrerbau.

Dear Grand Admiral,

As, on account of the non-appearance of all the divisions, our position seems hopeless, the Fuehrer dictated last night the enclosed political testament.

Heil Hitler.
Yours,

M.Bormann

9 The meeting of East and West, and the closeness of an end to hostilities, brought together in uneasy comradeship the generals of the Soviet and United States armies, obliged for political reasons to be friendly, but in most cases deeply distrustful of each other. Here General Bradley meets Koniev in the Soviet general's headquarters.

7

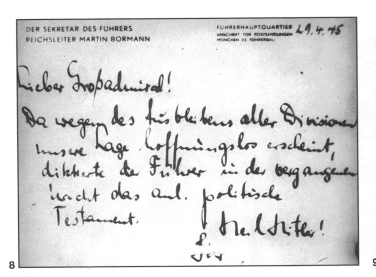

8

9

Victory in Europe

There was no lack of determination or morale on the German side in this last great defence against the hated Bolshevik invader. But in a war of attrition, the Soviet armies could not fail to win, and the beginning of the end for the Germans came on April 19th when the German 9th Army collapsed. Suddenly, Zhukov was through a breach in the line and in Strausberg, only 22 miles from Hitler's bunker. Konev, meanwhile had crossed the Spree at Spremberg and was in Saxony, receiving orders to turn North to support Zhukov.

On April 22nd, the two Soviet armies met at Konigs Wusterhausen, to the South-East of Berlin, and the German 9th Army was encircled. Two days later, Berlin itself was totally surrounded. Hitler, personally in charge of the defence of the city, but by now living in a world of fantasy, had despatched Field-Marshal Keitel and Colonel-General Jodl to command the counter-attacks that were totally to annihilate the Soviet invaders. Meanwhile he and Dr. Josef Goebbels, in the latter's capacity as Gauleiter of Berlin, would organise the 90,000 boys and old men of the *Volkssturm* and hold off the Russian armies indefinitely.

In response to an extraordinary order requiring him to come to the defence of Berlin, General Wenck and the 12th Army gave way to the Western Allies on the Elbe, and headed for Berlin. At Potsdam, it acquired the remains of the 9th Army that had escaped the Russians, and, on 29th April, approached the city as Zhukov's armies began the last great push to break the city's defenders. 25,000 guns rained

1 The end of the war in Europe and the events immediately preceding it had brought to the gaze of a horrified public worldwide, including Germany itself, the true nature of the Nazi regime over which Hitler had presided. Men who had fought across half the width of Europe because it was their job and their duty, now saw what they had been fighting to crush. These sad figures were inmates of Buchenwald concentration camp, when it was relieved by the US Army.

2 The sheer horror of the concentration camps and the crimes that were perpetrated in them shocked the most hardened soldiers and pressmen. The condition of the prisoners at Buchenwald was the result, not of neglect, but of a positive policy of starvation.

3 The concentration camp at Vught, where two ranks of barbed wire and a moat, surveyed by watch-towers manned by *SS* guards armed with machine guns, were more than enough to keep starving and disease-racked prisoners in the camp where most met their death.

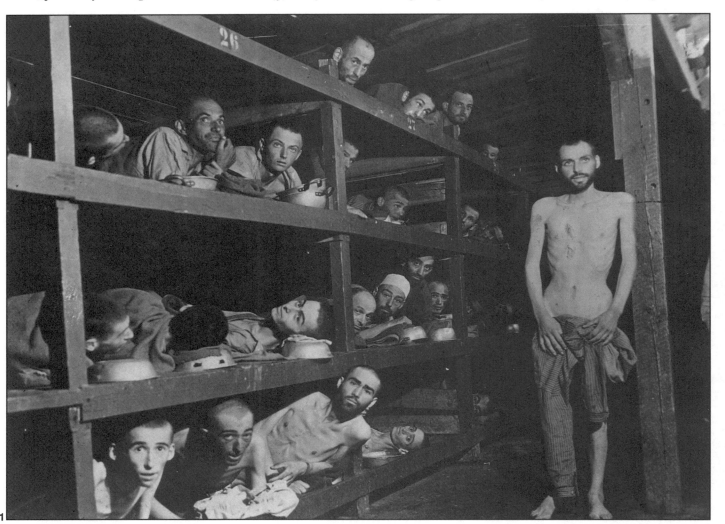

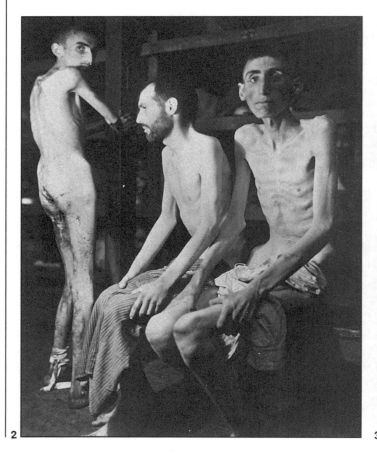

Stutthof

Neuengamme
Papenburg
Westerbork
Vught
Bergen-Belsen
Sachsenhausen
Oranienburg
Ravensbrück

NETH.

Dora-Nordhausen
Torgau
Buchenwald

BEL.

LUX.

GERMANY

Flossenbürg

Theresienstadt

BOHEMIA-MORAVIA

Natzviller

FRANCE
Landsberg
Dachau
Mauthausen

SWITZ.

ITALY

AUSTRIA

Grossrosen

Chelmno

Treblinka

POLAND

Sobibor

Majdenek

Belzec

Auschwitz-Birkenau

Plaszow

SLOVAKIA

RUMANIA

HUNGARY

| ☐ | Concentration Camps |
| ○ | Extermination Camps |

SWEDEN

DENMARK

NORTH SEA

BALTIC SEA

LATVIA

LITHUANIA

EAST PRUSSIA

4 Inside the camp at Vught, as at others of *Reichsfuehrer-SS* Himmler's camps, appalled Allied investigators discovered the equipment of mass murder. On this table, in the room next to the ovens of the crematorium, bodies of prisoners gassed in the gas-chambers were laid so that their gold teeth could be extracted. Then the corpse was opened and filled with tar so that it would burn more efficiently. Note the drainage channels in the surface of the table.

5 An American soldier examines the discarded clothing of executed concentraion camp inmates. The 'N.N.' marking stands for 'Nacht und Nebel' (literally 'Night and Fog') indicating that the prisoner was considered a dangerous political opponent of the Nazi Party. Few 'N.N' prisoners survived the camps.

over 25,000 tons of shells on the besieged capital in one week. Wenck and the 12th Army could do nothing, and were roundly defeated. The Russians had Berlin.

The End of Hitler

Adolf Hitler, now a prematurely aged sick man whose appearance shocked all who saw him, had no intention of allowing himself to be captured by the Soviet troops whom he loathed, and to whose nation he had brought such dreadful suffering and losses. He had come in six years from a zenith of conquest, the equal of which Europe had never before seen, to total disaster and the destruction of his adopted land. His Thousand Year Reich, born of the Germanic myths, of the injustices of Versailles, of the desires of the German people for the greatness that they believed themselves heir to, had been grossly perverted to the service of hideously inhuman ideas and practices.

Hitler's philosophy, so clearly set out in *Mein Kampf* in 1924 and 1927, and yet totally ignored by those who had allowed his rise to European power to go unchecked, had been directly responsible for the deaths of six million Jews, 20 million Russians, and millions more Allied civilians and soldiers. To Adolf Hitler must go the distinction of having caused more human deaths and suffering than any other man in history.

Now, after marrying his mistress and confidante Eva Braun on April 29th, the one time ruler of Europe and his wife of a few hours mutually committed suicide on April 30th, 1945. Their bodies were taken to the garden of the Chancellery by those still loyal to them in the bunker and burned. Josef Goebbels, Reich Propaganda Minister and his wife Magda, who were also in the Fuehrer's bunker, poisoned their children and then commited suicide, he by the bullet, she by poison. Martin Bormann, Hitler's secretary and aide, disappeared,

1 Although the original caption to this picture states that it was taken on May 3rd 1945, the day on which a German delegation first came to Field-Marshal Montgomery's 21st Army Group headquarters to seek surrender terms, it was in fact probably taken on May 4th, when the hard talking took place. With staff officers are (group left), facing camera, Admiral von Friedeburg, next to him General Kunzel, next to him and hidden by the German staff officer in the foreground, Admiral Wagner. Field-Marshal Montgomery is at the right-hand end of the table. Note the characteristic Montgomery touches – two vases of flowers, a table lamp and attractive period chairs, all in a field headquarters.

2 On May 7th 1945, the unconditional surrender of all German armed forces was signed at General Eisenhower's headquarters in Rheims by Colonel-General Jodl.

3 On May 24th 1945, at 10 a.m., on General Eisenhower's orders, members of the last government of the Third Reich were arrested at Flensburg in preparation for their trial for war crimes. The arrest was carried out without force being necessary, and the only casualty was Admiral Friedeberg, who committed suicide by poison when the moment of arrest came. Left to right, being interviewed by Allied press in the courtyard at Flensburg: Minister for Armaments production (and Hitler's friend and architect) Albert Speer; Grand Admiral Doenitz, last Fuehrer of Hitler's Thousand-Year Reich, and Colonel-General Jodl.

5

6

7

4 Mighty 240mm howitzers of the US 9th Army stand silent at last as Sergeant Joiner of B Battery, 265th Field Artillery, sounds the Cease Fire along the Western Front. For these men, one simple fact was paramount. They had survived.

5 On June 10th 1945, Marshal Zhukov decorated Field-Marshal Montgomery and General Eisenhower with the Soviet Order of Victory. Just over a month later, on July 13th, Montgomery, representing King George VI, decorated both Marshal Rokossovsky and Marshal Zhukov with the Order of the Bath. This picture was taken after the investiture – Marshal Rokossovsky is on the left, Zhukov is on the right.

6 In Berlin for the Potsdam Conference between the victorious Allied powers, Winston Churchill toured the city. At the devastated Reich Chancellery, Soviet guides showed Mr Churchill Adolf Hitler's chair. Perhaps not surprisingly, the temptation to occupy his late adversary's seat was too much, and Winston Churchill sat gingerly, just for a moment, saying as he did so 'I have tracked the Nazi beast to his lair'. It should be emphasised that this picture of the shattered chair was taken before he sat down, not afterwards!

7 On 21st July 1945, Winston Churchill took the salute at the great Victory Parade in Berlin, and inspected men of most of the famous formations whose successes had brought Germany to defeat. Left to right are Field-Marshal Montgomery, Winston Churchill, Field-Marshal Alexander, who became Governor-General of Canada on July 31st, and Anthony Eden.

8 Winston Churchill, President Truman and Marshal Stalin, photographed after one of the sessions at Potsdam. President Truman still looks vaguely ill-at-ease in his comparatively new role as President among the experienced warlords.

believed killed by a Soviet tank attempting to escape from Berlin. Grand Admiral Doenitz, in Flensburg, learned that he had been named in Hitler's will as the new Fuehrer of Germany. Goering, Keitel, Jodl, Kesselring, Speer and the rest of the Nazi hierarchy were progressively over the following few weeks captured and sent to await either trial for war crimes, or their interrogation and appearance as witnesses at the Nuremberg War Crimes Tribunal.

The Surrender

But, before the leaders passed into captivity, the very last act of the war that the German Reich had begun with such bravura and style, and which had changed permanently the face of Europe, remained to be played out. On May 3rd, a deputation led by General E. Kinzel, Chief of Staff to Field-Marshal Busch, and Admiral von Friedeburg, the new head of the *Kriegsmarine* following Doenitz' elevation to his role as Head of State, presented themselves at the caravan that had been Field-Marshal Montgomery's travelling headquarters since 1943, and which was now on Luneburg Heath on the North German plain. They offered Montgomery the surrender of the German forces in the North of Germany, including those in retreat from Marshal Rokossovsky on the Eastern front. Rather disconcertingly, Montgomery dismissed them as he might have done an application for compassionate leave from his batman.

The next day, they were invited back, and were obliged to accede to terms of total and abject surrender, but only in respect of the forces facing Montgomery's 21st Army Group. The Allied Command in the West was resolved not to provide refuge from the advancing Soviet armies, something that Doenitz was anxious to achieve for as many as possible of his countrymen.

The final surrender ending the European war totally was signed on May 7th 1945 in a schoolroom at Rheims. Lieutenant-General

8

1 The final press conference picture at Potsdam had a certain poignancy, reflecting in the absence of both President Roosevelt and Winston Churchill a clear feeling that the war was over and a new age had arrived. Behind Clement Attlee, Britain's Socialist Prime Minister, President Truman and Marshal Stalin, are (left to right) Admiral Leahy, British Foreign Secretary Ernest Bevin, Secretary of State Byrnes and Soviet Foreign Minister Molotov.

2 Although the European war was technically over at the beginning of May, the surrender of German submarines, isolated military units and ships continued for weeks after the cessation of hostilities. Here, the German submarine *U-858* surrenders to the US Navy off Cape May on May 14th, becoming the first German warship to surrender in American waters.

3 In December 1945, General Anton Dostler became the first German High Command general to be tried by a US Court Martial and condemned to death.

Walter Bedell Smith of the US Army, deputising for General Eisenhower, read to the German representatives, Colonel-General Jodl, Admiral von Friedeburg and Major-General Oxenius of the *Luftwaffe* the full document which ordered the simultaneous cessation of hostilities on all fronts on May 8th at 11.01pm. The surrender document confirmed the total defeat of the armed forces of the Third Reich, and settled the terms of their yielding their arms and accepting Allied orders.

Colonel-General Jodl and his colleagues each signed on behalf of Germany, then General Bedell Smith added his signature. Next was Lieutenant-General Sir Frederick Morgan for Great Britain, General Sevez for France, and Major-General Susloporov for the USSR. Next day, a further act of surrender took place in Berlin when Field-Marshal Keitel, Admiral von Friedeburg and Colonel-General Stumpf signed a further document of unconditional surrender in the presence of Marshal Zhukov, General de Lattre de Tassigny, Air Chief Marshal Sir Arthur Tedder and General Spaatz.

The war in Europe was at last really over. To rejoicing not only in Britain, where the population of London danced in the streets all night on 'VE night', May 8th 1945, but also in the USA and in France was added total joy in tens of countries around the world. But there was another war to finish. Hardly had the excitement of the surrender passed before the Allies' near-total attention was focused on the Far East, where the war still raged on. This book will look at the immediately post-war events in Germany in the last chapter. Let us now return to the defeat of Japan.

CHAPTER 47

THE FINAL PUSH IN BURMA
THE END OF JAPANESE DOMINATION

The Burma war had, since May 1942 when the British Army had been driven out of Burma, been remote both from the European War, which it resembled so little as to be almost incomprehensible to the soldiers fighting in Europe, and from the American war against Japan, nearer at hand but totally different in character. The Japanese, having captured Burma and the road to Chiang Kai-shek's Nationalist China, were content to stay on the defensive. The successive British and Allied commanders felt on the one hand an obligation and a duty to attack, and on the other a sense of the futility of repeated offensives and counter-offensives that achieved little and could be predicted to do little more than cost lives.

The frustration of Churchill and the Allied political leaders with the moving stalemate of Burma had been echoed in repeated changes in command at all levels. These had culminated, after the Allies' disastrous performance during 1942 and 1943 in the Arakan coastal region of North-West Burma, in the total restructuring of the Allied command. General Wavell had, in 1943, become Viceroy of India, General Sir Claude Auchinleck had become Commander-in-Chief in India, and Admiral Lord Louis Mountbatten had been appointed Allied Supreme Commander, South-East Asia Command, based in Ceylon (now Sri Lanka). An 11th Army Group commanded by General Sir George Giffard had included a new 14th Army commanded by Lieutenant-General (as he then was) William Slim.

The new organisation had prospered, and the structure of the military organisation in India and Burma was overhauled from top to bottom. When the third Arakan offensive had been launched after the monsoon at the end of 1943, it had been a much tougher and better equipped Allied army that advanced down the Mayu peninsula to the heavily-fortified Maungdaw — Buthidaung line to join battle with the Japanese at the beginning of 1944. The Japanese 55th Division under

4

Lieutenant-General Hanaya had attacked the strung-out Allied army by their well-tried techniques of jungle infiltration and outflanking movements, mainly as a diversionary tactic to draw as much Allied strength as possible into the Arakan, and away from the other side of Burma. For it was there, the Japanese High Command had decided, that their main strategy for 1944 was to be concentrated in an attack west across the Chindwin hills towards Imphal.

The so-called 'Ha-Go' offensive by the Japanese had lasted three weeks in February 1944 before General Hanaya, recognising that XV Corps intended to hold out indefinitely, called it off as a battle he could not win. For the first time in the Burma war, the British and Commonwealth army had used air support, proved by the Chindits to be an effective and practical supply system, to maintain a full-scale siege and eliminate the need to withdraw in the face of attack. General

Slim's new Army had shown that the Japanese were not, after all, invincible. As for Hanaya, although he had lost the battle, he had achieved his greater objective. One Japanese division had succeeded in tying down more than six Allied divisions while the parallel 'U-Go' offensive against the British stronghold at Imphal was mounted. The new administrative and organisational structure of the 14th Army had, however, been shown to be the hinge of succesful defence; now it was to become the thin end of the wedge of victory.

The Japanese attack on Imphal began in earnest on March 8th 1944, forestalling the Allies' own intended advance to the Chindwin River. Lieutenant-General Yanagida's 33rd Japanese division crossed the Chindwin and advanced against the British IV Corps under General Scoones. Rather than attempt to fight the Japanese on their own ground, in the jungles through which they had proved themselves the superior soldiers, Slim instructed Scoones to withdraw to the plain, and bring the Japanese out into the open terrain in which they

5

4 Jungle fighters get a certain look to them after a few months of never knowing for sure where the enemy is or when to duck. These British troops (despite the slouch hats, they are British soldiers) were Chindits dropped by Colonel Cochrane's transports and gliders to cut Japanese supply lines in central Burma. They are carrying an injured soldier on a litter.

5 A picture taken early in the Burma war as Sir Reginald Dorman-Smith, Governor of Burma, listens to the tale of terror that was typical of the experiences of refugees fleeing before the Japanese onslaught. The man holding his child was a refugee from Rangoon.

6 General, later Field-Marshal, William Slim was a much-admired and respected commander who played a major part in the turning of the Burma stalemate into victory. Here he talks during an inspection to one of the men of the 14th Army who shared in the defeat of the Japanese in Burma, who were usually content to remain on the defensive once Burma and the road to Nationalist China had been taken.

6

The Final Push in Burma

were least effective. In doing this, the Allied commanders knew that if the Japanese succeeded in cutting the road to the railhead at Dimapur, the defenders of Imphal would be totally dependent on supply from the air. The Japanese in fact intended not only to cut the road but also to capture the railway, and thereby to block the supply route by which Chiang Kai-shek's arms and supplies reached General Stilwell's air force, which in turn ferried them 'over the hump' to China.

The Japanese commanders now made the same mistake, born of over-confidence nurtured by years of success, that they had made in the recent Arakan campaign. They gambled on the availability of the supplies at Imphal to feed their own army. They thus made an assumption of rapid victory that was not to be justified in the event. By the end of March 1944, the Japanese had succeeded in cutting the road to Dimapur, and were advancing on to the plain of Imphal from three sides. Allied air power now began to tell in purely military terms, as the 5th Indian Division was flown into Imphal from the

1 The arrival of Admiral Lord Louis Mountbatten as Allied Supreme Commander in Southeast Asia, and the shake-up of the military command structure, brought a breath of new optimism and a boost to morale among the soldiers in that theatre. Shortly after assuming his command in August 1943, Admiral Mountbatten met General Ho Yin-Chen, the Nationalist Chinese Minister of War.

2 General Sir Claude Auchinleck became Commander in Chief of British Forces in India in 1943.

3 After a frustratingly long period of stalemate and failure in Burma during 1942 and the first half of 1943, the Allies and their caption-writers were keen to generate whatever propaganda they could from the pictures of the Third Arakan Offensive in the Autumn of 1943. The caption to this picture of a Japanese motorised unit under attack claimed irrelevantly that the air blitz on Japanese communications reduced railway efficiency to thirty per cent.

Arakan, and the 7th Indian Division was brought by air to Dimapur.

Meanwhile, to the North, the parallel Japanese attack against the town of Kohima, which was the key to a pass to the Assam valley, had been stemmed by the defenders. They were a lean, hungry, small but determined force made up of a battalion of the Royal West Kent Regiment, a Nepalese battalion, a battalion of the Assam Rifles and every walking wounded and convalescent from the military hospital capable of firing a rifle. On April 4th, the Japanese 31st Division attacked viciously, driving them into an ever tighter perimeter, and eventually on to one hill. There, supported by bombing attacks from Allied aircraft, they held on tenaciously and stubbornly, supplied entirely from the air and denying the Japanese army passage through the pass to Assam, until they were relieved on April 20th.

Even after the relief of Kohima by the 161st Indian Brigade, there were still 60,000 British and Indian troops encircled at Imphal requiring all their supplies and food and ammunition to be dropped from the air. Mountbatten was desperately short of transport aircraft, and clung firmly to twenty American aircraft that he had 'borrowed' from Stilwell's 'Hump' air force, and had neglected to return, despite every encouragement from the Americans to do so. But to supply Imphal effectively, and starve the Japanese army into retreat, he needed seventy more transport aircraft quickly. Appeals to the Americans for yet more aircraft were unsuccessful – perhaps they suspected they might not get those back either – and it eventually fell to Churchill to pull strings and deprive Field Marshal Sir Harold Alexander of seventy of his transport aircraft from the Mediterranean.

As May ended and June began, the siege of Imphal continued unremittingly. The Japanese overall commander in the sector, Lieutenant-General Mutaguchi, secure in a distant hill station, instructed the commanders of his 15th and 33rd Japanese Divisions to fight on and not under any circumstances to retreat. In fact, the Japanese divisions were now desperately short of food and

4 During the Japanese Chindwin offensive in February 1944, these British troops were part of the army that successfully held the attack until the Japanese withdrew. In this picture the British soldiers are checking the Japanese dead to ensure that some were not feigning death in order to launch a suicide attack later.

5 The Japanese Army of the Second World War was relatively little photographed by comparison with the German, Soviet and Western Allied armies, all of whom relied extensively upon photography for propaganda purposes. This picture shows a Japanese army unit fording a river in Burma.

6 Down in the bushes something stirred – in this case a camouflaged Japanese Type 97 Te-Ke/Ke-Ke tankette. The Type 97 was a two-man light tank which was only twelve feet one inch long and five feet eleven inches wide, and in which the commander (top right) had the dubious privilege of having to load and fire the gun as well as direct operations. This particular example seems to be one of the minority of Type 97 tankettes which were fitted with a 7·7mm machine gun rather than the more usual 37mm gun. Already out of date and vulnerable at the outbreak of war, the Type 97 remained in service until Japan's surrender.

equipment, as a result of the Chindits having cut their supply lines, and were attacking fanatically as their strength ebbed. General Scoones, commanding IV Corps in the defence of Imphal, had been ordered to break out, but the effort of maintaining his line against suicide attacks aimed at capturing his food supplies was tying down a substantial part of the Corps. By the third week of June, the monsoon was in full spate, the Japanese had lost ground and were being squeezed by the British 2nd Division coming from Kohima, and it seemed that the end of the battle was in sight. But the monsoon conditions effectively prevented Allied air power from dominating the battle. Not until June 22nd did the British 2nd Division and the Indian 5th Division meet and open the road to Imphal. With some justification, Lord Louis Mountbatten predicted that the first major British victory in Burma was in sight.

General Slim ordered IV Corps and the divisions that had lifted the siege to pursue the two Japanese divisions, who, despite their privations – the 33rd were in far less difficulty with disease and starvation than the 15th Division – were fighting grimly on the roads to the South. But Allied air superiority, the increasing ravages of the monsoon and the devastation wrought by disease completed the Japanese defeat. Of the 88,000 Japanese soldiers who had crossed the Irawaddy to begin the attack, over 53,000 were dead, sick or wounded. Allied casualties at Imphal and Kohima totalled 16,700.

The victory at Imphal began the advance by Lieutenant-General Slim's 14th Army back to the Chindwin, which was crossed in December 1944. At the same time, the British 36th Division, a part of General Stilwell's Northern Combat Area Command, had fought its way South down the railway from Mogaung and was, at the turn of the year only 100 miles North of Mandalay. The 36th Division played a major role in limiting the options of the Japanese 15th Army by turning its flank as the 14th Army advanced. Now the final push to victory in Burma could begin.

The Final Push in Burma

The Road to Mandalay

As the 19th Indian Division made the 14th Army's first crossing of the Chindwin River early in December 1944, Lieutenant-General Slim, who had planned a campaign West of the Chindwin to eliminate the expected Japanese resistance in that area, suddenly found he had to revise his plans. Major-General Rees' 19th Indian Division made contact so quickly with the British 36th Division from the Northern Combat Area Command that it was apparent the Japanese had little intention of making a major stand East of the Chindwin river. Slim therefore decided to push for Mandalay, East of the Irawaddy, the great river that flows South to the strategically vital port of Rangoon, and which stood between the 14th Army and the regaining of Lashio and the Burma Road.

General Stopford's XXXIII Corps was to push as two columns from Kalewa via Yeu to the Irawaddy North of Mandalay, and via Monywa to the South of the city. The 19th Indian Division, already East of the river well North of Mandalay, would advance down the East bank to the objective, and IV Corps under Lieutenant-General

1

2

3

4

1 The Kachin Scouts, with a mixture of British, American and Burmese officers and NCOs, and colourfully-turbaned Kachin soldiers, were a special-purpose jungle commando group whose role was to find and destroy Japanese defensive positions ahead of conventionally-trained troops and engineers. Here, a British Lieutenant-Colonel and an American Captain discuss an operation with a Kachin Lieutenant during the building of the Ledo road.

2 A Kachin Lieutenant and two American NCOs lead a Kachin Scouts patrol along a river in Burma early in 1944. Note the interesting assortment of weapons – American carbines, a Bren gun, short-magazine Lee-Enfields and Lee-Enfield No. 4 rifles. The Kachin soldiers knew the jungle so well that they could spot camouflaged Japanese positions that were virtually invisible to Western eyes.

3 Lieutenant-General Stilwell was a tough, down-to-earth commander who talked straight and believed in sharing both the battle and his forthright opinions with his soldiers. Here he neatly sidesteps a Japanese shell crater as, rifle slung over his shoulder, he tours troop positions in North Central Burma.

4 A picture taken in June 1944 of Lieutenant-General Joseph Stilwell, the American Commander of US and Chinese troops in the Southeastern Asia theatre of war, with Admiral Lord Louis Mountbatten, Supreme Allied Commander. Stilwell's own posthumously published diaries reveal that the American had little respect or regard for Mountbatten, whom he referred to as 'Looie'. General Stilwell, here wearing a Chinese cap, frequently carried a rifle, as did General Slim.

Messervy would cross the Irawaddy well South-West of the city and strike East to take Meiktila, the most important road, rail and communications centre of the region. The advance went well. As February began, Stopford's XXXIII Corps was across the Irawaddy, and two weeks later IV Corps was in position for its Southern crossing. While the 14th Army was pushing forward, Commando units captured the island of Akyab and Ramree to provide sites for airfields necessary if the armies were to be supplied from the air in sufficient quantity.

To the North, General Stilwell's 140,000 troops of the Northern Combat Area Command were advancing southwards against stiff opposition from Lieutenant-General Honda's Japanese 33rd Army. On the Burmese coast, General Christison's XV Corps was fighting the Japanese 28th Army for an opportunity to get through the An and Taungup passes and hammer the Japanese communications to the rear of the army facing the other fronts. But for the Japanese Army's jungle experience and training, their position would have been precarious in the extreme. As it was, they were outnumbered, unable to call up any reserves, and constantly threatened by massive Allied air superiority.

As General Stopford's 20th Division of XXXIII Corps crossed the Irawaddy, the Japanese counter-attacked in force on February 12th, and although the division established a bridge-head, the battle raged for two weeks before the 20th could break out and continue the advance. During that time, the 2nd Division also crossed, some miles further North, and had a similarly difficult time, but between the two of them the 20th and the 2nd Divisions kept the much-depleted 15th Army busy while General Messervy's 7th Division crossed with only limited resistance on its way to take Meiktila. By February 20th, Messervy's IV Corps had consolidated its bridge-head sufficiently

5 Although it is on record that General Mark Clark once did sentry duty in his underpants during a clandestine visit to North Africa, not too many US generals were in the habit of doing their own cooking. Brigadier-General Frank Merrill, at thirty-nine the youngest general in the US Army in 1944, earned a place in military history, and maybe also in American folklore, as the leader of 'Merrill's Marauders', a commando band of saboteurs and fighters operating behind Japanese lines in the manner of Wingate's Chindits. Here, in early 1944, he demonstrates the crucial art of survival by frying pan. Although he was hospitalised for some weeks during the first half of 1944, his Marauders broke through and took Myitkyina on 4th August. Merrill later became Chief of Staff of the US 10th Army in the Pacific, and died in 1956.

6 A column of troops and pack animals of 'Merrill's Marauders' crossing a jungle stream during the advance into Northern Burma behind withdrawing Japanese forces late in 1944. The men are heavily laden for such arduous marching conditions, and needed to be extremely fit.

7 Men of 'Merrill's Marauders' who were wounded in the field were often flown out from jungle airstrips in light communications aircraft. Here, an injured man on a stretcher is prepared for his trip to a base hospital while watchful soldiers stand guard against the sniper attack at which the Japanese soldiers were supremely effective.

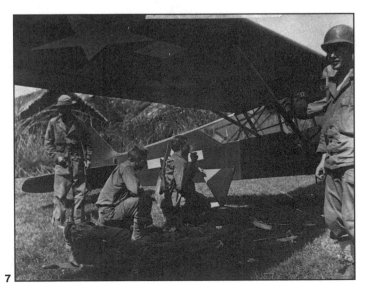

to make its move towards the target, 80 miles away. By the end of February, Major-General Cowan's 17th Division of IV Corps had reached Meiktila, and on March 1st, without wasting any time, they attacked. By March 3rd, Cowan had both the town and the airfield, which was absolutely vital for the Allied airborne supply operation. Despite many Japanese counter-attacks, Major-General Cowan, reinforced with an extra brigade, not only held on to Meiktila, but also launched a number of successful local forays that mopped up Japanese opposition.

While all this was happening in Meiktila, Stopford's divisions were advancing on Mandalay, and although the 19th Division ran into stiff opposition around Mandalay Hill, and the 2nd Division found the old town of Ava more difficult to take than expected, Slim found that overall the defence of Mandalay was lighter than had been anticipated. So he ordered a column of the 20th Division to bypass Mandalay and head South to Meiktila, and gave the 2nd Division the job of capturing the city. By March 20th Mandalay had fallen, and the Allies at last knew they were beating the Japanese at their own game.

The Final Push in Burma

In the North, General Stilwell's troops had been similarly successful, and had taken Hsenwi on March 1st, and the vital target of Lashio on March 6th. On March 24th, the Burma Road from Lashio to Mandalay was once again open to Allied traffic. The success of the campaign for Mandalay and Lashio was the swansong of the Northern Combat Area Command. On March 19th it was disbanded, and its Chinese divisions returned to the liberation of China's rice-growing areas from the Japanese.

The 14th Army had, since crossing the Irawaddy, lost some 10,600 killed, wounded and missing in the fighting. But they had gained a considerable prize. Now all eyes turned on Rangoon, the great port to the South.

The Sweep to Rangoon —
and the End of the War in Burma

The 14th Army had come a long way since Imphal. But Rangoon was a long hard fight ahead of them at the end of March 1945. One of the earliest and bloodiest actions of the campaign had come at Kangaw, two months earlier, while the campaign for Mandalay was in its early stages. Holding the An and Taungup passes, Lieutenant-General Miyazaki and his 54th Division sent a covering force to delay the advancing 81st and 82nd West African Divisions for as long as possible, and set about establishing full-scale defensive positions in two crucial areas. The principal defence was in the region of Kangaw, 40 miles East of Akyab, and only 10 miles East of the Myebon peninsula. The secondary force was in the town of Taungup. Since January 1945, the Allied navies had been in total control once more of the Bay of Bengal, and furthermore Akyab itself had been

1 Brigadier-General Haydon Boatner (left) of New Orleans, who was Chief of Staff to General Stilwell in Burma and Assam, photographed during discussions in the field with Air Marshal Sir John Baldwin, who, as Tactical Air Force Commander in Burma, played a major part in the Allies success in Assam in the spring of 1944.

2 Cooperation at unit level between the Nationalist Chinese and the Americans in Burma was usually harmonious under Stilwell's command, although Stilwell himself was not liked by Generalissimo Chiang Kai-Shek, whose personal lack of interest in fighting outside China did not endear itself to the American general. The Chinese leader's animosity towards Stilwell, and Stilwell's own outspoken disrespect for his Supreme Commander, eventually led to his being recalled in October 1944, and the command being divided between Major-General Albert C. Wedemeyer, in command of Chinese troops in the theatre, and Lieutenant-General Daniel I. Sultan, who took over command of American troops in India and Burma. In this picture a Chinese officer and two Americans are sizing up Japanese positions from a forward observation post.

recaptured. It was decided that the 3rd Commando Brigade would take Myebon with an amphibious landing, and open the way for the 74th Brigade to advance inland and cut the Japanese division's communications at Kangaw.

On January 12th, 42 Commando, Royal Marines, went ashore in style on the beaches of Myebon, closely followed by 5 Commando, who were supposed to be there, and by 1 and 44 Commandos who were supposed to be on quite a different beach but landed anyway. The next day, Myebon itself was taken, and by the 17th the whole peninsula was in Allied hands. The 74th Brigade set out for Kangaw, and the Commandos were withdrawn for their assault role. The plan at Kangaw was for the Commando Brigade to seize a bridge-head on the East bank of the River Diangbon Chaung two miles South-West of the town of Kangaw, and for the 51st Brigade to go through the bridgehead and join up with the 74th after their march overland from

Myebon. This would hem the Japanese force in on three sides. But surprise was vital.

On January 21st, a Royal Navy force of 50 assorted ships and craft anchored off the mouth of the Diangbon Chaung and bombarded the beaches, while aircraft of the RAF bombed Japanese positions. The Japanese did not see the attack coming, and were thrown completely off balance. Over two days, first 5 Commando, then Nos. 42 and 44 Royal Marine Commandos went ashore and established positions under heavy fire. The Japanese fought back toughly, bombarding the invaders with artillery and repelling attempts to take Kangaw. On the 26th January, the 51st and 53rd Brigades landed, bringing tanks to reinforce the Commandos.

General Miyazaki responded by bringing up his own reinforcements in the shape of 3 infantry battalions and an artillery battalion under Major-General Koga. On January 31st, they attacked

3 On December 15th 1944, the strategic northern Burmese town of Bhamo was recaptured by Chinese troops after a fierce battle lasting a month against an encircled Japanese garrison which refused to recognise defeat. This picture was taken in the final stages of the battle as Chinese troops moved into the town.

4 Heavy bombing by British and American aircraft played a major role in harassing Japanese supply lines to their retreating armies as 1944 gave way to 1945. This bridge across the Wam Chaung river was brought down by RAF bombs in January 1945.

5 The air offensive was extensive, not only in Burma, but also in other areas of Japanese-occupied Southeast Asia. These railway and jetty installations at Surasdhani, 600 miles north of Singapore, were bombed by RAF Liberators of Air Command Southeast Asia, which flew over 2,000 miles in heavy monsoon weather to make the attack.

6 A temple stands proud and little damaged amid the scorched ground of battle in the Burmese village of Ywathitgyi, in the Irrawaddy basin. British troops of General Slim's 14th Army took the village after fierce fighting as they advanced towards Mandalay.

7 The fierce and much-respected Gurkha troops of the British Army were well-suited to jungle warfare against the Japanese, and played a leading role in many actions. These Gurkhas, overseen by an Indian Army NCO, were marching into Mandalay, for long an objective that seemed unattainable, but which was captured by the British on March 20th 1945.

8 This Indian mortar company was supporting an infantry attack on Seywa during the drive on Meiktila.

9 Lieutenant-General Frank Messervy in 1945, when he was in command of IV Corps during the battles for Mandalay and Rangoon. In 1942, Messervy had become renowned as the commander of the British 7th Armoured Division, known as the 'Desert Rats'. It was his brilliant operation which resulted in the fall of Meiktila.

the Commando positions with everything they could muster, and for almost two days a fierce battle continued without respite, and without the Japanese taking the British positions. By the time the 74th Brigade arrived, the Commandos had killed more than 300 Japanese, had lost 66 killed and 259 wounded, and had won a posthumous Victoria Cross — that of Lieutenant Knowland of No.1 Commando. By mid February, the Japanese had withdrawn to the An pass, and Kangaw was won — a vital step in the campaign that began one month later to capture Rangoon.

Since November 1944, the 11th Army Group had been disbanded, and Lieutenant-General Slim and the 14th Army came under Lieutenant-General Sir Oliver Leese, in his new role as Commander, Allied Land Forces, South-East Asia. After the capture of Mandalay on March 20th, Mountbatten and Leese were anxious to complete the clearance of Japanese forces in Burma by advancing to Rangoon

The Final Push in Burma

1 Cutting a dashing figure aboard a mule is Lieutenant-General Daniel I. Sultan, the American commander in India and Burma, during a front-line visit in April 1945 to the Mars Task Force, an American infantry and artillery formation which had been fighting finally to clear the Burma-China road of Japanese troops.

2 The British commanders in Burma in 1945: (right to left) Lieutenant-General Sir Oliver Leese, who had commanded XXX Corps at Alamein and was now Commander in Chief Allied Land Forces in Southeast Asia; Lieutenant-General Sir Philip Christison, commander of XV (Indian) Corps; and a Brigadier who is not identified by the news agency caption.

3 May 1945, and Rangoon is only fifty miles from this battle-scarred scene at Pegu, on the wide Pegu river. Men of the 14th Army, in this as in almost every town formerly occupied by the Japanese, are mopping up suicidal Japanese snipers left to harry the advancing Allied troops.

4 British infantrymen tackle the hazardous task of hunting hidden Japanese positions among elephant grass under the cover of a Bren gun team. Many soldiers died in localised mopping-up operations of this sort because of the Japanese code by which death was preferable to surrender.

before the monsoon. General Slim was therefore instructed to drive southwards, again as a two-corps thrust. General Stopford's XXXIII Corps was to move down the Irawaddy valley to Prome and on to Rangoon; General Messervy and IV Corps were to follow the road through Pyabwe, Pyinmana, Toungoo and Pegu. The two Corps would, it was decided, move from airfield to airfield, being resupplied at each as it was captured. More than 3,000 local fighters, the Karens, were organised as a defence force in the hills to protect the flanks of the advancing Corps, which each had 350 miles to advance before reaching their goal.

The advance went smoothly, with only occasional serious hold-ups due to determined Japanese resistance. General Stopford captured Chauk on April 18th; Magwe and Yenangyaung on April 21st. His Corps reached Prome on May 3rd. General Messervy and IV Corps

took Pyinmana on April 19th, Toungoo on the 22nd and Pegu on May 1st. Messervy was now only 50 miles from Rangoon.

Meanwhile, Mountbatten, alarmed at the imminence of the rains of the monsoon, and its potential for delaying the end of the war in Burma, had decided to go ahead with an amphibious invasion of Rangoon. On April 27th, two naval forces set sail to support the operation. One, consisting of two battleships (one of them the French *Richelieu*), four cruisers and two escort carriers, bombarded targets in the Nicobar and Andaman Islands to prevent intervention from Japanese forces based on them. The other was made up of three destroyers and succeeded in sinking most of a small Japanese convoy carrying reinforcements and stores. Early in the morning of May 1st, a battalion of the 50th Gurkha Parachute Brigade was dropped at Elephant Point, where they overcame a small force of Japanese defenders, and cleared the way for landing craft to come up the river to Rangoon itself. During that day, an RAF Mosquito twin-engined fighter-bomber, flying over Rangoon jail, saw the immortal words 'Japs gone. Extract digit' painted on the roof. Knowing that only those with a sound grasp of RAF slang could have painted such words, the pilot, Wing-Commander Saunders, landed at a nearby airfield, which was deserted, made contact with the prisoners, and then, because his aircraft had been damaged while landing, took to the river in a motor boat to alert the landing troops that the Japanese had left. As he did so, the 26th Division came up river and took the city.

Thus was the victory in Burma finally won. To be sure, there were many small engagements between May and August, mainly in the appalling conditions of an unusually severe monsoon flood, but organised resistance by the Japanese had been broken, and they held no further major strategic Burmese locations. Lieutenant-General Slim, promoted full General, became Commander Allied Land Forces South-East Asia in succession to Leese, and, his reputation made, was set for a distinguished postwar career.

Only the final assault on the Japanese islands, and on Japan itself remained before the Second World War would finally be concluded.

5 Admiral Lord Louis Mountbatten watches Allied bombing and strafing of Japanese positions on an island 400 yards away during an inspection tour of the British 36th Division in the Schweli River area of Burma, April 1945.

6 Admiral Lord Louis Mountbatten and his staff photographed during a visit to a US B-29 bomber base in India. Greeting Admiral Mountbatten is Brigadier-General Kenneth Wolfe, Commanding General of 20th Bomber Command. On the left of the picture is Brigadier-General John Upston, Assistant Chief of Staff, Operations, 20th Bomber Command.

5

7 When the Japanese surrender in Southeast Asia eventually came at the end of August 1945, Lieutenant-General Takazo Numata (left) led the delegation that negotiated terms, accompanied by Rear-Admiral Kalgye Chudo. This picture was taken as they arrived at Mingaladon Airfield in Rangoon, where they signed a preliminary document, prior to the formal ceremony at which the surrender of all Japanese forces in Southeast Asia was finalised in Singapore on September 12th.

6

7

CHAPTER 48

THE LAST OF THE ISLANDS
IWO JIMA AND OKINAWA

As the US forces advanced across the Pacific, drawing closer to Japan with each successive island and archipelago, the resistance from the Japanese armies that they encountered became stronger rather than weaker. As the hopelessness of their military position became more apparent, so the Japanese commanders and their men relied more upon the ancient tenets of their culture and less upon the Western military wisdom that their nation had learned so quickly since the latter part of the nineteenth century. Instead of making rational decisions to retreat, or surrender, as any Western army would have done — and indeed did in Germany — when hopelessly outnumbered, outgunned and surrounded, the Japanese fought relentlessly to the point of starvation or the last bullet, and even then launched themselves into last bids for suicidal glory, desperately seeking to take as many as possible of their enemy with them to a certain death. The most difficult part of beating the Japanese was that they could not honourably acknowledge themselves to be beaten.

By the end of 1944, the US commanders had recognised this fact, and the horrifying potential for bloodshed that the Japanese attitude to war and defeat promised should America ever attempt an invasion

1 The anxiety of the commanders of US Air power in the Pacific theatre to deprive the Japanese of their fighter bases was a principal motivation for the costly assaults on Iwo Jima and Okinawa. On the left is General of the Army H.H. Arnold, Commanding General of US Army Air Forces, seen with Lieutenant-General George Kenny, who was in command of USAAF forces in the Pacific, at a press conference during the planning phase for the landings.

2 Morning on February 19th 1945, and for many of the US Marines who streamed ashore from these landing craft on to the beaches of Iwo Jima, it was to be their last morning. Although the quality of this action picture is poor, the first wave can be seen going over the ridge above the beach, closely followed by the men just leaving the landing craft.

3 The Marines are ashore on Iwo Jima, but only just. Unexpectedly fierce Japanese mortar and artillery fire has pinned down some of America's finest and most experienced soldiers, and many Marines lie dead on the ugly, black volcanic sand of the Iwo Jima beach. In the middle distance are landing craft and knocked out tanks.

5

6

7

4 Marine Corps mobile rocket units hammer home hit and run rocket attacks on Japanese positions during the protracted battle for every last inch of the tiny island of Iwo Jima. By keeping constantly on the move between salvoes, the rocket units were able to avoid the worst of Japanese counterfire.

5 Once the vital airfields of Iwo Jima had finally been captured, the US Army Air Force lost little time in making the maximum possible use of them. Here, torpedo bombers of the Fourth Aircraft Wing are lined up alongside Army and Navy aircraft on Motoyama Airfield No. 1 to help guard vital sea approaches to Iwo Jima. Knocked out Japanese anti-aircraft guns overlook an armada of American aircraft, ranging from B-29 Superfortress bombers to tiny, single-engined artillery-spotting planes.

6 A shot taken from one of the attacking aircraft during bombing by United States B-25 planes of the Fifth Air Force of a Japanese escort vessel. The success of the American aircraft in destroying and disabling significant numbers of Japanese ships had a major impact upon the ability of the Japanese defenders to hold the islands in the last months of the war.

7 A picture taken during the initial invasion of Okinawa as two Japanese aircraft attacking the American invasion fleet were shot down by anti-aircraft fire. Although the original news agency caption does not admit it, and the details are not clear even on the original print, it seems possible that some of the dense smoke is rising from a ship hit by a *kamikaze* attack. The allied censors were very sensitive about admitting the success of *kamikaze* raids at this time, for fear of alarming the US public unduly.

of mainland Japan. It was clear that Japan must be bombed into submission, but even this presented major obstacles. Although the capture of the Marianas brought Japan within effective range of the new US Boeing B-29 Superfortress bombers, the presence of substantial Japanese air bases on islands closer to Japan meant that the bombers could be intercepted and damaged en route. Without bases or emergency airstrips nearer to their target than their home base, damaged aircraft were likely to have to ditch in the vastness of the Pacific, which in turn usually meant the total loss of the aircraft and the death of the crew.

Thus it was primarily to secure vital airfields, both to prevent their use against US aircraft, and to make them available as emergency landing facilities, that the US Chiefs of Staff reluctantly ordered the assault in February 1945 on the tiny island of Iwo Jima — just over four and a half miles long by two and a half miles wide, but with two operational Japanese-built airfields, and a third airfield under construction. Not surprisingly, the commander of the Japanese troops on the island, Lieutenant-General Kuribayashi, was aware of its importance to the defence of Japan, and of its potential value to the US forces. He had been given orders as early as 1942 to prepare to defend Iwo Jima to the last, and had set his men to work on what became probably the most comprehensive and best-planned defensive system in the Pacific theatre of war. The island's eight square miles had 800 pillboxes and an incredible three miles of tunnels connecting them and the deep concrete shelters designed to protect the troops from an expected pre-invasion bombardment. Not only were the

beaches fully protected by guns with overlapping fields of fire, but there was a series of further defence lines with saturation coverage of the ground before them at carefully chosen intervals inland from the beaches. There were almost a thousand field guns, howitzers, anti-aircraft guns, rocket launchers and mortars. There were 20,000 light guns and machine-guns, with 22 million rounds of ammunition. Almost 21,000 Japanese troops were on the island by the time the American assault began. There were even 22 tanks — and all within less than five miles by three.

Of course, Allied intelligence knew quite a bit about this and was aware that the island was exceptionally heavily defended. Throughout the second half of 1944, from June through to January 1945, a constant air offensive was maintained in preparation for an assault that, in mid-1944, was probably going to be necessary and, by the end of the year was positively planned. What the American Intelligence men had not discovered and appreciated was the extent to which the defenders were protected by tunnels and deep shelters. Thus, the erroneous assumption was made that, by the time the three-day bombardment by the US Navy that preceded the invasion was completed, the Japanese defence would have been reduced to a fraction of its former power.

In fact, when the 4th and 5th Divisions of the US Marine Corps under General Holland Smith swarmed up the beaches of Iwo Jima just after 9 am on February 19th 1945, the ferocity of their reception was unprecedented. Withering machine-gun fire from emplacements in a wide arc before them mingled with mortar fire, and many

The Last of the Islands

Marines died there and then on the beaches. Using flame-throwers and explosives, tanks brought ashore in the second wave and every assault weapon available to them, the Marines managed by the end of the first day to isolate the Japanese troops defending Mount Suribachi, a 550 ft extinct volcano that dominates the topography of the little island, and thereby secure a beach-head.

Under any normal conditions, the US Marines might then have expected to mop up the defence of the hill and move on to other matters within a few hours, but the defensive positions around Mount Suribachi were so strong, and the Japanese defenders were so determined, that it was not until late on February 21st, two days later, that the hill was totally surrounded, and not until the 23rd that a patrol under Lieutenant Harold Shrier managed to take the summit and plant the Stars and Stripes.

On February 24th, the battle to take the airfields of Iwo Jima began. Despite an air strike, a naval bombardment lasting more than an hour and constant artillery fire, the deep thick concrete emplacements that protected the Japanese defenders held up, and the

advancing tanks of the 4th and 5th Divisions of the Marines, moving down the two side of the airfield, were once again extremely hard put to it to achieve any gains. The 4th Division advance was stopped by mines and guns; the 5th was just 500 yards nearer the Japanese positions after a day of fierce fighting. Next day, the newly-landed 3rd Division began their attempt to capture the plateau at the northern end of Iwo Jima. It took three days of determined fighting, culminating in the use of tanks with flame throwers to incinerate the Japanese in their bunkers, to break through the Japanese line.

By the 28th, the three divisions of the US Marines had captured all three airfields and were mopping up, but there remained a major fight ahead. Two hills, each honeycombed with tunnels built by the Japanese defenders, became the centre of costly battles, as the Japanese army fought fiercely and, as always, to the death. One of them, known as Hill 382, had an associated rocky outcrop christened by the Marines 'Turkey Knob'. Nearby was a natural hollow, filled with defence emplacements and hull-down Japanese tanks, which became known as 'The Amphitheatre.' It took ten days, and hundreds

of American casualties, just to capture those features, and it was not until March 10th that they were in American hands. Almost as long a time elapsed before the Marines captured Hill 362A, whose tunnels and surrounding rough ground gave the defenders a tremendous advantage. But on March 8th, that hill fell too. Even then the Japanese kept attacking, but their artillery was gone, and their last major effort was more in the nature of a mediaeval charge than a modern battle.

After March 10th, organised resistance on Iwo Jima was finished, but each isolated defensive position fought on to the bitter end, most of them to the death. Not until March 25th was the Battle for Iwo Jima finally over. It had taken more than a month, and the lives of almost 6,000 Marines — with more than 17,000 wounded — to capture the tiny island. Of the 21,000 Japanese on the island, only 216 were captured. The remainder died in accordance with their ancient code.

To put the Marine losses in perspective, the battle for Iwo Jima proved subsequently, by providing emergency airfields for American aircraft, to have saved nearly 25,000 aircrew from almost certain death. The Marines did not die in vain.

1 Not only large-calibre naval shells were used during the softening-up of the Okinawa beaches before the invasion – here, one of the rocket-firing LCIs of Vice-Admiral Kelly Turner's Amphibious Forces Pacific Fleet pours rockets into what were assumed to be Japanese positions. In the event, it proved that much of the effort and ammunition had been wasted on the wrong part of the island, and that the Japanese defenders were concentrated in the south.

2 Some of the ships of the US Fleet that took part in the supporting operations for the invasions of Iwo Jima and Okinawa in the early months of 1945. The picture was taken from the flight deck of an aircraft carrier – the folded wings of some of the carrier's aircraft can be seen at the bottom of the picture. More than 800 vessels of all types took part in the invasions.

3 The US Sixth Marine Division was commanded on Okinawa by this fine soldier, Major-General Lemuel C. Shepherd, Jr., who, as a Brigadier-General, had distinguished himself in command of the 1st Provisional Marine Brigade (4th and 22nd Marines) during the recapture of Guam in 1944. On June 4th, the Sixth Marine Division staged a daylight crossing of Naha Harbour and landed south of Naha on the west coast of Oroku peninsula, where they established a 1,200 yard beachhead before capturing Naha airfield.

4 Into the battle at Okinawa aboard a coast guard landing craft, after the first wave, goes Commander Jack Dempsey of the US Coast Guard – the same Jack Dempsey who had in 1919 become world heavyweight boxing champion by knocking out Willard, and who, in 1926, drew 120,757 spectators for his fight with Gene Tunney, still a record paid attendance at any fight. Already in his fiftieth year, Dempsey took part in several actions, and his presence was a valuable morale-booster for the men.

5 The 30,000 ton Japanese battleship *Hyuga* was badly damaged by air attacks on the 19th and 28th March 1945, and was effectively out of action from then until she was sunk in shallow water on 24th July 1945. The *Hyuga* was rebuilt and modified twice, and at the time of her destruction was armed with eight fourteen inch guns and sixteen five inch guns, plus light armament. She was originally commissioned in 1918.

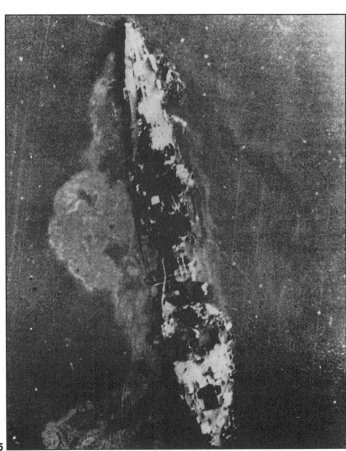

Okinawa

The next target was Okinawa, a much larger island some 60 miles long, and, although 18 miles wide at one point, a mere 2 miles wide at its narrowest. US Intelligence once again underestimated the enemy, this time as a result of being unable, because of the extreme range of Okinawa from any available US air base during the planning phase, to get adequate aerial reconnaissance pictures. The Intelligence estimate of Japanese army strength on the island was 65,000. In fact there were well over 100,000 defenders, including locally recruited soldiers and a force of auxiliaries whose function it was to transport ammunition and supplies and thereby relieve the front line troops of support duties and keep them in the fighting line. Lieutenant-General Ushijima, in command of the defenders, accepted from the outset that there would be no victory. His objective was simply to hold out for as long as he could, kill as many Americans as he could and delay an American advance on the Japanese mainland, only 350 miles away. He therefore decided to concentrate the bulk of his 32nd Army in the Southern part of the island, with its

four important airfields, and put up only a token defence in the northern part.

The newly designated US 10th Army that put 154,000 men into the struggle for Okinawa that began on April 1st 1945 was in fact made up of seven of the toughest and most battle-hardened divisions in the Pacific war — XIV Corps under General Hodge included the 7th and 96th Infantry Divisions, III Amphibious (Marine) Corps under Major-General Geiger was made up of the 1st and 6th Marine Divisions, and the reserve included the 27th and 77th Infantry Divisions and the 2nd Marine Division. The two Corps that made the initial landing totalled about 116,000 men. Just before the main Okinawa landing, the nearby islands of the Kerama Retto group were captured by the 77th Division under Major-General Bruce between March 26th and March 29th to prevent their being used as bases for counter-attacks.

Air attacks were made by carrier-borne US bombers on the airfields on Kyushu from which the Japanese might (if they had had sufficient fuel, which was doubtful) have launched fighter bomber

6 April 1945 – and a United States B-25 bomber of the 'Air Apaches' Group scores a direct hit on a Japanese frigate in the South China Sea. According to the original newsagency caption, the ship was literally blown to bits. Thousands of Japanese sailors lost their lives in attacks like these during the closing months of the war.

The Last of the Islands

raids on the invasion force. Vice-Admiral Blandy's Task Force 52 spent a week before the invasion both clearing the dense minefield off the Okinawa beaches and bombarding them with over 13,000 shells. More than 3,000 sorties were flown by fighter bombers from Blandy's Task Force against targets on Okinawa. In fact, it subsequently proved that much of this fire power had been wasted on areas North of the centre of the island in which there were relatively few Japanese defenders.

The bombardment from the sea continued right up to the time when the invasion fleet landed — only to find that the landing itself was virtually unopposed. More than 60,000 American troops were ashore at the end of the first day. At the same time as the first wave had landed in the morning, a dummy assault mounted by the 2nd Marine Division had diverted Japanese attention from the main landing by seeming to approach for an amphibious landing in the South, only to turn away again. This ruse was repeated on the second day, and helped to tie down the Japanese forces in the South while the beach-head was established.

Quickly, the Americans crossed the island, isolating the North from the South, still without significant Japanese opposition. Not until the 7th and 96th Infantry Divisions were sent South after learning from local inhabitants that the Japanese had concentrated in that area did the real battle for Okinawa begin. And what a battle it proved to be.

1 It was not only the Imperial Japanese Navy that was damaged by air strikes during the battles of the islands. The USS *Saratoga*, with her sister ship USS *Lexington* the world's fastest aircraft carrier until the *Midway* class was built, received seven hits during Japanese attacks off Iwo Jima. Here, crewmen work frantically to extinguish the flames as billowing clouds of smoke rise from the flight deck.

2 The 35,000 ton *Lexington*-class aircraft carrier USS *Saratoga* in the prewar era of biplanes — in August 1944, US Secretary of the Navy James V. Forrestal disclosed that the Fleet air strength had been multiplied twenty times since these prewar days.

3 As their true strength dwindled, the Japanese, like the allied armies, used dummy equipment to deceive airborne reconnaissance cameras. When US invasion forces captured the Okinawa airfields on April 1st, they discovered these dummy aircraft on Katena airstrip. These particular examples were made of wicker work – others were crudely assembled from old aircraft parts.

4 Once the American forces had secured the airfields on Okinawa, they were subjected to relentless and often suicidal attacks by Japanese aircraft, some of which actually attempted to land and carry out commando-type raids. Here, the bodies of two Japanese soldiers lie near a wrecked bomber on Yontan airfield. The aircraft had landed with its wheels retracted, and its occupants were killed as they attempted to destroy airfield installations with hand grenades. Four other aircraft were similarly destroyed on the same airfield.

On April 5th, the US troops ran into determined opposition, but were still able to advance, although with difficulty. By the 9th, the resistance was so fierce that both divisions were brought to a standstill before a heavily defended position on Kakazu Ridge. For days the Americans attacked the ridge and were driven back. The Japanese took appalling casualties. By April 12th, more than 5,500 Japanese had died, against 451 Americans, and on that sad day when President Roosevelt died (to the joy of Adolf Hitler in far-away Germany) the two infantry divisions were still stuck in front of Kakazu Ridge. Suddenly the Japanese counter-attacked, and for two fearsome days the American troops found themselves defending their hard-won positions against desperately determined Japanese soldiers. Each successive Japanese attack was held, and by the 14th April the front had settled down, with little change since the 12th. The Battle of Okinawa was beginning to assume something of the character of the Battles of the Somme.

Meanwhile, the 6th Marine Division had been sent to clear the Northern part of the island, a task which proved extremely difficult in the highly defensible narrow-necked Motobu Peninsula. General Geiger's troops spent twelve days in bloody battle before the peninsula was cleared, and even after it was declared secure parties of Japanese soldiers turned guerillas were harrying the US positions.

In the South, General Hodge had decided to try and bypass the Kakazu Ridge and thrust deep into the Japanese positions with an attack that began on April 19th and was a costly and bloody failure. Over 700 Americans died, and XXIV Corps was no farther forward. Next day they tried again, pushing towards Machinato airfield, and again the attack failed. For a week they strove to take the airfield, and

a terrible week it was. Not until April 27th was 'Item Pocket', as the area had become known, declared secure. During the preceding three days, Kakazu Ridge had at last fallen, but every day's fighting was gaining only yards, and still the Japanese seemed able to hold the Shuri region for ever.

On May 4th, after another week's desperate and largely fruitless battle, General Ushijima launched a Japanese counter-attack, attempting to split the US 10th Army in half with an amphibious landing to capture Tanabaru Ridge at the centre of the American army. By the 7th, his attack had failed totally, and the American commanders decided to attempt to 'wrong foot' the Japanese by attacking before they had had time to regroup. This time the American attack succeeded, although slowly, and by the third week of May several important hills had been taken and the Americans seemed poised to begin the encirclement of Japanese positions. But the weather suddenly turned against the attackers. Huge rainstorms made the island a quagmire and rendered the American attack many times more difficult. Nonetheless, the American troops persevered and gradually advanced on either side of the Japanese army. Recognising the probability of encirclement, General Ushijima now decided to evacuate the Shuri region altogether, and withdraw for a last stand in the extreme South of the island. Overnight on May 23rd/24th, the 32nd Army began to pull back under cover of a rearguard action, and by the end of the month, most of the Japanese forces were well South of their front line in the Shuri, which was still holding against the American offensive. When, on May 31st, the Shuri line collapsed, the Americans were disappointed to find that they had not, after all, encircled an army. The bird had flown.

Now began the last phase in Okinawa. Between June 12th and June 17th the Americans fought, against an enemy who seemed to be more ferocious than ever, to capture what was identified as the Yaeju – Dake position. Every machine-gun nest, every foxhole, had to be blasted with unimaginable force before the defenders gave up – usually because they were dead. By the 17th, the survivors were in a pocket only 8 miles by 8. After refusing an appeal to surrender and save his men's lives, Ushijima committed hara-kiri on the 21st June, and on the same day the last major Japanese position was taken. Isolated resistance continued until July 2nd 1945, when Okinawa was finally declared secure after one of the worst battles of the war for the Americans. Over 49,000 Americans had been killed or wounded, and 763 US aircraft had been lost. The Navy had lost 36 ships, and had had 368 damaged.

But the terrible toll of American life was as nothing to that of the lives of Japanese soldiers. Over 110,000 had died; only 7,400 prisoners were taken. In ten large-scale kamikaze suicide air attacks, 1,465 Japanese aircraft and piots had been hurled at US ships. A reputed 7,800 Japanese aircraft had been destroyed, and the Japanese Navy had lost 16 ships, including the giant battleship Yamato, sent on a useless and ineffective suicide mission and sunk by US aircraft before even coming within sight of Okinawa.

There remained only the homeland of Japan to defend. As the wearisome battle for Okinawa had ground to its close, the bomber offensive against mainland Japan was reaching its climax. The chilling horrors of nuclear war were, unknown to all but a select few, about to be unleashed for the first time in the Earth's history. It was an awe-inspiring moment.

5 Accompanied by the destroyer Barry and an oiler, the USS Albany, a 13,600 ton Oregon City class heavy cruiser, (right foreground) keeps station with an American aircraft carrier and other ships somewhere in the Pacific. The Albany was built towards the end of the war.

6 Although an amateur picture snatched in desperately difficult circumstances, this photograph catches the drama of a ship sinking. Following an attack by aircraft of the US Fifth Air Force, many of the crew of this Japanese escort vessel are clinging to lines and sliding down the battered hull of their ship as she sinks in the South China Sea.

CHAPTER 49

FINAL SURRENDER
THE AIR OFFENSIVE~ HIROSHIMA & NAGASAKI

Since October 1944, when the B-29 bombers of the US 21st Bomber Command had been moved up to bases in the Marianas from China and India, the bomber fleet had been able, albeit hazardously, to strike at targets in mainland Japan. The first large-scale raid on Tokyo was launched on November 24th 1944, but, because the Japanese were able to put up fighter intercepter forces from their bases on Iwo Jima and Okinawa, and because bombers had such a long trip home, losses were high. Moreover, the actual effectiveness of the raids was not great. The B-29s were using the high-level precision daylight bombing techniques that had always been favoured by the American Air Staff, and were doing relatively little damage. This was partly because the combination of high altitude and extreme range rendered the aircraft unable to carry more than a fraction of their maximum bomb load.

The final capture of Iwo Jima in March 1945, and the arrival of the innovative and adventurously inclined Major-General Curtis

the raid. The American bombers all returned, with the exception of one that ditched at take-off.

Two days later, after the American ground-crews had worked ceaselessly to repair the 20 aircraft damaged over Nagoya and the 42 that had limped back from Tokyo, the B-29s struck again, this time against the port and shipbuilding centre of Osaka. A total of 301 B-29s, each with six tons of bombs, left the Marianas; 274 found the target and dropped over 1,700 tons of bombs on it. Once again, they started a firestorm, although, because the Japanese people were far better prepared, many fewer inhabitants of Osaka died than had met their end in the Tokyo raid. Nearly 4,000 civilians were killed, and another 8,400 were injured. Over 8 square miles of the city were burnt out, with the loss of 119 major factories and almost 135,000 houses. On March 16th, the bombers hit Kobe, another port, and Japan's sixth largest city, destroying 500 industrial buildings and almost 66,000 houses, disabling Japan's submarine-building yard and

1 Grumman Avengers from a British aircraft carrier raiding Ishioaki airfield in May 1945. A prewar design, the Avenger was a versatile aircraft, capable of operating as a conventional light bomber or as a torpedo bomber, and, in either case, of carrying its bomb-load enclosed within its exceptionally deep fuselage.

2 Continued pressure on the remaining ships of the Japanese Imperial Navy and of the Japanese merchant marine was maintained as a vital part of the bombing campaign in 1945. Here, a Japanese destroyer in Muroran Bay, off Hokkaido, is being strafed by carrier-based aircraft of the US Pacific Fleet. One of the aircraft can be seen above and to the left of the ship.

LeMay as commander of the 21st Bomber Command, changed things dramatically. It was clear that the final assault on mainland Japan had to be from the air, and LeMay set about finding ways to maximise the effectiveness of the B-29 raids. Perhaps benefitting (at long last) from the experience of RAF Bomber Command over Germany during the previous two years, LeMay decided to try low-level night bombing with a mixture of incendiary and high explosive bombs. The technique was, if anything, more capable of bringing about destruction on a massive scale in Japan than it had been in Germany, since most Japanese houses were of relatively flimsy timber construction. After small-scale test raids on Nagoya in January and Kobe in February, the first full-scale night raid of the offensive was scheduled for the night of March 9th/10th. The target was Tokyo.

To prevent possible mayhem caused by crews unaccustomed to night raids firing at each other in the dark, the B-29s flew without ammunition for their machine-guns. The weight saving made it possible for each aircraft to carry an additional 3,200 pounds of bombs to the target, a significant addition which brought the average load per bomber for the low-level raid to about six tons. Between them that night, the 334 B-29 aircraft delivered about 2,000 tons of bombs from between 4,900 and 9,200 feet. The effect on Tokyo was awful and awe-inspiring. More than a quarter of a million buildings were destroyed; over a million people were made homeless; 83,000 people died; almost 41,000 were injured. Nearly 16 square miles of the city were burnt out in the fire storm that the raid raised, which had been visible to the crews of the returning bombers for more than 150 miles. Many of the crucial industrial plants supplying the Japanese war effort were destroyed beyond repair. Against this raid, the Japanese had been unable to put up fighters, and had found their anti-aircraft fire to be almost totally ineffective. Only 14 American bombers were lost; 42 more were damaged.

It seemed that LeMay had found the answer to crushing Japan. But when this success for the American bomber fleet was followed on March 11th with a similar raid on Nagoya, the centre of Japan's aircraft industry, the results were less devastating by far. Although more bombs were dropped, there was no firestorm, no general devastation, and no total destruction of industrial plants. In part, this was due to the still air of the night, but far more of the credit for saving a large part of the city went to the efficiency of the fire fighters, and the fact that their water supply continued to work through and after

killing nearly 3,000 people. Three days later, Nagoya was bombed again, this time with more than 1,800 tons of bombs including a significantly greater proportion of high explosive than had been used in the earlier raid. As a result, the fire-fighting on the ground was less effective, and a firestorm burned out 3·square miles.

The March raids had proved that strategic night bombing at low altitudes achieved dramatic results with relatively light losses. During April 1945, the wearisome and bloody campaign in Okinawa needed all the support the bombers could give, and the attacks on Japan ceased, giving the devastated cities a breathing space in which to begin the major task of clearing up. The last bodies of people killed in the first Tokyo raid of March 9th/10th were not found and removed until the second week of April, and the immensity of the task of restoring some semblance of civic order was daunting. But the experience of the American Army and Marine Corps in Okinawa was sufficient to convince both Curtis LeMay and his superiors that an amphibious invasion of mainland Japan should be considered only as a last resort. During April, the cities and industrial centres of Japan had been graded as targets according to their strategic significance, and in May the remorseless assault from the air began again with yet another raid on Nagoya, home of the Mitsubishi engineering and aircraft factories. LeMay now had more aircraft at his disposal, and

was able to send 472 B-29s to deliver more than 2,500 tons of bombs – but he sent them by day to bomb from a height of between 12,000 and 20,500 feet, carrying an average of 5.3 tons apiece. The force lost ten aircraft, and achieved less damage than had the earlier night raids. Two days later, the 21st Bomber Command attacked by night and at low level again, once more against Nagoya. This time the aircraft carried 8 tons each, and finally managed virtually to destroy the Mitsubishi aircraft works, with the loss of only 3 aircraft, all of which suffered mechanical failure rather than the effects of enemy action.

Through May and June the night attacks continued, raining destruction on the major cities and industrial centres of Japan. On May 25th, only two nights after a further raid on Tokyo had burned out over 5 square miles, the worst non-nuclear raid of the war on Japan totally destroyed 16.8 square miles of the city. By the end of June, 105.6 square miles of the total 257.2 square miles area of Japan's six largest cities had been burned out. More than half of Tokyo was in total ruins. Even so, in excess of sixty attacks were made between June 17th and August 14th. Yet still the spirit of Japan prevailed. Absolute devotion to the Emperor could only be overcome by the Emperor himself accepting surrender. How, the Allies asked themselves, does one persuade a god to accept defeat?

4

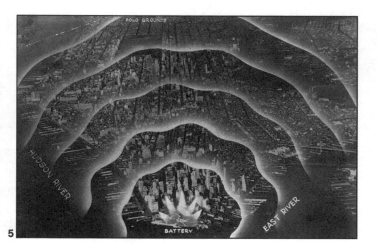
5

6

3 The image that marked the beginning of the nuclear age and an irretrievable change in the nature of warfare itself – the mushroom cloud of the world's second nuclear bombs, boiling into the clear morning sky above Nagasaki on August 9th 1945. This picture was taken from one of the three B-29 bombers that carried 'Fat Boy' to the doomed Japanese city.

4 The world's first nuclear weapon, which destroyed Hiroshima on August 6th 1945, looked like this – 'Little Boy', just 120 inches long and twenty-eight inches in diameter, with a weight of 9,000lbs and an explosive force equivalent to 20,000 tons of TNT. By the standards of modern nuclear armaments it was both primitive and relatively ineffective, yet it wrought destruction on a scale never before imagined.

5 As Americans struggled to grasp the scale of the explosions that were to bring an end to the war in Japan, this diagram was published in the US press demonstrating the effect of the Hiroshima bomb if it were dropped on Manhattan Island. Assuming that the bomb was dropped on the Battery at the southern tip of the island, and looking northward, its graphically illustrated waves of destruction would, stated the original government-approved caption, reduce the city to dust as far north as the polo grounds on 155th Street, rendering everybody in that area either dead or homeless.

6 The reality of Hiroshima looked a great deal worse than the attempts at diagrammatic representation of a hypothetical attack on New York. The vastness of the area over which a beautiful city was totally levelled was difficult for observers to comprehend – and even more difficult to understand for those who had lived through the mightiest explosion man had yet created.

The Nuclear Holocaust

In the strictest secrecy, the 'Manhattan' project had, as the conventional war progressed, created in America the world's first practical nuclear weapons. Two separate lines of weapons research had resulted in the USA having, by the spring of 1945, two entirely different types of atomic bomb. The first, a gun-assembly weapon known as 'Little Boy', was an oblong, parallel sided bomb containing, at one end of the casing, a quantity of Uranium 235 fissionable material that was just short of the critical mass, and, at the other, a gun 'loaded' with a segment of the same material. When the gun was fired, and the smaller piece of radio-active uranium was propelled into the larger, the total mass became critical and a massive explosion ensued. This was the bomb that was to create the devastation of Hiroshima.

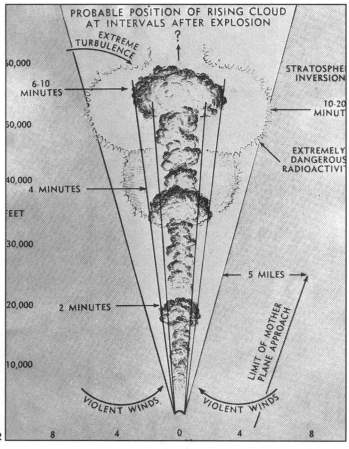

The other weapon, 'Fat Boy', used plutonium as its fissionable material, and relied upon the implosion principle for its detonation. A core made up of several separate units of plutonium was contained within a casing of TNT. When the conventional explosive was detonated, the plutonium was collapsed into one larger critical mass to create the nuclear blast. America's second bomb, dropped over Nagasaki, was of this type.

In June 1945, knowing that 'Little Boy' could be ready late in July, and that 'Fat Boy' could be operational at about the same time if tests in July proved that it worked, a meeting between President Truman and the US Chiefs of Staff discussed the disturbing question of whether the new weapon should or should not be used. The problem was not quite as straightforward as it has sometimes been made to seem. General George C. Marshall had calculated that, if mainland Japan was to be invaded as the means of ending the war, it would have to be tackled in two major campaigns, the first against the island of Kyushu, the second some months later against Honshu. He had worked out from Okinawa experience of the Japanese army's fanatical preparedness to die that the first of these attacks alone would cost the USA as many as 69,000 killed and wounded out of a proposed force of 190,000. What the losses arising from the final attack on Honshu would have been, once the Japanese army had reached the zenith of its suicidal zeal, nobody seems to have dared to calculate. Despite these figures, Marshall favoured holding back the atomic weapons, and the June meeting did in fact agree that the invasion of Kyushu would begin on November 1st 1945, and that the invasion of Honshu would be scheduled for March 1946.

A further school of thought held that there was no need either to use the nuclear weapons or to invade. Since Japan could shortly

1 The bomb which destroyed much of Nagasaki on August 9th was of a quite different type from that released over Hiroshima. 'Fat Boy', which relied for its operation upon the implosion by a charge of TNT of several separate segments of plutonium into one critical mass, weighed 10,000lbs, and was 128 inches long and sixty inches in diameter.

2 A diagram which was extensively published in the US and British press after the nuclear attacks on Japan showed how the violent uprush of searingly hot air and radioactive dust ascended and spread within minutes into the stratosphere, creating the characteristic mushroom cloud as it rose. Within only a few years it was realised that the spread of dangerous radioactivity was over a far greater area than had at first been supposed.

3 The point above which the bomb was detonated was known to the Americans as Point X. This picture was taken from a position just 550 feet from Point X, looking northwest across the devastated city of Hiroshima, soon after the explosion. The man with the bicycle, like everybody else in the world at that time, had no comprehension of the risk to his future wellbeing of just being in the intensely radioactive target area.

be totally surrounded and blockaded, it was argued, her own inability to feed her population without imports would ensure her defeat. But this argument did not gain ground, and by the time the Potsdam Conference issued its considered view, on July 26th, that Japan must either surrender unconditionally or accept 'prompt and utter destruction', the weapons were ready, and the Allies clearly intended that the Potsdam ultimatum was to be taken seriously. Despite appeals to the military government of Japan by Emperor Hirohito to accept surrender if the terms could be negotiated to include the continued existence of the Imperial Throne, Prime Minister Suzuki declined to consider the acceptance of defeat. The die was cast.

The 509th Composite Group of the USAAF, which had been based at North Field on Tinian Island in the Marianas since May, was put on readiness to deliver the new secret weapon on or after August 3rd. The uranium 235 necessary for the 'Little Boy' bomb had arrived on Tinian on July 26th. The crews of the 509th had been training for months, dropping large high explosive bombs with similar characteristics to the atomic weapons in raids over Japan. Now they waited for the clear weather that was obligatory for the dropping of the most terrible weapon man had yet devised.

On August 6th, the weather cleared, and Colonel Paul Tibbets,

commander of the 509th Group, rostered himself to fly the 'Enola Gay', the long range B-29 that he had named after his mother. Two other B-29 aircraft flew with him as observers. The target was Hiroshima. The 'Little Boy' bomb, armed during the flight to avoid danger to Tinian Island should an accident occur at take-off, weighed 9,000 lbs, and the 'Enola Gay' was, at 65 tons take-off weight, fully eight tons over the normal operational bombing weight for a B-29. Despite this, the take-off was uneventful, the flight to the Japanese mainland passed without incident, and when the lone B-29 whose task it was to check on weather conditions over the target signalled at 7.15am that it was clear, the three aircraft bringing the bomb began their approach to the target. By the time they arrived over the city at 8.06am, the earlier air raid warning triggered by the weather aircraft had been cancelled. People were on the streets, and the city continued to go about its business, undeterred by the three aircraft far above at over 31,000 feet. Survivors reported noticing that the two aircraft either side of the leading B-29 turned away unusually tightly and made off at speed after an object on a parachute was dropped.

Just 17 seconds after 8.15am, a mighty flash, followed by searing heat and an explosion like a hundred claps of thunder rolled together, followed by blast that lifted and disintegrated buildings, tramcars,

4 In this picture of Hiroshima a few days after the explosion, it is noticeable how well isolated buildings had withstood the effects of the bomb. Note, too, how the bridge has remained standing.

5 It was a cause for considerable discussion among observers of the aftermath of the Hiroshima and Nagasaki explosions that some buildings seemed to withstand the blast comparatively well, often for no very clear reason. This structure, which remained standing despite being quite near to the centre of the explosion, seems from the picture to be built, at least in part, of brick.

6 A Japanese army picture of a military policeman (extreme left) making notes shortly after the destruction of Hiroshima. To the right is a charred body, and in the background some of the many thousands of homeless survivors who wandered in the ruins of the city.

7 The surviving children of Hiroshima wore masks over their mouths and noses to provide some protection against the all-pervading smells of death and disease in which they had to live after the atomic bomb. The baggy trousers were typical of the children's wear of the time in Japan.

8 Some of the more obvious short-term injuries to be seen among the survivors of the Hiroshima blast were horrific. This man was suffering from burns caused by the searing heat of the flash when the atomic bomb exploded. Most patients afflicted with these injuries later also developed the symptoms of radiation sickness.

9 Remaining public buildings in and around Hiroshima were pressed into service as temporary hospitals and shelters for the injured. These burn victims were sheltered in the ruins of a bank. The photographer noted that all the burns had a pronounced reddish appearance.

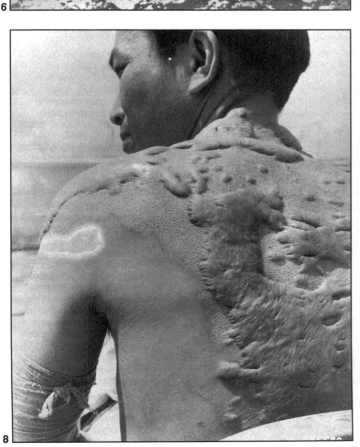

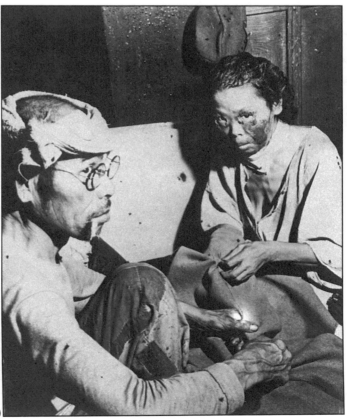

Final Surrender

expected on that front. As fuel and water were dropped from the air in a spectacular airlift operation, the advancing Russian Tank Army overcame the Japanese 80th Brigade, then the 107th Division, who fought on oblivious to Japan's total surrender on August 15th. The Russian 17th Army made similar progress, and by August 20th was over the Chinese border. All along the front, the armies of Soviet Russia rushed forward, overcoming all in their path. After 15th August, news of Japan's surrender gradually reached the Japanese armies in the field, many units of which simply failed to believe what they heard and fought on. But the progressive surrender of Japanese units speeded the Russian advance all along the Transbaikal Front, and by the 24th August, the Russian forces were in Mukden, Dairen and Port Arthur, and had avenged Russia's defeat by Japan in 1905. More to the point, Stalin had successfully grabbed some more territory before the war finally ended.

On the Far Eastern Front, the Japanese armies were better defended and more concentrated, and fought fiercely. Only the final surrender of Japan saved the Soviet troops from a protracted and bloody campaign of the sort the Americans had suffered throughout the long haul back across the Pacific. This was particularly true of the Russian landing on Sakhalin and in the Kurile Islands. Now Russia was able to support with arms captured from the Japanese

the Communist forces fighting the civil war in China against the Nationalist army of Chiang Kai-shek. Faced with this new peril, Chiang's future was bleak.

The Final Surrender

The devastation of the two atomic bombs, and the Russian declaration of war and offensive against Manchuria, convinced Emperor Hirohito of Japan that the time had come for a little rational Western thinking, and for his nation to surrender. For almost ten years, he had been effectively a puppet Emperor, unable to do more than accept the dictates of his 'advisers' and acquiesce in the rule of the military government. Now, when the military dictatorship had demonstrably failed, and Japan had been brought to her knees, he convened a meeting in the air-raid shelter of the Imperial Palace at midnight on August 9th 1945. There was a heated discussion. All agreed that any surrender must permit the Emperor to retain his throne and his sovereignty, but the military members of the government wanted also to ensure that there was no Allied occupation, and that Japanese war criminals would be tried by Japanese in Japan. When everyone had had their say, Hirohito, for the first time since the Thirties, took a decision. Japan would offer surrender on only the one condition — that the sovereign power of the Emperor would be retained.

1 Although the formal end of the Japanese war did not come until the signing of the surrender document in Tokyo bay on September 2nd 1945, individual Japanese surrenders were signed in several theatres of the Far Eastern war. Here, Major-General Keller E. Rockey, Commanding General of the Third Amphibious Marine Corps, signs documents accepting surrender of the Japanese forces in Tientsin on behalf of Generalissimo Chiang Kai-Shek.

2 The Emperor's instructions to all Japanese forces to lay down their arms were issued on August 14th, and on the 15th the Emperor broadcast to his people for the first time. These are ships of the Imperial Japanese Navy which assembled after surrender in Kure Bay, South of Hiroshima.

3 After the surrender there was considerable confusion in Japan, not least because the Japanese had been taught from the cradle that surrender was unthinkable – yet now the Emperor himself had instructed them to lay down their arms. These Japanese soldiers were assembled in a Tokyo street awaiting demobilisation.

5

6

7

4 General of the Army Douglas MacArthur, pictured for once without his dark glasses, shortly before he took up his peacetime role as Occupation Director in Tokyo. Like another great commander in another age and place, the Duke of Wellington, he demonstrated unexpected talent for the art of government after having proved his skills as a general.

5 The mere signing of a surrender document, while it stopped the war, did little to allay the sufferings of the people of the afflicted cities of mainland Japan. This Japanese family moved back to the site of their former home in Nagasaki, and, by the time this picture was taken in mid-September 1945, had set up home in a shack.

6 Even Hiroshima began to get back on its feet by the end of 1945, and the tramcars were running again before the end of the year. American troops were everywhere – in this picture a jeep full of Americans passes a queue of Hiroshima's inhabitants waiting for a ride.

7 Not all Japanese who had survived the war went home to freedom. This picture of Colonel Akira Nagahama was taken as he awaited trial for war crimes committed while he was Chief of the Japanese Secret Police in the Philippines.

8 Admiral Shigetora Shimada had been Naval Minister in the Japanese Cabinet at the time of the attack on Pearl Harbour, and earned the distinction, by a series of ill-planned and executed naval actions, of being one of the most universally disliked of Japan's military commanders. After the war he was tried for his crimes, and is pictured awaiting that trial.

The decision was cabled to the Allies. The US Secretary of State, James Byrnes, responded swiftly – only unconditional surrender was acceptable, and the Emperor was to be 'subject to' the Supreme Allied Commander. More heated discussion ensued in the Japanese Cabinet, and on August 14th a further meeting with the Emperor again elicited a decision made by him alone without deference to his government. Japan would accept the Allied conditions. Radio messages were sent forthwith to all Japanese armies and troops in the field telling them of the surrender and instructing them to lay down their arms. Most did. Some fought on. Many officers committed ritual *Hara kiri* rather than dishonour themselves by surrender.

To convince the Japanese population that the unthinkable had happened, Emperor Hirohito, for the first time in a reign spanning (since 1926) almost two decades, recorded a radio broadcast, and at noon on August 15th the Japanese population heard the voice of their Emperor, still officially a god, telling them that the war was at an end and that Japan was to be occupied.

On August 30th, the first of the occupation forces, a contingent of American and British troops, landed at Yokosuka. Three days later, on September 2nd, just one day and three hours short of six years after the first Allied declaration of war against Hitler by Britain in 1939, the Second World War came officially to an end when the formal surrender was signed aboard the battleship USS *Missouri* in Tokyo harbour. The newly appointed Foreign Minister of Japan, Mamoru Shigemitsu, and representatives of the Japanese armed services signed on behalf of their country. General Douglas MacArthur, and generals and admirals of the USA, Great Britain, China, Russia, the Netherlands, New Zealand, Canada, France and Australia signed on behalf of the Allies. There remained now only the rebuilding of a peacetime world.

8

CHAPTER 50

THE LEGACY OF WAR AND ITS POST WAR IMPACT

The end of the Second World War ushered in a period of world-wide political change. The invasions and counter-invasions of the aggressors and those who sought to liberate had brought forth from nations the world over an increased awareness of the meaning of freedom; of human rights; of the horrors of war. The bursting forth of Soviet socialism across Europe and Asia swept up in its wake proud nations whose history was as individual and as deserving of preservation as any on earth, and substituted a new tyranny for that which had so recently been defeated.

In the USA, the death in April of President Roosevelt, who had for so long believed that Stalin would not deceive him, brought to the Presidency Harry S. Truman, who recognised that the West had already been deceived, and that the USSR could be checked only by the nuclear deterrent. Truman dismissed Henry Morgenthau Jr, the Secretary of the Treasury whose extraordinary plan to pastoralise Germany into a purely agricultural community had come so close to being Allied policy. Under Truman, the USA took a more realistic view of Germany's future and sought to rebuild the economy of the new Federal Republic.

In Britain, Winston Churchill, having inspired and led Britain tirelessly through her most desperate hours, was remorselessly sacked and sent home to the country by a swing to Socialism apparently boosted by the votes of the returning servicemen. Just when Britain needed that leadership again, it got instead Clement Attlee; a worthy Prime Minister, an excellent administrator, but lacking in inspirational quality.

In India, General Wavell was replaced as Viceroy almost as soon as Attlee came to power, and it was to Admiral Lord Louis Mountbatten that the task of guiding India to independence fell, a task completed in 1947.

In Japan, General Douglas MacArthur administered the Allied occupation wisely and well, guiding the Japanese nation to a new alliance of traditional values and Western attitudes. MacArthur proved himself a considerable politician, pushing through radical changes in the Japanese constitution that outlawed war entirely, guaranteed political freedom and created a democratic state. The Emperor was stripped of all but his symbolic status, and formally renounced his divinity. The major Japanese war leaders were tried

1 This is the image of the end of the war in Germany that most remember – yet the reality was not the end of a war but the beginning of political division and brinkmanship which lasted into the eighties.

1

2

3

2 Berlin was divided into four sectors – American, British, Soviet and French – presided over by an Allied Control Commission. Each sector was in turn controlled by the troops of the relevant power, who exercised civil power over the German population.

3 Much of the ruined city of Berlin, including many of its most famous landmarks, remained as they were at the end of the war for years. This is the Kaiser Wilhelm Memorial Church in the Tauenzienstrasse.

4 A meeting of the Coordinating Committee of the Allied Control Authority for Germany in Berlin in December 1945. This was the principal executive authority, with far-reaching powers over the administration of postwar Germany. Its decisions were passed for ratification to the four Allied commanders, Eisenhower, Montgomery, Zhukov and Koenig.

for their crimes. Seven, including General Yamashita, General Tojo and General Homma, the perpetrator of the infamous 'Death March' in the Philippines, were hanged. Two — Prince Funimaro Konoye and General Honjo — beat the hangman and committed suicide.

In Germany — the part of that country the world was now obliged to become accustomed to calling West Germany — a War Crimes Tribunal was convened on a much larger scale. Under four-power jurisdiction, the Tribunal was to try the former leaders of Nazi Germany for having committed crimes against humanity. On October 18th 1945, the prosecutors issued indictments against twenty-one Nazis. Thirty days later, on November 20th, the accused faced their accusers in one of the few intact buildings left in Nuremberg. As in Japan, some of the war criminals beat the hangman. Hitler, Goebbels and Himmler were all dead long before their crimes were heard.

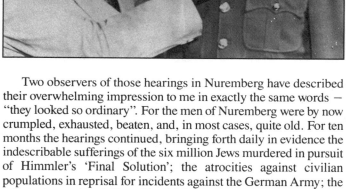

5 War memorabilia gradually became big business, both at the levels of commonplace souvenirs – badges, weapons etc – and in the serious collectors' markets. The final draft of the surrender of the German armed forces to Field-Marshal Montgomery on Luneberg Heath was sold at Sotheby's in London in 1977 for $3,100 to Mr Donald Wilson, a collector from Scotland, shown here with his acquisition.

6 As Christmas 1945 approached in Germany, many families were in considerable need, for a very large number of German soldiers were either dead or in captivity. Outside a railway station in Frankfurt a man sells calendars for 1946. Behind him, a poster appeals for gifts of clothing for the needy.

7 Returning heroes were decorated in recognition of their achievements and fortitude in the service of their country. General Jonathan Wainwright, who had been obliged to surrender after a heroic defence of Bataan and Corregidor in 1942, received from President Truman at a White House ceremony in September 1945 the highest award for valour that the United States of America can bestow – the Congressional Medal of Honor.

8 In the USA, the rejoicing and celebrations at the end of the war continued for months. In October 1945, much of the US Pacific Fleet was assembled in the Hudson River for review by President Truman, who inspected the fleet aboard the destroyer USS *Renshaw*, watched by thousands of spectators who jammed the shoreline.

Two observers of those hearings in Nuremberg have described their overwhelming impression to me in exactly the same words – "they looked so ordinary". For the men of Nuremberg were by now crumpled, exhausted, beaten, and, in most cases, quite old. For ten months the hearings continued, bringing forth daily in evidence the indescribable sufferings of the six million Jews murdered in pursuit of Himmler's 'Final Solution'; the atrocities against civilian populations in reprisal for incidents against the German Army; the callousness and brutality with which Hitler's Reich rightly became identified.

When it was all over, twelve of the accused were sentenced to death. Hermann Goering, Martin Bormann (in his absence) and Foreign Minister Joachim von Ribbentrop. Ernst Kaltenbrunner, who had succeeded 'Hangman Heydrich' as Protector of Bohemia and Moravia after Heydrich's assassination. Rosenberg, the party 'philosopher'. Hans Frank, the Nazi inquisitor in Poland. Julius Streicher, the Jew baiter of Nuremberg, probably the most unpleasant and sadistic of the Nazi hierarchy. The curiously colourless Frick, Plenipotentiary for Administration in Hitler's cabinet. Fritz Sauckel, the organiser of slave labour. Dr Arthur Seyss-Inquart, the quisling Governor of Austria. Keitel and Jodl. All were hanged in the early morning of October 16th 1946 – except for Goering, who succeeded in taking poison an hour before he was due to die, and Bormann, who has never been located and was probably already dead.

Three of the accused were acquitted – Hjalmar Schacht, who had attempted as Hitler's Economics Minister and President of the Reichsbank to keep the Fuehrer in touch with reality; Franz von Papen, once Chancellor of Germany; and Hans Fritsche. The remainder, including Albert Speer, Hitler's Armaments Minister, Rudolf Hess, who had flown to Britain in May 1941 to seek peace, and Grand Admiral Karl Doenitz, nominated by Hitler as his successor, were imprisoned for varying terms. Most were released in the Fifties. Only Hess remained in captivity, the lone prisoner in Berlin's Spandau Prison, until his controversial death by strangulation in 1987.

With the conclusion of the Nuremburg trials, it was as though the past ended and the future began. The Soviet Union, constantly aware of the enormous strategic advantage gained by the USA as a result of having the nuclear bomb, had begun in 1945 a campaign of espionage to obtain the necessary secrets. On July 10th 1949, Russia proved the effectiveness of both her espionage and her scientists by conducting a successful nuclear test. The age of the rival deterrents had arrived, years before Washington believed it possible.

Little more than a year earlier the USSR had reacted sharply and quite indefensibly to US action to revitalise the West German economy by abolishing Hitler's Reichsmark and introducing a new Deutschmark. Recognising that Berlin was isolated within Soviet dominated East Germany, Russia callously attempted

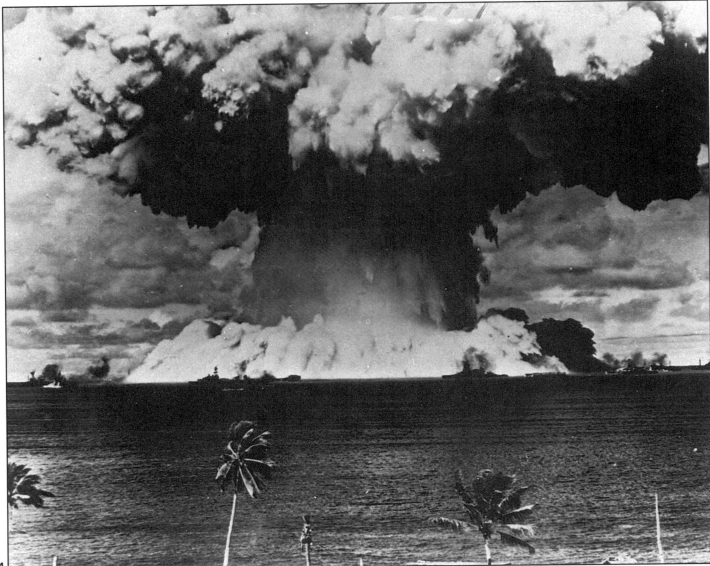

1 The lessons of German achievements in the field of guided weapons did not go unheeded, and the Allies had, even during the war, developed unmanned guided weapons of their own. This picture shows 'The Bat', claimed somewhat dubiously by the US Navy at the time to be 'the first fully automatic guided missile to be used in combat by any nation'. Launched in the air by US Navy Privateer patrol bombers outside the range of enemy anti-aircraft fire, and guided on to their targets by its own inbuilt radar, the Bat sank a number of Japanese ships towards the end of the war. Postwar development was more sophisticated, and the acquisition of Wernher von Braun, designer of the German V2 rocket, greatly assisted the US rocketry programme.

2 The postwar US government of President Truman was more realistic about the Soviet threat to the Western world than his predecessor had been, and the development of US arms continued. This shot was taken in 1946 aboard the USS *Helena*, a cruiser built after VJ day, the end of the Japanese war, and issued after it had been announced that US vessels had been given permission by the Royal Navy to anchor at Portsmouth, as part of the development of postwar defence co-operation between the USA and Great Britain.

3 The awareness of the need for Western defence brought about the development in the fifties of early warning systems to detect intrusions into Western airspace. The first early warning radar system to span the American continent was 'Pine Tree', and in 1955 the press were allowed to photograph this Pine Tree operations room in Eastern Canada.

4 It was inevitable after the birth of atomic war at Hiroshima and Nagasaki that the East and the West would both seek to develop ever more powerful atomic weapons, and that that development would imply test programmes. Before the full extent of the danger of testing nuclear devices in the atmosphere had been fully recognised, the USA had tested weapons in the Nevada Desert, Britain and France had tested them in the South Pacific, and the Soviet Union had exploded bombs in the vastness of the Eastern USSR. This is a test at Bikini Atoll.

to starve the population of West Berlin into submission to Russian domination by closing all land routes from West Germany to the former capital. The Allies could do nothing to reopen the roads and canals thus closed short of going to war with Russia, for there were 17 Red Army divisions between Berlin and the Western Zones of Occupation. But Russia had not and could not close the air lanes.

Thus began the Berlin Airlift, by which two and a quarter million Berliners were supplied with their every essential for almost a year before the Russians gave in, admitted defeat and reopened the land routes. By the time the airlift finished, the pilots and controllers had become so efficient that every day saw lifted into Berlin three times more supplies than the city needed for a day. The Russians learned from this a great lesson − the value of strategic military transport aircraft. One has only to reflect on the efficiency of their invasion of Afghanistan at Christmas 1979 to recognise how well the lesson was learned.

Even in the years immediately after the war, Russian influence

5 Control of the atomic bomb and of the nuclear age was an early and pressing political question, particularly in the United States. A Senate Special Committee was set up to discuss the problem. At a meeting of the committee in February 1946, are (left to right) Senator Brien McMahon, the Chairman, Senator Arthur Vandenberg, James McInerney of the Department of Justice and Major-General Leslie R. Groves, Director of the US Army's Atomic Bomb Project.

6 The end of the war did not end the spirit of the wartime RAF in Britain. This picture could almost date from the Battle of Britain, except for the late mark of the Spitfire fighters – which indicate that it was in fact taken at Biggin Hill in 1946.

7 Anglo-US cooperation, which had become so effective during the war years, continued after the war with an extensive US presence in Britain, and with the establishment of the North Atlantic Treaty Organisation – NATO. These B-29 Superfortresses arrived in June 1947 at RAF Marham, Norfolk, for a goodwill visit, and were escorted on the last leg of their journey by twin-engined Mosquito fighter-bombers of the RAF.

extended far beyond Berlin, Germany or indeed Europe. As soon as the Japanese were defeated by the advancing Red Army in Manchuria, the captured arms began to be ferried to Mao-Tse-Tung's communist revolutionaries in China. Although the USA tried repeatedly to find diplomatic means to reconcile Chiang Kai-shek and Mao, and did achieve, through a mission by General George C. Marshall, a truce between the two in 1946, by the end of 1949 Mao had smashed the Kuomintang, Chiang Kai-shek had retreated to his Formosan Nationalist stronghold (now Taiwan), and Mao was in control of what became known as Red China.

There next emerged what is now a familiar Soviet tactic designed to extend Russian domination − the supply of arms to a guerilla force. Many of those same captured Japanese arms, and many more of the genuine Russian article, found their way into North Korea, where the communists were seeking to overrun the (genuinely) democratic South. The Americans intervened forcefully and

successfully to contain the Communist attack, and prevented the loss of South Korea to the free world − but, when the stalemate armistice was signed at Panmunjom, it was the United Nations that enforced it.

Born of an idea hatched between Roosevelt and Churchill, christened by Roosevelt, and brought to maturity by a series of conferences at Dumbarton Oaks, Washington DC, during 1944, and at a meeting in San Francisco in April 1945, the United Nations had been already in existence by the end of the war. Because it was genuinely an organisation seeking to avoid unnecessary conflict, it was and, to a lesser extent is, a more successful policing body than the League of Nations, which had failed in so many crises during the Thirties. In the early years after the war, before its original political polarisation and intent was clouded and put out of balance by the procession of newly independent emergent countries of the Sixties and Seventies, the United Nations was an effective balance in the Cold War, and several times prevented the Cold War becoming

The Legacy of War

hot. But, as the Fifties succeeded the Forties, it was the balance of power rather than idealistic concepts that once more determined whether the peace was preserved. That balance, by 1949, was polarised as being between, on the one hand, the Soviet Union itself with the Soviet dominated countries that the USSR had overrun in the closing stages of the war, which now became known collectively as the Warsaw Pact nations, and, on the other, the North Atlantic Treaty Organisation, known as NATO. The Treaty was ratified on 4th April 1949, and brought together with the USA and Canada under a common umbrella of defence spending and planning eleven nations of Western Europe, to which were later added Greece and Turkey, which joined in 1952, and West Germany, which joined in 1955.

The emergence of NATO was perhaps the most significant single example of the mighty change in the position of the USA that the war had wrought. Before the Second World War, Britain had been a great imperial power, still wielding the influence and through it much of the wealth of the Victorian era. The USA was a determinedly neutral, isolationist nation. When America had thrown its means of production heart and soul into the war, it actually did the nation good. The standard of living in the United States rose sharply during the war; in other combatant countries it fell. British and British Commonwealth shipping losses reduced the size of their fleet from 40,000,000 tons to only 19,500,000 tons. The US merchant fleet quadrupled to 50,000,000 tons. Britain lost as a result of the war 35 times as much foreign invested capital as did the USA. The USA ended the war rich. Britain ended it poor.

Recognising this situation, the USA put its new-found wealth to the defence of the free world; and in particular to the defence of

1 In Eastern Europe, things were less rosy. In 1946, the value of the Hungarian pengö fell in a manner reminiscent of the great inflation of the German mark after the First World War. To post a letter cost the equivalent of $1,300,000,000 at prewar exchange rates! A man in Hungary who owned a block of flats, for which the rent was controlled at the 1939 level, found that the rent for the year on the whole block was not sufficient to buy a tram ticket. In this picture, the cigarette is being lit with a 1 Milliard pengö note, at 1939 rates worth $50,000,000.

2 In 1947, Lord Wavell was succeeded as Viceroy of India by Admiral Lord Louis Mountbatten, who was to guide India to independence as the two separate states of India and Pakistan. In this picture, Lord and Lady Mountbatten are greeted by Lord and Lady Wavell.

3 The growth in Soviet arms production accelerated with the coming of peace, whereas the building of armaments by the other powers was greatly slowed. In 1958, Marshal Budenny received from Marshal Voroschilov, President of the Supreme Soviet, decorations for his achievements in building the Red Army to new peaks of power and readiness after its struggles during the Second World War.

4 The grip of the Soviet Union on Eastern Europe after the war became tighter each year. Here Stalin and his Foreign Minister Molotov are seen in 1947, voting in what passed for an election in the one-party Soviet Union.

5

6

7

8

5 War soon returned to the Far East, with Britain fighting a protracted undeclared war against Communist guerillas in Malaya from 1948, and the emergence of the Korean War between South and North Korea, and then Red China, in 1950. Ceasefire talks aimed at ending the Korean War began in 1951, but dragged on for months without achieving anything. This was the North Korean/Chinese team at those talks, held at Kaesong. Their inscrutability suggests possible reasons for the failure of the talks.

6 In Japan, the dedication and energy of the Japanese people soon reasserted itself, and recovery began before 1945 was over. These Japanese Catholics are praying before the ruins of Nagasaki Cathedral.

7 Even in Hiroshima, worst-hit of all Japanese cities, a new city began to arise from the rubble, first in prefabricated buildings like these, photographed in 1946, then as a fine, modern city which thrives today. In this picture, the stark, scorched trees are reminders of the heat of the bomb a year before.

8 In the middle of 1946, the Philippines became independent after forty-eight years of American rule. On July 4th, appropriately, General of the Army Douglas MacArthur delivered the principal address at the ceremonies that marked the birth of the Republic of the Philippines, for which he had fought so hard during the recent war.

Western Europe. From being an isolationist power observing the doings of the British Empire with interest, America had become the most significant financial and international diplomatic force on earth. From that again sprang the space programme. For, as General Patton's 3rd Army had rushed through Southern Germany in the closing stages of the war, they had discovered a stockpile of complete and near complete V2 rockets. The US Army had also secured the services of Wernher von Braun, the brilliant chief scientist of Hitler's rocket programme. After a discreet interval, von Braun and his rockets were reunited in the USA, and from his continued work were developed the 'Gemini', 'Mercury' and 'Apollo' programmes which put Neil Armstrong and his successors on the moon.

When he set out to conquer Europe and subjugate Russia, Hitler sought to change the face of the world. He and his allies drew a large part of the world into war. He conquered; he over-reached himself; he was totally defeated. The evils of his regime were so great that almost any result was to be preferred to his success. But although his plans for the world were not to be, the pattern of political and military power was altered for the remainder of the twentieth century, and probably for the twenty-first, by the perverted genius of the Austrian corporal. His impact upon history, and upon our lives, has been greater than that of any other man since the ancients.

Index of Illustrations

Index of Illustrations

396

Index of Illustrations